Chrysler Sebring
Dodge Stratus & Avenger
Automotive Repair Manual

**by John A Wegmann
and John H Haynes**

Member of the Guild of Motoring Writers

Models covered:

Chrysler Sebring convertible and sedan (1995 through 2006)
Chrysler Sebring coupe (1995 through 2005)
Dodge Stratus sedan (2001 through 2006)
Dodge Stratus coupe (2001 through 2005)
Dodge Avenger (1995 through 2000)

Does not include information specific to Flexible Fuel Vehicles

(25040 - 9W19)   ABCDE

2

AUTOMOTIVE PARTS & ACCESSORIES ASSOCIATION MEMBER

Haynes Publishing Group
Sparkford Nr Yeovil
Somerset BA22 7JJ England

Haynes North America, Inc
859 Lawrence Drive
Newbury Park
California 91320 USA
www.haynes.com

Acknowledgements

We are grateful to the Chrysler Corporation for providing technical information and certain illustrations. Wiring diagrams produced exclusively for Haynes North America, Inc. by Valley Forge Technical Information Services. Technical writers who contributed to this project include Bob Henderson, Robert Maddox, Mike Stubblefield and Larry Warren.

© Haynes North America, Inc. 2002, 2006, 2012

With permission from J.H. Haynes & Co. Ltd.

A book in the Haynes Automotive Repair Manual Series

Printed in Malaysia

ISBN-13: 978-1-62092-001-5

Library of Congress Control Number: 2012942978

Contents

Haynes photographer, mechanic and author with a 1998 Dodge Avenger

About this manual

Its purpose

The purpose of this manual is to help you get the best value from your vehicle. It can do so in several ways. It can help you decide what work must be done, even if you choose to have it done by a dealer service department or a repair shop; it provides information and procedures for routine maintenance and servicing; and it offers diagnostic and repair procedures to follow when trouble occurs.

We hope you use the manual to tackle the work yourself. For many simpler jobs, doing it yourself may be quicker than arranging an appointment to get the vehicle into a shop and making the trips to leave it and pick it up. More importantly, a lot of money can be saved by avoiding the expense the shop must pass on to you to cover its labor and overhead costs. An added benefit is the sense of satisfaction and accomplishment that you feel after doing the job yourself.

Using the manual

The manual is divided into Chapters. Each Chapter is divided into numbered Sections, which are headed in bold type between horizontal lines. Each Section consists of consecutively numbered paragraphs.

At the beginning of each numbered Section you will be referred to any illustrations which apply to the procedures in that Section. The reference numbers used in illustration captions pinpoint the pertinent Section and the Step within that Section. That is, illustration 3.2 means the illustration refers to Section 3 and Step (or paragraph) 2 within that Section.

Procedures, once described in the text, are not normally repeated. When it's necessary to refer to another Chapter, the reference will be given as Chapter and Section number. Cross references given without use of the word "Chapter" apply to Sections and/or paragraphs in the same Chapter. For example, "see Section 8" means in the same Chapter.

References to the left or right side of the vehicle assume you are sitting in the driver's seat, facing forward.

Even though we have prepared this manual with extreme care, neither the publisher nor the author can accept responsibility for any errors in, or omissions from, the information given.

NOTE

A **Note** provides information necessary to properly complete a procedure or information which will make the procedure easier to understand.

CAUTION

A **Caution** provides a special procedure or special steps which must be taken while completing the procedure where the Caution is found. Not heeding a Caution can result in damage to the assembly being worked on.

WARNING

A **Warning** provides a special procedure or special steps which must be taken while completing the procedure where the Warning is found. Not heeding a Warning can result in personal injury.

Introduction to the Chrysler Sebring, Dodge Avenger and Stratus

The Chrysler Sebring models are available in convertible, coupe and four-door sedan body styles. The Dodge Avenger is only available as a coupe while the Stratus is offered in both coupe and four-door sedan type body styles. They feature transversely mounted engines offered in a variety of displacements: 2.0L and 2.4L four-cylinder engines and 2.5L, 2.7L and 3.0L V6 engines.

All models are equipped with an electronically controlled multi-port electronic fuel injection system.

The engine transmits power to the front wheels through either a five-speed manual transaxle or a four-speed automatic transaxle via independent driveaxles.

All models feature an all steel unibody design and independent front and rear suspension. The front suspension on all models - except 2001 and later coupes - incorporates a shock absorber/coil spring assembly with upper and lower control arms; 2001 and later coupe models use a MacPherson strut design. The rear suspension on all models utilizes a shock absorber/coil spring assembly and upper control arm in combination with a trailing arm and lateral links.

The standard power rack-and-pinion steering unit is mounted behind the engine on the front suspension crossmember.

All models are equipped with power assisted front disc and rear disc or drum brakes with an Anti-lock Brake System (ABS) available as an option.

Vehicle identification numbers

Modifications are a continuing and unpublicized process in vehicle manufacturing. Since spare parts manuals and lists are compiled on a numerical basis, the individual vehicle numbers are essential to correctly identify the component required.

Vehicle Identification Number (VIN)

This very important identification number is located on a plate attached to the dashboard inside the windshield on the driver's side of the vehicle **(see illustration)**. The VIN also appears on the Vehicle Certificate of Title and Registration. It contains information such as where and when the vehicle was manufactured, the model year and the body style.

VIN engine and model year codes

Two particularly important pieces of information found in the VIN are the engine code and the model year code. Counting from the left, the engine code letter designation is the 8th digit and the model year code designation is the 10th digit.

On the models covered by this manual the engine codes are:

1995
Sebring/Avenger coupe
Y	2.0L 4-cyl DOHC
N	2.5L V6 SOHC

1996
Sebring/Avenger coupe
Y	2.0L 4-cyl DOHC
N	2.5L V6 SOHC

Sebring convertible
X	2.4L 4-cyl DOHC
H	2.5L V6 SOHC

1997
Sebring/Avenger coupe
Y	2.0L 4-cyl DOHC
N	2.5L V6 SOHC

Sebring convertible
X	2.4L 4-cyl DOHC
H	2.5L V6 SOHC

1998
Sebring/Avenger coupe
Y	2.0L 4-cyl DOHC
N	2.5L V6 SOHC

Sebring convertible
X	2.4L 4-cyl DOHC
H	2.5L V6 SOHC

1999
Sebring/Avenger coupe
Y	2.0L 4-cyl DOHC
N	2.5L V6 SOHC

Sebring convertible
X	2.4L 4-cyl DOHC
H	2.5L V6 SOHC

2000
Sebring/Avenger coupe
N	2.5L V6 SOHC

Sebring convertible
H	2.5L V6 SOHC

2001
Sebring/Stratus coupe
G	2.4L 4-cyl SOHC
H	3.0L V6 SOHC

Sebring/Stratus sedan/convertible
Y	2.0L 4-cyl DOHC
X	2.4L 4-cyl DOHC
U	2.7L V6 DOHC

2002
Sebring/Stratus coupe
G	2.4L 4-cyl SOHC
H	3.0L V6 SOHC

Sebring/Stratus sedan/convertible
Y	2.0L 4-cyl DOHC
X	2.4L 4-cyl DOHC
R	2.7L V6 DOHC

2003
Y	2.0L 4-cyl DOHC
R	2.7L V6 DOHC
G, X	2.4L 4-cyl DOHC
H	3.0L V6 SOHC

2004 and 2005
J	2.4L 4-cyl PZEV
R	2.7L V6 DOHC
G, X	2.4L 4-cyl DOHC
Y	2.0L 4-cyl DOHC
H	3.0L V6 SOHC

2006
G, X	2.4L 4-cyl DOHC
R	2.7L V6 DOHC

On the models covered by this manual the model year codes are:

S	1995
T	1996
V	1997
W	1998
X	1999
Y	2000
1	2001
2	2002
3	2003
4	2004
5	2005
6	2006

Body Code Plate

The Body Code Plate is a stamped metal plate attached in the engine compartment. It contains more specific information about the manufacturing of the vehicle such as the paint code, trim code and vehicle order number, as well as the VIN.

Vehicle Safety Certification label

The Vehicle Safety Certification label is attached to the driver's side door end **(see illustration)**. The label contains the name of the manufacturer, the month and year of production, the Gross Vehicle Weight Rating (GVWR), the Gross Axle Weight Rating (GAWR) and the certification statement.

The Vehicle Identification Number (VIN) is stamped into a metal plate fastened to the dashboard on the driver's side - it's visible through the windshield

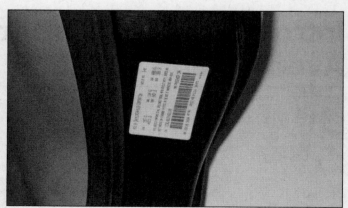

The Vehicle Safety Certification label is affixed to the driver's door pillar

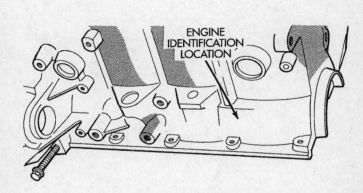

On 2.4L four-cylinder engines, the engine identification number is stamped on the left rear of the engine block (behind the starter motor)

The transaxle identification number can be found on the top of the case (as shown) or on the side the of the bellhousing

Engine identification numbers

The four-cylinder engine identification numbers can be found stamped on a machined pad on the transmission end of the engine block **(see illustration)**. V6 engine identification is located on the transmission end of the engine block just below the cylinder head.

Transaxle identification numbers

The transaxle identification information can be found on a bar code label located on the front of the transaxle **(see illustration)**.

Vehicle Emissions Control Information (VECI) label

The emissions control information label is found under the hood, normally on the radiator support or the bottom side of the hood. This label contains information on the emissions control equipment installed on the vehicle, as well as tune-up specifications (see Chapter 6 for more information).

Buying parts

Replacement parts are available from many sources, which generally fall into one of two categories - authorized dealer parts departments and independent retail auto parts stores. Our advice concerning these parts is as follows:

Retail auto parts stores: Good auto parts stores will stock frequently needed components which wear out relatively fast, such as clutch components, exhaust systems, brake parts, tune-up parts, etc. These stores often supply new or reconditioned parts on an exchange basis, which can save a considerable amount of money. Discount auto parts stores are often very good places to buy materials and parts needed for general vehicle maintenance such as oil, grease, filters, spark plugs, belts, touch-up paint, bulbs, etc. They also usually sell tools and general accessories, have convenient hours, charge lower prices and can often be found not far from home.

Authorized dealer parts department: This is the best source for parts which are unique to the vehicle and not generally available elsewhere (such as major engine parts, transmission parts, trim pieces, etc.).

Warranty information: If the vehicle is still covered under warranty, be sure that any replacement parts purchased - regardless of the source - do not invalidate the warranty!

To be sure of obtaining the correct parts, have engine and chassis numbers available and, if possible, take the old parts along for positive identification.

Maintenance techniques, tools and working facilities

Maintenance techniques

There are a number of techniques involved in maintenance and repair that will be referred to throughout this manual. Application of these techniques will enable the home mechanic to be more efficient, better organized and capable of performing the various tasks properly, which will ensure that the repair job is thorough and complete.

Fasteners

Fasteners are nuts, bolts, studs and screws used to hold two or more parts together. There are a few things to keep in mind when working with fasteners. Almost all of them use a locking device of some type, either a lockwasher, locknut, locking tab or thread adhesive. All threaded fasteners should be clean and straight, with undamaged threads and undamaged corners on the hex head where the wrench fits. Develop the habit of replacing all damaged nuts and bolts with new ones. Special locknuts with nylon or fiber inserts can only be used once. If they are removed, they lose their locking ability and must be replaced with new ones.

Rusted nuts and bolts should be treated with a penetrating fluid to ease removal and prevent breakage. Some mechanics use turpentine in a spout-type oil can, which works quite well. After applying the rust penetrant, let it work for a few minutes before trying to loosen the nut or bolt. Badly rusted fasteners may have to be chiseled or sawed off or removed with a special nut breaker, available at tool stores.

If a bolt or stud breaks off in an assembly, it can be drilled and removed with a special tool commonly available for this purpose. Most automotive machine shops can perform this task, as well as other repair procedures, such as the repair of threaded holes that have been stripped out.

Flat washers and lockwashers, when removed from an assembly, should always be replaced exactly as removed. Replace any damaged washers with new ones. Never use a lockwasher on any soft metal surface (such as aluminum), thin sheet metal or plastic.

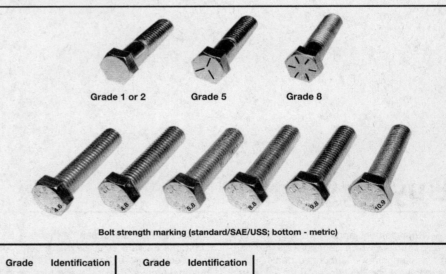

Grade 1 or 2   Grade 5   Grade 8

Bolt strength marking (standard/SAE/USS; bottom - metric)

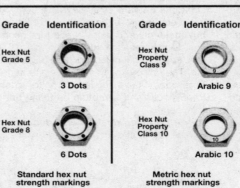

Grade	Identification
Hex Nut Grade 5	3 Dots
Hex Nut Grade 8	6 Dots

Standard hex nut strength markings

Grade	Identification
Hex Nut Property Class 9	Arabic 9
Hex Nut Property Class 10	Arabic 10

Metric hex nut strength markings

Class 10.9   Class 9.8   Class 8.8

Metric stud strength markings

00-1 HAYNES

Fastener sizes

For a number of reasons, automobile manufacturers are making wider and wider use of metric fasteners. Therefore, it is important to be able to tell the difference between standard (sometimes called U.S. or SAE) and metric hardware, since they cannot be interchanged.

All bolts, whether standard or metric, are sized according to diameter, thread pitch and length. For example, a standard 1/2 - 13 x 1 bolt is 1/2 inch in diameter, has 13 threads per inch and is 1 inch long. An M12 - 1.75 x 25 metric bolt is 12 mm in diameter, has a thread pitch of 1.75 mm (the distance between threads) and is 25 mm long. The two bolts are nearly identical, and easily confused, but they are not interchangeable.

In addition to the differences in diameter, thread pitch and length, metric and standard bolts can also be distinguished by examining the bolt heads. To begin with, the distance across the flats on a standard bolt head is measured in inches, while the same dimension on a metric bolt is sized in millimeters (the same is true for nuts). As a result, a standard wrench should not be used on a metric bolt and a metric wrench should not be used on a standard bolt. Also, most standard bolts have slashes radiating out from the center of the head to denote the grade or strength of the bolt, which is an indication of the amount of torque that can be applied to it. The greater the number of slashes, the greater the strength of the bolt. Grades 0 through 5 are commonly used on automobiles. Metric bolts have a property class (grade) number, rather than a slash, molded into their heads to indicate bolt strength. In this case, the higher the number, the stronger the bolt. Property class numbers 8.8, 9.8 and 10.9 are commonly used on automobiles.

Strength markings can also be used to distinguish standard hex nuts from metric hex nuts. Many standard nuts have dots stamped into one side, while metric nuts are marked with a number. The greater the number of dots, or the higher the number, the greater the strength of the nut.

Metric studs are also marked on their ends according to property class (grade). Larger studs are numbered (the same as metric bolts), while smaller studs carry a geometric code to denote grade.

It should be noted that many fasteners, especially Grades 0 through 2, have no distinguishing marks on them. When such is the case, the only way to determine whether it is standard or metric is to measure the thread pitch or compare it to a known fastener of the same size.

Standard fasteners are often referred to as SAE, as opposed to metric. However, it should be noted that SAE technically refers to a non-metric fine thread fastener only. Coarse thread non-metric fasteners are referred to as USS sizes.

Since fasteners of the same size (both standard and metric) may have different strength ratings, be sure to reinstall any bolts, studs or nuts removed from your vehicle in their original locations. Also, when replacing a fastener with a new one, make sure that the new one has a strength rating equal to or greater than the original.

Metric thread sizes	Ft-lbs	Nm
M-6	6 to 9	9 to 12
M-8	14 to 21	19 to 28
M-10	28 to 40	38 to 54
M-12	50 to 71	68 to 96
M-14	80 to 140	109 to 154

Pipe thread sizes		
1/8	5 to 8	7 to 10
1/4	12 to 18	17 to 24
3/8	22 to 33	30 to 44
1/2	25 to 35	34 to 47

U.S. thread sizes		
1/4 - 20	6 to 9	9 to 12
5/16 - 18	12 to 18	17 to 24
5/16 - 24	14 to 20	19 to 27
3/8 - 16	22 to 32	30 to 43
3/8 - 24	27 to 38	37 to 51
7/16 - 14	40 to 55	55 to 74
7/16 - 20	40 to 60	55 to 81
1/2 - 13	55 to 80	75 to 108

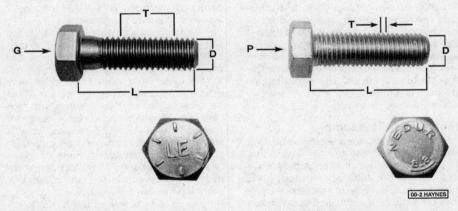

Standard (SAE and USS) bolt dimensions/ grade marks

G	Grade marks (bolt strength)
L	Length (in inches)
T	Thread pitch (number of threads per inch)
D	Nominal diameter (in inches)

Metric bolt dimensions/grade marks

P	Property class (bolt strength)
L	Length (in millimeters)
T	Thread pitch (distance between threads in millimeters)
D	Diameter

Tightening sequences and procedures

Most threaded fasteners should be tightened to a specific torque value (torque is the twisting force applied to a threaded component such as a nut or bolt). Overtightening the fastener can weaken it and cause it to break, while undertightening can cause it to eventually come loose. Bolts, screws and studs, depending on the material they are made of and their thread diameters, have specific torque values, many of which are noted in the Specifications at the beginning of each Chapter. Be sure to follow the torque recommendations closely. For fasteners not assigned a specific torque, a general torque value chart is presented here as a guide. These torque values are for dry (unlubricated) fasteners threaded into steel or cast iron (not aluminum). As was previously mentioned, the size and grade of a fastener determine the amount of torque that can safely be applied to it. The figures listed here are approximate for Grade 2 and Grade 3 fasteners. Higher grades can tolerate higher torque values.

Fasteners laid out in a pattern, such as cylinder head bolts, oil pan bolts, differential cover bolts, etc., must be loosened or tight-

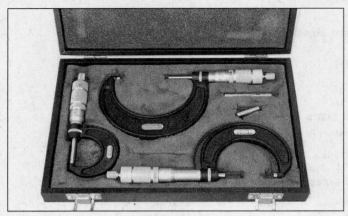

Micrometer set

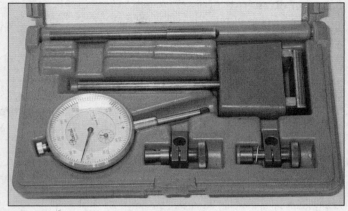

Dial indicator set

ened in sequence to avoid warping the component. This sequence will normally be shown in the appropriate Chapter. If a specific pattern is not given, the following procedures can be used to prevent warping.

Initially, the bolts or nuts should be assembled finger-tight only. Next, they should be tightened one full turn each, in a crisscross or diagonal pattern. After each one has been tightened one full turn, return to the first one and tighten them all one-half turn, following the same pattern. Finally, tighten each of them one-quarter turn at a time until each fastener has been tightened to the proper torque. To loosen and remove the fasteners, the procedure would be reversed.

Component disassembly

Component disassembly should be done with care and purpose to help ensure that the parts go back together properly. Always keep track of the sequence in which parts are removed. Make note of special characteristics or marks on parts that can be installed more than one way, such as a grooved thrust washer on a shaft. It is a good idea to lay the disassembled parts out on a clean surface in the order that they were removed. It may also be helpful to make sketches or take instant photos of components before removal.

When removing fasteners from a component, keep track of their locations. Sometimes threading a bolt back in a part, or putting the washers and nut back on a stud, can prevent mix-ups later. If nuts and bolts cannot be returned to their original locations, they should be kept in a compartmented box or a series of small boxes. A cupcake or muffin tin is ideal for this purpose, since each cavity can hold the bolts and nuts from a particular area (i.e. oil pan bolts, valve cover bolts, engine mount bolts, etc.). A pan of this type is especially helpful when working on assemblies with very small parts, such as the carburetor, alternator, valve train or interior dash and trim pieces. The cavities can be marked with paint or tape to identify the contents.

Whenever wiring looms, harnesses or connectors are separated, it is a good idea to

identify the two halves with numbered pieces of masking tape so they can be easily reconnected.

Gasket sealing surfaces

Throughout any vehicle, gaskets are used to seal the mating surfaces between two parts and keep lubricants, fluids, vacuum or pressure contained in an assembly.

Many times these gaskets are coated with a liquid or paste-type gasket sealing compound before assembly. Age, heat and pressure can sometimes cause the two parts to stick together so tightly that they are very difficult to separate. Often, the assembly can be loosened by striking it with a soft-face hammer near the mating surfaces. A regular hammer can be used if a block of wood is placed between the hammer and the part. Do not hammer on cast parts or parts that could be easily damaged. With any particularly stubborn part, always recheck to make sure that every fastener has been removed.

Avoid using a screwdriver or bar to pry apart an assembly, as they can easily mar the gasket sealing surfaces of the parts, which must remain smooth. If prying is absolutely necessary, use an old broom handle, but keep in mind that extra clean up will be necessary if the wood splinters.

After the parts are separated, the old gasket must be carefully scraped off and the gasket surfaces cleaned. Stubborn gasket material can be soaked with rust penetrant or treated with a special chemical to soften it so it can be easily scraped off. A scraper can be fashioned from a piece of copper tubing by flattening and sharpening one end. Copper is recommended because it is usually softer than the surfaces to be scraped, which reduces the chance of gouging the part. Some gaskets can be removed with a wire brush, but regardless of the method used, the mating surfaces must be left clean and smooth. If for some reason the gasket surface is gouged, then a gasket sealer thick enough to fill scratches will have to be used during reassembly of the components. For most applications, a non-drying (or semi-drying) gasket sealer should be used.

Hose removal tips

Warning: *If the vehicle is equipped with air conditioning, do not disconnect any of the A/C hoses without first having the system depressurized by a dealer service department or a service station.*

Hose removal precautions closely parallel gasket removal precautions. Avoid scratching or gouging the surface that the hose mates against or the connection may leak. This is especially true for radiator hoses. Because of various chemical reactions, the rubber in hoses can bond itself to the metal spigot that the hose fits over. To remove a hose, first loosen the hose clamps that secure it to the spigot. Then, with slip-joint pliers, grab the hose at the clamp and rotate it around the spigot. Work it back and forth until it is completely free, then pull it off. Silicone or other lubricants will ease removal if they can be applied between the hose and the outside of the spigot. Apply the same lubricant to the inside of the hose and the outside of the spigot to simplify installation.

As a last resort (and if the hose is to be replaced with a new one anyway), the rubber can be slit with a knife and the hose peeled from the spigot. If this must be done, be careful that the metal connection is not damaged.

If a hose clamp is broken or damaged, do not reuse it. Wire-type clamps usually weaken with age, so it is a good idea to replace them with screw-type clamps whenever a hose is removed.

Tools

A selection of good tools is a basic requirement for anyone who plans to maintain and repair his or her own vehicle. For the owner who has few tools, the initial investment might seem high, but when compared to the spiraling costs of professional auto maintenance and repair, it is a wise one.

To help the owner decide which tools are needed to perform the tasks detailed in this manual, the following tool lists are offered: *Maintenance and minor repair, Repair/overhaul* and *Special.*

The newcomer to practical mechanics

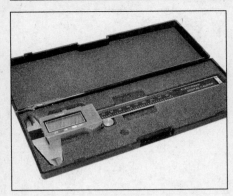

Dial caliper

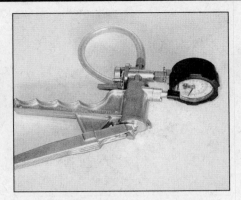

Hand-operated vacuum pump

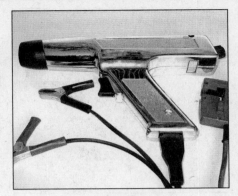

Timing light

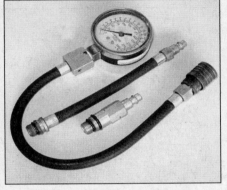

Compression gauge with spark plug hole adapter

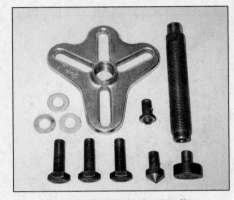

Damper/steering wheel puller

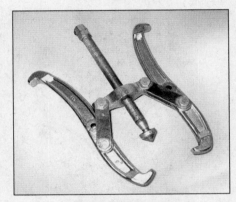

General purpose puller

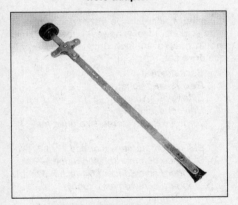

Hydraulic lifter removal tool

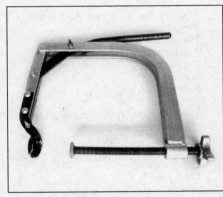

Valve spring compressor

Valve spring compressor

Ridge reamer

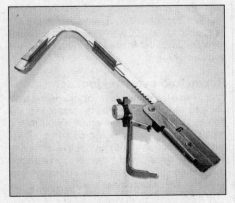

Piston ring groove cleaning tool

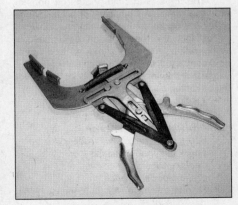

Ring removal/installation tool

Ring compressor

Cylinder hone

Brake hold-down spring tool

Torque angle gauge

Clutch plate alignment tool

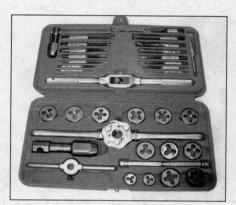

Tap and die set

should start off with the *maintenance and minor repair* tool kit, which is adequate for the simpler jobs performed on a vehicle. Then, as confidence and experience grow, the owner can tackle more difficult tasks, buying additional tools as they are needed. Eventually the basic kit will be expanded into the *repair and overhaul* tool set. Over a period of time, the experienced do-it-yourselfer will assemble a tool set complete enough for most repair and overhaul procedures and will add tools from the special category when it is felt that the expense is justified by the frequency of use.

Maintenance and minor repair tool kit

The tools in this list should be considered the minimum required for performance of routine maintenance, servicing and minor repair work. We recommend the purchase of combination wrenches (box-end and open-end combined in one wrench). While more expensive than open end wrenches, they offer the advantages of both types of wrench.

Combination wrench set (1/4-inch to 1 inch or 6 mm to 19 mm)
Adjustable wrench, 8 inch
Spark plug wrench with rubber insert
Spark plug gap adjusting tool
Feeler gauge set
Brake bleeder wrench
Standard screwdriver (5/16-inch x 6 inch)

Phillips screwdriver (No. 2 x 6 inch)
Combination pliers - 6 inch
Hacksaw and assortment of blades
Tire pressure gauge
Grease gun
Oil can
Fine emery cloth
Wire brush
Battery post and cable cleaning tool
Oil filter wrench
Funnel (medium size)
Safety goggles
Jackstands (2)
Drain pan

Note: *If basic tune-ups are going to be part of routine maintenance, it will be necessary to purchase a good quality stroboscopic timing light and combination tachometer/dwell meter. Although they are included in the list of special tools, it is mentioned here because they are absolutely necessary for tuning most vehicles properly.*

Repair and overhaul tool set

These tools are essential for anyone who plans to perform major repairs and are in addition to those in the maintenance and minor repair tool kit. Included is a comprehensive set of sockets which, though expensive, are invaluable because of their versatility, especially when various extensions and drives are available. We recommend the 1/2-inch drive over the 3/8-inch drive. Although the larger drive is bulky and more expensive, it has the

capacity of accepting a very wide range of large sockets. Ideally, however, the mechanic should have a 3/8-inch drive set and a 1/2-inch drive set.

Socket set(s)
Reversible ratchet
Extension - 10 inch
Universal joint
Torque wrench (same size drive as sockets)
Ball peen hammer - 8 ounce
Soft-face hammer (plastic/rubber)
Standard screwdriver (1/4-inch x 6 inch)
Standard screwdriver (stubby - 5/16-inch)
Phillips screwdriver (No. 3 x 8 inch)
Phillips screwdriver (stubby - No. 2)
Pliers - vise grip
Pliers - lineman's
Pliers - needle nose
Pliers - snap-ring (internal and external)
Cold chisel - 1/2-inch
Scribe
Scraper (made from flattened copper tubing)
Centerpunch
Pin punches (1/16, 1/8, 3/16-inch)
Steel rule/straightedge - 12 inch
Allen wrench set (1/8 to 3/8-inch or 4 mm to 10 mm)
A selection of files
Wire brush (large)
Jackstands (second set)
Jack (scissor or hydraulic type)

Note: *Another tool which is often useful is an electric drill with a chuck capacity of 3/8-inch and a set of good quality drill bits.*

Special tools

The tools in this list include those which are not used regularly, are expensive to buy, or which need to be used in accordance with their manufacturer's instructions. Unless these tools will be used frequently, it is not very economical to purchase many of them. A consideration would be to split the cost and use between yourself and a friend or friends. In addition, most of these tools can be obtained from a tool rental shop on a temporary basis.

This list primarily contains only those tools and instruments widely available to the public, and not those special tools produced by the vehicle manufacturer for distribution to dealer service departments. Occasionally, references to the manufacturer's special tools are included in the text of this manual. Generally, an alternative method of doing the job without the special tool is offered. However, sometimes there is no alternative to their use. Where this is the case, and the tool cannot be purchased or borrowed, the work should be turned over to the dealer service department or an automotive repair shop.

Valve spring compressor
Piston ring groove cleaning tool
Piston ring compressor
Piston ring installation tool
Cylinder compression gauge
Cylinder ridge reamer
Cylinder surfacing hone
Cylinder bore gauge
Micrometers and/or dial calipers
Hydraulic lifter removal tool
Balljoint separator
Universal-type puller
Impact screwdriver
Dial indicator set
Stroboscopic timing light (inductive pick-up)
Hand operated vacuum/pressure pump
Tachometer/dwell meter
Universal electrical multimeter
Cable hoist
Brake spring removal and installation tools
Floor jack

Buying tools

For the do-it-yourselfer who is just starting to get involved in vehicle maintenance and repair, there are a number of options available when purchasing tools. If maintenance and minor repair is the extent of the work to be done, the purchase of individual tools is satisfactory. If, on the other hand, extensive work is planned, it would be a good idea to purchase a modest tool set from one of the large retail chain stores. A set can usually be bought at a substantial savings over the individual tool prices, and they often come with a tool box. As additional tools are needed, add-on sets,

individual tools and a larger tool box can be purchased to expand the tool selection. Building a tool set gradually allows the cost of the tools to be spread over a longer period of time and gives the mechanic the freedom to choose only those tools that will actually be used.

Tool stores will often be the only source of some of the special tools that are needed, but regardless of where tools are bought, try to avoid cheap ones, especially when buying screwdrivers and sockets, because they won't last very long. The expense involved in replacing cheap tools will eventually be greater than the initial cost of quality tools.

Care and maintenance of tools

Good tools are expensive, so it makes sense to treat them with respect. Keep them clean and in usable condition and store them properly when not in use. Always wipe off any dirt, grease or metal chips before putting them away. Never leave tools lying around in the work area. Upon completion of a job, always check closely under the hood for tools that may have been left there so they won't get lost during a test drive.

Some tools, such as screwdrivers, pliers, wrenches and sockets, can be hung on a panel mounted on the garage or workshop wall, while others should be kept in a tool box or tray. Measuring instruments, gauges, meters, etc. must be carefully stored where they cannot be damaged by weather or impact from other tools.

When tools are used with care and stored properly, they will last a very long time. Even with the best of care, though, tools will wear out if used frequently. When a tool is damaged or worn out, replace it. Subsequent jobs will be safer and more enjoyable if you do.

How to repair damaged threads

Sometimes, the internal threads of a nut or bolt hole can become stripped, usually from overtightening. Stripping threads is an all-too-common occurrence, especially when working with aluminum parts, because aluminum is so soft that it easily strips out.

Usually, external or internal threads are only partially stripped. After they've been cleaned up with a tap or die, they'll still work. Sometimes, however, threads are badly damaged. When this happens, you've got three choices:

1) *Drill and tap the hole to the next suitable oversize and install a larger diameter bolt, screw or stud.*
2) *Drill and tap the hole to accept a threaded plug, then drill and tap the plug to the original screw size. You can also buy a plug already threaded to the original size. Then you simply drill a hole to the specified size, then run the threaded plug into the hole with a bolt and jam nut.*

Once the plug is fully seated, remove the jam nut and bolt.
3) *The third method uses a patented thread repair kit like Heli-Coil or Slimsert. These easy-to-use kits are designed to repair damaged threads in straight-through holes and blind holes. Both are available as kits which can handle a variety of sizes and thread patterns. Drill the hole, then tap it with the special included tap. Install the Heli-Coil and the hole is back to its original diameter and thread pitch.*

Regardless of which method you use, be sure to proceed calmly and carefully. A little impatience or carelessness during one of these relatively simple procedures can ruin your whole day's work and cost you a bundle if you wreck an expensive part.

Working facilities

Not to be overlooked when discussing tools is the workshop. If anything more than routine maintenance is to be carried out, some sort of suitable work area is essential.

It is understood, and appreciated, that many home mechanics do not have a good workshop or garage available, and end up removing an engine or doing major repairs outside. It is recommended, however, that the overhaul or repair be completed under the cover of a roof.

A clean, flat workbench or table of comfortable working height is an absolute necessity. The workbench should be equipped with a vise that has a jaw opening of at least four inches.

As mentioned previously, some clean, dry storage space is also required for tools, as well as the lubricants, fluids, cleaning solvents, etc. which soon become necessary.

Sometimes waste oil and fluids, drained from the engine or cooling system during normal maintenance or repairs, present a disposal problem. To avoid pouring them on the ground or into a sewage system, pour the used fluids into large containers, seal them with caps and take them to an authorized disposal site or recycling center. Plastic jugs, such as old antifreeze containers, are ideal for this purpose.

Always keep a supply of old newspapers and clean rags available. Old towels are excellent for mopping up spills. Many mechanics use rolls of paper towels for most work because they are readily available and disposable. To help keep the area under the vehicle clean, a large cardboard box can be cut open and flattened to protect the garage or shop floor.

Whenever working over a painted surface, such as when leaning over a fender to service something under the hood, always cover it with an old blanket or bedspread to protect the finish. Vinyl covered pads, made especially for this purpose, are available at auto parts stores.

Jacking and towing

Jacking

Warning: *The jack supplied with the vehicle should only be used for changing a tire or placing jackstands under the frame. Never work under the vehicle or start the engine while this jack is being used as the only means of support.*

The vehicle should be on level ground. Place the shift lever in Park, if you have an automatic, or Reverse if you have a manual transaxle. Block the wheel diagonally opposite the wheel being changed. Set the parking brake.

Remove the spare tire and jack from stowage. Remove the wheel cover and trim ring (if so equipped) with the tapered end of the lug nut wrench by inserting and twisting the handle and then prying against the back of the wheel cover. Loosen the wheel lug nuts about 1/4-to-1/2 turn each.

Place the scissors-type jack under the side of the vehicle and adjust the jack height until it fits in the notch in the vertical rocker panel flange nearest the wheel to be changed. There is a front and rear jacking point on each side of the vehicle **(see illustration)**.

Turn the jack handle clockwise until the tire clears the ground. Remove the lug nuts and pull the wheel off. Replace it with the spare.

Install the lug nuts with the beveled edges facing in. Tighten them snugly. Don't attempt to tighten them completely until the vehicle is lowered or it could slip off the jack. Turn the jack handle counterclockwise to lower the vehicle. Remove the jack and tighten the lug nuts in a diagonal pattern.

Install the cover (and trim ring, if used) and be sure it's snapped into place all the way around.

Stow the tire, jack and wrench. Unblock the wheels.

Towing

As a general rule, the vehicle should be towed with the front (drive) wheels off the ground. If they can't be raised, place them on a dolly. The ignition key must be in the ACC position, since the steering lock mechanism isn't strong enough to hold the front wheels straight while towing.

Vehicles equipped with an automatic transaxle can be towed from the front only with all four wheels on the ground, provided that speeds don't exceed 25 mph and the distance is not over 15 miles. Before towing, check the transmission fluid level (see Chapter 1). If the level is below the HOT line on the dipstick, add fluid or use a towing dolly.

Caution: *Never tow a vehicle with an automatic transaxle from the rear with the front wheels on the ground.*

When towing a vehicle equipped with a manual transaxle with all four wheels on the ground, be sure to place the shift lever in Neutral and release the parking brake.

Equipment specifically designed for towing should be used. It should be attached to the main structural members of the vehicle, not the bumpers, brackets or suspension.

Safety is a major consideration when towing and all applicable state and local laws must be obeyed. A safety chain system must be used at all times.

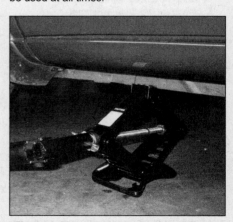

The jack fits over the rocker panel flange (there are two jacking points on each side of the vehicle, indicated by a notch in the rocker panel flange)

Booster battery (jump) starting

Observe these precautions when using a booster battery to start a vehicle:

a) *Before connecting the booster battery, make sure the ignition switch is in the OFF position.*
b) *Turn off the lights, heater and other electrical loads.*
c) *Your eyes should be shielded. Safety goggles are a good idea.*
d) *Make sure the booster battery is the same voltage as the dead one in the vehicle.*
e) *The two vehicles MUST NOT TOUCH each other!*

f) *Make sure the transaxle is in Neutral (manual) or Park (automatic).*
g) *If the booster battery is not a maintenance-free type, remove the vent caps and lay a cloth over the vent holes.*

On convertible and sedan models the battery is located in front of the left front wheel-well. Due to the lack of accessibility, remote battery connections are provided inside the engine compartment for jump-starting and easy battery disconnection **(see illustration)**. On coupe models, the battery is located in the conventional position in the engine compartment.

Connect the red colored jumper cable to the positive (+) terminal of booster battery and the other end to the positive (+) remote terminal inside the engine compartment (convertible and sedan models) or to the positive terminal of the battery (coupe models). Then connect one end of the black colored jumper cable to the negative (-) terminal of the booster battery and other end of the cable to the negative (-) remote terminal (convertible and sedan models) or to a good ground point on the engine of the disabled vehicle (coupe models) **(see illustration)**.

Start the engine using the booster battery then, with the engine running at idle speed disconnect the jumper cables in the reverse order of connection.

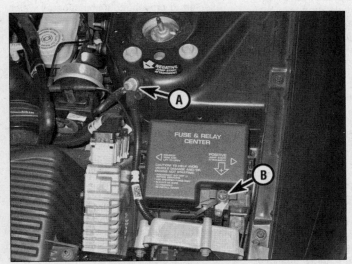

On convertible and sedan models, the remote battery terminals are located in the engine compartment and well marked - when connecting jumper cables connect the cable to the positive terminal (A) first, then the negative terminal (B)

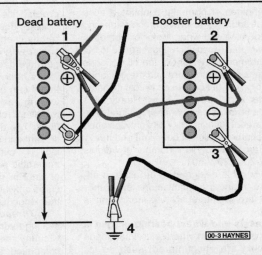

On coupe models make the booster cable connections in the numerical order shown (note that the negative cable of the booster battery is NOT attached to the negative terminal of the dead battery)

Automotive chemicals and lubricants

A number of automotive chemicals and lubricants are available for use during vehicle maintenance and repair. They include a wide variety of products ranging from cleaning solvents and degreasers to lubricants and protective sprays for rubber, plastic and vinyl.

Cleaners

Carburetor cleaner and choke cleaner is a strong solvent for gum, varnish and carbon. Most carburetor cleaners leave a dry-type lubricant film which will not harden or gum up. Because of this film it is not recommended for use on electrical components.

Brake system cleaner is used to remove brake dust, grease and brake fluid from the brake system, where clean surfaces are absolutely necessary. It leaves no residue and often eliminates brake squeal caused by contaminants.

Electrical cleaner removes oxidation, corrosion and carbon deposits from electrical contacts, restoring full current flow. It can also be used to clean spark plugs, carburetor jets, voltage regulators and other parts where an oil-free surface is desired.

Demoisturants remove water and moisture from electrical components such as alternators, voltage regulators, electrical connectors and fuse blocks. They are non-conductive and non-corrosive.

Degreasers are heavy-duty solvents used to remove grease from the outside of the engine and from chassis components. They can be sprayed or brushed on and, depending on the type, are rinsed off either with water or solvent.

Lubricants

Motor oil is the lubricant formulated for use in engines. It normally contains a wide variety of additives to prevent corrosion and reduce foaming and wear. Motor oil comes in various weights (viscosity ratings) from 0 to 50. The recommended weight of the oil depends on the season, temperature and the demands on the engine. Light oil is used in cold climates and under light load conditions. Heavy oil is used in hot climates and where high loads are encountered. Multi-viscosity oils are designed to have characteristics of both light and heavy oils and are available in a number of weights from 0W-20 to 20W-50.

Gear oil is designed to be used in differentials, manual transmissions and other areas where high-temperature lubrication is required.

Chassis and wheel bearing grease is a heavy grease used where increased loads and friction are encountered, such as for wheel bearings, balljoints, tie-rod ends and universal joints.

High-temperature wheel bearing grease is designed to withstand the extreme temperatures encountered by wheel bearings

in disc brake equipped vehicles. It usually contains molybdenum disulfide (moly), which is a dry-type lubricant.

White grease is a heavy grease for metal-to-metal applications where water is a problem. White grease stays soft under both low and high temperatures (usually from -100 to +190-degrees F), and will not wash off or dilute in the presence of water.

Assembly lube is a special extreme pressure lubricant, usually containing moly, used to lubricate high-load parts (such as main and rod bearings and cam lobes) for initial start-up of a new engine. The assembly lube lubricates the parts without being squeezed out or washed away until the engine oiling system begins to function.

Silicone lubricants are used to protect rubber, plastic, vinyl and nylon parts.

Graphite lubricants are used where oils cannot be used due to contamination problems, such as in locks. The dry graphite will lubricate metal parts while remaining uncontaminated by dirt, water, oil or acids. It is electrically conductive and will not foul electrical contacts in locks such as the ignition switch.

Moly penetrants loosen and lubricate frozen, rusted and corroded fasteners and prevent future rusting or freezing.

Heat-sink grease is a special electrically non-conductive grease that is used for mounting electronic ignition modules where it is essential that heat is transferred away from the module.

Sealants

RTV sealant is one of the most widely used gasket compounds. Made from silicone, RTV is air curing, it seals, bonds, waterproofs, fills surface irregularities, remains flexible, doesn't shrink, is relatively easy to remove, and is used as a supplementary sealer with almost all low and medium temperature gaskets.

Anaerobic sealant is much like RTV in that it can be used either to seal gaskets or to form gaskets by itself. It remains flexible, is solvent resistant and fills surface imperfections. The difference between an anaerobic sealant and an RTV-type sealant is in the curing. RTV cures when exposed to air, while an anaerobic sealant cures only in the absence of air. This means that an anaerobic sealant cures only after the assembly of parts, sealing them together.

Thread and pipe sealant is used for sealing hydraulic and pneumatic fittings and vacuum lines. It is usually made from a Teflon compound, and comes in a spray, a paint-on liquid and as a wrap-around tape.

Chemicals

Anti-seize compound prevents seizing, galling, cold welding, rust and corrosion in

fasteners. High-temperature anti-seize, usually made with copper and graphite lubricants, is used for exhaust system and exhaust manifold bolts.

Anaerobic locking compounds are used to keep fasteners from vibrating or working loose and cure only after installation, in the absence of air. Medium strength locking compound is used for small nuts, bolts and screws that may be removed later. High-strength locking compound is for large nuts, bolts and studs which aren't removed on a regular basis.

Oil additives range from viscosity index improvers to chemical treatments that claim to reduce internal engine friction. It should be noted that most oil manufacturers caution against using additives with their oils.

Gas additives perform several functions, depending on their chemical makeup. They usually contain solvents that help dissolve gum and varnish that build up on carburetor, fuel injection and intake parts. They also serve to break down carbon deposits that form on the inside surfaces of the combustion chambers. Some additives contain upper cylinder lubricants for valves and piston rings, and others contain chemicals to remove condensation from the gas tank.

Miscellaneous

Brake fluid is specially formulated hydraulic fluid that can withstand the heat and pressure encountered in brake systems. Care must be taken so this fluid does not come in contact with painted surfaces or plastics. An opened container should always be resealed to prevent contamination by water or dirt.

Weatherstrip adhesive is used to bond weatherstripping around doors, windows and trunk lids. It is sometimes used to attach trim pieces.

Undercoating is a petroleum-based, tar-like substance that is designed to protect metal surfaces on the underside of the vehicle from corrosion. It also acts as a sound-deadening agent by insulating the bottom of the vehicle.

Waxes and polishes are used to help protect painted and plated surfaces from the weather. Different types of paint may require the use of different types of wax and polish. Some polishes utilize a chemical or abrasive cleaner to help remove the top layer of oxidized (dull) paint on older vehicles. In recent years many non-wax polishes that contain a wide variety of chemicals such as polymers and silicones have been introduced. These non-wax polishes are usually easier to apply and last longer than conventional waxes and polishes.

Conversion factors

Length (distance)
Inches (in)	X	25.4	= Millimeters (mm)	X 0.0394	= Inches (in)
Feet (ft)	X	0.305	= Meters (m)	X 3.281	= Feet (ft)
Miles	X	1.609	= Kilometers (km)	X 0.621	= Miles

Volume (capacity)
Cubic inches (cu in; in^3)	X	16.387	= Cubic centimeters (cc; cm^3)	X 0.061	= Cubic inches (cu in; in^3)
Imperial pints (Imp pt)	X	0.568	= Liters (l)	X 1.76	= Imperial pints (Imp pt)
Imperial quarts (Imp qt)	X	1.137	= Liters (l)	X 0.88	= Imperial quarts (Imp qt)
Imperial quarts (Imp qt)	X	1.201	= US quarts (US qt)	X 0.833	= Imperial quarts (Imp qt)
US quarts (US qt)	X	0.946	= Liters (l)	X 1.057	= US quarts (US qt)
Imperial gallons (Imp gal)	X	4.546	= Liters (l)	X 0.22	= Imperial gallons (Imp gal)
Imperial gallons (Imp gal)	X	1.201	= US gallons (US gal)	X 0.833	= Imperial gallons (Imp gal)
US gallons (US gal)	X	3.785	= Liters (l)	X 0.264	= US gallons (US gal)

Mass (weight)
Ounces (oz)	X	28.35	= Grams (g)	X 0.035	= Ounces (oz)
Pounds (lb)	X	0.454	= Kilograms (kg)	X 2.205	= Pounds (lb)

Force
Ounces-force (ozf; oz)	X	0.278	= Newtons (N)	X 3.6	= Ounces-force (ozf; oz)
Pounds-force (lbf; lb)	X	4.448	= Newtons (N)	X 0.225	= Pounds-force (lbf; lb)
Newtons (N)	X	0.1	= Kilograms-force (kgf; kg)	X 9.81	= Newtons (N)

Pressure
Pounds-force per square inch (psi; lbf/in^2; lb/in^2)	X	0.070	= Kilograms-force per square centimeter (kgf/cm^2; kg/cm^2)	X 14.223	= Pounds-force per square inch (psi; lbf/in^2; lb/in^2)
Pounds-force per square inch (psi; lbf/in^2; lb/in^2)	X	0.068	= Atmospheres (atm)	X 14.696	= Pounds-force per square inch (psi; lbf/in^2; lb/in^2)
Pounds-force per square inch (psi; lbf/in^2; lb/in^2)	X	0.069	= Bars	X 14.5	= Pounds-force per square inch (psi; lbf/in^2; lb/in^2)
Pounds-force per square inch (psi; lbf/in^2; lb/in^2)	X	6.895	= Kilopascals (kPa)	X 0.145	= Pounds-force per square inch (psi; lbf/in^2; lb/in^2)
Kilopascals (kPa)	X	0.01	= Kilograms-force per square centimeter (kgf/cm^2; kg/cm^2)	X 98.1	= Kilopascals (kPa)

Torque (moment of force)
Pounds-force inches (lbf in; lb in)	X	1.152	= Kilograms-force centimeter (kgf cm; kg cm)	X 0.868	= Pounds-force inches (lbf in; lb in)
Pounds-force inches (lbf in; lb in)	X	0.113	= Newton meters (Nm)	X 8.85	= Pounds-force inches (lbf in; lb in)
Pounds-force inches (lbf in; lb in)	X	0.083	= Pounds-force feet (lbf ft; lb ft)	X 12	= Pounds-force inches (lbf in; lb in)
Pounds-force feet (lbf ft; lb ft)	X	0.138	= Kilograms-force meters (kgf m; kg m)	X 7.233	= Pounds-force feet (lbf ft; lb ft)
Pounds-force feet (lbf ft; lb ft)	X	1.356	= Newton meters (Nm)	X 0.738	= Pounds-force feet (lbf ft; lb ft)
Newton meters (Nm)	X	0.102	= Kilograms-force meters (kgf m; kg m)	X 9.804	= Newton meters (Nm)

Vacuum
Inches mercury (in. Hg)	X	3.377	= Kilopascals (kPa)	X 0.2961	= Inches mercury
Inches mercury (in. Hg)	X	25.4	= Millimeters mercury (mm Hg)	X 0.0394	= Inches mercury

Power
Horsepower (hp)	X	745.7	= Watts (W)	X 0.0013	= Horsepower (hp)

Velocity (speed)
Miles per hour (miles/hr; mph)	X	1.609	= Kilometers per hour (km/hr; kph)	X 0.621	= Miles per hour (miles/hr; mph)

Fuel consumption*
Miles per gallon, Imperial (mpg)	X	0.354	= Kilometers per liter (km/l)	X 2.825	= Miles per gallon, Imperial (mpg)
Miles per gallon, US (mpg)	X	0.425	= Kilometers per liter (km/l)	X 2.352	= Miles per gallon, US (mpg)

Temperature
Degrees Fahrenheit = (°C x 1.8) + 32

Degrees Celsius (Degrees Centigrade; °C) = (°F - 32) x 0.56

*It is common practice to convert from miles per gallon (mpg) to liters/100 kilometers (l/100km), where mpg (Imperial) x l/100 km = 282 and mpg (US) x l/100 km = 235

Safety first!

Regardless of how enthusiastic you may be about getting on with the job at hand, take the time to ensure that your safety is not jeopardized. A moment's lack of attention can result in an accident, as can failure to observe certain simple safety precautions. The possibility of an accident will always exist, and the following points should not be considered a comprehensive list of all dangers. Rather, they are intended to make you aware of the risks and to encourage a safety conscious approach to all work you carry out on your vehicle.

Essential DOs and DON'Ts

DON'T rely on a jack when working under the vehicle. Always use approved jackstands to support the weight of the vehicle and place them under the recommended lift or support points.

DON'T attempt to loosen extremely tight fasteners (i.e. wheel lug nuts) while the vehicle is on a jack - it may fall.

DON'T start the engine without first making sure that the transmission is in Neutral (or Park where applicable) and the parking brake is set.

DON'T remove the radiator cap from a hot cooling system - let it cool or cover it with a cloth and release the pressure gradually.

DON'T attempt to drain the engine oil until you are sure it has cooled to the point that it will not burn you.

DON'T touch any part of the engine or exhaust system until it has cooled sufficiently to avoid burns.

DON'T siphon toxic liquids such as gasoline, antifreeze and brake fluid by mouth, or allow them to remain on your skin.

DON'T inhale brake lining dust - it is potentially hazardous (see *Asbestos* below).

DON'T allow spilled oil or grease to remain on the floor - wipe it up before someone slips on it.

DON'T use loose fitting wrenches or other tools which may slip and cause injury.

DON'T push on wrenches when loosening or tightening nuts or bolts. Always try to pull the wrench toward you. If the situation calls for pushing the wrench away, push with an open hand to avoid scraped knuckles if the wrench should slip.

DON'T attempt to lift a heavy component alone - get someone to help you.

DON'T *rush or take unsafe shortcuts to finish a job.*

DON'T allow children or animals in or around the vehicle while you are working on it.

DO wear eye protection when using power tools such as a drill, sander, bench grinder, etc. and when working under a vehicle.

DO keep loose clothing and long hair well out of the way of moving parts.

DO make sure that any hoist used has a safe working load rating adequate for the job.

DO get someone to check on you periodically when working alone on a vehicle.

DO carry out work in a logical sequence and make sure that everything is correctly assembled and tightened.

DO keep chemicals and fluids tightly capped and out of the reach of children and pets.

DO remember that your vehicle's safety affects that of yourself and others. If in doubt on any point, get professional advice.

Steering, suspension and brakes

These systems are essential to driving safety, so make sure you have a qualified shop or individual check your work. Also, compressed suspension springs can cause injury if released suddenly - be sure to use a spring compressor.

Airbags

Airbags are explosive devices that can **CAUSE** injury if they deploy while you're working on the vehicle. Follow the manufacturer's instructions to disable the airbag whenever you're working in the vicinity of airbag components.

Asbestos

Certain friction, insulating, sealing, and other products - such as brake linings, brake bands, clutch linings, torque converters, gaskets, etc. - may contain asbestos or other hazardous friction material. Extreme care must be taken to avoid inhalation of dust from such products, since it is hazardous to health. If in doubt, assume that they do contain asbestos.

Fire

Remember at all times that gasoline is highly flammable. Never smoke or have any kind of open flame around when working on a vehicle. But the risk does not end there. A spark caused by an electrical short circuit, by two metal surfaces contacting each other, or even by static electricity built up in your body under certain conditions, can ignite gasoline vapors, which in a confined space are highly explosive. Do not, under any circumstances, use gasoline for cleaning parts. Use an approved safety solvent.

Always disconnect the battery ground (-) cable at the battery before working on any part of the fuel system or electrical system. Never risk spilling fuel on a hot engine or exhaust component. It is strongly recommended that a fire extinguisher suitable for use on fuel and electrical fires be kept handy in the garage or workshop at all times. Never try to extinguish a fuel or electrical fire with water.

Fumes

Certain fumes are highly toxic and can quickly cause unconsciousness and even death if inhaled to any extent. Gasoline vapor falls into this category, as do the vapors from some cleaning solvents. Any draining or pouring of such volatile fluids should be done in a well ventilated area.

When using cleaning fluids and solvents, read the instructions on the container carefully. Never use materials from unmarked containers.

Never run the engine in an enclosed space, such as a garage. Exhaust fumes contain carbon monoxide, which is extremely poisonous. If you need to run the engine, always do so in the open air, or at least have the rear of the vehicle outside the work area.

The battery

Never create a spark or allow a bare light bulb near a battery. They normally give off a certain amount of hydrogen gas, which is highly explosive.

Always disconnect the battery ground (-) cable at the battery before working on the fuel or electrical systems.

If possible, loosen the filler caps or cover when charging the battery from an external source (this does not apply to sealed or maintenance-free batteries). Do not charge at an excessive rate or the battery may burst.

Take care when adding water to a non maintenance-free battery and when carrying a battery. The electrolyte, even when diluted, is very corrosive and should not be allowed to contact clothing or skin.

Always wear eye protection when cleaning the battery to prevent the caustic deposits from entering your eyes.

Household current

When using an electric power tool, inspection light, etc., which operates on household current, always make sure that the tool is correctly connected to its plug and that, where necessary, it is properly grounded. Do not use such items in damp conditions and, again, do not create a spark or apply excessive heat in the vicinity of fuel or fuel vapor.

Secondary ignition system voltage

A severe electric shock can result from touching certain parts of the ignition system (such as the spark plug wires) when the engine is running or being cranked, particularly if components are damp or the insulation is defective. In the case of an electronic ignition system, the secondary voltage is much higher and could prove fatal.

Hydrofluoric acid

This extremely corrosive acid is formed when certain types of synthetic rubber, found in some O-rings, oil seals, fuel hoses, etc. are exposed to temperatures above 750-degrees F (400-degrees C). The rubber changes into a charred or sticky substance containing the acid. *Once formed, the acid remains dangerous for years. If it gets onto the skin, it may be necessary to amputate the limb concerned.*

When dealing with a vehicle which has suffered a fire, or with components salvaged from such a vehicle, wear protective gloves and discard them after use.

DECIMALS to MILLIMETERS

Decimal	mm	Decimal	mm
0.001	0.0254	0.500	12.7000
0.002	0.0508	0.510	12.9540
0.003	0.0762	0.520	13.2080
0.004	0.1016	0.530	13.4620
0.005	0.1270	0.540	13.7160
0.006	0.1524	0.550	13.9700
0.007	0.1778	0.560	14.2240
0.008	0.2032	0.570	14.4780
0.009	0.2286	0.580	14.7320
		0.590	14.9860
0.010	0.2540		
0.020	0.5080		
0.030	0.7620		
0.040	1.0160	0.600	15.2400
0.050	1.2700	0.610	15.4940
0.060	1.5240	0.620	15.7480
0.070	1.7780	0.630	16.0020
0.080	2.0320	0.640	16.2560
0.090	2.2860	0.650	16.5100
		0.660	16.7640
0.100	2.5400	0.670	17.0180
0.110	2.7940	0.680	17.2720
0.120	3.0480	0.690	17.5260
0.130	3.3020		
0.140	3.5560		
0.150	3.8100		
0.160	4.0640	0.700	17.7800
0.170	4.3180	0.710	18.0340
0.180	4.5720	0.720	18.2880
0.190	4.8260	0.730	18.5420
		0.740	18.7960
0.200	5.0800	0.750	19.0500
0.210	5.3340	0.760	19.3040
0.220	5.5880	0.770	19.5580
0.230	5.8420	0.780	19.8120
0.240	6.0960	0.790	20.0660
0.250	6.3500		
0.260	6.6040		
0.270	6.8580	0.800	20.3200
0.280	7.1120	0.810	20.5740
0.290	7.3660	0.820	21.8280
		0.830	21.0820
0.300	7.6200	0.840	21.3360
0.310	7.8740	0.850	21.5900
0.320	8.1280	0.860	21.8440
0.330	8.3820	0.870	22.0980
0.340	8.6360	0.880	22.3520
0.350	8.8900	0.890	22.6060
0.360	9.1440		
0.370	9.3980		
0.380	9.6520		
0.390	9.9060	0.900	22.8600
0.400	10.1600	0.910	23.1140
0.410	10.4140	0.920	23.3680
0.420	10.6680	0.930	23.6220
0.430	10.9220	0.940	23.8760
0.440	11.1760	0.950	24.1300
0.450	11.4300	0.960	24.3840
0.460	11.6840	0.970	24.6380
0.470	11.9380	0.980	24.8920
0.480	12.1920	0.990	25.1460
0.490	12.4460	1.000	25.4000

FRACTIONS to DECIMALS to MILLIMETERS

Fraction	Decimal	mm	Fraction	Decimal	mm
1/64	0.0156	0.3969	33/64	0.5156	13.0969
1/32	0.0312	0.7938	17/32	0.5312	13.4938
3/64	0.0469	1.1906	35/64	0.5469	13.8906
1/16	0.0625	1.5875	9/16	0.5625	14.2875
5/64	0.0781	1.9844	37/64	0.5781	14.6844
3/32	0.0938	2.3812	19/32	0.5938	15.0812
7/64	0.1094	2.7781	39/64	0.6094	15.4781
1/8	0.1250	3.1750	5/8	0.6250	15.8750
9/64	0.1406	3.5719	41/64	0.6406	16.2719
5/32	0.1562	3.9688	21/32	0.6562	16.6688
11/64	0.1719	4.3656	43/64	0.6719	17.0656
3/16	0.1875	4.7625	11/16	0.6875	17.4625
13/64	0.2031	5.1594	45/64	0.7031	17.8594
7/32	0.2188	5.5562	23/32	0.7188	18.2562
15/64	0.2344	5.9531	47/64	0.7344	18.6531
1/4	0.2500	6.3500	3/4	0.7500	19.0500
17/64	0.2656	6.7469	49/64	0.7656	19.4469
9/32	0.2812	7.1438	25/32	0.7812	19.8438
19/64	0.2969	7.5406	51/64	0.7969	20.2406
5/16	0.3125	7.9375	13/16	0.8125	20.6375
21/64	0.3281	8.3344	53/64	0.8281	21.0344
11/32	0.3438	8.7312	27/32	0.8438	21.4312
23/64	0.3594	9.1281	55/64	0.8594	21.8281
3/8	0.3750	9.5250	7/8	0.8750	22.2250
25/64	0.3906	9.9219	57/64	0.8906	22.6219
13/32	0.4062	10.3188	29/32	0.9062	23.0188
27/64	0.4219	10.7156	59/64	0.9219	23.4156
7/16	0.4375	11.1125	15/16	0.9375	23.8125
29/64	0.4531	11.5094	61/64	0.9531	24.2094
15/32	0.4688	11.9062	31/32	0.9688	24.6062
31/64	0.4844	12.3031	63/64	0.9844	25.0031
1/2	0.5000	12.7000	1	1.0000	25.4000

Troubleshooting

Contents

This section provides an easy reference guide to the more common problems which may occur during the operation of your vehicle. These problems and their possible causes are grouped under headings denoting various components or systems, such as Engine, Cooling system, etc. They also refer you to the chapter and/or section that deals with the problem.

Remember that successful troubleshooting is not a mysterious art practiced only by professional mechanics. It is simply the result of the right knowledge combined with an intelligent, systematic approach to the problem. Always work by a process of elimination, starting with the simplest solution and working through to the most complex - and never overlook the obvious. Anyone can run the gas tank dry or leave the lights on overnight, so don't assume that you are exempt from such oversights.

Finally, always establish a clear idea of why a problem has occurred and take steps to ensure that it doesn't happen again. If the electrical system fails because of a poor connection, check the other connections in the system to make sure that they don't fail as well. If a particular fuse continues to blow, find out why - don't just replace one fuse after another. Remember, failure of a small component can often be indicative of potential failure or incorrect functioning of a more important component or system.

Engine

1 Engine will not rotate when attempting to start

1 Battery terminal connections loose or corroded (Chapters 1 and 5).
2 Battery discharged or faulty (Chapter 1).
3 Automatic transaxle not completely engaged in Park (Chapter 7B) or clutch pedal not completely depressed (Chapter 8).
4 Broken, loose or disconnected wiring in the starting circuit (Chapters 5 and 12).
5 Starter motor pinion jammed in flywheel ring gear (Chapter 5).
6 Starter solenoid faulty (Chapter 5).
7 Starter motor faulty (Chapter 5).
8 Ignition switch faulty (Chapter 12).
9 Starter pinion or flywheel teeth worn or broken (Chapter 5).
10 Defective fusible link (see Chapter 12).

2 Engine rotates but will not start

1 Fuel tank empty.
2 Battery discharged (engine rotates slowly) (Chapter 5).
3 Battery terminal connections loose or corroded (Chapters 1 and 5).
4 Leaking fuel injector(s), faulty fuel pump, pressure regulator, etc. (Chapter 4).
5 Broken or stripped timing belt or chain (Chapter 2).

6 Ignition components damp or damaged (Chapter 5).
7 Worn, faulty or incorrectly gapped spark plugs (Chapter 1).
8 Broken, loose or disconnected wiring in the starting circuit (Chapter 5).
9 Broken, loose or disconnected wires at the ignition coil(s) or faulty coil(s) (Chapter 5).
10 Defective crankshaft sensor, camshaft sensor or PCM (see Chapter 6).

3 Engine hard to start when cold

1 Battery discharged or low (Chapter 1).
2 Malfunctioning fuel system (Chapter 4).
3 Faulty coolant temperature sensor or intake air temperature sensor (Chapter 6).
4 Fuel injector(s) leaking (Chapter 4).
5 Faulty ignition system (Chapter 5).
6 Defective MAP sensor (see Chapter 6).

4 Engine hard to start when hot

1 Air filter clogged (Chapter 1).
2 Fuel not reaching the fuel injection system (Chapter 4).
3 Corroded battery connections, especially ground (Chapters 1 and 5).
4 Faulty coolant temperature sensor or intake air temperature sensor (Chapter 6).

5 Starter motor noisy or excessively rough in engagement

1 Pinion or flywheel gear teeth worn or broken (Chapter 5).
2 Starter motor mounting bolts loose or missing (Chapter 5).

6 Engine starts but stops immediately

1 Loose or faulty electrical connections at ignition coil (Chapter 5).
2 Insufficient fuel reaching the fuel injector(s) (Chapters 4).
3 Vacuum leak at the gasket between the intake manifold/plenum and throttle body (Chapter 4).
4 Fault in the engine control system (Chapter 6).
5 Intake air leaks, broken vacuum lines (see Chapter 4).

7 Oil puddle under engine

1 Oil pan gasket and/or oil pan drain bolt washer leaking (Chapter 2).
2 Oil pressure sending unit leaking (Chapter 2).

3 Oil filter or adapter block leaking (Chapter 1).
4 Valve cover(s) leaking (Chapter 2).
5 Engine oil seals leaking (Chapter 2).

8 Engine lopes while idling or idles erratically

1 Vacuum leakage (Chapters 2 and 4).
2 Leaking EGR valve or EGR vacuum lines (Chapter 6).
3 Air filter clogged (Chapter 1).
4 Fuel pump not delivering sufficient fuel to the fuel injection system (Chapter 4).
5 Leaking head gasket (Chapter 2).
6 Timing chain or belt and/or sprockets worn (Chapter 2).
7 Camshaft lobes worn (Chapter 2).

9 Engine misses at idle speed

1 Spark plugs worn or not gapped properly (Chapter 1).
2 Faulty spark plug wires (Chapter 1).
3 Vacuum leaks (Chapters 2 and 4).
4 Faulty ignition coil(s) (Chapter 5).
5 Uneven or low compression (Chapter 2).
6 Faulty fuel injector(s) (Chapter 4).

10 Engine misses throughout driving speed range

1 Fuel filter clogged and/or impurities in the fuel system (Chapter 4).
2 Low fuel output at the fuel injector(s) (Chapter 4).
3 Faulty or incorrectly gapped spark plugs (Chapter 1).
4 Defective spark plug wires (Chapter 1 or 5).
5 Faulty emission system components (Chapter 6).
6 Low or uneven cylinder compression pressures (Chapter 2).
7 Burned valves (Chapter 2).
8 Weak or faulty ignition system (Chapter 5).
9 Vacuum leak in fuel injection system, throttle body, intake manifold or vacuum hoses (Chapter 4).

11 Engine stumbles on acceleration

1 Spark plugs fouled (Chapter 1).
2 Problem with fuel injection system (Chapter 4).
3 Fuel filter clogged (Chapter 4).
4 Fault in the engine control system (Chapter 6).
5 Intake air leak (Chapters 2 and 4).
6 EGR system malfunction (Chapter 6).

12 Engine surges while holding accelerator steady

1 Intake air leak (Chapter 4).
2 Fuel pump or fuel pressure regulator faulty (Chapter 4).
3 Problem with fuel injection system (Chapter 4).
4 Problem with the emissions control system (Chapter 6).

13 Engine stalls

1 Idle speed incorrect (Chapter 1).
2 Fuel filter clogged and/or water and impurities in the fuel system (Chapter 4).
3 Ignition components damp or damaged (Chapter 5).
4 Faulty emissions system components (Chapter 6).
5 Faulty or incorrectly gapped spark plugs (Chapter 1).
6 Faulty spark plug wires (Chapter 1).
7 Vacuum leak in the fuel injection system, intake manifold or vacuum hoses (Chapters 2 and 4).

14 Engine lacks power

1 Worn camshaft lobes (Chapter 2).
2 Burned valves or incorrect valve timing (Chapter 2).
3 Faulty spark plug wires or faulty coil(s) (Chapters 1 and 5).
4 Faulty or incorrectly gapped spark plugs (Chapter 1).
5 Problem with the fuel injection system (Chapter 4).
6 Plugged air filter (Chapter 1).
7 Brakes binding (Chapter 9).
8 Automatic transaxle fluid level incorrect (Chapter 1).
9 Clutch slipping (Chapter 8).
10 Fuel filter clogged and/or impurities in the fuel system (Chapter 4).
11 Emission control system not functioning properly (Chapter 6).
12 Low or uneven cylinder compression pressures (Chapter 2).
13 Restricted exhaust system or catalytic converter (Chapter 4).

15 Engine backfires

1 Emission control system not functioning properly (Chapter 6).
2 Faulty spark plug wires or coil(s) (Chapter 5).
3 Problem with the fuel injection system (Chapter 4).
4 Vacuum leak at fuel injector(s), intake manifold or vacuum hoses (Chapters 2 and 4).
5 Burned valves or incorrect valve timing (Chapter 2).

16 Pinging or knocking engine sounds during acceleration or uphill

1 Incorrect grade of fuel.
2 Problem with the engine control system (Chapter 6).
3 Fuel injection system faulty (Chapter 4).
4 Improper or damaged spark plugs or wires (Chapter 1).
5 EGR valve not functioning (Chapter 6).
6 Vacuum leak (Chapters 2 and 4).

17 Engine runs with oil pressure light on

1 Low oil level (Chapter 1).
2 Idle rpm below specification (Chapter 1).
3 Short in wiring circuit (Chapter 12).
4 Faulty oil pressure sender (Chapter 2).
5 Worn engine bearings and/or oil pump (Chapter 2).

18 Engine diesels (continues to run) after switching off

1 Idle speed too high (Chapter 1).
2 Excessive engine operating temperature (Chapter 3).
3 Excessive carbon deposits on valves and pistons (see Chapter 2)

Engine electrical system

19 Alternator light fails to come on when key is turned on

1 Warning light bulb defective (Chapter 12).
2 Fault in the printed circuit, dash wiring or bulb holder (Chapter 12).

20 Alternator light fails to go out

1 Faulty alternator or charging circuit (Chapter 5).
2 Alternator drivebelt defective or out of adjustment (Chapter 1).
3 Alternator voltage regulator fault (Chapter 5).

21 Battery will not hold a charge

1 The alternator drivebelt defective or not adjusted properly (slipping) (Chapter 1).
2 Battery electrolyte level low (not applicable on maintenance-free batteries) (Chapter 1).
3 Battery terminals loose or corroded (Chapters 1 and 5).

4 Alternator not charging properly (Chapter 5).
5 The wiring in the charging circuit is loose, broken or faulty (Chapter 5).
6 Short in vehicle wiring (Chapter 12).
7 The battery is internally defective (Chapters 1 and 5).

Fuel and emissions systems

22 CHECK ENGINE light remains on or is flashing

1 Light remains on:
a) *Fuel filler cap (gas cap) is not seated or tightened properly.*
b) *On-Board Diagnostic (OBD-II) computer has detected an emissions or fuel injection component fault (Chapter 6).*
2 Light is flashing:
a) *If the CHECK ENGINE light is flashing, severe catalytic converter damage has occurred and engine power loss will soon result. Take the vehicle to your nearest dealer service department or other qualified shop for immediate repair.*

23 Excessive fuel consumption

1 Dirty or clogged air filter element (Chapter 1).
2 Emissions system not functioning properly (Chapter 6).
3 The fuel injection system not functioning properly (Chapter 4).
4 Low tire pressure or incorrect tire size (Chapter 1).
5 Dragging brakes (Chapter 9).

24 Fuel leakage and/or fuel odor

1 Leaking fuel feed or return line (Chapters 1 and 4).
2 Fuel tank overfilled.
3 Clogged evaporative canister filter (Chapters 1 and 6).
4 Problem with fuel injection system (Chapter 4).

Cooling system

25 Overheating

1 There is insufficient coolant in the system (Chapter 1).
2 Water pump defective (Chapter 3).
3 Radiator core blocked or grille restricted (Chapter 3).
4 The thermostat is faulty (Chapter 3).
5 Electric cooling fan inoperative or the blades are broken (Chapter 3).
6 Radiator cap not maintaining proper pressure (Chapter 3).

26 Overcooling

1   The thermostat is faulty (Chapter 3).
2   The temperature gauge sending unit is inaccurate (Chapter 3)

27 External coolant leakage

1   Deteriorated/damaged hoses; loose clamps (Chapters 1 and 3).
2   Water pump defective (Chapter 3).
3   Leakage from radiator core or coolant reservoir (Chapter 3).
4   Engine drain or water jacket core plugs leaking (Chapter 2).

28 Internal coolant leakage

1   Leaking cylinder head gasket (Chapter 2).
2   Cracked cylinder bore or cylinder head (Chapter 2).

29 Coolant loss

1   Too much coolant in system (Chapter 1).
2   Coolant boiling away because of overheating (Chapter 3).
3   Internal or external leakage (Chapter 3).
4   Faulty pressure cap (Chapter 3).

30 Poor coolant circulation

1   Inoperative water pump (Chapter 3).
2   Restriction in cooling system (Chapters 1 and 3).
3   Thermostat sticking (Chapter 3).

Clutch

31 Pedal travels to floor - no pressure or very little resistance

1   Broken or disconnected clutch cable (Chapter 8).
2   Broken release bearing or fork (Chapter 8).
3   Faulty clutch master cylinder or release cylinder (Chapter 8).

32 Unable to select gears

1   Faulty transaxle (Chapter 7).
2   Faulty clutch disc or pressure plate (Chapter 8).
3   Broken or disconnected clutch cable (Chapter 8).
4   Faulty clutch master cylinder or release cylinder (Chapter 8).
5   Faulty release lever or release bearing (Chapter 8).
6   Faulty shift lever assembly or rods (Chapter 8).

33 Clutch slips (engine speed increases with no increase in vehicle speed)

1   Clutch plate worn (Chapter 8).
2   Clutch plate is oil soaked by leaking rear main seal (Chapter 8).
3   Clutch plate not seated (Chapter 8).
4   Warped pressure plate or flywheel (Chapter 8).
5   Weak clutch diaphragm springs (Chapter 8).
6   Clutch plate overheated. Allow to cool.
7   Faulty clutch self-adjusting mechanism (Chapter 8).

34 Grabbing (chattering) as clutch is engaged

1   Oil on clutch plate lining, burned or glazed facings (Chapter 8).
2   Worn or loose engine or transaxle mounts (Chapters 2 and 7).
3   Worn splines on clutch plate hub (Chapter 8).
4   Warped pressure plate or flywheel (Chapter 8).
5   Burned or smeared resin on flywheel or pressure plate (Chapter 8).

35 Transaxle rattling (clicking)

1   Release fork loose (Chapter 8).
2   Low engine idle speed (Chapter 1).

36 Noise in clutch area

1   Faulty throw-out bearing (Chapter 8).

37 Clutch pedal stays on floor

1   Broken release bearing or fork (Chapter 8).
2   Broken or disconnected clutch cable (Chapter 8).
3   Faulty clutch master cylinder or release cylinder (Chapter 8).

38 High pedal effort

1   Binding clutch cable (Chapter 8).
2   Pressure plate faulty (Chapter 8).

Manual transaxle

39 Knocking noise at low speeds

1   Worn driveaxle constant velocity (CV) joints (Chapter 8).
2   Worn side gear shaft counterbore in differential case (Chapter 7A).*

40 Noise most pronounced when turning

1   Differential gear noise (Chapter 7A).*

41 Clunk on acceleration or deceleration

1   Loose engine or transaxle mounts (Chapters 2 and 7A).
2   Worn differential pinion shaft in case.*
3   Worn side gear shaft counterbore in differential case (Chapter 7A).*
4   Worn or damaged driveaxle inboard CV joints (Chapter 8).

42 Clicking noise in turns

1   Worn or damaged outboard CV joint (Chapter 8).

43 Vibration

1   Rough wheel bearing (Chapters 1 and 10).
2   Damaged driveaxle (Chapter 8).
3   Out of round tires (Chapter 1).
4   Tire out of balance (Chapters 1 and 10).
5   Worn CV joint (Chapter 8).

44 Noisy in Neutral with engine running

1   Damaged input gear bearing (Chapter 7A).*
2   Damaged clutch release bearing (Chapter 8).

45 Noisy in one particular gear

1   Damaged or worn constant mesh gears (Chapter 7A).*
2   Damaged or worn synchronizers (Chapter 7A).*
3   Bent reverse fork (Chapter 7A).*
4   Damaged fourth speed gear or output gear (Chapter 7A).*
5   Worn or damaged reverse idler gear or idler bushing (Chapter 7A).*

46   Noisy in all gears

1   Insufficient lubricant (Chapters 1 and 7A).
2   Damaged or worn bearings (Chapter 7A).*
3   Worn or damaged input gear shaft and/or output gear shaft (Chapter 7A).*

47   Slips out of gear

1   Worn or improperly adjusted linkage (Chapter 7A).
2   Transaxle loose on engine (Chapter 7A).
3   Shift linkage does not work freely, binds (Chapter 7A).
4   Input gear bearing retainer broken or loose (Chapter 7A).*
5   Dirt between clutch cover and engine housing (Chapter 7A).
6   Worn shift fork (Chapter 7A).*

48   Leaks lubricant

1   Driveaxle seals worn (Chapter 7A).
2   Excessive amount of lubricant in transaxle (Chapters 1 and 7A).
3   Loose or broken input gear shaft bearing retainer (Chapter 7A).*
4   Input gear bearing retainer O-ring and/or lip seal damaged (Chapter 7A).*
5   Vehicle speed sensor O-ring leaking (Chapter 7A).

49   Hard to shift

1   Shift linkage loose or worn (Chapter 7A).
2   Crossover cable out of adjustment

Although the corrective action necessary to remedy the symptoms described is beyond the scope of this manual, the above information should be helpful in isolating the cause of the condition so that the owner can communicate clearly with a professional mechanic.

Automatic transaxle

Note: *Due to the complexity of the automatic transaxle, it is difficult for the home mechanic to properly diagnose and service this component. For problems other than the following, the vehicle should be taken to a dealer service department or other qualified transmission shop.*

50   Fluid leakage

1   Automatic transaxle fluid is a deep red color. Fluid leaks should not be confused with engine oil, which can easily be blown onto the transaxle by air flow.
2   To pinpoint a leak, first remove all built-up dirt and grime from the transaxle housing with degreasing agents and/or steam cleaning. Then drive the vehicle at low speeds so air flow will not blow the leak far from its source. Raise the vehicle and determine where the leak is coming from. Common areas of leakage are:

a)   *Pan (Chapters 1 and 7)*
b)   *Dipstick tube (Chapters 1 and 7)*
c)   *Transaxle oil cooler lines (Chapter 7)*
d)   *Speed sensor (Chapter 7)*
e)   *Driveaxle oil seals (Chapter 7).*

51   Transaxle fluid brown or has a burned smell

Transaxle fluid overheated - change fluid and filter (Chapter 1).

52   General shift mechanism problems

1   Chapter 7, Part B, deals with checking and adjusting the shift linkage on automatic transaxles. Common problems that may be attributed to poorly adjusted linkage are:

a)   *Engine starting in gears other than Park or Neutral.*
b)   *Indicator on shifter pointing to a gear other than the one actually being used.*
c)   *Vehicle moves when in Park.*

2   Refer to Chapter 7B for the shift linkage adjustment procedure.

53   Transaxle will not downshift with accelerator pedal pressed to the floor

The transaxle is electronically controlled. This type of problem - which is caused by a malfunction in the Transmission Control Module (TCM), a sensor or solenoid, or the circuit itself - is beyond the scope of this manual. Have the problem diagnosed by a dealer service department or other qualified automatic transmission shop.

54   Engine will start in gears other than Park or Neutral

Neutral start switch out of adjustment or malfunctioning (Chapter 7B).

55   Transaxle slips, shifts roughly, is noisy or has no drive in forward or reverse gears

There are many probable causes for the above problems, but the home mechanic should be concerned with only one possibility - fluid level. Before taking the vehicle to a repair shop, check the level and condition of the fluid and/or filter as described in Chapter 1. Correct the fluid level as necessary or change the fluid and filter if needed. If the problem persists, have a professional diagnose the cause.

Driveaxles

56   Clicking noise in turns

Worn or damaged outboard CV joint (Chapter 8).

57   Shudder or vibration during acceleration

1   Excessive toe-in (Chapter 10).
2   Incorrect spring heights (Chapter 10).
3   Worn or damaged inboard or outboard CV joints (Chapter 8).
4   Sticking inboard CV joint assembly (Chapter 8).

58   Vibration at highway speeds

1   Out of balance front wheels and/or tires (Chapters 1 and 10).
2   Out of round front tires (Chapters 1 and 10).
3   Worn CV joint(s) (Chapter 8).

Brakes

Note: *Before assuming that a brake problem exists, make sure that:*

a)   *The tires are in good condition and properly inflated (Chapter 1).*
b)   *The front end alignment is correct (Chapter 10).*
c)   *The vehicle weight is not loaded in an unequal manner.*

59   Vehicle pulls to one side during braking

1   Incorrect tire pressures (Chapter 1).
2   Front end out of alignment (have the front end aligned).
3   Front tire sizes or tread types not matched to one another.
4   Restricted brake lines or hoses (Chapter 9).
5   Malfunctioning/leaking brake wheel cylinder or caliper assembly (Chapter 9).
6   Loose suspension parts (Chapter 10).
7   Loose calipers (Chapter 9).
8   Excessive wear of brake shoe or pad material or disc/drum on one side.

60 Noise (high-pitched squeal when the brakes are applied)

Front disc brake pads worn out. The noise comes from the wear sensor rubbing against the disc (does not apply to all vehicles). Replace pads with new ones immediately (Chapter 9).

61 Brake roughness or chatter (pedal pulsates)

1 Excessive lateral runout (Chapter 9).
2 Uneven pad wear (Chapter 9).
3 Defective disc (Chapter 9).
4 If the vehicle is equipped with an anti-lock brake system (ABS), brake pedal pulsation and associated noises are normal when severe braking is required.

62 Excessive brake pedal effort required to stop vehicle

1 Malfunctioning power brake booster (Chapter 9).
2 Partial system failure (Chapter 9).
3 Excessively worn pads or shoes (Chapter 9).
4 Piston in caliper or wheel cylinder stuck or sluggish (Chapter 9).
5 Brake pads or shoes contaminated with oil or grease (Chapter 9).
6 Brake disc grooved and/or glazed (Chapter 1).
7 New pads or shoes installed and not yet seated. It will take a while for the new material to seat against the disc or drum.

63 Excessive brake pedal travel

1 Partial brake system failure (Chapter 9).
2 Insufficient fluid in master cylinder (Chapters 1 and 9).
3 Air trapped in system (Chapters 1 and 9).

64 Dragging brakes

1 Incorrect adjustment of brake light switch (Chapter 9).
2 Master cylinder pistons not returning correctly (Chapter 9).
3 Restricted brakes lines or hoses (Chapters 1 and 9).
4 Incorrect parking brake adjustment (Chapter 9).

65 Grabbing or uneven braking action

1 Malfunction of proportioning valve (Chapter 9).

2 Malfunction of power brake booster unit (Chapter 9).
3 Binding brake pedal mechanism (Chapter 9).

66 Brake pedal feels spongy when depressed

1 Air in hydraulic lines (Chapter 9).
2 Master cylinder mounting bolts loose (Chapter 9).
3 Master cylinder defective (Chapter 9).

67 Brake pedal travels to the floor with little resistance

1 Little or no fluid in the master cylinder reservoir caused by leaking caliper piston(s) (Chapter 9).
2 Loose, damaged or disconnected brake lines (Chapter 9).

68 Parking brake does not hold

Parking brake cables improperly adjusted (Chapters 1 and 9).

Suspension and steering systems

Note: *Before attempting to diagnose suspension and steering system problems, perform the following preliminary checks:*
a) *Tires for wrong pressure and uneven wear.*
b) *Steering universal joints from the column to the rack and pinion for loose connectors or wear.*
c) *Front and rear suspension and the rack and pinion assembly for loose or damaged parts.*
d) *Out-of-round or out-of-balance tires, bent rims and loose and/or rough wheel bearings.*

69 Vehicle pulls to one side

1 Mismatched or uneven tires (Chapter 10).
2 Broken or sagging coil springs (Chapter 10).
3 Wheel alignment out-of-specification (Chapter 10).
4 Front brake dragging (Chapter 9).
5 Tire pressure(s) incorrect (Chapter 1)

70 Abnormal or excessive tire wear

1 Wheel alignment out-of-specification (Chapters 1 and 10).
2 Sagging or broken coil springs (Chapter 10).
3 Tire out-of-balance (Chapter 10).
4 Worn shock absorber (Chapter 10).

5 Overloaded vehicle.
6 Tires not rotated regularly (Chapter 1).
7 Tire pressure(s) incorrect (Chapter 1).

71 Wheel makes a thumping noise

1 Blister or bump on tire (Chapter 10).
2 Faulty shock absorber(s) (Chapter 10).

72 Shimmy, shake or vibration

1 Tire or wheel out-of-balance or out-of-round (Chapter 10).
2 Loose or worn wheel bearings (Chapters 1, 8 and 10).
3 Worn tie-rod ends (Chapter 10).
4 Worn balljoints (Chapters 1 and 10).
5 Excessive wheel runout (Chapter 10).
6 Blister or bump on tire (Chapter 10).

73 Hard steering

1 Lack of lubrication at balljoints, tie-rod ends and rack and pinion assembly (Chapter 10).
2 Low power steering fluid level (Chapter 1).
3 Faulty power steering pump (Chapter 10).
4 Front wheel alignment out-of-specifications (Chapter 10).
5 Low tire pressure(s) (Chapter 1).

74 Poor returnability of steering to center

1 Lack of lubrication at balljoints and tie-rod ends (Chapter 10).
2 Binding in balljoints (Chapter 10).
3 Binding in steering column (Chapter 10).
4 Lack of lubricant in steering gear assembly (Chapter 10).
5 Front wheel alignment out-of-specifications (Chapter 10).

75 Abnormal noise at the front end

1 Lack of lubrication at balljoints and tie-rod ends (Chapters 1 and 10).
2 Damaged strut mounting (Chapter 10).
3 Worn control arm bushings or tie-rod ends (Chapter 10).
4 Loose stabilizer bar (Chapter 10).
5 Loose wheel nuts (Chapter 1).
6 Loose suspension bolts (Chapter 10)

76 Wander or poor steering stability

1 Mismatched or unevenly worn tires (Chapter 10).

2   Lack of lubrication at balljoints and tie-rod ends (Chapters 1 and 10).
3   Bad shock absorber(s) (Chapter 10).
4   Loose stabilizer bar (Chapter 10).
5   Broken or sagging coil springs (Chapter 10).
6   Wheels out of alignment (Chapter 10).
7   Tire pressure(s) incorrect (Chapter 1)

77 Erratic steering when braking

1   Wheel bearings worn (Chapter 10).
2   Broken or sagging coil springs (Chapter 10).
3   Leaking wheel cylinder or caliper (Chapter 10).
4   Warped discs or drums (Chapter 10).

78 Excessive pitching and/or rolling around corners or during braking

1   Loose stabilizer bar (Chapter 10).
2   Worn shock absorbers or mountings (Chapter 10).
3   Broken or sagging coil springs (Chapter 10).
4   Overloaded vehicle.

79 Suspension bottoms

1   Overloaded vehicle.
2   Worn shock absorbers (Chapter 10).

3   Incorrect, broken or sagging coil springs (Chapter 10).

80 Cupped tires

1   Front wheel or rear wheel alignment out-of-specifications (Chapter 10).
2   Worn shock absorbers (Chapter 10).
3   Wheel bearings worn (Chapter 10).
4   Excessive tire or wheel runout (Chapter 10).
5   Worn balljoints (Chapter 10).

81 Excessive tire wear on outside edge

1   Inflation pressures incorrect (Chapter 1).
2   Excessive speed during turns.
3   Front end alignment incorrect (excessive toe-in). Have professionally aligned.
4   Suspension arm bent or twisted (Chapter 10).

82 Excessive tire wear on inside edge

1   Inflation pressures incorrect (Chapter 1).
2   Front end alignment incorrect (toe-out). Have professionally aligned.
3   Loose or damaged steering components (Chapter 10).

83 Tire tread worn in one place

1   Tires out-of-balance.
2   Damaged or buckled wheel. Inspect and replace if necessary.
3   Defective tire (Chapter 1).

84 Excessive play or looseness in steering system

1   Wheel bearing(s) worn (Chapter 10).
2   Tie-rod end loose (Chapter 10).
3   Steering gear loose or worn (Chapter 10).
4   Worn or loose steering intermediate shaft (Chapter 10).

85 Rattling or clicking noise in steering gear

Steering gear loose or worn (Chapter 10).

Chapter 1
Tune-up and routine maintenance

Contents

Specifications

Recommended lubricants and fluids

Engine oil
    Type .... API "Certified for gasoline engines"
    Viscosity .... See accompanying chart
Manual transaxle lubricant
    Avenger and pre-2001 Sebring and Stratus .... MOPAR MS9417 MTX fluid (P/N 4773167)
    Sebring and Stratus (2001 on)
        2001 .... API classification GL-4 SAE 75W-90, 75W-85
        2002 .... MOPAR 4659920AB Type MS-9602
        2003 on .... MOPAR ATF+4 automatic transmission fluid

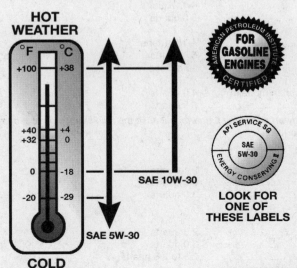

Engine oil viscosity chart - For best fuel economy and cold starting, select the lowest SAE viscosity grade for the expected temperature range

LOOK FOR ONE OF THESE LABELS

Recommended lubricants and fluids (continued)

Automatic transaxle fluid
    1995 through 1997
        Except Sebring Convertibles .... MOPAR ATF Plus or Diamond ATF SP
        Sebring Convertibles
            1996 .... MOPAR ATF Plus
            1997 .... MOPAR ATF+2
    1998 through 2000
        Except 1998 Sebring Convertible .... MOPAR ATF+3
        1998 Sebring Convertible .... MOPAR ATF+2
    2001 and later
        Except Sebring Coupe and Stratus Coupe.... .... MOPAR ATF+4 or ATF+4 Type 9602
        Sebring Coupe and Stratus Coupe.. Diamond ATF SPII, SPIIM or SPIII
Power steering fluid
    1995 through 1997 .... MOPAR ATF Plus or DEXRON II
    1998 through 2000 .... MOPAR ATF+3
    2001
        Except Stratus Coupe.. MOPAR Type MS-9933
        Stratus Coupe.. Dexron II
    2002 .... MOPAR Type MS-9602
    2003 and later .... MOPAR ATF+4
Brake and clutch fluid .... DOT type 3 or 4 brake fluid
If the fluid type on the dipstick differs from that listed here, use the type listed on the dipstick.
Engine coolant
    1995 through 2000.. 50/50 mixture of ethylene-glycol based antifreeze and water*
    2001 and later .... 50/50 mixture of Mopar @ 5 year/100,000 mile Formula
                                                                                                                (MS-9769) antifreeze coolant with HOAT
                                                                                                                (Hybrid Organic Additive Technology) and water

Parking brake mechanism grease.. White lithium-based grease NLGI no. 2
Chassis lubrication grease .... NLGI no. 2 LB grease
Hood, door and trunk hinge lubricant .... Engine oil
Hood latch and door check spring grease .... NLGI no. 2 multi-purpose grease
Key lock cylinder lubricant .... Graphite spray
Door latch striker lubricant.. Mopar Door Ease no. 3744859 or equivalent

Some models are filled with a 50/50 mixture of Mopar 5 year/100,000 mile coolant that shouldn't be mixed with other coolants. Refer to the coolant reservoir label under the hood to determine what type coolant you have. Always refill with the correct coolant.

Capacities*

Engine oil (including filter)
    1995 and 1996 models.. 4-1/2 quarts
    1997 and 1998 models
        Coupe .... 4-1/2 quarts
        Convertible
            2.4L four-cylinder engine.. 5.0 quarts
            2.5L V6 engine .... 4-1/2 quarts
    1999 and 2000 models
        2.0L four-cylinder and 2.5L V6 engine.................................. 4-1/2 quarts
        2.4L four-cylinder engine .... 5.0 quarts
    2001 and later
        Coupe .... 4-1/2 quarts
        Convertible and sedan models .... 5.0 quarts
Fuel tank .... 16 gallons
Automatic transaxle (drain and refill)
    2000 and earlier coupe models, all convertible and sedan models).. 4.0 quarts
    2001 and later coupe models.. 5.8 quarts
Note: On 2001 and later coupe models you'll have to buy an additional 6 quarts, because the fluid changing procedure requires flushing the system (the transaxle on these models does not have a fluid filter).
Manual transaxle
    2000 and earlier models
        Coupe .... 2.1 quarts
        Convertible.. 2.3 quarts
    2001 models.. 3.0 quarts
    2002 and later models
        Coupe
            Four-cylinder models.. 2.3 quarts
            V6 models .... 3.0 quarts
        Convertible and sedan.. 2.5 to 2.8 quarts
All capacities approximate. Add as necessary to bring to appropriate level.

Cooling system
   2.0L engine .... 8.5 quarts
   2.4L engine .... 9.0 quarts
   2.5L engine .... 10.5 quarts
   2.7L engine .... 9.5 quarts
   3.0L engine .... 8.5 quarts
All capacities approximate. Add as necessary to bring to appropriate level.

Brakes
Disc brake pad wear limit .... 1/8 inch
Drum brake shoe wear limit....................................... 1/16 inch
Parking brake lever travel
   Rear disc brake.. 3 to 5 clicks
   Rear drum brake .... 5 to 7 clicks

Ignition system
Spark plug type and gap*
   Type
      1995 through 2000
         2.0L four .... Champion RC9YC5
         2.5L V6 .... Champion RC10PYP4, NGK PFR5J-11 or Nippondenso PK16PR-P11
         2.4L VIN X .... Champion RC12YC5
      2001 and later convertibles and sedans
         2.4L VIN J PZEV .... Champion PLZTR4A-13
         2.4L VIN X .... Champion RE14MCC5
         2.7L .... Champion RE10PMC5
      2001 and later coupes
         2.4L four .... Champion RC10YC4, Denso K16PR-U11 or NGK BKR5E-11
         3.0L V6 .... Champion RC10PYP4, Denso PK20PR11 or NGK PFR6G-11
   Gap
      2.0L engine .... 0.048 to 0.053 inch
      2.4L SOHC VIN G... 0.039 to 0.043 inch
      2.4L DOHC VIN X... 0.048 to 0.053 inch
      2.4L PZEV VIN J... 0.046 to 0.051 inch
      2.5L engine .... 0.039 to 0.044 inch
      2.7L engine .... 0.048 to 0.053 inch
      3.0L engine .... 0.039 to 0.043 inch
Refer to the Vehicle Emission Control Information label in the engine compartment and follow the information on the label if it differs from that shown here.

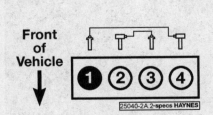

**Four-cylinder engine cylinder numbering
and coil pack/spark plug wire locations
(2.4L SOHC engine)**

**V6 engine cylinder numbering and
distributor cap terminal locations -
2.5L and 3.0L* V6 engines**

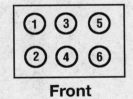

Cylinder location diagram - 2.7L V6 engine

On 2001 and later 3.0L V6 engines, refer to the numbers on the distributer cap for terminal locations

Ignition system (continued)

Spark plug wire resistance
2.0L and 2.4L four-cylinder engines
  Wire numbers 1 and 4 .... 3,500 to 4,900 ohms
  Wire numbers 2 and 3 .... 2,950 to 4,100 ohms
2.5L/3.0L V6 engine
  Minimum .... 250 ohms per inch
  (3,000 ohms per foot)
  Maximum .... 560 ohms per inch
  (6,700 ohms per foot)

Firing order
  Four-cylinder engines 1-3-4-2
  V6 engines 1-2-3-4-5-6

Front of Vehicle

30034-1-specs HAYNES

Four-cylinder engine cylinder numbering and coil terminal locations (2.0L and 2.4L DOHC engines)

Torque specifications

Ft-lbs (unless otherwise indicated)

Note: One foot pound (ft-lb) of torque is equivalent to 12 inch-pounds (in-lbs) of torque. Torque values below approximately 15 ft-lbs are expressed in inch-pounds, since most foot-pound torque wrenches are not accurate at these smaller values.

Automatic transaxle fluid pan bolts (2000 and earlier coupe models, all convertible and sedan models) .... 165 in-lbs
Automatic transaxle drain plug (2001 and later coupe models) 24
Drivebelt tensioner bolts
  2.0L DOHC 22
  2.7L V6 21
Drivebelt tensioner bolt 2.4L DOHC 40
Engine oil drain plug
  2000 and earlier models
    Four-cylinder engines 25
    V6 engines 29
  2001 models
    Coupe (all) 29
    Convertible and sedan
      2.0L four-cylinder engine 25
      2.4L four-cylinder and 2.7L V6 engines 20

Engine compartment layout (2001 sedan with a 2.4L DOHC four-cylinder engine)

1 Automatic transaxle fluid dipstick
2 Brake fluid reservoir
3 Battery negative remote terminal
4 Power Distribution Center (PDC) - fuses and relays
5 Battery positive remote terminal
6 Air filter housing
7 Engine oil dipstick
8 Upper radiator hose
9 Power steering fluid reservoir
10 Windshield washer fluid reservoir
11 Coolant reservoir
12 Engine coolant pressure/filler cap
13 Engine oil filler cap
14 Spark plugs

Torque specifications

Ft-lbs (unless otherwise indicated)

Note: One foot pound (ft-lb) of torque is equivalent to 12 inch-pounds (in-lbs) of torque. Torque values below approximately 15 ft-lbs are expressed in inch-pounds, since most foot-pound torque wrenches are not accurate at these smaller values.

Engine oil drain plug (continued)
  2002 and later models
    Coupe (all) 29
    Convertible and sedan (all).. 20
Manual transaxle drain plug 22
Spark plugs
  1999 and earlier models
    Four-cylinder engines 20
    V6 engines 18
  2000 models (all)... 18
  2001 models
    Coupe (all) 18
    Convertible and sedan
      2.0L four-cylinder engine.. 156 in-lbs
      2.4L four-cylinder engine.. 20
      2.7L V6 engine 15
  2002 and later models
    Coupe (all) 18
    Convertible and sedan
      2.0L four-cylinder engine.. 156 in-lbs
      2.4L four-cylinder engine.. 156 in-lbs
      2.7L V6 engine .... 156 in-lbs
Fuel filter fitting bolts (2000 and earlier coupe models only) 22
Wheel lug nuts
  Coupe models .... 65 to 80
  Convertible and sedan models... 100

Engine compartment layout (typical convertible and sedan 2.5L V6 engine shown)

1 Power steering fluid reservoir	6 Battery positive remote terminal	10 Spark plug boot
2 Brake fluid reservoir	7 Power Distribution Center (PDC) -	11 Engine oil filler cap
3 Transmission fluid dipstick	fuses and relays	12 Engine oil dipstick
4 Battery negative remote terminal	8 Upper radiator hose	13 Windshield washer reservoir
5 Air filter housing	9 Engine coolant pressure/filler cap	14 Engine coolant reservoir

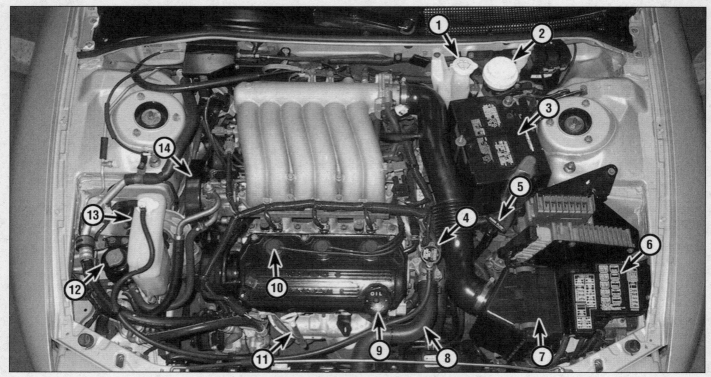

Engine compartment layout (typical coupe 2.5L V6 engine shown)

1	Windshield washer reservoir	6	Power Distribution Center (PDC) - fuses and relays	10	Spark plug boot
2	Brake fluid reservoir			11	Engine oil dipstick
3	Battery	7	Air filter housing	12	Power steering fluid reservoir
4	Engine coolant pressure/filler cap	8	Upper radiator hose	13	Engine coolant reservoir
5	Transmission fluid dipstick	9	Engine oil filler cap	14	Drivebelt

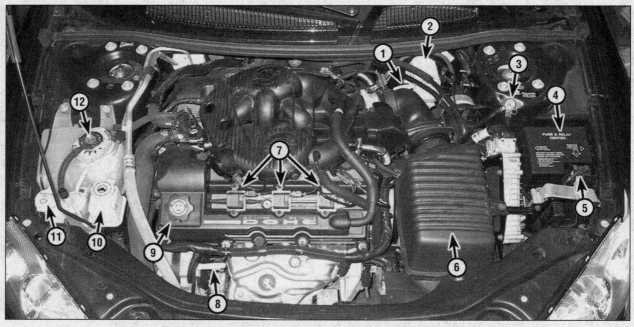

Engine compartment layout (convertible with 2.7L V6 engine)

1	Automatic transaxle fluid dipstick	5	Battery positive remote terminal	9	Engine oil filler cap
2	Brake fluid reservoir	6	Air filter housing	10	Power steering fluid reservoir
3	Battery negative remote terminal	7	Spark plugs (front bank, under ignition coils)	11	Windshield washer fluid reservoir
4	Power Distribution Center (PDC) - fuses and relays	8	Engine oil dipstick	12	Coolant expansion tank pressure cap

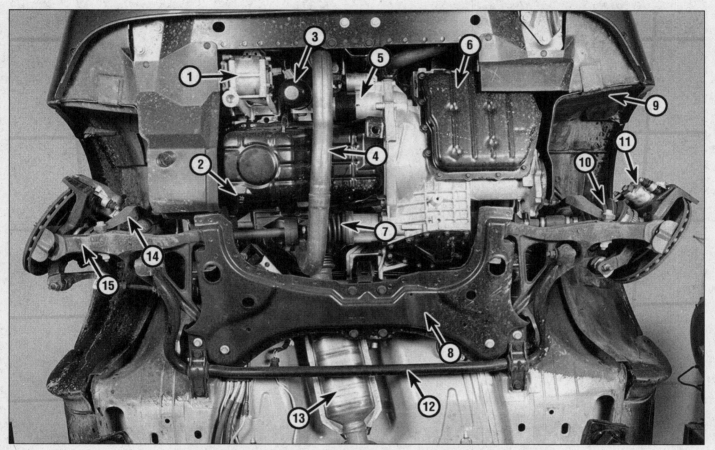

Typical engine compartment underside components (2.5L V6 engine shown)

1	Air conditioning compressor	6	Automatic transaxle fluid pan	11	Front brake caliper
2	Engine oil drain plug	7	Driveaxle inner CV joint boot	12	Front stabilizer bar
3	Engine oil filter	8	Front suspension crossmember	13	Catalytic converter
4	Exhaust crossover pipe	9	Battery location (in front of fenderwell)	14	Shock absorber damper fork
5	Starter motor	10	Driveaxle outer CV joint boot	15	Front suspension lower control arm

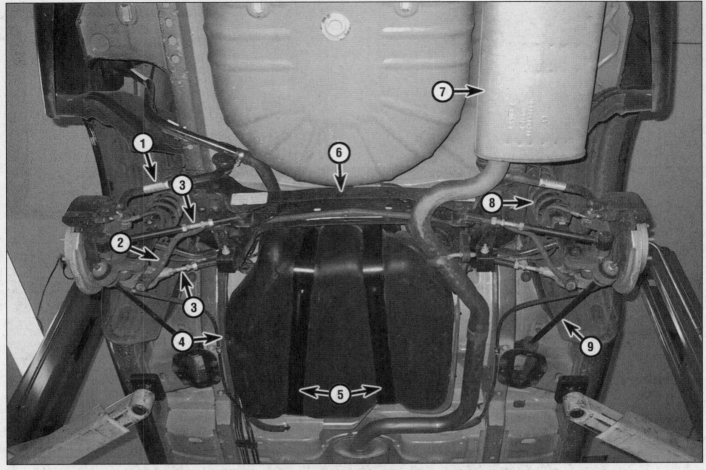

Typical rear underside components (convertible and sedan shown)

1	Rear suspension upper control arm	4	Fuel tank drain plug	7	Muffler
2	Rear stabilizer bar	5	Fuel tank retaining straps	8	Coil/shock absorber assembly
3	Lateral links	6	Rear suspension crossmember	9	Trailing arm

1 Chrysler Sebring, Dodge Stratus and Avenger Maintenance schedule

The following maintenance intervals are based on the assumption that the vehicle owner will be doing the maintenance or service work, as opposed to having a dealer service department do the work. Although the time/mileage intervals are loosely based on factory recommendations, most have been shortened to ensure, for example, that such items as lubricants and fluids are checked/changed at intervals that promote maximum engine/driveline service life. Also, subject to the preference of the individual owner interested in keeping his or her vehicle in peak condition at all times, and with the vehicle's ultimate resale in mind, many of the maintenance procedures may be performed more often than recommended in the following schedule. We encourage such owner initiative.

When the vehicle is new it should be serviced initially by a factory authorized dealer service department to protect the factory warranty. In many cases the initial maintenance check is done at no cost to the owner (check with your dealer service department for more information).

Every 250 miles or weekly, whichever comes first

Check the engine oil level; add oil as necessary (see Section 4)

Check the engine coolant level; add coolant as necessary (see Section 4)

Check the windshield washer fluid level (see Section 4)

Check the brake and clutch fluid level (see Section 4)

Check the tires and tire pressures (see Section 5)

Check the automatic transaxle fluid level (see Section 6)

Check the power steering fluid level (see Section 7)

Check the operation of all lights

Check the horn operation

Every 7500 miles or 6 months, whichever comes first

Change the engine oil and filter (see Section 8)*
Check and clean the battery and terminals (see Section 9)
Check the cooling system hoses and connections for leaks and damage (see Section 10)
Check the condition of all underhood hoses and connections (see Section 11)
Check the wiper blade condition (see Section 12)
Rotate the tires (see Section 13)
Check for free play in the steering linkage and balljoints (see Section 14)
Check the front suspension components (see Section 14)
Check the exhaust pipes and hangers (see Section 15)
Check the manual transaxle lubricant level (see Section 16)
Check the driveaxle boots (see Section 17)

Every 15,000 miles or 12 months, whichever comes first

All items listed above, plus:
Check the brake system (see Section 18)
Check the fuel system hoses and connections for leaks and damage (see Section 19)
Check the drivebelts and adjust if necessary (see Section 20)

Every 30,000 miles or 24 months, whichever comes first

All items listed above, plus:
Lubricate the suspension and steering balljoints (see Section 21)*
Replace the air filter element (see Section 22)*
Change the automatic transaxle fluid and filter (see Section 23)*
Change the manual transaxle lubricant (see Section 24)*
Drain and replace the engine coolant (unless filled with Mopar 5 year/100,000 mile coolant) (see Section 25)
Check the fuel evaporative emission control system and hoses (see Section 26)
Replace the spark plugs (non-platinum type) (see Section 27)
Check the spark plug wires (see Section 29)

Every 60,000 miles or 48 months, whichever comes first

All items listed above, plus:
Replace the drivebelts (see Section 20)
Check and replace, if necessary, the PCV valve (see Section 28)*
Replace spark plug wires (some 2.0L and 2.4L engines) (see Section 29)
Replace the fuel filter (2000 and earlier models) (see Section 30)

Every 100,000 miles or 84 months, whichever comes first

Drain and replace the engine coolant if filled with Mopar 5 year/100,000 mile coolant (see Section 25)
Replace the spark plugs (platinum-tipped spark plugs) (see Section 27)*
Replace the spark plug wires, distributor cap and rotor (2.5L/3.0L V6 engine) (see Section 29)*
Replace the timing belt on all but the 2.7L V6 engine (see Chapter 2)

This item is affected by "severe" operating conditions as described below. If the vehicle in question is operated under "severe" conditions, perform all maintenance procedures marked with an asterisk (*) at the intervals specified by the mileage headings below.

Consider the conditions "severe" if most driving is done . . .
In dusty areas
Towing a trailer
Idling for extended periods and/or low-speed operation
When outside temperatures remain below freezing and most trips are less than four miles
In heavy city traffic where outside temperatures regularly reach 90-degrees F or higher

Every 3000 miles

Change the engine oil and filter (see Section 8)

Every 15,000 miles

Lubricate the front and rear suspension and steering ball joints (see Section 21)
Check and replace, if necessary, the air filter element (see Section 22)
Change the automatic transaxle fluid and filter (see Section 23)
Change the manual transaxle lubricant (see Section 24)

Every 30,000 miles

Check and replace, if necessary, the PCV valve (see Section 28)

Every 75,000 miles

Replace the spark plugs (2.5L/3.0L V6 engines) (see Section 27)
Replace the spark plug wires (2.5L/3.0L V6 engines) (see Section 29)

2 Introduction

This Chapter is designed to help the home mechanic maintain the Chrysler Sebring, Dodge Stratus and Avenger models with the goals of maximum performance, economy, safety and reliability in mind.

Included is a master maintenance schedule, followed by procedures dealing specifically with each item on the schedule. Visual checks, adjustments, component replacement and other helpful items are included. Refer to the accompanying illustrations of the engine compartment and the underside of the vehicle for the locations of various components.

Adhering to the mileage/time maintenance schedule and following the step-by-step procedures, which is simply a preventive maintenance program, will result in maximum reliability and vehicle service life. Keep in mind that it's not possible for this comprehensive program to produce the same results if you maintain some items at the specified intervals but not others.

As you service the vehicle, you'll discover that many of the procedures can - and should - be grouped together because of the nature of the particular procedure you're performing or because of the close proximity of two otherwise unrelated components to one another.

For example, if the vehicle is raised, you should inspect the exhaust, suspension, steering and fuel systems while you're under the vehicle. When you're rotating the tires, it makes good sense to check the brakes, since the wheels are already removed. Finally, let's suppose you have to borrow or rent a torque wrench. Even if you only need it to tighten the spark plugs, you might as well check the torque of as many critical fasteners as time allows.

The first step in this maintenance program is to prepare before the actual work begins. Read through all the procedures you're planning, then gather together all the parts and tools needed. If it looks like you might run into problems during a particular job, seek advice from a mechanic or an experienced do-it-yourselfer.

Owner's Manual and VECI label information

Your vehicle owner's manual was written for your year and model and contains very specific information on component locations, specifications, fuse ratings, part numbers, etc. The Owner's Manual is an important resource for the do-it-yourselfer to have; if one was not supplied with your vehicle, it can generally be ordered from a dealer parts department.

Among other important information, the Vehicle Emissions Control Information (VECI) label contains specifications and procedures for applicable tune-up adjustments and, in some instances, spark plugs (see Chapter 6 for more information on the VECI label). The

information on this label is the exact maintenance data recommended by the manufacturer. This data often varies by intended operating altitude, local emissions regulations, month of manufacture, etc.

This Chapter contains procedural details, safety information and more ambitious maintenance intervals than you might find in manufacturer's literature. However, you may also find procedures or specifications in your Owner's Manual or VECI label that differ with what's printed here. In these cases, the Owner's Manual or VECI label can be considered correct, since it is specific to your particular vehicle.

3 Tune-up general information

The term "tune-up" is used in this manual to represent a combination of individual operations rather than one specific procedure.

The engine will be kept in relatively good running condition and the need for additional work will be minimized if the routine maintenance schedule is followed closely and frequent checks are made of fluid levels and high wear items, as suggested throughout this manual from the time the vehicle is new.

More likely than not, however, there will be times when the engine is running poorly due to lack of regular maintenance. This is even more likely if a used vehicle, which hasn't received regular and frequent maintenance checks, is purchased. In such cases, an engine tune-up will be needed outside of the regular routine maintenance intervals.

The first step in any tune-up or diagnostic procedure to help correct a poor running engine is a cylinder compression check. A compression check (see Chapter 2, Part D) will help determine the condition of internal engine components and should be used as a guide for tune-up and repair procedures. For instance, if a compression check indicates serious internal engine wear, a conventional tune-up will not improve the performance of the engine and would be a waste of time and money. Because of its importance, someone with the right equipment and the knowledge to use it properly should do the compression check.

The following procedures are those most often needed to bring a generally poor running engine back into a proper state of tune:

Minor tune-up

Check all engine related fluids (see Section 4)
Clean, inspect and test the battery (see Section 9)
Check all underhood hoses (see Section 11)
Check and adjust the drivebelts (see Section 20)
Check the air filter (see Section 22)
Service the cooling system (see Section 25)

4.2 The engine oil dipstick is located at the front (passenger's) side of the engine and is clearly marked (V6 engine shown)

Replace the spark plugs (see Section 27)
Check the PCV valve (see Section 28)
Inspect the spark plug wires (see Section 29)

Major tune-up

All items listed under Minor tune-up plus . . .
Check the fuel system (see Section 19)
Replace the air filter (see Section 22)
Check the charging system (see Chapter 5)

4 Fluid level checks (every 250 miles or weekly)

Note: *The following are fluid level checks to be done on a 250 mile or weekly basis. Additional fluid level checks can be found in specific maintenance procedures that follow. Regardless of the intervals, develop the habit of checking under the vehicle periodically for evidence of fluid leaks.*

1   Fluids are an essential part of the lubrication, cooling, brake and window washer systems. Because the fluids gradually become depleted and/or contaminated during normal operation of the vehicle, they must be replenished periodically. See *Recommended lubricants and fluids* at the beginning of this Chapter before adding fluid to any of the following components. **Note:** *The vehicle must be on level ground when fluid levels are checked.*

Engine oil

Refer to illustrations 4.2, 4.4 and 4.5

2   Engine oil level is checked with a dipstick that is located on the side of the engine facing the front of the vehicle **(see illustration)**. The dipstick extends through a tube and into the oil pan at the bottom of the engine.

3   The oil level should be checked before the vehicle has been driven, or about 5 minutes after the engine has been shut off. If

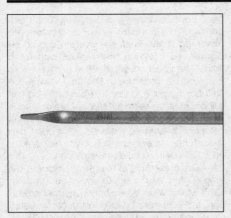

4.4 The oil level should be between the two marks, or near the top of the cross-hatched area, on the dipstick - if it isn't, add enough oil to bring the level up to or near the upper mark (do not overfill)

the oil is checked immediately after driving the vehicle, some of the oil will remain in the upper engine components, resulting in an inaccurate reading on the dipstick.

4   Pull the dipstick out of the tube and wipe all the oil off the end with a clean rag or paper towel. Insert the clean dipstick all the way back into the tube, then pull it out again. Note the oil level at the end of the dipstick. Add oil as necessary to bring the oil level to the second notch in the dipstick or to the top of the cross-hatched area, as applicable **(see illustration)**.

5   Oil is added to the engine after removing a cap located on the valve cover **(see illustration)**. The cap will be marked "Engine oil". Use a funnel to reduce spills as the oil is added.

6   Don't allow the level to drop below the lower notch or mark on the dipstick or engine damage may occur. On the other hand, don't overfill the engine by adding too much oil - it may result in oil aeration and loss of oil pressure and also could result in oil fouled spark plugs, oil leaks or seal failures.

7   Checking the oil level is an important preventive maintenance step. A consistently low oil level indicates oil leakage through damaged seals, defective gaskets or past worn rings or valve guides. If the oil looks milky in color or has water droplets in it, the block or head may be cracked and leaking coolant is entering the crankcase. The engine should be checked immediately. The condition of the oil should also be checked. Each time you check the oil level, slide your thumb and index finger up the dipstick before wiping off the oil. If you see small dirt or metal particles clinging to the dipstick, the oil should be changed (see Section 8).

Engine coolant
Refer to illustration 4.9

Warning: *Do not allow antifreeze to come in contact with your skin or painted surfaces of the vehicle. Flush contaminated areas immediately with plenty of water. Don't store new*

4.5 Turn the oil filler cap counterclockwise to remove it

coolant or leave old coolant lying around where it's accessible to children or pets – they're attracted by its sweet smell. Ingestion of even a small amount of coolant can be fatal! Wipe up garage floor and drip pan spills immediately. Keep antifreeze containers covered and repair cooling system leaks as soon as they're noticed.

8   All vehicles covered by this manual are equipped with a pressurized coolant recovery system. A white plastic coolant reservoir (all engines except the 2.7L V6) or expansion tank (2.7L V6 engine) is located on the right (passenger's) side of the engine compartment.

9   The coolant level in the tank should be checked regularly. **Warning:** *Do not remove the pressure cap or expansion tank cap to check the coolant level when the engine is warm!* The level in the tank varies with the temperature of the engine. When the engine is cold, the coolant level should be at or slightly above the COLD or MIN mark on the reservoir or expansion tank. Once the engine has warmed up, the level should be at or near the HOT or FULL mark. If it isn't, allow the engine to cool, then remove the cap from the tank and add a 50/50 mixture of ethylene glycol based antifreeze and water **(see illustration)**.

4.9 Maintain the coolant level near the upper line on the reservoir

Note: *Some models do not have a HOT mark on the tank.*

10   Drive the vehicle and recheck the coolant level. If only a small amount of coolant is required to bring the system up to the proper level, water can be used. However, repeated additions of water will dilute the antifreeze and water solution. In order to maintain the proper ratio of antifreeze and water, always top up the coolant level with the correct mixture. Don't use rust inhibitors or additives. An empty plastic milk jug or bleach bottle makes an excellent container for mixing coolant.

11   If the coolant level drops consistently, there may be a leak in the system. Inspect the radiator, hoses, filler cap, drain plugs and water pump (see Section 10). If no leaks are noted, have the pressure cap or expansion tank cap pressure tested by a service station.

12   If you have to remove the pressure cap or expansion tank cap, wait until the engine has cooled completely, then wrap a thick cloth around the cap and turn it to the first stop. If coolant or steam escapes, or if you hear a hissing noise, let the engine cool down longer, then remove the cap.

13   Check the condition of the coolant as well. It should be relatively clear. If it's brown or rust colored, the system should be drained, flushed and refilled. Even if the coolant appears to be normal, the corrosion inhibitors wear out, so it must be replaced at the specified intervals.

Windshield washer fluid
Refer to illustrations 4.14

14   The fluid for the windshield washer system is stored in a plastic reservoir. The reservoir level should be maintained about one inch below the filler cap. The reservoir is accessible after opening the hood and is located on the right (passenger's) side of the engine compartment next to the coolant recovery tank on some models **(see illustration)**. On other models it is located on the firewall.

15   In milder climates, plain water can be used in the reservoir, but it should be kept no more than two-thirds full to allow for expansion if the water freezes. In colder climates, use windshield washer system antifreeze,

4.14 Flip up the cap and add the washer fluid (convertible and sedan models shown)

4.17 Brake fluid level, indicated on the translucent white plastic brake fluid reservoir, should be kept at the upper (FULL or MAX) mark

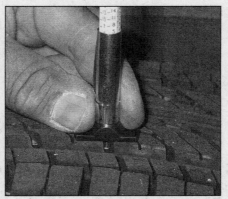

5.2 Use a tire tread depth indicator to monitor tire wear - they are available at auto parts stores or service stations and are relatively inexpensive

available at any auto parts store, to lower the freezing point of the fluid. Mix the antifreeze with water in accordance with the manufacturer's directions on the container. **Caution:** *DO NOT use cooling system antifreeze - it will damage the vehicle's paint. To help prevent icing in cold weather, warm the windshield with the defroster before using the washer.*

Brake and clutch fluid

Refer to illustration 4.17

Note: *Not all models equipped with a manual transaxle have a hydraulic clutch release system - some are cable actuated.*

16   The brake fluid reservoir is located on top of the brake master cylinder on the driver's side of the engine compartment near the firewall. The clutch fluid reservoir is mounted on the firewall, next to the brake master cylinder.

17   The fluid level should be maintained at

the upper (FULL or MAX) mark on either reservoir **(see illustration)**.

18   If additional fluid is necessary to bring the level up, use a rag to clean all dirt off the top of the reservoir to prevent contamination of the system. If any foreign matter enters the reservoir when the cap is removed, blockage in the system lines can occur. Also, make sure all painted surfaces around the reservoir are covered, since brake fluid will ruin paint. Carefully pour new, clean brake fluid obtained from a sealed container into the reservoir. Be sure the specified fluid is used; mixing different types of brake fluid can cause damage to the system. See *Recommended lubricants and fluids* at the beginning of this Chapter or your owner's manual.

19   At this time the fluid and the master cylinder should be inspected for contamination. Normally the brake hydraulic system won't

need periodic draining and refilling, but if rust deposits, dirt particles or water droplets are observed in the fluid, the system should be dismantled, cleaned and refilled with fresh fluid. Over time brake fluid will absorb moisture from the air. Moisture in the fluid lowers the fluid boiling point; if the fluid boils, the brakes will become ineffective. Normal brake fluid is clear in color. If the brake fluid is dark brown in color or is over three years old, it's a good idea to flush the system and refill it with new fluid.

20   Reinstall the fluid reservoir cap.

21   The brake fluid in the master cylinder will drop slightly as the brake shoes and pads at each wheel wear down during normal operation. If the master cylinder requires repeated replenishing to maintain the correct level, there is a leak in the brake system that should be corrected immediately. Check all brake lines and connections, along with the calipers, wheel cylinders and vacuum booster (see Section 18 and Chapter 9 for more information).

22   If you discover that the reservoir is empty or nearly empty, the system should be thoroughly inspected, refilled and then bled (see Chapter 8 for clutch system bleeding and Chapter 9 for brake system bleeding).

---

5   Tire and tire pressure checks (every 250 miles or weekly)

Refer to illustrations 5.2, 5.3, 5.4a, 5.4b and 5.8

1   Periodic inspection of the tires may spare you the inconvenience of being stranded with a flat tire. It can also provide you with vital information regarding possible problems in the steering and suspension systems before major damage occurs.

2   Original tires on this vehicle are equipped

5.3 This chart will help you determine the condition of the tires, the probable cause(s) of abnormal wear and the corrective action necessary

UNDERINFLATION

CUPPING

Cupping may be caused by:
- Underinflation and/or mechanical irregularities such as out-of-balance condition of wheel and/or tire, and bent or damaged wheel.
- Loose or worn steering tie-rod or steering idler arm.
- Loose, damaged or worn front suspension parts.

OVERINFLATION

INCORRECT TOE-IN OR EXTREME CAMBER

FEATHERING DUE TO MISALIGNMENT

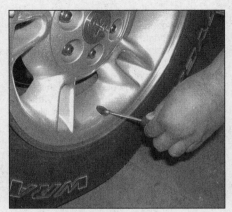

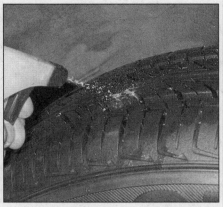

5.4a If a tire loses air on a steady basis, check the valve stem core first to make sure it's snug (special inexpensive wrenches are commonly available at auto parts stores)

5.4b If the valve stem core is tight, raise the corner of the vehicle with the low tire and spray a soapy water solution onto the tread as the tire is turned slowly - leaks will cause small bubbles to appear

5.8 To extend the life of the tires, check the air pressure at least once a week with an accurate gauge (don't forget the spare!)

with 1/2-inch wide bands that will appear when tread depth reaches 1/16-inch, at which point the tires can be considered worn out. Tread wear can be monitored with a simple, inexpensive device known as a tread depth indicator **(see illustration)**.

3   Note any abnormal tread wear **(see illustration)**. Tread pattern irregularities such as cupping, flat spots and more wear on one side than the other are indications of front end alignment and/or balance problems. If any of these conditions are noted, take the vehicle to a tire shop or service station to correct the problem.

4   Look closely for cuts, punctures and embedded nails or tacks. Sometimes a tire will hold air pressure for a short time or leak down very slowly after a nail has embedded itself in the tread. If a slow leak persists, check the valve stem core to make sure it's tight **(see illustration)**. Examine the tread for an object that may have embedded itself in the tire or for a "plug" that may have begun to leak (radial tire punctures are repaired with a plug that's installed in a puncture). If a puncture is suspected, it can be easily verified by

spraying a solution of soapy water onto the puncture area **(see illustration)**. The soapy solution will bubble if there's a leak. Unless the puncture is unusually large, a tire shop or service station can usually repair the tire.

5   Carefully inspect the inner sidewall of each tire for evidence of brake fluid leakage. If you see any, inspect the brakes immediately.

6   Correct air pressure adds miles to the life span of the tires, improves mileage and enhances overall ride quality. Tire pressure cannot be accurately estimated by looking at a tire, especially if it's a radial. A tire pressure gauge is essential. Keep an accurate gauge in the vehicle. The pressure gauges attached to the nozzles of air hoses at gas stations are often inaccurate.

7   Always check tire pressure when the tires are cold. Cold, in this case, means the vehicle has not been driven over a mile in the three hours preceding a tire pressure check. A pressure rise of four to eight pounds is not uncommon once the tires are warm.

8   Unscrew the valve cap protruding from the wheel or hubcap and push the gauge firmly onto the valve stem **(see illustration)**.

Compare the reading on the gauge to the recommended tire pressure shown on the placard on the driver's side door pillar. Be sure to reinstall the valve cap to keep dirt and moisture out of the valve stem mechanism. Check all four tires and, if necessary, add enough air to bring them up to the recommended pressure.

9   Don't forget to keep the spare tire inflated to the specified pressure (refer to your owner's manual or the tire sidewall). Note that the pressure recommended for the compact spare is higher than for the tires on the vehicle.

6   Automatic transaxle fluid level check (every 250 miles or weekly)

Refer to illustrations 6.3 and 6.4

1   Fluid inside the transaxle should be at normal operating temperature to get an accurate reading on the dipstick. This is done by driving the vehicle for several miles, making frequent starts and stops to allow the transaxle to shift through all gears.

2   Park the vehicle on a level surface and apply the parking brake. With the engine running, apply the brakes and place the gear selector lever momentarily in Reverse, then Drive and repeat the sequence again ending with the gear selector in the Park position.

3   With the engine still running, locate the transaxle fluid dipstick near the brake fluid reservoir. The dipstick has a "T" handle and is identified as "TRANS FLUID" **(see illustration)**. Remove the dipstick and wipe the fluid from the end with a clean rag.

4   Insert the dipstick back into the transaxle until the cap seats completely. Remove the dipstick again and note the fluid level on the end. The level should be in the area marked Hot (between the two upper holes in the dipstick) **(see illustration)**. If the fluid isn't hot (temperature approximately 100-degrees F), the level should be in the area marked Warm (between the two lower holes).

6.3 The automatic transaxle dipstick is located on the left (drivers) side of the engine compartment and is clearly marked

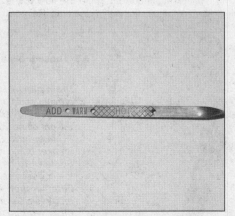

6.4 Check the fluid with the transaxle at normal operating temperature - the level should be kept in the HOT range, between the two upper holes

7.2 The power steering reservoir is located on the right (passenger's) side of the engine compartment and the fluid reservoir is translucent plastic - keep the level within the fill range (V6 engine shown)

7.5 The power steering fluid dipstick on most models' reservoir is marked on both sides for checking the fluid level (the arrow is pointing to the COLD level mark)

5   If the fluid level is at or below the ADD mark on the dipstick, add just enough of the specified fluid (see *Recommended lubricants and fluids* at the beginning of this Chapter) to raise the level to within the marks indicated for the appropriate temperature. Fluid should be slowly added into the dipstick tube, using a funnel to prevent spills.

6   DO NOT overfill the transaxle. Never allow the fluid level to go above the upper hole on the dipstick - it could cause internal transaxle damage. The best way to prevent overfilling is to add fluid a little at a time, driving the vehicle and checking the level between additions.

7   Use only transaxle fluid specified by the manufacturer. This information can be found in the *Recommended lubricants and fluids* Section at the beginning of this Chapter or in your owner's manual.

8   The condition of the fluid should also be checked along with the level. If it's a dark reddish-brown color, or if it smells burned, it should be changed. If you're in doubt about the condition of the fluid, purchase some new fluid and compare the two for color and odor.

7   Power steering fluid level check (every 250 miles or weekly)

Refer to illustrations 7.2 and 7.6

1   Unlike manual steering, the power steering system relies on hydraulic fluid that may, over a period of time, require replenishing.

2   The fluid reservoir for the power steering pump is located on the right (passenger's) side of the engine compartment **(see illustration)**.

3   The power steering fluid level can be checked with the engine either hot or cold.

4   On some models the power steering fluid reservoir is translucent and the level can be checked without removing the cap. On these models it's a simple matter to make sure the fluid level is within the proper range (see Step 7).

5   With the engine off, use a rag to clean the reservoir cap and the area around the cap. This will help prevent foreign material from falling into the reservoir when the cap is removed.

6   Turn and pull out the reservoir cap, which, on models without a translucent reservoir, has a dipstick attached to it. Wipe the fluid at the bottom of the dipstick with a clean rag. Reinstall

the cap to get a fluid level reading. Remove the cap again and note the fluid level. It should be at the appropriate mark on the dipstick in relation to the engine temperature.

7   If additional fluid is required, pour the specified type fluid (see *Recommended lubricants and fluids* at the beginning of this Chapter or your owner's manual) directly into the reservoir using a funnel to prevent spills.

8   If the reservoir requires frequent topping up, all power steering hoses, hose connections, the power steering pump and the steering gear should be carefully examined for leaks.

8   Engine oil and filter change (every 7500 miles or 6 months)

Refer to illustrations 8.3, 8.8, 8.13 and 8.18

1   Frequent oil changes are the most important preventive maintenance procedures that can be performed by the home mechanic. When engine oil ages, it gets diluted and contaminated, which ultimately leads to premature engine wear.

2   Although some sources recommend oil filter changes every other oil change, a new filter should be installed every time the oil is changed.

3   Gather together all necessary tools and materials before beginning this procedure **(see illustration)**. **Note:** *To avoid rounding off the corners of the drain plug, use a box-end type wrench or socket. In addition, you should have plenty of clean rags and newspapers handy to mop up any spills.*

4   Raise the front of the vehicle and support it securely on jackstands. **Warning:** *Never work under a vehicle that is supported only by a jack!*

5   If this is your first oil change on the vehicle, familiarize yourself with the locations of the oil drain plug and the oil filter. Since the engine and exhaust components will be warm during the actual work, it's a good idea to figure out any potential problems beforehand.

6   Allow the engine to warm up to normal operating temperature. If oil or tools are needed, use the warm-up time to gather everything necessary for the job. The correct

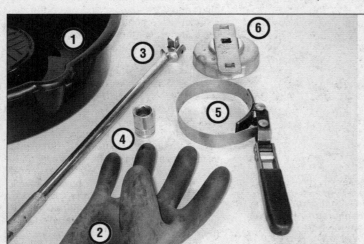

8.3 These tools are required when changing the engine oil and filter

1   ***Drain pan*** - *It should be fairly shallow in depth, but wide to prevent spills and capable of holding at least 5 quarts*
2   ***Rubber gloves*** - *When removing the drain plug and filter, you will get oil on your hands (the gloves will prevent burns)*
3   ***Breaker bar*** - *Sometimes the oil drain plug is tight, and a long breaker bar is needed to loosen it*
4   ***Socket*** - *To be used with the breaker bar or a ratchet (must be the correct size to fit the drain plug - six-point preferred)*
5   ***Filter wrench*** - *This is a metal band-type wrench, which requires clearance around the filter to be effective*
6   ***Filter wrench*** - *This type fits on the bottom of the filter and can be turned with a ratchet or breaker bar (different size wrenches are available for different types of filters)*

8.8 To avoid rounding off the corners, use the correct size box-end wrench or a socket to remove the engine oil drain plug

8.13 Since the oil filter is on very tight, you'll need a special wrench for removal (2.7L V6 engine shown)

type of oil to buy for your application can be found in the *Recommended lubricants and fluids* Section at the beginning of this Chapter or your owner's manual.

7   Move all necessary tools, rags and newspapers under the vehicle. Place a drain pan capable of holding at least 5 quarts under the drain plug. Keep in mind that the oil will initially flow from the engine with some force, so position the pan accordingly.

8   Being careful not to touch any of the hot exhaust components, use the breaker bar and socket or box-end wrench to remove the drain plug **(see illustration)**. Depending on how hot the oil is, you may want to wear gloves while unscrewing the plug the final few turns.

9   Allow the oil to drain into the pan. It may be necessary to move the pan further under the engine when the oil flow slows to a trickle.

10   After all the oil has completely drained, clean the plug thoroughly with a rag. Small metal particles may cling to it and would immediately contaminate the new oil.

11   Clean the area around the drain plug opening and reinstall the plug. Tighten it to the

torque listed in this Chapter's Specifications.

12   Next, carefully move the drain pan into position under the oil filter.

13   Now use the filter wrench to loosen the oil filter in a counterclockwise direction **(see illustration)**.

14   Sometimes the oil filter is on so tight it cannot be loosened, or it's positioned in an area inaccessible with a conventional filter wrench. Other type of tools which fit over the end of the filter and turned with a ratchet or breaker bar are available and may be better for removing the filter.

15   Completely unscrew the old filter. Be careful, it's full of oil. Empty the old oil inside the filter into the drain pan.

16   Compare the old filter with the new one to make sure they're identical.

17   Use a clean rag to remove all oil, dirt and sludge from the area where the oil filter seals on the engine. Check the old filter to make sure the rubber gasket isn't stuck to the engine mounting surface.

18   Apply a light coat of clean engine oil to the rubber gasket on the new oil filter **(see illustration)**.

19   Attach the new filter to the engine, following the tightening directions printed on the filter canister or packing box. Most filter manufacturers recommend against using a filter wrench due to the possibility of overtightening and damage to the seal.

20   Remove all tools and materials from under the vehicle, being careful not to spill the oil in the drain pan. Lower the vehicle.

21   Working inside the engine compartment, locate and remove the oil filler cap from the engine valve cover **(see illustration 4.5)**.

22   Using a funnel to prevent spills, pour the specified type and amount of new oil required (see the *Specifications* Section in the beginning of this Chapter) into the engine. Wait a few minutes to allow the oil to drain down to the pan, then check the level on the dipstick (see Section 4 if necessary). If the oil level is at or above the first notch or lower mark on

the dipstick, start the engine and allow the new oil to circulate.

23   Run the engine for only about a minute, then shut it off. Immediately look under the vehicle and check for leaks at the oil pan drain plug and around the oil filter. If either one is leaking, tighten it with a bit more force.

24   With the new oil circulated and the filter now completely full, wait a few minutes for the oil to drain back down into the pan then recheck the oil level on the dipstick. If necessary, add enough oil to bring the level to the second notch or upper mark on the dipstick. DO NOT overfill!

25   During the first few trips after an oil change, make it a point to check for leaks and keep a close watch on the oil level.

26   The old oil drained from the engine cannot be reused in its present state and should be disposed of. Check with your local auto parts store, disposal facility or environmental agency to see if they will accept the oil for recycling. After the oil has cooled it can be drained into a container (capped plastic jugs, topped bottles, milk cartons, etc.) for transport to one of these disposal sites. Don't dispose of the oil by pouring it on the ground or down a drain!

---

9   Battery check, maintenance and charging (every 7,500 miles or 6 months)

Warning: *Certain precautions must be followed when checking and servicing the battery. Hydrogen gas, which is highly explosive, is produced by the battery. Keep lighted tobacco, open flames, bare light bulbs or other possible sources of ignition away from the battery. Furthermore, the electrolyte inside the battery is sulfuric acid which is highly corrosive and can burn your skin and cause severe injury to your eyes. Always wear eye protection! It will also destroy clothing and ruin painted surfaces.*

8.18 Lubricate the oil filter gasket with clean engine oil before installing the filter on the engine

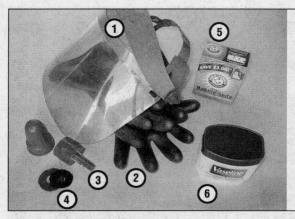

9.1a Tools and materials required for battery maintenance on "side post" batteries

1 *Face shield/safety goggles* - *When removing corrosion with a brush, the acidic particles can easily fly up into your eyes*
2 *Rubber gloves* - *Another safety item to consider when servicing the battery; remember that's acid inside the battery!*
3 *Battery terminal/cable cleaner* - *This wire brush cleaning tool will remove all traces of corrosion from the battery and cable*
4 *Treated felt washers* - *Placing one of these on each post, directly under the cable clamps, will help prevent corrosion*
5 *Baking soda* - *A solution of baking soda and water can be used to neutralize corrosion*
6 *Petroleum jelly* - *A layer of this on the battery posts will help prevent corrosion*

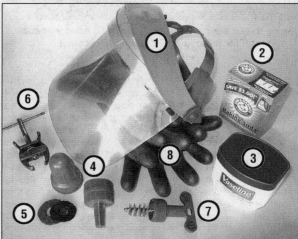

9.1b Tools and materials required for conventional "top post" type battery maintenance

1 *Face shield/safety goggles* - *When removing corrosion with a brush, the acidic particles can easily fly up into your eyes*
2 *Baking soda* - *A solution of baking soda and water can be used to neutralize corrosion*
3 *Petroleum jelly* - *A layer of this on the battery posts will help prevent corrosion*
4 *Battery post/cable cleaner* - *This wire brush cleaning tool will remove all traces of corrosion from the battery posts and cable clamps*
5 *Treated felt washers* - *Placing one of these on each post, directly under the cable clamps, will help prevent corrosion*
6 *Puller* - *Sometimes the cable clamps are very difficult to pull off the posts, even after the nut/bolt has been completely loosened. This tool pulls the clamp straight up and off the post without damage*
7 *Battery post/cable cleaner* - *Here is another cleaning tool which is a slightly different version of Number 4 above, but it does the same thing*
8 *Rubber gloves* - *Another safety item to consider when servicing the battery; remember that's acid inside the battery!*

Servicing

Refer to illustrations 9.1a and 9.1b

1   A routine preventive maintenance program for the battery in your vehicle is the only way to ensure quick and reliable starts. But before performing any battery maintenance, make sure that you have the proper equipment necessary to work safely around the battery **(see illustrations)**.

2   Prior to servicing the battery always turn the engine and all accessories off and disconnect the cable from the negative terminal of the battery.

3   On convertible and sedan models, the battery is the side terminal type and is located inside the wheel well of the left. On coupe models the battery is the conventional top post type and is located in the left side of the engine compartment.

4   On convertible and sedan models it will be necessary to remove the battery from the vehicle for service (see Chapter 5).

5   Inspect the external condition of the battery. Check the battery case for cracks or other damage.

Convertible and sedan models

Refer to illustrations 9.6a, 9.6b and 9.6c

6   On these models the terminals are located on the side of the battery. Clean the battery terminals and cable connections thoroughly with a wire brush or a terminal cleaner and a solution of warm water and baking soda **(see illustrations)**. Wash the terminals and the top of the battery case with the same solution but make sure that the solution doesn't get into the battery. When cleaning the cables, terminals

9.6a Use a side terminal battery brush (available at most auto parts stores) to clean up the terminal contact area

9.6b The side terminal battery brush includes a special ring-type portion used to clean the battery cable sealing recess around the terminal

9.6c After cleaning, the battery side terminal should have a clean, shiny surface like this

9.7a Battery terminal corrosion usually appears as light, fluffy powder

9.7b Removing the cable from a battery post with a wrench - sometimes special battery pliers are required for this procedure if corrosion has caused deterioration of the nut or bolt hex (always remove the ground cable first and hook it up last!)

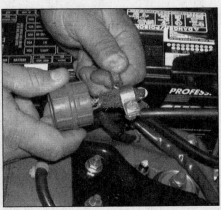

9.8a When cleaning the cable clamps, all corrosion must be removed

9.8b Regardless of the type of tool used on the battery post, a clean, shiny surface should be the result (the inside of the clamp is tapered to match the taper on the post, so don't remove too much material

and battery top, wear safety goggles and rubber gloves to prevent any solution from coming in contact with your eyes or hands. Wear old clothes too - even diluted, sulfuric acid splashed onto clothes will burn holes in them. Thoroughly wash all cleaned areas with plain water. On these models periodic inspection is difficult because of the battery and cables are located in the fenderwell, so while they are disconnected it's a good idea to check the cables for damage and corrosion and replace them if necessary.

Coupe models

Refer to illustrations 9.7a, 9.7b, 9.8a and 9.8b
7   If corrosion, which looks like white, fluffy deposits **(see illustration)** is evident, particularly around the terminals, the battery should be removed for cleaning. Loosen the cable clamp bolts with a wrench, being careful to remove the ground cable first, and slide them off the terminals **(see illustration)**. Then disconnect the hold-down clamp bolt and nut, remove the clamp and lift the battery from the engine compartment.
8   Clean the cable clamps thoroughly with a battery brush or a terminal cleaner and a solution of warm water and baking soda **(see illustration)**. Wash the terminals and the top of the battery case with the same solution but make sure that the solution doesn't get into the battery. When cleaning the cables, terminals and battery top, wear safety goggles and rubber gloves to prevent any solution from coming in contact with your eyes or hands. Wear old clothes too - even diluted, sulfuric acid splashed onto clothes will burn holes in them. If the terminals have been extensively corroded, clean them up with a terminal cleaner **(see illustration)**. Thoroughly wash all cleaned areas with plain water.
9   Inspect the battery carrier. If it's dirty or covered with corrosion, clean it with the same solution of warm water and baking soda and rinse it with clean water.
10   If the battery is a maintenance-type, it has removable cell caps which allow you to add water (use distilled water only) to the battery when the electrolyte level gets low.
11   If you are not sure what type of battery

you have (some maintenance-types have recessed cell caps that resemble maintenance-free batteries), one simple way to confirm your type of battery is to look for a built-in hydrometer. Most maintenance-free batteries have built-in hydrometers that indicate the state of charge by the color displayed in the hydrometer window, since measuring the specific gravity of the electrolyte is not possible. Also check for cut-outs near the cell caps - if the caps can be removed, cut-outs are usually provided to assist with prying off the caps.
12   If your battery is a maintenance-type, remove the cell caps and check the level of the electrolyte. It should be up to the split-ring inside the battery. If the level is low, add distilled water (distilled water is mineral-free, tap water contains minerals that will shorten the life of your battery) to bring the electrolyte up to the proper level.
13   Next, check the entire length of each battery cable for cracks, worn insulation and frayed conductors. Replace the cable(s) if necessary.
14   Install the battery (see Chapter 5).

Charging

Warning: *When batteries are being charged, hydrogen gas, which is very explosive and flammable, is produced. Do not smoke or allow open flames near a charging or a recently charged battery. Wear eye protection when near the battery during charging. Also, make sure the charger is unplugged before connecting or disconnecting the battery from the charger.*

15   Slow-rate charging is the best way to restore a battery that's discharged to the point where it will not start the engine. It's also a good way to maintain the battery charge in a vehicle that's only driven a few miles between starts. Maintaining the battery charge is particularly important in the winter when the battery must work harder to start the engine and

electrical accessories that drain the battery are in greater use.
16   It's best to use a one or two-amp battery charger (sometimes called a "trickle" charger). They are the safest and put the least strain on the battery. They are also the least expensive. For a faster charge, you can use a higher amperage charger, but don't use one rated more than 1/10th the amp/hour rating of the battery. Rapid boost charges that claim to restore the power of the battery in one to two hours are hardest on the battery and can damage batteries not in good condition. This type of charging should only be used in emergency situations.
17   The average time necessary to charge a battery should be listed in the instructions that come with the charger. As a general rule, a trickle charger will charge a battery in 12 to 16 hours.
18   On convertible and sedan models with the battery located inside the wheel well of the left front fender, remove the battery from the vehicle (see Chapter 5).
19   On maintenance-type batteries, remove the cell caps. Make sure the electrolyte level

is OK before beginning to charge the battery. Cover the holes with a clean cloth to prevent spattering electrolyte.

20   On batteries with the terminals located on the side, install bolts (with the appropriate thread size and pitch) in the terminals so the charger can be attached.

21   Connect the battery charger leads to the battery posts (positive to positive, negative to negative), then plug in the charger. Make sure it is set at 12 volts if it has a selector switch. If the battery charger does not have a built-in timer, it's a good idea to use one in case you forget - so you won't over charge the battery.

22   If you're using a charger with a rate higher than two amps, check the battery regularly during charging to make sure it doesn't overheat. If you're using a trickle charger, you can safely let the battery charge overnight after you've checked it regularly for the first couple of hours.

23   If the battery has removable cell caps, measure the specific gravity with a hydrometer every hour during the last few hours of the charging cycle. Hydrometers are available inexpensively from auto parts stores - follow the instructions that come with the hydrometer. Consider the battery charged when there's no change in the specific gravity reading for two hours and the electrolyte in the cells is outgassing (bubbling) freely. The specific gravity reading from each cell should be very close to the others. If not, the battery probably has a bad cell(s).

24   Most batteries with sealed tops have built-in hydrometers on the top that indicate the state of charge by the color displayed in the hydrometer window. Normally, a bright-colored hydrometer indicates a full charge and a dark hydrometer indicates the battery still needs charging. Check the battery manufacturer's instructions to be sure you know what the colors mean. **Note:** *It may be necessary to jiggle the battery to bring the test indicator fluid into view.*

25   If the battery has a sealed top and does not have a built-in hydrometer, you can hook up a voltmeter across the battery terminals to check the charge. A fully charged battery should read approximately 12.6 volts or higher.

26   Further information on the battery and jump starting can be found in Chapter 5 and at the front of this manual, respectively.

10   Cooling system check (every 7,500 miles or 6 months)

Refer to illustration 10.4
Warning: *The electric cooling fan(s) on these models can activate at any time the ignition switch is in the ON position. Make sure the ignition is OFF when working in the vicinity of the fan(s).*

1   Many major engine failures can be attributed to a faulty cooling system. If the vehicle is equipped with an automatic transaxle, a transmission fluid cooler is incorporated inside the radiator side tank.

2   The cooling system should be checked with the engine cold. Do this before the vehicle is driven for the day or after it has been shut off for three or four hours and the upper radiator hose feels cool to the touch.

3   Remove the cooling system pressure cap **(see illustration 4.9 and the underhood photos at the beginning of this Chapter)** and thoroughly clean the cap with water. Also clean the filler neck. All traces of corrosion and gum should be removed.

4   Carefully check the upper and lower radiator hoses along with the smaller diameter heater hoses. Inspect the entire length of each hose, replacing any that are cracked, swollen or deteriorated **(see illustration)**. Cracks may become more apparent when a hose is squeezed.

5   Also check that all hose connections are tight. If the vehicle came equipped with spring-type hose clamps which lose their tension over time, replace them with the more reliable screw-type clamps when new hoses are installed. A leak in the cooling system will usually show up as white or rust-colored deposits on the areas adjoining the leak.

6   Use compressed air, water or a soft brush to remove bugs, leaves, and other debris from the front of the radiator or air conditioning condenser. Be careful not to damage the delicate cooling fins, or cut yourself on them.

7   Finally, have the cap and system pressure tested. If you do not have a pressure tester available, most gas stations and repair shops will do this for a minimal charge.

11   Underhood hose check and replacement (every 7,500 miles or 6 months)

Warning: *Replacement of air conditioning hoses must be left to a dealer service department or air conditioning shop equipped to depressurize the system safely. Never remove air conditioning components or hoses until the system has been depressurized.*

General

1   High temperatures under the hood can cause the deterioration of the rubber and plastic hoses used for engine, accessory and emission systems operation. Periodic inspection should be made for cracks, loose clamps, material hardening and leaks.

2   Information specific to the cooling system hoses can be found in Section 10.

3   Some hoses use clamps to secure the hoses to fittings. Where clamps are used, check to be sure that they haven't lost their tension, allowing the hose to leak. Where clamps are not used, make sure the hose hasn't expanded and/or hardened where it slips over the fitting, allowing it to leak.

Vacuum hoses

4   It's quite common for vacuum hoses, especially those in the emissions system, to

Check for a chafed area that could fail prematurely.

Check for a soft area indicating the hose has deteriorated inside.

Overtightening the clamp on a hardened hose will damage the hose and cause a leak.

Check each hose for swelling and oil-soaked ends. Cracks and breaks can be located by squeezing the hose.

10.4 Hoses, like drivebelts, have a habit of failing at the worst possible time - to prevent the inconvenience of a blown radiator or heater hose, inspect them carefully as shown here

be color coded or identified by colored stripes molded into the hose. Various systems require hoses with different wall thickness, collapse resistance and temperature resistance. When replacing hoses, make sure the new ones are made of the same material as the original.

5   Often the only effective way to check a hose is to remove it completely from the vehicle. Where more than one hose is removed, be sure to label the hoses and their attaching points to insure proper reattachment.

6   Include plastic T-fittings in the check of vacuum hoses. Check the fittings for cracks and the hose where it fits over the fitting for enlargement, which could cause leakage.

7   A small piece of vacuum hose (1/4-inch inside diameter) can be used as a stethoscope to detect vacuum leaks. Hold one end

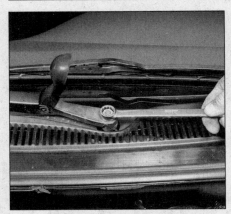

12.3a On convertible and sedan models, lift the cover and check the mounting nut for tightness

12.3b On coupe models, pry out the plastic cover for access to the wiper nut

of the hose to your ear and probe around vacuum hoses and fittings, listening for the "hissing" sound characteristic of a vacuum leak. **Warning:** *When probing with the vacuum hose stethoscope, be careful not to allow your body or the hose to come into contact with moving engine components such as the drivebelt, cooling fan, etc.*

Fuel hose

Warning: *Gasoline is extremely flammable, so take extra precautions when you work on any part of the fuel system. Don't smoke or allow open flames or bare light bulbs near the work area, and don't work in a garage where a gas-type appliance (such as a water heater or clothes dryer) is present. If you spill any fuel on your skin, rinse it off immediately with soap and water. When you perform any kind of work on the fuel system, wear safety glasses and have a Class B type fire extinguisher on hand. Before working on any part of the fuel system, relieve the fuel system pressure (see Chapter 4).*

8   Check all rubber fuel hoses for damage and deterioration. Check especially for cracks in areas where the hose bends and just before clamping points, such as where a hose attaches to the fuel injection system.
9   High quality fuel line, specifically designed for fuel injection systems, must be used for fuel line replacement. **Warning:** *Never use vacuum line, clear plastic tubing or water hose for fuel lines.*

Brake hoses

10   The hoses used to connect the brake calipers or wheel cylinders to the metal lines are subject to extreme working conditions. They must endure high hydraulic pressures, heat and still maintain flexibility. The brake hoses typically can be inspected without removing the wheels. Carefully examine each hose for leakage, cracks, bulging, delaminating and damage. If any damage is found, the hose must be replaced immediately (see Chapter 9).

Fuel and brake system metal lines

11   Sections of metal line are often used for fuel line between the fuel tank and fuel injection system. Carefully check to be sure the line has not been bent and crimped and that no cracks have started in the line.

12   If a section of metal fuel line must be replaced, only seamless steel tubing should be used, since copper and aluminum tubing do not have the strength necessary to withstand normal engine operating vibration.
13   Check the metal brake lines where they enter the master cylinder and brake proportioning or ABS unit (if equipped) for cracks in the lines or loose fittings. Any sign of brake fluid leakage calls for an immediate thorough inspection of the brake system.

12   Windshield wiper blade inspection and replacement (every 7,500 miles or 6 months)

Refer to illustrations 12.3a, 12.3b, 12.5a and 12.5b
1   The windshield wiper blade elements should be checked periodically for cracks and deterioration.
2   Road film can build up on the wiper blades and affect their efficiency, so they should be washed regularly with a mild detergent solution.
3   The action of the wiping mechanism can loosen the wiper arm retaining nuts, so they should be checked and tightened at the same time the wiper blades are checked **(see illustrations)**.
4   Lift the wiper blade assembly away from the windshield.
5   Press the release lever and slide the blade assembly out of the hook in the end of the wiper arm **(see illustrations)**. Carefully rest the wiper arm on the windshield.
6   The rubber wiper element is secured to the blade assembly at one end of the blade element channel. Compress the locking feature on the element so it clears the tangs on the blade assembly channel claw and then slide the element out of the frame.
7   Installation is the reverse of removal. Make sure the rubber element and blade assembly is securely attached.

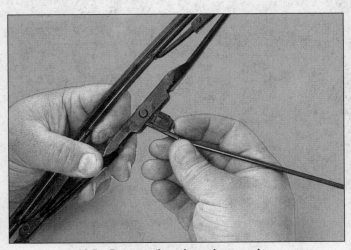

12.5a Depress the release lever and . . .

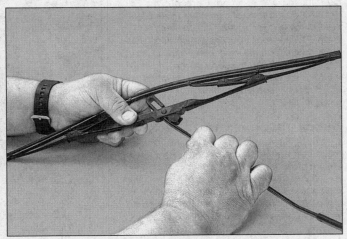

12.5b . . . slide the wiper element down out of the hook in the end of the arm

13   Tire rotation (every 7,500 miles or 6 months)

Refer to illustrations 13.2a and 13.2b

1   The tires should be rotated at the specified intervals and whenever uneven wear is noticed. Since the vehicle will be raised and the tires removed, this is a good time to check the brakes also (see Section 18).

2   Radial tires must be rotated in a specific pattern **(see illustrations)**. **Note:** *Most vehicles are sold with non-directional radial tires, but some performance tires are directional, and have an arrow on the sidewall indicating the direction they must turn when mounted on the vehicle.*

3   See the information in *Jacking and towing* at the front of this manual for the proper procedures to follow when raising the vehicle and changing a tire; however, if the brakes are to be checked, don't apply the parking brake as stated. Make sure the tires are blocked to prevent the vehicle from rolling. **Note:** *Prior to raising the vehicle, loosen all lug nuts a quarter turn.*

4   Preferably, the entire vehicle should be raised at the same time. This can be done on a hoist or by jacking up each corner of the vehicle and lowering it onto jackstands. Always use jackstands and make sure the vehicle is safely supported. **Warning:** *Never work under a vehicle that is supported only by a jack!*

5   After the tire rotation, check and adjust the tire pressures as necessary and tighten the wheel lug nuts to the torque listed in this Chapter's Specifications.

14   Steering and suspension check (every 7,500 miles or 6 months)

Note 1: *The steering linkage and suspension components should be checked periodically. Worn or damaged suspension and steering components can result in excessive and abnormal tire wear, poor ride quality and vehicle handling and reduced fuel economy. For detailed illustrations of the steering and suspension components, refer to Chapter 10.*

Note 2: *The front suspension on 2001 and later coupe models is a MacPherson strut design. The front suspension on all other models, as well as the rear suspension on all models, uses coil-over shock absorber assemblies.*

Shock absorber/strut check

1   Park the vehicle on level ground, turn the engine off and set the parking brake. Check the tire pressures.

2   Push down at one corner of the vehicle, then release it while noting the movement of the body. It should stop moving and come to rest in a level position within one or two bounces.

3   If the vehicle continues to move up-and-down or if it fails to return to its original posi-

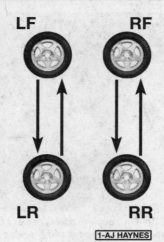

13.2a The recommended four-tire rotational pattern for *directional* radial tires

13.2b The recommended four-tire rotational pattern for *non-directional* radial tires

tion, a worn or weak shock absorber or strut assembly is probably the reason.

4   Repeat the above check at each of the three remaining corners of the vehicle.

5   Raise the vehicle and support it securely on jackstands.

6   Check the shock absorbers/struts for evidence of fluid leakage. A light film of fluid is no cause for concern. Make sure that any fluid noted is from the shocks and not from some other source. If leakage is noted, replace the shocks/struts as a set.

14.9 Front suspension components

1	*Upper control arm*	*5*	*Shock absorber damper fork*
2	*Coil spring*	*6*	*Tie-rod end*
3	*Steering knuckle*	*7*	*Lower control arm*
4	*Shock absorber*	*8*	*Steering gear boot*

14.10 Check for tie-rod end play by moving the wheel/tire front and rear, then move the top and bottom of the tire to check for play in the balljoints

7   Check the shocks/struts to be sure that they are securely mounted and undamaged. Check the upper mounts for damage and wear. If damage or wear is noted, replace the shocks/struts as a set (front or rear).
8   If the shocks or struts must be replaced, refer to Chapter 10 for the procedure.

Suspension and steering check

Refer to illustrations 14.9, 14.10 and 14.13
9   Raise the vehicle and support it securely on jackstands. **Warning:** *Never work under a vehicle that is supported only by a jack!* Visually inspect the steering and suspension components (front and rear) for damage and distortion. Look for damaged seals, boots and bushings and leaks of any kind. Examine the bushings where the lower control arm meets the chassis and on the stabilizer bar connections **(see illustration)**.
10   Clean the lower end of the steering knuckle. On all models except 2001 and later coupes, place a floor jack under the lower control arm and raise it slightly. Have an assistant grasp the lower edge of the tire and move the

wheel in-and-out while you look for movement at the steering knuckle-to-control arm balljoint **(see illustration)**. If there is any movement, the suspension balljoint(s) must be replaced.
11   Grasp each front tire at the front and rear edges, push in at the front, pull out at the rear and feel for play in the steering system components. If any freeplay is noted, check the tie-rod ends for looseness.
12   Additional steering and suspension system information and illustrations can be found in Chapter 10.
13   Inspect the steering gear boots for cracks as well as loose clamps **(see illustration)**. If you notice lubricant leaking from the boots, the rack seals have failed, in which case the steering gear will have to be replaced with a new or rebuilt unit, or overhauled by an automotive service technician.

15 Exhaust system check (every 7,500 or 6 months)

Refer to illustration 15.3
Note: *Perform the following procedure with the engine cold.*
1   Raise the vehicle and support it securely on jackstands. **Warning:** *Never work under a vehicle that is supported only by a jack!*
2   With the engine cold (at least three hours after the vehicle has been driven), check the complete exhaust system from its starting point at the engine to the end of the tailpipe.
3   Check the pipes and connections for signs of leakage and/or corrosion indicating a potential failure. Make sure that all brackets and hangers are in good condition and tight **(see illustration)**.
4   At the same time, inspect the underside of the body for holes, corrosion and open seams which may allow exhaust gases to enter the passenger compartment. Seal all body openings with silicone sealant or body putty.
5   Rattles and other noises can often be traced to the exhaust system, especially the mounts and hangers. Try to move the pipes, muffler and catalytic converter. If the compo-

nents can come into contact with the body, secure the exhaust system with new mounts.
6   This is also an ideal time to check the running condition of the engine by inspecting the very end of the tailpipe. The exhaust deposits here are an indication of the engine's state-of-tune. If the pipe is black and sooty or coated with white deposits, the engine may be in need of a tune-up (including a thorough fuel injection system inspection).

16 Manual transaxle lubricant level check (every 7500 miles or 6 months)

1   Manual transaxles do not have a fluid dipstick. The lubricant level is checked by removing the plug from the side of the transaxle case. The lubricant level should be checked with the engine cold and the vehicle level.
2   Raise the vehicle and support it securely on jackstands in a level position. **Warning:** *Never work under a vehicle that is supported only by a jack!*
3   Locate the metal or rubber plug on the left (driver's) side of the transaxle differential near the driveaxle shaft. Use a rag to clean it and the surrounding area. It may be necessary to remove the left inner fenderwell cover for access to the plug. Place a drain pan under the transaxle.
4   Use a socket or wrench (metal plug), or pliers or a screwdriver (rubber plug) to remove the plug. If oil begins to run out, let it find its own level (presuming the vehicle is relatively level). If oil does not run out, insert your finger to feel the lubricant level. It should be within 3/16-inch of the bottom of the plug hole.
5   If the transaxle requires additional lubricant, use a funnel with a rubber tube or a syringe to pour or squeeze the recommended lubricant into the plug hole to restore the level. If you overfill it, let the fluid run out until it is level with the plug hole. **Caution:** *Use only the specified transaxle lubricant - see* Recommended lubricants and fluids *at the beginning*

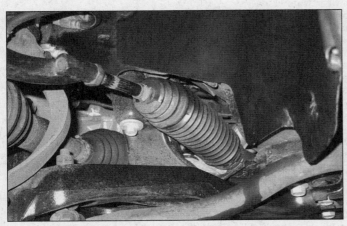

14.13 Check the steering rack tie-rod boot for damage

15.3 Check the exhaust system connections, clamps, mounting bolts, brackets and hangers for damage (arrows)

17.3 Check the inner and outer boot on each driveaxle for cracks and/or leaking grease

18.5a With the wheel off, measure the thickness of the inner pad lining material through the inspection hole

18.5b Measure the thickness of the outer brake pad from the metal backing

of this Chapter or your owner's manual. **Note:** *Most auto parts stores sell pumps that screw into the oil containers which make this job much easier and less messy.*

6   Install the plug, tighten it securely and lower the vehicle. Test drive it and check for leaks.

17   Driveaxle boot check (every 7,500 miles or 6 months)

Refer to illustration 17.3

1   If the driveaxle boots are damaged, letting grease out and water and dirt in, serious (not to mention costly) damage can occur to the CV joints. The boots should be inspected very carefully at the recommended intervals or anytime the vehicle is raised.

2   Raise the front of the vehicle and support it securely on jackstands. **Warning:** *Never work under a vehicle that is supported only by a jack!*

3   Place the transaxle in Neutral. While rotating the wheels, inspect the four driveaxle boots (two on each driveaxle) very carefully for cracks, tears, holes, deteriorated rubber and loose or missing clamps **(see illustration)**. If the boots are dirty, wipe them clean before beginning the inspection.

4   If damage or deterioration is evident, replace the boots and check the CV joints for damage (see Chapter 8).

5   Place the transaxle in Park or in-gear as applicable and lower the vehicle.

18   Brake system check (every 15,000 miles or 12 months)

Warning: *Dust created by the brake system is harmful to your health. Never blow it out with compressed air and don't inhale any of it. An approved filtering mask should be worn when working on brakes. Do not, under any circumstances, use petroleum-based solvents to clean brake parts. Use brake system cleaner only!*

1   The brakes should be inspected every time the wheels are removed or whenever a defect is suspected. Indications of a potential brake system problem include the vehicle pulling to one side when the brake pedal is depressed, noises coming from the brakes when they are applied, excessive brake pedal travel, a pulsating pedal and leakage of fluid, usually seen on the inside of the tire or wheel. **Note:** *It is normal for a vehicle equipped with an Anti-lock Brake System (ABS) to exhibit brake pedal pulsation's during severe braking conditions.*

Disc brakes
Refer to illustration 18.5a, 18.5b and 18.8

2   Disc brakes can be visually checked without removing any parts except the wheels. Remove the hub caps (if applicable) and loosen the front wheel lug nuts a quarter turn each.

3   Raise the front of the vehicle and place it securely on jackstands. **Warning:** *Never work under a vehicle that is supported only by a jack!*

4   Remove the front wheels. Now visible is the disc brake caliper which contains the pads. There is an outer brake pad and an inner pad. Both must be checked for wear. **Note:** *Usually the inner pad wears faster than the outer pad.*

5   Measure the thickness of the outer pad at each end of the caliper and the inner pad through the inspection hole in the caliper body **(see illustrations)**. Compare the measurement with the limit given in this Chapter's Specifications; if any brake pad thickness is less than specified, then all brake pads must be replaced (see Chapter 9).

6   If you're in doubt as to the exact pad thickness or quality, remove them for measurement and further inspection (see Chapter 9).

7   Check the disc for score marks, wear and burned spots. If any of these conditions exist, the disc should be removed for servicing or replacement (see Chapter 9).

8   Before installing the wheels, check all the brake lines and hoses for damage, wear, deformation, cracks, corrosion, leakage,

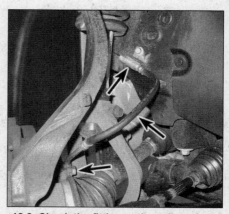

18.8 Check the fitting at the caliper, look along the brake hose for signs of cracking or fluid leakage, and check where the flexible brake hose meets the steel line on the chassis (arrows)

bends and twists, particularly in the vicinity of the rubber hoses and calipers **(see illustration)**.

9   Install the front wheels, lower the vehicle and tighten the wheel lug nuts to the torque given in this Chapter's Specifications.

Drum brakes
Refer to illustrations 18.14 and 18.17

10   Remove the hub caps (if applicable) and loosen the wheel lug nuts a quarter turn each.

11   Raise the rear of the vehicle and support it securely on jackstands. **Warning:** *Never work under a vehicle that is supported only by a jack!* Block the front wheels to prevent the vehicle from rolling, however, do not apply the parking brake or it will lock the drums in place. Remove the rear wheels.

12   Remove the brake drum as described in Chapter 9.

13   With the drum removed, carefully clean off any accumulations of dirt and dust using brake system cleaner. **Warning:** *DO NOT blow the dust out with compressed air and don't inhale any of it.*

14   Measure the thickness of the lining

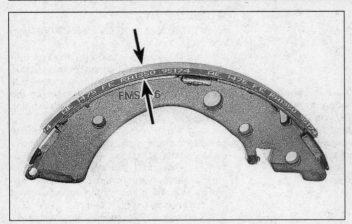

18.14 If the lining is bonded to the brake shoe, measure the lining thickness from the outer surface to the metal shoe; if the lining is riveted to the shoe, measure from the lining outer surface to the rivet head

18.17 Pull the boot away from the cylinder and check for fluid leakage

material on both leading and trailing brake shoes **(see illustration)**. Compare the measurement with the limit given in this Chapter's Specifications, if any brake shoe thickness is less than specified, then all brake shoes must be replaced (see Chapter 9).

15   Inspect the brake shoes for uneven wear patterns, cracks, glazing and delamination and replace if necessary. If the shoes have been saturated with brake fluid, oil or grease, this also necessitates replacement (see Chapter 9).

16   Make sure all the brake assembly springs are connected and in good condition.

17   Check the brake wheel cylinder for signs of fluid leakage. Carefully pry back the rubber dust boots on the wheel cylinder **(see illustration)**. Any leakage here is an indication that the wheel cylinders must be overhauled immediately (see Chapter 9). Also, check all hoses and connections for signs of leakage.

18   Clean the inside of the drum with brake system cleaner. Again, be careful not to breathe the dust.

19   Inspect the inside of the drum for cracks, score marks, deep scratches and "hard spots" which will appear as small discolored areas. If imperfections cannot be removed with fine emery cloth, the drum must be taken to an automotive machine shop for resurfacing.

20   Repeat the procedure for the remaining wheel.

21   Install the wheels, lower the vehicle and tighten the wheel lug nuts to the torque given in this Chapter's Specifications.

Parking brake

22   Slowly pull up on the parking brake and count the number of clicks you hear until the handle is up as far as it will go. The adjustment is correct if you hear the specified number of clicks (see this Chapter's Specifications). If you hear more or fewer clicks, it's time to adjust the parking brake (see Chapter 9).

23   An alternative method of checking the parking brake is to park the vehicle on a steep hill with the engine running (so you can apply

the brakes if necessary) with the parking brake set and the transaxle in Neutral. If the parking brake cannot prevent the vehicle from rolling, it needs adjustment (see Chapter 9).

---

19   Fuel system hoses and connections check (every 15,000 miles or 12 months)

Refer to illustration 19.5

Warning: *Gasoline is extremely flammable, so take extra precautions when you work on any part of the fuel system. Don't smoke or allow open flames or bare light bulbs near the work area, and don't work in a garage where a gas-type appliance (such as a water heater or clothes dryer) is present. If you spill any fuel on your skin, rinse it off immediately with soap and water. When you perform any kind of work on the fuel system, wear safety glasses and have a Class B type fire extinguisher on hand.*

1   If the smell of gasoline is noticed while driving, or after the vehicle has been parked in the sun, the fuel system and evaporative emissions control system (see Section 26) should be thoroughly inspected immediately.

2   The fuel system is under pressure even when the engine is off. Consequently, the fuel system must be depressurized before servicing the system (see Chapter 4). Even after depressurization, if any fuel lines are disconnected for servicing, be prepared to catch some fuel as it spills out. Plug all disconnected fuel lines immediately to prevent the tank from emptying itself.

3   Remove the gas tank filler cap and check for damage, corrosion and a proper sealing imprint on the gasket. Replace the cap with a new one if necessary.

4   Raise the vehicle and support it securely on jackstands. **Warning:** *Never work under a vehicle that is supported only by a jack!*

5   Inspect the gas tank and filler neck for punctures, cracks and other damage. The hose connection between the filler neck and

the tank is especially critical **(see illustration)**. Sometimes the filler neck hose will leak due to loose clamps or deteriorated rubber; problems a home mechanic can usually rectify.

6   Carefully inspect all rubber hoses and metal lines leading to-and-from the fuel tank. Check for loose connections, deteriorated hoses, crimped lines and damage of any kind. Follow the lines up to the front of the vehicle, carefully inspecting them all the way. Repair or replace damaged sections as necessary (see Chapter 4).

---

20   Drivebelt check, adjustment and replacement (every 15,000 miles or 12 months)

Warning: *The electric cooling fan(s) on these models can activate at any time the ignition switch is in the ON position. Make sure the ignition is OFF when working in the vicinity of the fan(s).*

Check

Refer to illustrations 20.2, 20.3 and 20.4

1   The drivebelts are located at the front of

19.5 Check the fuel filler neck-to-tank hose and clamp (arrow)

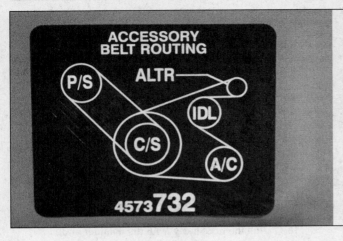

20.2 A drivebelt routing diagram sticker can be found under the hood, usually on the radiator support

Adjustment

Refer to illustrations 20.6a, 20.6b, 20.7a and 20.7b

5   If it is necessary to adjust the belt tension on models without an automatic adjuster, either to make the belt tighter or looser, it is done by moving the belt tensioner or the component, depending on which belt is being adjusted.

6   On some models, the adjustment is made by loosening adjustment and pivot bolts on the component, then moving the component in the required direction within its mounting bracket **(see illustrations)**. Hold the component in position and tighten the adjustment bolt, followed by the pivot bolt.

7   On some models the adjustment is made with a tensioner pulley. Loosen the locking and (on some models) pivot bolts on the tensioner, then turn the adjuster bolt until the desired tension is attained **(see illustrations)**. Tighten the locking and pivot bolts securely.

8   The 2.7L V6 engine also uses a tensioner, but has a 1/2-inch square drive hole into which a 1/2-inch drive extension, connected to a ratchet or breaker bar, can be inserted. To adjust the belt, loosen the tensioner bracket bolt and insert the extension into the square adjuster opening. Rotate the tensioner until the desired tension is achieved, then tighten the bracket bolt securely.

Replacement

Note: *Take the old belt(s) with you when purchasing new ones in order to make a direct comparison for length, width and design.*

All models except 2001 and later 4-cylinder convertibles and sedans

Refer to illustration 20.10

9   Follow the above procedures for drivebelt adjustment but slip the belt off the pulleys and remove it. Since belts tend to wear out more or less at the same time, it's a good idea to replace all of them at the same time.

the engine and play an important role in the operation of the vehicle and its components. Due to their function and material makeup, the belts are prone to failure after a period of time and should be inspected and adjusted periodically to prevent major damage. On 2001 and later convertible and sedan models with four-cylinder engines no adjustment is necessary because they are equipped with an automatic drivebelt tensioning system.

2   The number of belts used on a particular vehicle depends on the accessories installed. Drivebelts are used to turn the alternator, power steering pump, water pump, air pump and air-conditioning compressor. Depending on the pulley arrangement, more than one of these components may be driven by a single belt. On later models, a single self-adjusting serpentine drivebelt is used to drive all of the components.

3   With the engine turned off, open the hood and locate the drivebelts at the front of the engine. Use a flashlight to carefully check each belt. Check for a severed core, separation of the adhesive rubber on both sides of the core and for core separa-

tion from the belt side. Inspect the ribs for separation from the adhesive rubber and for cracking or separation of the ribs, torn or worn ribs or cracks in the inner ridges of the ribs **(see illustration)**. Also check for fraying and glazing, which gives the belt a shiny appearance. Inspect both sides of the belt by twisting the belt to check the underside. Use your fingers to feel the belt where you can't see it. If any of the above conditions are evident, replace the belt(s). **Note:** *Drivebelt inspection can be made easier by removing the accessory drivebelt splash shield located inside the right hand fenderwell.*

4   The tension of each belt is checked by pushing on it at a distance halfway between the pulleys. Apply about 10 pounds of force with your thumb and see how much the belt moves down (deflects). Measure the deflection with a ruler **(see illustration)**. The belt should deflect about 1/4-inch if the distance between pulleys is between 7 and 11 inches and around 1/2-inch if the distance is between 12 and 16 inches.

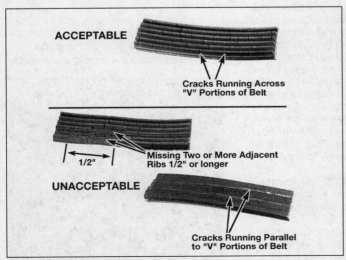

20.3 Here are some of the more common problems associated with drivebelts (check the belts very carefully to prevent an untimely breakdown)

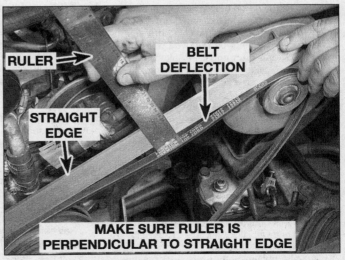

20.4 Measure drivebelt deflection with a straightedge and ruler - make sure the ruler is perpendicular to the straightedge

20.6a Power steering pump pivot bolt (upper arrow) and front locking bolt (lower arrow)

20.6b Power steering pump rear locking bolt (viewed from under the vehicle)

20.7a Here's one type of tensioner pulley; to adjust the belt, loosen the locking bolt (A), then turn the adjusting bolt (B) to achieve the proper tension

10   When installing the belt(s), make sure the belt is centered on the pulleys **(see illustration)**.

11   Adjust the belt(s) as described earlier in this Section.

2001 and later 4-cylinder convertibles and sedans

Alternator and air conditioning compressor drivebelt

Refer to illustration 20.12

12   The automatic tensioner must be released to allow drivebelt replacement. Insert a 3/8-inch drive ratchet or breaker bar into the belt tensioner opening and rotate it clockwise until the belt can be removed **(see illustration)**. Remove the belt and slowly release the tensioner. Install the new belt then rotate the tensioner clockwise to allow the belt to slip over it, then release the tensioner slowly until it contacts the drivebelt.

Power steering drivebelt

13   Remove the alternator and air conditioning compressor drivebelt.

14   After loosening the power steering pivot bolt, lock bolt and nut, rotate the pump toward the engine and remove the belt.

15   After installing the new belt, insert a 1/2-inch drive socket or breaker bar into the opening in the power steering pump bracket and rotate it clockwise to hold belt tension, then tighten the power steering pump adjusting nut/bolt and the pivot bolt.

16   Install the alternator and air conditioning compressor drivebelt.

Drivebelt tensioner replacement

Note: 2.0L DOHC four-cylinder and 2.7L V6 engines are equipped with a drivebelt tensioner that is secured to the engine using several bolts. On 2.4L DOHC four-cylinder engines, the tensioner is mounted with a single bolt. All other engines are equipped with adjusting brackets to tension the drivebelt.

17   Raise the vehicle and support it securely on jackstands.

18   Remove the inner fender splash shield (see Chapter 11).

19   Remove the drivebelt (see Steps 9 through 16).

20   Remove the drivebelt tensioner bolt(s).

21   Install the new tensioner and the tighten the bolts to the torque listed in this Chapter's Specifications.

22   Installation is the reverse of removal.

21   Chassis lubrication (every 30,000 miles or 24 months)

Refer to illustrations 21.1 and 21.5

1   A grease gun and a cartridge filled with the proper grease (see *Recommended lubricants and fluids*), graphite spray and an oil can filled with engine oil will be required to

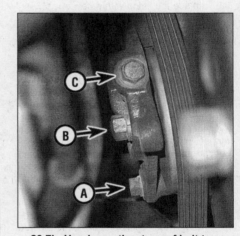

20.7b Here's another type of belt tensioner pulley; to adjust the belt, loosen the pivot bolt (A) and locking bolt (B), then turn the adjuster bolt (C) to achieve the proper tension

20.12 Rotate the tensioner pulley clockwise to release the tension on the belt (2001 and later convertibles and sedans with a four-cylinder engine)

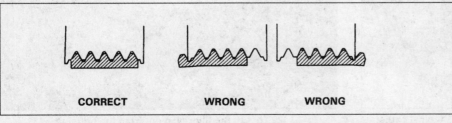

CORRECT   WRONG   WRONG

20.10 When installing a V-ribbed belt, make sure it is centered - it must not overlap either edge of the pulley

lubricate the chassis components **(see illus-tration)**.

2   Raise the vehicle and support it securely on jackstands. **Warning:** *Never work under a vehicle that is supported only by a jack!*

3   Before beginning, force a little grease out of the nozzle to remove any dirt from the end of the gun. Wipe the nozzle clean with a rag.

4   Armed with the grease gun and plenty of clean rags, begin lubricating the components. **Note:** *The tie-rod ends and front suspension lower control arm balljoints are not service-able.*

5   Wipe the grease fitting clean and push the nozzle firmly over it. Operate the lever on the grease gun to force grease into the fit-ting until it oozes out of the joint between the two components **(see illustration)**. If grease escapes around the grease gun nozzle, the fitting is clogged or the nozzle is not com-pletely seated on the fitting. Reattach the gun nozzle to the fitting and try again. If neces-sary, replace the fitting with a new one.

6   Lubricate the sliding contact and pivot points of the parking brake cable along with the cable guides and levers. This can be done by smearing some of the chassis grease onto the cable and related parts with your fingers. Be careful of frayed wires!

7   Lower the vehicle to the ground.

8   Open the hood and smear a little chas-sis grease on the hood latch mechanism and striker. Have an assistant pull the hood release lever from inside the vehicle as you lubricate the cable at the latch.

9   Lubricate all the hinges (door, hood, trunk, etc.) with the recommended lubricant (see *Recommended lubricants and fluids* at the beginning of this Chapter) to keep them in proper working order.

10   The key lock cylinders can be lubricated with spray-type graphite or silicone lubricant which is available at auto parts stores.

11   Lubricate the door weather-stripping with silicone spray. This will reduce chafing and retard wear.

12   Some components should not be lubri-

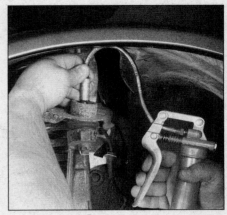

21.1 Materials required for chassis and body lubrication

1   **Engine oil** - *Light engine oil in a can like this can be used for door and hood hinges*

2   **Graphite spray** - *Used to lubricate lock cylinders*

3   **Grease** - *Grease, in a variety of types and weights, is available for use in a grease gun. Check the Specifications for your requirements*

4   **Grease gun** - *A common grease gun, shown here with a detachable hose and nozzle, is needed for chassis lubrication. After use, clean it thoroughly*

21.5 Greasing the front suspension upper control arm balljoint

22   Air filter replacement (every 30,000 miles or 24 months)

Refer to illustrations 22.2a, 22.2b, 22.3a, 22.3b, 22.4a and 22.4b

1   The air filter element is located in a hous-ing on the driver's side of the engine compart-ment.

2   On earlier models, unclip the latches securing the top cover of the air cleaner hous-ing and lift the filter element out. **(see illustra-tions)**.

3   On 2.7L V6 engines, detach the plastic tube connecting the fuel injection throttle body and the air cleaner and withdraw the element from the housing **(see illustration)**.

4   On later four-cylinder models, detach the clips, pull out the hose and filter assem-bly, then separate the filter from the hose **(see illustrations)**.

5   Inspect the inside of the air cleaner housing, top and bottom, for dirt, debris or damage. If necessary, clean the inside of the housing with a rag or shop vacuum as appli-cable. If the air cleaner housing is damaged and requires replacement, refer to Chapter 4.

cated for the following reasons. Some are permanently lubricated, some lubricants will cause component failure or the lubricants will be detrimental to the component's operating characteristics. Do not lubricate the follow-ing: air pump, generator bearings, drivebelts, drivebelt idler pulley, front wheel bearings, rubber bushings, starter motor bearings, sus-pension strut bearings, throttle control cable, throttle linkage ball bearings and water pump bearings.

22.2a To remove the air cleaner top cover on a typical earlier model, release the latches (arrows), lift the cover and disengage it from the locking lugs on the opposite side

22.2b Lift the filter element from the housing

22.3a On 2.7L V6 engines, loosen the hose clamp at the throttle body, disengage the tabs connecting the end of the plastic tube to the air cleaner housing . . .

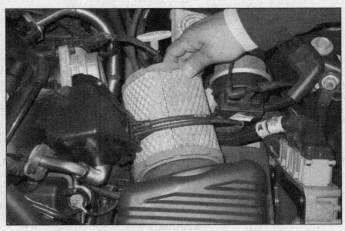

22.3b . . . then remove the air filter element from the housing

22.4a On later 2.4L four-cylinder models, detach the clips and withdraw the air hose and filter element from the housing . . .

22.4b . . . then detach the filter element from the hose

23 Automatic transaxle fluid and filter change (every 30,000 miles or 24 months)

1   The automatic transaxle fluid and filter (if equipped) should be changed and the magnet (if equipped) cleaned at the recommended intervals.
2   Raise the front of the vehicle and support it securely on jackstands. **Warning:** *Never work under a vehicle that is supported only by a jack!* Remove the transaxle splash shield.
3   Position a container capable of holding at least 5 quarts under the transaxle oil pan.

2000 and earlier coupe models, all convertible and sedan models
Refer to illustrations 23.4, 23.5a and 23.5b
4   Since the transaxle drain pan does not have a drain plug, this procedure can get a bit messy, so you should have plenty of clean rags and newspapers handy to mop up any

23.4 To drain the transaxle fluid, first loosen the bolts, then remove all the bolts except for two on the high side and two on the low side - after breaking the pan seal, remove the two bolts on the lower side and let the pan hang down to drain further

spills that may occur. If the drain pan you're using isn't very large in diameter, place it on a piece of plastic such as a trash bag to catch any splashing oil. Loosen only the pan bolts. Remove the bolts on each side of the pan leaving two bolts loosely in place on the upper and lower sides of the pan **(see illustration)**. Tap the corners of the pan using a soft-faced

mallet to break the seal and allow the fluid to drain into the container (the remaining bolts will prevent the pan from completely separating from the transaxle). Remove the 2 bolts from the lower side of the pan and let it hang down to drain further. After the pan has finished draining, remove the remaining bolts and detach the pan.

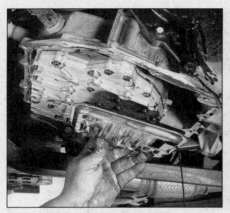

23.5a Remove the transaxle fluid filter . . .

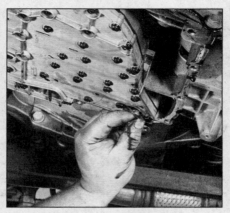

23.5b . . . and O-ring seal

23.16 On 2001 and later coupe models, disconnect the fluid cooler line a the radiator and direct it into the drain pan, then start the engine to pump the fluid out

5   Remove the filter and O-ring seal (if equipped) (see illustrations).
6   Carefully remove all traces of old sealant from the pan, transaxle body (be careful not to nick or gouge the sealing surfaces) and the bolts.
7   Clean the pan and the magnet located inside the pan with a clean, lint-free cloth moistened with solvent. Don't forget to place the magnet back in its proper location at the bottom of the pan.
8   Fit the new filter in place, with a new O-ring installed, on the transaxle valve body.
9   Apply a 1/8-inch bead of RTV sealant to the pan sealing surface (stay on the inboard side of the bolt holes) and to the underside of each bolt head.
10   Position the pan on the transaxle and install the bolts. Tighten them to the torque listed in this Chapter's Specifications following a criss-cross pattern. Work up to the final torque in three or four steps. Allow the RTV sealant time to dry according to the manufacturer's instructions.
11   Install the transaxle splash shield and secure it with the push-in fasteners.
12   Lower the vehicle and add four quarts of the specified fluid (see Recommended lubricants and fluids at the beginning of this Chapter) to the transaxle (see Section 6 if necessary). Start the engine and allow it to idle for at least two minutes while checking for leakage around the pan.
13   With the engine running and the brakes applied, move the shift lever through each of the gear positions and ending in Park. Check the fluid level on the dipstick. The level should be just up to the ADD mark. If necessary, add more fluid (a little at a time) until the level is just at the ADD mark (be careful not to overfill it).
14   Drive the vehicle until it reaches normal operating temperature. Recheck the fluid level and add as necessary until the fluid reaches the HOT range on the dipstick (see Section 6).
15   The old fluid drained from the transaxle cannot be reused in its present state and

should be disposed of. Check with your local auto parts store, disposal facility or environmental agency to see if they will accept the fluid for recycling. After the fluid has cooled it can be drained into a container (capped plastic jugs, topped bottles, milk cartons, etc.) for transport to one of these disposal sites. Don't dispose of the fluid by pouring it on the ground or down a drain!

2001 and later coupe models

Refer to illustration 23.16
16   Locate the oil cooler hose that connects to the metal tube at the radiator (see illustration). Disconnect the hose from the tube and point it into the drain pan. Cap off the metal tube to keep out dirt.
17   Apply the parking brake and block the front wheels. Have an assistant start the engine and let it idle in neutral while you watch the hose. Let the engine run until the fluid stops coming out, then shut the engine off immediately (but in any case, don't let the engine run longer than one minute).
18   Remove the drain plug from the transaxle and drain the fluid.
19   With the engine off, add new fluid to the transaxle through the dipstick tube (see Recommended fluids and lubricants for the recommended fluid type and capacity). Use a funnel to prevent spills. It is best to add a little fluid at a time. Allow the fluid time to drain into the transaxle.
20   Repeat Step 17 to pump more fluid into the drain pan, then drain a small amount from the drain plug and check it for contamination. If it's contaminated, add more fluid, then repeat Step 17 and this Step again.
21   Reconnect the fluid hose to the metal tube at the radiator.
22   Start the engine and let it idle for one to two minutes. Shift the selector into all positions from P through L, then shift into P and apply the parking brake.
23   With the engine idling, check the fluid level. It should be up to the Cold mark on the dipstick. Add fluid slowly to bring the level up if necessary.

24   Operate the vehicle to bring transmission temperature up to normal, then recheck level on the dipstick. It should be within the Hot range.
25   The old fluid drained from the transaxle cannot be reused in its present state and should be disposed of. Check with your local auto parts store, disposal facility or environmental agency to see if they will accept the fluid for recycling. After the fluid has cooled it can be drained into a container (capped plastic jugs, topped bottles, milk cartons, etc.) for transport to one of these disposal sites. Don't dispose of the fluid by pouring it on the ground or down a drain!

24   Manual transaxle - lubricant change (every 30,000 miles or 24 months)

Refer to illustrations 24.2a and 24.2b
Caution: Do not use Hypoid gear lube or engine oil in transaxles that specify Mopar ATF+4 automatic transaxle fluid. If the incorrect lubricant is used, it will result in increased shifting effort and internal transaxle damage.
1   Raise the vehicle and support it securely on jackstands in a level position. Warning: Never work under a vehicle that is supported only by a jack!
2   Using a box-end wrench or socket to prevent rounding off the plug corners, remove the drain plug. Drain the fluid into a suitable container capable of holding at least four quarts (see illustrations).
3   After the fluid has completely drained, install the drain plug and tighten it to the torque given in this Chapter's Specifications.
4   Fill the transaxle with the recommended lubricant (see Section 16).
5   The old oil drained from the transaxle cannot be reused in its present state and should be disposed of. Check with your local auto parts store, disposal facility or environmental agency to see if they will accept the oil for recycling. After the oil has cooled it can be

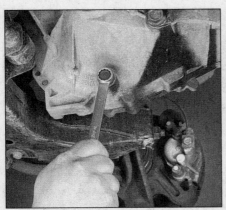

24.2a To avoid rounding off the corners, use the correct size box-end wrench or a socket to remove the manual transaxle oil drain plug . . .

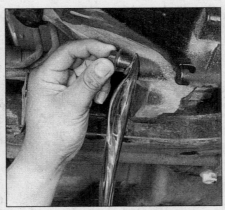

24.2b . . . and drain the lubricant

25.5 The drain fitting (arrow) is located at the bottom of the radiator on the right hand side (radiator removed for clarity)

drained into a container (capped plastic jugs, topped bottles, milk cartons, etc.) for transport to one of these disposal sites. Don't dispose of the oil by pouring it on the ground or down a drain!

25 Cooling system servicing (draining, flushing and refilling) (every 30,000 miles or 24 months)

Warning 1: *Do not allow coolant (antifreeze) to come in contact with your skin or painted surfaces of the vehicle. Flush contaminated areas immediately with plenty of water. Do not store new coolant or leave old coolant lying around where it's accessible to children or pets - they're attracted by its sweet smell. Ingestion of even a small amount of coolant can be fatal! Wipe up garage floor and drip pan spills immediately. Keep antifreeze containers covered and repair cooling system leaks as soon as they're noticed. Check with local authorities about the disposal of used antifreeze. Many communities have collection centers which will see that antifreeze is disposed of properly.*
Warning 2: *The electric cooling fan(s) on these models can activate at any time the ignition switch is in the ON position. Make sure the ignition is OFF when working in the vicinity of the fan(s).*
Note; *Some models are filled with Mopar 5 year/100,000 mile coolant that shouldn't be mixed with other coolants. Check the coolant reservoir/expansion tank under the hood to determine what type coolant you have. Always refill with the correct coolant.*
1   Periodically, the cooling system should be drained, flushed and refilled to replenish the coolant (antifreeze) mixture and prevent formation of rust and corrosion, which can impair the performance of the cooling system and cause engine damage. When the cooling system is serviced, all hoses and the radiator/expansion tank cap should be checked and replaced, if necessary.

Draining

Refer to illustration 25.5
2   At the same time the cooling system is serviced, all hoses and the radiator (pressure) cap should be inspected, tested and replaced if faulty (see Section 10).
3   With the engine cold, remove the pressure cap and set the heater control to maximum heat.
4   Move a large container capable of holding at least 12 quarts under the radiator drain fitting to catch the coolant mixture as it's drained.
5   Open the drain fitting located at the bottom of the radiator **(see illustration)**. Allow the coolant to completely drain out.

Flushing

Refer to illustrations 25.7 and 25.10
6   Once the system is completely drained, remove the thermostat from the engine (see Chapter 3). Then reinstall the thermostat

housing without the thermostat. This will allow the system to be thoroughly flushed.
7   Disconnect the upper radiator hose from the radiator, then place a garden hose in the upper radiator inlet and flush the system until the water runs clear at the upper radiator hose **(see illustration)**.
8   Severe cases of radiator contamination or clogging will require removing the radiator (see Chapter 3) and reverse flushing it. This involves inserting the hose in the bottom radiator outlet to allow the clean water to run against the normal flow, draining out through the top. A radiator repair shop should be consulted if further cleaning or repair is necessary.
9   When the coolant is regularly drained and the system refilled with the correct coolant mixture there should be no need to employ chemical cleaners or descalers.
10   Disconnect the coolant reservoir or expansion tank hose, remove the reservoir/

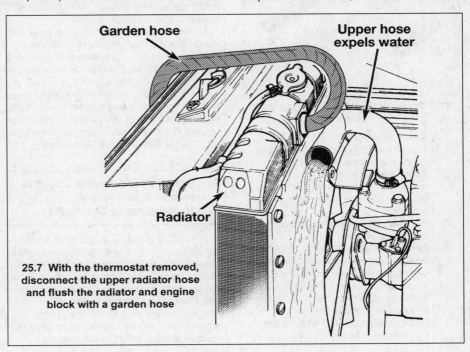

Garden hose

Upper hose expels water

Radiator

25.7 With the thermostat removed, disconnect the upper radiator hose and flush the radiator and engine block with a garden hose

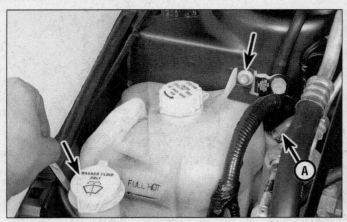

25.10 On convertible and sedan models, disconnect the hose (A) and remove the two mounting fasteners

25.13 Loosen the bleed valve (arrow); only 2001 and later models with a 2.0/2.4L four-cylinder or a 2.7L V6 engine have these

tank from the vehicle and flush it with clean water **(see illustration)**. Inspect it for damage and replace if necessary.

Refilling

Refer to illustration 25.13

11   Install the thermostat, the thermostat housing and connect the radiator hose (see Chapter 3).

12   Install the coolant reservoir/expansion tank, reconnect the hose and close the radiator drain fitting.

13   On 2001 and later models with a 2.0L/2.4L four-cylinder or 2.7L V6 engine, loosen the coolant bleed valve **(see illustration)**. On 2.7L V6 engines, pinch off the expansion tank-to-

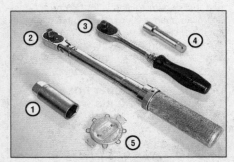

27.2 Tools required for changing spark plugs

1   ***Spark plug socket*** *- This will have special padding inside to protect the spark plug's porcelain insulator*

2   ***Torque wrench*** *- Although not mandatory, using this tool is the best way to ensure the plugs are tightened properly*

3   ***Ratchet*** *- Standard hand tool to fit the spark plug socket*

4   ***Extension*** *- Depending on model and accessories, you may need special extensions and universal joints to reach one or more of the plugs*

5   ***Spark plug gap gauge*** *- This gauge for checking the gap comes in a variety of styles. Make sure the gap for your engine is included*

reservoir hose. **Note:** *These models have two coolant tanks.* **Note:** *It's a good idea to attach a length of clear hose to the bleed valve and direct it into a container; this will prevent coolant from bubbling out and spilling on the drivebelts.*

14   Add the correct mixture of high-quality antifreeze/coolant and water in the ratio specified on the antifreeze container or in this Chapter's Specifications through the filler neck until it reaches the pressure cap seat (all except models with a 2.7L V6 engine) or to a point in between the MIN and MAX marks on the expansion tank (models with a 2.7L V6 engine) and a steady bubble-free stream of coolant flows from the bleed valve bolt (if equipped). Tighten the bleed valve bolt securely. If you're working on a model with a 2.7L V6 engine, install the pressure cap on the expansion tank.

15   On models without a 2.7L V6 engine, add the same coolant mixture to the reservoir until the level is between the FULL and ADD marks. Install the pressure cap.

16   Run the engine until normal operating temperature is reached (the fans will cycle on, then off), then allow the engine to cool. With the engine cold, add coolant as necessary to bring it up to the correct level.

17   Keep a close watch on the coolant level and the various cooling system hoses during the first few miles of driving and check for any coolant leaks. Tighten the hose clamps and add more coolant mixture as necessary.

26   Evaporative emissions control system check (every 30,000 miles or 24 months)

1   The function of the evaporative emissions control system is to prevent fuel vapors from escaping the fuel system and being released into the atmosphere. Vapors from the fuel tank are temporarily stored in a charcoal canister. The Powertrain Control Module (PCM) monitors the system and allows the vapors to be drawn into the intake manifold when the engine reaches normal operating temperature.

2   The charcoal canister on 1997 and earlier coupe models and 1999 and earlier convertible models is mounted to a bracket behind the right front bumper fascia. On 1998 and later coupe models and 2000 and later convertible and sedan models it's located above the fuel tank. The canister is maintenance-free and should last the life of the vehicle.

3   The most common symptom of a fault in the evaporative emissions system is a strong fuel odor in the engine compartment or at the rear (or inside of) the vehicle, depending on canister location, or raw fuel leaking from the canister. These indications are usually more prevalent in hot temperatures. All systems except for those installed on some early models are pressurized by a Leak Detection Pump (LDP) (refer to the vacuum diagram on the Vehicle Emission Control Information label under the hood). If normal system pressure cannot be achieved by the LDP, which indicates a leak, the PCM will store the appropriate fault code and illuminate the CHECK ENGINE light on the instrument panel. The most common cause of system pressure loss is a loose or poor-sealing gas cap.

4   For more information and replacement procedures see Chapter 6.

27   Spark plug check and replacement (see Maintenance schedule for intervals)

All models

Refer to illustrations 27.2, 27.5a and 27.5b

1   The spark plugs are located in the cylinder head.

2   In most cases the tools necessary for spark plug replacement include a spark plug socket which fits onto a ratchet (this special socket is padded inside to protect the porcelain insulators on the new plugs and hold them in place), various extensions and a feeler gauge to check and adjust the spark plug gap **(see illustration)**. A special plug wire removal tool is available for separating the wire boot from the spark plug, but it isn't absolutely nec-

27.5a Spark plug manufacturers recommend using a wire-type gauge when checking the gap - if the wire does not slide between the electrodes with a slight drag, adjustment is required

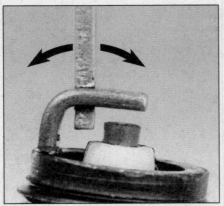

27.5b To change the gap, bend the side electrode only, as indicated by the arrows, and be very careful not to crack or chip the porcelain insulator surrounding the center electrode

27.7a First detach the spark plug wire from the coil pack . . .

essary. Since these engines are equipped with an aluminum cylinder head(s), a torque wrench should be used when tightening the spark plugs.

3   The best approach when replacing the spark plugs is to purchase the new spark plugs beforehand, adjust them to the proper gap and then replace each plug one at a time. When buying the new spark plugs, be sure to obtain the correct plug for your specific engine. This information can be found in the Specification Section at the front of this Chapter, in your owner's manual or on the Vehicle Emissions Control Information (VECI) label located under the hood. If differences exist between the sources, purchase the spark plug type specified on the VECI label as it was printed for your specific engine.

4   Allow the engine to cool completely before attempting to remove any of the plugs. During this cooling off time, each of the new spark plugs can be inspected for defects and the gaps can be checked.

5   The gap is checked by inserting the proper thickness gauge between the electrodes at the tip of the plug (see illustration). The gap between the electrodes should be as listed in this Chapter's Specifications or in your owner's manual. The wire should touch each of the electrodes. If the gap is incorrect, use the adjuster on the thickness gauge body to bend the curved side electrode slightly until the proper gap is obtained (see illustration). **Caution:** *The manufacturer recommends against checking the gap on platinum-tipped spark plugs; the platinum coating could be scraped off.* Also, at this time check for cracks in the spark plug body (if any are found, the plug must not be used). If the side electrode is not exactly over the center one, use the adjuster to align the two.

6   Cover the fender to prevent damage to the paint. Fender covers are available from auto parts stores but an old blanket will work just fine.

Four-cylinder engines

All except 2001 and later coupe models

Refer to illustrations 27.7a and 27.7b

7   **Note:** *Due to the short length of the spark plug wire, always disconnect the spark plug wire from the ignition coil pack first.* Disconnect the spark plug wire from any retaining clips. With the engine cool, disconnect one of the spark plug wires from the ignition coil pack **(see illustration)**. Pull only on the boot at the end of the wire; don't pull on the wire. Using a twisting motion, loosen the boot/wire at the valve cover, then withdraw the boot/wire from the valve cover **(see illustration)**. Proceed to Step 11.

2001 and later coupe models

8   These models use a combination of coil-over-plug ignition and spark plug wires. Cylinders 1 and 3 have spark plug wires that attach to coil-over plug assemblies on cylinders 2 and 4. Detach the spark plug wires from the coil assemblies on cylinders 2 and 4, then remove the spark plug wire boots as shown in **illustration 27.7b**. To remove the coil-over-

plug assemblies from cylinders 2 and 4, refer to **illustration 27.9**. Proceed to Step 11.

V6 engine

Refer to illustration 27.9

Note: *On 2.5L/3.0L V6 models, the manufacturer recommends replacing the spark plugs, spark plug wires, distributor cap and rotor at the same time. Refer to Section 29 for spark plug wire, distributor cap and rotor replacement.*

9   On 2.5L and 3.0L V6 models it will be necessary to remove the upper intake manifold for access to the spark plugs in the rear cylinder bank (see Chapter 2B). On 2.7L V6 engines with coil-over-plug ignition, disconnect the coil connector and remove the bolts, then lift the coil off for access to the spark plug **(see illustration)**. **Note:** *To prevent dirt or other foreign debris from entering the engine, place duct tape over the openings in the lower intake manifold.*

10   Detach any clips securing the spark plug wires. Using a twisting motion, loosen the boot/wire at the valve cover then withdraw the boot/wire from the valve cover **(see illustration 27.7b)**.

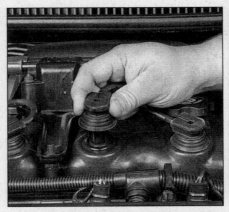

27.7b . . . then pull on the spark plug wire boot and twist it back-and-forth to detach it from the spark plug/valve cover

27.9 On coil-over-plug ignition systems, disconnect the electrical connector, then unscrew the bolts and remove the coil

27.12 Use a ratchet and extension to remove the spark plugs

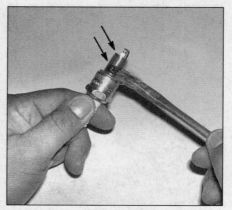

27.14 Apply a thin coat of anti-seize compound to the spark plug threads - DO NOT get any on the electrodes!

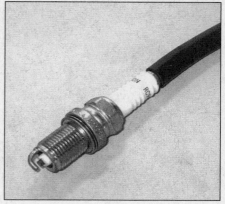

27.15 A length of snug fitting rubber hose will save time and prevent damaged threads when installing the spark plugs

All models

Refer to illustrations 27.12, 27.14 and 27.15

11   If compressed air is available, use it to blow any dirt or foreign material away from the spark plug area. **Warning:** *Wear eye protection!* The idea here is to eliminate the possibility of material falling into the cylinder through the spark plug hole as the spark plug is removed.

12   Place the spark plug socket over the plug and remove it from the engine by turning it in a counterclockwise direction **(see illustration)**.

13   Compare the spark plug with the chart on the inside back cover of this manual to get an indication of the overall running condition of the engine.

14   It's a good idea to lightly coat the threads of the spark plugs with an anti-seize compound **(see illustration)** to insure that the spark plugs do not seize in the aluminum cylinder head. Be careful not to get any of the anti-seize compound on the plug electrodes!

15   It's often difficult to insert spark plugs into their holes without cross-threading them. To avoid this possibility, fit a piece of rubber hose over the end of the spark plug **(see illustration)**. The flexible hose acts as a universal joint to help align the plug with the plug hole. Should the plug begin to cross-thread, the hose will slip on the spark plug, preventing thread damage. Install the spark plug and tighten it to the torque listed in this Chapter's Specifications.

16   Attach the plug wire or coil to the new spark plug, again using a twisting motion on the boot until it is firmly seated on the end of the spark plug. On four-cylinder engines, attach the other end to the ignition coil pack. Attach the spark plug wire to any retaining clips to secure the wires in their proper location on the valve cover.

17   Follow the above procedure for the remaining spark plugs, replacing them one at a time to prevent mixing up the spark plug wires.

18   On 2.5L/3.0L V6 models, replace the spark plug wires, distributor cap and rotor

(see Section 29). Remove the duct tape from the lower intake manifold and install the upper intake manifold (see Chapter 2B).

28 Positive Crankcase Ventilation (PCV) valve check and replacement (every 60,000 miles or 48 months)

Refer to illustrations 28.2 and 28.4

1   The PCV valve controls the amount of crankcase vapors allowed to enter the intake manifold. Inside the PCV valve is a spring loaded valve that opens in relation to intake manifold vacuum, which allows crankcase vapors to be drawn from the valve cover back into the engine combustion chamber.

2   The PCV valve on earlier four-cylinder engines is located in the rubber hose connected to the intake manifold plenum and the valve cover. On later four-cylinder engines the PCV valve is at top of the engine and connected to the manifold by a hose. On 2.5L/3.0L V6 models, it's located in the valve cover **(see illustration)**. On 2.7L V6 engines it's located on the top of the intake plenum.

3   Check the operation of the PCV valve by

disconnecting the valve or hose, depending on your particular application.

4   Start the engine and listen for a hissing sound coming from the PCV valve. Place your finger over the valve opening - you should feel vacuum **(see illustration)**. If there's no vacuum at the valve, check for a plugged hose, plenum port or valve. Replace any plugged or deteriorated hoses.

5   Check the spring-loaded pintle located inside the valve for freedom of movement by using a small screwdriver or equivalent to push the valve off its seat and see that it returns to the fully seated position. If the valve is sluggish or the inside of the valve is contaminated with gum and carbon deposits, the valve must be replaced.

6   To replace the valve, disconnect it from the intake manifold hose, valve cover, valve cover hose or intake plenum, as applicable.

7   When purchasing a replacement PCV valve, make sure it's for your particular vehicle and engine size. Compare the old valve with the new one to make sure they're the same.

8   Installation is the reverse of removal. Make sure the new PCV valve is installed with the closed end (plunger seat) towards the valve cover.

28.2 The PCV valve (arrow) is located in the valve cover on 2.5L/3.0L V6 engines

28.4 Feel for vacuum at the PCV valve with the engine idling and the hose off (2.7L V6 engine shown)

29 Spark plug wires, distributor cap and rotor check and replacement (see Maintenance schedule for intervals)

Note: *Distributor cap and rotor replacement applies to 2.5L and 3.0L V6 engines only.*

All models

1   The spark plug wires should be checked at the recommended intervals or whenever new spark plugs are installed.

2   Begin this procedure by making a visual check of the spark plug wires while the engine is running. In a darkened garage (make sure there is adequate ventilation) or at night while using a flashlight, start the engine and observe each plug wire. Be careful not to come into contact with any moving engine parts. If possible, use an insulated or non-conductive object to wiggle each wire. If there is a break in the wire, you will see arcing or a small blue spark coming from the damaged area. Secondary ignition voltage increases with engine speed and sometimes a damaged wire will not produce an arc at idle speed. Have an assistant press the accelerator pedal to raise the engine speed to approximately 2000 rpm. Check the spark plug wires for arcing as stated previously. If arcing is noticed, replace all spark plug wires.

Four-cylinder engines

3   Perform the following checks with the engine OFF. The wires should be inspected one at a time to prevent mixing up the order that is essential for proper engine operation.
Note: *Due to the short length of the spark plug wire, always disconnect the spark plug wire from the ignition coil pack first.*

4   With the engine cool, disconnect the spark plug wire from the ignition coil pack. Pull only on the boot at the end of the wire; don't pull on the wire itself. Use a twisting motion to free the boot/wire from the coil. Disconnect the same spark plug wire from the spark plug, using the same twisting method while pulling on the boot. Disconnect the spark plug wire from any retaining clips as necessary and remove it from the engine.

5   Check inside the boot for corrosion, which will look like a white, crusty powder (don't mistake the white dielectric grease used on some plug wire boots for corrosion protection).

6   Now push the wire and boot back onto the end of the spark plug. It should be a tight fit on the plug end. If not, remove the wire and use a pair of pliers to carefully crimp the metal connector inside the wire boot until the fit is snug.

7   Now push the wire and boot back into the end of the ignition coil terminal. It should be a tight fit in the terminal. If not, remove the wire and use a pair of pliers to carefully crimp the metal connector inside the wire boot until the fit is snug.

8   Now, using a cloth, clean each wire

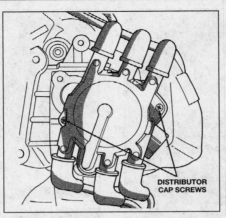

29.15 Distributor cap retaining screw locations (2.5L V6 engine)

along its entire length. Remove all built-up dirt and grease. As this is done, inspect for burned areas, cracks and any other form of damage. Bend the wires in several places to ensure that the conductive material inside hasn't hardened. Repeat the procedure for the remaining wires.

9   If new spark plug wires are required, purchase a complete set for your particular engine. The terminals and rubber boots should already be installed on the wires. Replace the wires one at a time to avoid mixing up the firing order and make sure the terminals are securely seated on the coil pack and the spark plugs.

10   Attach the plug wire to the new spark plug and to the ignition coil pack using a twisting motion on the boot until it is firmly seated. Attach the spark plug wire to any retaining clips to keep the wires in their proper location on the valve cover.

2.5L/3.0L V6 engines

Refer to illustration 29.15

Note: *On 2.5L/3.0L engines, the manufacturer recommends replacing the spark plugs, spark plug wires, distributor cap and rotor at the same time.*

11   Remove the upper intake manifold (see Chapter 2B).

12   To prevent dirt or other foreign debris from entering the engine, place duct tape over the openings of the lower intake manifold.

13   Remove the EGR tube from the EGR valve (see Chapter 6 if necessary).

14   Disconnect one spark plug wire from the distributor cap. Pull only on the boot at the end of the wire; don't pull on the wire itself. Use a twisting motion to free the boot/wire from the distributor. Install the removed wire into the new distributor cap in the exact same location. Repeat this procedure until all spark plug wires are installed in the new cap.

15   Loosen the 2 screws and remove the old distributor cap **(see illustration)**. Remove the rotor.

16   Install the new rotor and distributor cap (with spark plug wires attached).

30.1 The fuel filter (arrow) on convertible models is tucked up behind the fuel tank and mounted to the frame above the rear suspension crossmember

17   Replace the spark plugs as described in Section 27, except do not reattach the spark plug wires to the retaining clips.

18   Replace the spark plug wires one at a time to avoid mixing up the firing order and make sure the terminals are securely seated on the distributor cap and the spark plugs. Install the plug wires using a twisting motion on the boot until it is firmly seated. Attach the spark plug wire to any retaining clips as required.

19   Using a new gasket, install the EGR tube onto the EGR valve (see Chapter 6). Tighten the bolts to the torque given in the Specification Section of Chapter 6.

20   Remove the duct tape from the lower intake manifold.

21   Install the upper intake manifold (see Chapter 2B).

30 Fuel filter replacement (every 60,000 miles or 48 months)

Note: *The manufacturer does not suggest periodic fuel filter replacement on 2001 and later models because the fuel filters are integrated with the fuel pump assembly. See Chapter 4 if the fuel filter requires replacement due to a fuel restriction or fuel contamination problem.*
Warning: *Gasoline is extremely flammable, so take extra precautions when you work on any part of the fuel system (see the **Warning** in Chapter 4, Section 2).*

Convertible models
Removal

Refer to illustration 30.1

1   The in-line fuel filter mounts to the frame above the rear of the fuel tank, near the filler neck **(see illustration)**.

2   Remove the fuel tank filler cap to relieve fuel tank pressure.

3   Perform the fuel pressure relief procedure (see Chapter 4).

30.19 The fuel filter (arrow) on coupe models is mounted behind the fuel tank

30.21 Use an open end wrench to steady the filter while unscrewing the fuel fitting bolts (coupe models)

4   Disconnect the negative battery cable from the ground stud on the left shock tower (see Chapter 5).
5   Remove the rear seat (see Chapter 11). Locate the fuel pump wiring harness 4-pin connector and disconnect it from the wiring harness. Follow the fuel pump wiring to the grommet at the base of the rear seat. Tie a length of string to the fuel pump wiring harness and secure the other end somewhere in the trunk (this will allow you to easily retrieve the wiring harness). Push the grommet through the floorpan and feed the wiring and 4-pin connector through the hole.
6   Raise the vehicle and support it securely on jackstands.
7   Position an approved gasoline container under the fuel tank drain plug. If necessary, use a funnel to prevent spilling fuel. **Warning:** *The fuel tank capacity is 16 gallons. Unless the fuel tank is almost empty, be prepared to collect a significant amount of fuel. Do not leave the fuel tank draining operation unattended. Be prepared to replace the drain plug in case the fuel tank capacity exceeds the container capacity.* Remove the drain plug (see Chapter 4) and drain the fuel into the container.
8   After the fuel has finished draining, rein-

stall the drain plug and tighten it securely.
9   Support the fuel tank with a floor jack. Place a piece of wood between the jack head and the fuel tank to protect the tank.
10   Remove the driver's side fuel tank strap (the long strap).
11   Loosen, but do not remove, the passenger side fuel tank strap so the fuel tank filler neck just touches the rear suspension crossmember. **Caution:** *Do not let the weight of the fuel tank rest on the filler neck! Support it with the jack at all times.*
12   Label and disconnect the quick-connect fuel line fittings connecting the fuel filter to the fuel system. See Chapter 4 for fuel line quick-connect fitting information.
13   Detach the fuel filter from its mounting and remove it from the vehicle.

Installation

14   Installation is the reverse of removal.
15   Connect the fuel line quick-connect fittings and verify they are securely assembled by trying to pull them apart.
16   Tighten the fuel tank strap bolts to the torque listed in the Chapter 4 Specifications.
17   Pressurize the system and check for leaks.

Coupe and sedan models

Refer to illustrations 30.19 and 30.21
18   Raise the vehicle, support it securely on jackstands. **Note:** *On some models, it will be necessary to remove the rear bumper cover (see Chapter 11).*
19   The fuel filter is located on the engine compartment firewall or on the frame above the rear of the fuel tank **(see illustration)**.
20   Perform the fuel pressure relief procedure (see Chapter 4). Disconnect the cable from the negative terminal of the battery.
21   Use an open end wrench to hold the filter, then unscrew the fitting bolts and detach the fuel lines **(see illustration)**. **Note:** *Have spare rags or a container to catch or wipe up the extra fuel that will spill from the filter.* Discard the sealing washers (new ones must be used during installation).
22   Remove the bracket bolt and detach the filter and bracket. Note the direction that the filter is facing.
23   Make sure the new filter is installed so that it's facing the proper direction as noted above. Using new sealing washers, connect the inlet and outlet lines, then tighten the fitting bolts to the torque listed in this Chapter's Specifications.
24   Pressurize the system and check for leaks.

Chapter 2 Part A
Four-cylinder engines

Contents

Specifications

2.0L DOHC engine

General
Bore	3.445 inches
Stroke	3.267 inches
Compression ratio	9.6:1
Displacement	122 cubic inches (2.0 liters)
Firing order	1-3-4-2

Camshaft
Bearing bore diameter	1.024 to 1.025 inches
Bearing journal diameter	1.0217 to 1.0224 inches
Bearing clearance	0.0027 to 0.0028 inch
Endplay	0.006 inch
Lobe lift	
Intake	0.324 inch
Exhaust	0.276 inch

Cylinder head
Cylinder head warpage	
Head gasket surface	0.004 inch maximum
Exhaust manifold mounting surfaces	0.006 inch maximum

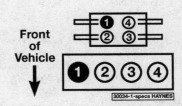

Front of Vehicle

Cylinder numbering and coil terminal location (2.0L DOHC and 2.4L DOHC engines)

2.0L DOHC engine (continued)

Intake and exhaust manifolds
Warpage limit... 0.006 inch maximum

Oil pump
Cover warpage limit.. 0.003 inch
Inner rotor thickness (minimum)... 0.301 inch
Outer rotor thickness (minimum).. 0.301 inch
Outer rotor diameter (minimum)... 3.148 inch
Rotor-to-pump cover clearance (maximum)......................... 0.004 inch
Outer rotor-to-housing clearance (maximum)...................... 0.015 inch
Inner rotor-to-outer rotor lobe clearance (maximum)........... 0.008 inch
Pressure relief spring free length....................................... 2.39 inches (approximate)

Torque specifications*   **Ft-lbs** (unless otherwise indicated)
Note: *One foot pound (ft-lb) of torque is equivalent to 12 inch-pounds (in-lbs) of torque. Torque values below approximately 15 ft-lbs are expressed in inch-pounds, since most foot-pound torque wrenches are not accurate at these smaller values.*
Camshaft bearing cap bolts
    Caps 2 through 5... 108 inch-lbs
    Caps 1 and 6... 20
Camshaft timing belt sprocket bolt 75
Crankshaft damper bolt... 105
Cylinder head bolts (in sequence - **see illustration 14.14a**)
    Step 1
        Bolts 1 through 6.. 24
        Bolts 7 through 10.. 20
    Step 2
        Bolts 1 through 6.. 48
        Bolts 7 through 10.. 20
    Step 3
        Bolts 1 through 6.. 48
        Bolts 7 through 10.. 20
    Step 4.. Tighten all fasteners an additional 90-degrees (1/4 turn)
Exhaust manifold-to-cylinder head bolts.............................. 17
Exhaust manifold-to-exhaust pipe bolts.............................. 33
Flywheel/driveplate-to-crankshaft bolts 70
Intake manifold bolts/nuts
    Lower intake manifold-to-intake manifold plenum
      (upper intake manifold) bolts .... N/A
    Lower intake manifold-to-cylinder head bolts/nuts............ 17
Oil pan bolts... 108 inch-lbs
Oil pump
    Oil pump mounting bolts 17
    Cover screws .... 108 inch-lbs
    Pick-up tube bolt 20
    Relief valve cap.. 39
Timing belt
    Cover bolts
        Upper bolt .... 107 inch-lbs
        Lower bolt 21
    Timing belt tensioner assembly bolts
        1995 through 1997
            Timing belt tensioner bolts 23
            Tensioner pulley bolt...................................... 50
        1998 and later... 21
Valve cover bolts .... 108 inch-lbs
Refer to Part D for additional torque specifications

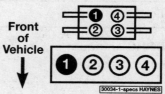

Front of Vehicle

Cylinder numbering and coil terminal location (2.0L DOHC and 2.4L DOHC engines)

2.4L DOHC engine

General
Bore... 3.445 inches
Stroke.. 3.976 inches
Compression ratio
    1995 through 2001... 9.4:1
    2002 and later.. 9.5:1
Displacement.. 148 cubic inches (2.4 liters)
Firing order 1-3-4-2

Camshaft

Bearing bore diameter	1.024 to 1.025 inches
Bearing journal diameter	1.021 to 1.023 inches
Bearing clearance	0.0027 to 0.003 inch
Endplay	0.0019 to 0.0066 inch
Lobe lift	
Intake	0.324 inch
Exhaust	
1996 through 2002	0.256 inch
2003 and later	0.259 inch

Cylinder head

Head gasket surface warpage limit	0.004 inch maximum
Exhaust manifold mounting surface warpage limit	0.006 inch maximum

Intake and exhaust manifolds

Warpage limit	0.006 inch maximum

Oil pump

Cover warpage limit	0.001 inch
Inner rotor thickness (minimum)	
1996 through 2002	0.370 inch
2003 and later	0.421 inch
Outer rotor thickness (minimum)	
1996 through 2002	0.370 inch
2003 and later	0.421 inch
Outer rotor diameter (minimum)	
1996 through 2002	3.148 inches
2003 and later	3.383 inches
Rotor-to-pump cover clearance (maximum)	0.004 inch
Outer rotor-to-housing clearance (maximum)	0.015 inch (maximum)
Inner rotor-to-outer rotor lobe clearance (maximum)	0.008 inch (maximum)
Pressure relief spring free length	2.39 inches (approximate)

Torque specifications*

Ft-lbs (unless otherwise indicated)

Note: *One foot pound (ft-lb) of torque is equivalent to 12 inch-pounds (in-lbs) of torque. Torque values below approximately 15 ft-lbs are expressed in inch-pounds, since most foot-pound torque wrenches are not accurate at these smaller values.*

Alternator drivebelt idler pulley bolt	40
Camshaft bearing cap bolts **(see illustration 10.19 for bolt tightening sequence)**	
M6 bolts	105 in-lbs
M8 bolts	21
Camshaft sprocket bolt	
1996 through 2001	75
2002 and later	85
Crankshaft damper bolt	
1996 through 2001	105
2002 and later	100
Cylinder head bolts (in sequence - **see illustration 14.4a**)	
1996 through 2005 except PZEV VIN J engines	
Step 1	25
Step 2	50
Step 3	50
Step 4	Tighten an additional 90-degrees
2005 PZEV VIN J engines and 2006	
Step 1	25
Step 2	60
Step 3	60
Step 4	Tighten an additional 90-degrees
Driveplate-to-crankshaft bolts	70
Exhaust manifold-to-cylinder head bolts	16.5
Exhaust manifold-to-exhaust pipe bolts	21
Intake manifold bolts	
1996 through 1999	105 in-lbs
2001 and later	21
Oil pan bolts	105 in-lbs
Oil pump	
Attaching bolts	21
Cover screws	105 in-lbs
Pick-up tube bolt	
1996 through 1999	21
2001	20
2002 and later	16.5
Relief valve cap bolt	30

2.4L DOHC engine (continued)

Torque specifications (continued)*   Ft-lbs (unless otherwise indicated)

Note: *One foot pound (ft-lb) of torque is equivalent to 12 inch-pounds (in-lbs) of torque. Torque values below approximately 15 ft-lbs are expressed in inch-pounds, since most foot-pound torque wrenches are not accurate at these smaller values.*

Structural collar assembly	
1996 through 1998 **(see illustration 15.5a)**	
Bolts 1, 2 and 3	75
Bolts 4, 5, 6, 7 and 8	45
Front torque bracket-to-bending strut bolts	24
Front engine mount through bolt	45
1999 **(see illustration 15.5b)**	
Pre-torque two center collar-to-oil pan bolts (No. 2 bolts)	25 in-lbs
Structural collar-to-transaxle bolts (No. 1 bolts)	80
Final torque: all structural collar-to-oil pan bolts (No. 2 bolts)	21
2001 and later **(see illustration 15.5c)**	
Bolts 1, 2 and 3	75
Bolts 4 and 5	35
Bolts 6 and 7	45
Thermostat housing bolts	See Chapter 3
Timing belt	
Cover bolts	
1996 through 1999	
Outer-cover bolts	40 in-lbs
Inner cover bolts	105 in-lbs
2001	
Outer cover bolts	40 in-lbs
Inner cover bolts	
M6 bolts	40 in-lbs
M8 bolts	21
2002 and later	
Outer cover bolts	
2002	80 in-lbs
2003 and later	50 in-lbs
Inner cover bolts	
M6 bolts	105 in-lbs
M8 bolts	21
Idler pulley bolt	45
Tensioner assembly	
Tensioner pulley bolt	
1996 through 2002	21
2003 and later	18
Tensioner mounting bolt	45
Valve cover bolts	105 in-lbs

*Refer to Part D for additional torque specifications

2.4L SOHC engine

General

Bore	3.41 inches
Stroke	3.94 inches
Compression ratio	9.5:1
Displacement	143.4 cubic inches (2.4 liters)
Firing order	1-3-4-2

Camshaft

Lobe height	
Intake	
Standard	1.472 inches
Service limit	1.452 inches
Exhaust	
Manual transaxle	
Standard	1.462 inches
Service limit	1.443 inches
Automatic transaxle	
Standard	1.450 inches
Service limit	1.430 inches
Camshaft journal diameter	1.8 inches

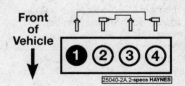

Four-cylinder engine cylinder numbering and coil pack/spark plug wire locations (2.4L SOHC engine)

Cylinder head
Warpage limit
    Standard.. 0.002 inch
    Service limit.. 0.007 inch
Resurfacing limit (combined head and block).. 0.007 inch

Intake and exhaust manifolds
Warpage limit... 0.008 inch

Timing belt
Automatic tensioner pushrod movement (@ 22 to 44 lbs pressure) .... 0.040 inch or less
Automatic tensioner protrusion.. 0.15 to 0.18 inch
Balance-shaft belt deflection .... 0.2 to 0.3 inch

Oil pump
Side clearance
    Drive gear.. 0.004 to 0.006 inch
    Driven gear.. 0.003 to 0.004 inch

Torque specifications*   **Ft-lbs** (unless otherwise indicated)
Note: *One foot pound (ft-lb) of torque is equivalent to 12 inch-pounds (in-lbs) of torque. Torque values below approximately 15 ft-lbs are expressed in inch-pounds, since most foot-pound torque wrenches are not accurate at these smaller values.*
Balance shaft sprocket bolt 33
Balance shaft belt tensioner bolt .... 168 in-lbs
Camshaft sprocket bolt... 65
Crankshaft pulley bolts 18
Crankshaft sprocket bolt... 87
Cylinder head bolts** (in sequence - **see illustration 14.14b**)
    Step 1.. 58
    Step 2.. Loosen completely
    Step 3.. 15
    Step 4.. Tighten 1/4-turn
    Step 5.. Tighten 1/4-turn further
Exhaust manifold bolts/nuts
    Upper nuts.. 22
    Lower nuts.. 36
Exhaust pipe-to-exhaust manifold bolts/nuts....................................... 37
Flywheel or driveplate bolts.. 98
Front case (oil pump housing) bolts 17
Front case (oil pump housing) plug 17
Intake manifold-to-engine nuts/bolts... 14
Intake manifold stay (support bracket) bolts.. 23
Oil filter bracket bolts .... 168 inch-lbs
Oil pan bolts/nuts... 61 inch-lbs
Oil pressure switch .... 168 inch-lbs
Oil pump pick-up tube mounting bolts .... 168 inch-lbs
Oil pump driven gear-to-balance shaft flange bolt................................ 27
Oil pump cover
    Screws.. 87 inch-lbs
    Bolts .... 144 inch-lbs
Oil pump driven gear bolt 27
Oil pump relief valve plug 33
Timing belt front cover bolts
    Upper cover bolts... 117 in-lbs
    Lower cover bolts
        Bolts without washers .... 96 in-lbs
        Bolts with washers.. 78 in-lbs
Timing belt assembly
    Automatic tensioner mounting bolt... 17
    Tensioner pulley bolt 36
Valve cover bolts .... 31 inch-lbs

Refer to Part D for additional torque specifications.

**Apply engine oil to the threads.*

1   General information

This Part of Chapter 2 is devoted to in-vehicle engine repair procedures. Information concerning engine removal and installation can be found in Part D of this Chapter.

The following repair procedures are based on the assumption that the engine is installed in the vehicle. If the engine has been removed from the vehicle and mounted on a stand, many of the steps outlined in this Part of Chapter 2 will not apply.

The Specifications included in this Part of Chapter 2 apply only to the procedures contained in this Part.

There are three types of four-cylinder engines installed in the models covered in this book: 2.0L double overhead camshaft (DOHC), 2.4L DOHC and 2.4L single overhead camshaft (SOHC) engine. The 2.4L engines incorporate two balance shafts that are installed below the crankshaft. For service information on the balance shafts, refer to Part D of this Chapter.

2   Repair operations possible with the engine in the vehicle

Many major repair operations can be accomplished without removing the engine from the vehicle.

Clean the engine compartment and the exterior of the engine with some type of degreaser before any work is done. It will make the job easier and help keep dirt out of the internal areas of the engine.

Depending on the components involved, it may be helpful to remove the hood to improve access to the engine as repairs are performed (refer to Chapter 11 if necessary). Cover the fenders to prevent damage to the paint. Special pads are available, but an old bedspread or blanket will also work.

If vacuum, exhaust, oil or coolant leaks develop, indicating a need for gasket or seal replacement, the repairs can generally be made with the engine in the vehicle. The intake and exhaust manifold gaskets, oil pan gasket, camshaft and crankshaft oil seals and cylinder head gasket are all accessible with the engine in place.

Exterior engine components, such as the intake and exhaust manifolds, the oil pan, the oil pump, the water pump, the starter motor, the alternator, the distributor and the fuel system components can be removed for repair with the engine in place.

Since the camshaft(s) and cylinder head can be removed without pulling the engine, valve component servicing can also be accomplished with the engine in the vehicle. Replacement of the timing belt and sprockets is also possible with the engine in the vehicle.

In extreme cases caused by a lack of necessary equipment, repair or replacement of piston rings, pistons, connecting rods and rod bearings is possible with the engine in the vehicle. However, this practice is not recommended because of the cleaning and preparation work that must be done to the components involved.

3   Top Dead Center (TDC) for number one piston - locating

1   Top Dead Center (TDC) is the highest point in the cylinder that each piston reaches as it travels up-and-down when the crankshaft turns. Each piston reaches TDC on the compression stroke and again on the exhaust stroke, but TDC generally refers to piston position on the compression stroke. The cast-in timing mark arrow on the crankshaft timing belt pulley installed on the front of the crankshaft is referenced to the number one piston at TDC when the arrow is straight up, or at "12 o'clock", and aligned with the cast-in timing mark arrow on the oil pump housing (see Section 7).

2   Positioning a specific piston at TDC is an essential part of many procedures such as camshaft(s) removal, rocker arm removal, timing belt and sprocket replacement.

3   In order to bring any piston to TDC, the crankshaft must be turned using one of the methods outlined below. When looking at the front of the engine, normal crankshaft rotation is clockwise. **Warning:** *Before beginning this procedure, be sure to set the emergency brake, place the transmission in Park or Neutral and disable the ignition system by disconnecting the primary electrical connector from the ignition coil pack.*

a)   *The preferred method is to turn the crankshaft with a large socket and breaker bar attached to the crankshaft balancer hub bolt that is threaded into the front of the crankshaft.*

b)   *A remote starter switch, which may save some time, can also be used. Attach the switch leads to the S (switch) and B (battery) terminals on the starter solenoid. Once the piston is close to TDC, discontinue with the remote switch and use a socket and breaker bar as described in the previous paragraph.*

c)   *If an assistant is available to turn the ignition switch to the Start position in short bursts, you can get the piston close to TDC without a remote starter switch. Use a socket and breaker bar as described in Paragraph a) to complete the procedure.*

4   Remove all of the spark plugs as this will make it easier to rotate the engine by hand.

5   Insert a compression gauge (screw-in type with a hose) in the number 1 spark plug hole. Place the gauge dial where you can see it while turning the crankshaft pulley hub bolt. **Note:** *The number one cylinder is located at the front (timing belt end) of the engine.*

6   Turn the crankshaft clockwise until you see compression building up on the gauge - you are on the compression stroke for that cylinder. If you did not see compression build up, continue with one more complete revolution to achieve TDC for the number one cylinder.

7   Remove the compression gauge. Through the number one cylinder spark plug hole insert a length of wooden dowel or plastic rod and slowly push it down until it reaches the top of the piston. **Caution:** *Don't insert a metal or sharp object into the spark plug hole as the piston crown may be damaged.*

8   With the dowel or rod in place on top of the piston crown, slowly rotate the crankshaft clockwise until the dowel or rod is pushed upward, stops, and then starts to move back down. At this point, rotate the crankshaft slightly counterclockwise until the dowel or rod has reached it upper most travel. At this point the number one piston is at the TDC position.

9   On 2.0L DOHC engines, remove the timing belt cover; on 2.4L DOHC and 2.4L SOHC engines, remove the upper timing belt cover (see Section 7). Then check the alignment of the camshaft timing marks **(see illustration 7.13)**. At this point the camshaft(s) timing marks should be aligned. If not repeat this procedure until alignment is correct.

10   After the number one piston has been positioned at TDC on the compression stroke, TDC for any of the remaining cylinders can be located by turning the crankshaft 180-degrees (1/2-turn) at a time and following the firing order (refer to the Specifications).

4   Valve cover - removal and installation

Removal

1   Disconnect the battery cable from the negative battery terminal or from the remote ground terminal (see Chapter 5).

2   Remove the ignition coil pack from the valve cover (see Chapter 5).

3   Clearly label and then detach any electrical wiring harnesses which connect to or cross over the valve cover.

4   Disconnect the PCV valve hose and breather hose from the valve cover (see Chapter 6).

5   Remove the valve cover bolts in the reverse order of the tightening sequence **(see illustration 4.12)** and then lift off the cover. If the cover sticks to the cylinder head, tap on it with a soft-face hammer or place a wood block against the cover and tap on the wood with a hammer. **Caution:** *If you have to pry between the valve cover and the cylinder head, be extremely careful not to gouge or nick the gasket surfaces of either part. A leak could develop after reassembly.*

6   Remove the valve cover perimeter rubber seal. Thoroughly clean the valve cover and remove all traces of old gasket material. Gasket removal solvents are available from auto parts stores and may prove helpful. After cleaning the surfaces, degrease them with a rag soaked in lacquer thinner or acetone.

4.9 After applying a small amount of red Loctite No. 271, or equivalent, to the lower end of the tube, install it and then carefully tap the tube into place until it seats on the cylinder head (2.4L SOHC engine only)

4.10 Remove and inspect each spark plug tube seal for deterioration and hardness; install new seals as a set and make sure that they're correctly seated in the cover (SOHC valve cover shown, DOHC valve covers similar)

Spark plug tube replacement (SOHC engine only)

Refer to illustration 4.9

7   Grasp spark plug tube with locking pliers, carefully twist back and forth and remove the tube from cylinder head.

8   Clean locking agent from tube receptacle

in cylinder head with solvent and dry.

9   Apply a small amount of red Loctite No. 271, or equivalent, around the lower end of the tube and install the tube into the cylinder head. Carefully tap the tube into the receptacle with a wood block and mallet. Tap the tube in until it seat against the cylinder head (see illustration).

Installation

Refer to illustrations 4.10, 4.11a, 4.11b and 4.12

10   Inspect the spark plug tube seals (see illustration) for deterioration and hardness. Replace them if necessary.

11   Install a new gasket on the cover, using RTV sealant to hold it in place (see illustrations). On DOHC models, apply RTV sealant to the camshaft cap corners and the top edges of the half-round seal. Place the cover on the engine and install the cover bolts.

12   Tighten the bolts in the proper sequence to the torque listed in this Chapter's Specifications (see illustration). The remaining steps are the reverse of removal. When finished, run the engine and check for oil leaks.

5   Intake manifold - removal and installation

1   Relieve the fuel system pressure (see Chapter 4), then disconnect the cable from the negative battery terminal or from the remote ground terminal (see Chapter 5).

2.0L DOHC engine

Removal

2   Drain the cooling system (see Chapter 1).

3   On vehicles with cruise control, disconnect the vacuum hoses from the cruise control reservoir (located behind the engine, under the intake manifold), remove the three reservoir retaining nuts (one on top, two on bottom) and then remove the cruise control reservoir.

4   Remove the air intake duct between the air filter housing and the throttle body (see Chapter 4).

5   Disconnect and remove the PCV and breather hoses (see Chapter 6).

6   Disconnect the accelerator cable, and the cruise control cable, if equipped, from the throttle body (see Chapter 4). Then detach the accelerator cable bracket from the intake manifold plenum.

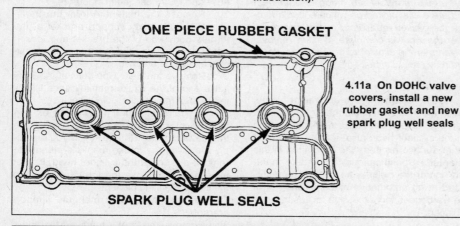

ONE PIECE RUBBER GASKET

SPARK PLUG WELL SEALS

4.11a On DOHC valve covers, install a new rubber gasket and new spark plug well seals

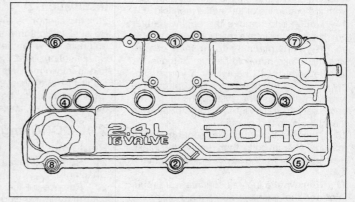

4.11b On SOHC valve covers, apply a light coat of RTV sealant onto the cover sealing surface and then install the new gasket

4.12 Valve cover bolt tightening sequence (DOHC engine shown, SOHC engine similar except that it doesn't have two center bolts)

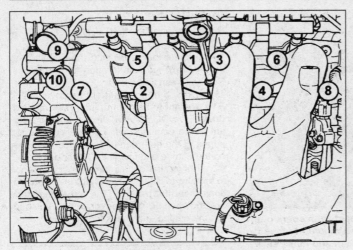

5.32a Intake manifold fastener tightening sequence (1995 through 1999 2.4L DOHC engine)

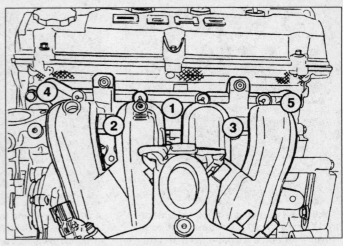

5.32b Intake manifold fastener tightening sequence (2001 and later 2.4L DOHC engine)

7   Unplug the electrical connectors from the Throttle Position Sensor (TPS) and from the Idle Air Control (IAC) motor (see Chapter 6) and then unplug the control harness connector from the alternator wiring harness connector.

8   Detach the two control harness clips from the plenum and then set the control harness aside.

9   Unplug the electrical connectors from the Manifold Absolute Pressure (MAP) sensor and from the Intake Air Temperature (IAT) sensor (see Chapter 6).

10   Clearly label and disconnect all vacuum hoses and lines from the air intake plenum. Also disconnect the brake booster vacuum hose from the plenum.

11   Remove the EGR pipe flange bolts and disconnect the EGR pipe flange from the plenum (see Chapter 6).

12   Unplug the electrical connectors from the fuel injectors, then disconnect the fuel supply and return lines from the fuel rail (see Chapter 4).

13   Unbolt the two intake manifold stays (support brackets) from the cylinder head and from the underside of the intake manifold.

14   Unbolt and remove the engine-hanger bracket from the intake manifold.

15   If you're planning to *replace* or *service* the intake manifold plenum, remove the throttle body (see Chapter 4). If you're simply removing the intake manifold plenum to remove or service the cylinder head, it's not necessary to remove the throttle body from the intake manifold plenum.

16   Remove the intake manifold-to-intake manifold plenum bolts, then remove the intake manifold plenum (the upper half of the manifold).

17   Remove the fuel rail, fuel pressure regulator and fuel injectors as a single assembly (see Chapter 4).

18   Remove the intake manifold bolts and nuts, then remove the intake manifold (the lower half of the manifold) from the engine.

If it sticks, tap the manifold with a soft-face hammer or carefully pry it from the head. **Caution:** *Do not pry between gasket sealing surfaces.* Remove the intake manifold gasket by carefully scraping all traces of gasket material from both the cylinder head and the intake manifold. **Caution:** *The cylinder head and intake manifold are made of aluminum and are easily nicked or gouged. Don't damage the gasket surfaces or a leak may result after the work is complete. Gasket removal solvents are available from auto parts stores and may prove helpful.*

Inspection

19   Using a straightedge and feeler gauge, check the intake manifold mating surface for warpage. Check the intake manifold surface on the cylinder head also. If the warpage on either surface exceeds the limit listed in this Chapter's Specifications, the intake manifold and/or the cylinder head must be resurfaced at an automotive machine shop or, if the warpage is too excessive for resurfacing, replaced.

Installation

20   Installation is the reverse of removal. Be sure to tighten the intake manifold bolts and nuts to the torque listed in this Chapter's Specifications and tighten the intake manifold-to-intake manifold plenum bolts securely. Refill the cooling system (see Chapter 1). When you're done, be sure to run the engine and check for air, coolant and/or fuel leaks.

2.4L DOHC engine

Removal

21   Remove the air inlet resonator (see Chapter 4).

22   Remove the fuel rail, fuel pressure regulator and fuel injectors as a single assembly (see Chapter 4).

23   Disconnect the accelerator cable and, if equipped, the cruise control and kickdown

cables from the throttle lever arm (see Chapter 4).

24   Unplug the electrical connectors from the Idle Air Control (IAC) motor, the Throttle Position Sensor (TPS) and the Intake Air Temperature (IAT) sensor (see Chapter 6).

25   Disconnect the leak detection pump hose and PCV hose (see Chapter 6).

26   Remove the fasteners from the transaxle-to-throttle body support bracket at the throttle body end of the bracket and *loosen* - but don't remove - the fastener at the transaxle end of the bracket.

27   Remove the EGR pipe bolts at the EGR valve and at the intake manifold (see Chapter 6), then remove the EGR pipe.

28   If you're planning to *replace* or *service* the intake manifold plenum, remove the throttle body (see Chapter 4). If you're simply removing the intake manifold plenum to remove or service the cylinder head, it's not necessary to remove the throttle body from the intake manifold plenum.

29   Remove the intake manifold support bracket.

30   Remove the intake manifold fasteners and washers, then remove the intake manifold and the manifold gasket.

Inspection

31   Refer to Step 19.

Installation

Refer to illustrations 5.32a and 5.32b

32   Using a new manifold gasket, install the intake manifold and tighten the intake manifold fasteners gradually and evenly in the indicated sequence **(see illustrations)** to the torque listed in this Chapter's Specifications.

33   Installation is otherwise the reverse of removal.

2.4L SOHC engine

Removal

34   Drain the cooling system (see Chapter 1).

35   Remove the filter housing (see Chapter 4).

36   Remove the throttle body (see Chapter 4). **Note:** *On most vehicles, it's not necessary to remove the throttle body in order to remove the intake manifold unless the intake manifold is being replaced. But on this particular design, the throttle body must be removed in order to provide sufficient clearance to remove the fuel rail from the intake manifold.*

37   Remove the thermostat housing assembly (see Chapter 3).

38   Disconnect the EVAP canister purge hose from the underside of the intake manifold.

39   Disconnect the power brake booster vacuum hose from the intake manifold.

40   Unplug the electrical connectors from the ignition coil (see Chapter 5), the fuel injectors (see Chapter 4), the manifold differential pressure sensor and the evaporative emission purge solenoid valve (see Chapter 6), then set the wiring harness aside. Also unplug the electrical connector from the Exhaust Gas Recirculation (EGR) valve (see Chapter 6) and set the harness aside.

41   Disconnect the fuel supply and return hoses from the fuel rail (see Chapter 4) and set them aside.

42   Remove the engine oil dipstick, then remove the dipstick tube retaining bolt and remove the tube.

43   Disconnect and remove the PCV hose (see Chapter 6).

44   Remove the two fuel return pipe retaining bolts and remove the fuel return pipe.

45   Remove the EGR valve (see Chapter 6).

46   Remove the fuel rail, fuel pressure regulator and fuel injectors as a single assembly (see Chapter 4). Remove the fuel rail mounting bolt insulators and store them in a plastic bag.

47   Unbolt and remove the three vacuum pipes from the intake manifold.

48   Remove the manifold differential pressure sensor, the Evaporative Emission (EVAP) purge solenoid valve and the EGR solenoid valve and vacuum control valve (see Chapter 6).

49   Remove the intake manifold stay bolts and remove the stay (the support bracket underneath the manifold).

50   Remove the intake manifold fasteners, then remove the intake manifold and discard the old manifold gasket.

Inspection

51   Refer to Step 19.

Installation

52   Using a new intake manifold gasket, place the intake manifold in position, install and hand-tighten the fasteners. Then, working from the center outward, gradually and evenly tighten them to the torque listed in this Chapter's Specifications.

53   The remainder of installation is the reverse of removal. Refill the cooling system (see Chapter 1).

6   Exhaust manifold - removal and installation

Warning: *Allow the engine to cool completely before beginning this procedure.*

2.0L DOHC engine

Removal

1   Drain the engine coolant (see Chapter 1).

2   Remove the air intake duct (see Chapter 4).

3   Disconnect the upper radiator hose from water outlet fitting (see Chapter 3).

4   Unbolt and detach the control wiring harness bracket from the valve cover.

5   Unbolt and remove the water pipe assembly.

6   Remove the engine oil dipstick.

7   Unscrew the bolts and remove the upper heat shield from the exhaust manifold.

8   Unbolt and remove the engine hanger bracket.

9   Set the parking brake and block the rear wheels. Raise the vehicle and support it securely on jackstands.

10   Working from under the vehicle, disconnect the air hose from the pulsed secondary air injection valve and remove the pulsed secondary air injection valve from the exhaust pipe (see Chapter 6).

11   Apply penetrating oil to the threads of the exhaust manifold-to-exhaust pipe studs and allow it to soak in for awhile Then remove the exhaust pipe-to-exhaust manifold flange nuts and separate the exhaust pipe from the exhaust manifold.

12   Unscrew the bolts and remove the lower heat shield from the exhaust manifold.

13   Unscrew the bolts and nuts and remove the exhaust manifold.

14   Remove the exhaust manifold gasket.

Inspection

15   Inspect the exhaust manifold for cracks and any other obvious damage. If the manifold is cracked or damaged in any way, replace it.

16   Using a wire brush, clean up the threads of the exhaust manifold bolts and inspect the threads for damage. Replace any bolts that have thread damage.

17   Using a scraper, remove all traces of gasket material from the mating surfaces and inspect them for wear and cracks. **Caution:** *When removing gasket material from any surface, especially aluminum, be very careful not to scratch or gouge the gasket surface. Any damage to the surface may result in a leak after reassembly. Gasket removal solvents are available from auto parts stores and may prove helpful.*

18   Using a straightedge and feeler gauge, inspect the exhaust manifold mating surface for warpage. Check the exhaust manifold surface on the cylinder head also. If the warpage on any surface exceeds the limits listed in this Chapter's Specifications, the exhaust manifold and/or cylinder head must be replaced or resurfaced at an automotive machine shop.

Installation

19   Coat the threads of the exhaust manifold bolts and studs with an anti-seize compound. Install a new gasket, install the manifold and install the fasteners. Tighten the bolts and nuts in several stages, working from the center out, to the torque listed in this Chapter's Specifications.

20   The remainder of installation is the reverse of removal. Refill the cooling system (see Chapter 1). When you're done, be sure to run the engine and check for exhaust leaks.

2.4L DOHC engine

Removal

Refer to illustrations 6.23a, 6.23b and 6.25

21   Raise the vehicle and place it securely on jackstands.

22   Disconnect the exhaust pipe from the exhaust manifold (see Chapter 4). **Note:** *On some models, it might be necessary to remove the exhaust system to create sufficient clearance to remove the manifold.*

23   Remove the exhaust manifold heat shield **(see illustrations)**.

24   Unplug the electrical connector for the oxygen sensor, then remove the oxygen sensor from the exhaust manifold (see Chapter 6).

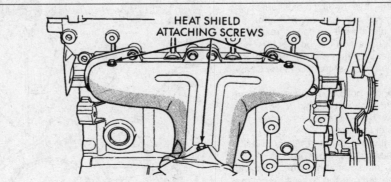

6.23a To detach the heat shield from the exhaust manifold on 1995 through 1999 2.4L DOHC engines, remove these three screws

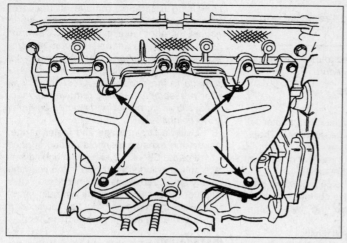

6.23b To detach the heat shield from the exhaust manifold on 2001 and later 2.4L DOHC engines, remove these four bolts (arrows)

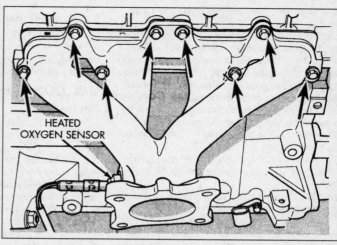

6.25 To detach the exhaust manifold on a 1995 through 1999 2.4L DOHC engine, remove the oxygen sensor (see Chapter 6), then remove these bolts

25   Unscrew the mounting bolts (see illustration) and remove the exhaust manifold and the old manifold gasket.

Inspection
26   Refer to Steps 15 through 18.

Installation
Refer to illustration 6.27
27   Using a new exhaust manifold gasket (and NO sealant), install the exhaust manifold and tighten the mounting bolts to the torque listed in this Chapter's Specifications. On 1995 through 1999 models, starting in the center, work out toward the ends of the manifold, gradually and evenly tightening the bolts to the specified torque. On 2001 and later models, tighten the bolts in the indicated sequence (see illustration).
28   The remainder of installation is the reverse of removal.

2.4L SOHC engine
Removal
29   Raise the vehicle and place it securely on jackstands.
30   Remove the exhaust manifold-to-exhaust pipe flange nuts, then detach the exhaust pipe from the exhaust manifold (see Chapter 4). Remove and discard the old flange gasket.
31   Unplug the electrical connector from the oxygen sensor, then remove the oxygen sensor from the exhaust manifold (see Chapter 6).
32   Unscrew the bolts and remove the heat shield from the exhaust manifold.
33   Unscrew the bolts and remove the exhaust manifold bracket.
34   Loosen the two exhaust manifold bolts that secure the engine hanger bracket.
35   Remove the exhaust manifold nuts and washers, then remove the exhaust manifold and discard the old exhaust manifold gasket.

Inspection
36   Refer to Steps 15 through 18.

Installation
37   Using a new exhaust manifold gasket, place the exhaust manifold in position and install and hand-tighten the exhaust manifold mounting nuts. Then, working from the center and working your way toward the ends of the manifold, gradually and evenly tighten the nuts to the torque listed in this Chapter's Specifications.
38   The remainder of installation is the reverse of removal.

---

7   Timing belt - removal, inspection and installation

Refer to illustrations 7.6 and 7.7
Caution 1: *If the timing belt failed with the engine operating, damage to the valves may*

have occurred. Remove the camshaft(s) and pressurize each cylinder with compressed air (see Section 13) to confirm damage (if a cylinder won't hold air, the valves are most likely bent).
Caution 2: *Do not try to turn the crankshaft with a camshaft sprocket bolt and do not rotate the crankshaft counterclockwise.*
Caution 3: *Do not turn the crankshaft or camshaft(s) after the timing belt has been removed. Doing so will damage the valves from contact with the pistons.*
1   Position the number one piston at Top Dead Center (see Section 3).
2   Disconnect the battery cable from the negative battery terminal or from the remote ground terminal (see Chapter 5).
3   Remove the accessory drivebelts (see Chapter 1).
4   Set the parking brake and block the rear wheels. Raise the front of the vehicle and support it securely on jackstands.

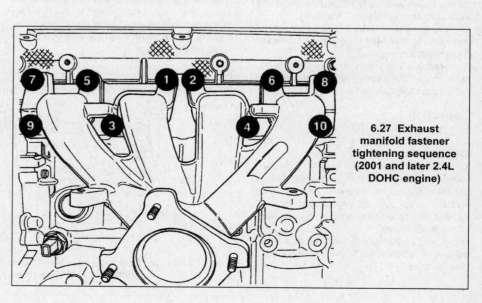

6.27 Exhaust manifold fastener tightening sequence (2001 and later 2.4L DOHC engine)

7.6 Insert a large screwdriver or bar through the opening in the pulley and wedge it against the engine block, then loosen the bolt with a socket and breaker bar

7.7 Install a 3-jaw puller onto the damper pulley, position the center post of the puller on the crankshaft end (use the proper insert to keep from damaging the crankshaft threads), tighten the puller and remove the pulley from the crankshaft

7.12 Remove the two lower bolts (arrows) that attach the timing belt outer cover to the engine

5   Remove the right (passenger-side) inner fender splash shield, if equipped.

6   Loosen the large bolt in the center of the crankshaft damper pulley. It might be very tight; to break it loose insert a large screwdriver or bar through the opening in the pulley to keep the pulley stationary and loosen the bolt with a socket and breaker bar **(see illustration)**.

7   Install a 3-jaw puller onto the damper pulley and remove the pulley from the crankshaft **(see illustration)**. Use the proper insert to keep the puller from damaging the crankshaft bolt threads. If the pulley is difficult to remove, tap the center bolt of the puller with a brass mallet to break it loose. Reinstall the bolt with a spacer so you can rotate the crankshaft later.

2.0L DOHC engine
Removal
Refer to illustrations 7.12, 7.13 and 7.14
Caution: *The timing system is complex. Severe engine damage will occur if you make any mistakes. Do not attempt this procedure unless you are highly experienced with this type of repair. If you are at all unsure of your abilities, consult an expert. Double-check all your work and be sure everything is correct before you attempt to start the engine.*

8   Remove the coolant reservoir (see Chapter 3).

9   Remove the power steering pump and the power steering pump bracket (see Chapter 10).

10   Support the engine with a floor jack under the oil pan. Place a wood block on the jack head to prevent the floor jack from denting or damaging the oil pan.

11   Remove the right (passenger-side) engine mount and engine mount bracket (see Section 19).

12   Remove the two lower timing cover bolts **(see illustration)** and the single upper bolt and then remove the timing belt cover.

13   Before removing the timing belt, make sure that the camshaft sprocket timing marks are aligned **(see illustration)**. **Note:** *If you plan to reuse the timing belt, paint an arrow on it to indicate the direction of rotation (clockwise).*

14   Remove the timing belt tensioner mounting bolts **(see illustration)** and remove the tensioner. **Note:** *The tensioner plunger will extend when the assembly is removed.*

15   Carefully slip the timing belt off the sprockets and set it aside. If you plan to reuse the timing belt, place it in a plastic bag - do not allow the belt to come in contact with any type of oil or water at this will greatly shorten belt life.

16   If you're planning to replace a camshaft seal, it will be necessary to remove the camshaft sprockets, the timing belt tensioner pulley and the rear timing belt cover (see Section 9).

17   Inspect the oil pump seal for leaks and replace it if necessary (see Section 16).

Inspection
Refer to illustration 7.19
18   Rotate the tensioner pulley and idler pulley by hand and move them side-to-side to detect roughness and excess play. Visually inspect the sprockets for any signs of damage and wear. Replace parts as necessary.

19   Inspect the timing belt for cracks, separation, wear, missing teeth and oil contamination. Replace the belt if it's in questionable condition **(see illustration)**. If the timing belt is excessively worn or damaged on one side, it might be due to incorrect tracking (misalignment). If the belt looks like it was misaligned, be sure to replace the belt tensioner assembly.

20   Check the automatic tensioner for leaks or any obvious damage to the body.

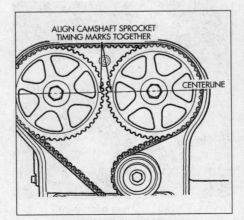

7.13 Camshaft timing mark details (DOHC models)

7.14 Remove the timing belt tensioner mounting bolts (arrows) and then remove the tensioner

7.19 Carefully inspect the timing belt; bending it backwards will often make wear or damage more apparent

Installation

Refer to illustrations 7.21a, 7.21b, 7.21c, 7.23a, 7.23b, 7.23c and 7.27

Caution: *Before starting the engine, carefully rotate the crankshaft by hand through at least two full revolutions (use a socket and breaker bar on the crankshaft pulley center bolt). If you feel any resistance, STOP! There is something wrong - most likely, valves are contacting the pistons. You must find the problem before proceeding. Check your work and see if any updated repair information is available.*

21   The tensioner pin must be compressed into the tensioner housing prior to installation. Place the tensioner in the vise so the surface with the hole faces up. Slowly compress the tensioner, then install a 5/64-inch Allen wrench or similar tool through the body to retain the plunger in this position until it is installed **(see illustrations)**. Remove the tensioner from the vise.

22   Confirm that the camshaft sprocket timing marks are aligned **(see illustration 7.13)**.

23   Position the crankshaft timing sprocket as follows **(see illustrations)**:

a) *Initially align the TDC mark on the sprocket with the arrow on the oil pump housing.*

b) *Back it off counterclockwise 3 teeth Before Top Dead Center (BTDC).*

c) *Rotate the crankshaft timing sprocket clockwise to 1/2-tooth BTDC.*

24   Install the timing belt as follows; first place the belt onto the crankshaft sprocket, maintaining tension on the belt, wrap it around the water pump sprocket, idler pulley (DOHC models) and camshaft sprocket, then slip the belt onto the tensioner pulley.

25   To take the slack out of the timing belt, rotate the crankshaft timing sprocket clockwise to align the marks (TDC); make sure the camshaft sprocket timing marks remain aligned.

26   Install the tensioner assembly - don't tighten the bolts at this time.

27   Place a torque wrench on the center bolt of the tensioner pulley and apply 250 inch-lbs of torque. With the torque applied to the ten-

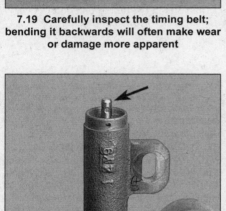

7.21a The tensioner pin (arrow) must be compressed into the tensioner housing prior to installation

7.21b Place the tensioner in the vise so the hole (arrow) faces up

7.21c Compress the pin with the vise and place a small Allen wrench (arrow), or something similar, through the hole to keep the pin retracted for reassembly on the engine

7.23a Using a box-end wrench, rotate the crankshaft timing sprocket until the TDC mark on the sprocket is aligned with the arrow on the oil pump housing (arrow) . . .

7.23b . . . then back it off counterclockwise 3 teeth BTDC (arrows)

7.23c Rotate the crankshaft timing sprocket clockwise to 1/2-tooth BTDC (arrows)

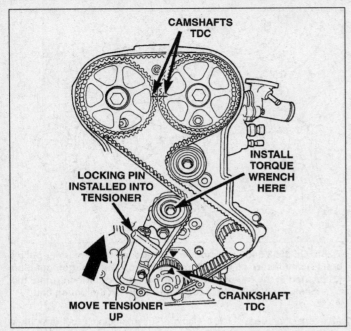

7.27 Using a torque wrench on the tensioner pulley, apply 250 inch-lbs of torque, move the tensioner up against the tensioner pulley bracket and tighten the tensioner mounting bolts

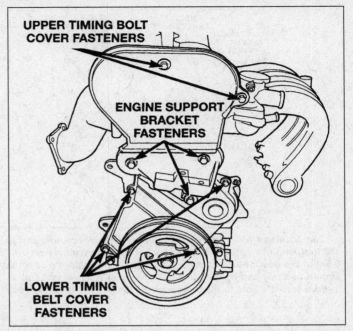

7.33 Remove the upper and lower timing belt cover fasteners and then remove the covers, then remove the right engine mount support bracket bolts (arrows) and remove the bracket

sioner pulley, move the tensioner up against the tensioner pulley bracket and tighten the tensioner bolts to the torque listed in this Chapter's Specifications **(see illustration)**. Remove the torque wrench.

28   Release the Allen wrench or pin from the tensioner. The timing belt tension is correct when the pin can be withdrawn and reinserted easily. Double check that the timing marks on both the camshaft sprocket(s) and crankshaft sprocket are still aligned at TDC.

29   Using the bolt in the center of the crankshaft sprocket, turn the crankshaft clockwise through two complete revolutions. **Caution:** *If you feel resistance while turning the crankshaft - STOP, the valves may be hitting the pistons from incorrect valve timing. Stop and re-check the valve timing.* **Note:** *The camshaft and crankshaft sprocket marks will align every two revolutions of the crankshaft. Recheck the alignment of the timing marks; If they do not align properly, loosen the tensioner, slip the belt off the camshaft sprocket, realign the marks, reinstall the belt, and recheck the alignment.*

30   Reinstall the remaining parts in the reverse order of removal.

31   Start the engine and road test the vehicle.

2.4L DOHC engine

Removal

Refer to illustrations 7.33, 7.35, 7.36a, 7.36b, 7.39, 7.40 and 7.41

Caution: *The timing system is complex. Severe engine damage will occur if you make any mistakes. Do not attempt this procedure unless you are highly experienced with this type of repair. If you are at all unsure of your abilities, consult an expert. Double-check all*

your work and be sure everything is correct before you attempt to start the engine.

32   Remove the alternator belt idler pulley bolt and remove the pulley (right below the alternator).

33   Remove the upper and lower timing belt cover fasteners **(see illustration)** and remove the covers.

34   Remove the right (passenger-side) engine mount (see Section 19) and remove the engine mount support bracket **(see illustration 7.33)**. **Note:** *Make sure the engine is supported with a piece of wood and a floor jack placed under the oil pan. The wood will prevent the floor jack from denting or damaging the oil pan.*

35   Before removing the timing belt, make sure that the camshaft timing marks are

aligned and that the TDC mark on the crankshaft timing belt sprocket is aligned with the stationary index mark on the oil pump housing **(see illustration)**. Note that the crankshaft timing belt sprocket TDC mark is located on the trailing edge of the sprocket tooth. If you don't align the trailing edge of the sprocket tooth with the TDC mark on the oil pump housing, the camshaft timing marks won't be aligned.

36   Release tension on the timing belt. **Note:** *2003 and later 2.4L DOHC engines are equipped with an updated timing belt tensioner that uses a spring tang and setting notch to adjust the timing belt tension.*

a) *On 1996 through 2002 engines, insert a 6 mm Allen wrench into the belt tensioner and insert the long end of a 1/8-inch or a 3 mm Allen wrench into the small hole*

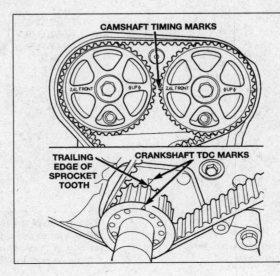

7.35 Before removing the timing belt, make sure that the camshaft timing marks are aligned and that the TDC mark on the crankshaft timing belt sprocket is aligned with the stationary index mark on the oil pump housing (note that the crankshaft timing belt sprocket TDC mark is located on the *trailing edge* of the sprocket tooth)

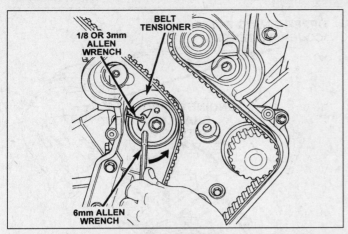

7.36a Insert an Allen wrench into the belt tensioner and insert the long end of a smaller Allen wrench into the small hole on the front of the tensioner; rotate the tensioner counterclockwise and simultaneously and lightly push in the smaller Allen wrench until it slides into the hole in the tensioner (1996 through 2002 models)

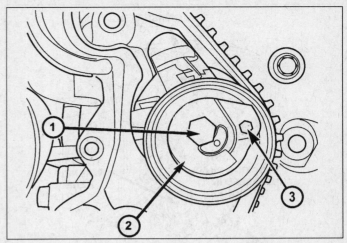

7.36b On 2003 and later models, first loosen the tensioner pulley bolt (1) and insert a 6 mm Allen wrench into the hexagon opening (3) located in the top plate (2) of the belt tensioner then rotate the tensioner clockwise to release tension on the timing belt

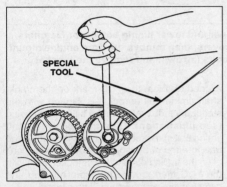

7.39 Using a suitable holding tool, remove the camshaft sprocket bolts

located on the front of the tensioner (**see illustration**). *Then, using the 6 mm Allen wrench as a lever, rotate the tensioner COUNTERCLOCKWISE and simultaneously and lightly push in the 1/8-inch or 3 mm Allen wrench until it slides into the locking hole in the tensioner.*

b) *On 2003 and later engines, insert a 6 mm Allen wrench into the hexagon opening on the top plate of the tensioner (**see illustration**). Then, using the 6 mm Allen wrench as a lever, rotate the tensioner CLOCKWISE until the tension is off the timing belt and it can be removed easily.*

37   Remove the timing belt.

38   Remove the timing belt idler pulley bolt, then remove the timing belt idler pulley.

39   Using a suitable holding tool (**see illustration**), remove the camshaft sprocket bolts, then remove the camshaft sprockets.

40   Remove the rear timing belt cover fasteners (**see illustration**) and then remove the rear cover.

41   Remove the lower timing belt tensioner bolt (**see illustration**) and then remove the tensioner assembly.

Inspection
42   Refer to Steps 18 through 20.

Installation
Refer to illustrations 7.48 and 7.50
Caution: *Before starting the engine, carefully rotate the crankshaft by hand through at least two full revolutions (use a socket and breaker*

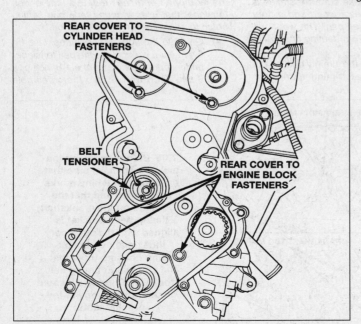

7.40 Remove the rear timing belt cover fasteners (arrows) and then remove the rear cover

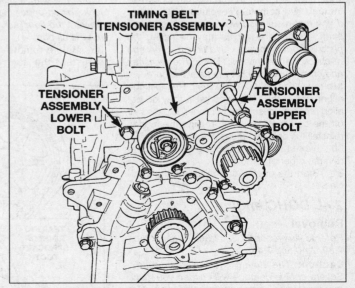

7.41 Remove the lower timing belt tensioner bolt, then remove the tensioner assembly; when installing the tensioner assembly, use one of the engine support bracket M10 bolts in the upper bolt hole to position the tensioner while torquing the lower bolt

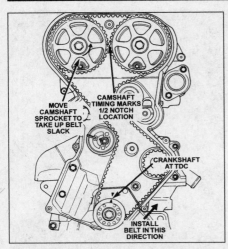

7.48 Turn the exhaust camshaft sprocket clockwise so the timing mark on the exhaust sprocket is slightly below the timing mark on the intake camshaft sprocket; when installing the belt, start at the crankshaft sprocket and thread the belt around the water pump sprocket, idler pulley, cam sprockets and tensioner pulley

bar on the crankshaft pulley center bolt). If you feel any resistance, STOP! There is something wrong - most likely, valves are contacting the pistons. You must find the problem before proceeding. Check your work and see if any updated repair information is available.

43 Place the timing belt tensioner in position on the front of the engine and then install the lower mounting bolt to hold it in place, but don't tighten the lower bolt yet. Install an engine bracket mounting bolt (M10) in the upper tensioner bolt hole **(see illustration 7.41)** and then screw it in five to seven turns. Tighten the lower tensioner bolt to the torque listed in this Chapter's Specifications and then remove the upper bolt.

44 Install the rear timing belt cover and tighten the cover fasteners securely.

45 Install the timing belt idler pulley and tighten the bolt to the torque listed in this Chapter's Specifications.

46 Install the camshaft sprockets and tighten the sprocket bolts to the torque listed in this Chapter's Specifications. Be sure to prevent the camshafts from turning as shown in **illustration 7.39**.

47 Make sure that the TDC mark on the crankshaft timing belt sprocket is still aligned with the stationary index mark on the oil pump housing **(see illustration 7.35)**.

48 Turn the exhaust camshaft sprocket clockwise so the timing mark on the exhaust sprocket is slightly below the timing mark on the intake camshaft sprocket **(see illustration)**.

49 Install the timing belt as follows: Start at the crankshaft sprocket, then thread the belt onto the water pump sprocket, the idler pulley, the camshaft sprockets and then finally the tensioner **(see illustration 7.48)**. Now take up tension by moving the exhaust camshaft sprocket counterclockwise until the timing marks on the two cam sprockets are realigned.

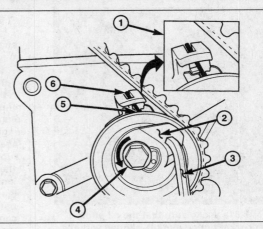

7.50 Timing belt tensioner details (2003 and later models)

1 Setting notch and spring tang alignment details
2 Top plate
3 6 mm Allen wrench
4 Lock bolt
5 Setting notch
6 Spring tang

50 Reset the tension on the timing belt:

a) On 1996 through 2002 models, remove the 3 mm Allen wrench from the timing belt tensioner to release the tensioner against the timing belt. Install then grip the 6 mm Allen wrench to prevent the tensioner from rotating, and torque the tensioner bolt to this Chapter's Specifications **(see illustration 7.48)**.

b) On 2003 and later models, insert a 6 mm Allen wrench into the hexagon opening located on the top plate of the belt tensioner pulley. Using the 6 mm Allen wrench as a lever, rotate the belt tensioner counterclockwise until there is tension on the timing belt. Continue to rotate the tension until the setting notch is aligned with the spring tang **(see illustration)**. Grip the Allen wrench to prevent the tensioner from rotating, and torque the tensioner bolt to this Chapter's Specifications. Recheck the tensioner alignment marks. If they are incorrect, loosen the bolt and repeat the procedure.

51 Rotate the crankshaft two complete revolutions and verify the TDC marks on the crankshaft sprocket and the oil pump housing are still aligned and the timing marks on the camshaft sprockets are still aligned. If they're not, go back to Step 49 and reinstall the belt.

52 Install the right engine mount and support bracket. Tighten all fasteners securely.

53 Install the upper and lower timing belt covers and tighten the fasteners to the torque listed in this Chapter's Specifications.

54 Install the alternator drivebelt idler pulley and tighten the idler pulley bolt to the torque listed in this Chapter's Specifications.

55 Install the crankshaft vibration damper pulley, install the washer and pulley bolt and then tighten the pulley bolt to the torque listed in this Chapter's Specifications.

56 The remainder of installation is the reverse of removal.

2.4L SOHC engine

Removal

Timing belt

Refer to illustrations 7.60, 7.61a, 7.61b and 7.63

Caution: The timing system is complex.

Severe engine damage will occur if you make any mistakes. Do not attempt this procedure unless you are highly experienced with this type of repair. If you are at all unsure of your abilities, consult an expert. Double-check all your work and be sure everything is correct before you attempt to start the engine.

Note: There are two timing belts on the 2.4L SOHC engine: The longer belt (the outer belt) is the timing belt; it drives the oil pump sprocket (which, in turn, drives the front balance shaft) and the camshaft. The shorter belt (located behind the timing belt) is also driven by the crankshaft; it drives the rear balance shaft. When you replace one belt, always replace the other belt at the same time.

57 Support the engine with a floor jack under the oil pan. Place a wood block on the jack head to prevent the floor jack from denting or damaging the oil pan.

58 Remove the four upper timing belt upper cover bolts and then remove the upper timing belt cover. Note the position of the wiring harness clips that are secured by the upper timing cover bolts.

59 Remove the lower timing cover bolts and then remove the lower timing cover.

60 Rotate the crankshaft in a clockwise direction until the timing mark on the camshaft sprocket is aligned with the stationary index mark on the engine **(see illustration)**.

7.60 Rotate the crankshaft in a clockwise direction until the timing mark on the camshaft sprocket is aligned with the stationary index mark on the engine

7.61a Make sure that the oil pump sprocket timing mark is aligned with the stationary mark on the engine

7.61b To verify that the front balance shaft is in the correct position, and to lock the shaft in this position until the timing belt is reinstalled, remove the plug on the side of the engine block and then insert a screwdriver or a long punch through the hole in the block and into the hole in the balance shaft (oil pan removed so you can see how the tool passes through the balance shaft)

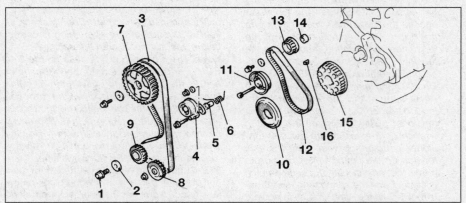

7.63 An exploded view of the timing belt assembly (2.4L SOHC engine)

1	Crankshaft sprocket bolt	9	Crankshaft sprocket
2	Special washer	10	Belt guide
3	Timing belt	11	Balance shaft belt tensioner
4	Timing belt tensioner	12	Balance shaft belt
5	Tensioner spacer	13	Rear balance shaft sprocket
6	Tensioner spring	14	Spacer
7	Camshaft sprocket	15	Crankshaft sprocket
8	Oil pump sprocket	16	Key

61   Verify that the oil pump sprocket timing mark is aligned with the stationary mark **(see illustration)**. The oil pump, of course, is not timed, but the balance shafts are, and the front balance shaft is driven by the oil pump driven gear. There are timing marks on the oil pump drive and driven gears, but you can't see them unless the pump is removed. To verify that the front balance shaft is in the correct position - and to lock the shaft in this position until the timing belt is reinstalled - remove the plug on the side of the engine block and insert an 8 mm Phillips head screwdriver or drift through the hole in the block **(see illustration)**. When the shaft is in the correct position, the screwdriver will go about 2-1/2 inches into the hole in the block (the screwdriver goes over the top of the balance shaft, preventing it from turning). **Caution:** *Do NOT remove the screwdriver until the timing belt and balance belt have been reinstalled.*

62   If you're going to reuse the timing belt, put an arrow on the belt indicating the (clockwise) direction of rotation to ensure that it will be reinstalled in the same direction.

63   Loosen the timing belt tensioner pulley bolt and push the tensioner pulley toward the water pump to create slack in the belt. Make sure that the timing marks are still aligned, and then remove the timing belt.

Balance shaft belt

Refer to illustrations 7.64 and 7.66

64   To reuse the balance shaft belt, put an arrow on the belt indicating the (clockwise) direction of rotation to ensure it will be reinstalled in the same direction **(see illustration)**.

65   If you're planning to replace the rear balance shaft seal, you'll need to remove the rear balance shaft sprocket to do so. Try to loosen the bolt now, before removing the balance shaft belt. The tensioned belt helps to hold the sprocket while you're breaking the nut loose. If you're unable to loosen the nut this way, wait until after you have removed the balance belt and then, using a sprocket holding tool or a strap wrench, try again (see Step 67).

66   Make sure that the timing marks on the crankshaft sprocket and the rear balance

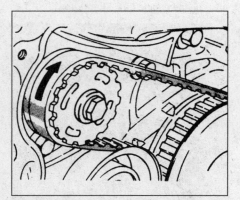

7.64 If you're going to reuse the balance shaft belt, put an arrow on the belt indicating the (clockwise) direction of rotation to ensure that it will be reinstalled in the same direction

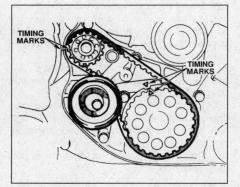

7.66 Before loosening the balance shaft belt tensioner pulley, make sure that the timing marks on the crankshaft sprocket and the balance shaft sprocket are aligned with their respective stationary marks on the engine

shaft sprocket are aligned with their respective stationary marks on the engine **(see illustration)**. Then loosen the tensioner pulley bolt, swing the tensioner in a counterclockwise direction and remove the balance shaft belt.

67 If you were unable to remove the balance shaft sprocket in Step 65, hold the balance shaft sprocket with a suitable sprocket holding tool or strap wrench, then loosen and remove the sprocket bolt and the sprocket.

68 If you're planning to replace the crankshaft front oil seal, remove the Crankshaft Position (CKP) sensor (see Chapter 6) and remove the outer crankshaft sprocket, the CKP sensing blade and the rear crank sprocket. To loosen the crankshaft sprocket bolt, remove the flywheel/driveplate inspection cover and wedge a screwdriver into the starter ring gear teeth. Remove the bolt and washer, and then pull off the outer sprocket (the timing belt sprocket), remove the sensing blade and then remove the rear sprocket (the rear balance shaft drive sprocket). **Caution:** *Note that the concave side of the CKP sensing blade faces toward the engine. When installing the CKP sensing blade, make sure that it is oriented correctly.*

Inspection

69 Refer to Steps 18 through 20.

Installation

Balance shaft belt

Refer to illustration 7.73

70 If the crankshaft sprockets were removed, degrease both sides of the crankshaft sensing blade and the crank sprockets and clean out the bolt hole in the nose of the crank with degreaser as well. Degreasing these areas will help prevent the crankshaft sprocket bolt from loosening, which might allow the sensing blade to waver slightly, which would affect the output signal from the CKP sensor. Be sure to install the CKP sensing blade between the inner and outer crankshaft sprockets, with its concave side facing toward the engine. Tighten the crankshaft sprocket bolt to the torque listed in this Chapter's Specifications.

71 If you remove the rear balance shaft sprocket to replace the seal, install the sprocket and tighten the sprocket retaining nut to the torque listed in this Chapter's Specifications.

72 Make sure that the timing marks on the crankshaft sprocket and the balance shaft sprocket are still correctly aligned **(see illustration 7.66)**, then install the balance shaft belt. After installing the balance shaft belt, make sure that the tension side (the upper run) of the belt has no slack.

73 Install the balance shaft belt tensioner pulley and bolt, but don't tighten the bolt completely at this time. First, make sure that the center of the tensioner pulley for the balance shaft belt is located to the left of the pulley **(see illustration)**. Holding up the tensioner in this position with one hand to tension the belt, tighten the tensioner pulley bolt to the torque listed in this Chapter's Specifi-

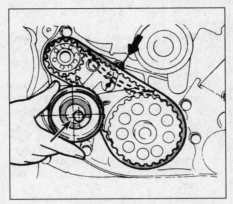

7.73 Before tensioning the balance shaft belt, make sure that the center of the tensioner pulley is located to the left of the pulley bolt; check the tension at the indicated point (arrow) on the upper run of the belt

cations. **Note:** *After tightening the bolt, use your index finger and press firmly on the balance shaft belt. The belt should deflect about 1/4-inch.*

Timing belt

Refer to illustration 7.75

Caution: *Before starting the engine, carefully rotate the crankshaft by hand through at least two full revolutions (use a socket and breaker bar on the crankshaft pulley center bolt). If you feel any resistance, STOP! There is something wrong - most likely, valves are contacting the pistons. You must find the problem before proceeding. Check your work and see if any updated repair information is available.*

74 Make sure that the timing mark on the camshaft sprocket is still aligned with the mark on the valve cover and that the timing marks on the crankshaft and oil pump sprockets are also still aligned **(see illustrations 7.60, 7.61a and 7.66)**. When aligning the oil pump sprocket marks, it is critical that the weighted part of the balance shaft is facing down. If you used a screwdriver or punch to verify that the balance shaft was in the correct position before removing the timing belt, the shaft is still in the correct position. But, if you didn't insert the screwdriver into the balance shaft, or if you removed it and then accidentally turned the oil pump sprocket, then you can no longer be sure which direction the weighted part of the shaft is facing. It's possible that the balance shaft weight could be facing up, even with the timing marks aligned. If this happens, severe engine vibration will result. If you find yourself in this predicament, try the following check: Before installing the timing belt, slightly rock the oil pump sprocket by hand and, watching closely, note whether the sprocket has a tendency to remain stationary (return to the timing-marks-aligned position) when the sprocket is rotated. If it does, this means that the balance shaft is CORRECTLY timed. If the sprocket has a tendency to rotate clockwise when spun lightly, the shaft is INCORRECTLY

7.75 Once the tensioner plunger is compressed, insert a small Allen wrench or rod through the hole in the tensioner body and into the hole in the plunger to keep the plunger retracted until the timing belt is installed

timed. If there is any doubt about whether or not the balance shaft is in the correct position, insert a screwdriver through the hole in the left side of the cylinder block **(see illustration 7.61b)**. Make sure the screwdriver extends about 2-1/2 inches into the hole and then verify that the sprocket cannot be rotated with the screwdriver in place. Now you can be sure the timing is correct. If the screwdriver can only be inserted about one inch into the hole, the timing is not correct. Rotate the sprocket until the marks are aligned again and insert the screwdriver again. It should now go in the full 2-1/2 inches. The balance shaft is now in the correct position.

75 The automatic tensioner should have a fair amount of resistance. Here's an easy way to test the tensioner before preparing it for installation: Grasp the tensioner firmly and press the plunger against a hard surface (like the engine block). You shouldn't be able to compress the plunger more than 0.04 inch (3/64-inch). If the plunger compresses much more than that, or is easily compressed, replace it with a new unit. To prepare the tensioner for installation, place it in a vise **(see illustration 7.21b)** and compress the plunger until the hole in the tensioner body and the hole in the plunger are aligned. **Caution:** *Make sure that the tensioner is in a level position when it is in the vise. Also, put a washer over the plug on the bottom of the tensioner to prevent the vise from contacting the plug.* When the holes are lined up, insert a small Allen wrench or rod through the holes to keep the plunger retracted during installation **(see illustration)**.

76 Install the automatic tensioner on the engine, install the tensioner mounting bolts and tighten them to the torque listed in this Chapter's Specifications. Make sure that the plunger remains in the compressed position (leave the Allen wrench or rod in place for now).

77 Install the tensioner pulley on the tensioner arm, install the pulley bolt and then tighten the bolt finger tight. Don't remove the

pin from the automatic tensioner yet.

78 Make sure the timing marks on the camshaft, oil pump sprocket and crankshaft sprocket are still correctly aligned **(see illustrations 7.60, 7.61a and 7.66)**

79 Remove the plug on the side of the block and insert a Phillips screwdriver or a long punch through the hole **(see illustration 7.61b)**. If the tool can still be inserted into the hole about 2-1/2 inches, the timing marks are still correctly aligned. If the tool cannot be inserted more than one inch, the oil pump sprocket must be reset. When it's positioned correctly, reinstall the screwdriver and keep it there until the timing belt is installed.

80 Install the timing belt in the following sequence:

a) *Start at the crankshaft sprocket.*
b) *Then go around the oil pump sprocket.*
c) *Then go around the camshaft sprocket*
d) *Then go around the tensioner pulley.*
e) *Set the tensioner pulley so that the two holes in the pulley hub are below the pulley bolt and horizontal, lightly push the tensioner pulley against the timing belt and temporarily tighten the pulley bolt just enough to hold the tensioner pulley in this position.*
f) *Remove the screwdriver from the engine block hole and install the plug.*

81 Adjust the timing belt tension in the following sequence:

a) *Turn the crankshaft 90-degrees (1/4-turn) in a counterclockwise direction, then turn it clockwise until the timing marks are realigned.*
b) *Loosen the tensioner pulley bolt and attach the special tool (No. MD998752, or a suitable equivalent; see your dealer parts department about this tool) to an inch-pound torque wrench.* **Note:** *Your torque wrench must be capable of measuring small increments between 0 and 40 inch-lbs. Apply 30 inch-lbs. to the tensioner.*
c) *While holding tension on the timing belt tensioner, tighten the tensioner pulley bolt to the torque listed in this Chapter's Specifications.*
d) *Remove the special tool.*
e) *Pull the Allen wrench or rod out of the automatic tensioner.*
f) *Rotate the crankshaft two complete (clockwise) turns and then wait about 15 minutes to allow the plunger in the automatic tensioner to fully extend.* **Caution:** *If you feel resistance while turning the crankshaft, the valves may be hitting the pistons from incorrect valve timing. Stop and re-check the valve timing.*
g) *Wait 15 minutes and measure how far the tensioner plunger protrudes from the tensioner body (the distance between the automatic tensioner body and the tensioner arm). It should be between 5/32 and 3/16-inch (3.8 to 4.5 mm).*
h) *Verify that all timing marks are still aligned.*

82 If the protrusion of the tensioner plunger is incorrect, repeat the belt adjustment procedure.

83 Install the timing belt covers and tighten the fasteners to the torque listed in this Chapter's Specifications. Note that the timing belt cover bolts come in different lengths; make sure they're reinstalled in the correct holes.

84 The remainder of installation is the reverse of removal.

85 Start the engine and road test the vehicle.

8 Crankshaft front oil seal - replacement

Refer to illustrations 8.2, 8.3, 8.5 and 8.6
Caution: *Do not rotate the camshaft(s) or crankshaft when the timing belt is removed or damage to the engine may occur.*

1 Remove the timing belt cover(s) and then remove the timing belt(s) (see Section 7).

2 Pull the crankshaft sprocket from the crankshaft with a bolt-type gear puller **(see illustration)**. Remove the Woodruff key. **Caution:** *If you are replacing the crank front seal on a 2.4L SOHC engine, note that there are two crankshaft sprockets - one for the timing belt and one for the balance shaft belt. On this engine, be careful when working around the sensing blade for the Crankshaft Position (CKP) sensor.*

3 Wrap the tip of a small screwdriver with tape. Working from below the right inner fender, use the screwdriver to pry the seal out of its bore **(see illustration)**. Take care to prevent damaging the oil pump assembly, the crankshaft and the seal bore.

4 Thoroughly clean and inspect the seal bore and sealing surface on the crankshaft. Minor imperfections can be removed with emery cloth. If there is a groove worn in the crankshaft sealing surface (from contact with the seal), installing a new seal will probably not stop the leak.

5 Lubricate the new seal with engine oil and drive the seal into place with a hammer and a appropriate size socket **(see illustration)**.

6 The remaining steps are the reverse of removal. **Note:** *Position the crankshaft sprocket with the word FRONT facing out* **(see illustration)**. **Caution:** *If you are working on a 2.4L SOHC engine, be careful when installing the crank sprockets and the CKP sensing blade, which is installed between the two sprockets. Make sure that you follow the procedure in Section 7 for degreasing the*

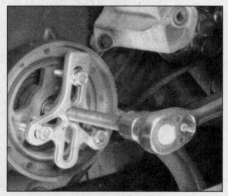

8.2 Attach a bolt-type gear puller to the crankshaft sprocket and remove the sprocket from the crankshaft

8.3 Working from below the right inner fender, use the screwdriver to pry the seal out of its bore

8.5 Lubricate the new seal with engine oil and drive the seal into place with a hammer and socket

8.6 Position the crankshaft sprocket with the word FRONT facing out and install it onto the crankshaft

9.5 Carefully pry the camshaft seal out of the bore - DO NOT nick or scratch the camshaft or seal bore

9.7 Gently tap the new seal into place with the spring side toward the engine

9.9 When installing a camshaft sprocket, make sure the pin in the camshaft is aligned with the hole in the sprocket (arrows)

sensing blade and the sprockets.

7   Reinstall the timing belt(s) and timing belt covers (see Section 7).

8   Run the engine and check for oil leaks.

9   Camshaft oil seal - replacement

Refer to illustrations 9.5, 9.7 and 9.9

Caution: *Do not rotate the camshaft(s) or crankshaft when the timing belt is removed or damage to the engine may occur.*

1   Remove the timing belt covers and timing belt (see Section 7).

2   Rotate the crankshaft counterclockwise until the crankshaft sprocket is three notches BTDC **(see illustration 7.23b)**. This will prevent engine damage if the camshaft sprocket is inadvertently rotated during removal.

3   If the engine is equipped with a rear timing belt cover, remove the upper part.

4   Remove the camshaft sprocket bolt(s) **(see illustration 7.39)**. Then, using two large screwdrivers, lever the sprocket(s) off the camshaft.

5   Note how far the seal is seated in the bore, then carefully pry it out with a small

screwdriver **(see illustration)**. Don't scratch the bore or damage the camshaft in the process (if the camshaft is damaged, the new seal will end up leaking).

6   Clean the bore and coat the outer edge of the new seal with engine oil or multi-purpose grease. Also lubricate the seal lip.

7   Using a socket with an outside diameter slightly smaller than the outside diameter of the seal **(see illustration)**, carefully drive the new seal into place with a hammer. Make sure it's installed squarely and driven in to the same depth as the original. If a socket isn't available, a short section of pipe will also work.

8   If the engine is equipped with a rear timing belt cover, install the upper part (see Section 7).

9   Install the camshaft sprocket, aligning the pin in the camshaft with the hole in the sprocket **(see illustration)**. Use an appropriate tool to hold the camshaft sprocket(s) while tightening the bolt(s) to the torque listed in this Chapter's Specifications.

10   Reinstall the timing belt (see Section 7).

11   Run the engine and check for oil leaks at the camshaft seal.

10   Camshaft(s) - removal, inspection and installation

2.0L and 2.4L DOHC engines
Removal

Refer to illustrations 10.4 and 10.5

1   Remove the valve cover (see Section 4).

2   Remove the timing belt (see Section 7).

3   Remove the camshaft sprockets **(see illustration 7.39)** and the rear timing belt cover.

4   The camshaft bearing caps are identified with their numbered location in the cylinder head **(see illustration)**.

5   Remove the outside bearing caps at each end of the camshafts, Remove the remaining camshaft bearing caps. Loosen the bolts a little at a time to prevent distorting the camshafts, in the sequence shown **(see illustration)**. When the bearing caps have all been loosened enough for removal, they may still be difficult to remove. Use the bearing cap bolts for leverage and move the cap back and forth to loosen the cap from the cylinder head. If they are still difficult to remove you can tap

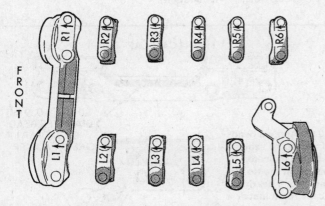

10.4 Note the camshaft bearing cap location numbers - they must be reinstalled in the same location in the cylinder head

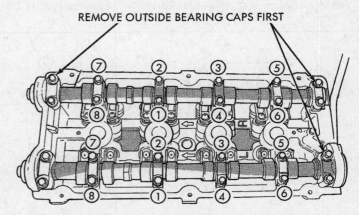

10.5 First, remove the outside bearing caps, then remove the remaining camshaft bearing caps in the sequence shown

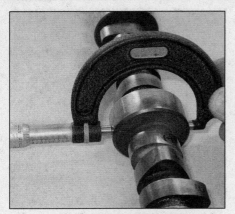

10.9 Measure the camshaft bearing journal diameters with a micrometer

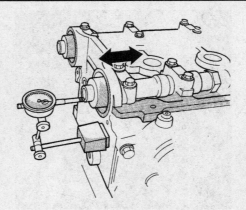

10.14 Measure the camshaft endplay with a dial indicator positioned on the sprocket end of the camshaft as shown

10.17 Prior to installing each camshaft, lubricate the bearing journals, thrust surfaces and lobes with assembly lube or clean engine oil

them gently with a soft face mallet until they can be lifted off. **Caution:** *Store them in order so they can be returned to their original locations, with the same side facing forward.*
6   Carefully lift the camshafts out of the cylinder head. Mark the camshafts INTAKE and EXHAUST. They cannot be mixed-up.
7   Remove the front seal from each camshaft. **Note:** *It would be prudent to inspect the rocker arms and lash adjusters at this time* (see Section 11).

Inspection
Refer to illustration 10.9
8   Clean the camshaft(s) and the gasket surface. Inspect the camshaft for wear and/or damage to the lobe surfaces, bearing journals, and seal contact surfaces. Inspect the camshaft bearing surfaces in the cylinder head and bearing caps for scoring and other damage.
9   Measure the camshaft bearing journal diameters **(see illustration)**. Measure the inside diameter of the camshaft bearing surfaces in the cylinder head, using a telescoping gauge (temporarily install the bearing caps). Subtract the journal measurement from the bearing measurement to obtain the camshaft bearing oil clearance. Compare this clearance

with the value listed this Chapter's Specifications. Replace worn components as required.
10   Replace the camshaft if it fails any of the above inspections. **Note:** *If the lobes are worn, replace the rocker arms and lash adjusters along with the camshaft.* The cylinder head may need to be replaced, if the camshaft bearing surfaces in the head are damaged or excessively worn.
11   Clean and inspect the cylinder head (see Chapter 2D).

Camshaft endplay measurement
Refer to illustration 10.14
12   Lubricate the camshaft(s) and cylinder head bearing journals with clean engine oil.
13   Place the camshaft in its original location in the cylinder head. **Note:** *Do not install the rocker arms for this check.* Install the rear bearing cap and tighten the bolts to the torque listed in this Chapter's Specifications.
14   Install a dial indicator on the cylinder head and place the indicator tip on the camshaft at the sprocket end **(see illustration)**.
15   Use a screwdriver to carefully pry the camshaft fully to the rear until it stops. Zero the dial indicator and pry the camshaft fully to the front. The amount of indicator travel is the camshaft endplay. Compare the endplay with

the tolerance given in this Chapter's Specifications. If the endplay is excessive, check the camshaft and cylinder head bearing journals for wear. Replace as necessary.

Installation
Refer to illustrations 10.17, 10.19, and 10.20
16   Install the valve lash adjusters and rocker arms (see Section 11).
17   Clean the camshaft and bearing journals and caps. Liberally coat the journals, lobes, and thrust portions of the camshaft with assembly lube or engine oil **(see illustration)**.
18   Carefully install the camshafts in the cylinder head in their original location. Temporarily install the camshaft sprockets and rotate the camshafts so that their timing marks align **(see illustration 7.13)**. Make sure the crankshaft is positioned with the crankshaft sprocket timing mark at three teeth BTDC. **Caution:** *If the pistons are at TDC when tightening the camshaft bearing caps, damage to the engine may occur.*
19   Install the bearing caps, except for the No. 1 and No. 6 (left side) end caps **(see illustration 10.4)**. Tighten the bolts in several steps, in the sequence shown to the torque listed in this Chapter's Specifications **(see illustration)**.

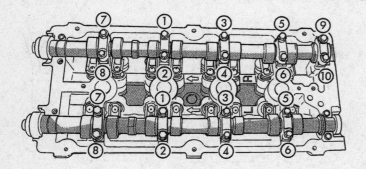

10.19 Except for the No. 1 and No. 6 end caps, install the bearing caps and tighten the bolts in the indicated sequence

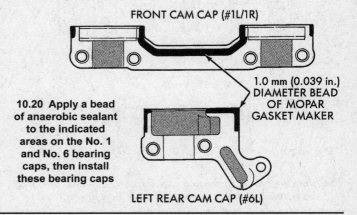

10.20 Apply a bead of anaerobic sealant to the indicated areas on the No. 1 and No. 6 bearing caps, then install these bearing caps

FRONT CAM CAP (#1L/1R)

1.0 mm (0.039 in.) DIAMETER BEAD OF MOPAR GASKET MAKER

LEFT REAR CAM CAP (#6L)

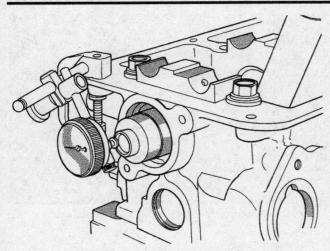

10.32 Measure the camshaft endplay with a dial indicator positioned on the sprocket end of the camshaft

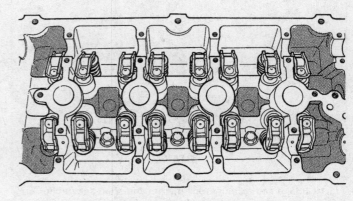

11.3 After the camshafts have been removed, remove the rocker arms and lift off the valve lash adjusters; be sure to keep the rocker arms and lash adjusters in order so they can be returned to their original locations

20 Apply a small bead of anaerobic sealant (approximately 1/8-inch) to the No. 1 and No. 6 (left side) bearing caps **(see illustration)**. Install the bearing caps and tighten the bolts to the torque listed in this Chapter's Specifications.

21 Install new camshaft oil seals (see Section 9).

22 Install the timing belt, covers, and related components (see Section 7).

23 Install the valve cover (see Section 4).

2.4L SOHC engine
Removal
24 Remove the valve cover (see Section 4).

25 Remove the camshaft cover and the timing belt (see Section 7).

26 Remove the timing belt sprocket **(see illustration 7.39)**.

27 Remove the rocker arm assemblies (see Section 11).

28 Remove the Camshaft Position (CMP) sensor (see Chapter 6), remove the CMP sensor housing bolts and then remove the CMP sensor housing.

29 Carefully remove the camshaft through the opening in the rear of the cylinder head. Be careful not to damage the camshaft lobes or bearing journals during removal.

Inspection
Refer to illustration 10.32

30 Thoroughly clean the camshaft. Inspect the camshaft lobes, bearing journals and seal contact surfaces for wear and damage. Also inspect the camshaft bearing surfaces in the cylinder head for scoring and other damage.

31 Measure the camshaft bearing journal diameters **(see illustration 10.9)**. Measure the inside diameter of the camshaft bearing surfaces in the cylinder head, using a telescoping gauge. Subtract the journal measurement from the bearing measurement to obtain the camshaft bearing oil clearance. Compare this clearance with this Chapter's Specifications.

32 Lubricate the camshaft journals with clean engine oil, install the camshaft in the cylinder head, then install the CMP sensor housing. Set up a dial indicator and measure the camshaft endplay **(see illustration)**. Compare your measurement with the value listed in this Chapter's Specifications.

33 Replace the camshaft if it fails any of the above inspections. **Note:** *If the lobes are worn, replace the rocker arms along with the camshaft.* Cylinder head replacement may be necessary if the camshaft bearing surfaces in the head are damaged or excessively worn or if the endplay is excessive.

Installation
34 Very carefully clean the camshaft and bearing journals. Liberally coat the journals, lobes and thrust portions of the camshaft with assembly lube or engine oil.

35 Carefully install the camshaft in the cylinder head.

36 Install a new camshaft oil seal (see Section 9).

37 Install the CMP sensor housing and the CMP sensor (see Chapter 6).

38 Install the rocker arm shaft assembly (see Section 11).

39 Install the timing belt and covers (see Section 7).

40 Install the valve cover (see Section 4).

11 Rocker arm assembly - removal, inspection and installation

2.0L and 2.4L DOHC engines
Removal
Refer to illustration 11.3

1 Remove the valve cover (see Section 4).

2 Remove both camshafts (see Section 10).

3 Once the camshafts have been removed, the rocker arms can be lifted off **(see illustration)**. **Caution:** *Each rocker arm*

must be placed back in the same location it was removed from, so mark each rocker arm or place them in a container (such as an egg carton) so they won't get mixed up. The lash adjusters can remain in the head at this time, unless they are being replaced (see Section 12).

Inspection
Refer to illustration 11.4

4 Inspect the rocker arm tip, roller and lash adjuster pocket for wear **(see illustration)**. Replace them if evidence of wear or damage is found.

5 Carefully inspect each lash adjuster for signs of wear and damage, particularly on the ball tip that contacts the rocker arm. The lash adjusters become clogged as they age, so it's a good idea to replace them if you're concerned about their condition or if the engine is making valve "tapping" noises.

Installation
6 Installation is the reverse of removal. When reinstalling the rocker arms, make sure that you install them at the same locations from which they were removed.

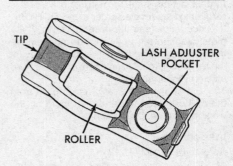

11.4 Inspect the roller, tip and lash-adjuster contact area for score marks and pitting

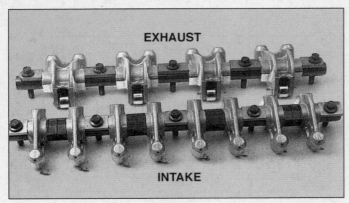

11.10 Intake and exhaust rocker arms and shaft assemblies are unique - don't intermix any of the parts

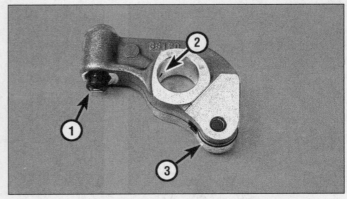

11.12 Rocker arm/valve lash adjuster assembly

1   *Valve lash adjuster*   3   *Roller*
2   *Rocker shaft bore*

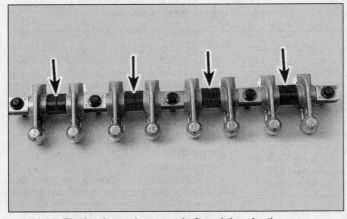

11.16 The intake rocker arm shaft and the plastic spacers (arrows) must be installed in the correct location

11.18 Both rocker arm shafts must be positioned with their notches (arrows) facing out, away from each other

2.4L SOHC engine

Removal

Refer to illustration 11.10

7   Remove the valve cover (see Section 4).

8   Prior to removing the rocker arm shafts, mark the front shaft as the intake rocker arm shaft and the rear shaft as the exhaust. **Caution:** *Do not interchange the rocker arms onto a different shaft as this could lead to premature wear.*

9   Loosen each rocker arm shaft bolt 1/4-turn at a time until the spring pressure is relieved, in the *reverse* order of the TIGHTEN-ING sequence **(see illustration 11.19)**. Completely loosen the bolts, but do not remove them, since leaving them in place will prevent the assembly from falling apart when it is lifted off the cylinder head.

10   Lift off the rocker arm assemblies from the cylinder head and then set them on the workbench **(see illustration)**.

Inspection

Refer to illustration 11.12

11   Disassemble the rocker arm shaft components **(see illustration 11.10)**. **Caution:** *Prior to disassembly, mark the rocker arm shafts, rocker arms, shaft retainers and plastic*

shaft spacers (intake only) to ensure that all the parts are reassembled in the same locations from which they were removed. To keep the rocker arms and related parts in order, it's a good idea to remove them and put them onto two pieces of wire (like coat hangers) in the order in which they're removed. Mark each wire (which serves as the rocker shaft) with respect to the front of the engine.

12   Inspect the rocker arms for wear **(see illustration)**. Replace them if evidence of wear or damage is found.

13   Inspect the rocker shafts and all parts on the shafts. Look for wear and scoring on the shafts. Replace all damaged parts.

Installation

Refer to illustrations 11.16, 11.18 and 11.19

14   Prior to installation, make sure that each lash adjuster is at least partially full of oil.

15   When reassembling the parts, make sure that they all go back on in the same locations they were removed from.

16   Make sure the plastic spacers are installed on the intake rocker arm shaft in the correct location **(see illustration)**.

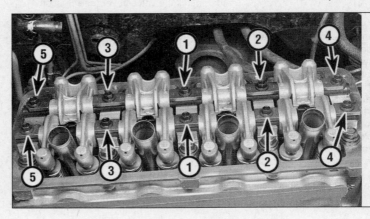

11.19 Rocker arm shaft bolt TIGHTENING sequence (SOHC models)

17   To prevent internal damage, rotate the crankshaft to position the crankshaft timing belt sprocket at the 3 teeth BTDC before installing the rocker arm shafts, **(see illustration 7.23b)**.

18   Install the rocker arm assemblies with the notch in each rocker arm shaft located at the timing belt end of the engine, facing out, away from each other **(see illustration)**.

19   Tighten the rocker arm bolts in sequence **(see illustration)** to the torque listed in this Chapter's Specifications.

20   The remainder of installation is the reverse of removal. Run the engine and check for oil leaks and proper operation when you're done.

12   Valve lash adjusters - removal, inspection and installation

2.0L and 2.4L DOHC engines

1   Remove the camshafts (see Section 10).

2   Remove the rocker arms (see Section 11).

3   If the lash adjusters aren't already removed from the head, lift them out now. **Caution:** *Be sure to keep the adjusters in order so they can be placed back in the same location in the cylinder head it was removed from.*

4   Inspect each adjuster carefully for signs of wear and damage, particularly on the ball tip that contacts the rocker arm. Since the lash adjusters frequently become clogged, we recommend replacing them if you're concerned about their condition or if the engine is exhibiting valve "tapping" noises.

5   The lash adjusters must be partially full of engine oil - indicated by little or no plunger action when the adjuster is depressed. If there's excessive plunger travel, place the lash adjuster into clean engine oil and pump the plunger until the plunger travel is eliminated. **Note:** *If the plunger still travels within the lash adjuster when full of oil it's defective and the lash adjuster must be replaced.*

6   When re-starting the engine after replacing the adjusters, the adjusters will normally make "tapping" noises. After warm-up, raise the speed of the engine from idle to 3,000 rpm for one minute. If the adjuster(s) do not become silent, replace the defective ones.

2.4L SOHC engine

Note: *The valve lash adjuster is an integral part of each rocker arm and can't be replaced separately.*

7   Remove the rocker arm shafts (see Section 11). Don't remove the rocker arms from the shafts.

8   Turn the rocker arm assembly upside down on the workbench. Inspect each lash adjuster carefully for signs of wear and damage, particularly on the surface that contacts the valve tip. Since the lash adjusters frequently become clogged, we recommend replacing the rocker arm/lash adjuster assem-

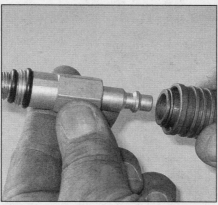

13.4   This is what the air hose adapter that threads into the spark plug hole looks like - they're easily available from auto parts stores

bly if you're concerned about their condition or if the engine is exhibiting valve "tapping" noises.

9   If any are removed, assemble the rocker arms onto their shaft(s) (see Section 11).

10   The lash adjusters must be partially full of engine oil - indicated by little or no plunger action when the adjuster is depressed. If there's excessive plunger travel, place the rocker arm assembly into clean engine oil and pump the plunger until the plunger travel is eliminated. **Note:** *If the plunger still travels within the rocker arm when full of oil it's defective and the rocker arm assembly must be replaced.*

11   When re-starting the engine after replacing the rocker arm/lash adjusters, the adjusters will normally make "tapping" noises. After warm-up, raise the speed of the engine from idle to 3,000 rpm for one minute. If the adjuster(s) do not become silent, replace the defective rocker arm/lash adjuster(s).

13   Valve springs, retainers and seals - replacement

Refer to illustrations 13.4, 13.7, 13.8, 13.13 and 13.15

Note: *Broken valve springs and defective valve stem seals can be replaced without removing the cylinder heads. Two special tools and a compressed air source are normally required to perform this operation, so read through this Section carefully and rent or buy the tools before beginning the job.*

1   Remove the valve cover (see Section 4).

2   Remove the spark plug from the cylinder which has the defective component. If all of the valve stem seals are being replaced, all of the spark plugs should be removed.

3   Turn the crankshaft until the piston in the affected cylinder is at top dead center on the compression stroke (refer to Section 3). If you're replacing all of the valve stem seals, begin with cylinder number one and work on the valves for one cylinder at a time. Move from cylinder-to-cylinder following the firing

13.7   Use needle-nose pliers (shown) or a small magnet to remove the valve spring keepers - be careful not to drop them down into the engine!

order sequence (see this Chapter's Specifications).

4   Thread an adapter into the spark plug hole **(see illustration)** and connect an air hose from a compressed air source to it. Most auto parts stores can supply the air hose adapter. **Note:** *Many cylinder compression gauges utilize a screw-in fitting that may work with your air hose quick-disconnect fitting.*

5   Remove the camshaft(s) and the rocker arm assembly (see Sections 10 and 11).

6   Apply compressed air to the cylinder. **Warning:** *The piston may be forced down by compressed air, causing the crankshaft to turn suddenly. If the wrench used when positioning the number one piston at TDC is still attached to the bolt in the crankshaft nose, remove it as it could cause damage or injury when the crankshaft moves.*

7   Stuff clean shop rags into the cylinder head holes above and below the valves to prevent parts and tools from falling into the engine, then use a valve spring compressor to compress the spring. Remove the keepers with small needle-nose pliers or a magnet **(see illustration)**.

8   Remove the spring retainer and valve spring, then remove the valve guide seal/spring seat assembly **(see illustration)**. Cau-

13.8   Remove the valve guide seal with a pair of pliers

tion: *If air pressure fails to hold the valve in the closed position during this operation, the valve face and/or seat is probably damaged. If so, the cylinder head will have to be removed for additional repair operations.*

9   Wrap a rubber band or tape around the top of the valve stem so the valve won't fall into the combustion chamber, then release the air pressure.

10   Inspect the valve stem for damage. Rotate the valve in the guide and check the end for eccentric movement, which would indicate that the valve is bent.

11   Move the valve up-and-down in the guide and make sure it doesn't bind. If the valve stem binds, either the valve is bent or the guide is damaged. In either case, the head will have to be removed for repair.

12   Pull up on the valve stem to close the valve, reapply air pressure to the cylinder to retain the valve in the closed position, then remove the tape or rubber band from the valve stem.

13   Lubricate the valve stem with engine oil and install a new valve guide seal/spring seat assembly. Tap into place with deep socket **(see illustration)**.

14   Install the spring in position over the valve.

15   Install the valve spring retainer. Compress the valve spring and carefully position the keepers in the groove. Apply a small dab of grease to the inside of each keeper to hold it in place if necessary **(see illustration)**.

16   Remove the pressure from the spring tool and make sure the keepers are seated.

17   Disconnect the air hose and remove the adapter from the spark plug hole.

18   Install the camshaft(s) and rocker arm assembly (SOHC model) (see Sections 10 and 11).

19   Install the spark plug(s) and connect the wire(s).

20   Refer to Section 4 and install the valve cover.

21   Start and run the engine, then check for oil leaks and unusual sounds coming from the valve cover area.

14   Cylinder head - removal and installation

Warning: *Allow the engine to cool completely before beginning this procedure.*

Removal

Refer to illustrations 14.4, 14.10a and 14.10b

1   Position the number one piston at Top Dead Center (see Section 3).

2   Disconnect the battery cable from the negative battery terminal or from the remote ground terminal (see Chapter 5).

3   Drain the cooling system and remove the spark plugs (see Chapter 1).

4   Remove the intake manifold (see Section 5). Cover the intake ports with duct tape to keep out debris **(see illustration)**.

5   If necessary, remove the exhaust mani-

13.13 Gently tap the new seal into place with a hammer and a deep socket

fold (see Section 6). **Note:** *On some models, the exhaust manifold is easier to remove after the cylinder head is removed.*

6   Remove the ignition system components (see Chapter 5).

7   Remove the timing belt (see Section 7).

8   Remove the valve cover (see Section 4).

9   Loosen the cylinder head bolts, 1/4-turn at a time, in the reverse of the tightening

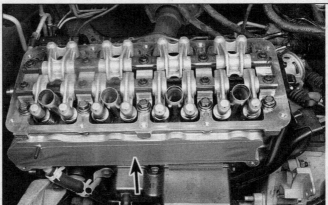

14.10a Carefully lift the cylinder head straight up and place the head on wood blocks to prevent damage to the sealing surfaces

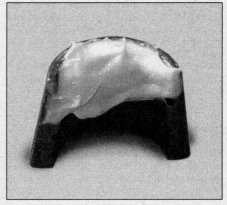

13.15 Apply a small dab of grease to each keeper before installation to hold it in place on the valve stem until the spring is released

sequence **(see illustration 14.14a or 14.14b)** until they can be removed by hand. **Note:** *Write down the location of the different length bolts so they will be reinstalled in the correct location.*

10   Carefully lift the cylinder head **(see illustration)** straight up and place the head on

14.4 Cover the intake ports with duct tape (arrow) to keep out debris before removing the cylinder head

14.10b If the head sticks to the engine block, dislodge it by placing a wood block against the head casting and tapping the wood with a hammer or by prying the head with a prybar placed carefully on a casting protrusion

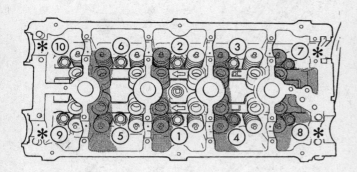

14.14a Cylinder head bolt TIGHTENING sequence (2.0L and 2.4L DOHC engines)

14.14b Cylinder head bolt TIGHTENING sequence (2.4L SOHC engine)

wood blocks to prevent damage to the sealing surfaces. If the head sticks to the engine block, dislodge it by placing a wood block against the head casting and tapping the wood with a hammer or by prying the head with a prybar placed carefully on a casting protrusion **(see illustration)**. **Caution:** *The cylinder head is aluminum, so you must be very careful not to gouge the sealing surfaces.* **Note:** *It's a good idea to have the head checked for warpage, even if you're just replacing the gasket.*

11   Special gasket removal solvents that soften gaskets and make removal much easier are available at auto parts stores. Remove all traces of old gasket material from the block and head. Do not allow anything to fall into the engine. Clean and inspect all threaded fasteners and be sure the threaded holes in the block are clean and dry.

Installation
Refer to illustrations 14.14a and 14.14b

12   Place a new gasket and the cylinder head in position on the engine block.

13   Apply clean engine oil to the cylinder head bolt threads prior to installation. The four short bolts (4.330 inch long) are to be installed in each corner of the cylinder head.

14   Tighten the cylinder head bolts in several stages in the recommended sequence **(see illustrations)** to the torque listed in this Chapter's Specifications. **Note:** *The final step in the tightening procedure requires you to tighten the bolts a specific number of degrees. An angle-torque gauge, that fits on your torque wrench, is available at most auto parts stores and is highly recommended for this procedure. If the tool is not available, paint marks on the bolt heads and tighten them in sequence until the mark is the specified number of degrees from the starting point.*

15   Reinstall the timing belt (see Section 7).

16   Reinstall the remaining parts in the reverse order of removal.

17   Refill the cooling system and change the engine oil and filter (see Chapter 1). Rotate the crankshaft clockwise slowly by hand through six complete revolutions. Recheck the camshaft timing marks (see Section 7).

18   Start the engine and run it until normal operating temperature is reached. Check for leaks and proper operation.

15   Oil pan - removal and installation

Removal
Refer to illustrations 15.4, 15.5a, 15.5b, 15.5c, 15.8a, 15.8b, 15.8c, 15.9a, 15.9b and 15.10

1   Disconnect the battery cable from the negative battery terminal or from the remote ground terminal (see Chapter 5).

2   Raise the vehicle and support it securely on jackstands.

3   Drain the engine oil (see Chapter 1).

4   On 1995 through 1999 2.0L DOHC engines, remove the rear plate. On 2002 2.0L DOHC engines, remove the structural collar **(see illustration)**.

5   On 1998 2.4L DOHC engines, disconnect the front engine torque bracket from the bending strut and insulator mount (see Section 19). On 1996 through 1999 2.4L DOHC engines, remove the engine support module (see Section 19). On 2001 and later 2.4L DOHC engines, remove the through-bolt from the front engine mount (see Section 19). On all 2.4L DOHC engines, remove the structural

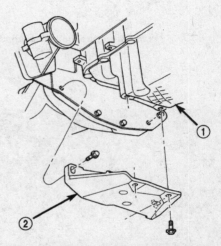

15.4 Structural collar installation details (2002 2.0L DOHC engine)

1   Oil pan
2   Structural collar

collar and the bending strut or torque reaction bracket **(see illustrations)**.

6   On 2.4L SOHC engines, remove the front exhaust pipe (see Chapter 4).

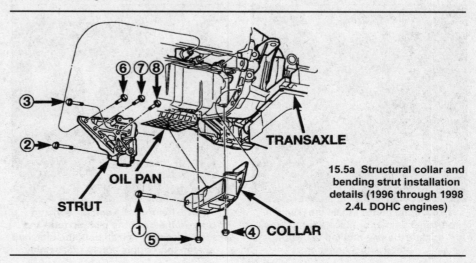

15.5a Structural collar and bending strut installation details (1996 through 1998 2.4L DOHC engines)

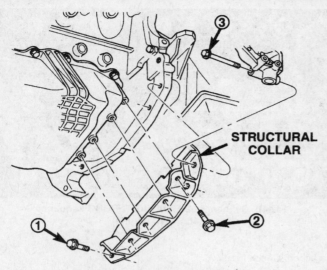

15.5b Structural collar installation details
(1999 2.4L DOHC engine)

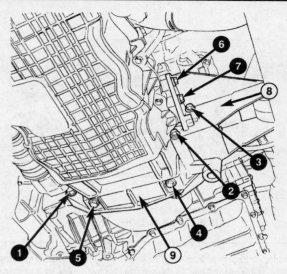

15.5c Structural collar installation details (2001 and later
2.4L DOHC engine)

1 through 7	Bolt tightening sequence
8	Torque reaction bracket
9	Structural collar

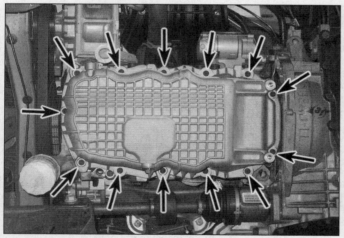

15.8a Using a criss-cross pattern, loosen and remove the
oil pan bolts (arrows) . . .

15.8b . . . and then lower the pan carefully (there might still be
some residual oil in the pan)

15.8c If the pan is stuck, tap it with a
soft-face hammer or place a wood block
against the pan and tap the wood
block with a hammer

15.9a Remove the bolt (arrow) and
remove the oil pump pick-up tube and
screen assembly - clean both the tube and
screen thoroughly before reassembly

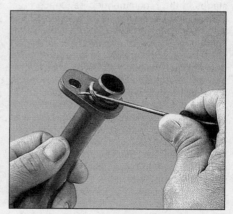

15.9b Install a new seal at the oil pump
pick-up tube mounting flange

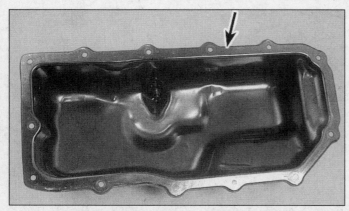

15.10 Thoroughly clean the oil pan and sealing surfaces on the engine block and oil pan (arrow) with a scraper to remove all traces of old gasket material

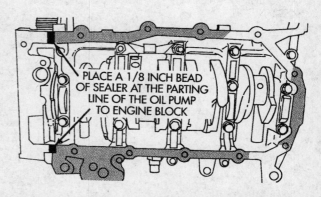

PLACE A 1/8 INCH BEAD OF SEALER AT THE PARTING LINE OF THE OIL PUMP TO ENGINE BLOCK

15.11 Apply a 1/8-inch bead of RTV sealant to the cylinder block-to-oil pump assembly joint at the oil pan flange

7   Remove the flywheel/driveplate inspection cover.

8   Remove the mounting bolts and lower the oil pan from the vehicle (see illustrations). If the pan is stuck, tap it with a soft-face hammer (see illustration) or place a wood block against the pan and tap the wood block with a hammer. **Caution:** *If you're wedging something between the oil pan and the engine block to separate the two, be extremely careful not to gouge or nick the gasket surface of either part; an oil leak could result.*

9   Remove the oil pump pickup tube and screen assembly (see illustration) and clean both the tube and screen thoroughly. Install the pick-up tube and screen with a new seal (see illustration).

10   Thoroughly clean the oil pan and sealing surfaces on the block and pan (see illustration). Use a scraper to remove all traces of old gasket material. Gasket removal solvents are available at auto parts stores and may prove helpful. Check the oil pan sealing surface for distortion. Straighten or replace as necessary. After cleaning and straightening (if necessary), wipe the gasket surfaces of the pan and block clean with a rag soaked in lacquer thinner or acetone.

Installation

Refer to illustration 15.11

11   Apply a 1/8-inch bead of RTV sealant at the cylinder block-to-oil pump assembly joint at the oil pan flange (see illustration). Install a new oil pan gasket.

12   Place the oil pan into position and install the bolts finger tight. Working side-to-side from the center out, tighten the bolts to the torque listed in this Chapter's Specifications.

13   On 1995 through 1999 2.0L DOHC engines, install the rear plate and tighten the bolts securely. On 2002 2.0L DOHC engines, install the structural collar (see illustration 15.4) and then tighten the bolts securely.

14   On 1996 through 1998 2.4L DOHC engines, install the structural collar and the torque reaction bracket (see illustration 15.5a) as follows:

a)   *Place the collar in position between the transaxle and the oil pan and then install and hand-tighten the collar-to-transaxle bolt (bolt 1).*

b)   *Install and then hand-tighten the collar-to-oil pan bolt (bolt 4).*

c)   *Place the bending strut in position, install bolt 3 in the upper transaxle hole and then hand-tighten it.*

d)   *Install bolt 2 through the strut and collar and then hand-tighten it.*

e)   *Install the strut-to-cylinder block bolt (bolt 6) and then hand-tighten it.*

f)   *Install the other collar-to-oil pan bolt and then hand-tighten it.*

g)   *Tighten the collar-to-transaxle bolts (bolts 1, 2 and 3) to the torque listed in this Chapter's Specifications.*

h)   *Install the strut-to-cylinder block bolts (bolts 7 and 8) and hand-tighten them.*

i)   *Tighten bolts 4 through 8 to the torque listed in this Chapter's Specifications.*

15   On 1999 2.4L DOHC engines, install the structural collar and the torque reaction bracket (see illustration 15.5b) as follows:

a)   *Holding the collar in a vertical position, insert it between the bending brace and the transaxle, and then rotate the free end of the collar to the rear until it's in the correct position for installation.*

b)   *Install two of the collar-to-oil pan bolts (No. 2 bolts) and then tighten them to about 25 in-lbs.*

c)   *Install the collar-to-transaxle bolts (No. 1 and 3 bolts) and then tighten them to the torque listed in this Chapter's Specifications.*

d)   *Install the rest of the collar-to-oil pan bolts (No. 2 bolts). Starting with the two center bolts, work your way out toward the ends of the collar, gradually and evenly tightening the bolts to the torque listed in this Chapter's Specifications.*

16   On 2001 and later 2.4L DOHC engines, install the structural collar and the torque reaction bracket (see illustration 15.5c) as follows:

a)   *Place the collar in position between the transaxle and the oil pan and then install and hand-tighten bolt No. 1.*

b)   *Install and then hand-tighten the collar-to-oil pan bolts (bolt Nos. 4 and 5).*

c)   *Place the torque reaction bracket in position and then install and hand-tighten bolts 2 and 3.*

d)   *Tighten bolts 1, 2 and 3 to the torque listed in this Chapter's Specifications.*

e)   *Install bolts 6 and 7 through the torque reaction bracket and into the block and then hand-tighten them.*

f)   *Tighten bolts 4 and 5 to the torque listed in this Chapter's Specifications.*

g)   *Tighten bolts 6 and 7 the torque listed in this Chapter's Specifications.*

h)   *Install the front engine mount through-bolt (see Section 19) and then tighten it securely.*

17   On 1996 through 1999 2.4L DOHC engines, install the engine support module (see Section 19) as follows:

a)   *Install the through-bolt at the front mount, but don't tighten it yet.*

b)   *Install the lower radiator support.*

c)   *Install the bolts that attach the engine support module to the lower radiator support.*

d)   *Install the upper bolt at the rear support bracket.*

e)   *Install the through-bolt at the rear mount (see Section 19) and then tighten it securely.*

f)   *Tighten the through-bolt at the front mount securely.*

18   On 1998 2.4L DOHC engines, reconnect the front engine torque bracket to the bending strut and insulator mount (see Section 19). On 2001 and later 2.4L DOHC engines, install the through-bolt in the front engine mount (see Section 19) and then tighten it securely.

19   The remainder of installation is the reverse of removal.

20   Refill the crankcase with the correct quantity and grade of oil, run the engine and check for leaks.

21   Road test the vehicle and check for leaks again.

16.5a Remove the oil pump assembly mounting bolts (arrows) and remove the assembly

16.5b If the pump doesn't come off by hand, tap it gently with a soft-faced hammer or pry gently on a casting protrusion

16 Oil pump - removal, inspection and installation

Removal

Refer to illustrations 16.5a, 16.5b, 16.6a, 16.6b and 16.6c

1   Disconnect the battery cable from the negative battery terminal or from the remote ground terminal (see Chapter 5).
2   Raise the vehicle and place it securely on jackstands.
3   Remove the oil pan and pick-up tube/ strainer assembly (see Section 15).
4   Remove the timing belt and the crank-shaft sprocket (see Section 7).
5   Remove the bolts and detach the oil pump assembly from the engine **(see illustration)**. **Caution:** *If the pump doesn't come off by hand, tap it gently with a soft-faced hammer or pry on a casting boss* **(see illustration)**.
6   Remove the mounting screws and remove the cover **(see illustration)**. Remove the inner and outer rotor from the body **(see illustrations)**. **Caution:** *Be very careful with these parts. Close tolerances are critical in creating the correct oil pressure. Any nicks or other damage will require replacement of the*

16.6a Remove the cover mounting screws (arrows) . . .

16.6b . . . and the cover

complete pump assembly.
7   If necessary, replace the crankshaft front seal within the oil pump body (see Section 8).

Inspection

Refer to illustrations 16.9a, 16.9b, 16.10a, 16.10b, 1610c, 16.10d and 16.10e

8   Clean all components including the block surfaces with solvent, then inspect all surfaces for excessive wear and/or damage.

9   Disassemble the relief valve, unscrew the cap bolt and remove the bolt, washer, spring and relief valve **(see illustrations)**. Check the oil pressure relief valve piston sliding surface and valve spring. If either the spring or the valve is damaged, they must be replaced as a set. If no damage is found reassemble the relief valve parts. Make sure to install the relief valve into the pump body with the grooved end going in first. Coating the parts with oil, and reinstall them in the oil

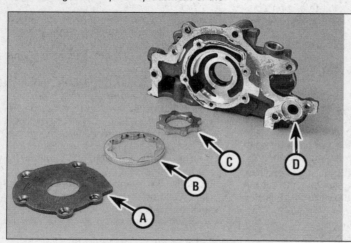

16.6c Arrangement of oil pump components

A   Cover
B   Outer rotor
C   Inner rotor
D   Oil pump body

16.9a Unscrew the oil pressure relief valve cap from the body

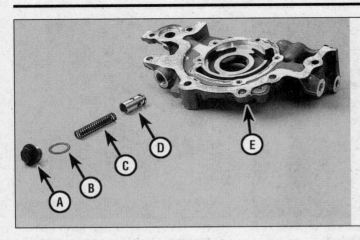

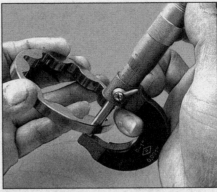

16.9b Oil pressure relief valve components

A Cap
B Gasket
C Spring
D Relief valve
E Oil pump body

16.10a Measure the outer rotor thickness

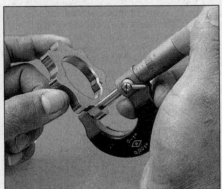

16.10b Measure the inner rotor thickness

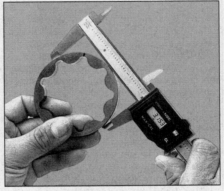

16.10c Use a caliper and measure the outer diameter of the outer rotor

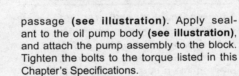

16.10d Use a feeler gauge and measure the outer rotor-to-case clearance

pump body. Tighten the cap bolt securely.

10 Check the clearance of the oil pump components with a micrometer and a feeler gauge **(see illustrations)** and compare the results to this Chapter's Specifications.

Installation

Refer to illustrations 16.12a and 16.12b

11 Lubricate the housing and the inner and outer rotors with clean engine oil and install both rotors in the body. Install the cover and tighten the cover screws securely. Prime the oil pump with clean engine oil.

12 Install a new O-ring in the oil discharge

passage **(see illustration)**. Apply sealant to the oil pump body **(see illustration)**, and attach the pump assembly to the block. Tighten the bolts to the torque listed in this Chapter's Specifications.

13 Install the crankshaft sprocket and the timing belt (see Section 7).

14 Install the pick-up tube/strainer assembly and oil pan (see Section 15).

15 Install a new oil filter and engine oil (see Chapter 1).

16 Start the engine and check for oil pressure and leaks.

17 Recheck the engine oil level.

17 Flywheel/driveplate - removal and installation

Removal

Refer to illustrations 17.4 and 17.5

1 Raise the vehicle and support it securely on jackstands, then refer to Chapter 7 and remove the transaxle assembly.

2 If the vehicle has a manual transaxle, remove the pressure plate and clutch disc (see Chapter 8). Now is a good time to check/replace the clutch components.

16.10e Place a precision straightedge over the rotors and measure the clearance between the rotors and the cover

16.12a Install a new O-ring seal in the oil pump body - apply clean engine oil to the seal

16.12b Apply a bead of anaerobic sealant to the housing sealing surface as shown

17.4 Mark the relative position of the flywheel or driveplate to the crankshaft and, using an appropriate tool to hold the flywheel, remove the bolts

17.5 Remove the flywheel/driveplate from the crankshaft

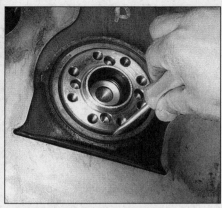

18.2 Carefully pry the crankshaft seal out of the bore - DO NOT nick or scratch the crankshaft or seal bore

3   To ensure correct alignment during reinstallation, mark the position of the flywheel/driveplate to the crankshaft before removal.

4   Remove the bolts that secure the flywheel/driveplate to the crankshaft **(see illustration)**. A tool is available a most auto parts stores to hold the flywheel/driveplate while loosening the bolts. If the tool is not available, wedge a screwdriver in the ring gear teeth to jam the flywheel.

5   Remove the flywheel/driveplate from the crankshaft **(see illustration)**. Since the flywheel is fairly heavy, be sure to support it while removing the last bolt.

6   Clean the flywheel to remove grease and oil. To inspect the flywheel, see Chapter 8.

7   Clean and inspect the mating surfaces of the flywheel/driveplate and the crankshaft. If the crankshaft rear main seal is leaking, replace it before reinstalling the flywheel/driveplate (see Section 18).

18.4 Position the new seal with the words THIS SIDE OUT facing out, toward the rear of the engine. Gently drive the seal into the cylinder block until it is flush with the outer surface of the block. Do not drive it past flush or there will be an oil leak - the seal must be flush

Installation

8   Position the flywheel/driveplate against the crankshaft. Align the previously applied match marks. Before installing the bolts, apply thread locking compound to the threads.

9   Hold the flywheel/driveplate with the holding tool, or wedge a screwdriver in the ring gear teeth to keep the flywheel/driveplate from turning as you tighten the bolts to the torque listed in this Chapter's Specifications.

10   The remainder of installation is the reverse of the removal procedure.

18   Rear main oil seal - replacement

Refer to illustrations 18.2 and 18.4

1   The one-piece rear main oil seal is pressed into a bore machined into the rear main bearing cap and engine block. Remove the transaxle (see Chapter 7), the clutch components, if equipped (see Chapter 8) and the flywheel or driveplate (see Section 17).

2   **Note:** *Observe that the oil seal is installed flush with the outer surface of the block.* Pry out the old seal with a 3/16-inch flat blade screwdriver **(see illustration)**. **Caution:** *To prevent an oil leak after the new seal is installed, be very careful not to scratch or otherwise damage the crankshaft sealing surface or the bore in the engine block.*

3   Clean the crankshaft and seal bore in the block thoroughly and de-grease these areas by wiping them with a rag soaked in lacquer thinner or acetone. Do not lubricate the lip or outer diameter of the new seal - it must be installed as it comes from the manufacturer.

4   Position the new seal onto the crankshaft. **Note:** *When installing the new seal, if so marked, the words THIS SIDE OUT on the seal must face out, toward the rear of the engine.* Using an appropriate size driver and pilot tool, drive the seal into the cylinder block until it is flush with the outer surface of the block. If the seal is driven in past flush, there will be a oil leak. Check that the seal is flush **(see illustration)**.

5   The remainder of installation is the reverse of removal.

19   Engine mounts - check and replacement

1   Engine mounts seldom require attention, but broken or deteriorated mounts should be replaced immediately or the added strain placed on the driveline components may cause damage or wear.

Check

2   During the check, the engine must be raised slightly to remove the weight from the mounts.

3   Raise the vehicle and support it securely on jackstands, then position a jack under the engine oil pan. Place a large wood block between the jack head and the oil pan to prevent oil pan damage, then carefully raise the engine just enough to take the weight off the mounts. **Warning:** *DO NOT place any part of your body under the engine when it's supported only by a jack!*

4   Check the mounts to see if the rubber is cracked, hardened or separated from the metal backing. Sometimes the rubber will split right down the center.

5   Check for relative movement between the mount plates and the engine or frame (use a large screwdriver or pry bar to attempt to move the mounts). If movement is noted, lower the engine and tighten the mount fasteners.

6   Rubber preservative may be applied to the mounts to slow deterioration.

Replacement

Refer to illustrations 19.9a, 19.9b, 19.9c, 19.9d, 19.9e, 19.9f, 19.9g, 19.9h, 19.9i and 19.9j

7   Disconnect the battery cable from the negative battery terminal, then raise the vehicle and support it securely on jackstands (if not already done).

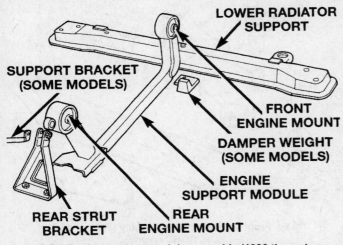

SUPPORT BRACKET (SOME MODELS)

LOWER RADIATOR SUPPORT

FRONT ENGINE MOUNT

DAMPER WEIGHT (SOME MODELS)

ENGINE SUPPORT MODULE

REAR ENGINE MOUNT

REAR STRUT BRACKET

19.9a Engine support module assembly (1996 through 1999 2.4L DOHC engine)

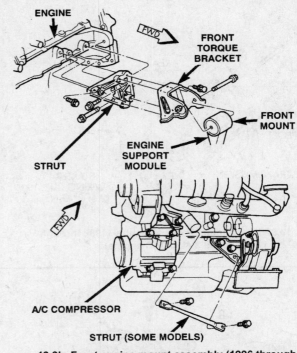

ENGINE

FRONT TORQUE BRACKET

FRONT MOUNT

ENGINE SUPPORT MODULE

STRUT

A/C COMPRESSOR

STRUT (SOME MODELS)

19.9b Front engine mount assembly (1996 through 1999 2.4L DOHC engine)

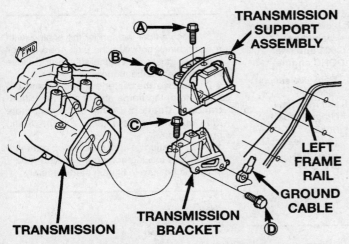

Ⓐ Ⓑ Ⓒ Ⓓ

TRANSMISSION SUPPORT ASSEMBLY

LEFT FRAME RAIL

GROUND CABLE

TRANSMISSION

TRANSMISSION BRACKET

19.9c Typical left engine mount assembly (1996 through 1999)

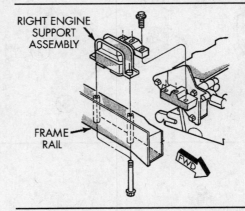

RIGHT ENGINE SUPPORT ASSEMBLY

FRAME RAIL

19.9d Typical right engine mount assembly (1996 through 1999)

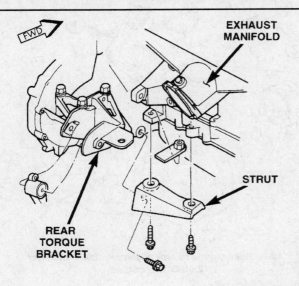

EXHAUST MANIFOLD

STRUT

REAR TORQUE BRACKET

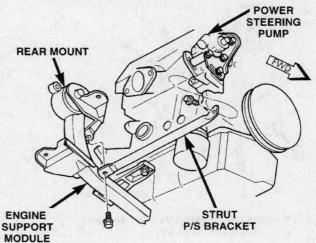

POWER STEERING PUMP

REAR MOUNT

ENGINE SUPPORT MODULE

STRUT P/S BRACKET

19.9e Rear engine mount assembly (2.0L DOHC engine)

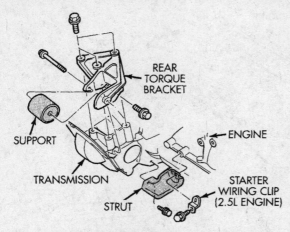

19.9f Rear engine mount assembly (1996 through 1999 2.4L DOHC engine)

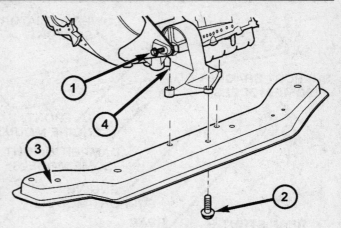

19.9g Front engine mount assembly (2001 and later 2.4L DOHC engine)

1	Horizontal through-bolt	3	Lower radiator
2	Vertical bolts		crossmember
		4	Front engine mount

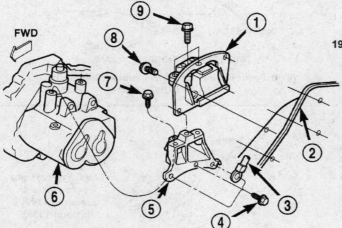

19.9h Left engine mount assembly (2001 and later DOHC engine)

1   Transaxle support assembly
2   Left frame rail
3   Ground cable
4   Bolt D
5   Transaxle bracket
6   Transaxle
7   Bolt C
8   Bolt B
9   Bolt A

8   Place a floor jack under the engine (with a wood block between the jack head and oil pan) and raise the engine slightly to relieve the weight from the mounts.

9   Remove the fasteners and detach the mount from the frame and engine **(see illustrations)**. **Caution:** *Do not disconnect more than one mount at a time, except during engine removal.*

10   Installation is the reverse of removal. Use thread locking compound on the mount bolts and be sure to tighten them securely.

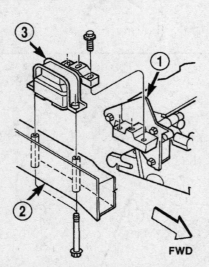

19.9i Right engine mount assembly (2001 and later 2.4L DOHC engine)

1	Engine support bracket	3	Right engine mount
2	Frame rail		

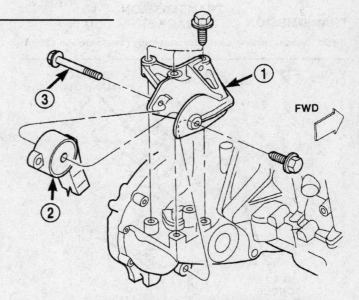

19.9j Rear engine mount assembly (2001 and later 2.4L DOHC engine)

1	Rear torque bracket	3	Through-bolt
2	Rear engine mount		

Chapter 2 Part B
2.5L and 3.0L V6 engines

Contents

Specifications

2.5L engine

General

Bore	3.29 inches
Stroke	2.99 inches
Displacement	152.4 cubic inches (2.5 liters)
Cylinder numbers (drivebelt end-to-transaxle end)	
Front cylinder bank (radiator side)	2-4-6
Rear cylinder bank (firewall side)	1-3-5
Firing order	1-2-3-4-5-6
Compression ratio	
1995 through 1997	9.5:1
1998 through 2000	
Federal	9.4:1
California	9.0:1

Camshaft

Cam lobe height	
Intake	
Standard	1.4795 inches
Service limit	1.4598 inches
Exhaust	
Standard	1.4547 inches
Service limit	1.4350 inches
Cam journal diameter	1.7689 inches

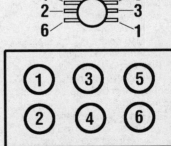

Cylinder numbering and spark plug wire terminal locations. On 2001 and later 3.0L V6 engines, refer to the numbers on the distributer cap for terminal locations

2.5L engine (continued)

Cylinder head
Cylinder head gasket surface warpage limit.................................... 0.008 inch

Intake and exhaust manifolds
Intake manifold warpage limit.. 0.008 inch
Exhaust manifold warpage limit.. 0.012 inch

Oil pump
Body clearance
    Standard... 0.0039 to 0.0071 inch
    Service limit.. 0.0138 inch
Side clearance.. 0.0016 to 0.0039 inch
Tip clearance .... 0.0024 to 0.0071 inch

Torque specifications   Ft-lbs (unless otherwise indicated)
Note: *One foot-pound (ft-lb) of torque is equivalent to 12 inch-pounds (in-lbs) of torque. Torque values below approximately 15 foot-pounds are expressed in inch-pounds, because most foot-pound torque wrenches are not accurate at these smaller values.*

Camshaft sprocket bolt.. 65
Camshaft thrust case bolts.. 113 in-lbs
Crankshaft pulley/vibration damper bolt 134
Crankshaft rear main seal retainer bolts................................... 96 in-lbs
Cylinder head bolts (in sequence - see illustration 13.24)......... 80
EGR pipe bolts 17
Exhaust manifold
    1995 through 1997
        Exhaust manifold-to-cylinder head nuts........................ 22
        Exhaust manifold-to-cross-under exhaust pipe bolts.................. 36
    1998 through 2000
        Federal
            Exhaust manifold-to-cylinder head nuts 22
            Exhaust manifold-to-cross-under exhaust pipe bolts 36
        California
            Exhaust manifold heat shield bolts.................................... 120 in-lbs
            Exhaust manifold-to-cylinder head nuts 36
            Exhaust manifold-to-cross-under exhaust pipe bolts 36
Flywheel/driveplate bolts 68
Intake manifold
    Upper intake manifold bolts/nuts.. 168 in-lbs
    Lower intake manifold nuts **(see illustration 5.24)**
        Step 1: Front bank nuts .... 61 in-lbs
        Step 2: Rear bank nuts.. 15.5
        Step 3: Front bank nuts 15.5
        Step 4: Repeat Steps 2 and 3... 15.5
Oil pan bolts... 50 in-lbs
Oil pump
    Mounting bolts
        M8 bolts .... 120 in-lbs
        M10 bolts 30
    Cover retaining bolts .... 84 in-lbs
    Pick-up tube bolts.. 156 in-lbs
    Relief valve cap bolt 33
Rocker arm shaft bolts... 23
Timing belt
    Timing belt cover bolts
        Upper timing cover
            Upper bolts... 96 in-lbs
            Lower bolt... 120 in-lbs
        Lower timing cover.. 96 in-lbs
    Auto-tensioner retaining bolts 17
    Tensioner arm retaining bolt.. 33
    Tensioner pulley bolt 35
Valve cover bolts .... 30 in-lbs

Refer to Part D for additional torque specifications

3.0L engine

General

Bore	3.59 inches
Stroke	2.99 inches
Displacement	181 cubic inches
Firing order	1-2-3-4-5-6
Compression ratio	9.0:1
Oil pressure (at curb idle speed)	11.6 psi (minimum)
Cylinder numbers (drivebelt end-to-transaxle end)	
Rear (firewall side)	1-3-5
Front (radiator side)	2-4-6

Camshaft

Cam lobe height	
Intake	
Standard	1.485 inches
Minimum	1.465 inches
Exhaust	
Standard	1.462 inches
Minimum	1.443 inches
Cam journal diameter	1.8 inches

Intake and exhaust manifolds

Intake manifold warpage limit	0.008 inch
Exhaust manifold warpage limit	0.008 inch

Oil pump

Body clearance	
Standard	0.004 to 0.007 inch
Service limit	0.013 inch
Side clearance	0.002 to 0.003 inch
Tip clearance	0.003 to 0.007 inch

Torque specifications   Ft-lbs (unless otherwise indicated)

Note: *One foot pound (ft-lb) of torque is equivalent to 12 inch-pounds (in-lbs) of torque. Torque values below approximately 15 ft-lbs are expressed in inch-pounds, since most foot-pound torque wrenches are not accurate at these smaller values.*

Camshaft sprocket bolt	65
Crankshaft pulley/vibration damper bolt	134
Crankshaft rear main seal retainer bolts	
Cylinder head bolts (in sequence - see illustration 13.24)	
Step 1	80
Step 2	Back off bolts to 0
Step 3	80
Exhaust manifold	
Exhaust manifold heat shield bolts	120 in-lbs
Exhaust manifold-to-cylinder head nuts	33
Exhaust pipe-to-exhaust manifold nuts	26
Flywheel/driveplate mounting bolts*	55
Intake manifold	
Upper intake manifold bolts/nuts	156 in-lbs
Lower intake manifold nuts **(see illustration 5.54)**	
Step 1 (rear nuts)	56 in-lbs
Step 2 (front nuts)	16
Step 3 (rear nuts)	16
Step 4 (front nuts)	16
Step 5 (rear nuts)	16
Oil pan bolts	
Lower oil pan-to-upper pan bolts	96 in-lbs
Upper oil pan bolts	
Upper pan-to-block bolts	52 in-lbs
Upper pan-to-transaxle bolts	26 in-lbs
Oil pump	
Mounting bolts	
M88 bolts	122 in-lbs
M10 bolts	30

* Apply a thread locking compound to the threads prior to installation

3.0L engine (continued)

Torque specifications (continued)　　　　　　　　　　Ft-lbs (unless otherwise indicated)

Note: *One foot pound (ft-lb) of torque is equivalent to 12 inch-pounds (in-lbs) of torque. Torque values below approximately 15 ft-lbs are expressed in inch-pounds, since most foot-pound torque wrenches are not accurate at these smaller values.*

Oil pump (continued)	
Cover retaining bolts	87 in-lbs
Pick-up tube bolts	168 in-lbs
Relief valve plug	33
Rocker arm shaft bolts	23
Timing belt	
Timing belt cover bolts	
Upper timing cover	
Front cylinder bank	117 in-lbs
Rear cylinder bank	96 in-lbs
Lower timing cover	96 in-lbs
Auto-tensioner retaining bolts	17
Tensioner arm retaining bolt	33
Tensioner pulley bolt	36
Valve cover bolts	31 in-lbs

1　General information

This Part of Chapter 2 is devoted to in-vehicle engine repair procedures. Information concerning engine removal and installation can be found in Part D of this Chapter.

The following repair procedures are based on the assumption that the engine is installed in the vehicle. If the engine has been removed from the vehicle and mounted on a stand, many of the steps outlined in this Part of Chapter 2 will not apply.

The Specifications included in this Part of Chapter 2 apply only to the procedures contained in this Part.

2　Repair operations possible with the engine in the vehicle

Many major repair operations can be accomplished without removing the engine from the vehicle.

Clean the engine compartment and the exterior of the engine with some type of degreaser before any work is performed. It will make the job easier and help keep dirt out of the internal areas of the engine.

Depending on the components involved, it may be helpful to remove the hood to improve access to the engine as repairs are performed (refer to Chapter 11 if necessary). Cover the fenders to prevent damage to the paint. Special pads are available, but an old bedspread or blanket will also work.

If vacuum, exhaust, oil or coolant leaks develop, indicating a need for gasket or seal replacement, the repairs can generally be made with the engine in the vehicle. The intake and exhaust manifold gaskets, oil pan gasket, camshaft and crankshaft oil seals and cylinder head gasket are all accessible with the engine in place.

Exterior engine components, such as the intake and exhaust manifolds, the oil pan, the oil pump, the water pump, the starter motor, the alternator, the distributor and the fuel system components can be removed for repair with the engine in place.

Since the camshafts and cylinder head can be removed without pulling the engine, valve component servicing can also be accomplished with the engine in the vehicle. Replacement of the timing belt and sprockets is also possible with the engine in the vehicle.

In extreme cases caused by a lack of necessary equipment, repair or replacement of piston rings, pistons, connecting rods and rod bearings is possible with the engine in the vehicle. However, this practice is not recommended because of the cleaning and preparation work that must be done to the components involved.

3　Top Dead Center (TDC) for number one piston - locating

Note: *The crankshaft timing marks on both engines aren't visible until after the timing belt cover has been removed. The number one cylinder can be positioned at TDC by using this procedure without removing the timing belt cover.*

1　Top Dead Center (TDC) is the highest point in the cylinder that each piston reaches as it travels up-and-down when the crankshaft turns. Each piston reaches TDC on the compression stroke and again on the exhaust stroke, but TDC generally refers to piston position on the compression stroke. The cast-in timing mark arrow on the crankshaft timing belt pulley installed on the front of the crankshaft is referenced to the number one piston at TDC when the arrow is straight up, or at "12 o'clock", and aligned with the cast-in timing mark arrow on the oil pump housing (see Section 7).

2　Positioning a specific piston at TDC is an essential part of many procedures such as camshaft(s) removal, rocker arm removal, timing belt and sprocket replacement.

3　In order to bring any piston to TDC, the crankshaft must be turned using one of the methods outlined below. When looking at the front of the engine, normal crankshaft rotation is clockwise. **Warning:** *Before beginning this procedure, be sure to set the emergency brake, place the transmission in Park or Neutral and disable the ignition system by disconnecting the primary electrical connector from the ignition coil pack.*

a) *The preferred method is to turn the crankshaft with a large socket and breaker bar attached to the crankshaft balancer hub bolt that is threaded into the front of the crankshaft.*

b) *A remote starter switch, which may save some time, can also be used. Attach the switch leads to the S (switch) and B (battery) terminals on the starter solenoid. Once the piston is close to TDC, discontinue with the remote switch and use a socket and breaker bar as described in the previous paragraph.*

c) *If an assistant is available to turn the ignition switch to the Start position in short bursts, you can get the piston close to TDC without a remote starter switch. Use a socket and breaker bar as described in Paragraph a) to complete the procedure.*

4　Remove all spark plugs as this will make it easier to rotate the engine by hand.

5　Insert a compression gauge (screw-in

4.4 To detach the breather hose between the valve covers on a 2.5L engine, loosen these hose clamps (arrows) and then pull the hose off both valve cover pipes

4.5 If you're removing the rear valve cover on a 2.5L engine, remove these nuts (arrows) and then detach these emissions vacuum lines

type with a hose) in the number 1 spark plug hole. Place the gauge dial where you can see it while turning the crankshaft balancer hub bolt. **Note:** *The number one cylinder is located at the front (timing belt end) of the engine, on the rear cylinder bank..*

6   Turn the crankshaft clockwise until you see compression building up on the gauge - you are on the compression stroke for that cylinder. If you did not see compression build up, continue with one more complete revolution to achieve TDC for the number one cylinder.

7   Remove the compression gauge. Through the number one cylinder spark plug hole insert a section of wooden dowel or plastic rod and slowly push it down until it reaches the top surface of the piston crown. **Caution:** *Don't insert a metal or sharp object into the spark plug hole as the piston crown may be damaged.*

8   With the dowel or rod in place on top of the piston crown, slowly rotate the crankshaft clockwise until the dowel or rod is pushed

upward, stops, and then starts to move back down. At this point, rotate the crankshaft slightly counterclockwise until the dowel or rod has reached it upper most travel. At this point the number one piston is at the TDC position.

9   After the number one piston has been positioned at TDC on the compression stroke, TDC for any of the remaining cylinders can be located by turning the crankshaft 120-degrees (1/3-turn) at a time and following the firing order (refer to the Specifications).

---

4   Valve cover - removal and installation

Removal

Refer to illustrations 4.4, 4.5, 4.6a, 4.6b, 4.7 and 4.8

1   Disconnect the cable from the negative battery terminal or the remote ground terminal (see Chapter 5).

2   If you're going to remove the *rear* valve

cover, remove the upper intake manifold (see Section 5).

3   Clearly label and then disconnect the spark plug wires (see Chapter 1). Also label and then disconnect any electrical harnesses that connect to or cross over the valve cover.

4   Disconnect the breather hose and the PCV hose from the valve cover (see Chapter 6). On some 2.5L engines, there's a breather hose connecting the front and rear valve covers **(see illustration)** If equipped, remove it.

5   If you're removing the rear valve cover on a 2.5L engine, detach the emission vacuum lines from the cover **(see illustration)**.

6   Remove the valve cover bolts **(see illustrations)** and then lift off the cover. If the cover sticks to the cylinder head, tap on it with a soft-face hammer or place a wood block against the cover and tap on the wood with a hammer. **Caution:** *If you have to pry between the valve cover and the cylinder head, be extremely careful not to gouge or nick the gasket surfaces of either part. A leak could develop after reassembly.*

4.6a Front valve cover mounting bolts (arrows) (2.5L engine shown, 3.0L engine similar)

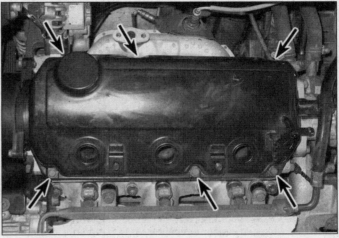

4.6b Rear valve cover mounting bolts (arrows) (2.5L engine shown, 3.0L engine similar)

7   Remove the spark plug tube seals. Even if they look OK, they should be replaced **(see illustration)**.

8   Remove the old gasket **(see illustration)**. Thoroughly clean the valve cover and remove all traces of old gasket material. Gasket removal solvents are available from auto parts stores and may prove helpful. After cleaning the surfaces, degrease them with a rag soaked in lacquer thinner or acetone.

Installation

9   Install the new spark plug seals onto the tubes.

10   Install a new gasket on the cover, using anaerobic RTV sealant to hold it in place.

11   Tighten the valve cover bolts in 3 steps to the torque listed in this Chapter's Specifications using a criss-cross pattern starting in the middle of the cover and working outwards.

12   The remaining installation steps are the reverse of removal. When complete, run the engine and check for oil leaks.

Spark plug tube replacement

13   Remove the applicable valve cover (see above).

4.7 Remove the spark plug tube seals and, even if they look okay, replace them

14   Grasp the spark plug tube firmly with locking pliers, carefully twist it back and forth and simultaneously pull up, then remove the tube from the cylinder head.

15   Clean the locking agent from the tube and the recess in the cylinder head with solvent, and then dry it thoroughly.

4.8 Remove the old valve cover gasket and then clean off all traces of old gasket material

16   Apply a small amount of Loctite No. 271, or equivalent, around the lower end of the tube and install the tube into the cylinder head. Carefully tap the tube into the recess with a wood block and mallet until it is fully seated in the cylinder head.

5   Intake manifold - removal and installation

2.5L engine
Upper intake manifold
Removal

Refer to illustrations 5.4a, 5.4b, 5.4c, 5.4d, 5.5, 5.6, 5.7a, 5.7b and 5.7c

1   Disconnect the cable from the negative battery terminal or the remote ground terminal (see Chapter 5).

2   Remove the air intake duct from the throttle body (see Chapter 4). If you're going to *replace* the upper intake manifold, remove the throttle body (see Chapter 4). If you're just removing the upper intake manifold to get to

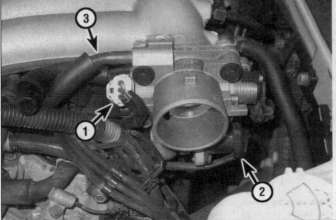

5.4a On the left side of the upper intake manifold, disconnect the Throttle Position Sensor (TPS) connector (1), the Idle Air Control (IAC) connector (2) and the vacuum hose (3) (2.5L engine)

5.4b On the right side of the upper intake manifold, disconnect the Manifold Absolute Pressure (MAP) sensor connector (1), the Intake Air Temperature (IAT) sensor connector (2) and the oxygen sensor connector (3) (2.5L engine)

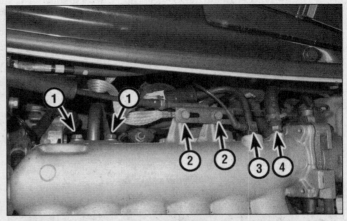

5.4c On the rear side of the upper intake manifold, remove the EGR pipe bolts (1) and the accelerator cable guide bolts (2) and then disconnect the EGR vacuum line (3) and the brake booster hose (4) (2.5L engine) (note the ground strap that's secured by the accelerator cable guide bolt — don't forget to reattach the ground when installing the manifold)

5.4d On the front side of the upper intake manifold, remove the harness clip bolts (arrows) and then detach the harnesses and set them aside (2.5L engine)

the lower intake manifold, or to perform some other service procedure, it's not necessary to remove the throttle body.

3   Disconnect the accelerator cable and cruise control cable (if applicable) from the throttle body (see Chapter 4 if necessary).

4   Clearly label and then disconnect all hoses, vacuum lines, wiring harnesses and cable brackets from the throttle body and from the intake manifold **(see illustrations)**.

5   Remove the bolts securing the upper intake manifold to the right and left side sup-port brackets **(see illustration)**.

6   Disconnect the EGR pipe from the intake manifold if you haven't already done so in Step 4 **(see illustration)**.

7   Loosen the upper intake manifold bolts in a criss-cross pattern 1/4 turn at a time until they can be removed by hand. Remove the upper intake manifold from the engine **(see illustrations)**. If it sticks, tap the manifold with a soft-face hammer or carefully pry it from the lower intake manifold. **Caution:** *Do not pry between gasket sealing surfaces.*

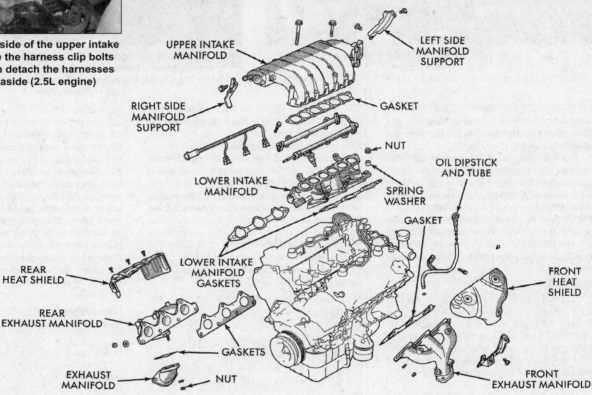

5.5 An exploded view of typical intake and exhaust system assemblies

5.6 To detach the EGR pipe from the upper intake manifold on a convertible, remove the two flange bolts

5.7a Starting in the center and working outwards, remove the upper intake manifold mounting bolts in a criss-cross pattern . . .

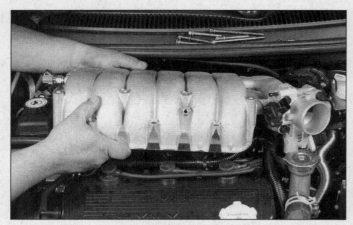

5.7b . . . then remove the manifold from the engine (convertible models)

5.7c To remove the upper intake manifold on a coupe or sedan, remove these bolts (arrows), starting in the center and working out in a criss-cross pattern

8   To minimize the chance of gasket debris or other contamination from getting into the engine, place clean rags into the lower intake manifold passages.

9   Remove all traces of gasket material from both the upper and lower intake manifold by carefully scraping them using a suitable gasket scraper. **Caution:** *The intake manifold components are made of aluminum and are easily nicked or gouged. Do not damage the gasket surfaces or a leak may result after the work is complete. Gasket removal solvents are available from auto parts stores and may prove helpful.*

Inspection

10   Using a precision straightedge and feeler gauge, check the upper and lower intake manifold mating surfaces for warpage **(see illustration 5.22)**. If the warpage on any surface exceeds the limits listed in this Chapter's Specifications, the discrepant intake manifold must be replaced or resurfaced by an automotive machine shop.

Installation

11   Remove the rags from the lower intake manifold. Use a shop vacuum to remove any contamination that may be present.

12   Install the upper intake manifold, using a new gasket. Tighten the bolts in 3 stages, working from the center out, to the torque listed in this Chapter's Specifications.

13   Install the EGR pipe using new gaskets. Tighten the bolts to the torque listed in this Chapter's Specifications.

14   The remaining installation steps are the reverse of removal **(see illustrations 5.4a, 5.4b, 5.4c and 5.4d)**.

Lower intake manifold

Removal

15   Relieve the fuel pressure (see Chapter 4).

16   Remove the upper intake manifold (see above).

17   Remove the fuel rail and injector assembly (see Chapter 4).

18   Loosen the intake manifold nuts in the *reverse* order of the tightening sequence **(see illustration 5.24)**, 1/4 turn at a time until they can be removed by hand. Remove the washers.

19   Remove the lower intake manifold from the engine. If it sticks, tap the manifold with a soft-face hammer or carefully pry it from the heads. **Caution:** *Do not pry between gasket*

sealing surfaces.

20   To minimize the chance of gasket debris or other contamination from getting into the engine, stuff clean rags into the intake manifold inlet ports.

21   Remove all traces of gasket material from the upper and lower intake manifold and cylinder heads by carefully scraping them using a suitable gasket scraper. **Caution:** *The intake manifold components and cylinder heads are made of aluminum and are easily nicked or gouged. Do not damage the gasket surfaces or a leak may result after the work is complete. Gasket removal solvents are available from auto parts stores and may prove helpful.*

Inspection

Refer to illustration 5.22

22   Using a precision straightedge and feeler gauge, check the upper and lower intake manifold gasket surfaces for warpage **(see illustration)**. Check the gasket surface on the cylinder head also. If the warpage on any surface exceeds the limits listed in this Chapter's Specifications, the discrepant component must be replaced or resurfaced by an automotive machine shop.

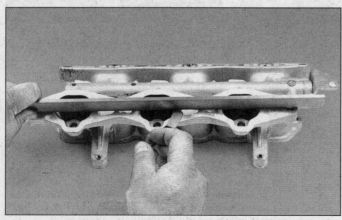

5.22 Check the lower intake manifold gasket surface for warpage

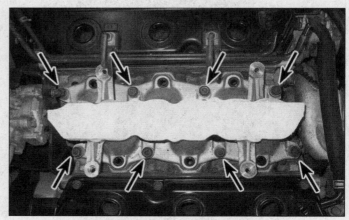

5.24 Lower intake manifold nuts

Installation

Refer to illustration 5.24

23 Remove the rags from the cylinder head intake passages. Use a shop vacuum to remove any contamination that may be present.

24 Install the lower intake manifold, using a new gaskets. Tighten the nuts in three stages, in the sequence shown **(see illustration)** to the torque listed in this Chapter's Specifications.

25 Install the fuel rail (see Chapter 4).

26 Install the upper intake manifold, using a new gasket. Tighten the bolts in three stages, working from the center out, to the torque listed in this Chapter's Specifications.

27 Install the EGR pipe using new gaskets. Tighten the bolts to the torque listed in this Chapter's Specifications.

28 The remainder of installation is the reverse of removal **(see illustrations 5.4a, 5.4b, 5.4c and 5.4d)**.

3.0L engine

Upper intake manifold

Removal

Refer to illustrations 5.39

29 Relieve the fuel pressure (see Chapter 4).

30 Disconnect the cable from the negative battery terminal or the remote ground terminal (see Chapter 5).

31 Remove the air intake duct from the throttle body (see Chapter 4).

32 Disconnect the accelerator cable and cruise control cable (if applicable) from the throttle body (see Chapter 4).

33 If you're going to *replace* the upper intake manifold, remove the throttle body (see Chapter 4). If you're just removing the upper intake manifold to get to the lower intake manifold or to perform some other service procedure, it's not necessary to remove the throttle body.

34 Remove the strut tower bar (see Chapter 10).

35 Clearly label and then disconnect all vacuum hoses, pipes and lines (see Chapter 6 if necessary).

36 Clearly label and then disconnect the following fuel, electrical and emission control electrical connectors and components (see Chapter 4, 5 or 6):

a) *Manifold Absolute Pressure (MAP) sensor connector*
b) *Control wiring harness and power steering wiring harness combination connector*
c) *Exhaust Gas Recirculation (EGR) solenoid valve connector*
d) *Evaporative emission (EVAP) purge solenoid valve connector*
e) *Knock sensor connector*
f) *Crankshaft Position (CKP) sensor connector*
g) *Right heated oxygen sensor connector*
h) *Fuel injector connector*
i) *Distributor connector*

5.39 To remove the upper intake manifold on a 3.0L engine, remove these bolts (arrows)

j) *Control wiring harness and injector wiring harness combination connector*
k) *EGR solenoid valve, evaporative emission purge solenoid valve and vacuum valve*
l) *EGR valve and EGR pipe*
m) *Manifold differential pressure sensor*

37 Remove the power steering pump drivebelt (see Chapter 1) and then remove the power steering pump bracket stay (see Chapter 10).

38 Remove the bolts securing the upper intake manifold to the right and left side support brackets. The support brackets are bolted to the rear cylinder head. The left bracket has four bolts (two to the manifold and two to the head) and the right bracket has three (one to the manifold and two to the head).

39 Remove the upper intake manifold bolts **(see illustration)**, remove the upper intake manifold and then remove the manifold gasket. If it sticks, tap the manifold with a soft-face hammer or carefully pry it from the lower intake manifold. **Caution:** *Do not pry between gasket sealing surfaces.*

40 To minimize the chance of gasket debris or other contamination from getting into the engine, place clean rags into the lower intake manifold passages.

41 Remove all traces of gasket material from both the upper and lower intake manifold by carefully scraping them using a suitable gasket scraper. **Caution:** *The intake manifold components are made of aluminum and are easily nicked or gouged. Do not damage the gasket surfaces or a leak may result after the work is complete. Gasket removal solvents are available from auto parts stores and may prove helpful.*

Inspection

42 Using a precision straightedge and feeler gauge, check the upper and lower intake manifold mating surfaces for warpage **(see illustration 5.22)**. If the warpage on any surface exceeds the limits listed in this Chapter's Specifications, the discrepant intake manifold must be replaced or resurfaced by an automotive machine shop.

Installation

43 Remove the rags from the lower intake manifold. Use a shop vacuum to remove any contamination that may be present.

44 Install the upper intake manifold, using a new gasket. Tighten the bolts in 3 stages, working from the center out, to the torque listed in this Chapter's Specifications.

45 The remainder of installation is the reverse of removal.

Lower intake manifold

Removal

46 Relieve the fuel pressure (see Chapter 4).

47 Remove the upper intake manifold (see above).

48 Remove the fuel rail and injector assembly (see Chapter 4).

49 Loosen the intake manifold nuts in the *reverse* order of the tightening sequence **(see illustration 5.54 and this Chapter's Specifications)**, 1/4 turn at a time until they can be removed by hand. Remove the washers.

50 Remove the lower intake manifold from the engine. If it sticks, tap the manifold with a soft-face hammer or carefully pry it from the heads. **Caution:** *Do not pry between gasket sealing surfaces.*

51 To minimize the chance of gasket debris or other contamination from getting into the engine, place clean rags into the cylinder head intake passages.

52 Remove all traces of gasket material from the upper and lower intake manifold and cylinder heads by carefully scraping them using a suitable gasket scraper. **Caution:** *The intake manifold components and cylinder heads are made of aluminum and are easily nicked or gouged. Do not damage the gasket surfaces or a leak may result after the work is complete. Gasket removal solvents are available from auto parts stores and may prove helpful.*

Inspection

53 Using a precision straightedge and feeler gauge, check the upper and lower intake manifold gasket surfaces for warpage. Check the

gasket surface on the cylinder head also. If the warpage on any surface exceeds the limits listed in this Chapter's Specifications, the discrepant component must be replaced or resurfaced by an automotive machine shop.

Installation

Refer to illustration 5.55

54   Remove the rags from the cylinder head intake passages. Use a shop vacuum to remove any contamination that may be present.

55   Install the lower intake manifold, using a new gaskets. Tighten the nuts **(see illustration)** in five stages, following the sequence listed in this Chapter's Specifications, to the final torque.

56   Install the fuel rail and fuel injector assembly (see Chapter 4).

57   Install the upper intake manifold, using a new gasket (see above).

58   The remainder of installation is the reverse of removal.

---

6   Exhaust manifold - removal and installation

Warning: *Allow the engine to cool completely before beginning this procedure.*

Note: *This procedure can be used to remove one or both of the exhaust manifolds as required.*

2.5L engine

Front exhaust manifold

Removal

Refer to illustrations 6.4, 6.5, 6.7, 6.8 and 6.9

1   Disconnect the negative battery cable from the negative battery terminal or the remote ground terminal (see Chapter 5).

2   Remove the engine cooling fan and shroud assembly (see Chapter 3).

3   Raise the vehicle and place it securely on jackstands.

4   Disconnect the cross-under pipe from the exhaust manifold **(see illustration)**. Be extremely careful not to damage the oxygen

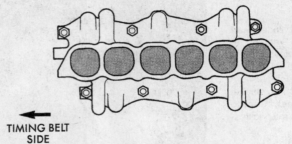

5.55 Lower intake manifold nuts (arrows) on the 3.0L engine; the "rear" nuts are the ones next to the rear cylinder head (the head next to the firewall) and the "front" nuts are those next to the front cylinder head (the one next to the radiator)

TIMING BELT SIDE

sensor in the upper end of the cross-under pipe. It's not a bad idea to unplug the sensor connector (see Chapter 6) and set it aside, out of the way, so the harness isn't accidentally damaged.

5   Remove the engine oil dipstick tube **(see illustration)**.

6   On some models, the alternator and upper alternator mounting bracket may be in the way. If so, remove the alternator and the alternator mounting bracket (see Chapter 5).

7   If the exhaust manifold is bolted to the exhaust manifold **(see illustration)**, remove it. On later models, the heat shield is permanently spot-welded onto the manifold, and

cannot be removed.

8   Remove the exhaust manifold support bracket **(see illustration)**.

9   To make removal easier, apply penetrating oil to the exhaust manifold and manifold-to-pipe fasteners. Wait awhile for the penetrating oil to soak into the threads between the exhaust manifold nuts and the manifold studs. Remove the exhaust manifold mounting nuts **(see illustration)**, and then remove the exhaust manifold and the manifold gasket.

10   Using a wire brush, clean the exhaust manifold studs, replacing any that show thread damage.

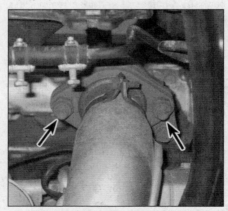

6.4 To disconnect the cross-under pipe from the front exhaust manifold, remove these two nuts (arrows)

6.5 To disconnect the engine oil dipstick tube from the cylinder head, remove this bolt (arrow)

6.7 To detach the heat shield from the front exhaust manifold, remove these bolts (arrows) (not all heat shields are removable - some are spot-welded to the manifold)

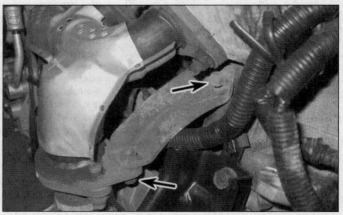

6.8 To remove the front exhaust manifold support bracket, remove these two bolts (arrows)

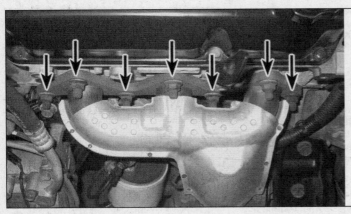

6.9 To remove the front (or the rear) exhaust manifold from the cylinder head, remove these nuts (arrows) (front exhaust manifold shown, rear manifold identical)

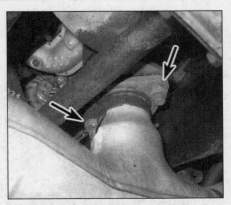

6.19 To disconnect the cross-under pipe from the rear exhaust manifold, remove these two nuts (arrows)

11   Using a scraper, remove all traces of gasket material from the exhaust manifold, cylinder head, and exhaust pipe mating surfaces and inspect them for wear and cracks. **Caution:** *When removing gasket material from any surface, especially aluminum, be very careful not to scratch or gouge the gasket surface. Any damage to the surface may a leak after reassembly. Gasket removal solvents are available from auto parts stores and may prove helpful.*

Inspection
12   Using a precision straightedge and feeler gauge, check the exhaust manifold gasket surfaces for warpage. Check the surface on the cylinder head also. If the warpage on any surface exceeds the limits listed in this Chapter's Specifications, the exhaust manifold and/or cylinder head must be replaced or resurfaced by an automotive machine shop.

Installation
13   Install a new exhaust manifold gasket on the cylinder head.
14   Apply Loctite No. 271 to the exhaust manifold mounting stud threads.
15   Install the manifold, washers and nuts. Tighten the nuts in three stages, working from the center out, to the torque listed in this Chapter's Specifications.
16   The remainder of installation is the

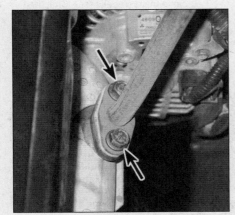

6.21 To disconnect the EGR pipe from the rear exhaust manifold, remove these two bolts (arrows)

reverse of removal. Install a new gasket between the exhaust manifold and the cross-under pipe. Tighten the nuts to the torque listed in this Chapter's Specifications.
17   Run the engine and check for exhaust leaks.

Rear exhaust manifold
Removal
Refer to illustrations 6.19 and 6.21
18   Raise the vehicle and place it securely on jackstands.
19   Disconnect the cross-under pipe from the front exhaust manifold **(see illustration 6.4)** and from the rear exhaust manifold **(see illustration)**.
20   Disconnect the cross-under pipe from the downstream catalytic converter, if possible (see Chapter 4) and them remove the cross-under pipe. It may be necessary to remove the entire exhaust system, because on some models the cross-under pipe cannot be disconnected from the catalytic converter. (You *have to remove* the cross-under pipe before you can remove the rear exhaust manifold because the manifold must be removed from *below*. There isn't enough room to remove it from above, unless the engine is removed from the vehicle.)
21   Disconnect the Exhaust Gas Recirculation (EGR) pipe from the rear exhaust manifold **(see illustration)**.
22   If the heat shield is bolted to the rear exhaust manifold, remove it. Before attempting to remove the rear manifold heat shield, disconnect the electrical connector from the oxygen sensor, if the sensor is installed in the exhaust manifold (see Chapter 6).
23   Remove the power steering pump and the power steering pump mounting bracket (see Chapter 10) if it's in the way.
24   Remove the exhaust manifold nuts **(see illustration 6.9)** and then remove the exhaust manifold and the manifold gasket.

Inspection
25   Refer to Step 12 above.

Installation
26   Install a new exhaust manifold gasket on the cylinder head.
27   Apply Loctite No. 271 to the exhaust manifold mounting stud threads.

28   Install the manifold, washers and nuts. Tighten the nuts in three stages, working from the center out, to the torque listed in this Chapter's Specifications.
29   The remainder of installation is the reverse of removal. Install a new gasket between the exhaust manifold and the cross-under pipe. Tighten the nuts to the torque listed in this Chapter's Specifications.
30   Run the engine and check for exhaust leaks.

3.0L engine
Removal
Refer to illustrations 6.35, 6.37, 6.38 and 6.40
31   Disconnect the cable from the negative battery terminal or the remote ground terminal (see Chapter 5).
32   Remove the front exhaust pipe/catalytic converter assembly (see Chapter 4).
33   Remove the air cleaner (see Chapter 4).
34   Remove the strut tower crossbar, if equipped.
35   Remove the engine oil dipstick tube and the front engine lifting bracket **(see illustration)**. If the vehicle is equipped with an automatic transaxle, remove the automatic trans-

6.35 To detach the dipstick tube from the cylinder head, remove this bolt (left arrow); then unbolt and remove the front engine lifting bracket (right arrow)

6.37 To detach the EGR pipe from the intake manifold, remove these two bolts (arrows); to detach the other end of the EGR pipe (not shown) from the rear exhaust manifold, back off the fitting at the lower end of the pipe and then unscrew the pipe

mission fluid level dipstick tube.

36   Disconnect the electrical connector for the upstream oxygen sensor (see Chapter 6).

37   If you're removing the rear exhaust manifold, disconnect the EGR pipe from the intake manifold **(see illustration)**, back off the threaded fitting at the lower end of the pipe and then unscrew the pipe from the exhaust manifold. If the EGR pipe-to-exhaust manifold fitting is difficult to loosen, apply some penetrating oil to the fitting, wait awhile and then try again.

38   Remove the upper and lower exhaust manifold heat shields **(see illustration)**. On the front exhaust manifold, there are two heat shields: the upper shield (shown in the accompanying illustration) and the lower shield (which must be removed from below). On the rear exhaust manifold, there are four heat shields: the upper shield, the left shield,

6.38 To detach the upper heat shield from the front exhaust manifold, remove these bolts (arrows) and then carefully slide the oxygen sensor harness and electrical connector through the hole in the shield

the right shield and the lower shield (which must be removed from below).

39   To make removal easier, apply penetrating oil to the exhaust manifold and to the manifold-to-upstream catalytic converter fasteners.

40   Detach the upstream catalytic converter from the manifold **(see illustration)**.

41   Unscrew the exhaust manifold mounting nuts **(see illustration 6.9)**, remove the exhaust manifold and then remove and discard the old manifold gasket.

42   Using a wire brush, clean the exhaust manifold studs, replacing any that show thread damage.

43   Using a scraper, remove all traces of gasket material from the exhaust manifold, cylinder head, and exhaust pipe mating surfaces and inspect them for wear and cracks. **Caution:** *When removing gasket material from any surface, especially aluminum, be very careful not to scratch or gouge the gasket surface. Any damage to the surface may cause a leak after reassembly. Gasket removal solvents are available from auto parts stores and may prove helpful.*

Inspection

44   Using a precision straightedge and feeler gauge, check the exhaust manifold gasket surfaces for warpage. Check the surface on the cylinder head also. If the warpage on any surface exceeds the limits listed in this Chapter's Specifications, the exhaust manifold and/or cylinder head must be replaced or resurfaced by an automotive machine shop.

Installation

45   Install a new exhaust gasket on the cylinder head.

46   Apply Loctite No. 271 to the exhaust manifold mounting stud threads.

47   Install the manifold, washers and nuts. Tighten the nuts in three stages, working from the center out, to the torque listed in this Chapter's Specifications.

48   The remaining installation steps are the reverse of removal. Install a new gasket(s) between the exhaust manifold and exhaust pipe(s). Tighten the nuts to the torque listed in this Chapter's Specifications.

49   Run the engine and check for exhaust leaks.

7   Timing belt - removal, inspection and installation

Caution: *If the timing belt failed with the engine operating, damage to the valves may have occurred. Perform an engine compression check after belt replacement to determine if any valve damage is present.*

Removal

> **** CAUTION ****
> The timing system is complex. Severe engine damage will occur if you make any mistakes. Do not attempt this procedure unless you are highly experienced with this type of repair. If you are at all unsure of your abilities, consult an expert. Double-check all your work and be sure everything is correct before you attempt to start the engine.

Refer to illustrations 7.4a, 7.4b, 7.6, 7.7, 7.11a, 7.11b, 7.12 and 7.13

Caution: *Do not turn the crankshaft or camshafts after the timing belt has been removed, as this will damage the valves from contact with the pistons. Do not try to turn the crankshaft with the camshaft sprocket bolt(s) and do not rotate the crankshaft counterclockwise as viewed from the timing belt end of the engine.*

Note: *In order to perform this procedure, you'll need a special tool (MD 998767) to tension the timing belt. This tool number is available from automotive specialty tool companies such as Miller Special Tools.*

1   Position the number one piston at Top Dead Center (see Section 3) and then disconnect the cable from the negative battery terminal or the remote ground terminal (see Chapter 5).

2   Raise the vehicle, place it securely on jackstands, remove the right front wheel and then remove the drivebelt splash shield (see Chapter 11).

3   Remove the drivebelts (see Chapter 1).

4   Loosen the large bolt in the center of the crankshaft damper/pulley. It might be very tight, to break it loose insert a large screw-

6.40 To detach the upstream catalytic converter from the exhaust manifold, remove these three nuts (arrows) (front exhaust manifold-to-catalyst flange shown, rear manifold-to-catalyst flange similar)

7.4a To keep the crankshaft from turning, insert a large screwdriver or bar through the opening in the damper/pulley and wedge it against the engine block, then loosen the bolt with a socket and breaker bar

7.4b Remove the damper/pulley from the crankshaft

driver or bar through the opening in the pulley to keep the crankshaft stationary, then loosen the bolt with a socket and breaker bar. Remove the bolt, washer and damper/pulley from the crankshaft **(see illustrations)**.

5   After removing the crankshaft pulley, reinstall the crankshaft bolt using an appropriate spacer (this will enable you to turn the crankshaft later).

6   Remove the upper-left timing belt cover **(see illustration)**.

7   Remove the lower timing belt cover **(see illustration)**.

8   Detach the power steering pump bracket from the engine (see Chapter 10 if necessary).

9   Remove the upper-right timing belt cover **(see illustration 7.6)**.

10   Remove the right (passenger side) engine mount and the mounting bracket from the engine (see Section 18). **Note:** *Make sure the engine is supported with a floor jack*

placed under the oil pan. Place a wood block on the jack head to prevent the floor jack from denting or damaging the oil pan.

11   Make sure the timing marks on the crankshaft sprocket and camshaft sprockets align with their respective marks before removing the timing belt **(see illustrations)**.

12   If you plan to reuse the timing belt, paint

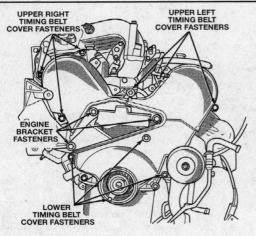

7.6 Timing belt cover bolt locations (2.5L engine shown, 3.0L engine similar)

7.7 Remove the bolts (arrows) that attach the timing belt lower cover to the engine (2.5L engine shown, 3.0L engine similar)

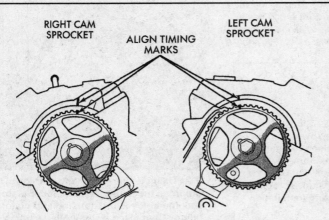

7.11a Verify that the camshaft sprocket timing marks are aligned with their respective marks on the rear timing belt covers

7.11b Crankshaft timing belt sprocket and oil pump housing timing marks (arrows)

7.12 Paint an arrow on the timing belt in the direction of rotation (clockwise) so it may be reinstalled in the same direction

7.13 Timing belt tensioner mounting bolts (arrows)

7.18 Carefully inspect the timing belt for damage or wear - bending it backwards will often make defects more apparent

an arrow on it to indicate the direction of rotation (clockwise) **(see illustration)**.

13   Loosen the timing belt tensioner mounting bolts and then remove the tensioner **(see illustration)**. **Note:** *The tensioner piston will extend when the assembly is removed.*

14   Carefully slip the timing belt off the sprockets and set it aside. If you plan to reuse the timing belt, place it in a plastic bag - do not allow the belt to come in contact with any type of oil or water as this will greatly shorten belt life.

Inspection
Refer to illustration 7.18

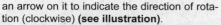

15   With the timing belt covers removed, now is a good time to inspect the front crankshaft and camshaft seals for leakage. If leakage is evident, replace them (see Sections 8 and 9, respectively).

16   Inspect the water pump for evidence of leakage (usually indicated by a trail of wet or dried coolant). Check the pulley for excessive radial play and bearing roughness. Replace if necessary (see Chapter 3).

17   Rotate the tensioner pulley and idler pulley by hand and move them side-to-side to detect bearing roughness and/or excessive play. Visually inspect all timing belt sprockets for any signs of damage or wear. Replace as necessary.

18   Inspect the timing belt for cracks, sepa-

ration, wear, missing teeth and oil contamination **(see illustration)**. Replace the belt if it's in questionable condition or the engine mileage is close to that referenced in the *Maintenance Schedule* (see Chapter 1).

19   Check the timing belt tensioner unit for leaks or any other obvious damage, replace if necessary.

Installation

> **✱✱ CAUTION ✱✱**
>
> Before starting the engine, carefully rotate the crankshaft by hand through at least two full revolutions (use a socket and breaker bar on the crankshaft pulley center bolt). If you feel any resistance, STOP! There is something wrong - most likely, valves are contacting the pistons. You must find the problem before proceeding. Check your work and see if any updated repair information is available.

Refer to illustrations 7.22, 7.24, 7.25 and 7.27

20   Confirm that the timing marks on both camshaft sprockets are aligned with their respective marks on the rear timing belt covers **(see illustration 7.11a)**. Reposition the camshafts if required. **Caution:** *If it is necessary to rotate the camshafts to align the timing marks, first rotate the crankshaft slightly coun-*

terclockwise *(three notches on the sprocket) to ensure the valves do not contact the pistons.*

21   Position the crankshaft sprocket with the timing marks aligned **(see illustration 7.11b)**.

22   Install the timing belt as follows; first place the belt onto the right camshaft sprocket (the one towards the rear of the vehicle) and clamp it to the sprocket, while maintaining tension on the belt, wrap it under the water pump pulley and place it onto the left sprocket camshaft sprocket. Secure the timing belt to the left camshaft sprocket **(see illustration)**. Continue to wrap the timing belt over the idler pulley, around the crankshaft sprocket and finishing with the tensioner pulley. Remove the clamps from the camshaft sprockets.

23   Make sure the timing belt is tight between the left camshaft sprocket and the crankshaft sprocket, all the slack is at the tensioner pulley and all the timing marks are aligned.

24   Before installation, the timing belt tensioner piston must be compressed into the tensioner housing. Place the tensioner in a vise so the surface with the pin hole is fac-

7.22 Binder clips (arrows) can be used to retain the timing belt in position on the camshaft sprockets during installation

7.24 Using a vise (lined with soft-jaws), compress the timing belt tensioner piston until the holes in the housing and piston align. Then place a small Allen wrench (arrow) or drill bit, through the holes to keep the piston in position for installation

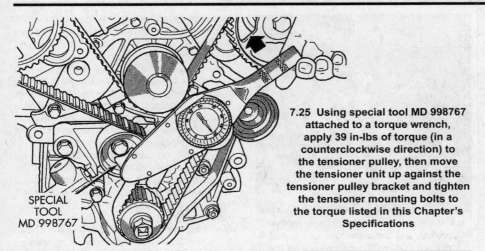

7.25 Using special tool MD 998767 attached to a torque wrench, apply 39 in-lbs of torque (in a counterclockwise direction) to the tensioner pulley, then move the tensioner unit up against the tensioner pulley bracket and tighten the tensioner mounting bolts to the torque listed in this Chapter's Specifications

shaft. Recheck the alignment of the timing marks **(see illustrations 6.11a and 6.11b)**. If the marks do not align properly, remove the timing belt tensioner, slip the belt off the camshaft sprockets, realign the marks, reinstall the belt and tensioner, then check the alignment again.

29 After crankshaft rotation, recheck the timing belt tension by inserting the tensioner piston retaining pin (Allen wrench or drill bit) back into the tensioner. If the retaining pin cannot be inserted and withdrawn freely, readjust the timing belt tension and repeat Steps 24 through 29.

30 The remaining installation steps are the reverse of removal. Tighten the crankshaft damper/pulley bolt to the torque listed in this Chapter's Specifications.

ing up. Slowly compress the tensioner using the vise, then install an appropriate size Allen wrench or drill bit through the body and into the piston to retain the piston in this position **(see illustration)**. Remove the tensioner from the vise.

25 Using the special tool "MD 998767"

7.27 If the timing belt tension is set correctly, the tensioner piston retaining pin (arrow) (an Allen wrench in this case) can be removed and installed easily

engaged in the tensioner pulley, have an assistant apply 39 in-lbs of torque in a counterclockwise direction **(see illustration)**.

26 With the torque applied to the tensioner pulley, install the tensioner assembly. Move the tensioner up against the tensioner pulley bracket and tighten the mounting bolts to the torque listed in this Chapter's Specifications. Remove the torque wrench and special tool from the tensioner pulley.

27 Remove the Allen wrench or drill bit retaining the piston from the tensioner. The timing belt tension is correct when the tensioner piston retaining pin (Allen wrench or drill bit) can be withdrawn and reinserted easily **(see illustration)**. Verify that the timing marks on the camshaft sprockets and crankshaft sprocket are still aligned with their respective timing marks **(see illustrations 6.11a and 6.11b)**.

28 Using the bolt in the center of the crankshaft sprocket, slowly turn the crankshaft clockwise two complete revolutions. **Caution:** *If you feel strong resistance while turning the crankshaft - STOP, the valves may be hitting the pistons from incorrect valve timing. Stop and re-check the valve timing.* **Note:** *The camshafts and crankshaft sprocket marks will align every two revolutions of the crank-*

8 Crankshaft front oil seal - replacement

Refer to illustrations 8.2, 8.3 and 8.5

Caution: *Do not rotate the camshafts or crankshaft when the timing belt is removed or damage to the engine may occur.*

1 Remove the timing belt (see Section 7).

2 Remove the crankshaft timing belt sprocket using a gear puller. Remove the Woodruff key from the crankshaft keyway **(see illustration)**.

3 Wrap the tip of a small screwdriver with vinyl tape. Carefully use the screwdriver to pry the seal out of its bore **(see illustration)**. Take care to prevent damaging the oil pump assembly, the crankshaft and the seal bore.

4 Thoroughly clean and inspect the seal bore and sealing surface on the crankshaft. Minor imperfections can be removed with fine emery cloth. If there is a groove worn in the crankshaft sealing surface (from contact with the seal), installing a new seal will probably not stop the leak.

5 Lubricate the new seal with engine oil and using a hammer and the appropriate size socket, drive the seal into the bore until it's flush with the oil pump housing **(see illustration)**.

8.2 After removing the timing belt sprocket, remove the Woodruff key (arrow) from the crankshaft

8.3 Using a hooked tool or screwdriver, carefully pry the crankshaft front seal out of its bore - DO NOT nick or scratch the crankshaft or seal bore

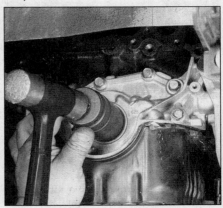

8.5 Lubricate the new seal with clean engine oil and drive it into place using a hammer and socket

9.3 To hold the camshaft while removing the sprocket bolt, use an old piece of timing belt wrapped around the sprocket and a chain wrench as shown

9.4 Using a hooked tool or screwdriver, carefully pry the camshaft seal out of the bore - DO NOT nick or scratch the camshaft or seal bore

head until it's flush with the face of the cylinder head. If a socket isn't available, a short section of pipe will also work. **Note:** *If engine location makes it difficult to use a hammer to install the camshaft seal, fabricate a seal installation tool from a piece of pipe cut to the appropriate length, a bolt and a large washer* **(see illustration)**. *Place the section of pipe over the seal and thread the bolt into the camshaft. The seal can now be pressed into the bore by tightening the bolt.*

7   Install the camshaft sprocket, aligning the pin in the camshaft with the hole in the sprocket. Using an appropriate tool to hold the camshaft sprocket, tighten the camshaft sprocket bolt to the torque listed in this Chapter's Specifications.

8   Install the timing belt (see Section 7).

9   Run the engine and check for oil leaks.

6   Install the Woodruff key into the slot in the crankshaft. Place the crankshaft timing belt sprocket onto the crankshaft with the timing belt retaining lip facing inward (toward the engine).

7   The remaining installation steps are the reverse of removal. Tighten the crankshaft pulley bolt to the torque listed in this Chapter's Specifications.

8   Start the engine and check for oil leaks.

9   Camshaft oil seal - replacement

Refer to illustrations 9.3, 9.4, 9.6a and 9.6b

Caution: *Do not rotate the camshafts or crankshaft when the timing belt is removed or damage to the engine may occur.*

1   Remove the timing belt (see Section 7).

2   Rotate the crankshaft counterclockwise until the crankshaft sprocket is three notches BTDC. This will prevent engine damage if the camshaft sprocket is inadvertently rotated during removal.

3   While keeping the camshaft from rotating, remove the camshaft sprocket bolt. Then using two large screwdrivers, lever the sprocket off the camshaft. **Note:** *A strap-type damper/pulley holder tool is available at most auto parts stores and is recommended for this procedure, however, if you are not going to reuse the old timing belt, you can wrap a piece of it around the sprocket and use a chain wrench to hold the sprocket in place as shown* **(see illustration)**.

4   Carefully pry out the camshaft oil seal using a small hooked tool or screwdriver **(see illustration)**. Don't scratch the bore or damage the camshaft in the process (if the camshaft is damaged, the new seal will end up leaking).

5   Clean the bore and coat the outer edge of the new seal with engine oil or multi-purpose grease. Also lubricate the seal lip.

6   Using a socket with an outside diameter slightly smaller than the outside diameter of the seal and a hammer **(see illustration)**, carefully drive the new seal into the cylinder

10   Rocker arm and hydraulic valve lash adjuster assembly - removal, inspection and installation

Removal

1   Disconnect the cable from the negative battery terminal or the remote ground terminal (see Chapter 5).

2   Position the number one piston at Top Dead Center (see Section 3).

3   Remove the valve cover(s) as required (see Section 4).

4   Prior to removing the rocker arm shafts, identify each rocker arm and shaft as to its proper location (cylinder number and intake or exhaust). **Caution:** *Do not interchange the rocker arms onto a different shaft or shaft assemblies onto a different location as this could lead to premature wear.*

5   Loosen the rocker arm shaft bolts 1/4-turn at a time, until they can be loosened by hand, in the *reverse* order of the tightening sequence **(see illustration 10.17)**. Completely loosen the bolts, but do not remove

9.6a Using a hammer and the appropriate size socket, drive the camshaft seal into the bore until it is flush with the cylinder head

9.6b If the space is too confined to use a hammer to drive the seal in place, fabricate a tool using a bolt, washer and section of pipe. Place the section of pipe over the seal and thread the bolt into the camshaft to press the seal into the bore

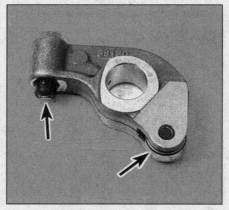

10.8 Visually inspect the hydraulic lash adjuster and roller (arrows) for damage and excessive play - check the rocker arm shaft bore for score marks or excessive wear

10.14 The intake rocker arm shaft springs (arrows) must be installed as shown

10.17 Rocker arm shaft bolt TIGHTENING sequence

them, leaving them in place will prevent the assembly from falling apart when it is lifted off the cylinder head.

6   Lift the rocker arms and shaft assemblies from the cylinder head and set them on the workbench. **Note:** *The hydraulic valve lash adjusters may become dislodged from the rocker arms during shaft removal. If required, secure the adjusters in place with vinyl tape.*

7   On 2.5L engines, it's okay to disassemble the rocker arm shaft components, but pay close attention to the relationship of the parts to each other. **Note:** *To keep the rocker arms and related parts in order, it's a good idea to remove them and put them onto two lengths of wire (such as unbent coat hangers) in the same order as they're removed, marking each wire (which simulates the rocker shaft) as to which end would be the front of the engine. On 3.0L engines, do NOT disassemble the rocker arm and shaft assemblies. They must be inspected and, if any damage or wear is evident, replaced as a single assembly.*

Inspection

Refer to illustration 10.8

Note: *The valve lash adjuster is an integral part of each rocker arm and cannot be replaced separately. If defective, both must be replaced.*

8   Visually check the rocker arms for excessive wear or damage **(see illustration)**. Replace them if evidence of wear or damage is found.

9   Inspect each lash adjuster carefully for signs of wear and damage, particularly on the surface that contacts the valve tip. Use a small diameter wire to check the oil holes for restrictions.

10   Since the lash adjusters frequently become clogged, we recommend replacing the rocker arm/lash adjuster assembly if you're concerned about their condition or if the engine is exhibiting valve "tapping" noises.

11   Inspect all rocker arm shaft components. Look for cracks, worn or scored surfaces or other damage. Replace any parts found to be damaged or worn excessively.

Installation

Refer to illustrations 10.14 and 10.17

12   Prior to installation, the lash adjusters must be partially full of engine oil - indicated by little or no plunger action when the adjuster is depressed. If there's excessive plunger travel, place the rocker arm assembly into clean engine oil and pump the plunger until the plunger travel is eliminated. **Note:** *If the plunger still travels within the rocker arm when full of oil it's defective and the rocker arm assembly must be replaced.*

13   Install the rocker arms (and springs - intake shafts only) onto the shafts, making sure they are reinstalled in their original locations.

14   On the intake rocker arm shafts, make sure that the springs are installed on the shaft in the correct locations **(see illustration)**.

15   On the right (rear) cylinder head, install the rocker arm assemblies with the flat at the end of each rocker arm shaft located at the timing belt end of the engine and positioned toward their respective valves.

16   On the left (front) cylinder head, install the rocker arm assemblies with the flat at the end of each rocker arm shaft located at the transaxle end of the engine and positioned toward their respective valves.

11.5 On the left (front) cylinder head, remove the thrust cover and carefully withdraw the camshaft

17   Tighten the rocker arm shaft bolts in sequence shown **(see illustration)** in three steps to the torque listed in this Chapter's Specifications.

18   The remaining installation steps are the reverse of removal. Run the engine and check for oil leaks and proper operation.

19   When re-starting the engine after replacing the rocker arm/lash adjusters, the adjusters will normally make "tapping" noises due to air in the lubrication system. To bleed air from the lash adjusters, start the engine and allow it to reach operating temperature, slowly raise the speed of the engine from idle to 3,000 rpm and back to idle over a one minute period. If, after several attempts, the adjuster(s) do not become silent, replace the defective rocker arm/lash adjuster assembly.

11   Camshafts - removal, inspection and installation

Note: *The camshaft(s) cannot be removed with the cylinder head(s) installed on the engine.*

Removal

Refer to illustration 11.5

1   Remove the rocker arm shaft assemblies (see Section 10).

2   If you are removing the camshaft from the rear cylinder head, remove the distributor (see Chapter 5).

3   Remove the cylinder head (see Section 13).

4   On the right cylinder head, carefully withdraw the camshaft from the distributor opening in the rear of the cylinder head. **Caution:** *Do not damage the camshaft lobes or bearing journals during removal.* **Note:** *If you are removing both camshafts, identify each one as it is removed from the cylinder head so that it may be installed back in its original location.*

5   On the left (front) cylinder head, remove the thrust case from the rear of the cylinder head and withdraw the camshaft **(see illustration)**. **Caution:** *Do not damage the camshaft*

11.10 Check the camshaft lobes for wear with a micrometer

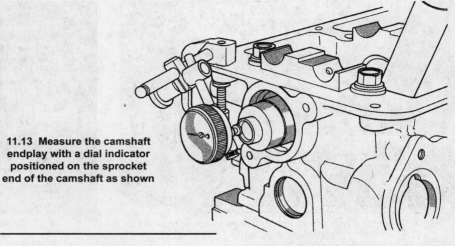

11.13 Measure the camshaft endplay with a dial indicator positioned on the sprocket end of the camshaft as shown

lobes or bearing journals during removal.
6   Remove the camshaft seal(s) from the cylinder head(s) (see Section 9).

Inspection

Refer to illustration 11.10
7   Using a suitable scraper, remove all traces of gasket material from all gasket surfaces. **Caution:** *When removing gasket material from any surface, especially aluminum, be very careful not to scratch or gouge the gasket surface. Any damage to the surface may a leak after reassembly. Gasket removal solvents are available from auto parts stores and may prove helpful.*
8   Thoroughly clean the camshaft(s) with a rag soaked in lacquer thinner or acetone. Visually inspect the camshaft(s) for wear and/or damage to the lobe surfaces, bearing journals and seal contact surfaces. Visually inspect the camshaft bearing surfaces in the cylinder head(s) for scoring and other damage. Cylinder head replacement may be necessary if the camshaft bearing surfaces in the head are damaged or excessively worn.
9   Replace any component that fails the above inspections.
10   Using a micrometer, check the camshaft lobes for excessive wear by measuring the center of the lobe (the area the rocker arm roller rides on) and comparing it with the edges of the lobes (the area the rocker arm roller does not ride on) **(see illustration)**. If any wear is indicated, check the corresponding rocker arm, replace the camshaft and rocker arms if necessary.

Camshaft endplay measurement

Refer to illustration 11.13
11   Lubricate the camshaft(s) and cylinder head bearing journals with clean engine oil.
12   Carefully insert the camshaft into the cylinder head and install the thrust case or distributor as applicable. Tighten the bolts to the torque listed in this Chapter's Specifications.
13   Install a dial indicator set up on the cylinder head and place the indicator tip on the camshaft at the sprocket end **(see illustration)**.

14   Using a screwdriver, carefully pry the camshaft to the rear of the cylinder head until it stops. Zero the dial indicator and pry the camshaft forward. The amount of indicator travel is the camshaft endplay. Compare the endplay measurement with the tolerance listed in this Chapter's Specifications. If the endplay is excessive, check the camshaft and cylinder head thrust bearing surfaces for wear and replace components as necessary.

Installation

Refer to illustration 11.15
15   Very carefully clean the camshaft and bearing journals. Liberally coat the bearing journals, lobes and thrust bearing surfaces of the camshaft with engine assembly lube or engine oil **(see illustration)**.
16   Carefully insert the camshaft into the cylinder head. On the left side cylinder head, install the thrust case, using a new O-ring, and tighten the bolts to the torque listed in this Chapter's Specifications.
17   Install a new camshaft oil seal in the cylinder head (see Section 9).
18   Inspect the cylinder head bolts and install the cylinder head(s) (see Section 13). Torque the cylinder head bolts as described in Section 12.
19   If removed, install the distributor using a new O-ring (see Chapter 5). Tighten the mounting nuts to the torque listed in the Chapter 5 Specifications.
20   The remaining installation steps are the reverse of removal. Start the engine and check for leaks and proper operation.

12   Valve springs, retainers and seals - replacement

Refer to illustrations 12.5, 12.7, 12.8, 12.13 and 12.15
Note: *Broken valve springs and defective valve stem seals can be replaced without removing the cylinder heads. Two special tools and a compressed air source are normally required to perform this operation, so*

11.15 Prior to installing the camshaft, lubricate the bearing journals, thrust surfaces and lobes with engine assembly lube or clean engine oil

read through this Section carefully and rent or buy the tools before beginning the job.
1   Remove the appropriate valve cover (see Section 4).
2   Remove the rocker arm assemblies (see Section 10).
3   Remove the spark plugs from that head (see Chapter 1).
4   Turn the crankshaft until the piston in the affected cylinder is at Top Dead Center on the compression stroke (see Section 3). If you're replacing all of the valve stem seals, begin with cylinder number one and work on the valves for one cylinder at a time. Move from cylinder-to-cylinder following the firing order sequence (see this Chapter's Specifications).
5   Thread an adapter into the spark plug hole **(see illustration)** and connect an air hose from a compressed air source to it. Most auto parts stores can supply the air hose adapter. **Note:** *Many cylinder compression gauges utilize a screw-in fitting that may work with your air hose quick-disconnect fitting.*
6   Apply compressed air to the cylinder. **Warning:** *The piston may be forced down by compressed air, causing the crankshaft to turn suddenly. If the wrench used when positioning*

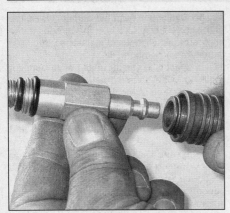

12.5 This is what an air hose adapter that threads into the spark plug hole looks like; hose adapters are readily available from auto parts stores

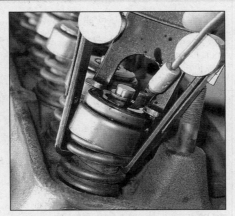

12.7 Use a small magnet (shown) or needle-nose pliers to remove the valve spring keepers - be careful not to drop them down into the engine!

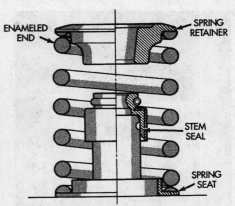

12.8 Cut-away view of the valve seal and spring components

the number one piston at TDC is still attached to the crankshaft pulley bolt, it could cause damage or injury when the crankshaft moves.

7   Stuff clean shop rags into the cylinder head holes above and below the valves to prevent parts and tools from falling into the engine, then use a valve spring compressor tool to compress the spring. Remove the keepers with small needle-nose pliers or a magnet **(see illustration)**.

8   Remove the spring retainer and valve spring. Next, using pliers remove the valve guide seal and then lift off spring seat **(see illustration)**. **Caution:** *If air pressure fails to hold the valve in the closed position during this operation, the valve face and/or seat is probably damaged. If so, the cylinder head will have to be removed for additional repair operations.*

9   Wrap a rubber band or tape around the top of the valve stem so the valve won't fall into the combustion chamber, then release the air pressure.

10   Inspect the valve stem for damage. Rotate the valve in the guide and check the end for eccentric movement, which would

indicate that the valve is bent.

11   Move the valve up-and-down in the guide and make sure it doesn't bind. If the valve stem binds, either the valve is bent or the guide is damaged. In either case, the head will have to be removed for repair.

12   Pull up on the valve stem to close the valve, reapply air pressure to the cylinder to retain the valve in the closed position, then remove the tape or rubber band from the valve stem.

13   Install the valve spring seat. Lubricate the valve stem with clean engine oil and place the new valve guide seal. Tap it into place with deep socket **(see illustration)**.

14   Install the spring in position over the valve.

15   Install the valve spring retainer. Compress the valve spring and carefully position the keepers in the groove. Apply a small dab of grease to the inside of each keeper to hold it in place if necessary **(see illustration)**.

16   Remove the pressure from the spring tool and make sure the keepers are seated.

17   Disconnect the air hose and remove the adapter from the spark plug hole. Repeat the

procedure for any other defective valves.

18   Install the rocker arm assemblies (see Section 10).

19   Install the spark plug and connect the wire(s).

20   Install the valve cover (see Section 4).

21   Start and run the engine, then check for oil leaks and unusual sounds coming from the valve cover area.

13   Cylinder head - removal and installation

Caution: *Allow the engine to cool completely before beginning this procedure.*

Removal

Refer to illustrations 13.11, 13.18, 13.19a and 13.19b

1   Disconnect the cable from the negative battery terminal or the remote ground terminal (see Chapter 5).

2   Position the number one piston at Top Dead Center (see Section 3).

3   Remove the upper and lower intake manifolds (see Section 5).

4   Drain the cooling system, remove the spark plugs and spark plug wires (see Chapter 1). **Note:** *Leave the plug wires attached to the distributor cap.*

5   If you are removing the rear cylinder head, remove the distributor (see Chapter 5).

6   Remove the thermostat housing (see Chapter 3).

7   Remove rocker arm shaft assemblies (see Section 10).

8   If you are removing the right (rear) cylinder head, remove the bolts securing the power steering reservoir and hoses to the cylinder head and position them out of the way (see Chapter 10).

9   Disconnect the power steering pump bracket from the engine (see Chapter 10).

10   Remove the exhaust manifold(s) (see Section 6).

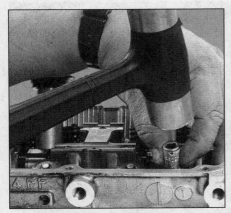

12.13 Gently tap the new seal onto the valve guide with a hammer and deep socket

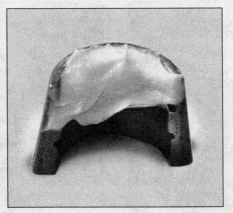

12.15 Apply a small dab of grease to each keeper before installation to hold it in place on the valve stem until the spring is released

13.11 EGR solenoid/transducer assembly (upper arrow) and EGR valve (lower arrow) - remove the EGR solenoid/transducer and engine lifting bracket as an assembly

11   If you are removing the left (front) cylinder head, remove the EGR solenoid/transducer assembly and EGR valve from the rear of the cylinder head **(see illustration)**.

12   Remove the timing belt (see Section 7).

13   Remove camshaft sprocket(s) (see Section 9).

14   Clearly label and disconnect any hoses, lines, brackets or electrical connections that may interfere with cylinder head removal.

15   Loosen the cylinder head bolts, 1/4-turn at a time, in the *reverse* order of the tightening sequence **(see illustration 13.24)** until they can be removed by hand.

16   Carefully lift the cylinder head straight up and place it on wood blocks to prevent damage to the sealing surfaces. If the head sticks to the engine block, dislodge it by placing a wood block against the head casting and tapping the wood with a hammer or by prying the head with a prybar placed carefully on a casting protrusion. **Note:** *If further disassembly of the cylinder head is required, refer to Part C of this Chapter.*

17   Remove all traces of old gasket material from the block and head. Special gasket removal solvents that soften gaskets and make removal much easier are available at auto parts stores. **Caution:** *The cylinder head is aluminum, be very careful not to gouge the sealing surfaces.* When working on the block, place clean shop rags into the cylinders to help keep out debris. Use a vacuum to remove any contamination from the engine. Use a tap of the correct size to chase the threads in the engine block. Clean and inspect all threaded fasteners for damage.

18   Inspect the cylinder head bolt threads for "necking," where the diameter of threads narrow due to bolt stretching **(see illustration)**. If any cylinder head bolt exhibits damage or necking, it must be replaced.

19   Using a precision straightedge and feeler gauge, check all gasket surfaces for warpage **(see illustrations)**. If the warpage on any surface exceeds the limits listed in this Chapter's Specifications, the discrepant component must be replaced or resurfaced by an automotive machine shop.

20   Refer to Part C of this Chapter for cleaning and inspection of the cylinder head.

Installation

Refer to illustrations 13.22, 13.23 and 13.24

21   Install the camshaft(s) if removed (see Section 11).

22   Place a new gasket on the engine block **(see illustration)**. Use no sealer unless indicated by the gasket manufacturer. Note any directions printed on the gasket such as "Front" or "This side up." Place the cylinder

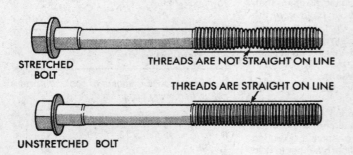

13.18 Place a precision straightedge along the cylinder head bolt thread profile as shown, if any part of the bolt threads are not on the straightedge, the bolt is stretched and must be replaced

13.19a Checking the cylinder head-to-engine block gasket surface for warpage

13.19b Checking the engine block head gasket surface for warpage

13.22 When installing the head gasket onto the block, make sure all passages in the block align with the holes in the gasket

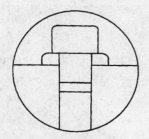

13.23 Install the head bolt washers as shown

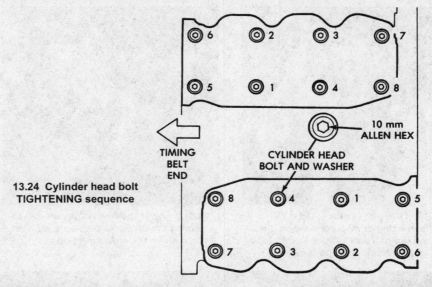

13.24 Cylinder head bolt TIGHTENING sequence

TIMING BELT END

10 mm ALLEN HEX

CYLINDER HEAD BOLT AND WASHER

head(s) in position on the engine block.

23 Install the washers onto the cylinder head bolts as shown (see illustration). Apply clean engine oil to the cylinder head bolt threads and install them into the cylinder head.

24 Tighten the cylinder head bolts in the sequence shown (see illustration) progressing in three stages to the torque listed in this Chapter's Specifications.

25 The remaining installation steps are the reverse of removal.

26 Refill the cooling system and check all fluid levels (see Chapter 1 if necessary).

27 Start the engine and let it run until normal operating temperature is reached. Check for leaks and proper operation.

14 Oil pan - removal and installation

Removal

Refer to illustrations 14.5, 14.7a, 14.7b, 14.8, 14.10, 14.11a, 14.11b, 14.12, 14.13a and 14.13b

1 Disconnect the cable from the negative battery terminal or the remote ground terminal (see Chapter 5).

2 Raise the vehicle and support it securely on jackstands.

3 Remove the accessory drivebelt splash shield (see Chapter 1).

4 Drain the engine oil (see Chapter 1).

14.5 Engine oil dipstick tube mounting bolt (arrow) - exhaust manifold heat shield removed for clarity

5 Remove the dipstick tube (see illustration).

6 Remove the starter motor (see Chapter 5).

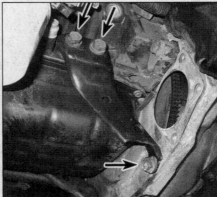

14.7a To detach the front engine-to-transmission support bracket, remove these bolts (arrows)

7 Remove the engine-to-transmission support brackets (see illustrations).

8 Remove the flywheel/driveplate inspection cover (see illustration).

14.7b To detach the rear engine-to-transmission support bracket, remove these bolts (arrows)

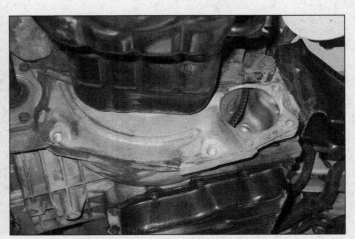

14.8 After removing the starter motor and the engine-to-transmission support brackets, remove the flywheel/driveplate inspection cover

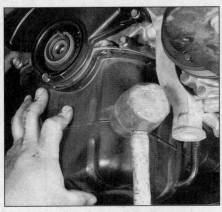

14.10 If the pan is stuck, tap it with a soft-face hammer or place a wood block against the pan and tap the wood block with a hammer to jar it loose

14.11a Lower the front of the oil pan to access the oil pump pick-up tube and remove the mounting bolts . . .

14.11b . . . then remove the oil pump pick up tube from the pump body

14.12 With the oil pump pick up tube removed, the oil pan can then be withdrawn over the engine support module (arrow)

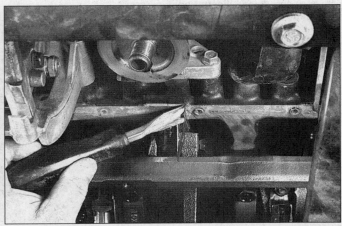

14.13a Thoroughly clean the oil pan and engine block gasket surfaces with a scraper to remove all traces of old gasket material

9   On 2.5L engines, remove the exhaust manifold cross-under pipe (see Section 6). On 3.0L engines, remove the front exhaust pipe/catalytic converter assembly (see Chapter 4).

10   Remove the mounting bolts and separate the oil pan from the engine block enough to facilitate oil pump pickup tube removal. If the pan is stuck, tap it with a soft-face hammer **(see illustration)** or place a wood block against the pan and tap the wood block with a hammer. **Caution:** *If you're wedging something between the oil pan and the engine block to separate them, be extremely careful not to gouge or nick the gasket surface of either part; an oil leak could result.*

11   Remove the oil pump pickup tube and screen assembly **(see illustrations)**.

12   Remove the oil pan from the vehicle **(see illustration)**.

13   Thoroughly clean all gasket sealing surfaces. Use a scraper to remove all traces of old gasket material **(see illustrations)**. Gasket removal solvents are available at auto parts stores and may prove helpful. Check the oil

pan sealing surface for distortion. Straighten or replace as necessary. After cleaning and straightening (if necessary), wipe the gasket surfaces of the pan and block clean with a rag soaked in lacquer thinner or acetone.

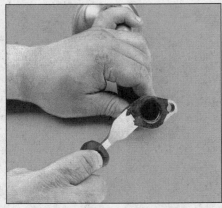

14.13b Remove the old gasket from the oil pump pick up tube

Installation

Refer to illustration 13.14

14   Apply a 1/8-inch bead of RTV sealant to the oil pan as shown **(see illustration)**. Also

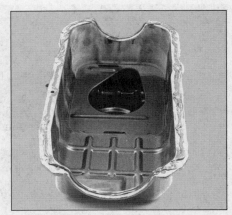

14.14 Apply a 1/8-inch bead of RTV sealant to the oil pan sealing surface as shown - stay on the inside of the bolt holes

15.7 Remove the oil pump assembly mounting bolts (arrows) and detach it from the engine - bolt (A) also secures the air conditioning compressor bracket (if equipped)

15.8 The oil filter passage O-ring seals (arrows) may remained attached to the engine block

apply a light coating of RTV sealant to the underside of the oil pan bolt heads.

15   Place the oil pan into position under the engine block and install the oil pump pick-up tube. Tighten the bolts to the torque listed in this Chapter's Specifications.

16   Place the oil pan against the engine block and install the bolts. Working from the center and proceeding outward in a criss-cross pattern, tighten the oil pan bolts to the torque listed in this Chapter's Specifications.

17   The remaining installation steps are the reverse of removal.

18   Lower the vehicle and fill the crankcase with the proper quantity and grade of engine oil (see *Recommended lubricants and fluids* at the beginning of Chapter 1) and run the engine, checking for leaks. Road test the vehicle and check for leaks again.

15   Oil pump - removal, inspection and installation

Removal

Refer to illustrations 15.7, 15.8, 15.9 and 15.10

1   Disconnect the cable from the negative battery terminal or the remote ground terminal (see Chapter 5).

2   Raise the vehicle and support it securely on jackstands.

3   Remove the drivebelts (see Chapter 1).

4   Remove the timing belt (see Section 7) and crankshaft sprocket and Woodruff key (see Section 8).

5   Remove the oil pan (see Section 14).

6   If equipped, remove the air conditioning compressor bracket from the engine and position it out of the way.

7   Remove the bolts and detach the oil pump assembly from the engine (see illustration). Caution: *If the pump doesn't come off by hand, tap it gently with a soft-faced hammer or pry on a casting boss.*

8   Remove the oil filter passage O-ring seals and discard them. They may stick to the engine block as shown (see illustration) or remain in the oil pump housing.

9   Remove the oil pump rotor cover (see illustration).

10   New rotors are manufactured with arrows on them which are aligned at installation. If both arrows are not clearly visible (see illustration), use a permanent marker to match-mark the rotors so they can be installed back in their original position. Remove the inner and outer rotor from the body. Caution: *Be very careful with these components. Close tolerances are critical in creating the correct oil pressure. Any nicks or other damage will require replacement of the complete pump assembly.*

15.9 Remove the rotor cover mounting screws (arrows)

15.10 The alignment mark has worn off the inner rotor on this oil pump; in this case, use a permanent marker to match-mark the rotors for reinstallation; to remove the oil pressure relief spring, remove this bolt (A)

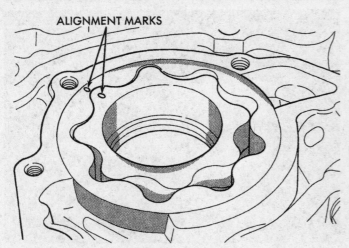

ALIGNMENT MARKS

15.16a Install the rotors into the oil pump body with the match marks aligned

15.16b Use a feeler gauge to measure the inner rotor-to-outer rotor lobe clearance

11   Using a hammer and drift, carefully and evenly drive the crankshaft front seal from the oil pump housing and discard it.

12   Disassemble the oil pressure relief valve assembly, taking note of the way the relief valve piston is installed. Unscrew the cap bolt **(see illustration 15.10)** and then remove the bolt, washer, spring and relief valve.

13   Thoroughly clean all gasket sealing surfaces. Use a scraper to remove all traces of old gasket material. Gasket removal solvents are available at auto parts stores and may prove helpful. Check the oil pan sealing surface for distortion. Straighten or replace as necessary. After removing the residual gasket material, wipe the gasket surfaces of the oil pan and block clean with a rag soaked in lacquer thinner or acetone.

Inspection
Refer to illustrations 15.16a, 15.16b, 15.16c, and 15.16d

14   Clean all oil pump components with solvent and inspect them for excessive wear and/or damage. Replace as required. **Note:**

If either rotor is damaged, they must be replaced as a set.

15   Inspect the oil pressure relief valve piston sliding surface and valve spring for damage. **Note:** *If either the spring or the valve is damaged, they must be replaced as a set.*

16   Install the rotors into the pump housing with the match-marks aligned **(see illustration)**. Check the oil pump rotor clearances using a precision straightedge and feeler gauges **(see illustrations)**. Compare the results to the tolerances listed in this Chapter's Specifications. Replace both rotors if any clearance is out of tolerance.

Installation
Refer to illustration 15.19

17   Lubricate the relief valve piston, piston bore and spring with clean engine oil. Install the relief valve piston into the bore maintaining original orientation followed by the spring and cap bolt. Tighten the cap bolt to the torque listed in this Chapter's Specifications. **Note:** *If the relief valve piston is installed incorrectly,*

serious engine damage could occur.

18   Lubricate the oil pump rotor recess in the housing and the inner and outer rotors with clean engine oil. Install the rotors into the pump housing with the match-marks aligned **(see illustration 15.16a)**. Next, fill the rotor cavity with clean engine oil and install the cover. Tighten the cover screws to the torque listed in this Chapter's Specifications.

19   Install new O-ring seals in the oil pump passages located on the pump body **(see illustration)**. If necessary, apply a light coating of grease on the O-rings to hold them in place.

20   Install the new crankshaft front seal into the oil pump housing (see Section 8).

21   Apply a 1/8 inch bead of RTV sealant to the oil pump body sealing surface, and position the pump assembly on the block aligning the inner rotor and crankshaft drive flats. Install the mounting bolts.

22   If equipped, install the air conditioning bracket onto the engine (one bolt secures both the air conditioning bracket and the oil pump housing).

15.16c Measuring the outer rotor-to-pump body clearance

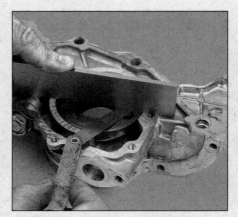

15.16d Place a precision straightedge over the rotors and measure the clearance between the rotors and the straightedge to determine the rotor-to-cover clearance

15.19 Install new O-ring seals on the oil filter passages (arrows)

16.5 Remove the flywheel/driveplate from the crankshaft

17.3 Carefully pry the crankshaft seal out of the bore - DO NOT nick or scratch the crankshaft or seal bore

23   Tighten the oil pump attaching bolts (see illustration 15.7) to the torque listed in this Chapter's Specifications.
24   Install the Woodruff key, crankshaft timing belt sprocket (see Section 8) and timing belt (see Section 7).
25   Install the oil pan (see Section 14).
26   If applicable, install a new oil filter (see Chapter 1).
27   The remaining installation steps are the reverse of removal.
28   Lower the vehicle and fill the crankcase with the proper quantity and grade of oil (see *Recommended lubricants and fluids* Section in Chapter 1).
29   Connect the negative battery cable to the ground stud.
30   After the sealant has cured per the manufacturer's directions, start the engine and check for leaks.

16   Driveplate - removal and installation

Removal

Refer to illustration 16.5
1   Raise the vehicle and support it securely on jackstands.
2   Remove the transaxle assembly (see Chapter 7).
3   To ensure correct alignment during reinstallation, match-mark the backing plate and driveplate to the crankshaft before removal.
4   Remove the bolts securing the driveplate to the crankshaft. A tool is available a most auto parts stores to hold the driveplate while loosening the bolts, if the tool is not available, wedge a screwdriver in the ring gear teeth to jam the driveplate.
5   Remove the driveplate from the crankshaft (see illustration).
6   Clean the driveplate to remove any grease and oil. Inspect it for cracks, distortion and missing or excessively worn ring gear teeth. Replace if necessary.

7   Clean and inspect the mating surfaces of the driveplate and the crankshaft. Check the crankshaft rear main seal for leakage; if leakage is evident replace it before reinstalling the driveplate (see Section 17).

Installation
8   Position the driveplate and backing plate against the crankshaft. Align the previously applied match marks. Before installing the bolts, apply thread locking compound to the threads.
9   Hold the driveplate with the special holding tool, or wedge a screwdriver in the ring gear teeth to keep the driveplate from turning as you tighten the bolts to the torque listed in this Chapter's Specifications.
10   The remaining installation steps are the reverse of removal.

17   Rear main oil seal - replacement

Refer to illustrations 17.3, 17.6 and 17.12
1   The crankshaft rear main oil seal is pressed into a retainer and bolted to the rear of the engine block.
2   Remove the driveplate (see Section 16).
3   The crankshaft rear main oil seal can be renewed without removing the oil pan or seal retainer. However, this method is NOT recommended because the lip of the seal is quite stiff and it's possible to cock the seal in the retainer bore or damage it during installation. If you want to take the chance, carefully and evenly pry out the old seal using a 3/16 flat blade screwdriver - do not to damage the crankshaft sealing surface (see illustration). Apply a light coating of clean engine oil to the crankshaft seal journal and the lip of the new seal then carefully tap the new seal into place using a hammer and socket. The seal lip is stiff, so carefully work it onto the seal journal of the crankshaft with a smooth object like the rounded end of a socket extension as you tap the seal into place (see illustration 17.12).

Don't force it or you may damage the seal.
4   The following method is recommended and requires removal of the oil pan (see Section 14).
5   Remove the mounting bolts from the crankshaft rear seal retainer and separate the retainer from the engine block.
6   Using a hammer and drift, carefully drive the old seal out of the retainer and discard it (see illustration).
7   Thoroughly clean all gasket sealing surfaces. Use a scraper to remove all traces of old gasket material. Gasket removal solvents are available at auto parts stores and may prove helpful. Check the oil pan sealing surface for distortion. Straighten or replace as necessary. After removing the residual gasket material, wipe the gasket surfaces clean using a rag soaked in lacquer thinner or acetone.
8   Thoroughly clean and inspect the seal bore and sealing surface on the crankshaft. Minor imperfections can be removed with fine emery cloth. If there is a groove worn in the crankshaft sealing surface (from contact with the seal), installing a new seal will probably not stop the leak.
9   Install the new seal into the retainer

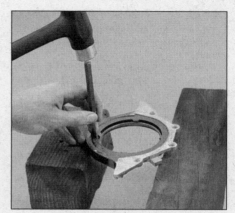

17.6 With the seal retainer supported on wood blocks, use a hammer and drift to drive the seal out of the retainer

17.12 Using a rounded object like a socket extension, carefully work the seal onto the crankshaft

using a socket (or block of wood) and a hammer. Drive it in until it's flush with the retainer.

10   Apply a 1/8 inch bead of RTV sealant to the retainer gasket sealing surface.

11   Lubricate the lip of the new seal and the crankshaft sealing surface with a light coat of clean engine oil.

12   Place the seal retainer in position on the engine block and install the mounting bolts. The seal lip is stiff, so carefully work it onto the seal journal of the crankshaft with a smooth object like the rounded end of a socket extension as you tap the seal into place **(see illustration)**. Don't force it or you may damage the seal. Tighten the bolts to the torque listed in this Chapter's Specifications.

13   Install the oil pan (see Section 14).

14   The remaining installation steps are the reverse of removal.

18   Engine mounts - check and replacement

1   Engine mounts seldom require attention, but broken or deteriorated mounts should be replaced immediately or the added strain placed on the driveline components may cause damage or wear.

Check

2   During the check, the engine must be raised slightly to relieve the weight from the mounts.

3   Raise the vehicle and support it securely on jackstands, then position a jack under the engine oil pan. Place a large wood block between the jack head and the oil pan to prevent oil pan damage, then carefully raise the engine just enough to take the weight off the mounts. **Warning:** *DO NOT place any part of your body under the engine when it's supported only by a jack!*

4   Inspect the mounts to see if the rubber is cracked, hardened or separated from the metal backing. Sometimes the rubber will split right down the center.

5   Check for relative movement between the mount plates and the engine or frame

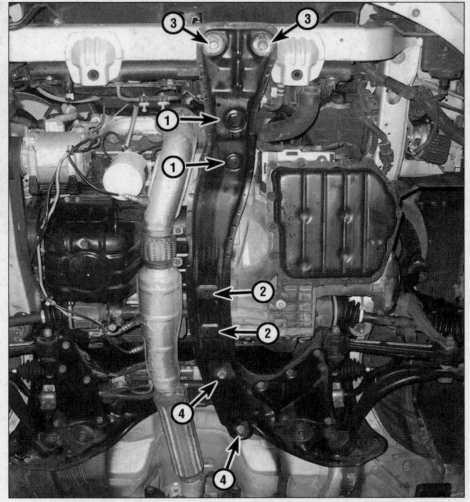

18.9a To detach the center member, remove the bolts (1) from the front engine mount bracket, remove the bolts (2) from the rear engine mount bracket, remove the front bolts (3) that attach the center member to the lower radiator crossmember and then remove the bolts (4) that attach the center member to the front suspension crossmember (coupe models)

(use a large screwdriver or pry bar to attempt to move the mounts). If movement is noted, lower the engine and tighten the mount fasteners.

6   Rubber preservative may be applied to the mounts to slow deterioration.

Replacement

Refer to illustrations 18.9a, 18.9b, 18.9c, 18.9d, 18.9e, 18.10a, 18.10b, 18.10c, 18.10d, 18.10e and 18.10f

7   Disconnect the cable from the negative battery terminal or the remote ground terminal (see Chapter 5).

8   Then raise the vehicle and support it securely on jackstands.

9   On coupe models, a center member runs longitudinally underneath the engine between the lower radiator crossmember and the front suspension crossmember **(see illustration)**. It's not necessary to remove this center member to replace either the front or rear engine

mount, but the bolts that attach the front and rear mounts to the center member are located inside holes in the underside of the center member. For some procedures, such as removing the oil pan, you will need to remove the center member. When removing any of the engine mounts - front, rear, left (transaxle) or right engine mount - be sure to place a floor jack under the engine (with a wood block between the jack head and oil pan) and raise the engine slightly to relieve the weight from the mount to be replaced. Remove the fasteners **(see illustrations)** and then detach the mount from the engine or transaxle and then, if you're going to replace the mount, detach it from the vehicle. **Caution:** *Do not disconnect more than one mount at a time, except during engine/transaxle removal.*

10   On 1996 through 1999 convertible models, an "engine support module" **(see illustration)** runs longitudinally under the engine between the lower radiator support and the

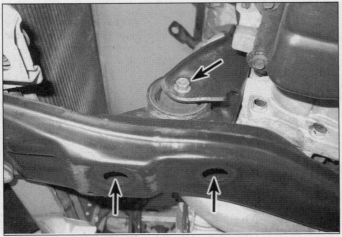

18.9b To disconnect the engine from the front engine mount, remove this through-bolt (upper arrow) and nut (not visible in this photo); to remove the front mount from the crossmember, remove the two bolts (lower arrows) from the underside of the crossmember (coupe models)

18.9c To disconnect the engine from the rear engine mount, remove this through-bolt (1); to remove the rear mount, remove these three bolts (2) (coupe models)

18.9d To disconnect the engine/transaxle assembly from the left engine/transaxle mount, remove the through-bolt and nut (1); to remove the left engine/transaxle mount, remove these three bolts (2) (coupe models)

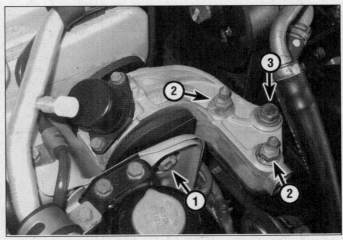

18.9e To disconnect the engine from the right engine mount, remove this through-bolt (1); to remove the right engine mount, remove these two nuts (2) and this bolt (3) (coupe models)

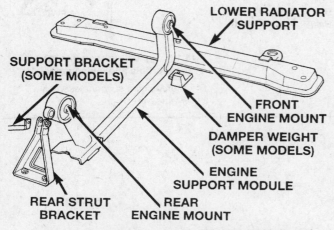

18.10a Engine support module assembly (1996 through 1999 convertible models)

LOWER RADIATOR SUPPORT

SUPPORT BRACKET (SOME MODELS)

FRONT ENGINE MOUNT

DAMPER WEIGHT (SOME MODELS)

ENGINE SUPPORT MODULE

REAR STRUT BRACKET

REAR ENGINE MOUNT

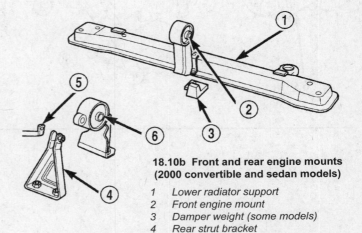

18.10b Front and rear engine mounts (2000 convertible and sedan models)

1   Lower radiator support
2   Front engine mount
3   Damper weight (some models)
4   Rear strut bracket
5   Support bracket (some models)
6   Rear engine mount

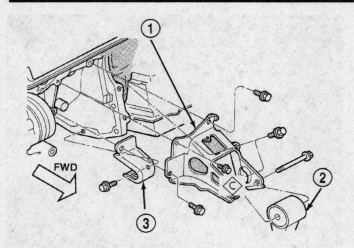

18.10c Typical front engine mount bracket (convertible and sedan models)

1   Front torque bracket
2   Front mount/engine support module
3   Strut

18.10d Typical rear engine mount bracket (convertible and sedan models)

1   Rear torque bracket
2   Engine
3   Transaxle
4   Rear mount/engine support module

rear strut bracket. On these models, the front and rear engine mounts are an integral part of the engine support module. On 2000 convertible and sedan models, there is no support module, but the front and rear mounts **(see illustration)** are similar. When removing any of the engine mounts - front, rear, left (trans-

axle) or right engine mount - be sure to place a floor jack under the engine (with a wood block between the jack head and oil pan) and raise the engine slightly to relieve the weight from the mount to be replaced. Remove the fasteners **(see illustrations)** and then detach the mount from the engine or transaxle and then,

if you're going to replace the mount, detach it from the vehicle. **Caution:** *Do not disconnect more than one mount at a time, except during engine/transaxle removal.*

11   Installation is the reverse of removal. Use thread locking compound on the mount fasteners and be sure to tighten them securely.

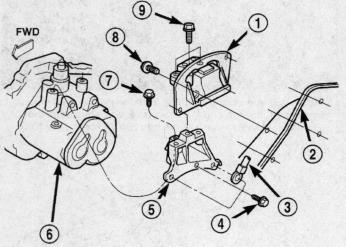

18.10e Typical left engine/transaxle mount (convertible and sedan models)

1   Transaxle support assembly
2   Left frame rail
3   Ground cable
4   Bolt
5   Transaxle bracket
6   Transaxle
7   Bolt
8   Bolt
9   Bolt

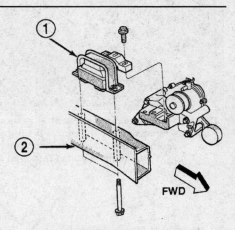

18.10f Typical right engine mount (convertible and sedan models)

1   Right engine support assembly
2   Frame rail

Chapter 2 Part C
2.7L V6 engine

Contents

Specifications

General

Bore	3.386 inches
Stroke	3.091 inches
Displacement	167 cubic inches (2.7 liters)
Cylinder numbers (front to rear)	
Front cylinder bank (radiator side)	2-4-6
Rear cylinder bank (firewall side)	1-3-5
Firing order	1-2-3-4-5-6
Compression ratio	9.67:1

Camshaft

Camshaft bore diameter	0.9469 to 0.9476 inch
Camshaft journal diameter	0.9441 to 0.9449 inch
Camshaft bearing oil clearance	
Standard	0.0020 to 0.0035 inch
Service limit	0.0051 inch
Camshaft endplay	0.0051 to 0.011 inch
Camshaft lobe wear	
Standard	0.001 inch
Service limit	0.010 inch

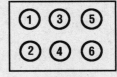

Front

Cylinder identification diagram

Cylinder head/intake and exhaust manifolds

Distortion (for cylinder head-to-block and for intake and exhaust manifold surfaces)

Standard...	Less than 0.002 inch
Service limit..	0.008 inch

Oil pump

Cover warpage limit...	0.001 inch
Inner and outer rotor thickness..	0.3731 to 3741 inch
Outer rotor diameter (minimum)	3.5109 inches
Outer rotor-to-housing clearance (maximum)......................	0.015 inch
Inner rotor-to-outer rotor lobe clearance............................	0.008 inch
Oil pump housing-to-rotor side clearance............................	0.003 inch

Torque specifications   Ft-lbs (unless otherwise indicated)

Note: *One foot pound (ft-lb) of torque is equivalent to 12 inch-pounds (in-lbs) of torque. Torque values below approximately 15 ft-lbs are expressed in inch-pounds, since most foot-pound torque wrenches are not accurate at these smaller values.*

Camshaft sprocket bolts...	21
Camshaft bearing cap bolts..	105 in-lbs
Crankshaft pulley bolt...	125
Cylinder head bolts (in sequence - see illustration 11.26)	
Step 1 (tighten bolts 1 through 8)......................................	35
Step 2 (tighten bolts 1 through 8)......................................	50
Step 3 (tighten bolts 1 through 8)......................................	50
Step 4 (tighten bolts 1 through 8)......................................	Tighten an additional 90-degrees (1/4-turn)
Step 5 (tighten bolts 9 through 11).....................................	21
Exhaust manifold	
Exhaust manifold bolts..	16.5
Exhaust manifold heat shield bolts....................................	105 in-lbs
Exhaust manifold-to-catalytic converter V-band clamp	100 in-lbs
Flywheel/driveplate bolts	70 to 75
Intake manifold bolts (upper and lower)	105 in-lbs
Oil pan	
Oil pan bolts	21
Oil pan nuts	105 in-lbs
Oil pump	
Oil pick-up tube mounting bolts...	21
Oil pump mounting bolts	21
Oil pump cover bolts	105 in-lbs
Rear main oil seal retainer bolts	105 in-lbs
Primary timing chain	
Timing chain cover bolts	
M6 bolts	105 in-lbs
M10 bolts	40
Timing chain tensioner retaining plate bolts.......................	105 in-lbs
Timing chain guide access plugs	15
Timing chain guide bolts	21
Timing chain tensioner arm pivot bolt	21
Secondary timing chain (camshaft timing chain) tensioner bolts............	105 in-lbs
Transaxle-to-oil pan structural collar bolts.............................	40
Valve cover bolts	105 in-lbs

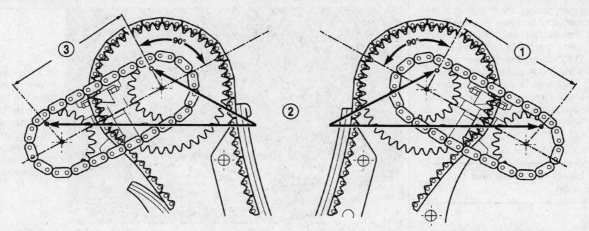

3.6 To bring the No. 1 piston to TDC, turn the crankshaft clockwise until the camshaft timing marks are at a 90-degree angle to the gasket mating surface of the cylinder heads

1   *12 pins between the timing marks of the camshaft sprockets on the front cylinder head*

2   *Camshaft timing marks*

3   *12 pins between the timing marks of the camshaft sprockets on the rear cylinder head*

1   General information

This Part of Chapter 2 is devoted to in-vehicle repair procedures for the 2.7L V6 engine. This engine has an aluminum block with six cylinders arranged in a "V" shape at a 60-degree angle between the two banks. The double-overhead-camshaft (DOHC) aluminum cylinder heads are equipped with replaceable valve guides and seats. Stamped steel rocker arms with an integral roller bearing actuate the valves.

All information concerning engine removal and installation and engine block and cylinder head overhaul information is in Part D of this Chapter.

The following repair procedures are based on the assumption that the engine is installed in the vehicle. If the engine has been removed from the vehicle and mounted on a stand, many of the steps outlined in this Part of Chapter 2 will not apply.

The Specifications included in this Part of Chapter 2 apply only to the procedures contained in this Part.

2   Repair operations possible with the engine in the vehicle

Many major repair operations can be accomplished without removing the engine from the vehicle.

Clean the engine compartment and the exterior of the engine with some type of degreaser before any work is done. It will make the job easier and help keep dirt out of the internal areas of the engine.

Depending on the components involved, it may be helpful to remove the hood to improve access to the engine as repairs are performed (refer to Chapter 11, if necessary). Cover the fenders to prevent damage to the paint. Special pads are available, but an old bedspread or blanket will also work.

If vacuum, exhaust, oil or coolant leaks develop, indicating a need for gasket or seal replacement, the repairs can generally be made with the engine in the vehicle. The intake and exhaust manifold gaskets, oil pan gasket, crankshaft oil seals and cylinder head gaskets are all accessible with the engine in place.

Exterior engine components, such as the intake and exhaust manifolds, the oil pan, the oil pump, the water pump (see Chapter 3), the starter motor, the alternator and the fuel system components (see Chapter 4) can be removed for repair with the engine in place.

Since the cylinder heads can be removed without pulling the engine, valve component servicing can also be accomplished with the engine in the vehicle. Replacement of the camshafts, timing chains and sprockets are also possible with the engine in the vehicle.

In extreme cases caused by a lack of necessary equipment, repair or replacement of piston rings, pistons, connecting rods and rod bearings is possible with the engine in the vehicle. However, this practice is not recommended because of the cleaning and preparation work that must be done to the components involved.

3   Top Dead Center (TDC) for number one piston - locating

Refer to illustration 3.6

1   Top Dead Center (TDC) is the highest point in the cylinder that each piston reaches as it travels up the cylinder bore. Each piston reaches TDC on the compression stroke and again on the exhaust stroke, but TDC generally refers to piston position on the compression stroke.

2   Positioning the piston(s) at TDC is an essential part of many procedures such as valve timing, camshaft and timing chain/sprocket removal.

3   Before beginning this procedure, be sure to place the transaxle in Neutral and apply the parking brake or block the rear wheels. Also, disable the ignition system by disconnecting the primary electrical connectors at the ignition coil packs and remove the spark plugs (see Chapter 1).

4   In order to bring any piston to TDC, the crankshaft must be turned using one of the methods outlined below. When looking at the front of the engine, normal crankshaft rotation is clockwise.

a) *The preferred method is to turn the crankshaft with a socket and ratchet attached to the bolt threaded into the front of the crankshaft. Apply pressure on the bolt in a clockwise direction only. Never turn the bolt counterclockwise.*

b) *A remote starter switch, which may save some time, can also be used. Follow the instructions included with the switch. Once the piston is close to TDC, use a socket and ratchet as described in the previous paragraph.*

c) *If an assistant is available to turn the ignition switch to the Start position in short bursts, you can get the piston close to TDC without a remote starter switch. Make sure your assistant is out of the vehicle, away from the ignition switch, then use a socket and ratchet as described in Paragraph (a) to complete the procedure.*

5   Remove the valve covers (see Section 4).

6   Rotate the crankshaft using one of the methods described above until the timing marks on the intake camshaft sprockets are at a 90-degree angle from the cylinder head cover sealing surfaces of both cylinder heads **(see illustration)**. The number one piston should now be at TDC on the exhaust stroke.

7   If the primary timing chain or one of the exhaust cam drive chains has recently been replaced, or removed and installed, there's an easy way to *verify* that the number one piston is in fact at TDC. Count the number of chain pins between the timing marks **(see illustration 3.6)**. If there are 12 pins, the timing is correct. If there are more or less than 12 pins between the timing marks, the valves are not correctly timed, and they must be re-timed (see Section 7).

4   Valve cover - removal and installation

Removal

Refer to illustrations 4.2, 4.3, 4.5, 4.7 and 4.8

1   Disconnect the cable from the remote ground terminal (see Chapter 5).
2   The wiring harness is attached to small pins on top of the front valve cover bolts by small plastic clips **(see illustration)**. To detach the harness, simply pull off the harness clips.
3   Disconnect the breather hose from the valve cover **(front breather hose, see illustration 4.2; rear breather hose, see accompanying illustration)**.
4   Remove the upper intake manifold (see Section 9) and then cover the lower intake manifold with rags to keep out dirt.
5   Disconnect the ground harness from the valve cover stud **(see illustration)**.
6   Remove the ignition coils from the spark plugs (see Chapter 5).
7   Disconnect the electrical connector from the ignition coil capacitor **(see illustration)**. (The capacitor is a radio noise-suppression device.)
8   Remove the valve cover bolts and nuts **(see illustration)**.
9   Detach the valve cover. **Note:** *If the cover sticks to the cylinder head, use a block of wood and a hammer to dislodge it. If the cover still won't come loose, pry on it carefully, but don't distort the sealing flange.*

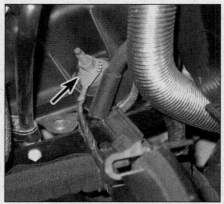

4.2 To detach the wiring harness from the front valve cover, pull off these small harness clips (upper arrows); then disconnect the breather hose (lower arrow)

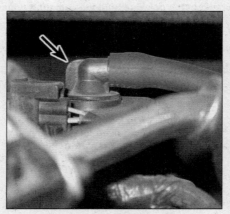

4.3 If you're removing the rear valve cover, disconnect the breather hose (arrow) from the cover

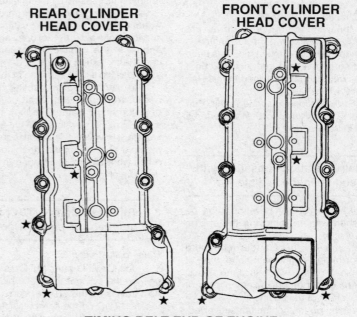

4.5 Disconnect the ground harness (arrow) from the valve cover stud (rear valve cover ground harness shown)

REAR CYLINDER HEAD COVER   **FRONT CYLINDER HEAD COVER**

TIMING BELT END OF ENGINE

4.8 Valve cover bolt and nut locations (stars indicate locations of nuts and double-ended studs)

4.7 Disconnect the electrical connector (arrow) from the ignition coil capacitor (a radio noise suppression device)

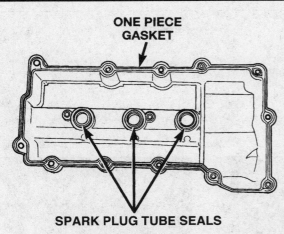

ONE PIECE GASKET

SPARK PLUG TUBE SEALS

4.11 Inspect the spark plug tube seals and replace them if necessary

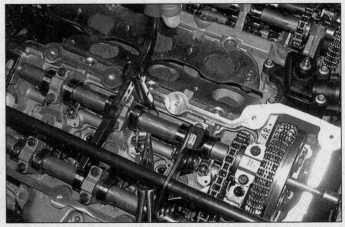

5.5 Using a shaft-mount type valve spring compressor, depress the valve spring just enough to remove the rocker arm

Installation

Refer to illustration 4.11

10   The mating surfaces of each cylinder head and valve cover must be perfectly clean when the covers are installed. Use a gasket scraper to remove all traces of sealant or old gasket material, then clean the mating surfaces with lacquer thinner or acetone (if there's sealant or oil on the mating surfaces when the cover is installed, oil leaks may develop). Be extra careful not to nick or gouge the mating surfaces with the scraper.

11   Inspect the spark plug tube seals **(see illustration)**. Replace them if they're cracked or flattened, or if the rubber has hardened. Make sure the spark plug tube seals are in position before installing the valve cover.

12   Clean the mounting bolt threads with a die if necessary to remove any corrosion and restore damaged threads. Use a tap to clean the threaded holes in the heads.

13   Place the valve cover and new gasket in position, then install the bolts and nuts. Tighten the bolts in several steps to the torque listed in this Chapter's Specifications.

14   The remainder of installation is the reverse of removal.

15   When you're done, start the engine and check carefully for oil leaks.

5   Rocker arms and hydraulic lash adjusters - removal, inspection and installation

Refer to illustrations 5.5, 5.7 and 5.8

Note: *A universal shaft-type valve spring compressor available from most aftermarket specialty tool manufacturers will be required for this procedure. The only other alternative to accomplishing this task without the use of this special tool is to remove the timing chains and the camshafts which requires major disassembly of the engine and surrounding components.*

1   Before beginning this procedure, be sure to place the transaxle in Park (automatic

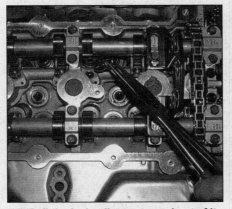

5.7 Pull the lash adjuster up and out of its bore to remove it from the cylinder head

transaxle) or Neutral (manual transaxle) and apply the parking brake or block the rear wheels. Also, disable the ignition system by disconnecting the primary electrical connectors at the ignition coils and remove the spark plugs (see Chapter 1).

2   Remove the upper intake manifold (see Section 9) and the valve cover(s) (see Section 4).

3   Rotate the engine with a socket and ratchet attached to the crankshaft pulley bolt until the cam lobe for the rocker arm to be removed is located on its base circle. Turn the crankshaft in a clockwise direction only.

4   Before the rocker arms and lash adjusters are removed, arrange to label and store them, so they can be kept separate and reinstalled on the same valve they were removed from.

5   Mount the valve spring compressor on the cylinder head. Depress the valve spring just enough to release tension on the rocker arm to be removed. Once tension on the rocker arm is relieved, the rocker arm can be removed by simply pulling it out **(see illustration)**.

6   If you're replacing or removing all of the rockers arms or lash adjusters, begin with cylinder number one and work on the rocker

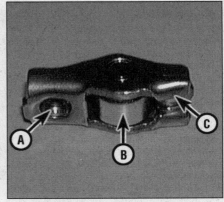

5.8 Inspect the rocker arms at the following locations

A   *Lash adjuster pocket*
B   *Roller*
C   *Valve stem seat*

arms for one cylinder at a time. Move from cylinder-to-cylinder following the firing order sequence (see this Chapter's Specifications). Remember to keep the rocker arm and lash adjuster for each valve together so they can be reinstalled in the same locations

7   Once the rocker arms are removed, the lash adjusters can be pulled out of the cylinder head and stored with the corresponding rocker arm **(see illustration)**.

8   Inspect each rocker arm for wear, cracks and other damage. Make sure the rollers turn freely and show no signs of wear. Also check the pivot area for wear, cracks and galling **(see illustration)**.

9   Inspect the lash adjuster contact surfaces for wear or damage. Make sure the lash adjusters move up and down freely in their bores on the cylinder head without excessive side-to-side play.

10   Installation is the reverse of removal with the following exceptions: Always install the lash adjusters first and make sure they're at least partially full of oil before installation. This is indicated by little or no lash adjuster plunger travel.

6　Valve springs, retainers and seals - replacement

Refer to illustrations 6.5, 6.7a, 6.7b, 6.8, 6.13 and 6.15

Note: *Broken valve springs and defective valve stem seals can be replaced without removing the cylinder heads. Two special tools and a compressed air source are normally required to perform this operation, so read through this Section carefully. The universal shaft-type valve spring compressor required for the tight valve spring pockets of this vehicle may not be available at all tool rental yards, so check on the availability before beginning the job.*

1　Remove the upper intake manifold (see Section 9) and valve cover(s) (see Setion 4).

2　Refer to Section 7 and remove the primary timing chain, then remove the camshafts (see Section 8) and the rocker arms from the affected cylinder head.

3　Remove the spark plug from the cylinder that has the defective component. If all of the valve stem seals are being replaced, all of the spark plugs should be removed.

4　Turn the crankshaft until the piston in the affected cylinder is at Top Dead Center on the compression stroke (refer to Section 3). If you're replacing all of the valve stem seals, begin with cylinder number one and work on the valves for one cylinder at a time. Move from cylinder-to-cylinder following the firing order sequence (see this Chapter's Specifications).

5　Thread a long adapter into the spark plug hole and connect an air hose from a compressed air source to it **(see illustration)**. Most auto parts stores can supply the air hose adapter. **Note:** *Because of the length of the spark plug tubes, it will be necessary to use a long spark plug adapter with a length of hose attached (as used on many cylinder compression gauges) utilizing a quick-disconnect fitting to hook to your air source.*

6　Apply 90 to 100 psi of compressed air to the cylinder. **Warning:** *The piston may be forced down by the compressed air, causing the crankshaft to turn suddenly. If the wrench used when positioning the number one piston at TDC is still attached to the bolt in the crankshaft nose, it could cause damage or injury when the crankshaft moves.*

7　Stuff shop rags into the cylinder head holes around the valves to prevent parts and tools from falling into the engine, then use a valve spring compressor to compress the spring. Remove the valve stem locks with small needle-nose pliers or a magnet **(see illustrations)**. **Note:** *The valves should be held in place by the air pressure. If the valve faces or seats are in poor condition, leaks may prevent air pressure from retaining the valves. If the valves cannot hold air, the cylinder head should be removed for a valve job at a machine shop.*

8　Remove the spring retainer and valve spring, then remove the valve stem seal **(see illustration)**.

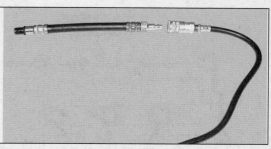

6.5 You'll need an air hose adapter this long to reach down into the spark plug tubes - they're commonly available from auto parts stores

6.7a Compress the valve spring enough to release the valve stem locks . . .

6.7b . . . and lift them out with a magnet or needle-nose pliers

9　Wrap a rubber band or tape around the top of the valve stem so the valve won't fall into the combustion chamber, then release the air pressure.

10　Inspect the valve stem for damage. Rotate the valve in the guide and check the end for eccentric movement, which would indicate that the valve is bent.

11　Move the valve up-and-down in the guide and make sure it doesn't bind. If the valve stem binds, either the valve is bent or the guide is damaged. In either case, the head will have to be removed for repair.

12　Reapply air pressure to the cylinder to retain the valve in the closed position, then remove the tape or rubber band from the valve stem.

13　Lubricate the valve stems with engine oil and install the valve spring seat/valve seal assembly over the top of the valves stems. Using the stem of the valves as a guide, slide the seals down to the top of each valve guide. Using a hammer and a deep socket or seal installation tool, gently tap each seal into place until it's completely seated on the guide **(see illustration)**. Don't twist or cock the seals during installation or they won't seal properly on the valve stems. Make sure the garter spring is still in place around the top of the seal.

14　Install the spring and retainer in position over the valve. Compress the valve spring only enough to install the keepers in the valve stem.

15　Position the keepers in the valve stem

6.8 A pair of pliers will be required to remove the valve stem seal from the valve guide

6.13 Using a deep socket and hammer, gently tap the new seal onto the valve guide only until seated

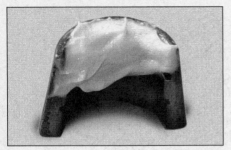

6.15 Apply a small dab of grease to each valve stem lock as shown here before installation - it will hold them in place on the valve stem as the spring is released

7.11 Timing chain cover and gasket

1. *Gasket*
2. *Timing chain cover*
3. *M6 bolt*
4. *M10 bolt*

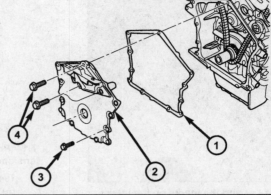

groove. Apply a small dab of grease to the inside of each keeper to hold it in place if necessary **(see illustration)**. Remove the pressure from the spring tool and make sure the keepers are seated.

16 Disconnect the air hose and remove the adapter from the spark plug hole.

17 Repeat the above procedure on the remaining cylinders, following the firing order sequence (see the Specifications). Bring each piston to top dead center on the compression stroke before applying air pressure.

18 Install the rocker arms. Refer to Section 8 and install the camshafts then refer to Section 7 and install the primary timing chain.

19 Refer to Section 4 and install the valve covers.

20 Install the spark plug(s), ignition coils and the upper intake manifold referring to the appropriate sections as necessary.

21 Start and run the engine, then check for oil leaks and unusual sounds coming from the valve cover area.

7 Timing chain and sprockets - removal, inspection and installation

Note 1: *Special tools are necessary to complete this procedure. Read through the entire procedure and obtain the special tools before beginning work.*

Note 2: *Because of work necessary to get at the timing chain and replace it, and because the water pump is in this area, it is recommended that the water pump be thoroughly inspected and replaced if necessary during this procedure (see Chapter 3).*

Note 3: *The 2.7L engine utilizes three timing chains to produce proper valve timing. The primary timing chain runs around the crankshaft sprocket, the water pump and around two intake camshaft sprockets. This chain synchronizes the valve timing with the crankshaft and pistons, while two secondary timing chains run around separate intake and exhaust camshaft sprockets to synchronize the intake and exhaust camshaft events.*

Note 4: *To check timing chain stretch, remove the rear valve cover and inspect the maximum extension of the primary chain tensioner through the cylinder head opening. If the max-*

imum wear indicator groove on the tensioner is visible, the timing drive system is worn beyond it limits and should be replaced.

Removal

> ### ** CAUTION **
> The timing system is complex. Severe engine damage will occur if you make any mistakes. Do not attempt this procedure unless you are highly experienced with this type of repair. If you are at all unsure of your abilities, consult an expert. Double-check all your work and be sure everything is correct before you attempt to start the engine.

Refer to illustrations 7.11, 7. 12a, 7.12b, 7.12c, 7.14, 7.16a, 7.16b, 7.17a, 7.17b and 7.19

1 Relieve the fuel system pressure (see Chapter 4) and then disconnect the cable from the remote ground terminal (see Chapter 5).

2 Drain the cooling system (see Chapter 1) and remove the coolant reservoir (see Chapter 3).

3 Loosen the right front wheel lug nuts. Raise the vehicle, place it securely on jackstands and remove the right front wheel. Remove the accessory drivebelt splash shield.

4 Remove the serpentine accessory drive-

belt (see Chapter 1), then remove the drivebelt tensioner/bracket assembly.

5 Remove the crankshaft pulley (see Section 12).

6 Detach the heater hose from the right front frame rail area, then remove the screws that secure the heater supply tube to the right front frame rail. Set the heater supply tube aside.

7 Remove the upper intake manifold (see Section 9) and the valve covers (see Section 4).

8 Remove the spark plugs (see Chapter 1).

9 Place a floor jack underneath the engine oil pan. Put a block of wood between the jack head and the oil pan to protect the pan, and then raise the jack just enough to prevent the engine from dropping when the right engine mount is removed.

10 Remove the right engine mount (see Section 18).

11 Remove the timing chain cover bolts, then remove the cover **(see illustration)**. Note that various types and sizes of bolts are used. To ensure that they're reinstalled in the correct location, mark each bolt or make a sketch to help remember where they go.

12 Rotate the engine until the crankshaft sprocket timing mark is aligned with the mark on the oil pump housing and the colored links on the chain are aligned with the timing marks on the camshaft sprockets and the crankshaft sprocket **(see illustrations)**.

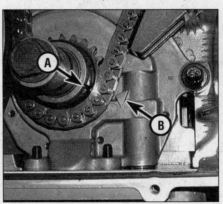

7.12a Make sure the mark on the crankshaft sprocket (A) aligns with the colored link on the primary timing chain and the mark on the oil pump housing (B)

7.12b Also verify that the mark on the intake camshaft sprocket on the front cylinder head is flanked by two colored links. . .

7.12c . . . and the marks on the intake camshaft sprocket on the rear head are aligned with the colored link on the primary chain

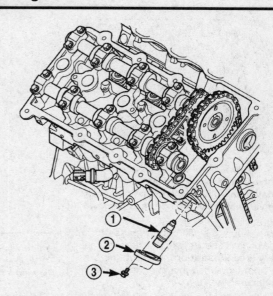

7.14 Primary timing chain tensioner mounting details

1　Tensioner
2　Retaining plate
3　Bolt

7.16a Primary timing chain guide access plugs (arrows) (front cylinder head)

Caution: *When aligning the timing marks, always rotate the engine by turning the crankshaft. Never rotate the engine by turning a camshaft sprocket.*

13　Unbolt the power steering pump and bracket and set them aside (see Chapter 10). Do NOT disconnect the power steering fluid hoses.

14　Remove the primary timing chain tensioner from the right rear cylinder head **(see illustration).**

15　Remove the Camshaft Position (CMP) sensor (see Chapter 6).

16　Remove the timing chain guide access plugs **(see illustrations)** from both cylinder heads.

7.16b An exploded view of the timing chain assembly

1　Camshaft damper (if equipped)
2　Timing chain guide
3　Timing chain guide access plug (rear cylinder head)
4　Camshaft Position (CMP) sensor
5　Primary timing chain
6　Crankshaft sprocket
7　Timing chain guide
8　Timing chain tensioner arm
9　Timing chain tensioner
10　Camshaft sprockets
11　Timing chain guide

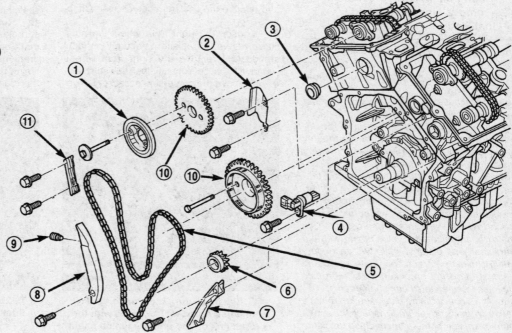

7.17a A 3/8-inch drive extension and ratchet inserted into the end of the camshaft hub is used as leverage while the sprocket bolts are loosened - make note of the vibration damper-to-camshaft sprocket alignment hole (arrow)

7.17b Left (front) camshaft sprocket retaining bolts (arrows)

17   Remove the retaining bolts from the primary camshaft sprockets **(see illustrations)**. **Caution:** *Pressure from the valve springs will make the camshafts rotate clockwise as the bolts are removed. Do not rotate the crankshaft or camshaft separately after the primary timing chain is loosened or removed as piston or valve damage may occur. The only exception to this rule is when the camshafts must be rotated counterclockwise slightly, to realign the primary camshaft sprockets with the camshafts during installation.*

18   Pull the primary sprockets off the camshaft hubs one at a time, lower the sprocket(s) into the cylinder head opening until the chain can be displaced from around the sprocket, then remove the primary camshaft sprockets from the engine. Note that the left (front) primary camshaft sprocket is identified by the camshaft position sensor ring which is mounted on the front of the sprocket by two nuts. It is not necessary to remove the sensor ring from the sprocket during this procedure unless damage to the sensor ring or sprocket has occurred. Also note that the right (rear) primary camshaft sprocket is identified by a vibration damper which is mounted in front of the sprocket. Make note of the alignment holes on the damper and the right (rear) primary sprocket as these two components will separate as the sprocket is removed from the camshaft. Always install the damper in the same position from which it was removed.

19   Detach the primary timing chain guides and tensioner arm **(see illustration)**.

20   Remove the primary timing chain. **Note:** *If you want to inspect, remove or replace the secondary timing chains, go to Section 8. They can't be removed without removing the camshafts, so they're included with camshaft removal and installation.* If the crankshaft sprocket needs to be replaced or if the sprocket needs to be removed for other procedures, such as oil pump removal, proceed to Step 41.

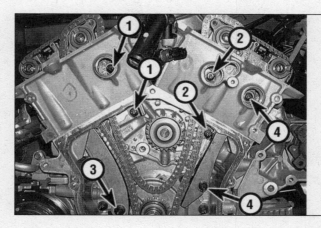

Inspection

21   Inspect the camshaft, water pump and crankshaft sprockets for wear on the teeth and keyways. Inspect the chains for cracks or excessive wear of the rollers. Inspect the facing of the chain guides and tensioner arm for excessive wear. If any of the components show signs of excessive wear they must be replaced.

Installation

> **** CAUTION ****
> Before starting the engine, carefully rotate the crankshaft by hand through at least two full revolutions (use a socket and breaker bar on the crankshaft pulley center bolt). If you feel any resistance, STOP! There is something wrong - most likely, valves are contacting the pistons. You must find the problem before proceeding. Check your work and see if any updated repair information is available.

Refer to illustrations 7.28, 7.31a, 7.31b, 7.31c, 7.32a, 7.32b, 7.32c and 7.37

22   If you removed the crankshaft sprocket,

7.19 Primary timing chain guide mounting details

1   *Upper timing chain guide mounting bolts (rear cylinder head)*
2   *Upper timing chain guide mounting bolts (front cylinder head)*
3   *Tensioner arm pivot bolt*
4   *Lower timing chain guide mounting bolts*

install it (see Steps 43 and 44). Make sure that the crankshaft sprocket is still aligned with the mark on the oil pump housing **(see illustration 7.12a)**.

23   If you removed either or both of the upper (shorter) chain guides **(see illustration 7.16b)**, install them and tighten the bolts to the torque listed in this Chapter's Specifications.

24   If you purchased a new timing chain, verify that you have the correct timing chain for your vehicle by counting the number of links in the chain and by comparing the new chain with the old chain. Also compare the position of the colored links in the new chain with the position of the colored links in the old chain. Before installing the primary timing chain, align the camshaft sprocket mark on the left (front) cylinder head, between the two light colored links on the chain **(see illustration 7.12b)**. Then lower the sprocket and chain assembly down through the chain tunnel in the front cylinder head and reposition the sprocket onto the intake camshaft hub. Don't install the sprocket bolts at this time. Allow the camshaft sprockets to "float" on the cam hub until the primary timing chain is installed and all the timing marks are aligned. Then you can move the sprockets to make final adjustments in relation to the chain, if necessary, without moving the camshafts.

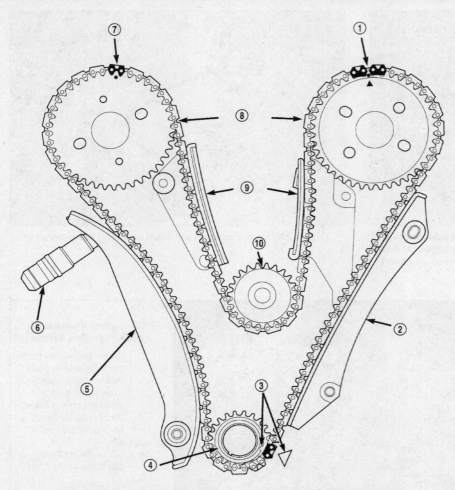

7.28 Primary timing chain alignment marks and installation details

1   *Intake camshaft timing marks (front cylinder head)*
2   *Front lower timing chain guide*
3   *Crankshaft sprocket timing marks*
4   *Crankshaft sprocket*
5   *Timing chain tensioner arm*
6   *Timing chain tensioner*
7   *Intake camshaft timing marks (rear cylinder head)*
8   *Intake camshaft sprockets*
9   *Upper chain guides*
10 *Water pump sprocket*

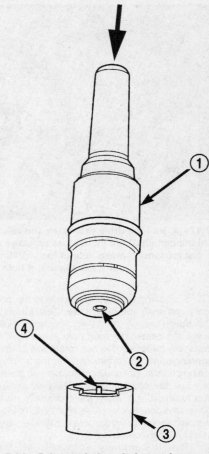

7.31a Primary timing chain tensioner - oil purging details

1   *Tensioner body*
2   *Check ball*
3   *Special tool (8186)*
4   *Pin*

25 Align the colored link on the timing chain with the timing marks on the crankshaft sprocket and on the oil pump housing **(see illustration 7.12a)**, then install the chain onto the crankshaft sprocket.

26 Loop the timing chain around the water pump sprocket.

27 Align the timing mark on the rear intake camshaft sprocket with the colored link on the timing chain, install the sprocket on the intake cam hub and install the camshaft vibration damper (if equipped).

28 Verify that all the timing marks are still correctly aligned **(see illustration)**.

29 Install the front lower chain guide and the tensioner arm **(see illustration 7.16b)**, then tighten the chain guide bolt and tension arm bolt to the torque listed in this Chapter's Specifications.

30 Install the chain guide access plugs and

then tighten them to the torque listed in this Chapter's Specifications.

31 Using the special tensioner tool (No. 8186), purge the oil from the tensioner as follows: Insert the *check ball end* of the tensioner into the *shallow end* of the special tool. Make sure that the pin in the special tool is aligned with the check ball in the tensioner **(see illustration)**. Then, using hand pressure, slowly depress the tensioner until you can't depress it any further **(see illustrations)**. The oil is now purged from the tensioner.

32 After purging the oil from the tensioner, reset the tensioner as follows: Insert the plunger end of the tensioner into the deep end of the special tool and then depress the plunger until it locks into place **(see illustrations)**. Once the tensioner is reset it will be about 1-1/2 inches shorter. If you have difficulty resetting the tensioner, there might

still be some oil inside; go back to the previous step and make sure that all oil has been purged from the tensioner. **Caution:** *Failure to reset the tensioner correctly can cause the tensioner to jam after it has been installed.*

33 Install the tensioner and tighten the tensioner retaining plate bolts to the torque listed in this Chapter's Specifications.

34 To install the camshaft sprocket retaining bolts, insert a 3/8-inch drive extension and ratchet into the rear intake camshaft hub and then rotate the camshaft in a counterclockwise direction until the bolt holes in the camshaft sprocket are aligned with the bolt holes in the camshaft hub. After hand tightening the rear intake cam bolts, repeat this step for the front intake cam sprocket bolts.

35 Leaving the 3/8-inch extension and ratchet inserted into the camshaft hub for leverage, tighten the camshaft sprocket bolts to the torque listed in this Chapter's Specifications.

36 Rotate the engine clockwise just enough remove any slack from the front side of the timing chain.

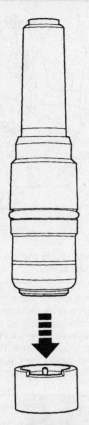

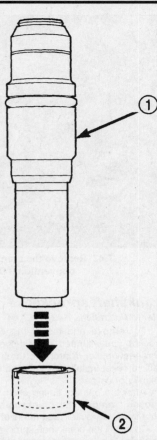

7.31b To purge the oil from the primary timing chain tensioner, insert the *check-ball end* of the timing chain tensioner into the *shallow end* of the special tool . . .

7.31c . . . and then depress the tensioner until you can't compress it any further

7.32a To reset the primary timing chain tensioner, insert the *plunger end* of the tensioner into the *deep end* of the special tool . . .

37   Verify that the timing marks on the camshaft and crankshaft sprockets are still aligned with the colored links on the chain (**see illustration 7.28**), then release the primary timing chain tensioner from its reset position (**see illustration**).

38   Remove all traces of old sealant from the timing chain cover and the cover bolts.

39   Apply a bead of RTV sealant to the timing chain cover gasket and sealing surfaces. Place the timing chain cover in position on the

engine, install the bolts in their original locations and tighten the bolts to the torque listed in this Chapter's Specifications.

40   The remainder of installation is the reverse of removal.

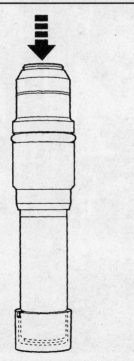

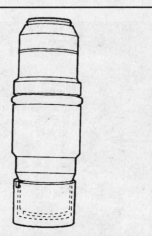

7.32b . . . push down on the check-ball end of the tensioner . . .

7.32c . . . until the plunger locks into place and resets itself (the plunger should be about 1-1/2 inches shorter when fully retracted)

7.37 With all slack removed from the left side of the chain and the colored links on the chain aligned with their respective marks on the sprockets, engage the tensioner by pushing the tensioner arm inward slightly, then release the tensioner arm to extend the tensioner

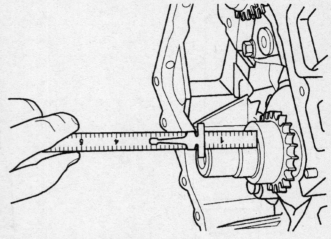

**7.42 Remove the crankshaft sprocket with a
conventional three jaw puller**

**7.44 Install the crankshaft sprocket 1-17/32 inches from the
end of the crankshaft snout**

Crankshaft sprocket

Refer to illustrations 7.42 and 7.44

41   To remove and install the crankshaft sprocket, you will need several special tools: a three-jaw puller, a propane torch or crankshaft sprocket installation tool and a machinist's ruler or caliper.

42   After the primary timing chain has been removed, remove the crankshaft sprocket with a three-jaw puller **(see illustration)**.

43   To install the crankshaft sprocket it will be necessary to purchase a sprocket installation tool or a common household propane torch. If a sprocket installation tool is purchased follow the installation procedures outlined in the tools instructions and install the sprocket to the correct depth (see Step 44). If a propane torch is chosen simply place the sprocket in a vise and heat the sprocket hub for several minutes until the sprocket has expanded enough to slide over the crankshaft. **Warning:** *After heating the sprocket always handle the sprocket with a pair of pliers or other insulated tool to avoid serious injury and never heat an object when gasoline or other volatile chemicals are present.*

44   Using a machinist ruler or dial caliper install the sprocket on the crankshaft to the correct depth (1-17/32 inches) by measuring from the end of the crankshaft to the face of the crankshaft sprocket **(see illustration)**.

8   Camshafts - removal and installation

Removal

Refer to illustrations 8.4, 8.5 and 8.6

Note: *Always check the camshaft endplay before removing the cams and always inspect the camshafts thoroughly after removing them. Do not install damaged or excessively worn camshafts.*

1   Remove the valve covers (see Section 4).

2   Remove the primary timing chain and the primary chain camshaft sprockets (see Section 7).

3   Camshaft endplay is controlled by the primary timing chain sprocket flange on the intake camshafts and by a thrust flange on the exhaust cams. Using a dial indicator with a magnetic base, place the tip of the dial indicator on the intake camshaft sprocket flange or exhaust cam thrust flange. Zero the indicator, then lever the cam back and forth with a pry-bar placed between a cam lobe and a bearing cap and measure the camshaft endplay. Compare your measurements with the camshaft endplay listed in this Chapter's Specifications. If the indicated cam endplay exceeds the service limit on either cam, replace the cam.

4   Remove the retaining bolts from the secondary timing chain tensioner **(see illustration)**.

5   Verify the markings on the camshaft bearing caps. The caps should be marked from 1 to 5, and with an "I" or an "E", to indicate intake or exhaust. Also verify that there are arrow marks on the caps indicating the front of the engine **(see illustration)**. Loosen the camshaft bearing caps in two or three steps, in the reverse order of the tightening sequence **(see illustration 8.18)**. **Caution:** *Keep the caps in order. They must go back in the same location they were removed from.*

**8.4 Secondary timing chain tensioner
retaining bolts (arrows) (right cylinder
head shown, left cylinder head similar)**

**8.5 Verify that the camshaft bearing caps
are marked to ensure correct reinstallation**

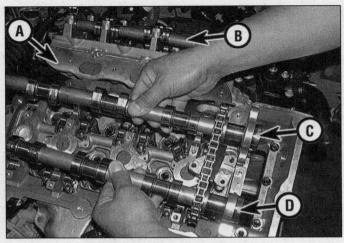

8.6 Camshaft installation details

A   Intake manifold location
B   Intake camshaft (left cylinder head)
C   Intake camshaft (right cylinder head)
D   Exhaust camshaft (right cylinder head)

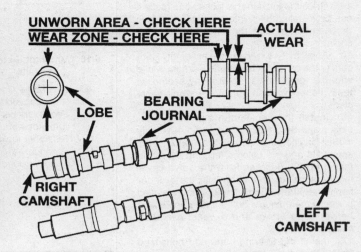

8.10 Camshaft lobe wear is the difference between the worn area (in the center of the lobe) and the unworn area (edge of the lobe)

6   Detach the bearing caps, then remove the camshafts, secondary timing chain and the secondary tensioner as an assembly from the cylinder head. Make a note that the intake camshafts have a flanged hub at the front and the exhaust camshafts do not. Also note that the intake camshafts are installed in the cylinder head (towards the center of the engine) next to the intake manifold and the exhaust camshafts are installed (towards the sides of the engine) next to the exhaust manifolds **(see illustration)**.

7   Remove the secondary tensioner and the secondary timing chain from the camshafts (see Section 7).

Inspection

Refer to illustration 8.10

8   Inspect the camshaft secondary timing chain sprocket teeth for excessive wear. If the teeth on either cam sprocket are damaged or worn, replace the camshaft. Inspect the chains for cracks or excessive wear of the rollers. Inspect the facing of the secondary chain tensioners for excessive wear. If the chains show signs of excessive wear, replace them.

9   Clean the camshafts and inspect them for wear and/or damage to the lobe surfaces, bearing journals and seal contact surfaces. Inspect the camshaft bearing surfaces in the cylinder head and in the bearing caps for scoring and other damage. Inspect the cylinder head oiling holes. Make sure that none of them are clogged.

10   Measure the camshaft lobe wear by measuring the difference in height between the edges and the center of each lobe **(see illustration)**. Also measure the camshaft journal diameter of all camshaft journals. Compare your measurements with the values listed in this Chapter's Specifications. If a camshaft fails either inspection, replace it.

11   If the cam lobes are worn, replace the

rocker arms and lash adjusters along with the camshaft. If the camshaft bearing surfaces in the head are damaged or excessively worn, the cylinder head may have to be replaced. Have it inspected by an automotive machine shop.

Installation

Refer to illustrations 8.13a, 8.13b, 8.16 and 8.18

12   Install the secondary timing chain(s) over the camshaft sprockets while aligning the colored links on the chain with the marks on the secondary camshaft sprockets in a 12 o'clock position. **Note:** The colored links on the chain must face outward toward the front of the engine.

13   Using a paperclip, fabricate a U-shaped tool to use as a tensioner locking pin. Then place the secondary tensioner in a vise and compress the tensioner until the U-shaped

tool can be inserted into the locking holes on the tensioner. This places the tensioner in the locked position so it can be reinstalled **(see illustration)**. **Note:** Some tensioners have a two piece design. On these models it will be necessary to separate the tensioner halves first and drain the oil from the tensioner housing before compressing the tensioner in a vise and inserting the locking pin. Be careful not to remove any of the internal tensioner components when the halves are separated **(see illustration)**.

8.13a Compress the secondary tensioner in a vise until a fabricated paperclip can be inserted into the secondary tensioner locking holes

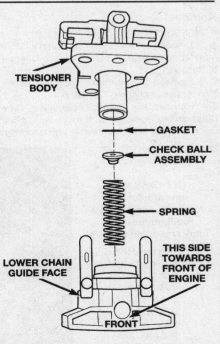

8.13b An exploded view of the two-piece secondary tensioner

14   Once the tensioner is locked into place it can be installed back into the place between the camshafts and the secondary timing chain.

15   Apply moly-based engine assembly lubricant to the camshaft lobes and journals. Make sure the rocker arms are properly seated on their respective lash adjuster and the valve stem tip.

16   Install the camshafts, secondary tensioner and the timing chain as an assembly in their original position with the marks on the sprockets and the colored links on the chain facing up (90 degrees from the valve cover mating surface) and inline with the cylinder bank **(see illustration)**. **Note:** *When installed correctly there should be 12 timing chain pins between the intake and exhaust camshaft marks.*

17   Install the bearing caps and bolts and tighten them hand tight.

18   Tighten the bearing cap bolts in several steps, to the torque listed in this Chapter's Specifications, using the correct tightening sequence **(see illustration)**.

19   Tighten the tensioner mounting bolts to the torque listed in this Chapter's Specifications and remove the tensioner locking pin.

20   Install the primary timing chain and camshaft sprockets (see Section 7).

21   The remainder of installation is the reverse of removal.

---

9   **Intake manifold - removal and installation**

Upper intake manifold (plenum)

Removal

Refer to illustrations 9.3, 9.6 and 9.7

1   Disconnect the negative battery cable from the remote ground terminal (see Chapter 5, Section 1).

2   Remove the air intake duct and the air cleaner assembly (see Chapter 4).

3   Remove the throttle cable shield **(see illustration)**, remove the throttle and speed control cables from the throttle arm and from

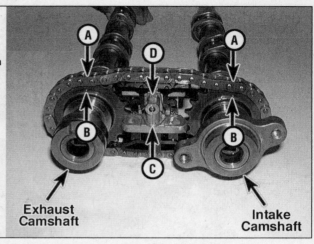

8.16 Camshaft installation details

A   Secondary timing chain colored links
B   Secondary camshaft sprocket marks
C   Tensioner locking pin
D   Secondary timing chain tensioner

Exhaust Camshaft   **Intake Camshaft**

8.18 Camshaft bearing cap TIGHTENING sequence

the throttle cable bracket and then remove the throttle cable bracket (see Chapter 4).

4   Remove the EGR upper tubes **(see illustration 9.3)**.

5   Disconnect the vapor purge hose, the brake booster hose, the speed control servo and the PCV hose.

6   Disconnect the Throttle Position Sensor (TPS) and the Idle Air Control (IAC) motor (see Chapter 6). Disconnect the Manifold Absolute Pressure (MAP) sensor and the Manifold Tun-

ing Valve (MTV) **(see illustration)**.

7   Remove the upper throttle body support bracket bolt **(see illustration)**.

8   Remove the upper manifold attaching bolts in the opposite sequence for tightening them **(see illustration 9.12)** and then remove the upper manifold.

9   Remove and discard the old gasket. Clean off any old gasket material from the gasket mating surfaces.

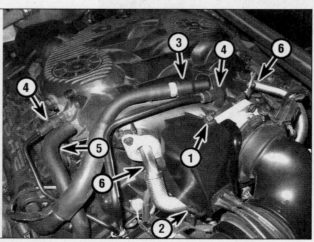

9.3 Label and disconnect the following components required for upper intake manifold removal

1   Throttle cable shield mounting bolt
2   Throttle cable shield retaining clip
3   PCV hose
4   Vacuum hoses
5   Breather hose
6   EGR tubes

9.6 Disconnect the Manifold Absolute Pressure (MAP) sensor connector (1) and the Manifold Tuning Valve (MTV) (2)

9.7 Remove the upper throttle body support bracket bolt (arrow)

9.12 Upper intake manifold (plenum) TIGHTENING sequence

Inspection

10   Inspect the gasket mating surfaces of the lower and upper intake manifolds. Look for cracks and other damage. Inspect all passages for clogging. If any passages are clogged, blow them out with compressed air. If the upper intake manifold is damaged in any way, replace it.

Installation

Refer to illustration 9.12

11   Make sure that the gasket mating surfaces of the upper and lower intake manifolds are clean. Install a new gasket. Make sure that the fuel injector wiring harness is correctly positioned and doesn't interfere with upper manifold installation.

12   Place the upper intake manifold in position on the lower intake manifold, install the manifold bolts and gradually and slowly tighten them in the correct sequence **(see illustration)** to the torque listed in this Chapter's Specifications.

13   The remainder of installation is the reverse of removal.

Lower intake manifold

Removal

14   Relieve the system fuel pressure (see Chapter 4).

15   Remove the upper intake manifold (see above).

16   Remove the fuel rail and injectors (see Chapter 4).

17   Loosen the lower intake manifold mounting bolts/nuts in 1/4-turn increments until they can be removed by hand In the reverse order of the tightening sequence **(see illustration 9.23)**.

18   Remove the lower intake manifold. The manifold will probably be stuck to the cylinder heads and force may be required to break the gasket seal. **Caution:** *Don't pry between the manifold and the heads or damage to the gasket sealing surfaces may occur, leading to vacuum leaks.*

Inspection

19   Refer to the inspection procedure for the upper intake manifold (see Step 10).

Installation

Refer to illustration 9.23

20   Clean and inspect the lower intake manifold-to-cylinder head sealing surfaces.

21   Place a new gasket in position and then position the lower manifold on the engine. To make sure that the gaskets and manifold are aligned correctly over the cylinder heads, install one of the rear manifold bolts and screw it in two or three turns. This will position the manifold correctly.

22   Install the fuel rail and injectors onto the cylinder heads and the lower manifold. Install the fuel rail retaining bolts into the manifold loosely to ensure correct gasket/manifold alignment, then install the remaining lower intake manifold bolts.

23   Following the recommended tightening sequence, tighten the bolts, in several steps, to the torque listed in this Chapter's Specifications **(see illustration)**.

24   The remainder of the installation is the reverse of the removal procedure. Run the engine and check for fuel, vacuum and coolant leaks.

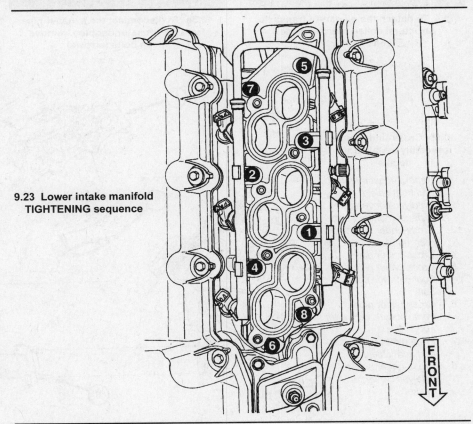

9.23 Lower intake manifold TIGHTENING sequence

10.2 To remove the upstream oxygen sensor (center arrow) from the exhaust manifold, trace the sensor electrical harness to the connector and unplug it, and then unscrew the sensor with an oxygen sensor socket (see Chapter 6); to detach the heat shield from the exhaust manifold, remove these four nuts (arrows)

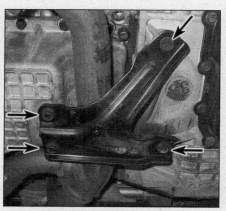

10.4 To detach the oil pan-to-transaxle structural collar, remove these bolts (arrows)

10.5a To disconnect the exhaust pipe from the cross-under pipe, remove these bolts (arrows)

10 Exhaust manifold - removal and installation

Warning: *The engine must be completely cool before beginning this procedure.*

Front exhaust manifold

Refer to illustrations 10.2, 10.4, 10.5a, 10.5b and 10.6

1   Disconnect the cable from the remote ground terminal (see Chapter 5, Section 1).

2   Disconnect the electrical connector from the upstream oxygen sensor **(see illustration)**, then remove the upstream sensor from the front exhaust manifold (see Chapter 6). Also remove the heat shield.

3   Raise the vehicle and place it securely on jackstands.

4   Remove the oil pan-to-transaxle structural collar **(see illustration)**.

5   Remove the downstream oxygen sensor (see Chapter 6). Disconnect the exhaust pipe from the cross-under pipe **(see illustration)**, remove the fasteners that attach the cross-under pipe to the catalytic converters **(see illustration)**, then remove the cross-under pipe.

6   Remove the front catalytic converter from the front exhaust manifold **(see illustration)**.

7   Apply penetrating lubricant to the exhaust manifold bolts and allow it to soak into the threads for awhile before trying to remove the manifold bolts. Remove the exhaust manifold bolts and the exhaust manifold. Remove and discard the old manifold gasket.

8   Clean the manifold mating surfaces to remove all traces of old gasket material, then inspect the manifold for cracks, discoloration

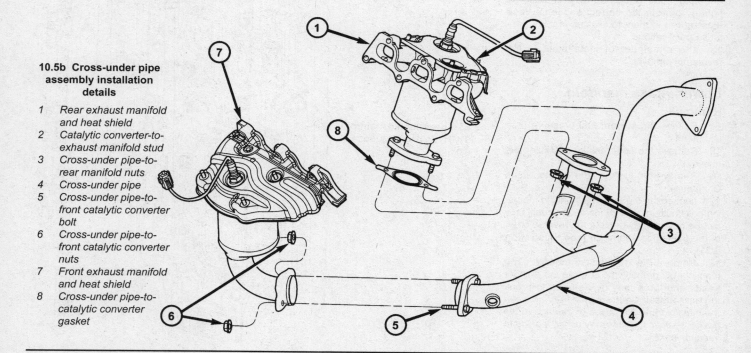

10.5b Cross-under pipe assembly installation details

1   *Rear exhaust manifold and heat shield*
2   *Catalytic converter-to-exhaust manifold stud*
3   *Cross-under pipe-to-rear manifold nuts*
4   *Cross-under pipe*
5   *Cross-under pipe-to-front catalytic converter bolt*
6   *Cross-under pipe-to-front catalytic converter nuts*
7   *Front exhaust manifold and heat shield*
8   *Cross-under pipe-to-catalytic converter gasket*

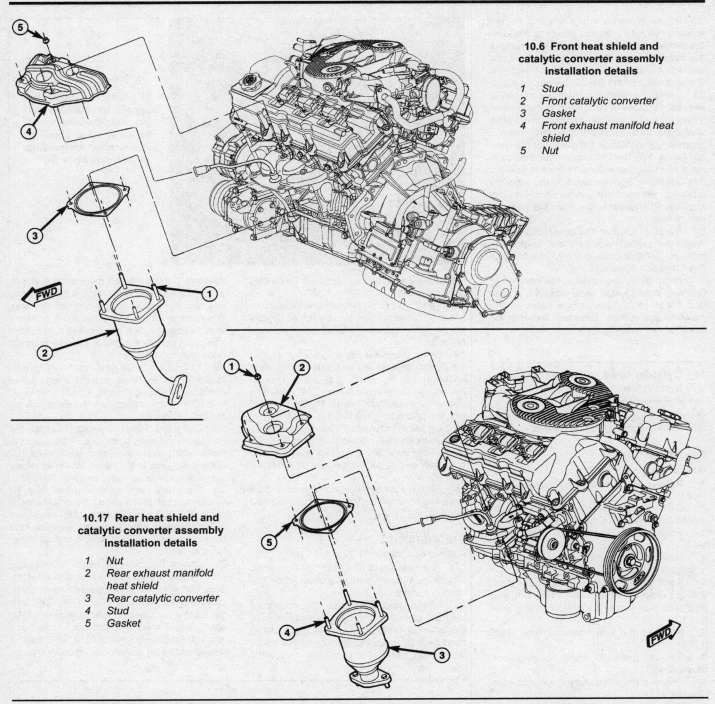

10.6 Front heat shield and catalytic converter assembly installation details

1   Stud
2   Front catalytic converter
3   Gasket
4   Front exhaust manifold heat shield
5   Nut

10.17 Rear heat shield and catalytic converter assembly installation details

1   Nut
2   Rear exhaust manifold heat shield
3   Rear catalytic converter
4   Stud
5   Gasket

and distortion. Measure distortion with a precision straightedge held against the mating flange and then compare your measurement to the cylinder head distortion listed in this Chapter's Specifications. If the manifold distortion exceeds the service limit, take the manifold to an automotive machine shop for resurfacing.

9   Place a new manifold gasket in position, install the exhaust manifold and then tighten the exhaust manifold bolts to the torque listed in this Chapter's Specifications.

10   Installation is otherwise the reverse of removal. When you're done, start the engine and check for exhaust leaks between the manifold and cylinder head and between the manifold and catalytic converter.

Rear exhaust manifold
Refer to illustration 10.17

11   Disconnect the cable from the remote ground terminal (see Chapter 5, Section 1).

12   Remove the air intake duct and the air cleaner housing (see Chapter 4).

13   Detach the EGR pipe from the exhaust manifold and from the EGR valve (see Chapter 6). Discard the old gaskets.

14   Raise the vehicle and place it securely on jackstands.

15   Remove the exhaust pipe (see Chapter 4).

16   Remove the cross-under pipe (see Step 5).

17   Remove the rear catalytic converter **(see illustration)**.

18   Disconnect the electrical connector from the upstream oxygen sensor and then remove the upstream sensor from the rear exhaust manifold (see Chapter 6).

19   Remove the rear exhaust manifold heat shield **(see illustration 10.17)**.

20   Apply penetrating lubricant to the exhaust manifold bolts and allow it to soak into the threads for awhile before trying to remove the manifold bolts. Remove the rear exhaust manifold bolts and the rear exhaust manifold. Remove and discard the old manifold gasket.

21   Clean the manifold mating surfaces to remove all traces of old gasket material, then inspect the manifold for cracks, discoloration and distortion. Measure distortion with a precision straightedge held against the mating flange and then compare your measurement to the cylinder head distortion listed in this Chapter's Specifications. If the manifold distortion exceeds the service limit, take the manifold to an automotive machine shop for resurfacing.

22   Place a new manifold gasket in position, install the exhaust manifold and tighten the exhaust manifold bolts to the torque listed in this Chapter's Specifications.

23   Installation is otherwise the reverse of removal. When you're done, start the engine and check for exhaust leaks between the manifold and cylinder head and between the manifold and catalytic converter.

11   Cylinder head - removal and installation

Warning: *The engine must be completely cool before beginning this procedure.*

Removal

Refer to illustrations 11.7

1   Relieve the fuel pressure (see Chapter 4).

2   Disconnect the cable from the remote ground terminal (see Chapter 5).

3   Drain the cooling system (see Chapter 1).

4   Remove the upper and lower intake manifolds (see Section 9).

5   Remove the exhaust cross-under pipe, the upstream catalytic converters and the front and rear exhaust manifolds (see Section 10).

6   Remove the valve covers (see Section 4).

7   Remove the water outlet housing **(see illustration)**.

8   Remove the accessory drivebelts (see Chapter 1).

9   Remove the crankshaft damper pulley (see Section 12).

10   Remove the timing chain cover and the primary timing chain (see Section 7). **Caution:** *Do NOT rotate the crankshaft during the remainder of this procedure.*

11   Remove the secondary timing chains and the camshafts from the cylinder head (see Section 8).

12   Remove the rocker arms and hydraulic lash adjusters from the cylinder head (see Section 5). Before the rocker arms and lash adjusters are removed, arrange to label and store them, so they can be kept separate and

11.7 Unscrew the heater supply tube retaining bolts (A), slide the tube out of the water outlet housing, then remove the housing retaining bolts (B)

reinstalled on the same valve from which they were removed.

13   Label and remove any remaining items attached to the cylinder head, such as coolant fittings, ground straps, cables, hoses, wires or brackets.

14   Using a breaker bar and socket, loosen the cylinder head bolts in 1/4-turn increments until they can be removed by hand. Loosen the bolts in the reverse order of the tightening sequence **(see illustration 11.26)** to avoid warping or cracking the head.

15   Lift the cylinder head off the engine block with the exhaust manifold attached. If it's stuck, very carefully pry up at the transaxle end, beyond the gasket surface, at a casting protrusion.

16   Remove all external components from the head to allow for thorough cleaning and inspection.

Installation

Refer to illustrations 11.21 and 11.26

17   The mating surfaces of the cylinder head and block must be perfectly clean when the head is installed.

18   Use a gasket scraper to remove all traces of carbon and old gasket material from the cylinder head and engine block being careful not to gouge the aluminum, then clean the mating surfaces with lacquer thinner or

acetone. If there's oil on the mating surfaces when the head is installed, the gasket may not seal correctly and leaks could develop. When working on the block, stuff the cylinders with clean shop rags to keep out debris. Use a vacuum cleaner to remove material that falls into the cylinders.

19   Check the block and head mating surfaces for nicks, deep scratches and other damage. If damage is slight, it can be removed with a file; if it's excessive, machining may be the only alternative.

20   Use a tap of the correct size to chase the threads in the head bolt holes, then clean the holes with compressed air - make sure that nothing remains in the holes. **Warning:** *Wear eye protection when using compressed air!*

21   Measure each cylinder head bolt for stretching **(see illustration)**. If the diameter of the bolt threads has necked down anywhere in the threaded area, the bolts have exceeded the maximum amount of stretch and will need to be replaced.

22   Check the cylinder head for warpage with a feeler gauge and a precision straightedge and compare your measurements to the cylinder head distortion listed in this Chapter's Specifications. Check the head gasket, intake and exhaust manifold surfaces. If the head is distorted beyond the service limit, have it resurfaced by an automotive machine shop.

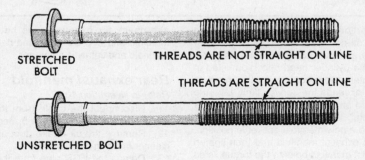

STRETCHED BOLT — THREADS ARE NOT STRAIGHT ON LINE

UNSTRETCHED BOLT — THREADS ARE STRAIGHT ON LINE

11.21 Place a metal ruler or straightedge against the cylinder head bolt threads to check if the bolts have stretched

11.26 Cylinder head bolt TIGHTENING sequence

12.4 Use a strap wrench or a chain-type wrench (shown) to hold the crankshaft pulley while removing the center bolt; if you use a chain wrench, wrap a section of old drivebelt or rag around the crankshaft pulley to protect the V-groove

23   Position the new cylinder head gasket over the dowel pins on the block noting which direction on the gasket faces up.

24   Carefully set the head over the dowels on the block without disturbing the gasket.

25   Before installing the head bolts, apply a small amount of clean engine oil to the threads and hardened washers (if equipped). The chamfered side of the washers must face the bolt heads.

26   Install the bolts in their original locations and tighten them finger tight. Then tighten all the bolts in several steps, following the indicated sequence (see illustration), to the torque listed in this Chapter's Specifications.

27   Installation is otherwise the reverse of removal.

28   Refill the cooling system and change the engine oil and filter (see Chapter 1).

29   Start the engine and check for oil and coolant leaks.

12   Crankshaft pulley - removal and installation

Refer to illustrations 12.4, 12.5 and 12.6

1   Disconnect the negative battery cable from the remote ground terminal.

2   Refer to Chapter 3 and remove the upper radiator crossmember, the cooling fan assembly and the radiator.

3   Remove the drivebelts (see Chapter 1) and position the belt tensioner away from the crankshaft pulley.

4   Use a strap wrench around the crankshaft pulley to hold it while using a breaker bar and socket to remove the crankshaft pulley center bolt (see illustration).

5   Pull the damper off the crankshaft with a puller (see illustration). **Caution:** *The jaws of the puller must only contact the hub of the pulley - not the outer ring.* **Note:** A long Allen-

head bolt should be inserted into the crankshaft nose for the puller's tapered tip to push against to prevent damage to the crankshaft threads.

6   Check the surface on the pulley hub that the oil seal rides on. If the surface has been grooved from long-time contact with the seal, a press-on sleeve may be available to renew the sealing surface (see illustration). This sleeve is pressed into place with a hammer and a block of wood and is commonly available at auto parts stores for various applications.

7   Lubricate the pulley hub with clean engine oil and reinstall the crankshaft pulley. Use a vibration damper installation tool to press the pulley onto the crankshaft.

8   Install the crankshaft pulley retaining bolt and tighten it to the torque listed in this Chapter's Specifications.

9   The remainder of installation is the reverse of removal.

12.5 Use a three-jaw puller to remove the crankshaft pulley; note that the puller jaws are pulling on the pulley hub, not on the outer edge

12.6 If the sealing surface of the pulley hub has a wear groove from contact with the seal, repair sleeves are available at most auto parts stores

13 Crankshaft front oil seal - replacement

Refer to illustrations 13.2 and 13.4

1   Remove the crankshaft pulley from the engine (see Section 12).

2   Carefully pry the seal out of the cover with a seal removal tool or a large screwdriver **(see illustration)**. **Caution:** *Be careful not to scratch, gouge or distort the area that the seal fits into or an oil leak will develop.*

3   Clean the bore to remove any old seal material and corrosion. Position the new seal in the bore with the seal lip (usually the side with the spring) facing IN (toward the engine). A small amount of oil applied to the outer edge of the new seal will make installation easier.

4   Drive the seal into the bore with a seal driver or large socket and hammer until it's completely seated **(see illustration)**. Select a socket that's the same outside diameter as the seal and make sure the new seal is pressed into place until it bottoms against the cover flange.

5   Lubricate the seal lips with engine oil and reinstall the crankshaft pulley.

6   The remainder of installation is the reverse of the removal. Run the engine and check for oil leaks.

14 Oil pan - removal and installation

Removal

Refer to illustrations 14.6 and 14.7

1   Disconnect the cable from the remote ground terminal (see Chapter 5).

2   Apply the parking brake and block the rear wheels. Raise the vehicle and place it securely on jackstands.

3   Drain the engine oil and remove the oil filter (see Chapter 1). Remove the oil dipstick tube.

4   Remove the oil pan-to-transaxle structural collar **(see illustration 10.4)**.

5   Remove the downstream oxygen sensor

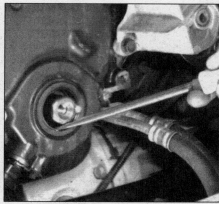

13.2 Pry out the crankshaft front seal very carefully with a seal removal tool or screwdriver; be careful not to nick or gouge the seal bore or the crankshaft

(see Chapter 6), disconnect the exhaust pipe from the cross-under pipe **(see illustration 10.5a)**, remove the fasteners that attach the cross-under pipe to the catalytic converters **(see illustration 10.5b)** and then remove the cross-under pipe.

6   Remove the torque converter access cover **(see illustration)**.

7   Remove the lower air conditioning compressor bracket bolt. Remove the oil pan bolts **(see illustration)**, then carefully separate the oil pan from the block. Don't pry between the block and the pan or damage to the sealing surfaces could occur and oil leaks may develop. Instead, pry at the casting protrusion at the front of the pan **(see illustration)**.

Installation

8   Clean the pan with solvent and remove all old sealant and gasket material from the block and pan mating surfaces. Clean the mating surfaces with lacquer thinner or acetone and make sure the bolt holes in the block are clear. Check the oil pan flange for distortion, particularly around the bolt holes.

13.4 Use a seal driver or a large socket to drive the new seal into the cover

9   Apply a bead of RTV sealant to the oil pan rail parting lines at the front cover and at the rear main oil seal retainer. Install the gasket on the block.

10   Place the oil pan in position on the block and install the nuts and bolts.

11   After the fasteners are installed, tighten them to the torque listed in this Chapter's Specifications. Starting at the center, follow a criss-cross pattern and work up to the final torque in three steps.

12   The remainder of installation is the reverse of removal.

13   Install the oil filter, refill the engine with oil (see Chapter 1), warm up the engine to its normal operating temperature and then check for leaks.

15 Oil pump - removal, inspection and installation

Removal

Refer to illustrations 15.3 and 15.4

1   Refer to Section 7 and remove the primary timing chain and the crankshaft

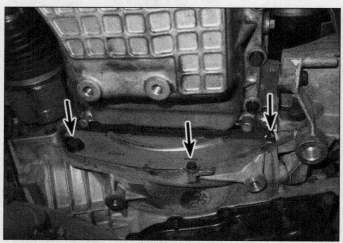

14.6 To remove the torque converter access cover, remove these bolts (arrows)

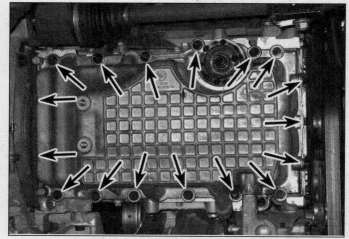

14.7 To detach the oil pan from the block, remove these bolts and nuts (arrows)

15.3 Oil pump pick-up tube mounting bolts (arrows)

15.4 Oil pump housing retaining bolts (arrows)

sprocket. **Note:** *Before removing the crank-shaft sprocket verify that the crankshaft sprocket marks align with the marks on the oil pump housing and do not rotate the crank-shaft from this position at any time during this procedure. This position is approximately 60-degrees after TDC.*

2   Remove the oil pan (see Section 14).

3   Remove the oil pump pick-up tube **(see illustration)**.

4   Remove the oil pump-to-engine block bolts from the front of the engine **(see illustration)**.

5   Gently pry the oil pump housing outward enough to clear the dowel pins on the engine block and remove it from the engine.

Inspection

Refer to illustrations 15.6, 15.8, 15.9a 15.9b, 15.9c, 15.9d, 15.9e and 15.9f

6   Remove the screws holding the front cover on the oil pump housing **(see illustration)**.

7   Clean all components with solvent, then inspect them for wear and damage.

8   Remove the oil pressure regulator cap, washer, spring and valve **(see illustration)**. Check the oil pressure regulator valve sliding

15.6 Remove the screws (arrows) and lift the cover off

surface and valve spring. If either the spring or the valve is damaged, they must be replaced as a set. Small burrs can be removed with 400-grit wet sandpaper and oil. The spring should measure approximately 1.95 inches long and should also have 23 to 25 pounds of pressure when compressed to 1.34 inches.

9   Check the clearance of the following oil pump components with a feeler gauge and a

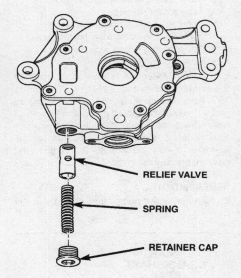

RELIEF VALVE

SPRING

RETAINER CAP

15.8 Oil pressure relief valve components

micrometer or dial caliper **(see illustrations)** and compare the measurements to the clear-ance listed in this Chapter's Specifications:

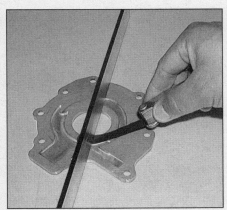

15.9a Place a straightedge across the oil pump cover and check it for warpage with a feeler gauge

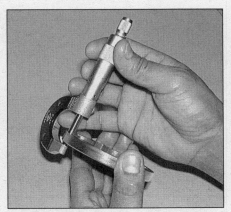

15.9b Use a micrometer or dial caliper to check the thickness and the diameter of the outer rotor

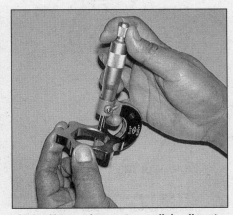

15.9c Use a micrometer or dial caliper to check the thickness of the inner rotor

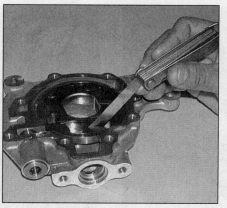

15.9d Check the outer rotor-to-housing clearance

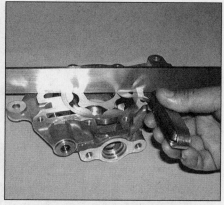

15.9e Check the clearance between the tips of the inner and outer rotors

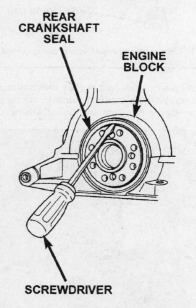

15.9f Using a straightedge and feeler gauge, check the side clearance between the surface of the oil pump and the inner and outer rotors

a) *Cover flatness*
b) *Outer rotor diameter and thickness*
c) *Inner rotor thickness*
d) *Outer rotor-to-body clearance*
e) *Inner rotor-to-outer rotor tip clearance*
f) *Cover-to-inner rotor side clearance*
g) *Cover-to-outer rotor side clearance*

If any clearance is excessive, replace the entire oil pump assembly.

10   Pack the pump with petroleum jelly to prime it. Assemble the oil pump and tighten all fasteners to the torque listed in this Chapter's Specifications. Install the oil pressure regulator valve, spring and washer, then tighten the oil pressure regulator valve cap.

Installation

11   To install the pump, turn the flats in the

rotor so they align with the flats on the crankshaft.
12   Install the pump-to-block bolts and tighten them to the torque listed in this Chapter's Specifications.
13   The remainder of installation is the reverse of removal.

16   Driveplate - removal and installation

1   Raise the vehicle and support it securely on jackstands.
2   Remove the transaxle (see Chapter 7). **Warning:** *The engine must be supported from above with an engine hoist or a suitable support fixture before working underneath the vehicle with the transaxle removed.*
3   Now would be a good time to check and replace the transaxle front pump seal (see Chapter 7).
4   Use paint or a center-punch to make alignment marks on the driveplate and crankshaft to ensure correct alignment during reinstallation.
5   Remove the bolts that secure the driveplate to the crankshaft. If the crankshaft turns, jam a large screwdriver or prybar through the

driveplate to keep the crankshaft from turning, then remove the driveplate retaining bolts.
6   Pull straight back on the driveplate to detach it from the crankshaft.
7   Installation is the reverse of removal. Be sure to align the matching paint marks. Before installing the driveplate retaining bolts, use thread locking compound on the bolt threads. Working in a criss-cross pattern, tighten the driveplate retaining bolts to the torque listed in this Chapter's Specifications.

17   Rear main oil seal - replacement

Refer to illustrations 17.2, 17.4 and 17.5

1   All models use a one-piece rear main oil seal which is installed in a bolt-on housing. Replacing this seal requires removal of the transaxle, torque converter and driveplate. Refer to Chapter 7 for the transaxle removal procedures.
2   The seal can be removed by prying it out of the housing by inserting a screwdriver, being careful not to nick the crankshaft surface (**see illustration**). Wrap the screwdriver tip with tape to avoid damage. Be sure to note how far it's recessed into the housing

REAR CRANKSHAFT SEAL

ENGINE BLOCK

SCREWDRIVER

17.2 Pry the seal out very carefully with a seal removal tool or screwdriver - if the crankshaft is damaged, the new seal will leak!

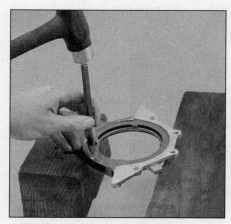

17.4 The seal can also be driven out of the housing with the housing removed

17.5 Use a block of wood to drive the new seal into the housing

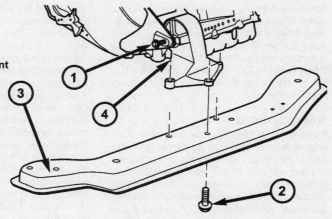

18.1a Front engine mount assembly

1 Through-bolt
2 Crossmember-to-engine mount bolts
3 Lower radiator crossmember
4 Front engine mount

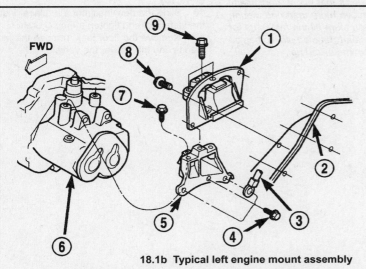

18.1b Typical left engine mount assembly

1 Transaxle support (mount) assembly
2 Left frame rail
3 Ground cable
4 Transaxle bracket-to-frame rail bolts
5 Transaxle bracket
6 Transaxle
7 Transaxle bracket-to-transaxle bolt
8 Transaxle support assembly-to-frame rail bolts
9 Transaxle support assembly-to-transaxle bracket bolts

bore before removal so the new seal can be installed to the same depth. Preferably, a seal installation tool is needed to press the new seal back into place. If the proper seal installation tool is unavailable, use a large socket, section of pipe or a blunt tool and carefully drive the new seal into place. The lip is stiff so carefully work it onto the seal journal of the crankshaft. Don't rush it or you may damage the seal.

3   The rear main seal housing can also be removed to change the seal, but whenever the housing is removed from the block a new seal and gasket must be installed.

4   If the housing is removed, place it on two blocks of wood and use a small punch to drive out the old seal **(see illustration)**.

5   Clean the housing thoroughly, then apply a thin coat of engine oil to the new seal. Set the seal squarely into the recess of the housing, then, using a piece of wood and a hammer, press the seal into place **(see illustration)**.

6   Carefully slide the seal over the crankshaft and bolt the seal housing to the block. Be sure to use a new gasket.

7   The remainder of installation is the reverse of the removal procedure.

18   Engine mounts - check and replacement

Refer to illustrations 18.1a, 18.1b, 18.1c and 18.1d

1   There are four engine mounts: front, left, right and rear. The front mount **(see illustration)** attaches the engine to the lower radiator crossmember. The left mount **(see illustration)** attaches the transaxle to the left frame rail. The right mount **(see illustration)** attaches the engine to the right frame rail. The rear mount **(see illustration)** attaches the transaxle to the suspension crossmember.

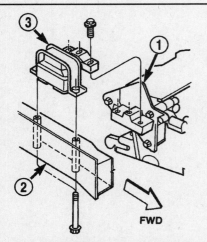

18.1c Right engine mount assembly

1 Engine support bracket
2 Right frame rail
3 Right engine mount

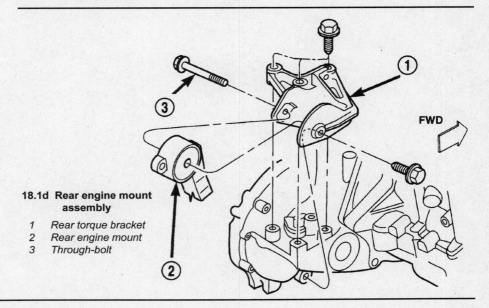

18.1d Rear engine mount assembly

1 Rear torque bracket
2 Rear engine mount
3 Through-bolt

Check

2   Raise the vehicle and support it securely on jackstands.

3   Before checking the engine mounts, raise the engine slightly with a floor jack to remove the weight from the mounts. Position a floor jack under the oil pan. Place a block of wood between the jack head and the oil pan, then carefully raise the engine/transaxle assembly just enough to take the weight off the mounts. **Warning:** *DO NOT place any part of your body under the engine when it's supported only by a jack!*

4   Inspect each mount to see if the rubber insulator is cracked, hardened or separated from the metal plates. If a rubber insulator is damaged in any way, replace it.

5   Check for relative movement between the two brackets of each mount (one is bolted to the engine or transaxle, the other is bolted to the vehicle). Insert a large screwdriver or prybar between the rubber insulator and each bracket and then try to lever the two brackets apart. Even new rubber insulators are somewhat flexible but it shouldn't be easy to pry apart the two brackets. If the brackets of a mount are easy to pry apart, the insulator is no longer doing its job. Replace it (see below).

6   Apply rubber preservative to the mounts to slow deterioration.

Replacement

Note: *Most of the time, the only part of an engine mount that must be replaced is the rubber insulator. The brackets on the engine or transaxle and on the vehicle are not normally replaced. However, you might need to remove an entire engine mount and bracket assembly when removing or installing the engine or transaxle. If that event, particularly if you have to remove more than one mount, make sure that you store all the fasteners for each mount in a clearly labeled plastic bag so that they don't become mixed up.*

7   Raise the vehicle and support it securely on jackstands.

8   Place a floor jack under the engine oil pan, put a block of wood between the jack head and the pan, and then raise the engine just enough to take the weight of the engine/transaxle assembly off the engine mount you're going to replace. (You'll know if you didn't raise the engine enough, or raised it too much, when you try to remove the engine mount fasteners in the next Step, because the fasteners, especially through-bolts, will be very difficult or impossible to remove.)

9   Remove the fasteners attaching the rubber insulator to the engine or transaxle bracket and to the bracket that's bolted to the vehicle **(see illustration 18.1a, 18.1b, 18.1c or 18.1d)**.

10   Slide the new insulator into place, install the fasteners and tighten them securely.

11   Remove the floor jack, remove the jackstands and then lower the vehicle.

Chapter 2 Part D
General engine overhaul procedures

Contents

Specifications

General

Displacement	
2.0L four-cylinder engine	121.8 cubic inches
2.4L DOHC four-cylinder engine	148 cubic inches
2.4L SOHC four-cylinder engine	143.4 cubic inches
2.5L V6 engine	152 cubic inches
3.0L V6 engine	181.4 cubic inches
2.7L V6 engine	167 cubic inches
Bore and Stroke	
2.0L four-cylinder engine	3.445 x 3.267 inches
2.4L DOHC four-cylinder engine	3.445 x 3.976 inches
2.4L SOHC four-cylinder engine	3.41 x 3.94 inches
2.5L V6 engine	3.29 x 2.99 inches
3.0L V6 engine	3.59 x 2.99 inches
2.7L V6 engine	3.386 x 3.091 inches
Cylinder compression pressure (at 250 to 400 rpm)	
2.0L and 2.4L DOHC four-cylinder engines	
Standard	170 to 225 psi
Minimum	100 psi
Maximum difference between cylinders	25 percent
2.4L SOHC four-cylinder engine	
Standard	185 psi
Minimum	139 psi
2.5L V6 engine	
1995 through 1997	
Standard	185 psi
Minimum	139 psi
1998 on	
Standard	
Federal	211 psi
California	202 psi
Minimum	
Federal	192 psi
California	154 psi
Maximum difference between cylinders	14 psi
3.0L V6 engine	
Standard	119 psi
Minimum	83 psi
Maximum difference between cylinders	14 psi
2.7L V6 engine	
Minimum	100 psi
Maximum difference between cylinders	25 percent

General (continued)

Oil pressure (engine warmed up)
  2.0L and 2.4L DOHC four-cylinder engines
    At idle... 4 psi (minimum)*
    At 3000 rpm.. 25 to 80 psi
  2.4L SOHC four-cylinder engine (at idle)........................... 11.4 psi (minimum)
  2.5L V6 engine
    Coupe (at idle)... 11.4 psi (minimum)
    Convertible
      At idle .... 6 psi (minimum)
      At 3000 rpm.. 35 to 72 psi
  3.0L V6 engine (at idle)... 11.6 psi (minimum)
  2.7L V6 engine
    At idle.. 5 psi (minimum)*
    At 3000 rpm.. 45 to 105 psi

* If oil pressure at idle is less than the specified minimum, do NOT run engine at 3000 rpm.

Torque specifications

Ft-lbs (unless otherwise indicated)

Note: *One foot-pound (ft-lb) of torque is equivalent to 12 inch-pounds (in-lbs) of torque. Torque values below approximately 15 foot-pounds are expressed in inch-pounds, because most foot-pound torque wrenches are not accurate at these smaller values.*

Connecting rod bearing cap bolts/nuts
  2.0L and 2.4L DOHC four-cylinder engine, 2.7L V6 engine
    Step 1 20
    Step 2 .... Tighten an additional 1/4-turn
  2.4L SOHC four-cylinder engine
    Step 1 .... 168 in-lbs
    Step 2 .... Tighten an additional 1/4-turn
  2.5L V6 engine 37
  3.0L V6 engine 38
Balance shaft carrier-to-engine bolts...................................... 40
Balance shaft chain tensioner and guide fasteners................. 105 in-lbs
Balance shaft gear cover stud (double-ended)........................ 105 in-lbs
Balance shaft rear cover bolts .... 105 in-lbs
Balance shaft sprocket bolts.. 21
Main bearing cap bolts
  2.0L four-cylinder engine
    1995 through 1999
      Bedplate bolts... 21
      Main bearing cap bolts 55
    2002 on
      Bedplate bolts... 25
      Main bearing cap bolts 60
  2.4L DOHC four-cylinder engine
    Bedplate bolts
      1996 through 2002 22
      2003 and later 21
    Main bearing cap bolts
      1996 through 2002
        Step 1 30
        Step 2 .... Tighten an additional 1/4 turn
      2003 and later 55
  2.4L SOHC four-cylinder engine
    Step 1 18
    Step 2 .... Tighten an additional 1/4-turn
  2.5L and 3.0L V6 engines 69
  2.7L V6 engine
    Tie bolts 21
    Inner main bearing cap bolts
      Step 1 15
      Step 2... Tighten an additional 1/4-turn
    Outer main bearing cap bolts
      Step 1 20
      Step 2... Tighten an additional 1/4-turn

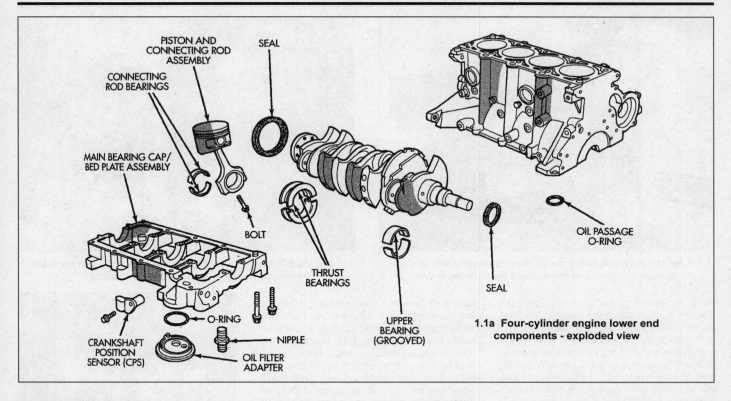

1.1a Four-cylinder engine lower end components - exploded view

1   General information - engine overhaul

Refer to illustrations 1.1a, 1.1b, 1.2, 1.3, 1.4, 1.5, 1.6 and 1.7

Included in this portion of Chapter 2 are general information and diagnostic testing procedures for determining the overall mechanical condition of your engine **(see illustrations 1.1a and 1.1b)**.

The information ranges from advice concerning preparation for an overhaul and the purchase of replacement parts and/or components to detailed, step-by-step procedures covering removal and installation.

The following Sections have been written to help you determine whether your engine needs to be overhauled and how to remove and install it once you've determined it needs to be rebuilt. For information concerning in-vehicle engine repair, see Chapter 2A, 2B or 2C.

The Specifications included in this Part are general in nature and include only those necessary for testing the oil pressure and checking the engine compression. Refer to Chapter 2A, 2B or 2C for additional engine Specifications.

It's not always easy to determine when, or if, an engine should be completely overhauled, because a number of factors must be considered.

High mileage is not necessarily an indication that an overhaul is needed, while low mileage doesn't preclude the need for an overhaul. Frequency of servicing is probably the most important consideration. An engine that's had regular and frequent oil and filter changes, as well as other required maintenance, will most likely give many thousands of miles of reliable service. Conversely, a neglected engine may require an overhaul very early in its service life.

Excessive oil consumption is an indication that piston rings, valve seals and/or valve guides are in need of attention. Make sure that oil leaks aren't responsible before deciding that the rings and/or guides are bad. Perform a cylinder compression check to deter-

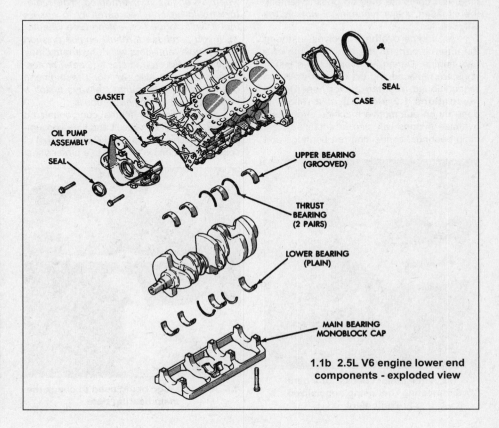

1.1b 2.5L V6 engine lower end components - exploded view

1.2 An engine block being bored. An engine rebuilder will use special machinery to recondition the cylinder bores

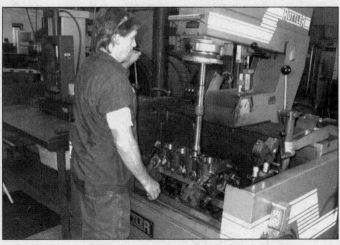

1.3 If the cylinders are bored, the machine shop will normally hone the engine on a machine like this

mine the extent of the work required (see Section 3). Also check the vacuum readings under various conditions (see Section 4).

Check the oil pressure with a gauge installed in place of the oil pressure sending unit and compare it to this Chapter's Specifications (see Section 2). If it's extremely low, the bearings and/or oil pump are probably worn out.

Loss of power, rough running, knocking or metallic engine noises, excessive valve train noise and high fuel consumption rates may also point to the need for an overhaul, especially if they're all present at the same time. If a complete tune-up doesn't remedy the situation, major mechanical work is the only solution.

An engine overhaul involves restoring the internal parts to the specifications of a new engine. During an overhaul, the piston rings are replaced and the cylinder walls are reconditioned (rebored and/or honed) **(see illustrations 1.2 and 1.3)**. If a rebore is done by an automotive machine shop, new oversize pistons will also be installed. The main bearings, connecting rod bearings and

camshaft bearings are generally replaced with new ones and, if necessary, the crankshaft may be reground to restore the journals **(see illustration 1.4)**. Generally, the valves are serviced as well, since they're usually in less-than-perfect condition at this point. While the engine is being overhauled, other components, such as the distributor, starter and alternator, can be rebuilt as well. The end result should be a like new engine that will give many trouble free miles. **Note:** *Critical cooling system components such as the hoses, drivebelts, thermostat and water pump should be replaced with new parts when an engine is overhauled. The radiator should be checked carefully to ensure that it isn't clogged or leaking (see Chapter 3). If you purchase a rebuilt engine or short block, some rebuilders will not warranty their engines unless the radiator has been professionally flushed. Also, we don't recommend overhauling the oil pump - always install a new one when an engine is rebuilt.*

Overhauling the internal components on today's engines is a difficult and time-consuming task which requires a significant amount of specialty tools and is best left to a professional

1.4 A crankshaft having a main bearing journal ground

engine rebuilder **(see illustrations 1.5, 1.6 and 1.7)**. A competent engine rebuilder will handle the inspection of your old parts and offer advice concerning the reconditioning or replacement of the original engine, never purchase parts or have machine work done on other components until the block has been thoroughly inspected by a professional machine shop. As a general rule, time is the primary cost of an over-

1.5 A machinist checks for a bent connecting rod, using specialized equipment

1.6 A bore gauge being used to check the main bearing bore

1.7 Uneven piston wear like this indicates a bent connecting rod

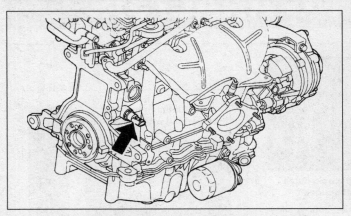

2.2a On 2.0L and 2.4L DOHC four-cylinder engines, the oil pressure sending unit (arrow) is located on the rear of the block, at the transaxle end of the engine

2.2b On 2.5L and 3.0L V6 engines, the oil pressure sending unit (arrow) is located on the oil filter housing

haul, especially since the vehicle may be tied up for a minimum of two weeks or more. Be aware that some engine builders only have the capability to rebuild the engine you bring them while other rebuilders have a large inventory of rebuilt exchange engines in stock. Also be aware that many machine shops could take as much as two weeks time to completely rebuild your engine depending on shop workload. Sometimes it makes more sense to simply exchange your engine for another engine that's already rebuilt to save time.

2   Oil pressure check

Refer to illustrations 2.2a, 2.2b, 2.2c, 2.2d and 2.3

1   Low engine oil pressure can be a sign of an engine in need of rebuilding. A "low oil pressure" indicator (often called an "idiot light") is not a test of the oiling system. Such indicators only come on when the oil pressure is dangerously low. Even a factory oil pressure gauge in the instrument panel is only a relative indication, although much better for driver information than a warning light. A better test is with a mechanical (not electrical) oil pressure gauge.

2   Locate the oil pressure indicator sending unit on the engine block:

a) *On 2.0L and 2.4L DOHC four-cylinder engines, the oil pressure sending unit is located at the left end of the rear side of the block* **(see illustration)**.

b) *On 2.4L SOHC four-cylinder engines, the sending unit is located at the left end of the rear side of the block.*

c) *On 2.5L and 3.0L V6 engines, the sending unit is located on the oil filter housing* **(see illustration)**, *on the front side of the block.*

d) *On 2.7L V6 engines, the sending unit is located at the left end of the rear side of the block. To access it, remove the heat shield* **(see illustrations)**.

3   Unscrew and remove the oil pressure sending unit and then screw in the hose for your oil pressure gauge **(see illustration)**. If necessary, install an adapter fitting. Use Teflon tape or thread sealant on the threads of the adapter and/or the fitting on the end of your gauge's hose.

4   Connect an accurate tachometer to the engine, according to the tachometer manufacturer's instructions.

5   Check the oil pressure with the engine running (normal operating temperature) at the specified engine speed, and compare it to this Chapter's Specifications. If it's extremely low, the bearings and/or oil pump are probably worn out.

3   Cylinder compression check

Refer to illustration 3.6

1   A compression check will tell you what mechanical condition the upper end of your engine (pistons, rings, valves, head gaskets) is in. Specifically, it can tell you if the compression is down due to leakage caused by worn piston rings, defective valves and seats or a blown head gasket. **Note:** *The engine must be at normal operating temperature and the battery must be fully charged for this check.*

2   Begin by cleaning the area around the

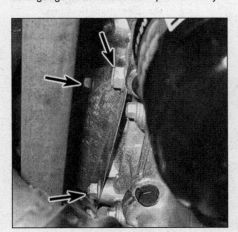

2.2c To access the oil pressure sending unit on 2.7L V6 engines, remove these three bolts (arrows), remove the heat shield . . .

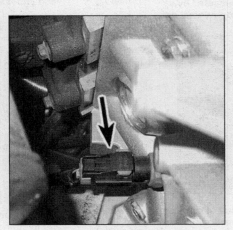

2.2d . . . to expose the oil pressure sending unit (arrow)

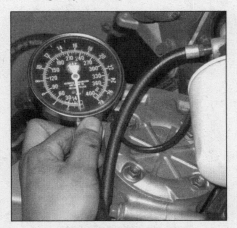

2.3 To check the oil pressure, unscrew the sending unit and screw in an oil pressure gauge in its place (2.5L V6 engine shown)

ENGINE BEARING ANALYSIS

Debris

Babbitt bearing embedded with debris from machinings

Microscopic detail of debris

Microscopic detail of gouges

Overplated copper alloy bearing gouged by cast iron debris

Aluminum bearing embedded with glass beads

Microscopic detail of glass beads

Damaged lining caused by dirt left on the bearing back

Misassembly

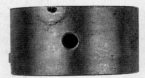

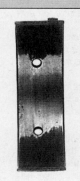

Result of a lower half assembled as an upper - blocking the oil flow

Excessive oil clearance is indicated by a short contact arc

Polished and oil-stained backs are a result of a poor fit in the housing bore

Result of a wrong, reversed, or shifted cap

Overloading

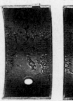

Damage from excessive idling which resulted in an oil film unable to support the load imposed

Damaged upper connecting rod bearings caused by engine lugging; the lower main bearings (not shown) were similarly affected

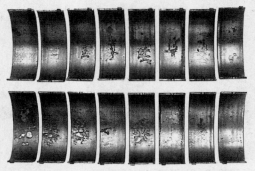

The damage shown in these upper and lower connecting rod bearings was caused by engine operation at a higher-than-rated speed under load

Misalignment

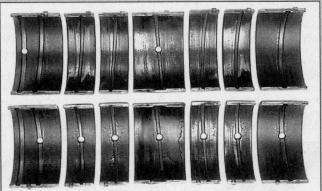

A warped crankshaft caused this pattern of severe wear in the center, diminishing toward the ends

A poorly finished crankshaft caused the equally spaced scoring shown

A tapered housing bore caused the damage along one edge of this pair

A bent connecting rod led to the damage in the "V" pattern

Lubrication

Result of dry start: The bearings on the left, farthest from the oil pump, show more damage

Result of a low oil supply or oil starvation

Severe wear as a result of inadequate oil clearance

Corrosion

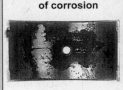

Microscopic detail of corrosion

Corrosion is an acid attack on the bearing lining generally caused by inadequate maintenance, extremely hot or cold operation, or inferior oils or fuels

Microscopic detail of cavitation

Example of cavitation - a surface erosion caused by pressure changes in the oil film

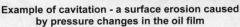

Damage from excessive thrust or insufficient axial clearance

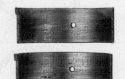

Bearing affected by oil dilution caused by excessive blow-by or a rich mixture

spark plugs before you remove them (compressed air should be used, if available). The idea is to prevent dirt from getting into the cylinders as the compression check is being done.

3   Remove all of the spark plugs from the engine (see Chapter 1).

4   Block the throttle wide open.

5   Disable the ignition system by disconnecting the primary (low voltage) electrical connectors from the coil packs (see Chapter 5). The fuel pump circuit should also be disabled (see Chapter 4).

6   Install a compression gauge in the spark plug hole **(see illustration)**.

7   Crank the engine over at least seven compression strokes and watch the gauge. The compression should build up quickly in a healthy engine. Low compression on the first stroke, followed by gradually increasing pressure on successive strokes, indicates worn piston rings. A low compression reading on the first stroke, which doesn't build up during successive strokes, indicates leaking valves or a blown head gasket (a cracked head could also be the cause). Deposits on the undersides of the valve heads can also cause low compression. Record

the highest gauge reading obtained.

8   Repeat the procedure for the remaining cylinders and compare the results to this Chapter's Specifications.

9   Add some engine oil (about three squirts from a plunger-type oil can) to each cylinder, through the spark plug hole, and repeat the test.

10   If the compression increases after the oil is added, the piston rings are definitely worn. If the compression doesn't increase significantly, the leakage is occurring at the valves or head gasket. Leakage past the valves may be caused by burned valve seats and/or faces or warped, cracked or bent valves.

11   If two adjacent cylinders have equally low compression, there's a strong possibility that the head gasket between them is blown. The appearance of coolant in the combustion chambers or the crankcase would verify this condition.

12   If one cylinder is slightly lower than the others, and the engine has a slightly rough idle, a worn lobe on the camshaft could be the cause.

13   If the compression is unusually high, the combustion chambers are probably coated with carbon deposits. If that's the case, the cylinder head(s) should be removed and decarbonized.

14   If compression is way down or varies greatly between cylinders, it would be a good idea to have a leak-down test performed by an automotive repair shop. This test will pinpoint exactly where the leakage is occurring and how severe it is.

3.6 Use a compression gauge with a threaded fitting for the spark plug hole, not the type that requires hand pressure to maintain the seal

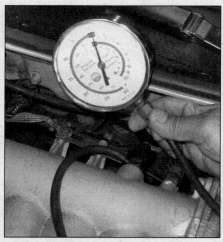

4.4 A simple vacuum gauge can be handy in diagnosing engine condition and performance

4   Vacuum gauge diagnostic checks

Refer to illustrations 4.4 and 4.6

1   A vacuum gauge provides inexpensive but valuable information about what is going on in the engine. You can check for worn rings or cylinder walls, leaking head or intake manifold gaskets, incorrect carburetor adjustments, restricted exhaust, stuck or burned valves, weak valve springs, improper ignition or valve timing and ignition problems.

2   Unfortunately, vacuum gauge readings are easy to misinterpret, so they should be used in conjunction with other tests to confirm the diagnosis.

3   Both the absolute readings and the rate of needle movement are important for accurate interpretation. Most gauges measure vacuum in inches of mercury (in-Hg). The following references to vacuum assume the diagnosis is being performed at sea level. As elevation increases (or atmospheric pressure decreases), the reading will decrease. For every 1,000 foot increase in elevation above approximately 2000 feet, the gauge readings will decrease about one inch of mercury.

4   Connect the vacuum gauge directly to the intake manifold vacuum, not to ported (throttle body) vacuum **(see illustration)**. Be sure no hoses are left disconnected during the test or false readings will result.

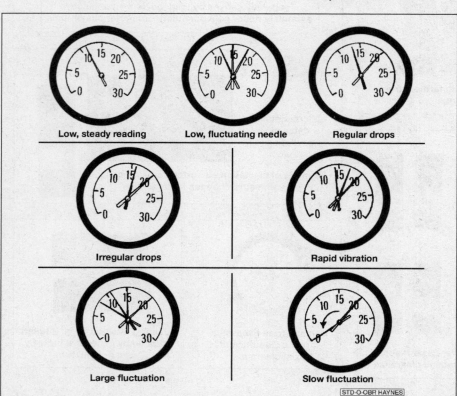

Low, steady reading   Low, fluctuating needle   Regular drops

Irregular drops   Rapid vibration

Large fluctuation   Slow fluctuation

STD-O-OBR HAYNES

4.6 Typical vacuum gauge readings

5   Before you begin the test, allow the engine to warm up completely. Block the wheels and set the parking brake. With the transmission in Park, start the engine and allow it to run at normal idle speed. **Warning:** *Keep your hands and the vacuum gauge clear of the fans.*

6   Read the vacuum gauge; an average, healthy engine should normally produce about 17 to 22 in-Hg with a fairly steady needle **(see illustration)**. Refer to the following vacuum gauge readings and what they indicate about the engine's condition:

7   A low steady reading usually indicates a leaking gasket between the intake manifold and cylinder head(s) or throttle body, a leaky vacuum hose, late ignition timing or incorrect camshaft timing. Check ignition timing with a timing light and eliminate all other possible causes, utilizing the tests provided in this Chapter before you remove the timing chain cover to check the timing marks.

8   If the reading is three to eight inches below normal and it fluctuates at that low reading, suspect an intake manifold gasket leak at an intake port or a faulty fuel injector.

9   If the needle has regular drops of about two-to-four inches at a steady rate, the valves are probably leaking. Perform a compression check or leak-down test to confirm this.

10   An irregular drop or down-flick of the needle can be caused by a sticking valve or an ignition misfire. Perform a compression check or leak-down test and read the spark plugs.

11   A rapid vibration of about four in-Hg vibration at idle combined with exhaust smoke indicates worn valve guides. Perform a leak-down test to confirm this. If the rapid vibration occurs with an increase in engine speed, check for a leaking intake manifold gasket or head gasket, weak valve springs, burned valves or ignition misfire.

12   A slight fluctuation, say one inch up and down, may mean ignition problems. Check all the usual tune-up items and, if necessary, run the engine on an ignition analyzer.

13   If there is a large fluctuation, perform a compression or leak-down test to look for a weak or dead cylinder or a blown head gasket.

14   If the needle moves slowly through a wide range, check for a clogged PCV system, incorrect idle fuel mixture, carburetor/throttle body or intake manifold gasket leaks.

15   Check for a slow return after revving the engine by quickly snapping the throttle open until the engine reaches about 2,500 rpm and let it shut. Normally the reading should drop to near zero, rise above normal idle reading (about 5 in-Hg over) and then return to the previous idle reading. If the vacuum returns slowly and doesn't peak when the throttle is snapped shut, the rings may be worn. If there is a long delay, look for a restricted exhaust system (often the muffler or catalytic converter). An easy way to check this is to temporarily disconnect the exhaust ahead of the suspected part and redo the test.

5   Engine rebuilding alternatives

The do-it-yourselfer is faced with a number of options when purchasing a rebuilt engine. The major considerations are cost, warranty, parts availability and the time required for the rebuilder to complete the project. The decision to replace the engine block, piston/connecting rod assemblies and crankshaft depends on the final inspection results of your engine. Only then can you make a cost effective decision whether to have your engine overhauled or simply purchase an exchange engine for your vehicle. Some of the rebuilding alternatives include:

Individual parts - If the inspection procedures reveal that the engine block and most engine components are in reusable condition, purchasing individual parts and having a rebuilder rebuild your engine may be the most economical alternative. The block, crankshaft and piston/connecting rod assemblies should all be inspected carefully by a machine shop first.

Short block - A short block consists of an engine block with a crankshaft and piston/connecting rod assemblies already installed. All new bearings are incorporated and all clearances will be correct. The existing camshafts, valve train components, cylinder head and external parts can be bolted to the short block

with little or no machine shop work necessary.

Long block - A long block consists of a short block plus an oil pump, oil pan, cylinder head, valve cover, camshaft and valve train components, timing sprockets and chain or gears and timing cover. All components are installed with new bearings, seals and gaskets incorporated throughout. The installation of manifolds and external parts is all that's necessary.

Low mileage used engines - Some companies now offer low mileage used engines which is a very cost effective way to get your vehicle up and running again. These engines often come from vehicles which have been in totaled in accidents or come from other countries which have a higher vehicle turn over rate. A low mileage used engine also usually has a similar warranty like the newly remanufactured engines.

Give careful thought to which alternative is best for you and discuss the situation with local automotive machine shops, auto parts dealers and experienced rebuilders before ordering or purchasing replacement parts.

6   Engine removal - methods and precautions

Refer to illustrations 6.1, 6.2, 6.3, 6.4 and 6.5

If you've decided that an engine must be removed for overhaul or major repair work, several preliminary steps should be taken. Read all removal and installation procedures carefully prior to committing this job. Some engines are removed by lowering to the floor and then raising the vehicle sufficiently to slide it out; this will require a vehicle hoist.

Locating a suitable place to work is extremely important. Adequate work space, along with storage space for the vehicle, will be needed. If a shop or garage isn't available, at the very least a flat, level, clean work surface made of concrete or asphalt is required. Cleaning the engine compartment and engine before beginning the removal procedure will help keep tools clean and organized **(see illustrations 6.1 and 6.2)**.

6.1 After tightly wrapping water-vulnerable components, use a spray cleaner on everything, with particular concentration on the greasiest areas, usually around the valve cover and lower edges of the block. If one section dries out, apply more cleaner

6.2 Depending on how dirty the engine is, let the cleaner soak in according to the directions and then hose off the grime and cleaner. Get the rinse water down into every area you can get at; then dry important components with a hair dryer or paper towels

An engine hoist or A-frame will also be necessary. Make sure the equipment is rated in excess of the combined weight of the engine and transaxle. Safety is of primary importance, considering the potential hazards involved in lifting the engine out of the vehicle.

If the engine is being removed by a novice, a helper should be available. Advice and aid from someone more experienced would also be helpful. there are many instances when one person cannot simultaneously perform all of the operations required when lifting the engine out of the vehicle.

Plan the operation ahead of time. Arrange for or obtain all of the tools and equipment you'll need prior to beginning the job **(see illustrations 6.3, 6.4 and 6.5)**. some

6.3 Get an engine hoist that's strong enough to easily lift your engine in and out of the engine compartment - an adapter, like the one shown here (arrow), can be used to change the angle of the engine as it's being removed or installed

6.4 Get an engine stand sturdy enough to firmly support the engine while you're working on it - stay away from three-wheeled models - they have a tendency to tip over more easily (get a four-wheeled unit)

of the equipment necessary to perform engine removal and installation safely and with relative ease are (in addition to an engine hoist) a heavy duty floor jack, complete sets of wrenches and sockets as described in the front of this manual, wooden blocks and plenty of rags and cleaning solvent for mopping up spilled oil, coolant and gasoline. If the hoist must be rented, make sure that you arrange for it in advance and perform all of the operations possible without it beforehand. This will save you money and time.

Plan for the vehicle to be out of use for quite a while. A machine shop will be required to perform all of the work which is beyond the scope of the home mechanic. These shops often have a busy schedule, so it would be a good idea to consult them before removing the engine in order to accurately estimate the amount of time required to rebuild or repair components that may need work.

Always be extremely careful when removing and installing the engine. Serious injury can result from careless actions. Plan ahead, take your time and a job of this nature, although major, can be accomplished successfully.

---

7   Engine (coupe models only) - removal and installation

Removal

Refer to illustrations , 7.6, 7.11, 7.17, 7.21a, 7.21b, 7.22 and 7.26

Warning 1: *The models covered by this manual are equipped with Supplemental Restraint systems (SRS), more commonly known as airbags. Always disable the airbag system before working in the vicinity of any airbag system components to avoid the possibility of accidental deployment of the airbag, which could cause personal injury (see Chapter 12).*

Warning 2: *Gasoline is extremely flammable, so take extra precautions when you work on any part of the fuel system. Don't smoke or allow open flames or bare light bulbs near the work area, and don't work in a garage where a gas-type appliance (such as a water heater or a clothes dryer) is present. Since gasoline is carcinogenic, wear latex gloves when there's a possibility of being exposed to fuel, and, if you spill any fuel on your skin, rinse*

it off immediately with soap and water. Mop up any spills immediately and do not store fuel-soaked rags where they could ignite. The fuel system is under constant pressure, so, if any fuel lines are to be disconnected, the fuel pressure in the system must be relieved first (see Chapter 4 for more information). When you perform any kind of work on the fuel system, wear safety glasses and have a Class B type fire extinguisher on hand.

Warning 3: *The air conditioning system is under high pressure! If you have to disconnect air conditioning hoses for engine removal, first have a dealer service department or service station discharge the system. Carefully note the routing of air conditioning system refrigerant lines before beginning engine removal to see if line disconnection, and therefore professional discharging, is necessary.*

Note: *The following procedure applies only to coupe models. On convertible and sedan models, the engine and transaxle must be removed as a single assembly from underneath the vehicle, using a special cradle, which is then rolled out from under the vehicle. This cradle is an expensive device, and can only be used under a vehicle that has been raised on a vehicle hoist, not jackstands. Engine removal on these models is therefore beyond the scope of the average home mechanic.*

1   Look carefully at the air conditioning system plumbing. If some of the plumbing, particularly rigid pipes, looks like it's going to impede engine removal and installation, have the system discharged by an automotive air conditioning shop before proceeding. If you're not sure whether the air conditioning system is going to be in the way, consult a dealer service department or an automotive air conditioning shop. If the air conditioning system plumbing can simply be unbolted and set aside, it's not necessary to have it discharged.

2   Relieve the fuel system pressure (see Chapter 4).

3   Disconnect the cable from the negative battery terminal or the remote ground terminal (see Chapter 5).

4   Remove the hood (see Chapter 11) and then cover the fenders and cowl. Special pads are available to protect the fenders, but an old bedspread or blanket will also work.

5   Remove the air cleaner assembly and the air intake duct (see Chapter 4).

6.5 A clutch alignment tool is necessary if you plan to install a rebuilt engine mated to a manual transmission

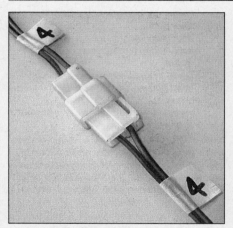

7.6 Label both ends of each wire and hose before disconnecting it - do the same for vacuum hoses

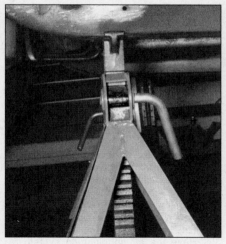

7.11 Place sturdy jackstands under the frame of the vehicle and set them both at uniform height

7.17 If you're planning to replace the block, be sure to remove the compressor bracket bolts (arrows) and then remove the bracket (2.7L V6 shown, four-cylinder engine compressor brackets similar)

6   Label all vacuum lines, emissions system hoses, wiring connectors and ground straps to ensure correct reinstallation, then disconnect them. Pieces of masking tape with numbers or letters written on them work well **(see illustration)**. So does colored electrical tape. If there's any possibility of confusion, make a sketch of the engine compartment and clearly label the lines, hoses and wires.

7   Disconnect the fuel lines running from the engine to the chassis (see Chapter 4). Plug or cap all open fittings/lines. **Warning:** *Gasoline is extremely flammable, so extra precautions must be taken when working on any part of the fuel system. DO NOT smoke or allow open flames or bare light bulbs near the vehicle. Also, don't work in a garage if a natural gas-type appliance is present.*

8   Disconnect the throttle cable from the throttle linkage (see Chapter 4). On models with an automatic transaxle, disconnect the throttle valve cable (see Chapter 7B).

9   Remove the cooling fan, shroud and radiator (see Chapter 3).

10   Remove the drivebelts (see Chapter 1).

11   Raise the vehicle and place it securely on jackstands **(see illustration)**.

12   Remove the engine under cover(s).

13   Drain the engine oil and then remove the oil filter (see Chapter 1).

14   Drain the cooling system (see Chapter 1).

15   Label and detach all coolant hoses from the engine.

16   Remove the alternator (see Chapter 5).

17   On air-conditioned models, unbolt the compressor (see Chapter 3) and set it aside. Do not disconnect the hoses unless absolutely necessary (see **Warning 3**). If you're going to be replacing the block, now is a good time to remove the compressor bracket **(see illustration)**.

18   Remove the part of the exhaust system that's routed underneath the engine, between the exhaust manifold(s) and the downstream catalytic converter (see Chapter 4).

19   Remove the starter motor (see Chapter 5).

20   Remove the transaxle (see Chapter 7).

21   Locate the lifting brackets on the engine **(see illustrations)**.

22   Roll the hoist into position and then attach it to the lifting brackets with a couple pieces of heavy-duty chain **(see illustration)**. Take up the slack in the sling or chain, but don't lift the engine. **Warning:** *DO NOT place any part of your body under the engine when it's supported only by a hoist or other lifting device.*

23   Remove the engine mount fasteners (see the "Engine mount" section in Chapter 2A or 2B).

24   Recheck to be sure nothing is still connecting the engine to the transaxle or vehicle. Disconnect anything still remaining.

7.22 Attach the chains securely to the engine lifting hooks and then take up the slack until there is slight tension on the chain

7.21a Typical front lifting hook (arrow)

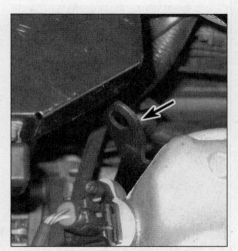

7.21b Typical rear lifting hook (arrow)

7.26 Use long high-strength bolts (arrows) to hold the engine block on the engine stand - make sure they are tight before resting all the weight on the stand

25   Raise the engine slightly and then inspect it thoroughly once more to make sure that *nothing* is still attached, then slowly raise the engine out of the engine compartment. Check carefully to make sure nothing is hanging up.

26   Remove the flywheel/driveplate (see Chapter 2A or 2B) and then mount the engine on an engine stand **(see illustration)**.

27   Inspect the engine and transaxle mounts (see the "Engine mount" section in Chapter 2A or 2B). If they're worn or damaged, replace them.

Installation

28   Install the flywheel/driveplate (see Chapter 2A or 2B).

29   If you're working on a vehicle with manual transaxle, install the clutch and pressure plate (see Chapter 8). Now is a good time to install a new clutch.

30   Carefully lower the engine into the engine compartment and then reattach it to the engine mounts (see the "Engine mounts" section in Chapter 2A or 2B).

31   Install the transaxle (see Chapter 7).

9.1 Before you try to remove the pistons, use a ridge reamer to remove the raised material (ridge) from the top of the cylinders

If you're working on a manual transaxle equipped vehicle, apply a film of high-temperature grease to the input shaft and guide it into the clutch disc splines until the bellhousing is flush with the engine block. If you're working on a vehicle with an automatic transaxle, guide the torque converter into the crankshaft following the procedure outlined in Chapter 7B. Install the transaxle-to-engine bolts and tighten them securely. **Caution:** *DO NOT use the bolts to force the transaxle and engine together!*

32   Reinstall the remaining components in the reverse order of removal.

33   Add coolant, oil and transaxle fluid as needed (see Chapter 1).

34   Run the engine and check for leaks and proper operation of all accessories, then install the hood and test drive the vehicle.

35   Have the air conditioning system recharged and leak tested, if it was discharged.

8   Engine overhaul - disassembly sequence

1   It's much easier to remove the external components if it's mounted on a portable engine stand. A stand can often be rented quite cheaply from an equipment rental yard. Before the engine is mounted on a stand, the flywheel/driveplate should be removed from the engine.

2   If a stand isn't available, it's possible to remove the external engine components with it blocked up on the floor. Be extra careful not to tip or drop the engine when working without a stand.

3   If you're going to obtain a rebuilt engine, all external components must come off first, to be transferred to the replacement engine. These components include:

> *Emissions-related components*
> *Distributor (if equipped)*
> *Spark plug wires and spark plugs*
> *Ignition coils*

9.3 Checking the connecting rod endplay (side clearance)

> *Thermostat and housing assembly*
> *Water pump*
> *Fuel injection components*
> *Intake/exhaust manifolds*
> *Oil filter*
> *Engine mounts and mount brackets*
> *Clutch and flywheel (models with manual transaxle)*
> *Driveplate (models with automatic transaxle)*

Note: *When removing the external components from the engine, pay close attention to details that may be helpful or important during installation. Note the installed position of gaskets, seals, spacers, pins, brackets, washers, bolts and other small items.*

4   If you're going to obtain a short block (assembled engine block, crankshaft, pistons and connecting rods), then remove the timing belt or chain, cylinder head, oil pan, oil pump pick-up tube, oil pump and water pump from your engine so that you can turn in your old short block to the rebuilder as a core. See *Engine rebuilding alternatives* for additional information regarding the different possibilities to be considered.

9   Pistons and connecting rods - removal and installation

Removal

Refer to illustrations 9.1, 9.3, 9.4 and 9.6

Note: *Prior to removing the piston/connecting rod assemblies, remove the cylinder head and oil pan (see Chapter 2A, 2B or 2C).*

1   Use your fingernail to feel if a ridge has formed at the upper limit of ring travel (about 1/4-inch down from the top of each cylinder). If carbon deposits or cylinder wear have produced ridges, they must be completely removed with a special tool **(see illustration)**. Follow the manufacturer's instructions provided with the tool. Failure to remove the ridges before attempting to remove the piston/connecting rod assemblies may result in piston breakage.

2   After the cylinder ridges have been removed, turn the engine so the crankshaft is facing up.

3   Before the main bearing cap assembly and connecting rods are removed, check the connecting rod endplay with feeler gauges. Slide them between the first connecting rod and the crankshaft throw until the play is removed **(see illustration)**. Repeat this procedure for each connecting rod. The endplay is equal to the thickness of the feeler gauge(s). Check with an automotive machine shop for the endplay service limit. If the play exceeds the service limit (a typical endplay should measure from 0.005 to 0.015-inch), new connecting rods will be required. If new rods (or a new crankshaft) are installed, the endplay may fall under the minimum allowable. If it does, the rods will have to be machined to restore it. If necessary, consult an automotive machine shop for advice.

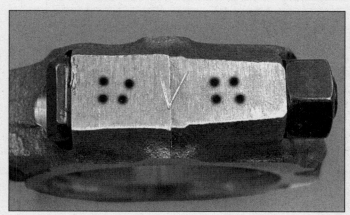

9.4 If the connecting rods and caps are not marked, use a center punch or numbered impression stamps to mark the caps to the rods by cylinder number (for example, this would be the No. 4 connecting rod)

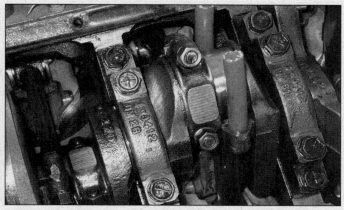

9.6 On V6 engines, push a short section of plastic or rubber hose over the connecting rod studs to prevent damage to the crankshaft journals during piston/rod removal

4   Check the connecting rods and caps for identification marks (see illustration). If they aren't plainly marked, use a small center-punch to make the appropriate number of indentations on each rod and cap (1, 2, 3, etc., depending on the cylinder they're associated with).
5   Loosen each of the connecting rod cap nuts or bolts 1/2-turn at a time until they can be removed by hand. Remove the number one connecting rod cap and bearing insert. Don't drop the bearing insert out of the cap.
6   If you are removing the rods from a V6 engine, slip a short length of plastic or rubber hose over each connecting rod stud to protect the crankshaft journal and cylinder wall as the rod is removed (see illustration).
7   Remove the bearing insert and push the connecting rod/piston assembly out through the top of the engine. Use a wooden or plastic hammer handle to push on the upper bearing surface in the connecting rod. If resistance is felt, double-check to make sure that all of the ridge was removed from the cylinder.
8   Repeat the procedure for the remaining cylinders. Note: If the connecting rod caps are secured by bolts (instead of nuts), discard the old rod cap bolts. Use new bolts when

reassembling the engine.
9   After removal, reassemble the connecting rod caps and bearing inserts in their respective connecting rods and install the cap bolts finger tight. Leaving the old bearing inserts in place until reassembly will help prevent the connecting rod bearing surfaces from being accidentally nicked or gouged.
10   The pistons and connecting rods are now ready for inspection and overhaul at an automotive machine shop.

Piston ring installation
Refer to illustrations 9.13, 9.14, 9.15, 9.19a, 9.19b, 9.21 and 9.22
11   Before installing the new piston rings, the ring end gaps must be checked. It's assumed that the piston ring side clearance has been checked and verified correct.
12   Lay out the piston/connecting rod assemblies and the new ring sets so the ring sets will be matched with the same piston and cylinder during the end gap measurement and engine assembly.
13   Insert the top (number one) ring into the first cylinder and square it up with the cylinder walls by pushing it in with the top of the piston (see illustration). The ring should be near the bottom of the cylinder, at the lower

limit of ring travel.
14   To measure the end gap, slip feeler gauges between the ends of the ring until a gauge equal to the gap width is found (see illustration). The feeler gauge should slide between the ring ends with a slight amount of drag. A typical end gap should fall between 0.010 and 0.020-inch for compression rings, and up to 0.030-inch for the oil ring steel rails. If the gap is larger or smaller than specified, double-check to make sure you have the correct rings before proceeding.
15   If the gap is too small, it must be enlarged or the ring ends may come in contact with each other during engine operation, which can cause serious damage to the engine. The end gap can be increased by filing the ring ends very carefully with a fine file. Mount the file in a vise equipped with soft jaws, slip the ring over the file with the ends contacting the file face and slowly move the ring to remove material from the ends. When performing this operation, file only by pushing the ring from the outside end of the file towards the vise (see illustration).
16   Excess end gap isn't critical unless it's greater than approximately 0.040-inch. Again, double-check to make sure you have the correct ring type and that you are referencing the

9.13 Install the piston ring into the cylinder then push it down into position using a piston so the ring will be square in the cylinder

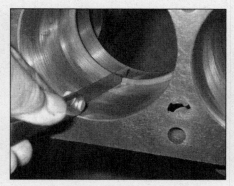

9.14 With the ring square in the cylinder, measure the ring end gap with a feeler gauge

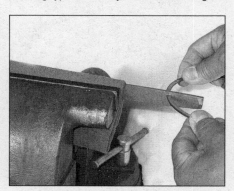

9.15 If the ring end gap is too small, clamp a file in a vise as shown and file the piston ring ends - be sure to remove all raised material

9.19a Installing the spacer/expander in the oil ring groove

9.19b DO NOT use a piston ring installation tool when installing the oil control side rails

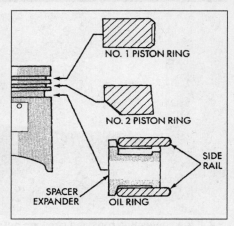

9.21 Piston ring assembly details

correct section and category of specifications.

17   Repeat the procedure for each ring that will be installed in the first cylinder and for each ring in the remaining cylinders. Remember to keep rings, pistons and cylinders matched up.

18   Once the ring end gaps have been checked/corrected, the rings can be installed on the pistons.

19   The oil control ring (lowest one on the piston) is usually installed first. It's composed of three separate components. Slip the spacer/expander into the groove **(see illustration)**. If an anti-rotation tang is used, make sure it's inserted into the drilled hole in the ring groove. Next, install the upper side rail in the same manner **(see illustration)**. Don't use a piston ring installation tool on the oil ring side rails, as they may be damaged. Instead, place one end of the side rail into the groove between the spacer/expander and the ring land, hold it firmly in place and slide a finger around the piston while pushing the rail into the groove. Finally, install the lower side rail.

20   After the three oil ring components have been installed, check to make sure that both the upper and lower side rails can be rotated

smoothly inside the ring grooves.

21   The number two (middle) ring is installed next. It's usually stamped with a mark which must face up, toward the top of the piston. Do not mix up the top and middle rings, as they have different cross-sections **(see illustration)**. **Note:** *Always follow the instructions printed on the ring package or box - different manufacturers may require different approaches.*

22   Use a piston ring installation tool and make sure the identification mark is facing the top of the piston, then slip the ring into the middle groove on the piston **(see illustration)**. Don't expand the ring any more than necessary to slide it over the piston.

23   Install the number one (top) ring in the same manner. Make sure the mark is facing up. Be careful not to confuse the number one and number two rings **(see illustration 9.21)**.

24   Repeat the procedure for the remaining pistons and rings.

Installation

25   Before installing the piston/connecting rod assemblies, the cylinder walls must be perfectly clean, the top edge of each cylinder

bore must be chamfered, and the crankshaft must be in place.

26   Remove the cap from the end of the number one connecting rod (refer to the marks made during removal). Remove the original bearing inserts and wipe the bearing surfaces of the connecting rod and cap with a clean, lint-free cloth. They must be kept spotlessly clean.

Connecting rod bearing oil clearance check

Refer to illustrations 9.30, 9.35, 9.37, 9.38 and 9.41

27   Clean the back side of the new upper bearing insert, then lay it in place in the connecting rod. Make sure the tab on the bearing fits into the recess in the rod. Don't hammer the bearing insert into place and be very careful not to nick or gouge the bearing face. Don't lubricate the bearing at this time.

28   Clean the back side of the other bearing insert and install it in the rod cap. Again, make sure the tab on the bearing fits into the recess in the cap, and don't apply any lubricant. It's critically important that the mating surfaces of the bearing and connecting rod are perfectly clean and oil free when they're assembled.

29   On V6 engines, slip a short section of

9.22 Use a piston ring installation tool to install the 2nd and top rings - be sure the directional mark on the piston ring(s) is facing toward the top of the piston

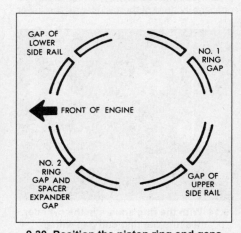

9.30 Position the piston ring end gaps as shown

GAP OF LOWER SIDE RAIL

NO. 1 RING GAP

FRONT OF ENGINE

NO. 2 RING GAP AND SPACER EXPANDER GAP

GAP OF UPPER SIDE RAIL

9.35 Use a plastic or wooden hammer handle to push the piston into the cylinder

9.37 Place Plastigage on each connecting rod bearing journal parallel to the crankshaft centerline

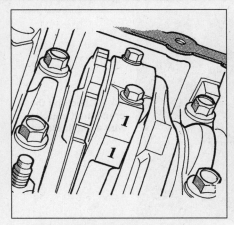

9.38 Install the connecting rod cap making sure the cap and rod identification numbers match

9.41 Use the scale on the Plastigage package to determine the bearing oil clearance - be sure to measure the widest part of the Plastigage and use the correct scale; it comes with both standard and metric scales

plastic or rubber hose over the connecting rod studs to avoid damaging the cylinder wall or crankshaft journal **(see illustration 9.6)**.

30   Position the piston ring gaps at 90-degree intervals around the piston as shown **(see illustration)**.

31   Lubricate the piston and rings with clean engine oil and attach a piston ring compressor to the piston. Leave the skirt protruding about 1/4-inch to guide the piston into the cylinder. The rings must be compressed until they're flush with the piston.

32   Rotate the crankshaft until the number one connecting rod journal is at BDC (bottom dead center) and apply a liberal coat of engine oil to the cylinder walls.

33   With the weight designation mark, or arrow, on top of the piston facing the front (timing belt end) of the engine, gently insert the piston/connecting rod assembly into the number one cylinder bore and rest the bottom edge of the ring compressor on the engine block. **Note:** *The connecting rod also has a mark on it that must face the front (timing belt end) of the engine if it faces the opposite direction, the piston and connecting rod have been assembled improperly.*

34   Tap the top edge of the ring compressor to make sure it's contacting the block around its entire circumference.

35   Gently tap on the top of the piston with the end of a wooden or plastic hammer handle **(see illustration)** while guiding the end of the connecting rod into place on the crankshaft journal. The piston rings may try to pop out of the ring compressor just before entering the cylinder bore, so keep some downward pressure on the ring compressor. Work slowly, and if any resistance is felt as the piston enters the cylinder, stop immediately. Find out what's hanging up and fix it before proceeding. Do not, for any reason, force the piston into the cylinder - you might break a ring and/or the piston.

36   Once the piston/connecting rod assembly is installed, the connecting rod bearing oil clearance must be checked before the rod

cap is permanently installed.

37   Cut a piece of the appropriate size Plastigage slightly shorter than the width of the connecting rod bearing and lay it in place on the number one connecting rod journal, parallel with the journal axis **(see illustration)**.

38   Clean the connecting rod cap bearing face and install the rod cap. Make sure the mating mark on the cap is on the same side as the mark on the connecting rod **(see illustration)**. **Note:** *Check to make sure the identification mark on the connecting rod faces toward the front (timing belt) end of the engine.*

39   Install the old rod bolts or nuts, at this time, and tighten them to the torque listed in this Chapter's Specifications, working up to it in three steps. **Note:** *Use a thin-wall socket to avoid erroneous torque readings that can result if the socket is wedged between the rod cap and the bolt or nut. If the socket tends to wedge itself between the fastener and the cap, lift up on it slightly until it no longer contacts the cap. DO NOT rotate the crankshaft at any time during this operation.*

40   Remove the fasteners and detach the rod cap, being very careful not to disturb the Plastigage. Discard the cap bolts at this time as they cannot be reused. **Caution:** *On four-cylinder engines, new connecting rod bolts must be installed.*

41   Compare the width of the crushed Plastigage to the scale printed on the Plastigage envelope to obtain the oil clearance **(see illustration)**. The connecting rod oil clearance is usually about 0.001 to 0.002 inch. Consult an automotive machine shop for the clearance specified for the rod bearings on your engine.

42   If the clearance is not as specified, the bearing inserts may be the wrong size (which means different ones will be required). Before deciding that different inserts are needed, make sure that no dirt or oil was between the bearing inserts and the connecting rod or cap when the clearance was measured. Also, recheck the journal diameter. If the Plastigage was wider at one end than the other, the

journal may be tapered. If the clearance still exceeds the limit specified, the bearing will have to be replaced with an undersize bearing. **Caution:** *When installing a new crankshaft always use a standard size bearing.*

Final installation

43   Carefully scrape all traces of the Plastigage material off the rod journal and/or bearing face. Be very careful not to scratch the bearing - use your fingernail or the edge of a plastic card.

44   Make sure the bearing faces are perfectly clean, then apply a uniform layer of clean moly-base grease or engine assembly lube to both of them. You'll have to push the piston into the cylinder to expose the face of the bearing insert in the connecting rod.

45   **Caution:** *If the connecting rod caps are secured to the rods with bolts (instead of nuts), install new connecting rod cap bolts. Do NOT reuse old bolts - they have stretched and cannot be reused.* Slide the connecting rod back into place on the journal, install the rod cap, install the nuts or new bolts and tighten them to the torque listed in this Chapter's Specifications. Again, work up to the torque in three steps.

46   Repeat the entire procedure for the remaining pistons/connecting rods.

47   The important points to remember are:

a)   *Keep the back sides of the bearing inserts and the insides of the connecting rods and caps perfectly clean when assembling them.*

b)   *Make sure you have the correct piston/rod assembly for each cylinder.*

c)   *The mark on the piston must face the front (timing belt or chain end) of the engine.*

d)   *Lubricate the cylinder walls liberally with clean oil.*

e)   *Lubricate the bearing faces when installing the rod caps after the oil clearance has been checked.*

10.1 Checking the crankshaft endplay with a dial indicator

10.3 Checking the crankshaft endplay with feeler gauges at the thrust bearing journal

48 After all the piston/connecting rod assemblies have been correctly installed, rotate the crankshaft a number of times by hand to check for any obvious binding.

49 As a final step, check the connecting rod endplay again, as described in Step 3. If it was correct before disassembly and the original crankshaft and rods were reinstalled, it should still be correct. If new rods or a new crankshaft were installed, the endplay may be inadequate. If so, the rods will have to be removed and taken to an automotive machine shop for resizing.

10 Crankshaft - removal and installation

Removal

Refer to illustrations 10.1 and 10.3

Note: *The crankshaft can be removed only after the engine has been removed from the vehicle. It's assumed that the flywheel or driveplate, crankshaft pulley, timing belt or chain, oil pan, oil pump body, oil filter and piston/connecting rod assemblies have already been removed. On V6 engines, the rear main oil seal retainer must be unbolted and separated from the block before proceeding with crankshaft removal.*

1 Before the crankshaft is removed, measure the endplay. Mount a dial indicator with the indicator in line with the crankshaft and touching the end of the crankshaft as shown **(see illustration)**.

2 Pry the crankshaft all the way to the rear and zero the dial indicator. Next, pry the crankshaft to the front as far as possible and check the reading on the dial indicator. The distance traveled is the endplay. A typical crankshaft endplay will fall between 0.003 to 0.010-inch. If it's greater than that, check the crankshaft thrust surfaces for wear after its removed. If no wear is evident, new main bearings should correct the endplay.

3 If a dial indicator isn't available, feeler gauges can be used. Gently pry the crankshaft all the way to the front of the engine. Slip feeler gauges between the crankshaft and the front face of the thrust bearing or washer to determine the clearance **(see illustration)**.

4 On 2.4L engines, remove the balance shaft (see Section 11).

5 Loosen the main bearing cap assembly bolts 1/4-turn at a time each, until they can be removed by hand. Gently tap the main bearing cap assembly with a soft-face hammer around the perimeter of the assembly. Pull the main bearing cap assembly straight up and off the cylinder block. On 2.0L four-cylinder engines, remove the oil filter passage O-ring seal and

the three main bearing cap assembly locating dowels. Try not to drop the bearing inserts if they come out with the assembly.

6 Carefully lift the crankshaft out of the engine. It may be a good idea to have an assistant available, since the crankshaft is quite heavy and awkward to handle. With the bearing inserts in place inside the engine block and main bearing caps, reinstall the main bearing cap assembly onto engine block and tighten the bolts finger tight. Make sure you install the main bearing cap assembly on V6 models with the arrow facing the front (timing belt end) of the engine.

Installation

7 Crankshaft installation is the first step in engine reassembly. It's assumed at this point that the engine block and crankshaft have been cleaned, inspected and repaired or reconditioned.

8 Position the engine block with the bottom facing up.

9 Remove the mounting bolts and lift off the main bearing cap assembly.

10 If they're still in place, remove the original bearing inserts from the block and the main bearing cap assembly. Wipe the bearing surfaces of the block and main bearing cap

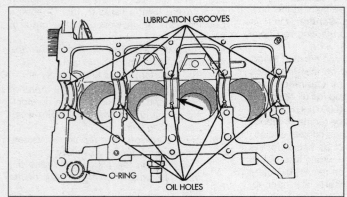

10.11a On four-cylinder engines, install the upper bearings (with grooves and holes) into the engine block. Be sure to align the oil holes and install the thrust bearing in the center bearing position (arrow)

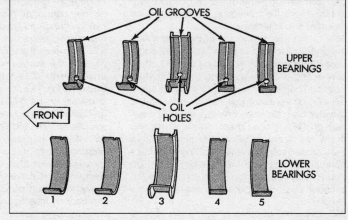

10.11b Main bearing installation details - four-cylinder engines

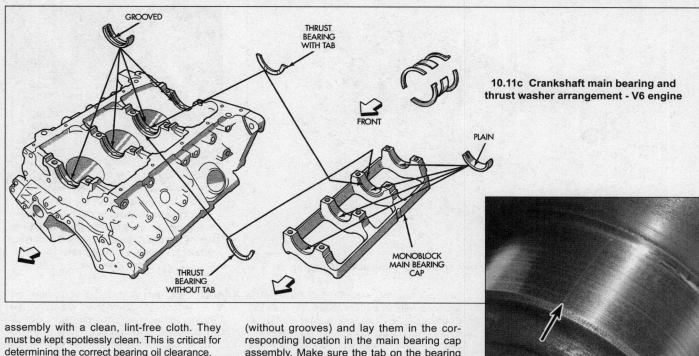

10.11c Crankshaft main bearing and thrust washer arrangement - V6 engine

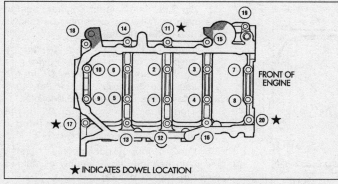

10.17 Place the Plastigage (arrow) onto the crankshaft bearing journal as shown

assembly with a clean, lint-free cloth. They must be kept spotlessly clean. This is critical for determining the correct bearing oil clearance.

Main bearing oil clearance check

Refer to illustrations 10.11a, 10.11b, 10.11c, 10.17, 10.19a, 10.19b, 10.19c and 10.21

11   Without mixing them up, clean the back sides of the new upper main bearing inserts (with grooves and oil holes) and lay one in each main bearing saddle in the block. Each upper bearing has an oil groove and oil hole in it. **Caution:** *The oil holes in the block must line up with the oil holes in the upper bearing inserts.* The thrust bearing insert or thrust washers (V6 engine) must be installed in the No. 3 bearing position **(see illustrations)**. V6 engines have two two-piece thrust washers which are installed on each side of the No. 3 bearing. Install the thrust washers with the grooved side toward the crankshaft (plain sides should be facing each other). Install the thrust washers so that one set has a tab located in the block and the other set's tab is in the main bearing cap assembly. Clean the back sides of the lower main bearing inserts

(without grooves) and lay them in the corresponding location in the main bearing cap assembly. Make sure the tab on the bearing insert fits into the recess in the block or main bearing cap assembly. **Caution:** *Do not hammer the bearing insert into place and don't nick or gouge the bearing faces. DO NOT apply any lubrication at this time.*

12   Clean the faces of the bearing inserts in the block and the crankshaft main bearing journals with a clean, lint-free cloth.

13   Check or clean the oil holes in the crankshaft, as any dirt here can go only one way - straight through the new bearings.

14   Once the crankshaft is clean, carefully lay it in position in the cylinder block.

15   Before the crankshaft can be permanently installed, the main bearing oil clearance must be checked. **Note:** *On four-cylinder engines, the crankshaft position sensor must be removed prior to main bearing oil clearance check* (see Chapter 6).

16   On 2.0L four-cylinder engines, make sure the three locating dowels are in place on the cylinder block. This is necessary for proper alignment of the main bearing cap assembly to

the cylinder block and crankshaft.

17   Cut several pieces of the appropriate size Plastigage (they must be slightly shorter than the width of the main bearing journal) and place one piece on each crankshaft main bearing journal, parallel with the journal axis as shown **(see illustration)**.

18   Clean the faces of the bearing inserts in the main bearing cap assembly, then install the assembly onto the crankshaft and cylinder block. DO NOT disturb the Plastigage. Make sure you install the main bearing cap assembly on V6 models with the arrow facing the front (timing belt end) of the engine.

19   Apply clean engine oil to all bolt threads prior to installation, then install all bolts finger-tight. Tighten main bearing cap assembly bolts in the sequence shown **(see illustrations)** progressing in three steps, to the torque listed

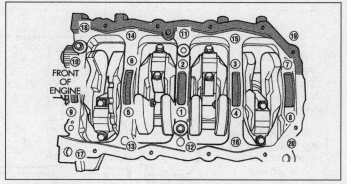

10.19a Main bearing cap assembly bolt tightening sequence - 2.0L four-cylinder engine

10.19b Main bearing cap assembly bolt tightening sequence - 2.4L four-cylinder engine

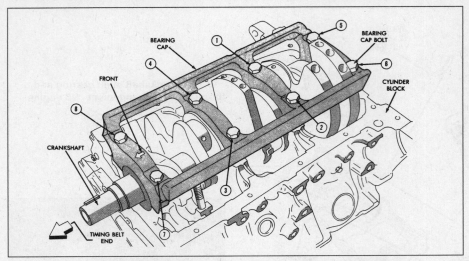

10.19c Main bearing cap assembly bolt tightening sequence - V6 engine

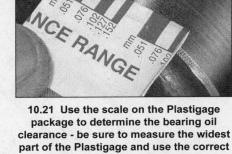

10.21 Use the scale on the Plastigage package to determine the bearing oil clearance - be sure to measure the widest part of the Plastigage and use the correct scale; it comes with both standard and metric scales

in this Chapter's Specifications. DO NOT rotate the crankshaft at any time during this operation.

20 Remove the bolts in the *reverse* order of the tightening sequence and carefully lift the main bearing cap assembly straight up and off the block. Do not disturb the Plastigage or rotate the crankshaft. If the main bearing cap assembly is difficult to remove, tap it gently from side-to-side with a soft-face hammer to loosen it.

21 Compare the width of the crushed Plastigage on each journal to the scale printed on the Plastigage envelope to determine the main bearing oil clearance **(see illustration)**. A typical main bearing oil clearance should fall between 0.0015 to 0.0023-inch. Check with an automotive machine shop for the endpay service limits.

22 If the clearance is not acceptable, the bearing inserts may be the wrong size (which means different ones will be required). Before deciding if different inserts are needed, make sure that no dirt or oil was between the bearing inserts and the cap assembly or block when the clearance was measured. If the Plastigage was wider at one end than the other, the crankshaft journal may be tapered. If the clearance still exceeds the limit speci-

fied, the bearing insert(s) will have to be replaced with an undersize bearing insert(s). **Caution:** *When installing a new crankshaft always install a standard bearing insert set.*

23 Carefully scrape all traces of the Plastigage material off the main bearing journals and/or the bearing insert faces. Be sure to remove all residue from the oil holes. Use your fingernail or the edge of a plastic card - don't nick or scratch the bearing faces.

Final installation

Refer to illustration 10.27

24 Carefully lift the crankshaft out of the cylinder block.

25 Clean the bearing insert faces in the cylinder block, then apply a thin, uniform layer of moly-base grease or engine assembly lube to each of the bearing surfaces. Be sure to coat the thrust faces as well as the journal face of the thrust bearing. **Caution:** *Be sure to install the thrust bearing inserts or thrust washers (V6 engine) in the No. 3 journal* **(see illustrations 10.11a, 10.11b and 10.11c).**

26 On 2.0L four-cylinder engines, install a new oil filter passage O-ring seal and make sure the three locating dowels are in place on the cylinder block. The dowels are necessary for proper alignment of the main bearing cap

assembly to the cylinder block and crankshaft.

27 On four-cylinder engines, clean the main bearing cap assembly-to-cylinder block mating surfaces. They must be free of any oil residue. Apply a 1/16-inch bead of anaerobic sealant (Mopar Torque Cure Gasket Maker, or equivalent) to the cylinder block as shown **(see illustration)**. **Caution:** *Use ONLY anaerobic sealant meeting the manufacturers specifications or engine damage may occur.*

28 Make sure the crankshaft journals are clean, then lay the crankshaft back in place in the cylinder block.

29 Clean the bearing insert faces in the main bearing cap assembly, then apply the same lubricant to them. **Caution:** *On four-cylinder engines, DO NOT get any lubricant on the main bearing cap assembly-to-cylinder block mating surfaces as it will inhibit the sealing ability of the anaerobic sealant.*

30 Hold the bearing inserts in place and install the main bearing cap assembly onto the crankshaft and cylinder block. On four-cylinder engines, push the assembly down until it contacts the locating dowels.

31 Prior to installation, apply clean engine oil to all bolt threads wiping off any excess, then install all bolts finger-tight. On 2.0L four-cylinder engines, install baffle studs in positions 12, 13 and 16 **(see illustration 10.19a)**.

32 On 2.0L four-cylinder engines, tighten the main bearing cap assembly as follows **(see illustration 10.19a)**:

a) *Tighten bolts 11, 17 and 20 until the assembly contacts the engine block.*

b) *Tighten bolts 1 through 10 in the sequence shown, in 3 steps to the torque listed in this Chapter's Specifications.*

c) *Tighten bolts 11 through 20 in the sequence shown to the torque listed in this Chapter's Specifications.*

33 On 2.4L four-cylinder engines, tighten the main bearing cap assembly as follows **(see illustration 10.19b)**:

a) *Tighten bolts 11, 17 and 20 until the assembly contacts the engine block.*

10.27 On four-cylinder engines, apply a 1/16-inch bead of anaerobic sealant (Mopar Torque Cure Gasket Maker, or equivalent) to the engine block as shown

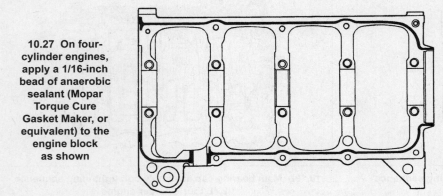

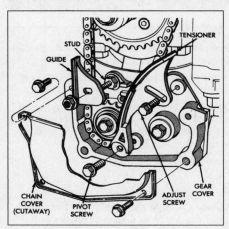

11.2 Balance shaft chain cover, guide and tensioner

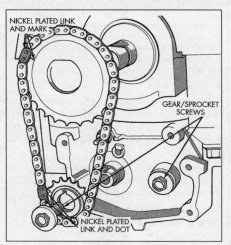

11.4 Balance shaft chain, crankshaft and balance shaft sprockets assembly details

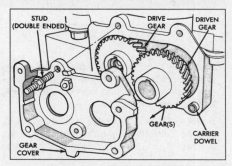

11.5 Remove the double ended stud and separate the gear cover from the balance shaft carrier

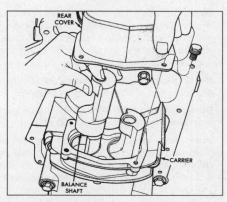

11.6 Remove the rear cover from the carrier and withdraw the balance shafts

b) *To ensure correct thrust bearing alignment, rotate the crankshaft until the No. 4 piston is at TDC.*

c) *Carefully pry the crankshaft all the way towards the rear of the block and then towards the front of the block.*

d) *Wedge an appropriate tool such as a block of wood, between the engine block and the crankshaft counterweight to hold the crankshaft in the most forward position.* **DO NOT** *drive the wedge between the main bearing cap assembly and the crankshaft.*

e) *Tighten bolts 1 through 10 in the sequence shown, in 3 steps to the torque listed in this Chapter's Specifications - except DO NOT tighten the bolts the additional 1/4-turn.*

f) *Remove the wedge and tighten bolts 1 through 10 in the sequence shown, the additional 1/4-turn.*

g) *Tighten bolts 11 through 20 in the sequence shown to the torque listed in this Chapter's Specifications.*

34 On V6 engines, tighten the main bearing cap assembly bolts in the sequence shown **(see illustration 10.19c)** progressing in three steps, to the torque listed in this Chapter's Specifications.

35 After tightening the main bearing cap assembly, tap the ends of the crankshaft forward and backward with a lead or brass hammer to seat the main bearing and crankshaft thrust surfaces.

36 Rotate the crankshaft a number of times by hand to check for any obvious binding. It should rotate with a running torque of 50 in-lbs or less (without the pistons/connecting rods installed). If the running torque is too high, correct the problem at this time.

37 Recheck the crankshaft endplay with a feeler gauge or a dial indicator. The endplay should be correct if the crankshaft thrust faces aren't worn or damaged and new bearings have been installed.

38 Install the new rear main oil seal (see Chapter 2A, 2B or 2C).

11 Balance shafts (2.4L four-cylinder engine only) - removal, inspection and installation

Note: *This procedure assumes that the engine has been removed from the vehicle and the driveplate, timing belt, oil pan and oil pump have also been removed (see Chapter 2A).*

Removal

Refer to illustrations 11.2, 11.4, 11.5 and 11.6

1 The balance shafts are installed in a carrier that is mounted to the lower part of the engine block **(see illustration 1.1a)**. The shafts are interconnected through two gears which rotate them in opposite directions. These gears are driven by a chain from the crankshaft and are designed to rotate at a 2:1 ratio with the crankshaft (one turn of the crankshaft equals two turns of the balance shafts). This motion will counterbalance certain reciprocating masses within the engine.

2 Remove the chain cover, guide and tensioner from the engine block **(see illustration)**.

3 While keeping the crankshaft from rotating, remove the balance shaft bolts. **Caution:** *If the rocker arm shaft assemblies have not been removed, DO NOT rotate the crankshaft as valve damage could occur.* **Note:** *A block of wood placed tightly between the engine block and the crankshaft counterbalance will prevent crankshaft rotation.*

4 Remove the balance shaft chain sprocket, chain and crankshaft chain sprocket **(see illustration)**. Use two prybars to work the sprocket back and forth until it is free from the crankshaft. **Note:** *The carrier assembly may be removed from the main bearing cap assembly at this time, if balance shaft removal is not required.*

5 Remove the special stud (double-ended) from the gear cover. Remove the gear cover, and balance shaft drive and

driven gears **(see illustration)**.

6 Remove the rear cover from the carrier and withdraw the balance shafts **(see illustration)**.

7 Remove the bolts that retain the carrier to the main bearing cap assembly, and separate the carrier from the engine.

Inspection

8 Clean all components with solvent and dry thoroughly. Inspect all components for damage and wear. Pay special attention to the chain, sprocket and gear teeth and the bearing surfaces of the carrier and balance shafts. Replace defective parts as necessary.

Installation

Refer to illustrations 11.12 and 11.15

9 Install the balance shaft carrier onto the main bearing cap assembly and tighten the bolts to the torque listed in this Chapter's Specifications.

10 Lubricate the balance shafts with clean engine oil and insert them into the carrier.

11 Install the rear cover and tighten the bolts to the torque listed in this Chapter's Specifications.

12 Rotate the balance shafts until both shaft keyways are parallel and facing toward the crankshaft. Install the short hub drive gear on the sprocket driven shaft and the long hub gear on the gear driven shaft. After installation, the timing marks (dots) should be together and the keyways positioned as

COMMON ENGINE OVERHAUL TERMS

B

Backlash - The amount of play between two parts. Usually refers to how much one gear can be moved back and forth without moving the gear with which it's meshed.

Bearing Caps - The caps held in place by nuts or bolts which, in turn, hold the bearing surface. This space is for lubricating oil to enter.

Bearing clearance - The amount of space left between shaft and bearing surface. This space is for lubricating oil to enter.

Bearing crush - The additional height which is purposely manufactured into each bearing half to ensure complete contact of the bearing back with the housing bore when the engine is assembled.

Bearing knock - The noise created by movement of a part in a loose or worn bearing.

Blueprinting - Dismantling an engine and reassembling it to EXACT specifications.

Bore - An engine cylinder, or any cylindrical hole; also used to describe the process of enlarging or accurately refinishing a hole with a cutting tool, as to bore an engine cylinder. The bore size is the diameter of the hole.

Boring - Renewing the cylinders by cutting them out to a specified size. A boring bar is used to make the cut.

Bottom end - A term which refers collectively to the engine block, crankshaft, main bearings and the big ends of the connecting rods.

Break-in - The period of operation between installation of new or rebuilt parts and time in which parts are worn to the correct fit. Driving at reduced and varying speed for a specified mileage to permit parts to wear to the correct fit.

Bushing - A one-piece sleeve placed in a bore to serve as a bearing surface for shaft, piston pin, etc. Usually replaceable.

C

Camshaft - The shaft in the engine, on which a series of lobes are located for operating the valve mechanisms. The camshaft is driven by gears or sprockets and a timing chain. Usually referred to simply as the cam.

Carbon - Hard, or soft, black deposits found in combustion chamber, on plugs, under rings, on and under valve heads.

Cast iron - An alloy of iron and more than two percent carbon, used for engine blocks and heads because it's relatively inexpensive and easy to mold into complex shapes.

Chamfer - To bevel across (or a bevel on) the sharp edge of an object.

Chase - To repair damaged threads with a tap or die.

Combustion chamber - The space between the piston and the cylinder head, with the piston at top dead center, in which air-fuel mixture is burned.

Compression ratio - The relationship between cylinder volume (clearance volume) when the piston is at top dead center and cylinder volume when the piston is at bottom dead center.

Connecting rod - The rod that connects the crank on the crankshaft with the piston. Sometimes called a con rod.

Connecting rod cap - The part of the connecting rod assembly that attaches the rod to the crankpin.

Core plug - Soft metal plug used to plug the casting holes for the coolant passages in the block.

Crankcase - The lower part of the engine in which the crankshaft rotates; includes the lower section of the cylinder block and the oil pan.

Crank kit - A reground or reconditioned crankshaft and new main and connecting rod bearings.

Crankpin - The part of a crankshaft to which a connecting rod is attached.

Crankshaft - The main rotating member, or shaft, running the length of the crankcase, with offset throws to which the connecting rods are attached; changes the reciprocating motion of the pistons into rotating motion.

Cylinder sleeve - A replaceable sleeve, or liner, pressed into the cylinder block to form the cylinder bore.

D

Deburring - Removing the burrs (rough edges or areas) from a bearing.

Deglazer - A tool, rotated by an electric motor, used to remove glaze from cylinder walls so a new set of rings will seat.

E

Endplay - The amount of lengthwise movement between two parts. As applied to a crankshaft, the distance that the crankshaft can move forward and back in the cylinder block.

F

Face - A machinist's term that refers to removing metal from the end of a shaft or the face of a larger part, such as a flywheel.

Fatigue - A breakdown of material through a large number of loading and unloading cycles. The first signs are cracks followed shortly by breaks.

Feeler gauge - A thin strip of hardened steel, ground to an exact thickness, used to check clearances between parts.

Free height - The unloaded length or height of a spring.

Freeplay - The looseness in a linkage, or an assembly of parts, between the initial application of force and actual movement. Usually perceived as slop or slight delay.

Freeze plug - See Core plug.

G

Gallery - A large passage in the block that forms a reservoir for engine oil pressure.

Glaze - The very smooth, glassy finish that develops on cylinder walls while an engine is in service.

H

Heli-Coil - A rethreading device used when threads are worn or damaged. The device is installed in a retapped hole to reduce the thread size to the original size.

I

Installed height - The spring's measured length or height, as installed on the cylinder head. Installed height is measured from the spring seat to the underside of the spring retainer.

J

Journal - The surface of a rotating shaft which turns in a bearing.

K

Keeper - The split lock that holds the valve spring retainer in position on the valve stem.

Key - A small piece of metal inserted into matching grooves machined into two parts fitted together - such as a gear pressed onto a shaft - which prevents slippage between the two parts.

Knock - The heavy metallic engine sound, produced in the combustion chamber as a result of abnormal combustion - usually detonation. Knock is usually caused by a loose or worn bearing. Also referred to as detonation, pinging and spark knock. Connecting rod or main bearing knocks are created by too much oil clearance or insufficient lubrication.

L

Lands - The portions of metal between the piston ring grooves.

Lapping the valves - Grinding a valve face and its seat together with lapping compound.

Lash - The amount of free motion in a gear train, between gears, or in a mechanical assembly, that occurs before movement can begin. Usually refers to the lash in a valve train.

Lifter - The part that rides against the cam to transfer motion to the rest of the valve train.

M

Machining - The process of using a machine to remove metal from a metal part.

Main bearings - The plain, or babbit, bearings that support the crankshaft.

Main bearing caps - The cast iron caps, bolted to the bottom of the block, that support the main bearings.

O

O.D. - Outside diameter.

Oil gallery - A pipe or drilled passageway in the engine used to carry engine oil from one area to another.

Oil ring - The lower ring, or rings, of a piston; designed to prevent excessive amounts of oil from working up the cylinder walls and into the combustion chamber. Also called an oil-control ring.

Oil seal - A seal which keeps oil from leaking out of a compartment. Usually refers to a dynamic seal around a rotating shaft or other moving part.

O-ring - A type of sealing ring made of a special rubberlike material; in use, the O-ring is compressed into a groove to provide the sealing action.

Overhaul - To completely disassemble a unit, clean and inspect all parts, reassemble it with the original or new parts and make all adjustments necessary for proper operation.

P

Pilot bearing - A small bearing installed in the center of the flywheel (or the rear end of the crankshaft) to support the front end of the input shaft of the transmission.

Pip mark - A little dot or indentation which indicates the top side of a compression ring.

Piston - The cylindrical part, attached to the connecting rod, that moves up and down in the cylinder as the crankshaft rotates. When the fuel charge is fired, the piston transfers the force of the explosion to the connecting rod, then to the crankshaft.

Piston pin (or wrist pin) - The cylindrical and usually hollow steel pin that passes through the piston. The piston pin fastens the piston to the upper end of the connecting rod.

Piston ring - The split ring fitted to the groove in a piston. The ring contacts the sides of the ring groove and also rubs against the cylinder wall, thus sealing space between piston and wall. There are two types of rings: Compression rings seal the compression pressure in the combustion chamber; oil rings scrape excessive oil off the cylinder wall.

Piston ring groove - The slots or grooves cut in piston heads to hold piston rings in position.

Piston skirt - The portion of the piston below the rings and the piston pin hole.

Plastigage - A thin strip of plastic thread, available in different sizes, used for measuring clearances. For example, a strip of plastigage is laid across a bearing journal and mashed as parts are assembled. Then parts are disassembled and the width of the strip is measured to determine clearance between journal and bearing. Commonly used to measure crankshaft main-bearing and connecting rod bearing clearances.

Press-fit - A tight fit between two parts that requires pressure to force the parts together. Also referred to as drive, or force, fit.

Prussian blue - A blue pigment; in solution, useful in determining the area of contact between two surfaces. Prussian blue is commonly used to determine the width and location of the contact area between the valve face and the valve seat.

R

Race (bearing) - The inner or outer ring that provides a contact surface for balls or rollers in bearing.

Ream - To size, enlarge or smooth a hole by using a round cutting tool with fluted edges.

Ring job - The process of reconditioning the cylinders and installing new rings.

Runout - Wobble. The amount a shaft rotates out-of-true.

S

Saddle - The upper main bearing seat.

Scored - Scratched or grooved, as a cylinder wall may be scored by abrasive particles moved up and down by the piston rings.

Scuffing - A type of wear in which there's a transfer of material between parts moving against each other; shows up as pits or grooves in the mating surfaces.

Seat - The surface upon which another part rests or seats. For example, the valve seat is the matched surface upon which the valve face rests. Also used to refer to wearing into a good fit; for example, piston rings seat after a few miles of driving.

Short block - An engine block complete with crankshaft and piston and, usually, camshaft assemblies.

Static balance - The balance of an object while it's stationary.

Step - The wear on the lower portion of a ring land caused by excessive side and back-clearance. The height of the step indicates the ring's extra side clearance and the length of the step projecting from the back wall of the groove represents the ring's back clearance.

Stroke - The distance the piston moves when traveling from top dead center to bottom dead center, or from bottom dead center to top dead center.

Stud - A metal rod with threads on both ends.

T

Tang - A lip on the end of a plain bearing used to align the bearing during assembly.

Tap - To cut threads in a hole. Also refers to the fluted tool used to cut threads.

Taper - A gradual reduction in the width of a shaft or hole; in an engine cylinder, taper usually takes the form of uneven wear, more pronounced at the top than at the bottom.

Throws - The offset portions of the crankshaft to which the connecting rods are affixed.

Thrust bearing - The main bearing that has thrust faces to prevent excessive endplay, or forward and backward movement of the crankshaft.

Thrust washer - A bronze or hardened steel washer placed between two moving parts. The washer prevents longitudinal movement and provides a bearing surface for thrust surfaces of parts.

Tolerance - The amount of variation permitted from an exact size of measurement. Actual amount from smallest acceptable dimension to largest acceptable dimension.

U

Umbrella - An oil deflector placed near the valve tip to throw oil from the valve stem area.

Undercut - A machined groove below the normal surface.

Undersize bearings - Smaller diameter bearings used with re-ground crankshaft journals.

V

Valve grinding - Refacing a valve in a valve-refacing machine.

Valve train - The valve-operating mechanism of an engine; includes all components from the camshaft to the valve.

Vibration damper - A cylindrical weight attached to the front of the crankshaft to minimize torsional vibration (the twist-untwist actions of the crankshaft caused by the cylinder firing impulses). Also called a harmonic balancer.

W

Water jacket - The spaces around the cylinders, between the inner and outer shells of the cylinder block or head, through which coolant circulates.

Web - A supporting structure across a cavity.

Woodruff key - A key with a radiused backside (viewed from the side).

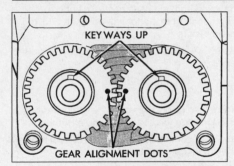

11.12 After gear installation, the balance shaft keyways should be parallel and facing the crankshaft, and the gear alignment marks should be together as shown

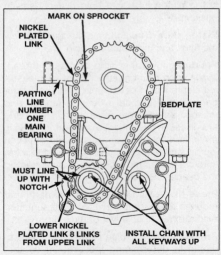

11.15 The timing mark on the crankshaft sprocket, nickel plated links, notch and the yellow dot on balance shaft sprocket must be aligned for correct timing

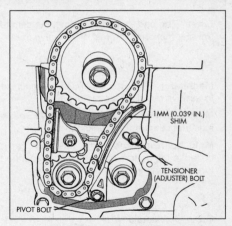

11.20 With the shim in place, apply approximately 5.5 to 6.5 lbs of pressure to the chain tensioner, then tighten the bolt to the torque listed in this Chapter's Specifications

shown **(see illustration)**.

13   Install the gear cover and tighten the double-ended stud to the torque listed in this Chapter's Specifications.

14   Install the sprocket onto the crankshaft with the timing mark facing out, be careful not to cock the sprocket as it's being installed.

15   Position the crankshaft so the timing mark on the chain sprocket is aligned with the parting line on the left side of the number 1 main bearing cap, as shown **(see illustration)**.

16   Place the chain onto the crankshaft sprocket so that the nickel plated link of the chain is located at the timing mark on the crankshaft sprocket **(see illustration 11.15)**.

17   Install the balance shaft sprocket into the chain so that the timing mark on the sprocket (yellow dot) mates with the nickel plated link on the chain (8 links from the upper nickel plated link) **(see illustration 11.15)**.

18   Slide the balance shaft sprocket onto the balance shaft. If the sprocket is difficult to install on the balance shaft, it may be necessary to loosen the rear cover and push the balance shaft slightly out of the carrier to facilitate sprocket installation. **Note:** *The timing mark on the balance shaft sprocket and the nickel plated link should align with the notch on the side of the gear cover* **(see illustration 11.15)**.

19   Install the balance shaft bolts. While keeping the crankshaft from rotating, tighten the balance shaft bolts to the torque listed in this Chapter's Specifications. **Note:** *A block of wood placed tightly between the engine block and the crankshaft counterbalance will prevent crankshaft rotation.*

Chain tensioning

Refer to illustration 11.20

20   Install the chain tensioner loosely. Place a 0.039 x 2.75 inch shim (a feeler gauge cut to the appropriate size can be used) between the tensioner and the chain **(see illustration)**. Push the tensioner up against the chain. Apply firm pressure (approximately 5.5 to 6.5 lbs) directly behind the adjustment slot to remove the slack.

21   With pressure applied, tighten the top tensioner bolt first, then the bottom pivot bolt.

Tighten the bolts to the torque listed in this Chapter's Specifications. Remove the shim.

22   Place the chain guide onto the double-ended stud, making sure the tab on the guide fits into the slot on the gear cover. Tighten the nut to the torque listed in this Chapter's Specifications.

23   Install the chain cover and tighten the bolts securely.

12   Engine overhaul - reassembly sequence

1   Before beginning engine reassembly, make sure you have all the necessary new parts, gaskets and seals as well as the following items on hand:

Common hand tools
A 1/2-inch drive torque wrench
New engine oil
Gasket sealant
Thread locking compound

2   If you obtained a short block it will be necessary to install the cylinder head(s), the oil pump and pick-up tube, the oil pan, the water pump, the timing belt or chain and timing cover, and the valve cover(s) (see Chapter 2A, 2B or 2C). In order to save time and avoid problems, the external components must be installed in the following general order:

Thermostat and housing cover
Water pump
Intake and exhaust manifolds
Carburetor or fuel injection components
Emission control components
Distributor (if equipped)
Spark plug wires and spark plugs
Ignition coils
Oil filter
Engine mounts and mount brackets
Clutch and flywheel (manual transaxle)
Driveplate (automatic transaxle)

13   Initial start-up and break-in after overhaul

Warning: *Have a fire extinguisher handy when starting the engine for the first time.*

1   Once the engine has been installed in the vehicle, double-check the engine oil and coolant levels.

2   With the spark plugs out of the engine and the ignition system and fuel pump disabled, crank the engine until oil pressure registers on the gauge or the light goes out.

3   Install the spark plugs, hook up the plug wires and restore the ignition system and fuel pump functions.

4   Start the engine. It may take a few moments for the fuel system to build up pressure, but the engine should start without a great deal of effort.

5   After the engine starts, it should be allowed to warm up to normal operating temperature. While the engine is warming up, make a thorough check for fuel, oil and coolant leaks.

6   Shut the engine off and recheck the engine oil and coolant levels.

7   Drive the vehicle to an area with minimum traffic, accelerate from 30 to 50 mph, then allow the vehicle to slow to 30 mph with the throttle closed. Repeat the procedure 10 or 12 times. This will load the piston rings and cause them to seat properly against the cylinder walls. Check again for oil and coolant leaks.

8   Drive the vehicle gently for the first 500 miles (no sustained high speeds) and keep a constant check on the oil level. It is not unusual for an engine to use oil during the break-in period.

9   At approximately 500 to 600 miles, change the oil and filter.

10   For the next few hundred miles, drive the vehicle normally. Do not pamper or abuse it.

11   After 2000 miles, change the oil and filter again and consider the engine broken in.

Chapter 3
Cooling, heating and air conditioning systems

Contents

Specifications

General

System cap pressure rating	
Convertible and sedan (reservoir cap)................................	14 to 18 psi
Coupe (radiator cap)...............................	11 to 15 psi
Thermostat rating (opening temperature)	
Convertible and sedan	192 to 199 degrees F
Coupe	
Four-cylinder engines	195 degrees F
V6 engine...	180 degrees F
Cooling system capacity..	See Chapter 1
Refrigerant capacity	
Chrysler	
Sebring convertible and sedan	
1995 through 1999	1.75 pounds
2000 through 2002 convertible..................................	1.19 pounds
2001 and 2002 sedans.......................................	1.69 pounds
2003 and later	Refer to the underhood specification label
Sebring coupe	
1995 through 2000	1.54 to 1.63 pounds
2001 through 2005	1.25 pounds
Dodge	
Avenger	1.54 to 1.63 pounds
Stratus coupe..................................	0.96 pounds
Stratus sedan	
2000	1.19 pounds
2001 and 2002	1.69 pounds
2003 and later...........................	Refer to the underhood specification label

Torque specifications

Ft-lbs (unless otherwise indicated)

Note: *One foot pound (ft-lb) of torque is equivalent to 12 inch-pounds (in-lbs) of torque. Torque values below approximately 15 ft-lbs are expressed in inch-pounds, since most foot-pound torque wrenches are not accurate at these smaller values.*

Expansion valve mounting screws (convertibles and sedans)	100 in-lbs
Thermostat housing bolts	
2.0L DOHC VIN Y	
1995 through 1999	16
2001 and later	110 in-lbs
2.4L DOHC VIN X,J	110 in-lbs
2.4L SOHC VIN G	109 in-lbs
2.5L SOHC V6 VIN N and VIN H, 3.0L VIN H V6	168 in-lbs
2.7L SOHC VIN R V6	105 in-lbs
Water pump mounting bolts	
2.0L DOHC VIN Y	105 in-lbs
2.4L DOHC VIN X,J	105 in-lbs
2.4L SOHC VIN G	
M8 bolts	117 in-lbs
M10	17
2.5L SOHC VIN H V6	17
2.5L SOHC VIN N V6, 3.0L VIN H V6	
M8 bolts	17
M10 bolts	30
2.7L SOHC VIN R V6	105 in-lbs

1 General information

Engine cooling system

All vehicles covered by this manual employ a pressurized engine cooling system with thermostatically controlled coolant circulation. An impeller-type water pump mounted on the front of the engine pumps coolant through the engine. The pump mounts directly on the engine block. The coolant flows around the combustion chambers and toward the rear of the engine. Cast-in coolant passages direct coolant near the intake ports, exhaust ports, and spark plug areas.

A wax pellet-type thermostat is located in a housing near the front of the engine. During warm-up, the closed thermostat prevents coolant from circulating through the radiator. As the engine nears normal operating temperature, the thermostat opens and allows hot coolant to travel through the radiator, where it's cooled before returning to the engine.

The cooling system is sealed by a pressure-type cap, which raises the boiling point of the coolant and increases the cooling efficiency of the system. If the system pressure exceeds the cap pressure relief value, the excess pressure in the system forces the spring-loaded valve inside the cap off its seat and allows the coolant to escape through the overflow tube into a coolant reservoir. When the system cools the excess coolant is automatically drawn from the reservoir back into the radiator.

On coupe models, the coolant reservoir does double duty as both the point at which fresh coolant is added to the cooling system to maintain the proper fluid level and as a holding tank for overheated coolant. On this type of system, coolant that escapes past the pressure cap is saved and reused.

On convertible and sedan models, the coolant reservoir is a pressurized part of the cooling system. Do not remove the cap until the engine has cooled completely.

Heating system

The heating system consists of a blower fan and heater core located in the heater housing, with hoses connecting the heater core to the engine cooling system. Hot engine coolant is circulated through the heater core. When the heater mode on the heater/air conditioning control panel on the instrument panel is activated, a flap door opens to expose the heater core to the passenger compartment. A fan switch on the control panel activates the blower motor, which forces air through the core, heating the air.

Air conditioning system

The air conditioning system consists of a condenser mounted in front of the radiator, an evaporator mounted adjacent to the heater core, a compressor mounted on the engine, receiver/drier which contains a high pressure relief valve and the plumbing connecting all of the above components.

A blower fan forces the warmer air of the passenger compartment through the evaporator core, transferring the heat from the air to the refrigerant (sort of a "radiator in reverse"). The liquid refrigerant boils off into low pressure vapor, taking the heat with it when it leaves the evaporator.

2 Antifreeze - general information

Refer to illustration 2.4

Warning: *Do not allow antifreeze to come in contact with your skin or painted surfaces of the vehicle. Rinse off spills immediately with plenty of water. Antifreeze is highly toxic if ingested. Never leave antifreeze lying around in an open container or in puddles on the floor; children and pets are attracted by it's sweet smell and may drink it. Antifreeze is also flammable, so don't store or use it near open flames. Check with local authorities about disposing of used antifreeze. Many communities have collection centers which will see that antifreeze is disposed of safely. Never dump used anti-freeze on the ground or into drains.*
Note: *Non-Toxic coolant is available at local auto parts stores. Although the coolant is non-toxic when fresh, proper disposal is still required.*

The cooling system should be filled with a water/ethylene glycol based antifreeze solution, which will prevent freezing down to at least 20 degrees F, or lower if local climate requires it. It also provides protection against corrosion and increases the coolant boiling point.

The cooling system should be drained, flushed and refilled at the specified intervals (see Chapter 1). Old or contaminated anti-freeze solutions are likely to cause damage and encourage the formation of rust and scale in the system. Use distilled water with the antifreeze.

Before adding antifreeze, check all hose connections, because antifreeze tends to leak through very minute openings. Engines don't normally consume coolant, so if the level goes down, find the cause and correct it.

The exact mixture of antifreeze-to-water which you should use depends on the relative weather conditions. The mixture should contain at least 50 percent antifreeze, but should never contain more than 70 percent antifreeze. Consult the mixture ratio chart on the antifreeze container before adding coolant. Use a hydrometers (available at auto parts stores) to test the coolant **(see illustration)**. Use antifreeze that meets the vehicle manufacturer's specifications.

3 Thermostat - check and replacement

Warning: *Do not remove the coolant tank cap, drain the coolant or replace the thermostat until the engine has cooled completely.*

2.4 Use a hydrometer to test the coolant

Check

1   Before assuming the thermostat is to blame for a cooling system problem, check the coolant level, drivebelt tension (see Chapter 1) and temperature gauge operation.

2   If the engine seems to be taking a long time to warm up (based on heater output or temperature gauge operation), the thermostat is probably stuck open. Replace the thermostat with a new one.

3   If the engine runs hot, use your hand to check the temperature of the upper radiator hose. If the hose isn't hot, but the engine is, the thermostat is probably stuck closed, preventing the coolant inside the engine from escaping to the radiator. Replace the thermostat. **Caution:** *Don't drive the vehicle without a thermostat. The computer may stay in open loop and emissions and fuel economy will suffer.*

4   If the upper radiator hose is hot, it means that the coolant is flowing and the thermostat is open. Consult the Troubleshooting Section at the front of this manual for cooling system diagnosis.

Replacement

5   Disconnect the cable from the negative battery terminal or the remote ground terminal (see Chapter 5).

6   Drain the cooling system (see Chapter 1). If the coolant is relatively new and still in good condition, save it and reuse it.

All engines except 2.7L V6

Refer to illustrations 3.8, 3.10a, 3.10b, 3.11, 3.13a and 3.13b

7   Follow the upper radiator hose to the engine to locate the thermostat housing.

8   Loosen the hose clamp **(see illustration)**, then detach the hose from the fitting. If it's stuck, grasp it near the end with a pair of adjustable pliers and twist it to break the seal, then pull it off. If the hose is old or if it has deteriorated, cut it off and install a new one.

9   If the outer surface of the thermostat housing cover, which mates with the hose, is

3.8 The thermostat housing (arrow) is located at the right (timing belt) end of the cylinder head on 2.4L DOHC (shown) and on 2.0L DOHC engines; the thermostat assembly is at other end of the cylinder head on 2.4L SOHC engines)

already corroded, pitted, or otherwise deteriorated, it might be damaged even more by hose removal. If it is, replace the thermostat housing cover.

10   Remove the fasteners and detach the housing cover **(see illustrations)**. If the cover is stuck, tap it with a soft-face hammer to jar it loose. Be prepared for some coolant to spill as the gasket seal is broken.

11   Note how it's installed (which end is facing up, or out) and then remove the thermostat **(see illustration)**.

12   Remove all traces of old gasket material and sealant from the housing and cover with a gasket scraper.

13   Install a new rubber gasket on the thermostat **(see illustration)** and then install the thermostat in the housing, spring-end first. On

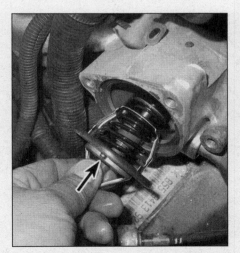

3.11 Before removing the thermostat, note how it's installed, with the spring facing in, toward the housing; also note the orientation of the "jiggle valve" (arrow) in relation to the housing

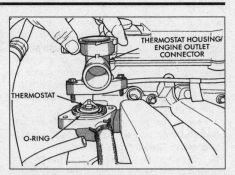

3.10a Typical four-cylinder thermostat installation details (2.4L DOHC engine shown, 2.0L DOHC engine similar; thermostat housing is at other end of the head on 2.4L SOHC engines)

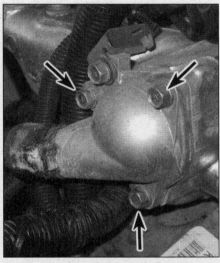

3.10b To remove the thermostat housing cover on a SOHC V6, remove these three bolts (arrows) (2.5L shown, 3.0L similar)

3.13a Be sure to install a new rubber O-ring type gasket on the thermostat, if equipped

housings that face out instead of up, make sure that you install the thermostat with the "jiggle valve" at 12 o'clock **(see illustration)**. If the thermostat housing cover uses a paper gasket, dip the new gasket in water and position it on the thermostat housing with the holes in the gasket aligned with the bolt holes in the housing.

14   Install the thermostat housing cover and bolts and then tighten the bolts to the torque listed in this Chapter's Specifications.

15   Reattach the hose to the thermostat housing cover. Make sure that the hose clamp is still tight. If it isn't, replace it.

16   Refill the cooling system (see Chapter 1).

17   Start the engine and allow it to reach normal operating temperature, then check for leaks and proper thermostat operation (as described in Steps 2 through 4). See Chapter 1 for the cooling system air-bleeding procedure.

2.7L V6 engine

Refer to illustrations 3.27 and 3.32

18   Raise the vehicle and place it securely on jackstands. Remove the right front wheel. Remove the accessory drivebelt splash shield (see Chapter 11).

19   Remove the accessory drivebelts (see Chapter 1).

20   Remove the lower alternator mounting bolt (see Chapter 5).

21   Lower the vehicle.

22   Disconnect the alternator electrical connectors (see Chapter 5).

23   Disconnect the electrical connectors from the air conditioning compressor.

24   Remove the oil dipstick and the dipstick tube. Plug the hole in the oil pan with a clean shop rag to prevent debris from entering the pan.

3.13b When installing the thermostat, make sure that the jiggle valve is at 12 o'clock

25   Remove the rest of the alternator mounting bolts and then remove the alternator (see Chapter 5).

26   Loosen the hose clamps and then disconnect the two hoses from the thermostat housing cover.

27   Remove the thermostat housing cover bolts and then remove the housing **(see illustration)**.

28   Note how the thermostat is installed, with the "jiggle valve" at the 12 o'clock position, and then remove the thermostat **(see illustration 3.27)**.

29   Remove all traces of sealant from the housing and cover with a gasket scraper.

30   Install the thermostat with the jiggle valve at the 12 o'clock position.

31   Install the thermostat housing cover and then tighten the bolts to the torque listed in this Chapter's Specifications.

32   Reattach the hoses to the thermo-

stat housing cover. Make sure that the hose clamps are still tight. If they aren't, replace them. Some of the hose clamps used on the 2.7L engine cooling system are the "low profile" type. A number or letter is stamped into the tongue **(see illustration)** of these clamps. If it's necessary to replace a clamp, make sure that you obtain an original equipment clamp with the same number.

33   The remainder of installation is the reverse of removal.

34   When you're done, refill the cooling system.

35   Start the engine and allow it to reach normal operating temperature, then check for leaks and proper thermostat operation (as described in Steps 2 through 4). See Chapter 1 for the cooling system air-bleeding procedure.

4   Engine cooling fans - check and replacement

Warning: *To avoid possible injury or damage, DO NOT operate the engine with a damaged fan. Do not attempt to repair fan blades - replace a damaged fan with a new one.*
Note: *Always be sure to check for blown fuses before attempting to diagnose an electrical circuit problem.*

Check

Refer to illustrations 4.1a, 4.1b, 4.3, and 4.4

1   If the engine is overheating and the cooling fan is not coming on when the engine temperature rises to an excessive level, unplug the fan motor electrical connector **(see illustrations)** and then connect the motor directly to the battery with fused jumper cables. If the fan motor doesn't come on, replace the motor.

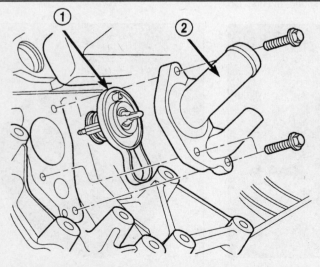

3.27 Thermostat housing cover and thermostat installation details (2.7L V6 engine)

1   *Thermostat and gasket*
2   *Thermostat housing cover*

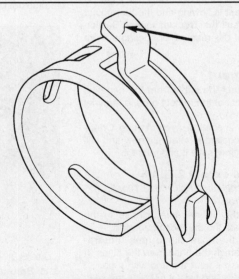

3.32 The 2.7L engine cooling system is equipped with special "low profile" clamps; if you have to replace one of these clamps, make sure that you obtain an original equipment clamp with the same number, which is located here (arrow)

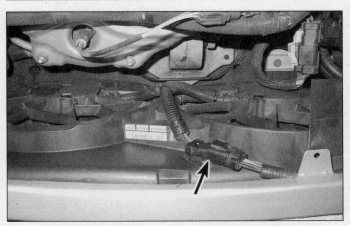

4.1a Typical radiator fan motor (and condenser fan motor) electrical connector (arrow) location (convertible and sedan models); if a single connector is used for both fan motors, note the color of the wires to each fan motor to determine which motor you're testing

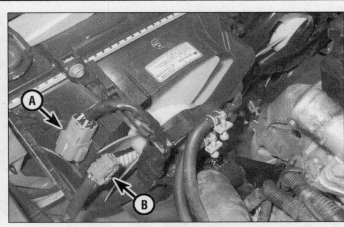

4.1b Typical radiator fan motor (and condenser fan motor) electrical connector halves (arrows) unplugged (coupe models); make sure that you connect the jumper cables to the *fan motor* side of the connector (A), not the harness side (B)

On air-conditioned vehicles, there is a separate fan for the condenser, but the two terminals (power and ground) for the condenser fan are located in the same electrical connector as the radiator fan motor terminals. If the radiator fan motor checks out okay, be sure to test the condenser fan motor.

2   If the radiator fan motor is okay, but it isn't coming on when the engine gets hot, one of the fan relays might be defective (there are two or three fan relays - low, high 1 and/or high 2 - on most models). A relay is used to control a circuit by turning it on and off in response to a control decision by the fan controller (a small microprocessor that turns the cooling fan relays on and off in response to engine coolant temperature) or by the Powertrain Control Module (PCM). These control circuits are fairly complex, and checking them should be left to a dealer service department. But sometimes the control system can be fixed by simply identifying and replacing a bad relay.

3   Locate the fan relays in the engine compartment fuse/relay box **(see illustration)**.

4   Pull out each relay and check its operation as follows: Most fan motor relays on these vehicles have four or five terminals (only four are used on relays with five or more terminals). Two terminals are for battery voltage and ground, respectively, and the other two are the control terminals. Using a pair of fused jumper cables, hook up battery voltage to the power terminal, connect the ground terminal to a good ground and verify that the relay clicks. If you hear this clicking sound, the relay is operating. **Caution:** *Don't apply battery voltage for more than a second or two or you might damage the relay.* To verify that the control side of the relay is functioning correctly, apply battery voltage through the power and ground terminals again and check continuity between the two control terminals with an ohmmeter. When the relay is energized, there should be continuity between the

control terminals. Then disconnect the jumper cables from the power and ground terminals and verify that there is no continuity between the two control terminals. If the relay passes these two tests, it's working correctly.

5   If the relays are okay, check all wiring and connections (see the Wiring Diagrams at the end of Chapter 12). If no obvious problems are found, the problem could be the Engine Coolant Temperature (ECT) sensor or the Powertrain Control Module (PCM), but further diagnosis should be done by a dealer service department or repair shop with the proper diagnostic equipment.

Replacement

Refer to illustrations 4.6, 4.8, 4.9, 4.10a, 4.10b, 4.10c, 4.10d, 4.11 and 4.12

6   On convertible and sedan models, remove the upper radiator crossmember **(see illustration)**.

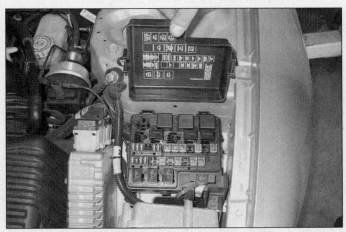

4.3 The fan motor relays are located inside the engine compartment fuse/relay box; depending on the model, there might be two or three relays (low, high 1 and/or high 2), but all the relays on a vehicle have the same terminals, so the test is the same for each relay

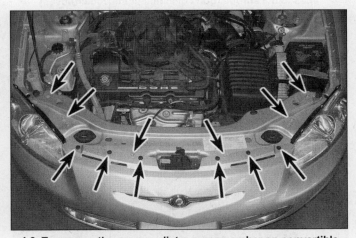

4.6 To remove the upper radiator crossmember on convertible and sedan models, disconnect the bumper cover from the crossmember by removing these six fasteners (lower arrows) and then remove these six crossmember bolts (upper arrows)

7   Disconnect the fan motor electrical connector **(see illustration 4.1a or 4.1b)**.

8   If the upper radiator hose is connected to the middle rather than the end of the radiator **(see illustration 4.8)**, it will be difficult or impossible to remove the engine cooling fan motor/shroud assembly from the engine compartment. Look at the upper radiator hose and decide whether the hose is in the way. If it is, drain the cooling system (see Chapter 1) and then disconnect the upper radiator hose from the radiator **(see illustration)**. If the coolant hose clamps are the constant-tension-spring type, loosen the hose clamp by squeezing the ends together. Hose clamp pliers such as the ones shown in the accompanying photo work best, but regular pliers will work too. Detach the hose from the radiator. If it's stuck, grasp it near the end with a pair of adjustable pliers and twist it to break the seal, then pull it off. If the hose is old or if it has deteriorated, cut it off and install a new one.

9   On some models with an automatic transaxle, the transaxle oil cooler lines are attached to the fan shroud, just to the right of the engine cooling fan motor. If your vehicle has a setup like this, detach the bracket that attaches the rigid lines to the fan shroud **(see illustration)**. It is NOT necessary to disconnect the oil cooler hoses from the lines to remove the fan shroud assembly.

10   Detach the wire harness from the fan shroud, remove the upper and lower fan shroud mounting bolts **(see illustrations)** and then carefully lift the fan motor and shroud out of the engine compartment as a single assembly.

11   To detach the fan blade from the motor, remove the nut or retaining clip from the motor shaft **(see illustration)**. Remove the fan blade from the motor.

12   To detach the motor from the shroud, remove the retaining nuts or screws **(see illustration)**. Remove the motor from the shroud.

13   Installation is the reverse of removal. **Note:** *When reinstalling the fan assembly,*

4.8 To disconnect the upper radiator hose from the radiator, loosen the hose clamp and then carefully pull off the hose (the special pliers used here are designed for this type of hose clamp, which is known as a constant-tension-spring type)

4.9 On some vehicles with an automatic transaxle, the transaxle cooler lines are secured to the fan shroud by a bracket; if your vehicle has this setup, remove the screw (arrow) that attaches the lines to the shroud (don't disconnect the cooler hoses)

4.10a Detach the fan motor wiring harness from any clips (lower arrows) that attach it to the fan shroud; to detach the upper end of the engine cooling fan shroud from the radiator, remove these bolts (upper arrows) (coupe model shown, convertible and sedan models similar)

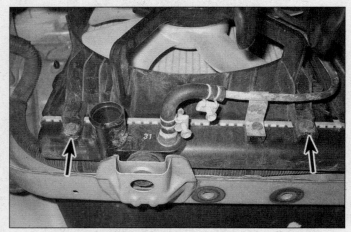

4.10b To detach the lower end of the engine cooling fan shroud from the radiator, remove these bolts (arrows) (coupe model shown, convertible and sedan models similar)

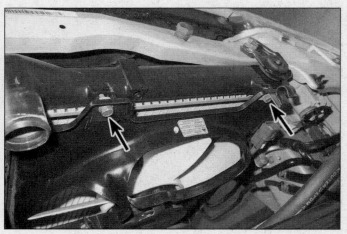

4.10c To detach the upper end of the condenser cooling fan shroud from the radiator, remove these bolts (arrows) (coupe model shown, convertible and sedan models similar)

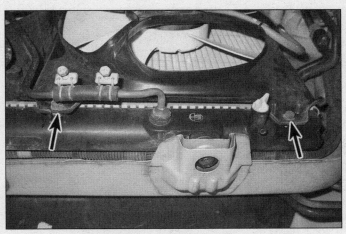

4.10d To detach the lower end of the condenser cooling fan shroud from the radiator, remove these bolts (arrows) (coupe model shown, convertible and sedan models similar)

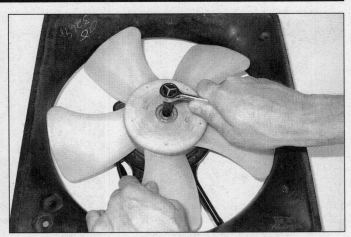

4.11 The fan blade is retained to the motor with either a nut or a clip (radiator fan shown, condenser fan similar)

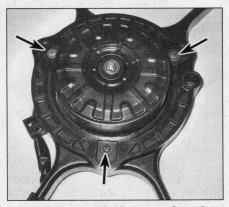

4.12 To remove the fan motor from the shroud, remove the three screws (arrows) (radiator fan motor shown, condenser fan motor similar)

make sure the rubber air shields around the assembly are still in place - without them, the cooling system may not work efficiently.

5 Radiator and coolant reservoir - removal and installation

Warning: *Wait until the engine is completely cool before beginning this procedure.*

Radiator

Removal

Refer to illustration 5.5a, 5.5b, 5.7a, 5.7b, 5.8a, 5.8b, 5.9, 5.10a, 5.10b and 5.11

1 Disconnect the cable from the negative battery terminal or the remote ground terminal (see Chapter 5).

2 Drain the cooling system (see Chapter 1). If the coolant is relatively new and in good condition, save it and reuse it.

3 On convertible and sedan models, remove the upper radiator crossmember **(see illustration 4.6)**.

4 Raise the vehicle and place it securely on jackstands.

5 If the overflow hose is connected to the thermostat housing, disconnect it from the thermostat housing, the upper radiator hose and the fan shroud **(see illustration)**. If the overflow hose is connected to the radiator filler neck, disconnect it from the filler neck. Remove the upper radiator hose **(see illustration 4.8)**. Loosen the hose clamp and then detach the lower coolant hose from the radiator **(see illustration)**. If the hose is stuck, grasp it near the end with a pair of adjustable pliers and twist it to break the seal, then pull it off. Be careful not to distort the radiator pipes. If the hoses are old or deteriorated, cut them off and install new ones.

6 On convertible and sedan models, remove the engine and condenser cooling fan/shroud assembly (see Section 4). On coupe models, it's not absolutely necessary to remove the fan and shroud assembly at this time; it can be removed with the radiator, and then separated from the radiator after removal from the engine compartment.

7 On models with an automatic transaxle, disconnect the transaxle cooler lines from the lower rear side of the radiator. On convert-

5.5a Loosen the hose clamp (upper right arrow) and disconnect the overflow hose from the thermostat housing, and then detach the hose from all clips (lower arrows) and set it aside (coupe model shown, convertible and sedan models similar)

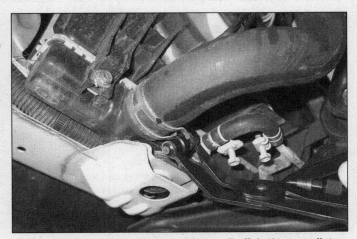

5.5b Loosen the hose clamp and then pull off the lower radiator hose (coupe model shown, convertible and sedan models similar)

5.7a   On convertible and sedan models, remove the bolt (arrow) that attaches the transaxle cooler lines to the left side of the radiator

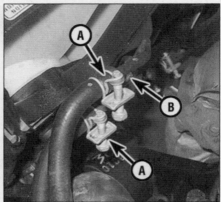

5.7b   On some coupe models with an automatic transaxle, the cooler hoses are connected to rigid lines next to the engine cooling fan; on these models, loosen the hose clamps (A), disconnect the hoses from the lines and then plug the lines; it's not necessary to remove the rigid lines from the fan shroud until after the radiator and shroud assembly has been removed, at which time you can detach the lines from the shroud by removing this screw (B)

5.8a   To detach the radiator from the body, remove these bolts (arrows) . . .

5.8b   . . . and these bolts (arrows) (coupe model shown)

ible and sedan models, remove the bolt that attaches the cooler line support bracket to the left side of the radiator **(see illustration)**. On some coupe models with an automatic, the transaxle oil cooler hoses are connected to rigid cooler lines from *above* (instead of the usual location, near the bottom of the radiator). The rigid lines are then routed down to a pair of hoses below, which in turn are connected to the cooler inlet and outlet tubes at the bottom of the radiator. If your vehicle has this setup, disconnect the transmission fluid cooler hoses up top from the rigid lines **(see illustration)** and then plug the lines. It's not necessary to detach the cooler line bracket from the fan shroud now; the rigid lines can come out with the radiator and fan shroud assembly and then can be removed on the work bench when you separate the fan shroud from the radiator.

8   Remove the radiator-to-body mounting bolts **(see illustrations)**.

9   On convertible and sedan models, remove the condenser-to-radiator mounting

screws **(see illustration)** and then disengage the condenser locating tabs from the radiator.

10   Carefully lift out the radiator and (on coupes) the fan and shroud as a single assembly **(see illustration)**. Don't spill coolant on the vehicle or scratch the paint. Make sure the rubber radiator insulators **(see illustration)** that fit on the bottom of the radiator and into sockets in the body remain in place in the body for proper reinstallation of the radiator.

11   On coupe models, remove the transaxle oil cooler lines, hoses and fittings and then remove the fan shrouds from the radiator **(see illustration)**.

12   Remove bugs and dirt from the radiator

with compressed air and a soft brush (don't bend the cooling fins). Inspect the radiator for leaks and damage. If it needs repair, have a radiator shop or a dealer service department do the work.

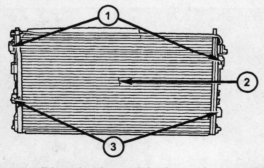

5.9   On convertible and sedan models, the condenser must be detached from the radiator before the radiator can be removed (unless you've discharged the air conditioning system and want to remove the condenser and radiator as a single assembly)

1   Air conditioning condenser locating tabs (must be disengaged from radiator)
2   Air conditioning condenser
3   Air conditioning condenser mounting screws (must be removed)

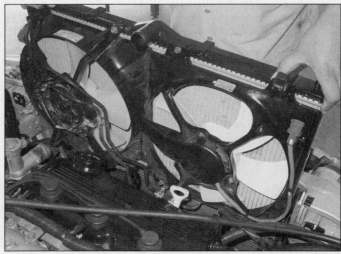

5.10a   Remove the radiator and (on coupes) the cooling fans and shroud as a single assembly

5.10b Make sure that the rubber insulators (arrows) don't come out with the radiator; if they do, inspect them to make sure that they're in good condition and then install them in their respective holes in the lower crossmember

5.11 After the radiator/fan assembly has been removed from a coupe model, remove the transaxle cooler fluid line bracket screw (1), disconnect the cooler lines, hoses and fittings (2) and then remove the fan shroud screws (arrows)

Installation
Refer to illustrations 5.13a and 5.13b

13   Inspect the rubber insulators in the lower crossmember **(see illustration 5.10b)** for cracks and deterioration. Make sure that they're free of dirt and gravel. When install-ing the radiator, make sure that it's correctly seated on the insulators **(see illustrations)** before fastening the top brackets.

14   Installation is otherwise the reverse of the removal procedure. After installation, fill the cooling system with the correct mixture of antifreeze and water (see Chapter 1).

15   Start the engine and check for leaks. Allow the engine to reach normal operating temperature, indicated by the upper radiator hose becoming hot. Recheck the coolant level and add more if required.

16   If you're working on an automatic trans-axle equipped vehicle, check and add fluid as needed.

Coolant reservoir

17   Drain the cooling system (see Chapter 1).

Coupe models
Refer to illustrations 5.18a and 5.18b

18   Disconnect the overflow hose from the reservoir **(see illustration)**. (It's not necessary to disconnect the vapor release hose unless you plan to replace the reservoir). Plug the hose(s) to prevent leakage. Lift the reservoir straight up to disengage it from its mounting bracket **(see illustration)**.

19   Clean out the reservoir with soapy water

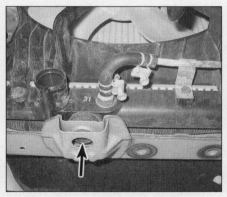

5.13a When installing the radiator, make sure that the left positioning pin is correctly seated in the left insulator (arrow) . . .

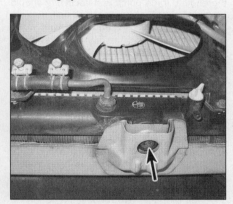

5.13b . . . and the that the right pin is seated in the right insulator (arrow) (coupe model shown)

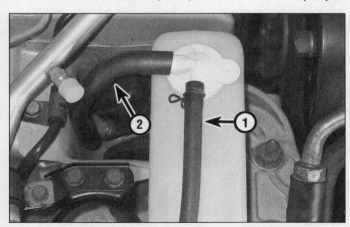

5.18a Disconnect the overflow hose (1). The vapor release hose (2) can stay in place

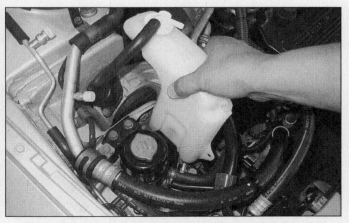

5.18b Lift the reservoir straight up to disengage it from its mounting bracket (coupe models)

5.21 Typical coolant reservoir on a convertible or sedan model (2.7L engine shown, four-cylinder engines similar)

1   *Power steering reservoir retaining screw*
2   *Air conditioning receiver/ drier retaining screw*
3   *Windshield washer fluid filler neck (attached to reservoir by a clip, not visible in this photo)*
4   *Overflow hose*
5   *Pressure cap*
6   *Hose to coolant outlet connector*

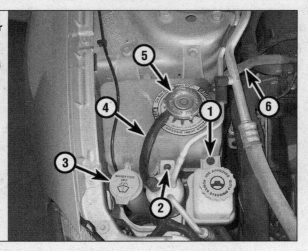

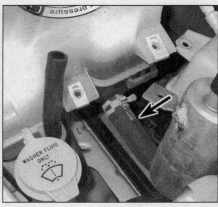

5.25 Lift up the reservoir far enough to loosen the hose clamp and disconnect the hose (arrow) connecting the reservoir to the radiator (convertible and sedan models)

and a brush to remove any deposits inside. Inspect the reservoir carefully for cracks. If you find a crack, replace the reservoir.
20   Installation is the reverse of removal.

Convertible and sedan models

Refer to illustrations 5.21 and 5.25
Warning: *The coolant reservoir on these models is a pressurized part of the cooling system. Allow the engine to cool completely before proceeding.*
21   Remove the power steering reservoir retaining screw **(see illustration)**.
22   Remove the air conditioning receiver/ drier retaining screw.
23   Detach the windshield washer fluid filler neck from its retaining clip on the coolant reservoir.
24   Disconnect the coolant overflow hose and the coolant outlet hose from the reservoir. Be prepared for coolant leakage; place a container under the reservoir.
25   Remove the coolant reservoir retaining screws and then lift up the reservoir enough to disconnect the hose between the reservoir and the radiator **(see illustration)**. Remove the coolant reservoir.
26   Clean out the reservoir with soapy water and a brush to remove any deposits inside. Inspect the reservoir carefully for cracks. If

you find a crack, replace the reservoir.
27   Installation is the reverse of removal.

6   Water pump - check

1   A failure in the water pump can cause serious engine damage due to overheating.
2   There are three ways to check the operation of the water pump while it's installed on the engine. If the pump is defective, it should be replaced with a new or rebuilt unit.
3   Water pumps are equipped with weep or vent holes. If a failure occurs in the pump seal, coolant will leak from the hole. In most cases you'll need a flashlight to find the hole on the water pump from underneath to check for leaks. **Note:** *Some small black staining around the weep hole is normal. If the stain is heavy brown or actual coolant is evident, replace the pump.*
4   If the water pump shaft bearings fail there may be a howling sound at the front of the engine while it's running. With the engine off, shaft wear can be felt if the water pump pulley is rocked up-and-down. Don't mistake drivebelt slippage, which causes a squealing sound, for water pump bearing failure.
5   A quick water pump performance check is to put the heater on. If the pump is failing, it

won't be able to efficiently circulate hot water all the way to the heater core as it should.

7   Water pump - replacement

Four-cylinder engines

Refer to illustration 7.5a, 7.5b and 7.8
1   Disconnect the cable from the negative battery cable or the remote ground terminal (see Chapter 5).
2   Drain the cooling system (see Chapter 1).
3   Remove the accessory drivebelts (see Chapter 1).
4   Remove the timing belt cover(s), the timing belt and, if applicable, the rear timing belt cover (see Chapter 2A).
5   Remove the bolts attaching the water pump to the engine block and remove the pump from the engine **(see illustrations)**. If the water pump is stuck, gently tap it with a soft-faced hammer to break the seal.
6   Clean the bolt threads and the threaded holes in the engine to remove the corrosion and sealant. Remove all traces of old gasket material from the sealing surfaces.

7.5a Using a criss-cross pattern, remove the six bolts (arrows) securing the water pump . . .

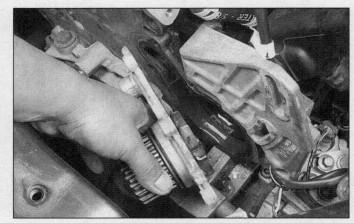

7.5b . . . and then the water pump from the engine; if necessary, tap it gently with a soft-faced hammer to break the seal

7.8 Remove the old O-ring seal, install a new one, then apply a thin film of RTV sealant to hold the seal in place during installation; make sure that the O-ring seal is correctly seated in the water pump and that it stays in place during pump installation

7   Compare the new pump to the old one to make sure that they're identical.

8   Install a new O-ring seal in the groove that lines the water pump body **(see illustration)** and then apply a thin film of RTV sealant to hold the seal in place during installation. **Caution:** *Make sure that the O-ring seal is*

correctly seated in the water pump groove to avoid a coolant leak. Carefully mate the pump to the engine.

9   Install the water pump bolts and then tighten them to the torque listed in this Chapter's Specifications. Don't overtighten the water pump bolts; doing so will damage the pump.

10   The remainder of installation is the reverse of removal. Refill the cooling system (see Chapter 1) when you're done. Then run the engine and check for leaks.

V6 engines
2.5L and 3.0L engines
Refer to illustrations 7.15 and 7.18

11   Disconnect the cable from the negative battery terminal or the remote ground terminal (see Chapter 5).

12   Drain the cooling system (see Chapter 1).

13   Remove the accessory drivebelts.

14   Remove the crankshaft damper/pulley, the timing belt covers and the timing belt (see Chapter 2B).

15   Remove the water pump mounting bolts **(see illustration)**.

16   Separate the pump from the water inlet pipe and remove the pump.

17   Clean all the gasket and O-ring surfaces on the pump and the water pipe inlet tube.

18   Install a new O-ring on the water inlet

pipe. Wet the O-ring with water to facilitate assembly **(see illustration)**.

19   Install a new gasket on the water pump and install the inlet opening over the water pipe. Press the water pipe into the pump housing.

20   Install the water pump mounting bolts and tighten the bolts to the torque listed in this Chapter's specifications.

21   The remainder of installation is the reverse of removal.

22   Refill the cooling system (see Chapter 1).

23   Operate the engine to check for leaks.

2.7L engine
Refer to illustrations 7.28 and 7.29

24   Disconnect the cable from the negative battery terminal or the remote ground terminal (see Chapter 5).

25   Drain the cooling system (see Chapter 1).

26   Remove the upper radiator crossmember **(see illustration 4.6)** and the cooling fan assembly (see Section 4).

27   Remove the timing chain and the chain guides (see Chapter 2C).

28   Remove the water pump bolts **(see illustration)** and then remove the water pump.

29   Install a new O-ring, wetting it with coolant for easier installation in the groove **(see illustration)**.

7.15 To remove the water pump on 2.5L and 3.0L engines, remove these bolts (arrows)

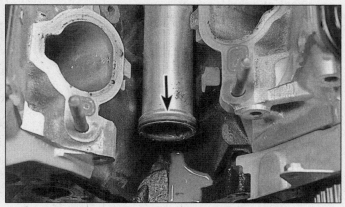

7.18 Install a new O-ring on the water inlet pipe (arrow) (2.5L and 3.0L engines) (intake manifold removed for clarity)

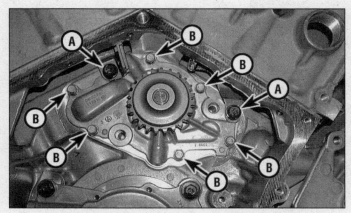

7.28 Remove the water pump retaining bolts (B) and the upper timing chain guide bolts (A) (2.7L engine)

7.29 Water pump O-ring installation details (2.7L engine)

9.1a Remove the glove box "stopper" . . .

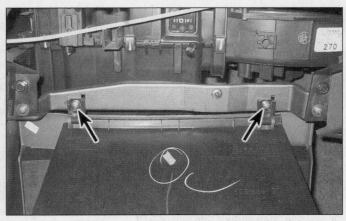

9.1b . . . remove these two screws (arrows) and then remove the glove box (coupe models)

30   Install the pump and then tighten the bolts to the torque listed in this Chapter's Specifications.
31   The remainder of installation is the reverse of removal.
32   Refill the cooling system (see Chapter 1).
33   Operate the engine to check for leaks.

---

8   Coolant temperature sending unit - check and replacement

Warning: *Wait until the engine is completely cool before beginning this procedure.*

Check

1   The coolant temperature indicator system consists of a warning light or a temperature gauge on the dash and a coolant temperature sending unit mounted on the engine. On the models covered by this manual, the Engine Coolant Temperature (ECT) sensor, which is an information sensor for the Powertrain Control Module (PCM), also functions as the coolant temperature sending unit.
2   If an overheating indication occurs,

check the coolant level in the system and then make sure all connectors in the wiring harness between the sending unit and the indicator light or gauge are tight.
3   When the ignition switch is turned to START and the starter motor is turning, the indicator light (if equipped) should come on. This doesn't mean the engine is overheated; it just means that the bulb is good.
4   If the light doesn't come on when the ignition key is turned to START, the bulb might be burned out, the ignition switch might be faulty or the circuit might be open.
5   As soon as the engine starts, the indicator light should go out and remain off, unless the engine overheats. If the light doesn't go out, the wire between the sending unit and the light could be grounded (see the Wiring Diagrams at the end of Chapter 12); the sending unit might be defective (have it checked by a dealer service department); or the ignition switch might be faulty (see Chapter 12). Check the coolant to make sure it's correctly mixed; plain water, with no antifreeze, or coolant that's mainly water, might have too low a boiling point to activate the sending unit (see Chapter 1).

Replacement

6   See Chapter 6.

---

9   Blower motor resistor and blower motor - replacement

Warning: *These models are equipped with airbags, always disable the airbag system before working in the vicinity of the impact sensors, steering column or instrument panel to avoid the possibility of accidental deployment of the airbag, which could cause personal injury (see Chapter 12).*

Coupe models
Blower motor resistor
Refer to illustrations 9.1a, 9.1b, 9.2 and 9.3
1   Remove the glove box "stopper" and then remove the glove box **(see illustrations)**.
2   Disconnect the electrical connector from the blower motor resistor **(see illustration)**.
3   Remove the blower motor resistor mounting screws **(see illustration)** and then remove the resistor from the joint duct (models without air conditioning) or from the evap-

9.2 Unplug the electrical connector from the blower motor resistor (coupe models)

9.3 To remove the blower motor resistor, remove these two screws (arrows) (coupe models)

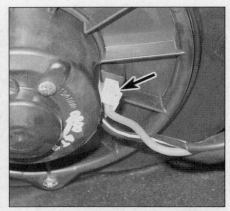

9.6 Unplug the electrical connector (arrow) from the blower motor (coupe models)

9.7 To remove the blower motor, remove these mounting screws (arrows) (coupe models)

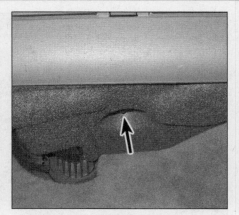

9.9 To remove the lower silencer panel, remove this fastener (arrow) (convertible and sedan models)

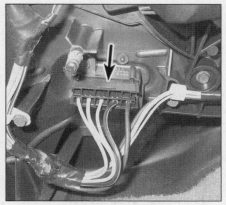

9.10 Unplug the electrical connector (arrow) from the blower motor resistor (convertible and sedan models)

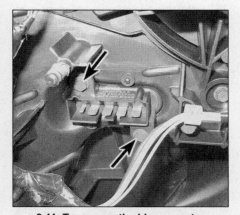

9.11 To remove the blower motor resistor, remove these two bolts (arrows) (convertible and sedan models)

orator housing (models with air conditioning).

4   Installation is the reverse of removal.

Blower motor

Refer to illustrations 9.6 and 9.7

5   Remove the glove box stopper and the glove box **(see illustrations 9.1a and 9.1b)**.

6   Disconnect the blower motor electrical connector **(see illustration)**.

7   Remove the blower motor mounting screws **(see illustration)** and then remove the blower motor.

8   Installation is the reverse of removal.

Convertible and sedan models

Blower motor resistor

Refer to illustrations 9.9, 9.10 and 9.11

9   Remove the lower right silencer panel **(see illustration)**.

10   Disconnect the electrical connector from the blower motor resistor **(see illustration)**.

11   Remove the blower motor resistor mounting bolts **(see illustration)** and then remove the blower motor resistor.

12   Installation is the reverse of removal.

Blower motor

Refer to illustrations 9.14 and 9.15

13   Remove the lower right silencer panel **(see illustration 9.9)**.

14   Disconnect the electrical connector from the blower motor **(see illustration)**.

15   Remove the blower motor mounting bolts

(see illustration) and then remove the blower motor.

16   Installation is the reverse of removal.

---

10   Heater/air conditioner control assembly - removal and installation

---

Warning: *These models are equipped with airbags, always disable the airbag system before working in the vicinity of the impact sensors, steering column or instrument panel to avoid the possibility of accidental deployment of the airbag, which could cause personal injury (see Chapter 12).*

1   Disconnect the cable from the negative battery terminal or the remote ground terminal (see Chapter 5).

Coupe models

Refer to illustrations 10.4, 10.6a, 10.6b, 10.6c and 10.7

2   Remove the center trim bezel (see Chapter 11).

3   Remove the radio (see Chapter 12).

4   Remove the heater/air conditioner con-

9.14 Unplug the electrical connector (arrow) from the blower motor (convertible and sedan models)

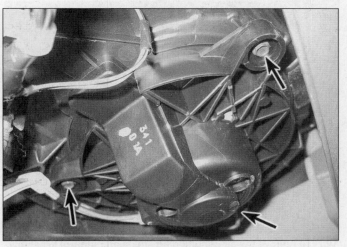

9.15 To remove the blower motor, remove these mounting bolts (arrows) (convertible and sedan models)

trol assembly retaining screws **(see illustration)**.

5   Remove the instrument panel (see Chapter 1).

6   Disconnect the control cables from the mode selector lever, from the temperature control lever and from the air selector lever **(see illustrations)**.

7   Disconnect the electrical connectors from the heater/air conditioner control assembly **(see illustration)** and then remove the assembly.

8   Installation is the reverse of removal.

Convertible and sedan models
1996 through 2000 models

Refer to illustrations 10.10, 10.11 and 10.15

9   Put the ignition key in the OFF position.

10   Remove the center trim bezel **(see illustration)**.

11   Remove the cluster hood bezel retaining screws in the trim bezel opening **(see illustration)**.

10.4 To detach the air conditioning and heater control assembly from the instrument panel, remove these screws (arrows) (coupe models)

12   Pry up the cluster hood bezel a few inches to expose the storage bin/cigarette lighter bezel and wiring.

13   Remove the storage bin/cigarette lighter bezel and wiring.

14   Remove the heater/air conditioner con-

trol assembly retaining screws **(see illustration 10.11)**.

15   Lower the heater/air conditioner control assembly into the storage bin/cigarette lighter bezel opening **(see illustration)** and then disconnect the electrical connectors from the

10.6a To disconnect the control cable from the vent control mode selector lever, which is located on the left side of the heater core case, simply pull the end of the cable off the lever pin (coupe models)

10.6b To disconnect the control cable from the temperature control lever, flip up the hinged cable guide (lower arrow), disengage the cable from the guide and then pull the end of the cable off the lever pin (upper arrow) (coupe models)

10.6c To disconnect the control cable from the fresh air/recycled air selector lever, disengage the cable from the cable guide (1) and then pull the end of the cable off the lever pin (2) (coupe models)

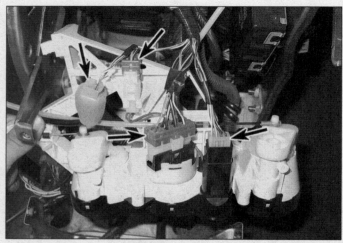

10.7 To remove the air conditioning and heater control assembly, unplug the electrical connectors (arrows) (coupe models)

10.10 To remove the center trim bezel, simply grasp it firmly and pull it off (1996 through 2000 convertible and sedan models)

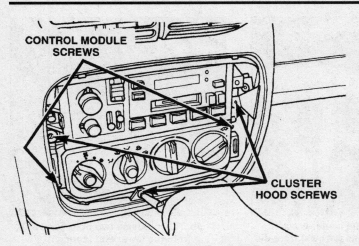

10.11 Heater and air conditioner control assembly installation details (1996 through 2000 convertible and sedan models)

1 *Control assembly retaining screws*
2 *Cluster hood bezel retaining screws*

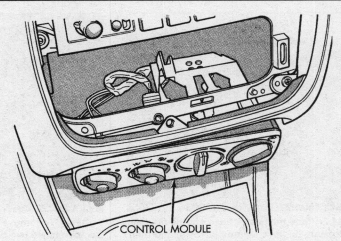

10.15 Lower the heater/air conditioner control assembly into the storage bin/cigarette lighter bezel opening to unplug the electrical connectors from the control assembly (1996 through 2000 convertible and sedan models)

backside of the control assembly.
16 Release the cable clips from the top of the control assembly; keep the cable clips for reassembly. Disconnect the temperature control cable and the recirculation control cable from their respective actuator levers on the backside of the control assembly. Remove the control assembly.
17 Installation is the reverse of removal.

2001 and later models
Refer to illustrations 10.18 and 10.20
18 Grasp the center trim bezel firmly and pull it out of the dash **(see illustration)**.
19 Disconnect the electrical connectors from the backside of the control assembly.
20 Remove the control assembly retaining screws **(see illustration)** and then detach the control assembly from the center bezel.
21 Installation is the reverse of removal.

11 Heater core - replacement

Warning 1: *All models are equipped with airbags, so to avoid the possibility of accidental deployment of the airbag, which could cause personal injury, always make sure that you disable the airbag system before working in the vicinity of the impact sensors, steering column or instrument panel (see Chapter 12).*
Warning 2: *On coupe models, the evaporator housing must be removed before the heater housing can be removed. On 2001 and later convertible and sedan models, the heating/ventilation/air conditioning (HVAC) housing must be removed before the heater core (or the air conditioning evaporator) can be removed. So if you are going to remove the heater core on any of these models, have the air conditioning system or by an*

automotive air conditioning shop BEFORE beginning this procedure. Do NOT loosen any refrigerant line fittings until the system has been discharged. The system is under high pressure and could cause a serious injury if opened while still pressurized. You will not be able to drive the vehicle to a dealer to have the system discharged once you have begun this procedure because the instrument panel must be removed and the vehicle will not be driveable.

Coupe models
Refer to illustrations 11.2, 11.4a, 11.4b, 11.5a, 11.5b, 11.6, 11.7a, 11.7b, 11.7c, 11.9, 11.10a, 11.10b, 11.11 and 11.12
1 Have the air conditioning system discharged by a dealer service department or by an automotive air conditioning shop before proceeding (see **Warning 2** above).

10.18 To remove the heater/air conditioner control assembly from the dash, simply grasp the center trim bezel firmly and pull

1 *Trim bezel positioning pins*
2 *Positioning pin grommets*
3 *Control assembly electrical connectors*

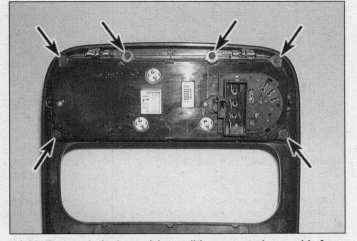

10.20 To detach the heater/air conditioner control assembly from the trim bezel, remove these screws (arrows)

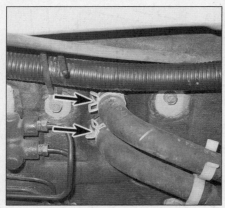

11.2 Trace the heater hoses to the firewall, loosen the hose clamps (arrows) and then disconnect the hoses from the heater core pipes (coupe model shown, other models similar)

11.4a To remove the center bracket, remove these two bolts (arrows) from the upper end of the bracket . .

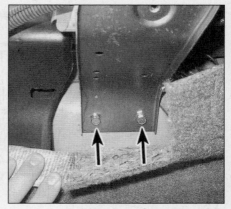

11.4b . . . and these two bolts (arrows) from the lower end (coupes)

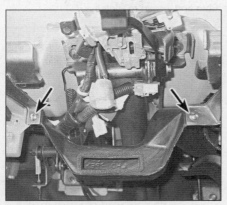

11.5a To remove the lap cooler duct, remove these two screws (arrows) . . .

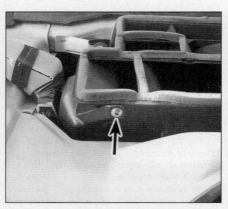

11.5b . . . and this screw (arrow) (coupes)

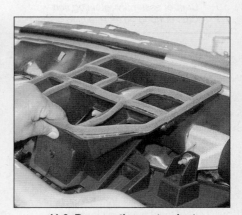

11.6 Remove the center duct assembly (coupes)

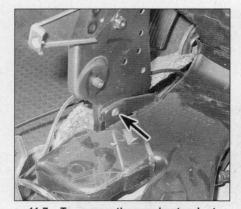

11.7a To remove the rear heater duct assembly, remove this screw (arrow) . . .

11.7b . . . remove this screw (arrow) from the right rear duct (carpet removed for clarity) . . .

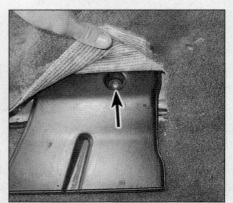

11.7c . . . remove this screw (arrow) from the left rear duct, disengage the left rear duct from the right rear duct (pull it off near the retaining screw shown in illustration 11.7a), pull the left duct out from underneath the carpet and then remove the right duct (coupes)

2   Drain the cooling system (see Chapter 1) and then disconnect the heater hoses from the heater core inlet and outlet pipes at the firewall **(see illustration)**.
3   Remove the instrument panel (see Chapter 11).
4   Remove the center bracket bolts **(see illustrations)** and then remove the center bracket.

5   Remove the lap cooler duct screws **(see illustrations)** and then remove the lap cooler duct.
6   Remove the center duct assembly **(see illustration)**.
7   Remove the left and right rear heater ducts **(see illustrations)**.
8   Remove the evaporator case (see Section 16).

9   Remove the foot distribution duct **(see illustration)**.
10   Remove upper and lower heater case mounting screws **(see illustrations)**.
11   Remove the heater core assembly

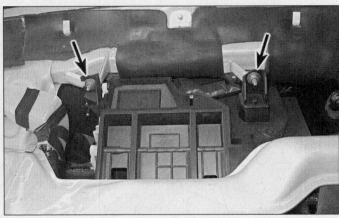

11.9 To remove the foot distribution duct, remove these two screws (arrows) (coupes)

11.10a To detach the heater housing from the vehicle, remove these two upper nuts (arrows) . . .

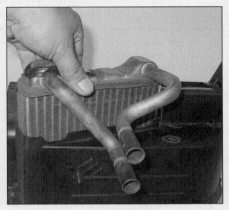

11.10b . . . and then remove these two lower nuts (arrows) (coupes)

11.11 To detach the heater core from the heater housing, remove these two screws (arrows) (coupes)

11.12 To remove the heater core from the heater housing, simply lift it straight up (coupes)

retaining screws **(see illustration)**.

12   Pull the heater core out of the housing **(see illustration)**.

13   If the old heater core has been leaking, remove the clips from the heater housing, separate the two halves of the housing and then clean the coolant from the housing.

14   Installation is the reverse of removal. Don't forget to reconnect the heater core inlet and outlet hoses at the firewall.

15   Refill the cooling system (see Chapter 1) when you're done.

Convertible and sedan models
1996 through 2000 models
Refer to illustrations 11.27a, 11.27b and 11.27c

16   Drain the cooling system (see Chapter 1) and then disconnect the heater hoses from the heater core inlet and outlet pipes at the firewall **(see illustration 11.2)**.

17   Remove the center trim bezel **(see illustration 10.10)**.

18   Remove the right instrument panel side trim (see Chapter 11).

19   Remove the two screws from the lower right support beam.

20   Remove the bolt from the instrument panel support at the A-pillar.

21   Remove the left instrument panel bezel (see Chapter 11).

22   Remove the lower left knee bolster (see Chapter 11).

23   Remove the center console screws at the instrument panel (see Chapter 11).

24   Remove the shift lever knob and then remove the shift lever bezel (see Chapter 7B).

25   Remove the rear half of the center console and then remove the front half of the console (see Chapter 11).

26   Remove the right instrument panel support strut.

27   Remove the heater core cover screws, remove the heater core cover and then remove the heater core **(see illustrations)**.

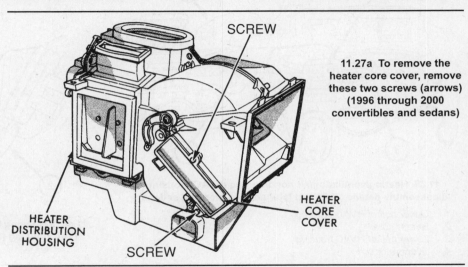

11.27a To remove the heater core cover, remove these two screws (arrows) (1996 through 2000 convertibles and sedans)

SCREW

HEATER DISTRIBUTION HOUSING

SCREW

HEATER CORE COVER

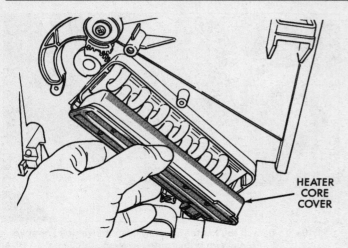

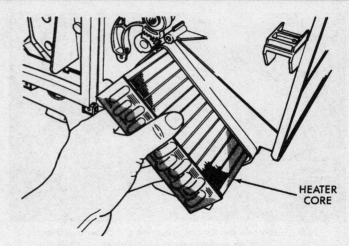

11.27b Remove the heater core cover (1996 through 2000 convertibles and sedans)

11.27c Pull the heater core out of the housing (1996 through 2000 convertibles and sedans)

28   If the heater core has been leaking, the heater core/evaporator housing must be removed and cleaned (see Section 16).

29   Installation is the reverse of removal. Don't forget to reconnect the heater core inlet and outlet hoses at the firewall.

30   Refill the cooling system (see Chapter 1) when you're done.

2001 and later models

Refer to illustrations 11.39 and 11.40

31   Have the air conditioning system discharged by a dealer service department or by an automotive air conditioning shop before proceeding (see **Warning 2** above).

32   Drain the cooling system (see Chapter 1) and then disconnect the heater hoses from the heater core inlet and outlet pipes at the firewall **(see illustration 11.2)**.

33   Referring to Section 16, remove the quick-connect clips from the air conditioning liquid and suction lines at the expansion valve

(see illustrations 16.16a and 16.16b) and then disconnect both lines from the expansion valve with a quick-connector kit (see illustrations 16.17a and 16.17b). Plug the air conditioning lines and the expansion valve to prevent moisture from entering the air conditioning system.

34   Remove the center console (see Chapter 11).

35   Remove the rear heat ducts.

36   Remove the nuts that secure the heating/ventilation/air conditioning (HVAC) housing to the firewall.

37   Remove the instrument panel and the HVAC housing as a single assembly (see Chapter 11) and then unbolt the HVAC housing from the instrument panel.

38   Remove the seal from the evaporator coil inlet and outlet pipes (see Section 16).

39   Separate the upper half of the HVAC housing from the lower half **(see illustration)**.

40   Pull the heater core out of the HVAC housing **(see illustration)**.

41   If the heater core has been leaking, remove the evaporator from the HVAC housing (see Section 16) and then clean out the housing.

42   Installation is the reverse of removal. Don't forget to reconnect the heater core inlet and outlet hoses at the firewall.

43   Refill the cooling system (see Chapter 1) when you're done.

12 Air conditioning and heating system - check and maintenance

Air-conditioning system

Refer to illustration 12.1

Warning: *The air conditioning system is under high pressure. Do not loosen any hose fittings or remove any components until after*

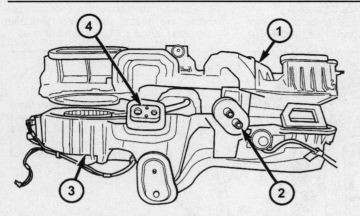

11.39 Heating/ventilation/air conditioning (HVAC) housing disassembly details (2001 and later convertibles and sedans)

1   Upper half of HVAC housing
2   Heater core
3   Lower half of HVAC housing
4   Evaporator coil

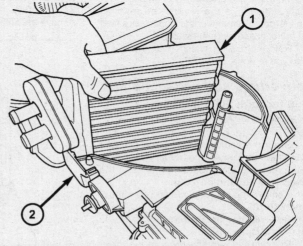

11.40 Removing the heater core (1) from the lower half of the HVAC housing (2) (2001 and later convertibles and sedans)

the system has been discharged by a dealer service department or service station. Always wear eye protection when disconnecting air conditioning system fittings.

1   The following maintenance checks should be performed on a regular basis to ensure the air conditioner continues to operate at peak efficiency.

a) *Check the compressor drivebelt. If it's worn or deteriorated, replace it (see Chapter 1).*

b) *Check the drivebelt tension and, if necessary, adjust it (see Chapter 1).*

c) *Check the system hoses. Look for cracks, bubbles, hard spots and deterioration. Inspect the hoses and all fittings for oil bubbles and seepage. If there's any evidence of wear, damage or leaks, replace the hose(s).*

d) *Inspect the condenser fins for leaves, bugs and other debris. Use a "fin comb" or compressed air to clean the condenser.*

e) *Make sure the system has the correct refrigerant charge.*

f) *Check the evaporator housing drain tube* (**see illustration**) *for blockage.*

2   It's a good idea to operate the system for about 10 minutes at least once a month, particularly during the winter. Long term non-use can cause hardening, and subsequent failure, of the seals.

3   Because of the complexity of the air conditioning system and the special equipment necessary to service it, in-depth troubleshooting and repairs are not included in this manual (refer to the *Haynes Automotive Heating and Air Conditioning Repair Manual*). However, simple checks and component replacement procedures are provided in this Chapter.

4   The most common cause of poor cooling is simply a low system refrigerant charge. If a noticeable drop in cool air output occurs, the following quick check will help you determine if the refrigerant level is low.

Checking the refrigerant charge

5   Warm the engine up to normal operating temperature.

6   Place the air conditioning temperature selector at the coldest setting and the blower at the highest setting. Open the doors (to make sure the air conditioning system doesn't cycle off as soon as it cools the passenger compartment).

7   With the compressor engaged - the clutch will make an audible click and the center of the clutch will rotate. If the compressor discharge line feels warm and the compressor inlet pipe feels cool, the system is properly charged.

8   Place a thermometer in the dashboard vent nearest the evaporator and operate the system until the indicated temperature is around 40 to 45 degrees F. If the ambient (outside) air temperature is very high, say 110 degrees F, the duct air temperature may be as high as 60 degrees F, but generally the air conditioning is 30-50 degrees F cooler than

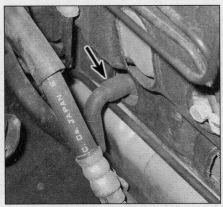

12.1 Look for the evaporator drain hose (arrow) on the firewall (coupe shown, other models similar); to remove it for cleaning (or for removing the evaporator) simply pull it off

the ambient air. **Note:** *Humidity of the ambient air also affects the cooling capacity of the system. Higher ambient humidity lowers the effectiveness of the air conditioning system.*

Adding refrigerant

Refer to illustrations 12.12 and 12.15

9   Buy an automotive charging kit at an auto parts store. A charging kit includes a 14-ounce can of refrigerant, a tap valve and a short section of hose that can be attached between the tap valve and the system low side service valve. Because one can of refrigerant may not be sufficient to bring the system charge up to the proper level, it's a good idea to buy an additional can. Make sure that one of the cans contains red refrigerant dye. If the system is leaking, the red dye will leak out with the refrigerant and help you pinpoint the location of the leak. **Caution:** *There are two types of refrigerant used in automotive systems; R-12 - which has been widely used on earlier models and the more environmentally-friendly R-134a used in all models covered by this manual. These two refrigerants (and their appropriate refrigerant oils) are not compatible and must never be mixed or components will be damaged. Use only R-134a refrigerant in the models covered by this manual.*

10   Hook up the charging kit by following the manufacturer's instructions. **Warning:** *DO NOT hook the charging kit hose to the system high side! The fittings on the charging kit are designed to fit* **only** *on the low side of the system.*

11   Back off the valve handle on the charging kit and screw the kit onto the refrigerant can, making sure first that the O-ring or rubber seal inside the threaded portion of the kit is in place. **Warning:** *Wear protective eyewear when dealing with pressurized refrigerant cans.*

12   Remove the dust cap from the low-side charging connection and attach the quick-connect fitting on the kit hose (**see illustration**).

13   Warm up the engine and turn on the air

12.12 Cans of R-134A refrigerant (available at auto parts stores) can be added to the low side of the air conditioning system with a simple recharging kit (coupe shown, other models similar)

12.15 Insert a thermometer in the center vent, turn on the air conditioning system and wait for it to cool down; depending on the humidity, the output air should be 30 to 40 degrees cooler than the ambient air temperature

conditioner. Keep the charging kit hose away from the fan and other moving parts. **Note:** *The charging process requires the compressor to be running. Your compressor may cycle off if the pressure is low due to a low charge. If the clutch cycles off, you can pull the low-pressure cycling switch plug and attach a jumper wire. This will keep the compressor ON.*

14   Turn the valve handle on the kit until the stem pierces the can, then back the handle out to release the refrigerant. You should be able to hear the rush of gas. Add refrigerant to the low side of the system until both the receiver-drier surface and the evaporator inlet pipe feel about the same temperature . Allow stabilization time between each addition.

15   If you have an accurate thermometer, place it in the center air conditioning vent (**see illustration**) and then note the temperature of the air coming out of the vent. A fully-charged system which is working correctly should cool

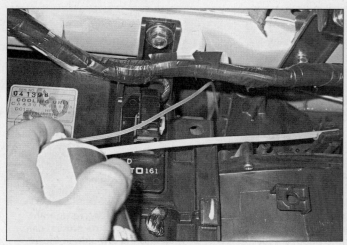

12.23a On coupes, remove the glove box (see Chapter 11) and then insert the nozzle of the disinfectant can into the evaporator housing by shoving it through the air recirculation door

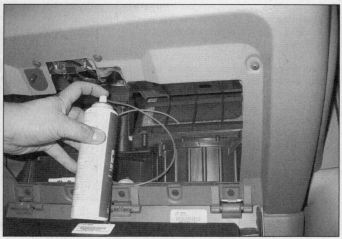

12.23b On convertibles and sedans, remove the glove box (see Chapter 11) and then insert the nozzle of the disinfectant can into the evaporator housing by shoving it through the air recirculation door

down to about 40 degrees F. Generally, an air conditioning system will put out air that is 30 to 40 degrees F cooler than the ambient air. For example, if the ambient (outside) air temperature is very high (over 100 degrees F), the temperature of air coming out of the registers should be 60 to 70 degrees F.

16   When the can is empty, turn the valve handle to the closed position and release the connection from the low-side port. Replace the dust cap. **Warning:** *Never add more than two cans of refrigerant to the system.*

17   Remove the charging kit from the can and store the kit for future use with the piercing valve in the UP position, to prevent inadvertently piercing the can on the next use.

Heating systems

18   If the carpet under the heater core is damp, or if antifreeze vapor or steam is coming through the vents, the heater core is leaking. Remove it (see Section 11) and install a new unit (most radiator shops will not repair a leaking heater core).

19   If the air coming out of the heater vents isn't hot, the problem could stem from any of the following causes:

a) *The thermostat is stuck open, preventing the engine coolant from warming up enough to carry heat to the heater core. Replace the thermostat (see Section 3).*

b) *There is a blockage in the system, preventing the flow of coolant through the heater core. Feel both heater hoses at the firewall. They should be hot. If one of them is cold, there is an obstruction in one of the hoses or in the heater core, or the heater control valve is shut. Detach the hoses and back flush the heater core with a water hose. If the heater core is clear but circulation is impeded, remove the two hoses and flush them out with a water hose.*

c) *If flushing fails to remove the blockage from the heater core, the core must be replaced (see Section 11).*

Eliminating air conditioning odors

Refer to illustrations 12.23a and 12.23b

20   Unpleasant odors that often develop in air conditioning systems are caused by the growth of a fungus, usually on the surface of the evaporator core. The warm, humid environment there is a perfect breeding ground for mildew to develop.

21   The evaporator core on most vehicles is difficult to access, and factory dealerships have a lengthy, expensive process for eliminating the fungus by opening up the evaporator case and using a powerful disinfectant and rinse on the core until the fungus is gone. You can service your own system at home, but it takes something much stronger than basic household germ-killers or deodorizers.

22   Aerosol disinfectants for automotive air conditioning systems are available in most auto parts stores, but remember when shopping for them that the most effective treatments are also the most expensive. The basic procedure for using these sprays is to start by running the system in the RECIRC mode for ten minutes with the blower on its highest speed. Use the highest heat mode to dry out the system and keep the compressor from engaging by disconnecting the wiring connector at the compressor (see Section 13).

23   Make sure that the disinfectant can comes with a long spray hose. Point the nozzle through the air recirculation door so that it protrudes inside the evaporator housing **(see illustrations)**, and then spray according to the manufacturer's recommendations. Try to cover the whole surface of the evaporator core, by aiming the spray up, down and sideways. Follow the manufacturer's recommendations for the length of spray and waiting

time between applications.

24   Once the evaporator has been cleaned, the best way to prevent the mildew from coming back again is to make sure your evaporator housing drain tube is clear **(see illustration 12.1)**.

13   Air conditioning compressor - removal and installation

Warning: *The air conditioning system is under high pressure. DO NOT disassemble any part of the system (hoses, compressor, line fittings, etc.) until after the system has been discharged by a dealer service department or by an automotive air conditioning shop.*
Note: *If you're replacing the compressor, also replace the filter-drier/receiver-drier (see Section 14).*

Removal

Refer to illustrations 13.3a, 13.3b, 13.3c, 13.3d, 13.4, 13.5a, 13.5b and 13.6

1   Have the system discharged (see the **Warning** above).

2   Disconnect the cable from the negative battery terminal or the remote ground terminal (see Chapter 5).

3   Remove the tensioner pulley retaining nut **(see illustration)**, slide the pulley down and then remove the drivebelt. Remove the tensioner pulley and then remove the pulley bearing dust cover **(see illustrations)**. Remove the adjusting bolt from the pulley retaining bolt **(see illustration)** and inspect the threads on both, particularly on the adjusting bolt. Make sure that both bolts are in good condition before re-using them.

4   Unplug the electrical connector **(see illustration)** from the compressor clutch.

5   Disconnect the refrigerant lines from the compressor **(see illustration)**. Plug the open

13.3a To release tension on the drivebelt and to release the tensioner pulley, remove this nut (lower arrow), loosen the adjuster bolt (upper arrow) enough to take tension off the drivebelt and then remove the belt (2.5L V6 tensioner assembly shown, other tensioners similar)

13.3b Remove the tensioner pulley . . .

13.3c . . . and then remove the pulley bearing dust cover

fittings to prevent entry of dirt and moisture. Be sure to remove and discard the old refrigerant line fitting O-rings **(see illustration)**.

6   Remove the compressor mounting bolts **(see illustration)** and then remove it from the vehicle.

Installation

7   If a new compressor is being installed, pour out the oil from the old compressor into a graduated container and add that amount of new refrigerant oil to the new compressor. Also follow any directions included with the new compressor.

8   The clutch might have to be transferred from the original compressor to the new unit.

9   Installation is the reverse of removal. Replace all O-rings with new ones specifically made for use with R-134a refrigerant and lubricate them with R-134a-compatible refrigerant oil.

10   Have the system evacuated, recharged and leak tested by the shop that discharged it.

13.3d Make sure that the threads on the pulley retaining bolt (lower arrow) and on the adjusting bolt (upper arrow) are in good condition before installing the tensioner pulley (2.5L V6 tensioner assembly shown, other tensioners similar)

14   Air conditioning receiver-drier - removal and installation

Warning: *The air conditioning system is under high pressure. DO NOT disassemble any part of the system (hose, compressor, line fittings,*

13.4 Unplug the compressor clutch electrical connector (arrow)

etc.) until after the system has been evacuated and the refrigerant recovered by a dealer service department or service station.
Caution: *Replacement filter-drier/receiver-drier units are so effective at absorbing moisture that they can quickly saturate upon exposure to the atmosphere. When installing a new unit, have all tools and supplies ready for quick reassembly to avoid having the system open any longer than necessary.*

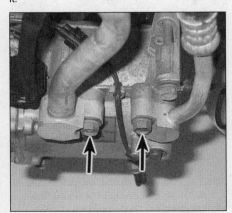

13.5a To detach the refrigerant lines from the compressor, remove these two bolts (arrows)

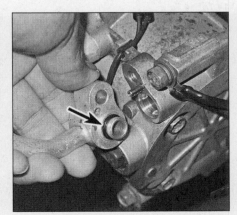

13.5b Be sure to discard the old O-ring (arrow) on each refrigerant line fitting

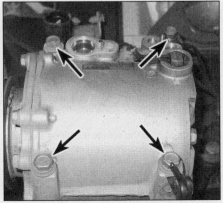

13.6 To detach the compressor from its mounting bracket, remove these bolts (arrows)

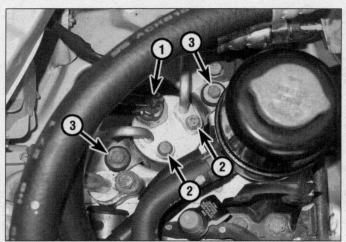

14.3 To remove the receiver-drier on coupe models, unplug the dual pressure switch electrical connector (1), remove the refrigerant line inlet and outlet fitting bolts (2) and then remove the receiver-drier mounting bolts (3)

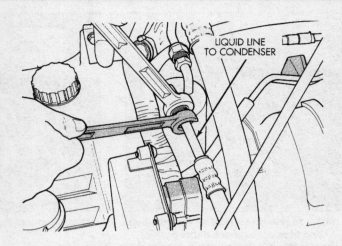

14.6a To disconnect the liquid line between the receiver-drier and the condenser on 1996 through 2000 convertible and sedan models, unscrew this fitting; be sure to use a back-up wrench to protect the line to the condenser from kinking

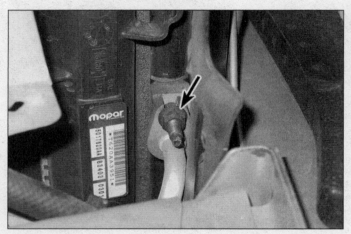

14.6b To disconnect the liquid line between the receiver-drier and the condenser on 2001 and later convertible and sedan models, remove this nut (arrow) and then pull off the fitting; be sure to discard and replace the old fitting O-ring

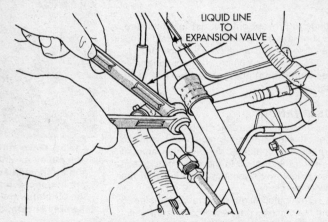

14.7a To disconnect the liquid line between the receiver-drier and the expansion valve on 1996 through 2000 convertible and sedan models, unscrew this fitting; be sure to use a back-up wrench to protect the line to the expansion valve from kinking

Removal

1   The receiver-drier acts as a reservoir for the system refrigerant. It's located on the right side of the engine compartment, next to the radiator and condenser.

2   Have the system discharged (see the **Warning** at the beginning of this Section).

Coupe models

Refer to illustration 14.3

3   Disconnect the dual pressure switch electrical connector **(see illustration)** from the receiver-drier.

4   Disconnect the refrigerant lines from the receiver-drier. Be sure to discard and replace the old O-rings in the fittings and then plug the open fittings to prevent entry of dirt and moisture.

5   Remove the bracket bolt at the base of the receiver/drier. Spread the aluminum clamp and remove the receiver/drier.

Convertible and sedan models

Refer to illustrations 14.6a, 14.6b, 14.7a, 14.7b, 14.7c

6   Disconnect the liquid line between the receiver-drier and the condenser. On 1996 through 2000 models, disconnect the fitting near the receiver-drier **(see illustration)**. On 2001 and later models, disconnect the line at the condenser **(see illustration)**. Plug the open fittings to prevent the entry of dirt and moisture.

7   Disconnect the liquid line between the receiver-drier and the expansion valve. On 1996 through 2000 models, disconnect the fitting near the receiver-drier **(see illustration)**. On 2001 and later models, disconnect the line at the expansion valve **(see illustration)**. Plug the open fittings to prevent the entry of dirt and moisture.

8   Remove the receiver-drier bracket bolt **(see illustration)** and then remove the receiver drier unit.

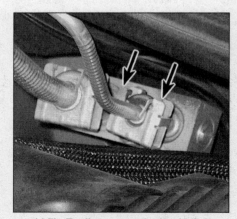

14.7b To disconnect the liquid line between the receiver-drier and the expansion valve on 2001 and later convertible and sedan models, pull down this clip (arrows) . . .

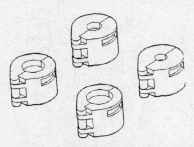

14.7c . . . and then disconnect the line from the expansion valve with a Quick Connector Kit (available at most auto parts stores) in accordance with the manufacturer's instructions

Installation

9   Installation is the reverse of removal. If a new receiver-drier is being installed add one ounce of refrigerant oil to it before installation.
10   Take the vehicle back to the shop that discharged it. Have the system evacuated, recharged and leak tested.

15 Air conditioning condenser - removal and installation

Warning: *The air conditioning system is under high pressure. Do not loosen any hose fittings or remove any components until after the system has been discharged by a dealer service department or service station. Always wear eye protection when disconnecting air conditioning system components.*
Note: *The receiver-drier should be replaced whenever the condenser is replaced (see section 14).*
1   Have the system discharged (see the **Warning** at the beginning of this Section).
2   Disconnect the cable from the negative battery terminal or the remote ground terminal (see Chapter 5).

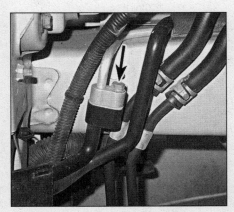

15.6b To disconnect this refrigerant liquid line, remove this bolt (arrow) (this line does not have a separate fitting on 1995 coupes; it shares the fitting shown in the previous illustration)

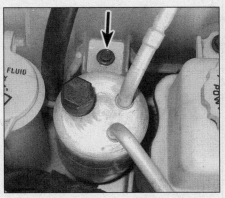

14.8 To detach the receiver-drier unit from a convertible or sedan, remove this bolt (arrow)

15.5b . . . and remove this bolt (arrow) from the right end (coupe models)

Coupe models

Refer to illustrations 15.5a, 15.5b, 15.6a, 15.6b, 15.6c and 15.7

3   Remove the radiator and condenser fan assemblies (see Section 4).
4   Remove the radiator (see Section 5).
5   Remove the upper insulator bolts **(see illustrations)**.
6   Disconnect the refrigerant liquid lines **(see illustrations)**. Be sure to remove and discard the old O-rings **(see illustration)**.
7   Remove the condenser mounting bolts

15.6c When disconnecting the refrigerant liquid line fittings, be sure to remove and discard the old O-rings (coupe models)

15.5a To detach the condenser from the upper crossmember, remove this bolt (arrow) from the left end of the crossmember . . .

15.6a To disconnect this refrigerant liquid line, remove this bolt (arrow) (on 1995 coupes, both refrigerant lines are disconnected at this fitting)

(see illustration) and then remove the condenser from the vehicle.
8   Be sure to inspect the rubber mounting bolt insulators for cracks and deterioration. Replace them if they're worn or damaged.

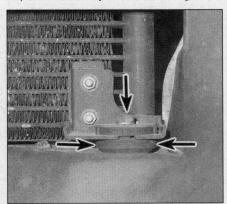

15.7 To detach the condenser assembly from the vehicle, remove this bolt (upper arrow) from each front corner of the condenser (left bolt shown); after removing the condenser, inspect each insulator (lower arrows) for cracks and deterioration and replace if necessary (coupe models)

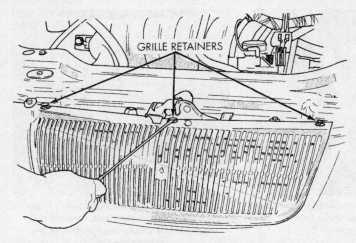

15.11 Remove the grille retainers (1996 through 2000 convertible and sedan models)

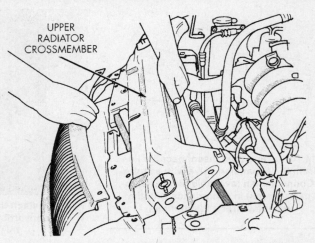

15.12 Remove the upper radiator crossmember (1996 through 2000 convertible and sedan models)

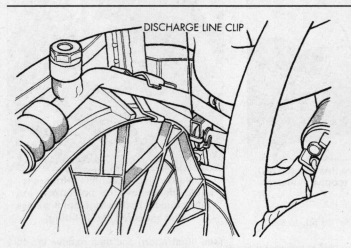

15.13a To disconnect the refrigerant lines from the condenser, pry off the retaining clip with a pair of pliers . . .

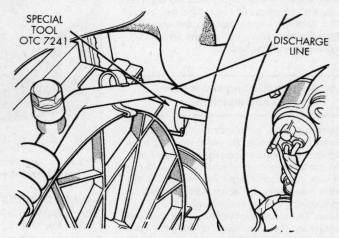

15.13b . . . and then install the special OTC tool (No. 7241, or a suitable equivalent, available at most auto parts stores) and disconnect the line (discharge line shown, other line similar) (1996 through 2000 convertible and sedan models)

9   Installation is the reverse of removal. If a new condenser is being installed add one ounce of refrigerant oil to it before installation.
10   Take the vehicle back to the shop that discharged it. Have the system evacuated, recharged and leak tested.

Convertible and sedan models
1996 through 2000 models
Refer to illustrations 15.11, 15.12, 15.13a, 15.13b and 15.15

11   Remove the upper grille retainers **(see illustration)**.
12   Remove the upper radiator crossmember **(see illustration)**.
13   Disconnect the refrigerant lines from the condenser **(see illustrations)**.
14   Remove the condenser line support bracket.
15   Remove the condenser mounting bolts **(see illustration)** and then remove the condenser.

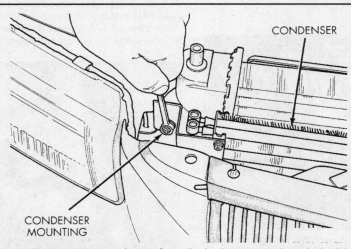

15.15 To detach the condenser from the body, remove these bolts (right bolt shown, other bolt at same location on left side) (1996 through 2000 convertible and sedan models)

15.20a Disconnect the transaxle cooler line bracket (right arrow) from the left side of the radiator and then disconnect the cooler line fitting bolt (left arrow) from the condenser (2001 and later convertible and sedan models)

15.20b Disconnect the transaxle cooler line fitting bolt (upper arrow) from the condenser; to disconnect the upper refrigerant line from the condenser, remove this nut (lower arrow) (2001 and later convertible and sedan models)

15.21 To disconnect the lower refrigerant line from the condenser, remove this nut (lower arrow); to detach the right end of the condenser from the radiator, remove this bolt (upper arrow) (2001 and later convertible and sedan models)

16   Installation is the reverse of removal. If a new condenser is being installed add one ounce of refrigerant oil to it before installation.

17   Take the vehicle back to the shop that discharged it. Have the system evacuated, recharged and leak tested.

2001 and later models

Refer to illustrations 15.20a, 15.20b, 15.21 and 15.22

18   Remove the front fascia (bumper cover) (see Chapter 11).

19   Remove the upper radiator crossmember **(see illustration 4.6)**.

20   Disconnect the transaxle cooler lines **(see illustrations)**.

21   Disconnect the refrigerant liquid lines **(upper line, see illustration 15.20b; lower line, see illustration)**.

22   Remove the condenser mounting bolts **(left bolt, see illustration; right bolt, see illustration 15.21)**.

23   Remove the condenser.

24   Installation is the reverse of removal. If a new condenser is being installed add one

ounce of refrigerant oil to it before installation. Be sure to use new O-rings when reconnecting the transaxle cooler line fittings and the refrigerant line fittings.

25   Take the vehicle back to the shop that discharged it. Have the system evacuated, recharged and leak tested.

---

16   Air conditioning evaporator and expansion valve - removal and installation

Warning 1: *These models are equipped with airbags, always disable the airbag system before working in the vicinity of the impact sensors, steering column or instrument panel to avoid the possibility of accidental deployment of the airbag, which could cause personal injury (see Chapter 12).*

Warning 2: *The air conditioning system is under high pressure. Do not loosen any hose fittings or remove any components until after the system has been discharged by a dealer*

service department or service station. Always wear eye protection when disconnecting air conditioning system components.

Note: *Evaporator removal on these models is a difficult undertaking for the home mechanic. It can be done, but it requires discharging the air conditioning system, disconnecting the passenger airbag system and many electrical connectors under the dash, and removing the complete instrument panel assembly. The air conditioning evaporator is contained in a two-piece housing which must be removed from under the dash and separated into two halves.*

Coupe models

Refer to illustrations 16.2, 16.3a, 16.3b, 16.5, 16.6, 16.8, 16.9a, 16.9b, 16.10, 16.11 and 16.12

1   Have the system discharged (see the **Warning** at the beginning of this Section).

2   Remove the cruise control reservoir from the firewall **(see illustration)** and then pull off the evaporator drain hose **(see illustration 12.1)**.

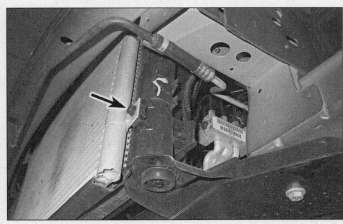

15.22 To detach the left end of the condenser from the radiator, remove this bolt (arrow) (2001 and later convertible and sedan models)

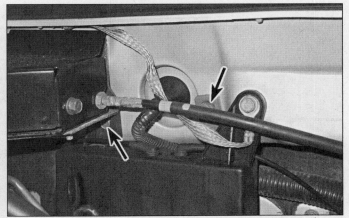

16.2 To detach the cruise control reservoir from the firewall, remove these two bolts when installing the reservoir - don't forget to reattach the ground strap to the firewall with the left bolt

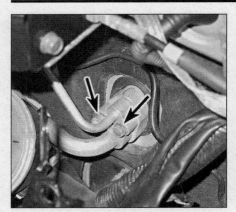

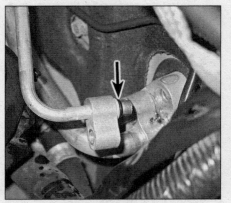

16.3a To disconnect the refrigerant lines from the evaporator, remove these two bolts (arrows)

16.3b Be sure to remove and discard the old O-ring (arrow) on each fitting; install new O-rings when reconnecting the lines to the evaporator

16.5 To remove the corner panel, remove these two screws (arrows) and then pull the panel back and slightly down (there's a positioning pin near the top of the panel that fits into a grommet on the instrument panel)

3   Disconnect the suction and liquid lines from the evaporator **(see illustrations)**. Remove and discard the old O-rings. Cap the lines to prevent dirt and moisture from entering the system.
4   Remove the glove box stopper and then remove the glove box **(see illustrations 9.1a and 9.1b)**.
5   Remove the corner panel **(see illustration)**.

6   Remove the glove box "under frame" **(see illustration)**.
7   Remove the instrument panel assembly (see Chapter 11).
8   Remove the evaporator housing mounting bolts **(see illustration)** and then carefully remove the housing.
9   Pry off all the evaporator housing clips

and then remove the insulation from the evaporator inlet and outlet flange **(see illustrations)**.
10   Pull apart the upper and lower halves of the evaporator housing **(see illustration)**.
11   Remove the fin thermo sensor from the

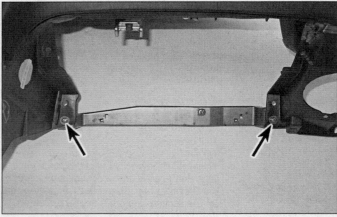

16.6 To remove the glove box under frame, remove these two screws (arrows)

16.8 To detach the evaporator housing, remove these bolts (arrows)

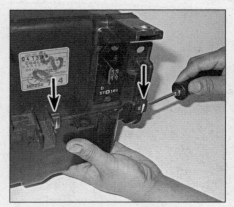

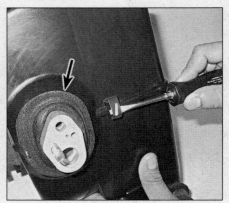

16.9a Pry off all of the evaporator housing clips (arrows) . . .

16.9b . . . and then carefully remove the insulation (arrow) from the evaporator inlet and outlet pipe flange

16.10 Pull apart the upper and lower halves of the evaporator housing

evaporator (see illustration).

12   Remove the expansion valve from the evaporator (see illustration). Remove the old O-rings from the expansion valve fittings.

13   Installation is the reverse of removal. Be sure to use new O-rings when installing the expansion valve. If a new evaporator is being installed, pour one ounce of new, R-134a-compatible refrigerant oil into it prior to installation.

14   Take the vehicle back to the shop that discharged it. Have the system evacuated, recharged and leak tested.

Convertible and sedan models

Expansion valve

Refer to illustrations 16.16a, 16.16b, 16.17a, 16.17b, 16.18 and 16.19

Note: *The expansion valve can be replaced without removing the evaporator from the vehicle or removed along with the evaporator.*

15   Have the system discharged (see the **Warning** at the beginning of this Section).

16   Remove the clips from the liquid line and from the suction line (see illustrations).

16.11 Remove the fin thermo sensor from the evaporator

17   Using a quick connect kit (special tool No. 7193), or an OTC tool (Nos. 7240/7242), or a suitable equivalent (available at most auto parts stores), disconnect the liquid line and the suction line from the expansion valve (see illustrations). Plug the air conditioning lines

16.12 To remove the expansion valve, unscrew these two fittings (arrows); be sure to discard the old O-rings in the fittings and use new O-rings when installing the expansion valve

to prevent and, if you're planning to re-use it, the expansion valve to prevent moisture from entering the air conditioning system.

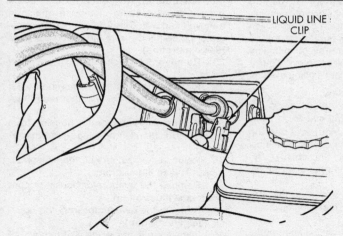

16.16a Remove the clip from the liquid line (convertibles and sedans)

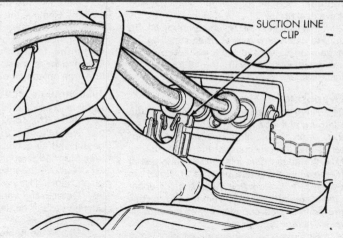

16.16b Remove the clip from the suction line (convertibles and sedans)

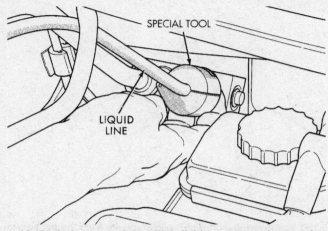

16.17a Using a special tool (available at auto parts stores), disconnect the liquid line (convertibles and sedans)

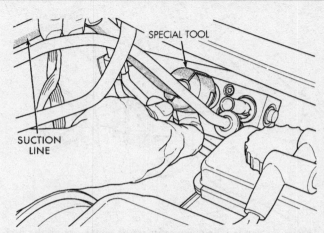

16.17b Using a special tool (available at auto parts stores), disconnect the suction line (convertibles and sedans)

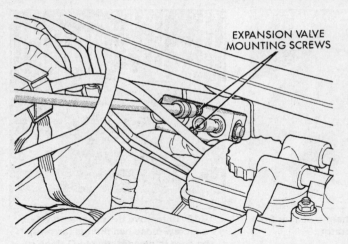

16.18 To detach the expansion valve from the evaporator, remove these two mounting screws (convertibles and sedans)

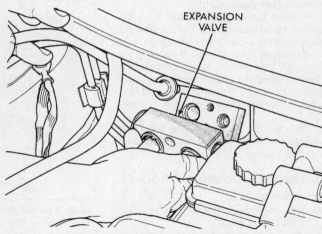

16.19 Remove the expansion valve from the evaporator and then remove the old gasket (convertibles and sedans)

18   Remove the expansion valve mounting screws (**see illustration**).
19   Remove the expansion valve (**see illustration**). and then remove the old expansion valve gasket.
20   Installation is the reverse of removal. Be sure to use a new gasket when installing the expansion valve and tighten the expansion valve mounting screws to the torque listed in this Chapter's Specifications.

Evaporator
21   Have the system discharged (see the **Warning** at the beginning of this Section).
22   Drain the cooling system (see Chapter 1) and then disconnect the heater hoses from the heater core inlet and outlet pipes at the firewall (**see illustration 11.2**). **Note:** *On vehicles equipped with a V6 engine, the upper intake manifold must be removed to access the heater hose connections at the firewall (see Chapter 2B).*
23   Remove the quick-connect clips from the air conditioning liquid and suction lines

at the expansion valve (**see illustrations 16.15a and 16.15b**) and then disconnect both lines from the expansion valve with a quick-connector kit (**see illustrations 16.16a and 16.16b**). Remove the expansion valve mounting screws and then separate the expansion valve from the evaporator (**see illustrations 16.18 and 16.19**). Plug the air conditioning lines and the expansion valve to prevent moisture from entering the air conditioning system.

1996 through 2000 models
Refer to illustration 16.28a, 16.28b, 16.30, 16.31a, 16.31b, 16.32, 16.33 and 16.34
24   Remove the center trim bezel and the heater and air conditioning control assembly (see Steps 10 through 16 in Section 10).
25   Remove the instrument panel assembly (see Chapter 11).
26   Detach any wiring harnesses that are attached to the heater/air conditioning housing.
27   Unbolt the heater/air conditioning housing from the firewall and then carefully remove

it from the vehicle.
28   Using a flat-blade screwdriver, pry up the locking tab on the evaporator probe cover (**see illustration**). Twist the evaporator probe access cover 1/4-turn clockwise and then remove the cover. Carefully pull out the evaporator probe needle from the evaporator core (**see illustration**).
29   Remove the recirculating door inlet cover.
30   Remove the clips that attach the heater and evaporator housings together (**see illustration**).
31   Separate the evaporator housing from the heater/distribution housing (**see illustrations**).
32   Remove the seal around the evaporator tube inlet (**see illustration**).
33   Remove the evaporator housing upper cover (**see illustration**).
34   Remove the evaporator from the housing (**see illustration**).
35   Installation is the reverse of removal. If a new evaporator is being installed, pour one

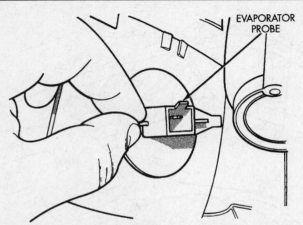

16.28a To remove the evaporator probe cover, pry up the tab and then turn the cover 1/4-turn clockwise (1996 through 2000 convertibles and sedans)

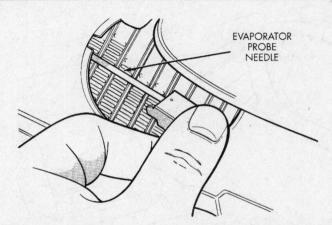

16.28b Remove the evaporator probe needle from the evaporator core (1996 through 2000 convertibles and sedans)

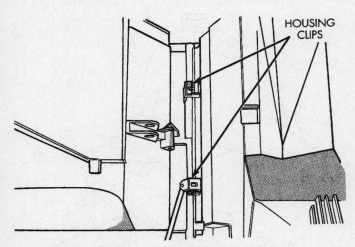

16.30 Remove the clips that attach the two housing sections (1996 through 2000 convertibles and sedans)

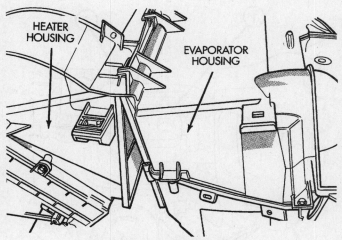

16.31a Pull the two sections apart . . .

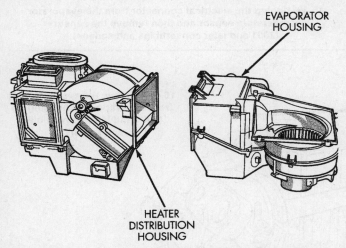

16.31b . . . and then separate the heater housing from the evaporator housing (1996 through 2000 convertibles and sedans)

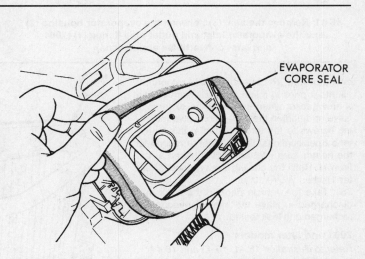

16.32 Remove the seal from the evaporator inlet and outlet flange (1996 through 2000 convertibles and sedans)

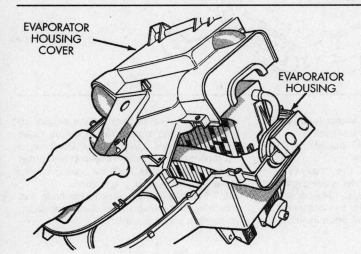

16.33 Remove the evaporator housing upper cover (1996 through 2000 convertibles and sedans)

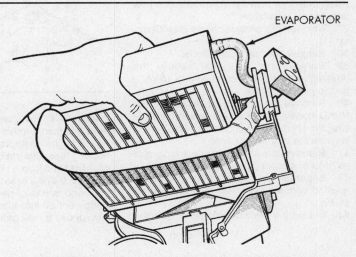

16.34 Remove the evaporator from the evaporator housing (1996 through 2000 convertibles and sedans)

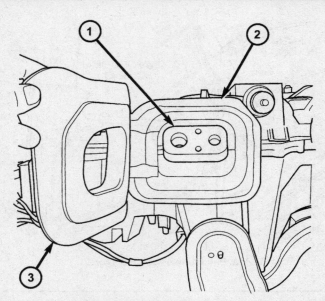

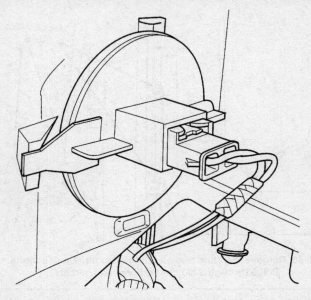

16.41 Remove the seal (3) between the evaporator housing (2) and the evaporator inlet and outlet pipe flange (1) (2001 and later convertibles and sedans)

16.43 Unplug the electrical connector from the evaporator temperature sensor and then remove the sensor (2001 and later convertibles and sedans)

ounce of new, R-134a-compatible refrigerant oil into it prior to installation. Be sure to use a new gasket when installing the expansion valve and tighten the expansion valve mounting screws to the torque listed in this Chapter's Specifications. Don't forget to reconnect the heater core inlet and outlet hoses at the firewall. Refill the cooling system (see Chapter 1) when you're done.

36   Take the vehicle back to the shop that discharged it. Have the system evacuated, recharged and leak tested.

2001 and later models

Refer to illustration 16.41, 16.43 and 16.44

Note: *When installing a new evaporator, always use a new gasket on the expansion valve* **(see illustration)** *and reinstall the temperature sensor from the old core into the new core before installation.*

37   Remove the center console (see Chapter 11).

38   Remove the rear heater ducts.

39   Remove the nuts that secure the heating/ventilation/air conditioning (HVAC) housing to the firewall.

40   Remove the instrument panel and the HVAC housing as a single assembly (see Chapter 11) and then unbolt the HVAC housing from the instrument panel.

41   Remove the seal from the evaporator coil inlet and outlet pipes **(see illustration)**.

42   Separate the upper half of the HVAC housing from the lower half **(see illustration 11.39)**.

43   Unplug the electrical connector from the

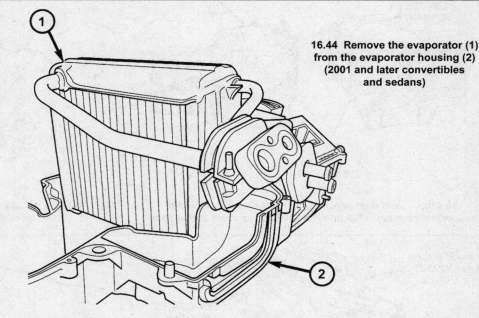

16.44 Remove the evaporator (1) from the evaporator housing (2) (2001 and later convertibles and sedans)

evaporator temperature sensor **(see illustration)** and then remove the sensor.

44   Pull the evaporator out of the HVAC housing **(see illustration)**.

45   Installation is the reverse of removal. If a new evaporator is being installed, pour one ounce of new, R-134a-compatible refrigerant oil into it prior to installation. Be sure to use a new gasket when installing the

expansion valve and tighten the expansion valve mounting screws to the torque listed in this Chapter's Specifications. Don't forget to reconnect the heater core inlet and outlet hoses at the firewall. Refill the cooling system (see Chapter 1) when you're done.

46   Take the vehicle back to the shop that discharged it. Have the system evacuated, recharged and leak tested.

Chapter 4
Fuel and exhaust systems

Contents

Specifications

General

Fuel pressure
  Convertible and sedan models
    1996 through 2000 models .... 47 to 51 psi
    2001 and later models .... 53 to 63 psi
  Coupe models .... 47 to 51 psi
Fuel system hold pressure (after five minutes) .... 21 psi minimum
Fuel injector resistance (approximate) @ 68-degrees F
  1995 through 2000 models
    Four-cylinder engines .... 11 to 15 ohms
    V6 engines .... 13 to 16 ohms
  2001 and later models .... 13 to 16 ohms

Torque specifications
Ft-lbs (unless otherwise indicated)

Note: *One foot pound (ft-lb) of torque is equivalent to 12 inch-pounds (in-lbs) of torque. Torque values below approximately 15 ft-lbs are expressed in inch-pounds, since most foot-pound torque wrenches are not accurate at these smaller values.*

Fuel rail mounting bolts
  2.0L DOHC 16
  2.4L DOHC
    1995 through 1999 16
    2001 and later .... 75 in-lbs
  2.5L V6 .... 106 in-lbs
  2.4L SOHC, 2.7L V6, 3.0L V6 .... 105 in-lbs
Fuel tank bolts
  1995 models 16
  1996 through 2000 models
    Coupes 19
    Convertibles 16
  2001 and later models
    Coupes 19
    Convertibles 40
Throttle body mounting bolts
  2.0L DOHC four-cylinder and 2.5L V6 engine 21
  2.4L SOHC four-cylinder and 3.0L V6 engine 14
  2.4L DOHC four-cylinder (2000 and earlier) engines 16
  2.4L DOHC four-cylinder (2001 and later) and 2.7L V6 engine .... 120 in-lbs

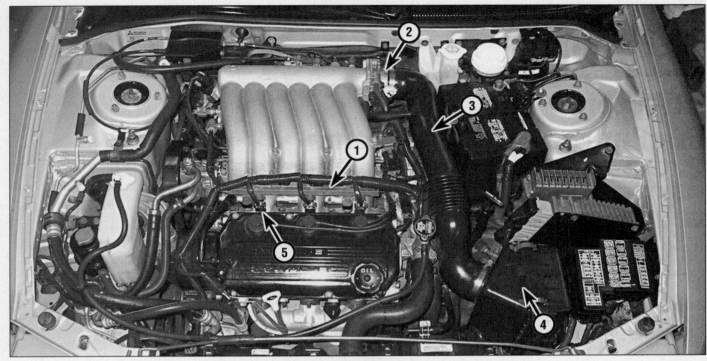

1.1a Typical fuel system components - 1998 coupe 2.5L V6 engine

| 1 | *Fuel rail* | 2 | *Throttle body* | 3 | *Air intake duct* | 4 | *Air filter housing* | 5 | *Fuel injector* |

1 General information

Sequential Electronic Fuel Injection system

Refer to illustrations 1.1a, 1.1b and 1.1c

The vehicles covered by this manual are equipped with a sequential Multi-Port Fuel Injection (MPFI) system **(see illustrations)**. This system uses timed impulses to sequentially inject the fuel directly into the intake ports of each cylinder. The injectors are controlled by the Powertrain Control Module (PCM). The PCM monitors various engine parameters and delivers the exact amount of fuel, in the correct sequence, to the intake ports. It also controls the engine idle speed via the idle air control motor which is mounted to the throttle body. This Chapter's information pertains to the air and fuel delivery components of the fuel injection system only. Refer to Chapter 6 for additional general information concerning the emissions and engine control systems.

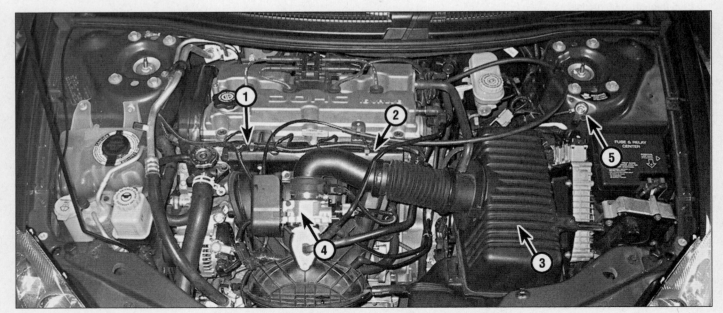

1.1b Typical fuel system components - 2001 2.4L DOHC engine

| 1 | *Fuel injector* | | 3 | *Air filter housing* | | 5 | *Remote ground terminal* |
| 2 | *Fuel rail* | | 4 | *Throttle body* | | | |

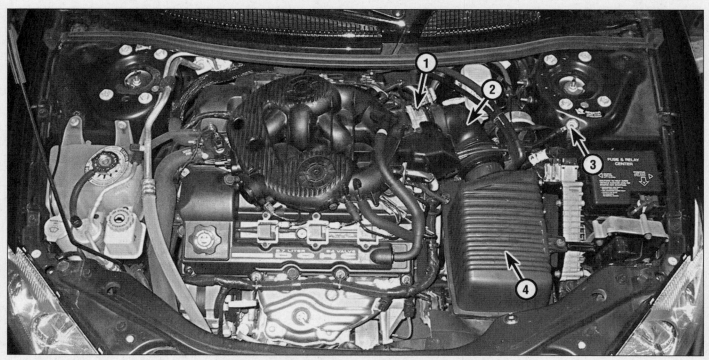

1.1c Typical fuel system components - 2001 2.7L V6

1 Throttle body	2 Air intake duct	3 Remote ground terminal	4 Air filter housing

Fuel pump and lines

All models are equipped with an electric fuel pump. The fuel pump is mounted in the fuel tank. On all coupe models, the fuel pump is accessible through a service hole access cover under the rear seat. On convertibles and sedan models, it is necessary to remove the fuel tank to gain access to the fuel pump. On 1995 through 2000 coupes, the fuel level sending unit is accessible through a separate service hole cover under the rear seat. On convertibles and all 2001 and later models, the fuel level sending unit is an integral component of the fuel pump and it must be removed from the fuel tank in the same manner.

The fuel pressure regulator is mounted in various locations on these models. 1995 models mount the fuel pressure regulator on the fuel rail. 1996 through 2000 coupes mount the fuel pressure regulator adjacent to the fuel tank near the fuel filter. 2001 and later coupes mount the fuel pressure regulator back on the fuel rail in the engine compartment. Convertible and sedan models mount the fuel pressure regulator in the tank with the fuel pump (fuel pump module).

The fuel filter is located in several different places depending upon year and model. Refer to Chapter 1 for all external fuel filter replacement procedures. The fuel filter is located inside the fuel tank along with the fuel pump on 2001 and later models. Fuel filter replacement on 2001 and later models is covered in the fuel pump replacement procedure in this chapter.

Only convertible and sedan models are equipped with a "returnless" fuel system. In this system, the fuel pressure regulator is part of the fuel pump/fuel level sending unit (fuel pump module) located in the fuel tank. Regulated fuel is sent to the inlet line and excess fuel is bled off directly into the fuel tank. Even though some coupe models are equipped with a fuel pressure regulator next to the fuel tank (external), this system is designed to return the fuel from the fuel pressure regulator back to the fuel tank and therefore is considered a "return" type fuel system.

Exhaust system

The exhaust system consists of the exhaust manifold(s), a catalytic converter, an exhaust pipe and a muffler. Each of these components is replaceable. For further information regarding the catalytic converter, refer to Chapter 6.

2   Fuel pressure relief procedure

Warning: *Gasoline is extremely flammable, so take extra precautions when you work on any part of the fuel system. Don't smoke or allow open flames or bare light bulbs near the work area, and don't work in a garage where a gas-type appliance (such as a water heater or a clothes dryer) is present. Since gasoline is carcinogenic, wear latex gloves when there's a possibility of being exposed to fuel, and if you spill any on your skin, rinse it off immediately with soap and water. Mop up any spills immediately and do not store fuel-soaked rags where they could ignite. The fuel*

system is under constant pressure, so, if any fuel lines are to be disconnected, the pressure must be relieved first. When you perform any kind of work on the fuel system, wear safety glasses and have a Class B type fire extinguisher on hand.

1   Remove the fuel filler cap to relieve the fuel tank pressure.

Coupes

Refer to illustration 2.3

2   Working inside the passenger compartment, remove the rear seat to access the fuel pump connector (see Section 5).

3   Locate the fuel pump electrical connector and disconnect it **(see illustration)**.

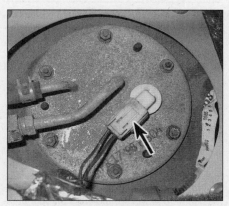

2.3 The fuel pump electrical connector (arrow) is located below the fuel pump access cover under the rear seat (coupe models)

4   Next, start the engine and allow it to run until it stops. This should only take a few seconds. Crank the engine again, to ensure the fuel pressure is completely relieved. Before working on any part of the fuel system, disconnect the cable from the negative battery terminal (see Chapter 5).

5   Even after the fuel pressure has been relieved, always lay a shop towel over any fuel connection that is to be separated to absorb the residual fuel that will leak out.

6   When you are finished working on the fuel system, reconnect the fuel pump electrical connector to the wiring harness.

Convertible and sedans

Refer to illustration 2.7

7   Locate the fuel pump relay in the relay/fuse center in the engine compartment **(see illustration)** and remove it.

8   Next, start the engine and allow it to run until it stops. This should only take a few seconds. Crank the engine again, to ensure the fuel pressure is completely relieved. Before working on any part of the fuel system, disconnect the battery cable from the remote ground terminal (see Chapter 5).

9   Even after the fuel pressure has been relieved, always lay a shop towel over any fuel connection that is to be separated to absorb the residual fuel that will leak out.

10   When you are finished working on the fuel system, install the fuel pump relay into the relay/fuse center.

All models

11   Connect the cable to the negative battery terminal or to the remote ground terminal (see Chapter 5).

12   Turn the ignition key to the ON position a few times to pressurize the system and check the serviced area for leaks.

13   Install the fuel filler cap and tighten it securely. **Note:** *If the fuel filler cap seal allows the fuel tank pressure to escape because of a damaged seal or it has not been tightened sufficiently, the CHECK ENGINE light will illuminate on the instrument panel.*

---

3   Fuel pump/fuel pressure - check

Warning: *Gasoline is extremely flammable, so take extra precautions when you work on any part of the fuel system (see the **Warning** in Section 2).*

Note 1: *Only convertible and sedans are equipped with a "returnless" fuel system. In this system the fuel pressure regulator is part of the fuel pump/fuel level sending unit located inside the fuel tank. Regulated fuel is sent to the inlet line and excess fuel is bled off directly into the fuel tank. Even though some coupes are equipped with a fuel pressure regulator next to the fuel tank, this system is designed to return the fuel from the fuel pressure regulator back to the fuel tank and therefore is considered a "return" type fuel system.*

Note 2: *The fuel pump will operate as long as*

2.7   The fuel pump relay is located in the fuse/relay center (Power Distribution Center) under the rectangular cover (convertible and sedan models)

the engine is cranking or running and the PCM is receiving ignition reference pulses from the electronic ignition system. If there are no reference pulses, the fuel pump will shut off after approximately 2 seconds.

Note 3: *To perform the fuel pressure check, you will need to obtain a fuel pressure gauge and adapter set (fuel line fittings). Also, On V6 engines and 2.4L SOHC four-cylinder engines, the fuel supply line is not equipped with a fuel pressure test port (Schrader valve fitting). A special fuel pressure test adapter must be installed between the fuel supply line and the fuel rail.*

General checks

1   If you suspect insufficient fuel delivery, check the following items first:

    a)   *Check the battery and make sure it's fully charged (see Chapter 5).*
    b)   *Check the fuel pump fuse.*
    c)   *Check the fuel filter for restriction.*
    d)   *Inspect all fuel lines to ensure that the problem is not simply a leak in a line.*

2   Verify the fuel pump actually runs. Place the transaxle in Park (automatic) or Neutral (manual) and apply the parking brake. Have an assistant turn the ignition switch to ON - you should hear a brief whirring noise (for approximately two seconds) as the pump comes on and pressurizes the system. **Note:** *The fuel pump is easily heard through the gas tank filler neck.* If there is no response from the fuel pump (makes no sound), check the fuel pump electrical circuit. If the fuel pump runs, but a fuel system problem is suspected, continue with the fuel pump pressure check.

3   If the pump does not turn on (makes no sound) with the ignition switch in the ON position, check the ignition fuse located in the engine compartment fuse center. Also, check the fuel pump relay and the ASD (automatic shutdown) relay. Refer to Chapter 12 for testing relays. **Note:** *These models are equipped with an ASD relay and a fuel pump relay. On some models, the ASD relay and the fuel pump relay are mounted together on the engine compartment firewall. On other*

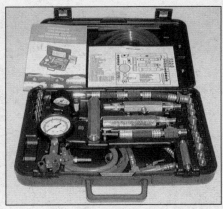

3.6a   This aftermarket fuel pressure testing kit contains all the necessary fittings and adapters, along with the fuel pressure gauge, to test most automotive fuel systems

models, the ASD relay and the fuel pump relay are mounted in the fuse/relay box in the engine compartment. 2001 and later models are equipped with an ignition failure sensor instead of an ASD relay.

4   If the relays are good and the fuel pump does not operate, check the fuel pump circuit. If the wiring and the connectors are good, replace the fuel pump (see Section 5).

Fuel pump pressure check

Refer to illustrations 3.6a, 3.6b, 3.6c and 3.6d

Warning: *Make sure the fuel pressure gauge hose is positioned away from the engine drivebelt before starting the engine.*

5   Perform the fuel pressure relief procedure (see Section 2).

6   Install a fuel pressure gauge **(see illustration):**

    a)   *On 2.0L and 2.4L DOHC four-cylinder engines, remove the cap from the fuel pressure test port (Schrader valve fitting) on the fuel rail and attach a fuel pressure gauge **(see illustration).***

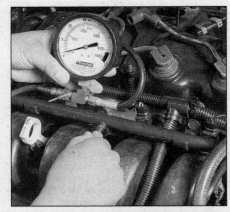

3.6b   On 2.0L and 2.4L DOHC engines, install the fuel pressure gauge onto the fuel rail test port

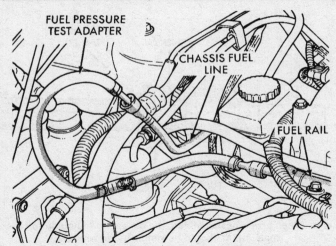

3.6c A special fuel pressure test adapter must be installed between the fuel supply line and the fuel rail (2.5L V6 engine shown)

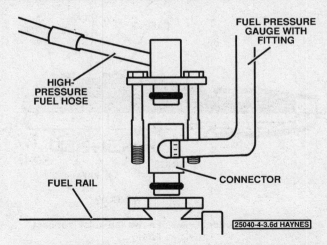

3.6d The fuel pressure gauge and connector mount between the fuel rail and the high pressure fuel line - note that the kit also contains extra long bolts to attach the connector to the fuel rail

b) *On V6 engines and 2.4L SOHC four-cylinder engines, the fuel supply line is not equipped with a fuel pressure test port (Schrader valve fitting). A special fuel pressure test adapter must be installed between the fuel supply line and the fuel rail. Disconnect the fuel supply line from the fuel rail (see Section 4) and install the fuel pressure test adapter between the supply line and the fuel rail* (see illustration). *Attach a fuel pressure gauge to the test adapter fitting.* **Note:** *Some models are equipped with a high pressure fuel line that is bolted to the fuel rail. Remove the fuel pressure line bolts and install the special adapter for the fuel pressure gauge* (see illustration).

Convertibles and sedans

7 Turn all the accessories Off and switch the ignition key On (engine not running). The fuel pump should run for approximately two seconds. Note the reading on the gauge. If the fuel pressure is higher than specified, replace the fuel pressure regulator. If the fuel pressure is too low, the fuel filter or in-tank strainer could be clogged, the lines could be restricted or leaking, a fuel injector could be leaking, or the fuel pressure regulator and/or fuel pump could be defective.

8 Start the engine and let it idle at normal operating temperature. The pressure should remain within the range listed in this Chapter's Specifications. If the pressure is lower than specified, check the items listed in Step 7. **Note:** *If no obvious problems are found, most likely the fuel pressure regulator and/or the fuel pump are defective. In this situation, it is recommended that both the fuel pressure regulator and fuel pump are replaced to prevent any future fuel pressure problems.*

1995 and 2001 and later coupes

9 Turn all the accessories Off and switch the ignition key On (engine not running). The fuel pump should run for approximately two

seconds. Note the reading on the gauge. If the fuel pressure is lower than specified, turn the key off, pinch off the fuel return line, then turn the key On again. **Caution:** *Use special pliers designed specifically for pinching a rubber fuel line (available at most auto parts stores). Use of any other type pliers may damage the fuel line.* **Caution:** *Do not allow the fuel pressure to rise above 85 psi or damage to the system may occur.* If the fuel pressure is now above the specified pressure, replace the fuel pressure regulator (see Section 6). If the fuel pressure is still lower than specified, check the fuel lines and the fuel filter for restrictions. If no restriction is found, remove the fuel pump assembly (see Section 5) and check the strainer for restrictions, also check the fuel pump wiring for high resistance. If no problems are found, replace the fuel pump.

10 If the fuel pressure recorded in Step 9 is higher than specified, check the fuel return line for restrictions. If no restrictions are found, replace the fuel pressure regulator (see Section 6).

11 Start the engine and let it idle at normal operating temperature. With the engine running, the fuel pressure should be 5 to 10 psi below the pressure recorded in Step 9. If it isn't, verify there is 12 to 14 in-Hg of vacuum present at the hose. If vacuum is not present at the hose, check the hose for a restriction or a break. If vacuum is present, reconnect the hose to the fuel pressure regulator. If the fuel pressure regulator does not decrease the fuel pressure with engine vacuum applied, replace the fuel pressure regulator.

1996 through 2000 coupes

12 Turn all the accessories Off and switch the ignition key On (engine not running). The fuel pump should run for approximately two seconds. Note the reading on the gauge. If the fuel pressure is above the specified pressure, replace the fuel pressure regulator (see Section 6). If the fuel pressure is lower than specified, check the fuel lines and the fuel fil-

ter for restrictions. If no restriction is found, remove the fuel pump assembly (see Section 5) and check the strainer for restrictions. If no problems are found, replace the fuel pump.

13 Start the engine and let it idle at normal operating temperature. The pressure should remain within the range listed in this Chapter's Specifications. If the pressure is lower than specified, check the items listed in Step 12. **Note:** *If no obvious problems are found, most likely the fuel pressure regulator and/or the fuel pump is defective. The fuel pressure regulator is mounted next to the fuel tank and cannot be removed and tested separately. In this situation, it is recommended that both the fuel pressure regulator and fuel pump are replaced to prevent any future fuel pressure problems.*

All models

14 Turn the engine off and check the gauge - the fuel pressure should hold steady. After five minutes, it should not drop below the minimum listed in this Chapter's Specifications. If it does drop, the fuel pump or fuel pressure regulator could be defective, or a fuel injector could be leaking.

15 After the testing is done, relieve the fuel pressure (see Section 2) and remove the fuel pressure gauge.

---

4 Fuel lines and fittings - repair and replacement

Warning: *Gasoline is extremely flammable, so take extra precautions when you work on any part of the fuel system (see the* **Warning** *in Section 2).*

General information

1 Always perform the fuel pressure relief procedure (see Section 2) before servicing fuel lines or fittings.

2 The fuel supply and vapor lines extend from the fuel tank to the engine compartment.

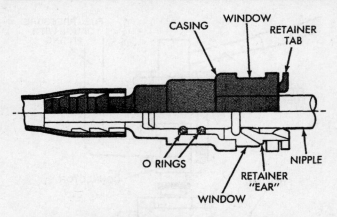

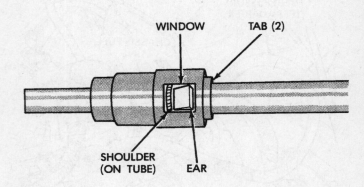

4.5a Cross-sectional view of a two-tab quick-connect fuel line fitting

4.5b When properly assembled, the tab ear and shoulder on the male fitting should be visible in the window

The lines are constructed of steel, plastic and rubber. They are secured to the underbody with clips and brackets. These lines should be inspected for leaks, kinks and dents anytime the vehicle is raised for service.

3   If evidence of dirt is found in the fuel system or fuel filter during service, the affected line should be disconnected and blown out. Check the fuel inlet strainer on the fuel pump for blockage or contamination (see Section 5).

Quick-connect fittings

4   These models use three different types of quick-connect fittings to join various fuel lines and components. The first type uses a single-tab retainer, the second type uses a two-tab retainer and the third type incorporates a plastic retainer ring (usually black in color) which connects/disconnects much like a common compressed air hose fitting. Some are equipped with safety latch clips. The fittings are equipped with non-serviceable O-ring seals located in the female part of the fitting. In the event the fitting or tubing becomes damaged or develops a leak, replace the entire fuel line/quick-connect fitting as an assembly. Always use original equipment parts, or parts that meet or exceed the original equipment standards.

Single and two-tab retainer fittings
Disassembly
Refer to illustrations 4.5a, 4.5b, 4.9a and 4.9b

5   These quick-connect fittings have one or two windows (depending on type) located in the side(s) of the female fitting. When the male fitting is inserted into the female, the tab(s) on the male engage in the window(s) and lock the fitting together **(see illustrations)**.

6   Perform the fuel pressure relief procedure (see Section 2).

7   Remove all fasteners, brackets or clips securing the lines as applicable.

8   Clean the area around the fitting to remove dirt and foreign debris.

9   Depress the retaining tab(s) on the quick-connect fitting and pull it apart **(see illustrations)**. **Note:** *The retaining tabs and shoulder should remain on the metal fuel line after separation.*

Assembly
10   Clean the male part of the fitting and

lightly lubricate it with clean engine oil.

11   Position the retaining tab ears on the tube so they align with the windows in the female fitting and push them together. You should hear the fitting snap into place as the retaining tab ears lock into the windows.

12   Verify the fitting is properly fastened by trying to pull the lines apart.

13   Secure the fuel line using any clips or brackets as applicable.

14   Pressurize the system and check for leaks.

Plastic retainer ring fittings
Disassembly
Refer to illustration 4.18

15   Perform the fuel pressure relief procedure (see Section 2).

16   Remove all fasteners, brackets or clips securing the lines as applicable.

17   Clean the area around the fitting to remove dirt and foreign debris.

18   Grasp the male line and push it in (towards the fitting). While applying pressure on the male line, press the plastic retainer ring into the female fitting and then pull the male line from the female fitting **(see illustra-**

4.9a Depress the plastic tabs on the male fitting . . .

4.9b . . . and separate the fitting - to assemble it, lubricate the male end with a small amount of clean engine oil, then push the fitting together until it locks into place - tug on it to ensure the connection is secure

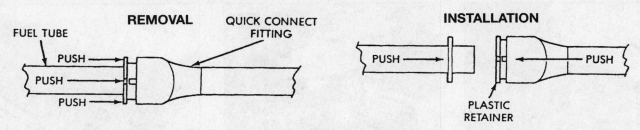

4.18 Plastic retainer ring type quick-connect fitting removal and installation

tion). **Note:** *The plastic retainer ring must be pushed into the female fitting squarely! If it gets cocked, the fitting will be difficult to separate. If necessary, use an open-end wrench applied to the plastic retainer to assist in evenly pressing it into the female fitting. The plastic retainer ring should remain attached to the female fitting after separation.*

Assembly

19   Clean the male part of the fitting and lightly lubricate it with clean engine oil.

20   Insert the male end into the female and push them together **(see illustration 4.18)**. You should hear the retainer ring snap into place as it locks the fitting together. Make sure the retainer ring is fully extended after assembly.

21   Verify the fitting is properly fastened by trying to pull the lines apart.

22   Secure the fuel line using any clips or brackets as applicable.

23   Pressurize the system and check for leaks.

Fuel lines - replacement

Steel tubing

24   If replacement of a metal line is required, disassemble the applicable quick-connect fittings as described above and remove the line from the vehicle. If the quick-connect fitting is damaged or leaks, replace the affected section of fuel line/quick-connect fittings as an assembly.

25   If the quick-connect fittings are acceptable, a new piece of steel tubing may be spliced-in to replace a damaged section by flaring the tubing ends and joining them with a union. Use tubing that meets or exceeds origi-

nal equipment standards. Do not use copper or aluminum tubing to replace steel tubing. These materials cannot withstand normal vehicle vibration. Do not use a rubber hose to replace a damaged section of steel tubing!

26   When installing the replacement section into the line, assemble the quick-connect fittings first, then tighten the unions. **Warning:** *Metal lines must never be allowed to rub against other components or each other. A minimum of 1/4-inch clearance must be maintained to prevent contact unless it is properly secured.*

27   After replacing the line or section, pressurize the system and check for leaks.

Plastic lines

28   If replacement of a plastic line is required, disassemble the applicable quick-connect fittings as described above and remove the line from the vehicle. The plastic lines used on these vehicles are not serviceable. If replacement is required, the affected section of fuel line/quick-connect fittings must be replaced as an assembly.

29   Install the new line onto the vehicle and assemble the quick-connect fittings as applicable (see above). Secure the line to the vehicle as required. **Warning:** *Plastic lines must never be allowed to rub against other components or each other. A minimum of 1/4-inch clearance must be maintained to prevent contact unless it is properly secured. Do not route plastic fuel lines within four inches of any part of the exhaust system or within ten inches of the catalytic converter.*

30   After replacing the line, pressurize the system and check for leaks.

Rubber hoses

Warning: *Only use hoses marked EFM/EFI. Replace with only original equipment hoses, or hoses that meet or exceed original equipment standards. Others may have a lower fatigue threshold.*

31   Perform the fuel pressure relief procedure (see Section 2).

32   Loosen the clamps securing the hose and remove it from the vehicle.

33   Installation is the reverse of removal. **Warning:** *Do not route rubber fuel hoses within four inches of any part of the exhaust system or within ten inches of the catalytic converter. Rubber hoses must never be allowed to rub against other components or each other. A minimum of 1/4-inch clearance must be maintained to prevent contact with other components unless it is properly secured.*

34   After replacing the hose, pressurize the system and check for leaks.

---

5   Fuel pump/fuel level sending unit - removal and installation

---

Warning: *Gasoline is extremely flammable, so take extra precautions when you work on any part of the fuel system (see the* **Warning** *in Section 2).*

Note: *The fuel filter is located in several different places depending upon year and model. Refer to Chapter 1 for all external fuel filter replacement procedures. The fuel filter is located inside the fuel tank along with the fuel pump on 2001 and later models.*

1   Relieve the fuel pressure (see Section 2).

2   Disconnect the cable from the negative battery terminal (see Chapter 5).

Coupes

1995 through 2000 models

Refer to illustrations 5.3, 5.5, 5.7, 5.8a, 5.8b, 5.8c, 5.9 and 5.10

3   Remove the rear seat, pull back the carpet and access the fuel pump service hole cover **(see illustration)**. **Note:** *There are two separate covers under the rear seat. The service hole cover on the passenger side of the vehicle is for the fuel pump while the service hole cover toward the center of the vehicle is for the fuel level sending unit.*

4   Remove the screws on the fuel pump service hole cover.

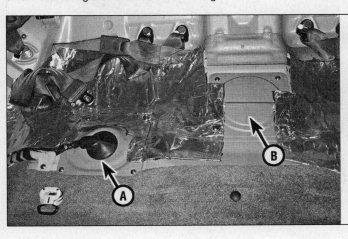

5.3 Location of the fuel pump assembly access hole cover (A) and the fuel level sending unit access hole cover (B)

5.5 Use two wrenches to disconnect the fuel lines

5.7 Lift the fuel pump assembly from the fuel tank. Slightly angle the assembly to avoid damaging the sending unit float arm

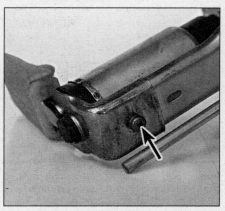

5.8a Remove the mounting screw (arrow) and separate the bracket from the frame

5   Disconnect the electrical connector. Disconnect the fuel line **(see illustration)**.

6   Remove the fuel pump retaining bolts.

7   Carefully withdraw the fuel pump assembly from the fuel tank **(see illustration)**.

8   Remove the fuel pump from the assembly (frame). Remove the screw from the bracket at the lower section of the frame **(see illustration)**. Remove the clip securing the inlet strainer to the pump **(see illustration)**. Remove the inlet strainer **(see illustration)**.

9   Remove the hose clamp and pull the lower end of the fuel pump loose from the bracket **(see illustration)**. Withdraw the pump from the hose.

10   Disconnect the electrical connector from the fuel pump **(see illustration)**. Separate the fuel pump from the frame.

11   Inspect the fuel strainer for contamination. If it is dirty, replace it.

12   Installation is the reverse of removal.

2001 and later models
Refer to illustrations 5.17

13   Remove the rear seat, pull back the carpet and access the fuel pump service hole cover (see Step 3).

14   Clean the top of the fuel tank around the fuel pump module to remove any dirt or debris.

15   Using a large pair of pliers,

remove the fuel pump module ring nut. **Caution:** *Do not apply too much pressure on the ring nut during removal or damage may result.*

16   Remove the fuel pump module from the tank. Angle the assembly slightly to avoid damaging the fuel level sending unit float arm. Do not damage the packing seal when removing the fuel pump module.

17   The electric fuel pump can be separated from the fuel pump module and replaced as a separate component **(see illustration)**. The serviceable parts on the fuel pump module are the fuel filter, the fuel inlet strainer and the fuel level sending unit.

18   For service procedures on the fuel pressure regulator, refer to Section 6. For service procedures on the fuel level sending unit, refer to Section 7.

19   Installation is the reverse of removal.

Convertibles and sedans
1995 through 2000 models
Refer to illustration 5.23

20   Remove the fuel tank from the vehicle (see Section 8).

21   Clean the top of the fuel tank around the fuel pump module to remove any dirt or debris.

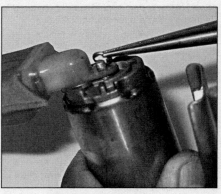

5.8b Remove the clip . . .

22   Using a large pair of pliers remove the fuel pump module ring nut. **Caution:** *Do not apply too much pressure on the ring nut during removal or damage may result.*

23   Remove the fuel pump module from the tank **(see illustration)**. Angle the assembly slightly to avoid damaging the fuel level sending unit float arm. Remove and discard the O-ring seal.

24   The electric fuel pump is not serviceable. In the event of failure, the complete assembly must be replaced. The only serviceable parts on the fuel pump module are the fuel inlet strainer, fuel pressure regulator and the fuel

5.8c . . . and detach the inlet strainer from the fuel pump

5.9 Remove the hose clamp

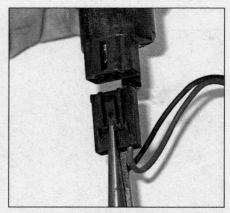

5.10 Unplug the electrical connector

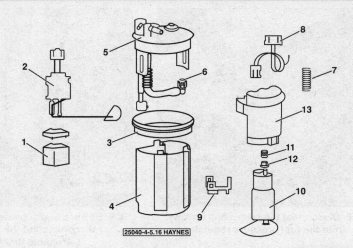

5.17 Exploded view of the fuel pump module and components on 2001 and later coupes

1   Thermistor case
2   Fuel level sending unit
3   Packing seal
4   Outer case
5   Fuel pump module (upper section)
6   O-ring
7   Spring
8   Fuel pump electrical connector
9   Bracket
10 Fuel pump
11 Grommet
12 Spacer
13 Fuel filter

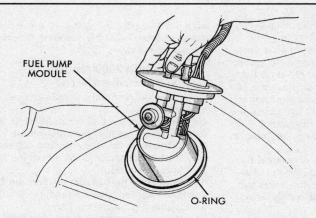

5.23 Be sure to slightly angle the fuel pump module to avoid damaging the fuel level sending unit (1998 convertible shown)

5.28 Disconnect the electrical connector (A) and the fuel line (B) from the fuel pump module

level sending unit. To replace the fuel pressure regulator, refer to Section 6. To replace the fuel level sending unit, refer to Section 7.

25   Installation is the reverse of removal. Be sure to use a new O-ring. When installing the fuel pump assembly, make sure that the locating tab on the underside of the pump mounting flange is aligned with the notch in the fuel tank. **Caution:** *Over-tightening the ring nut can cause the O-ring to leak.*

2001 and 2002 models

Refer to illustrations 5.28, 5.29, 5.30 and 5.34

Warning: *The fuel reservoir in the fuel pump module does not empty when the fuel tank is drained. This fuel will drain out when the fuel pump module is removed from the fuel tank - protect yourself accordingly.*

Caution: *Be sure to change the fuel pump module O-ring seal whenever the assembly is removed for service.*

Note: *The fuel pump module consists of the following components: fuel pump, fuel pressure regulator, fuel inlet strainer and fuel level sending unit. Note that the fuel filter is an integral component of the fuel pressure regulator on 2001 and later convertibles and sedans. Refer to Section 6 for the fuel pressure regulator/filter replacement procedure.*

26   Remove the fuel tank from the vehicle (see Section 8).

27   Clean the top of the fuel tank around the fuel pump module to remove any dirt or debris.

28   Disconnect the electrical connector and the fuel line from the fuel pump module **(see illustration)**.

29   Using a large pair of pliers, remove the

fuel pump module ring nut **(see illustration)**. **Caution:** *Do not apply too much pressure on the ring nut during removal or damage may result.*

30   Remove the fuel pump module from the tank **(see illustration)**. Angle the assembly slightly to avoid damaging the fuel level sending unit float arm. Remove and discard the O-ring seal.

5.29 Use a large pair of pliers to loosen the ring nut

5.30 Fuel pump module on a 2001 convertible

5.34 Align the notches (arrows) on the fuel tank with the tabs on the fuel pump module

6.8 Disconnect the return line (arrow) from the fuel pressure regulator

6.9 Be sure to use two wrenches when disconnecting the fuel lines from the fuel filter

31   The electric fuel pump is not serviceable. In the event of failure, the complete assembly must be replaced. The only serviceable parts on the fuel pump module are the fuel inlet strainer, the fuel pressure regulator and the fuel level sending unit. To replace the fuel pressure regulator, refer to Section 6. To replace the fuel level sending unit, refer to Section 7.

32   Clean the sealing area on the fuel tank.

33   Obtain the new fuel pump assembly O-ring seal/gasket, if equipped. Lightly lubricate the O-ring seal with clean engine oil and install it on the fuel tank opening.

34   Carefully insert the fuel pump module into the fuel tank.

a) *On 1995 through 2000 coupes, install the mounting screws and tighten them securely.*

b) *On all other models, align the tabs on the fuel pump module with the notches in the fuel tank* **(see illustration)**. *On 2001 and later coupes, align the arrow on the fuel pump cover with the arrow on the fuel tank.*

On convertibles and sedans and all 2001 and later models, while holding the fuel pump module in place, install the ring nut, tightening it securely. **Caution:** *Over-tightening the ring nut may result in a leak.* On convertibles and sedans, install the fuel tank (see Section 8).

35   The remaining installation steps are the reverse of removal.

2003 and later models

36   Remove the fuel tank (see Section 8).

37   Disconnect the fuel line quick-connect fitting (if you're unfamiliar with quick-connect fittings, see Section 4).

38   To disconnect the electrical connector from the fuel pump module, slide the connector lock to its unlocked position, then depress the release tab and pull off the connector.

39   Using a brass punch and hammer, carefully loosen the fuel pump lock ring.

40   Mark the orientation of the pump in relation to the fuel tank, then carefully remove the fuel pump assembly.

41 Remove and discard the old pump O-ring seal.

42   The electric fuel pump is not serviceable. In the event of failure, the complete assembly must be replaced. The only serviceable parts on the fuel pump module are the fuel inlet strainer, the fuel pressure regulator and the fuel level sending unit. To replace the fuel pressure regulator, refer to Section 6. To replace the fuel level sending unit, refer to Section 7.

43 Installation is the reverse of removal. Be sure to use a new O-ring seal. When installing the pump assembly, align the marks that you made prior to removal before tightening the lock ring.

---

6   Fuel pressure regulator - removal and installation

Warning: *Gasoline is extremely flammable, so take extra precautions when you work on any part of the fuel system (see the* **Warning** *in Section 2).*

1   Relieve the fuel system pressure (see Section 2).

2   Disconnect the cable from the negative battery terminal or the remote ground terminal (see Chapter 5).

Coupes

1995 and 2001 and later models

3   Remove the vacuum line from the fuel pressure regulator.

4   Disconnect the fuel line clamp and remove the fuel line (see Section 4).

5   Separate the fuel pressure regulator from the fuel rail:

a) *On 1995 four-cylinder engines, remove the snap ring from the body of the fuel pressure regulator and withdraw it from the fuel rail.*

b) *On all other engines, remove the mounting bolts from the fuel pressure regulator and separate it from the fuel rail.*

6   Installation is the reverse of removal. Be

sure to install new O-ring(s) on the fuel pressure regulator. Install the snap-ring or tighten the bolts securely.

1996 through 2000 models

Refer to illustrations 6.8 and 6.9

7   Raise the rear of the vehicle and secure it on jackstands.

8   Disconnect the fuel return line from the fuel pressure regulator **(see illustration)**.

9   Disconnect the fuel pressure regulator and the fuel connector junction from the fuel filter **(see illustration)**.

10   Disconnect the fuel inlet line from the fuel connector junction. Use a flare-nut wrench to avoid damaging the fuel line fitting.

11   Working on the bench, remove the fuel pressure regulator from the fuel connector junction.

12   Installation is the reverse of removal.

Convertible and sedans

13   Remove the fuel pump module from the fuel tank (see Section 5).

1995 through 2000 models

Refer to illustrations 6.14 and 6.16

14   Move the tabs on the fuel pressure regulator away from the body of the housing **(see illustration)**.

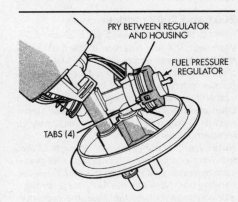

6.14 Spread the four tabs and remove the retainer

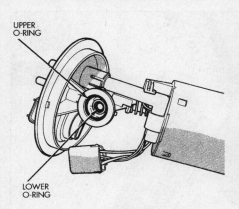

6.16 Apply a light coating of engine oil to the new O-ring seals and install them into the fuel pump module

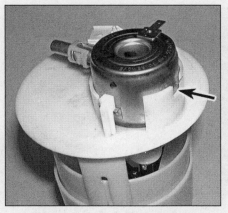

6.20 To remove the fuel pressure regulator/fuel filter, depress the locking tab (arrow), turn the assembly counterclockwise and pull it up

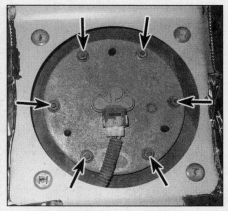

7.6 Remove the fuel level sending unit mounting nuts (arrows)

15 Pry the fuel pressure regulator out of the housing.

16 Replace both the upper and lower O-rings **(see illustration)**.

17 Lightly lubricate both O-rings with oil and push the fuel pressure regulator into the housing.

18 The remainder of the installation is the reverse of removal.

2001 and 2002 models

Refer to illustration 6.20

Note: *The fuel pump module consists of the following components: fuel pump, fuel pressure regulator, fuel inlet strainer and fuel level sending unit. Note that the fuel filter is an integral component of the fuel pressure regulator on 2001 and later convertibles and sedans.*

19 Remove the fuel line and the ground terminal from the fuel pressure regulator (see Section 5).

20 Press the locking tab in, turn the fuel pressure regulator/fuel filter counterclockwise and pull the unit straight up **(see illustration)**.

21 Separate the fuel pressure regulator/fuel filter from the fuel pump module.

22 Installation is the reverse of removal. Be sure to install new O-rings on the fuel pressure regulator/fuel filter.

23 Press the fuel pressure regulator/fuel filter assembly into the fuel pump module and lock it into place. Make sure the locking tab is seated in the slot.

24 The remainder of the installation is the reverse of removal.

2003 and later models

25 Remove the fuel pump/fuel level sending unit (see Section 5).

26 The fuel pressure regulator is mounted near the lower end of the fuel pump module, but it's retained in a similar fashion to the regulators on earlier pump modules.

27 To remove the fuel pressure regulator, carefully spread the four retainer tangs and pull out the regulator.

28 Remove the two pressure regulator O-rings and inspect them for cracks, tears and deterioration. If either of them is damaged, replace it.

29 Lightly lubricate the O-rings with clean engine oil and place them in position in the pressure regulator mounting hole. Then insert the regulator into the hole and push it in until it snaps into place.

30 Installation is otherwise the reverse of removal.

All models

31 When you are finished working on the fuel system and all fuel lines are installed correctly, turn the ignition key to the ON position a few times to pressurize the system and check the serviced area for leaks.

32 Connect the battery cable to the negative terminal or the remote ground terminal (see Chapter 5).

33 Install the fuel filler cap and tighten it securely. **Note:** *If the fuel filler cap seal allows the fuel tank pressure to escape because of a damaged seal or it has not been tightened sufficiently, the CHECK ENGINE light will illuminate on the instrument panel.*

7 Fuel level sending unit - replacement

Warning: *Gasoline is extremely flammable, so take extra precautions when you work on any part of the fuel system (see the* **Warning** *in Section 2).*

1 Relieve the fuel system pressure (see Section 2).

2 Disconnect the cable from the negative battery terminal or the remote ground terminal (see Chapter 5).

1995 through 2000 coupes

Refer to illustration 7.6

3 Remove the rear seat, pull back the carpet and access the fuel level sending unit ser-

vice hole cover (see Section 3). **Note:** *There are two separate covers under the rear seat. The service hole cover on the passenger side of the vehicle is for the fuel pump while the service hole cover toward the center of the vehicle is for the fuel level sending unit.*

4 Remove the fuel level sending unit service hole cover.

5 Disconnect the electrical connector for the fuel level sending unit.

6 Remove the fuel level sending unit retaining nuts from the fuel tank **(see illustration)**.

7 Carefully withdraw the fuel level sending unit assembly from the fuel tank.

8 Remove the fuel level sending unit retaining screws and separate it from the assembly.

9 Install the fuel level sending unit onto the frame. Installation is the reverse of removal.

2001 and later coupes

10 Remove the rear seat, pull back the carpet and access the fuel pump/fuel level sending unit service hole cover (see Section 3).

11 Remove the fuel pump module (see Section 5).

12 Disconnect the locking clips and separate the reservoir cup from the pump support assembly **(see illustration 5.17)**. Be careful not to damage the packing seal.

13 Disconnect the electrical connector for the fuel level sending unit.

14 Remove the fuel level sending unit along with the thermistor case located at the base of the assembly.

15 Install the fuel level sending unit into the module. Installation is the reverse of removal.

Convertibles and sedans
1995 through 2000 models

Refer to illustrations 7.18, 7.19, 7.20, 7.21, 7.22a and 7.22b

16 Remove the fuel tank (see Section 8).

17 Remove the fuel pump/fuel level sending unit assembly (see Section 5).

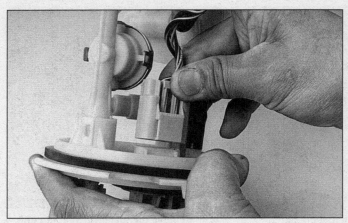

7.18 To disconnect the fuel pump/fuel level sending unit electrical connector, depress this release tab and pull off the connector

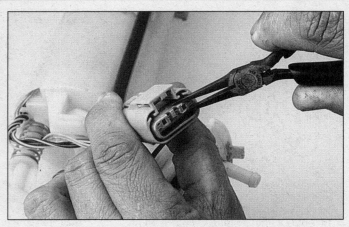

7.19 Remove the blue locking wedge from the electrical connector with needle-nose pliers

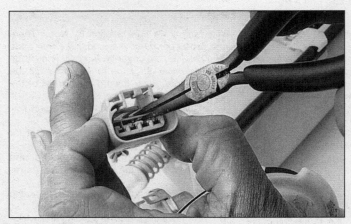

7.20 Lift the connector locking finger away from the fuel level sending unit wire terminals

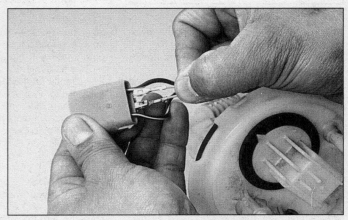

7.21 Using an awl, carefully push the leads out the backside of the electrical connector (if you have difficulty with this step, it's easier with factory tool C-4334 or a suitable equivalent)

18   Disconnect the fuel pump/fuel level sending unit electrical connector from the base of the fuel pump module flange **(see illustration)**.
19   Remove the blue locking wedge from the connector with a pair of needle-nose pliers **(see illustration)**.
20   Use a small screwdriver or needle-nose pliers to lift the connector locking finger away from the fuel level sending unit wire terminals **(see illustration)**.
21   Disengage the fuel level sending unit leads from the connector and pull them out the backside of the connector **(see illustration)**. (Use factory tool No. C-4334 or a suitable equivalent tool if necessary.)
22   To disengage the sending unit from the fuel pump module, insert a screwdriver between the module fuel reservoir and the top of the sending unit and carefully pry the sensor free **(see illustration)**, then slide off the sending unit **(see illustration)**.
23   Place the wires into the guide groove on the back side of the sending unit, route them through the module fuel reservoir and then slide the sensor up the channel until it snaps into place.
24   Install the wire terminals into the electrical connector, lock them into place with the

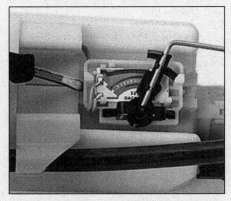

7.22a To detach the fuel level sending unit from the fuel pump module, insert a screwdriver between the module fuel reservoir and the top of the sending unit and pry it down slightly to disengage it . . .

blue locking wedge and verify that the terminals are correctly installed by gently pulling on the wires.
25   Installation is otherwise the reverse of removal.

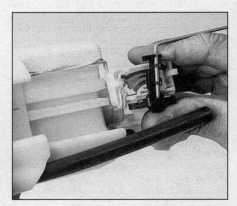

7.22b . . . then slide off the sending unit

2001 and 2002 models
Refer to illustrations 7.27, 7.28, 7.29a, 7.29b, 7.30 and 7.31
Note: *The fuel pump module consists of the following components: fuel pump, fuel pressure regulator, fuel inlet strainer and fuel level sending unit.*
26   Remove the fuel pump module (see Section 5).

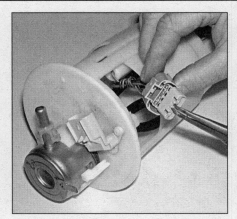

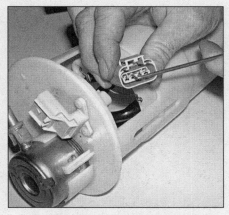

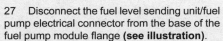

7.27   Disconnect the electrical connector (arrow) from the base of the fuel pump module flange (late model shown, early models similar)

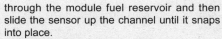

7.28   Use needle-nose pliers and carefully remove the locking collar

7.29a   Use a small screwdriver or pick, pry the locking fingers away from the terminals, then push the terminals into the connector

27   Disconnect the fuel level sending unit/fuel pump electrical connector from the base of the fuel pump module flange **(see illustration)**.
28   Use needle-nose pliers to remove the locking collar **(see illustration)**.
29   Use a small screwdriver or needle-nose pliers to lift the connector locking finger away from the fuel level sending unit wire terminals **(see illustration)** and then withdraw them from the module electrical connector **(see illustration)**. Note the wire colors and the position of each wire for correct assembly.
30   Unwrap the fuel level sensor wires from the fuel pump wires and separate them from the harness **(see illustration)**.
31   To remove the sending unit, insert a screwdriver between the module body and the top of the fuel level sending unit as shown and pry the sensor down slightly **(see illustration)**.
32   While guiding the sending unit wires through the module fuel reservoir opening, slide the sending unit out of the channel.
33   Place the wires into the guide groove on the back side of the sending unit, route them

through the module fuel reservoir and then slide the sensor up the channel until it snaps into place.
34   Install the wire terminals into the module connector in their proper locations.
35   Install the locking collar into the module connector.
36   Verify the wire terminals are properly installed in the module connector by gently pulling on the wires.
37   Connect the fuel level sending unit/fuel pump electrical connector to the base of the fuel pump module flange.
38   The remaining installation steps are the reverse of removal.

2003 and later models

Note: *Although the fuel pump/fuel level sending unit used on these models is a different unit, it's similar to the unit used on 1995 through 2000 models, particularly with respect to the fuel level sending unit. So if you're replacing the fuel level sending unit, refer to the illustrations accompanying Steps 18 through 22.*

39   Remove the fuel tank (see Section 8).
40   Remove the fuel pump/fuel level sending unit (see Section 5).
41   Disconnect the fuel pump/fuel level sending unit electrical connector from the base of the fuel pump/fuel level sending module **(see illustration 7.18)**.
42   Remove the blue locking wedge from the connector with a pair of needle-nose pliers **(see illustration 7.19)**.
43   Use a small screwdriver or needle-nose pliers to lift the connector locking finger away from the fuel level sending unit wire terminals **(see illustration 7.20)**.
44   Disengage the fuel level sending unit leads from the connector and pull them out the backside of the connector **(see illustration 7.21)**.
45   To disengage the sending unit from the fuel pump module, use a screwdriver to between the module fuel reservoir and the top of the sending unit and carefully pry the sensor free **(see illustration 7.22a)**, then slide off the sending unit **(see illustration 7.22b)**.
46   Installation is the reverse of removal.

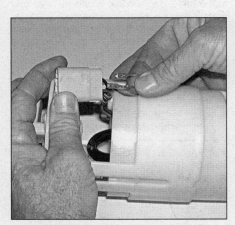

7.29b   Pull the two fuel level sending unit wires and terminals out of the connector

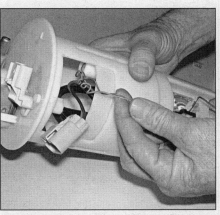

7.30   Unwrap the sending unit wires from around the fuel pump wires

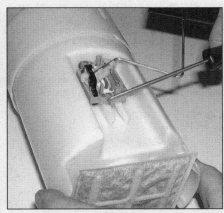

7.31   Using a screwdriver, pry the lock tab out of the notch and slide the fuel level sending unit down slightly to disengage the locking feature

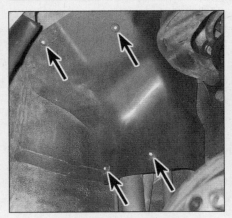

8.11 Remove the push-pin retainers (arrows) from the inner fender panel

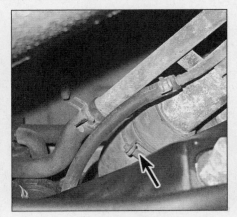

8.12 Loosen the filler pipe clamp (arrow)

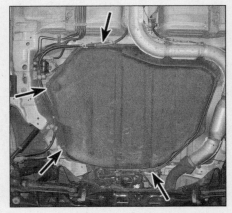

8.16a Location of the fuel tank mounting bolts - coupe models (typical)

8   Fuel tank - removal and installation

Warning: *Gasoline is extremely flammable, so take extra precautions when you work on any part of the fuel system (see the **Warning** in Section 2).*

Removal

1   Relieve the fuel system pressure (see Section 2).
2   Disconnect the cable from the negative battery terminal or the remote ground terminal (see Chapter 5).
3   Raise the vehicle and support it securely on jackstands.

Coupes
Note 1: *On 1995 through 2000 coupes, there are two separate covers under the rear seat. The service hole cover on the passenger side of the vehicle is for the fuel pump while the service hole cover toward the center of the vehicle is for the fuel level sending unit.*
Note 2: *On 2001 and later coupes, there is a single service hole cover under the rear seat for the fuel pump/fuel level sending unit assembly.*
4   Remove the rear seat, pull back the carpet and access the service hole cover for the fuel pump and/or the fuel level sending unit.
5   Disconnect the electrical connectors from the fuel pump and the fuel level sending unit and position them out of the way.

Convertible models
6   Working inside the trunk, fold back the trunk mat. Locate the fuel pump wiring harness 4-pin connector and disconnect it from the wiring harness.
7   Follow the fuel pump wiring to the grommet at the base of the rear seat. Push the grommet through the floorpan and feed the wiring and 4-pin connector through the hole. **Note:** *On some models it may be necessary to remove the rear seat for access to the grommet.*

All models
Refer to illustrations 8.11, 8.12, 8.16a and 8.16b
8   Disconnect the fuel line fittings from the fuel pump (see Section 4).
9   Position an approved gasoline container under the fuel tank drain plug. If necessary, use a funnel to prevent spilling fuel. **Warning:** *The fuel tank capacity is approximately 16 gallons. Unless the fuel tank is almost empty, be prepared to collect a significant amount of fuel. Do not leave the fuel tank draining operation unattended. Be prepared to reinstall the drain plug in case the fuel tank capacity exceeds the container capacity. Remove the drain plug and allow the fuel to drain. **Note:** Not all models are equipped with a fuel tank drain plug. Siphon the fuel from the tank using a special tool designed for siphoning fuel. **Warning:** Never start the siphoning action by mouth!*
10   After the fuel has finished draining, reinstall the drain plug and tighten it securely. **Warning:** *There will be approximately 1 to 2 gallons of fuel remaining inside the tank.*
11   Remove the inner fender panel **(see illustration)**.
12   Loosen the clamp and detach the filler neck hose **(see illustration)** and the vapor hose from the fuel tank. **Warning:** *There may be fuel inside the filler neck and hose; protect yourself accordingly.*
13   Remove the vapor hose from the rollover valve.
14   Remove the exhaust pipe, if necessary.
15   Support the fuel tank with a floor jack. Place a piece of wood between the jack head and the fuel tank to protect the tank.
16   Remove the fuel tank strap bolts or the fuel tank mounting bolts **(see illustrations)**. On some models, slightly lower the fuel tank and detach the EVAP canister purge line. Remove the hoses from the EVAP canister and disconnect the electrical connector from the leak detection pump (LDP) (see Chapter 6). **Note:** *Before disconnecting any lines or hoses, clearly label the hose and fitting so they can be reinstalled in their proper locations.*

8.16b Fuel tank strap bolts - convertible and sedan models (typical)

17   Lower the fuel tank and maneuver it out from under the vehicle.

Installation
18   Installation is the reverse of removal.
19   On convertible models, before installing the fuel tank, tie a length of string or wire to the fuel pump module wiring harness and route it through the hole in the trunk floorpan. As the fuel tank is raised into position, have an assistant pull the string to guide the wiring harness into place.
20   Tighten the fuel tank bolts or strap to the torque listed in this Chapter's Specifications.

9   Fuel tank cleaning and repair - general information

Warning: *Gasoline is extremely flammable, so take extra precautions when you work on any part of the fuel system (see the **Warning** in Section 2).*
1   The fuel tank on some models is made of plastic and is not repairable.
2   All repairs on metal fuel tanks should be carried out by a professional who has experience in this critical and potentially dangerous work. Even after cleaning and flushing of the fuel system, explosive fumes can remain and

10.1 Air inlet resonator-to-manifold bolts (2.5L V6 engine)

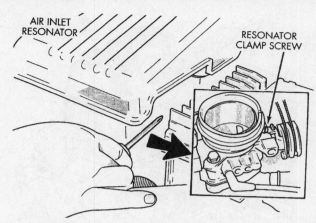

10.2a Removing the air inlet resonator clamp at the throttle body (2.4L DOHC engine)

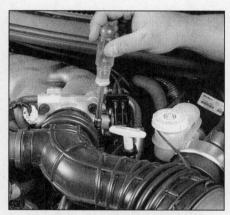

10.2b Remove the air inlet resonator clamp at the throttle body (2.5L V6 engine)

ignite during repair of the tank.
3   If the fuel tank is removed from the vehicle, do not place it in an area where sparks or open flames could ignite the fuel vapors escaping from the tank. Be especially careful inside a garage where a gas-type appliance is located, because it could cause an explosion.

10 Air filter housing and air inlet resonator - replacement

Air inlet resonator
Refer to illustrations 10.1, 10.2a, 10.2b and 10.3
Note 1: *Convertible models with the 2.4L DOHC (2000 and earlier) engine or the 2.5L V6 engine are equipped with an air inlet resonator. The air inlet resonator provides a chamber for intake air to gather and act as a reserve for hard acceleration (high intake volume). The air inlet resonator must be removed for throttle body, fuel rail, fuel injector, etc. service procedures.*
Note 2: *Coupe models with the 2.4L SOHC and 3.0L V6 engines are equipped with an air inlet resonator mounted on the side of the air filter housing. The air inlet resonator on these*

models must only be removed when the air filter housing is removed from the engine compartment.
1   Remove the air inlet resonator-to-manifold bolts **(see illustration)**.
2   Loosen the clamp and detach the air inlet resonator from the throttle body **(see illustrations)**.
3   Loosen the intake air duct clamp at the air cleaner housing **(see illustration)** and remove the air ducting with the air inlet resonator attached.
4   Installation is the reverse of removal. Make sure the air inlet resonator is free of dirt and contamination prior to installation.

Air filter housing
1995 through 2000 models
Refer to illustration 10.7
5   Loosen the intake air duct clamp and detach it from the air cleaner top cover **(see illustration 10.3)**.
6   Remove the air filter housing top cover and the air filter (see Chapter 1).
7   Remove the bolts from the air filter housing **(see illustration)**.
8   Remove the intake air duct from the front

of the air cleaner housing and lift the housing from the engine compartment.
9   Installation is the reverse of removal. Make sure the air filter housing is free of dirt and contamination prior to installation.

2001 and later models
Refer to illustrations 10.17a and 10.17b
10   Make sure the ignition key is in the Off position (it must remain in this position throughout the entire procedure to avoid setting a diagnostic trouble code).
11   Disconnect the electrical connector from the MAF sensor on the intake air duct, if equipped (see Chapter 6).
12   Disconnect the electrical connector from the IAT sensor on the intake air duct, if equipped (see Chapter 6).
13   Remove the fresh air inlet hose from the intake air duct, if equipped.
14   Loosen the intake air duct clamp and detach it from the air cleaner top cover **(see illustration)**.
15   Remove the air filter housing top cover and the air filter (see Chapter 1).
16   On 2.4L DOHC engines, remove the push pin and separate the air intake duct from the radiator support.

10.3 Loosen the intake air duct clamp at the air filter housing (2.5L V6 engine)

10.7 Remove the bolts from the air filter housing (arrows) (2.5L V6 engine shown)

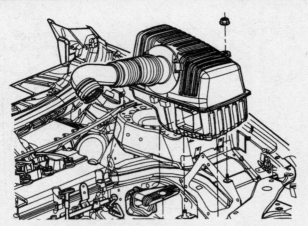

10.17a Remove the nuts from the bracket to detach the air filter housing (2.4L DOHC engine)

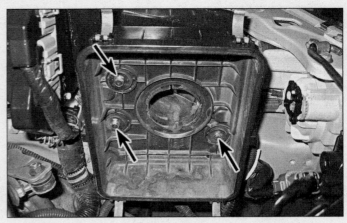

10.17b Remove the bolts (arrows) then remove the air filter housing from the engine (2.7L V6 engine)

17   Remove the air filter housing from the engine compartment:

a) *Some models are equipped with a large bracket that retains the air filter housing. Remove the nut(s) from the bracket that hold the air filter housing to the engine*

11.2 Disconnecting the accelerator cable from the throttle lever at the throttle body (2.5L V6 convertible engine)

compartment (**see illustration**).

b) *Some models mount the air filter housing directly to the interior of the engine compartment. Remove the bolts* (**see illustration**) *and lift the housing from the engine compartment.*

18   Lift the housing from the engine compartment. On some models, separate the lower intake duct from the housing.

19   Installation is the reverse of removal. Make sure the air filter housing is free of dirt and contamination prior to installation.

---

11   Accelerator cable - replacement and adjustment

Replacement

Refer to illustrations 11.2, 11.3a, 11.3b, 11.4, 11.5a and 11.5b

1   Access the throttle body:

a) *On convertible models, remove the air inlet resonator assembly and the intake air duct (see Section 10) from the engine compartment.*

b) *On all other models, remove the intake air duct from the throttle body (see Section 10).*

2   Rotate the throttle valve cam to the full throttle position and disconnect the accelerator cable from the slot in the throttle valve cam (**see illustration**).

3   Remove the accelerator cable from the bracket:

a) *On some engines, compress the cable retaining tabs and push the accelerator cable through the bracket* (**see illustration**).

b) *On some engines, compress the cable retaining tab and slide the cable out of the side of the bracket* (**see illustration**).

c) *On coupe models, unbolt the cable bracket from the upper intake manifold.*

4   Disconnect the accelerator cable from the firewall; on 2000 and earlier convertible models the cable and grommet can be pulled into the engine compartment (**see illustration**). 2001 and later convertible and sedan models use a circlip to retain the cable to the firewall (under the dash), and coupes use two

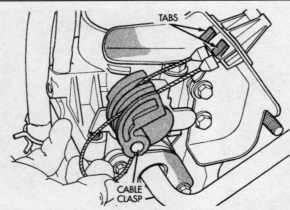

11.3a On models with a closed bracket, after detaching the cable from the throttle lever, compress the tab on the cable outer housing and push it through the bracket (2.4L DOHC engine)

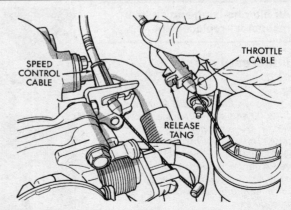

11.3b On models with a slotted bracket, compress the retaining tab on the cable housing and slide the cable from the bracket (convertible with a 2.5L V6 engine)

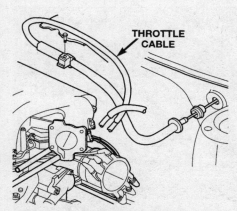

11.4 On 2000 and earlier convertibles, the accelerator cable is retained to the firewall by a grommet (2.5L V6 engine shown)

bolts to secure the cable housing to the firewall. **Note:** *On coupe models you'll have to remove the windshield washer reservoir for access to the cable housing-to-firewall bolts.*

5   At the accelerator pedal arm inside the vehicle, remove the accelerator cable from the accelerator pedal.

a) *On coupes, use pliers to grasp the cable end and pull slightly to disengage the accelerator cable from the pedal arm. Lift the accelerator cable through the slot in the pedal arm.*

b) *On 2000 and earlier convertibles, using a pair of pliers, squeeze the tabs on the accelerator cable retainer on the top side of the pedal to release the accelerator retainer. Push the accelerator cable through the pedal and lift the cable through the slot in the pedal arm* **(see illustration)**.

c) *On 2001 and later convertibles and sedans, using the tip of a screwdriver* **(see illustration)**, *pry the cable release clip from the accelerator pedal. Push the accelerator cable through the pedal and lift the cable through the slot in the pedal arm.*

6   Push the cable through the firewall into the engine compartment and remove it from the vehicle.

7   Installation is the reverse of removal.

Adjustment (coupes only)

Refer to illustration 11.8

8   To adjust the cable:

a) *Turn off the air conditioning system, the headlights and interior lights.*

b) *Start the engine and allow it to reach operating temperature.*

c) *Check the idle speed. Refer to the VECI label in the engine compartment.*

d) *Turn the engine off.*

e) *Check the cable deflection between the throttle lever and the cable casing. Deflection should be 0.04 to 0.08-inch (1 to 2 mm). If deflection is not within specifications, loosen the adjusting bolts and*

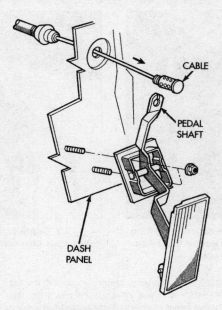

11.5a On 2000 and earlier convertibles, squeeze the tabs on the top of the cable retainer and push the cable through the pedal

slide the bracket as necessary until the deflection is as specified.

d) *After you have adjusted the accelerator cable, have an assistant help you verify that the throttle valve opens all the way when you depress the accelerator pedal to the floor and that it returns to the idle position when you release the accelerator. Verify the cable operates smoothly. It must not bind or stick.*

12 Fuel injection system - general information

The Electronic Fuel Injection (EFI) system consists of three sub-systems: air intake, electronic control and fuel delivery. The EFI system uses a Powertrain Control Module (PCM) along with several sensors to determine the proper air/fuel ratio under all operating conditions. **Refer to illustrations 1.1a, 1.1b and 1.1c** for component locations.

The fuel injection system and the emissions control system are closely linked in function and design. For additional information, refer to Chapter 6.

Air intake system

The air intake system consists of the air filter, the air ducts, air inlet resonator, the throttle body, the idle control system and the intake manifold.

The engine idle speed is controlled by the PCM via the Idle Air Control (IAC) motor. The IAC motor regulates the flow of air allowed to by-pass the throttle valve in the throttle body thereby increasing engine speed. The PCM uses information from various sensors

11.5b On 2001 and later convertibles and sedans, use the tip of a screwdriver to release the clip from the pedal arm

to determine the correct amount of airflow required to maintain the proper engine speed during engine warm-up and when a load is placed on the engine, such as engaging the air conditioning compressor, low speed steering or when an automatic transaxle is placed in gear.

Engine control system

For information on the engine control system, refer to Chapter 6.

Fuel delivery system

The fuel delivery system consists of the following components: an electric fuel pump, a fuel pressure regulator, a fuel filter, the fuel rail, the fuel injectors, various metal and plastic lines, the Automatic Shutdown (ASD) relay and the fuel pump relay.

All models are equipped with an electric fuel pump. The fuel pump is mounted in the fuel tank. On all coupes, the fuel pump is accessible through a service hole cover under the rear seat. On convertibles and sedan models, it is necessary to remove the fuel tank to gain access to the fuel pump. On 1995 through 2000 coupes, the fuel level sending unit is accessible through a separate service hole cover under the rear seat. On convertibles and all 2001 and later models, the fuel

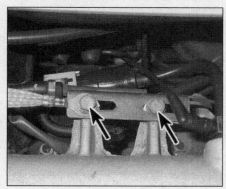

11.8 Loosen the adjusting bolts (arrows) to move the bracket into the correct position (coupe models)

13.7   Use a stethoscope to determine if the injectors are working properly - they should make a steady clicking sound that rises and falls with engine speed changes

13.8   Connect the probes of the ohmmeter to the injector terminals (arrows) and check the resistance of the fuel injector

level sending unit is an integral component of the fuel pump and it must be removed from the fuel tank in the same manner.

The fuel pressure regulator is mounted in various locations on these models. 1995 models mount the fuel pressure regulator on the fuel rail. 1996 through 2000 coupes mount the fuel pressure regulator adjacent to the fuel tank near the fuel filter. 2001 and later coupes mount the fuel pressure regulator back on the fuel rail in the engine compartment. Convertible and sedan models mount the fuel pressure regulator in the tank with the fuel pump (fuel pump module).

The fuel filter is located in several different places depending upon year and model. Refer to Chapter 1 for all external fuel filter replacement procedures. The fuel filter is located inside the fuel tank along with the fuel pump on 2001 and later models.

Only convertible and sedan models are equipped with a "returnless" fuel system. In this system, the fuel pressure regulator is part of the fuel pump/fuel level sending unit (fuel pump module) located in the fuel tank. Regulated fuel is sent to the inlet line and excess fuel is bled off directly into the fuel tank. Even though some coupe models are equipped with a fuel pressure regulator next to the fuel tank (external), this system is designed to return the fuel from the fuel pressure regulator back to the fuel tank and therefore is considered a "return" type fuel pressure system.

The fuel rail supplies the regulated fuel to each electronically controlled fuel injector. The injectors are solenoid types consisting of a solenoid, plunger, needle valve and housing. When the PCM sends a voltage signal to the fuel injector, the needle valve raises off its seat and lets metered fuel enter the intake manifold. The injection quantity is determined by the length of time which current is supplied to the injector.

The Automatic Shutdown (ASD) and the fuel pump relays are located either on the engine compartment firewall or in the fuse/relay center, which is located in the engine compartment on the left (driver's) side. The

ASD relay connects battery voltage to the fuel injectors and the ignition coil while the fuel pump relay connects battery voltage only to the fuel pump. If the PCM senses there is NO signal from the camshaft or crankshaft sensors while the ignition key is RUN or cranking, the PCM will de-energize both relays in approximately one second.

13   Fuel injection system - general check

Refer to illustrations 13.7 and 13.8
Warning: *Gasoline is extremely flammable, so take extra precautions when you work on any part of the fuel system (see the* **Warning** *in Section 2).*
1   Check all electrical connectors that are related to the system. Check the ground wire connections for tightness. Loose connectors and poor grounds can cause many problems that resemble more serious malfunctions.
2   Check to see that the battery is fully charged, as the control unit and sensors depend on an accurate supply voltage in order to properly meter the fuel.
3   Check the air filter element. A dirty or partially blocked filter will severely impede performance and economy (see Chapter 1).
4   Check the related fuses. If a blown fuse is found, replace it and see if it blows again. If it does, search for a wire shorted to ground in the harness.
5   Check the air intake duct to the intake manifold for leaks, which will result in an excessively lean mixture. Also check the condition of all vacuum hoses connected to the intake manifold and/or throttle body.
6   Remove the air intake duct from the throttle body and check for dirt, carbon, varnish, or other residue in the throttle body, particularly around the throttle plate. If it's dirty, clean it with carburetor cleaner spray, a toothbrush and shop towel.
7   With the engine running, place an automotive stethoscope against each injector, one at a time, and listen for a clicking sound that

indicates operation **(see illustration)**. If you don't have a stethoscope, you can place the tip of a long screwdriver against the injector and listen through the handle. If you hear the injectors operating but there is a misfire condition present, the electrical circuits are functioning, but the injectors may be dirty or fouled from carbon deposits - commercial cleaning products may help, or the injectors may require replacement.
8   If you can't hear the injector operating, disconnect the injector electrical connector and measure the resistance of each injector with an ohmmeter **(see illustration)**. Compare the measurement with the resistance value listed in this Chapter's Specifications. Replace any injector whose resistance value does not fall within the specifications.
9   If the injector was not operating but the resistance reading was within specifications, the PCM or the circuit to the injector may be faulty.

14   Throttle body - check, removal and installation

Check
Refer to illustrations 14.2a and 14.2b
1   Verify that the throttle linkage operates smoothly.
2   Remove the air intake duct from the throttle body and check for carbon and residue build-up. If it is dirty, clean it with aerosol carburetor cleaner and a tooth brush. Make sure the can specifically states that it is safe with oxygen sensor systems and catalytic converters **(see illustrations)**. **Caution:** *Do not clean the throttle position sensor (TPS) or Idle Air Control (IAC) valve with the solvent.*

Removal
Refer to illustrations 14.10a, 14.10b and 14.11
Warning: *Wait until the engine is completely cool before beginning this procedure.*
3   Disconnect the cable from the negative

14.2a The area inside the throttle body near the throttle plate (arrow) suffers from sludge build-up because the PCV hose vents vapor from the crankcase here

14.2b With the engine off, use aerosol carburetor cleaner (make sure it is safe for use with catalytic converters and oxygen sensors), a toothbrush and a rag to clean the throttle body - open the throttle plate so you can clean behind it

14.10a Throttle body mounting bolts (arrows) - 2.7L V6 engine. Note: *The bolt indicated by the lower left arrow secures the throttle cable bracket to the throttle body; it isn't actually a throttle body mounting bolt.*

battery terminal or the remote ground terminal (see Chapter 5).

4   Remove the air intake duct from the throttle body and the air filter housing cover (see Section 10).

5   Partially drain the cooling system (see Chapter 1) and remove the coolant hoses from the throttle body, if equipped.

6   Disconnect the canister purge vacuum hose from the throttle body.

7   Detach the accelerator cable and cruise control cable from the throttle valve lever (see Section 11).

8   Remove the throttle cable shield and the throttle cable bracket, if equipped, from the throttle body.

9   Disconnect the TPS and IAC connectors from the throttle body.

10   Remove the mounting bolts from the throttle body and then withdraw the throttle body and gasket from the manifold **(see illustrations)**.

11   The throttle body O-ring seal on 2.0L DOHC engines is reusable **(see illustration)**. Remove it from the manifold and inspect it for hardness and cracks. If visual inspection does

not reveal any defects, the O-ring seal may be reused.

12   On all other models, remove all traces of gasket material from the throttle body and manifold.

13   If necessary, clean the throttle body as outlined in Step 2.

Installation

14   Install the throttle body with a new gasket onto the intake manifold. **Note:** *2.0L DOHC engines may reuse the O-ring seal.*

15   Tighten the throttle body mounting bolts to the torque listed in this Chapter's Specifications.

16   The remaining installation steps are the reverse of removal. After installation, check to see that the throttle body operates freely.

15   Fuel rail and injectors - removal and installation

Warning: *Gasoline is extremely flammable,*

so take extra precautions when you work on any part of the fuel system (see the **Warning** in Section 2).

Removal

Refer to illustration 15.3

1   Relieve the fuel system pressure (see Section 2).

2   Disconnect the cable from the negative battery terminal or the remote ground terminal (see Chapter 5).

3   Detach the fuel supply line fitting (see Section 4) from the fuel rail **(see illustration)**. **Note:** *Some models are equipped with a return line attached at the fuel rail. Disconnect the return line and position it away from the fuel rail and surrounding components.*

Four-cylinder engines

Refer to illustration 15.7

4   Remove the intake duct from the throttle body and the air filter housing cover (see Section 10).

5   Disconnect the wiring harness electrical connectors from the fuel injectors. Clearly label and remove any vacuum hoses or elec-

14.10b Throttle body mounting bolts (arrows) - 2.5L V6 engine (coupe)

14.11 On 2.0L DOHC engines, the throttle body O-ring gasket (arrow) is reusable

15.3 Remove the fuel supply line mounting bolts (arrows) at the fuel rail - 2.5L V6 engine (coupe)

15.7 Fuel rail mounting bolts (arrows) - 2.0L DOHC engine

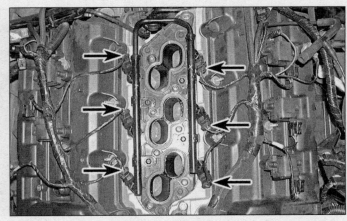

15.12 Disconnect the electrical connectors from the fuel injectors
(2.7L V6 shown)

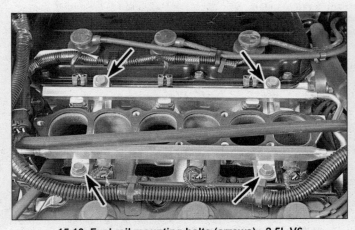

15.13 Fuel rail mounting bolts (arrows) - 2.5L V6
engine (convertible)

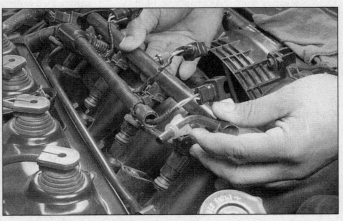

15.15a Removing the fuel rail/injectors - 2.0L DOHC engine

trical wiring that will interfere with the fuel rail removal.

6   On 2.4L SOHC engines, remove the throttle body (see Section 14).

7   Remove the fuel rail mounting bolts **(see illustration)**.

V6 engines

Refer to illustrations 15.12 and 15.13

8   Remove the intake duct from the throttle body (see Section 10).

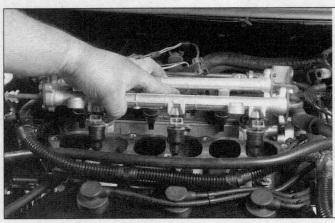

15.15b Removing the
fuel rail/injectors -
2.5L V6 engine

9   Disconnect the TPS, MAP sensor, IAC valve and IAT sensor connectors (see Chapter 6).

10   Remove the accelerator cable (see Section 11).

11   Remove the upper intake manifold (see Chapter 2B or 2C).

12   Disconnect the electrical connectors from the fuel injectors **(see illustration)**. Clearly label and remove any vacuum hoses or electrical wiring that will interfere with the

fuel rail removal.

13   Remove the fuel rail mounting bolts **(see illustration)**.

All models

Refer to illustrations 15.15a, 15.15b, 15.15c, 15.16a, 15.16b and 15.16c

14   Clean the injector-to-manifold area using compressed air (a can of compressed-gas duster like those used to blow out electrical components will work just as well) or spray-type carburetor cleaner to remove any dirt or debris from around the injectors.

15   Remove the fuel rail assembly, with the fuel injectors attached, from the engine **(see illustrations)**. **Note:** *On V6 engines, there are spacers located between the fuel rail and the lower intake manifold; if they become dislodged, make sure you reinstall them* **(see illustration)**.

16   Remove the retaining clips and withdraw the injectors from the fuel rail **(see illustrations)**. Remove the O-ring seals and discard them **(see illustration)**. **Note:** *Whether you're replacing an injector or a leaking O-ring seal, it's standard practice to replace all the O-ring seals on all the injectors at this time.*

15.15c On V6 engines, these plastic spacers must be installed between the fuel rail and the lower intake manifold

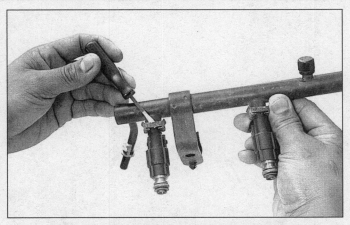

15.16a Using a screwdriver or pliers, remove the injector retaining clip securing the injector to the fuel rail . . .

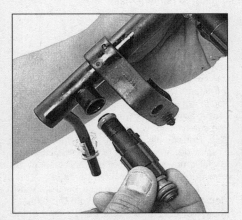

15.16b . . . then withdraw the injector from the fuel rail

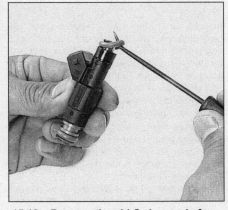

15.16c Remove the old O-ring seals from the fuel injector and discard them

Install the upper intake manifold (see Chapter 2B or 2C).

22 The remainder of the installation is the reverse of removal.

23 After the injector/fuel rail assembly installation is complete, turn the ignition switch to ON (engine not running). Repeat this two or three times, then check the fuel lines and the injectors for leaks.

16 Exhaust system servicing - general information

Refer to illustrations 16.1a, 16.1b, 16.3a and 16.3b

Warning: *Inspection and repair of exhaust system components should be done only after enough time has elapsed after driving the vehicle to allow the system components to cool completely. Also, when working under the vehicle, make sure it is securely supported on jackstands.*

1 The exhaust system consists of the exhaust manifold, the catalytic converter, the resonator, exhaust pipe, muffler and all brackets, hangers and clamps. The exhaust system is attached to the body with mounting brackets and rubber hangers (**see illustrations**).

Installation

17 Coat the new O-rings with clean engine oil and install them on the injectors, then insert each injector into its corresponding bore in the fuel rail. Install the injector retaining clips.

18 Install the injector and fuel rail assembly onto the intake manifold. Fully seat the injectors, then tighten the fuel rail mounting bolts to the torque listed in this Chapter's Specifications.

19 Connect the fuel lines and make sure they are securely installed.

20 Connect the electrical connectors to each injector, referring to the numbered tags.

21 On V6 engines, clean and inspect the upper-to-lower manifold gasket surfaces.

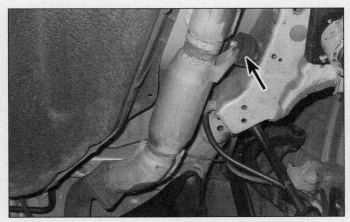

16.1a Inspect the exhaust system mounting brackets, clamps and rubber hangers for damage or improper installation

16.1b Be sure to replace the rubber hangers (arrow) at the rear of the exhaust system if they are severely deteriorated

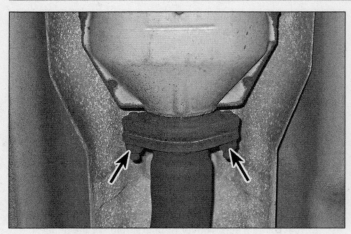

16.3a Spray penetrating oil to the nuts and studs (arrows) on the catalytic converter flange

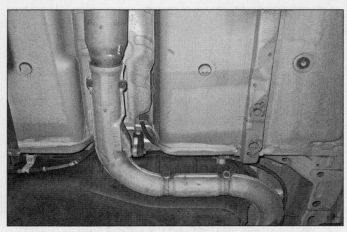

16.3b Spray the exhaust pipe heat shield fasteners before attempting to remove them

If any of the parts are improperly installed, excessive noise and vibration will be transmitted to the body.

Muffler and pipes

2   Conduct regular inspections of the exhaust system to keep it safe and quiet. Look for any damaged or bent parts, open seams, holes, loose connections, excessive corrosion or other defects which could allow exhaust fumes to enter the vehicle. Also check the catalytic converter when you inspect the exhaust system (see following). Deteriorated exhaust system components should not be repaired; they should be replaced with new parts.

3   Before trying to disassemble any exhaust components, spray the fasteners with a penetrating oil to help ease removal **(see illustrations)**. If the exhaust system components are extremely corroded or rusted together, welding equipment will probably be required to remove them. The convenient way to accomplish this is to have a muffler repair shop remove the corroded sections with a cutting torch. If, however, you want to save money by doing it yourself (and you don't have a welding outfit with a cutting torch), simply cut off the old components with a hacksaw. If you have compressed air, special pneumatic cutting chisels can also be used. If you decide to tackle the job at home, be sure to wear safety goggles to protect your eyes from metal chips and work gloves to protect your hands.

4   Here are some simple guidelines to follow when repairing the exhaust system:

a) *Work from the back to the front when removing exhaust system components.*

b) *Apply penetrating oil to the exhaust system component fasteners to make them easier to remove.*

c) *Use new gaskets, hangers and clamps when installing exhaust systems components.*

d) *Apply anti-seize compound to the threads of all exhaust system fasteners at reassembly.*

e) *Be sure to allow sufficient clearance between newly installed parts and all points on the underbody to avoid overheating the floor pan and possibly damaging the interior carpet and insulation. Pay particularly close attention to the catalytic converter and heat shield.*

Catalytic converter

Warning: *The converter gets extremely hot during operation, and can remain very hot for hours after the engine has been turned off. Make sure it has cooled down before you touch it.*

Note: *See Chapter 6 for more information on the catalytic converter.*

5   Periodically inspect the heat shield for cracks, dents and loose or missing fasteners.

6   Remove the heat shield and inspect the converter for cracks or other damage.

7   If the converter must be replaced, detach the exhaust system from the exhaust manifold. Loosen the rear band clamp at the resonator and separate the converter from the exhaust system.

8   Installation is the reverse of removal. Be sure to use new gaskets and tighten the fasteners securely.

Chapter 5
Engine electrical systems

Contents

Specifications

General

Engine firing order
  Four cylinder engines 1-3-4-2
  V6 engines 1-2-3-4-5-6
Ignition timing .... Not adjustable

Ignition system

Ignition coil resistance (approximate, at 70 to 80-degrees F)
  2.0L and 2.4L DOHC (1999 and earlier) engines
    Primary resistance .... 0.51 to 0.61 ohms
    Secondary resistance .... 11,000 to 13,500 ohms
  2.0L DOHC engine (2001 and later)
    Primary resistance .... Not available
    Secondary resistance .... Not available
  2.4L SOHC (2001 and later) engines
    Primary resistance .... Not available
    Secondary resistance .... 8,500 to 11,500 ohms
  2.4L DOHC (2001 and later) and 2.7L V6 engines
    Primary resistance .... Not available
    Secondary resistance .... Not available
  2.5L V6 engines
    Primary resistance .... 0.6 to 0.8 ohms
    Secondary resistance .... 12,000 to 18,000 ohms
  3.0L V6 engines
    Primary resistance .... 0.56 to 0.68 ohms
    Secondary resistance .... 9,400 to 12,800 ohms

Charging system

Charging voltage .... 13.5 to 15.0 volts
Standard amperage
  No load .... 10 amps or less
  With load .... 30 amps or more

Torque specifications   **Ft-lbs** (unless otherwise indicated)

Starter motor mounting bolts
  2.5L V6 coupe models 26
  All other models 40

1.1a Typical engine electrical system components - 1998 coupe, 2.5L V6 engine

1	*Distributor*	*2*	*Battery*	*3*	*Fuse/relay center*	*4*	*Ignition wires*

1   General information, precautions and battery disconnection

Refer to illustrations 1.1a, 1.1b and 1.1c

The engine electrical systems include all ignition, charging and starting components **(see Illustrations)**. Because of their engine-related functions, these components are discussed separately from body electrical devices such as the lights, the instruments, etc. (which are included in Chapter 12).

Precautions

Always observe the following precautions when working on the electrical system:

a) *Be extremely careful when servicing engine electrical components. They are easily damaged if checked, connected or handled improperly.*

b) *Never leave the ignition switched on for long periods of time when the engine is not running.*

c) *Never disconnect the battery cables while the engine is running.*

d) *Maintain correct polarity when connecting battery cables from another vehicle during jump starting - see the "Booster battery (jump) starting" section at the front of this manual.*

1.1b Typical engine electrical system components - 2001 sedan, 2.4L DOHC engine

1	*Alternator*	*2*	*Coil packs*	*3*	*Remote ground terminal*	*4*	*Fuse/relay center*

1.1c Typical engine electrical system components - 2001 convertible, 2.7L V6 engine

1	Coil/power transistor assembly	2	Remote ground terminal
3	Fuse/relay center	4	PCM

e) *Always disconnect the negative battery cable from the battery before working on the electrical system, but read the following battery disconnection procedure first.*

It's also a good idea to review the safety-related information regarding the engine electrical systems located in the *"Safety first!"* section at the front of this manual, before beginning any operation included in this Chapter.

Battery disconnection

Refer to illustration 1.4

The battery on these vehicles is located in two different places depending on the model; on coupes, the battery is located in the left rear corner of the engine compartment while on convertibles and sedans, the battery is located behind the left fender in front of the left front wheel. Since the battery terminals on convertibles and sedans cannot be easily accessed, the manufacturer has provided a remote ground terminal **(see illustration)** on the left strut tower and also a remote positive terminal for jump starting purposes. To disconnect the battery for service procedures requiring power to be cut from the vehicle, remove the nut and detach the negative cable from the ground stud on the strut tower (convertibles and sedans) or the negative battery terminal (coupes). On convertibles and sedans, press the hole mounted on the side of the cable onto the stud. This will isolate the cable end and prevent it from accidentally coming into contact with ground.

Several systems on the vehicle require battery power to be available at all times, either to ensure their continued operation (such as the radio, alarm system, power door

locks, windows, etc.) or to maintain control unit memories (such as that in the engine management system's Powertrain Control Module [PCM]) which would be lost if the battery were to be disconnected. Therefore, whenever the battery is to be disconnected, first note the following to ensure that there are no unforeseen consequences of this action:

a) *The engine management system's ECM will lose the information stored in its memory when the battery is disconnected. This includes idling and operating values, any fault codes detected and system monitors required for emissions testing. Whenever the battery is disconnected, the computer will require a certain period of time to "re-learn" the operating values (see Chapter 6).*

b) *On any vehicle with power door locks, it is a wise precaution to remove the key from the ignition and to keep it with you, so that it does not get locked inside if the power door locks should engage accidentally when the battery is reconnected!*

Devices known as "memory-savers" can be used to avoid some of the above problems. Precise details vary according to the device used. Typically, it is plugged into the cigarette lighter and is connected by its own wires to a spare battery; the vehicle's own battery is then disconnected from the electrical system, leaving the "memory-saver" to pass sufficient current to maintain audio unit security codes and ECM memory values, and also to run permanently live circuits such as the clock and radio memory, all the while isolating the battery in the event of a short-circuit occurring

while work is carried out.

Warning 1: *Some of these devices allow a considerable amount of current to pass, which can mean that many of the vehicle's systems are still operational when the main battery is disconnected. If a "memory-saver" is used, ensure that the circuit concerned is actually "dead" before carrying out any work on it!*

Warning 2: *If work is to be performed around any of the airbag system components, the battery must be disconnected and no "memory saver" can be used. If a memory-saver device is used, power will be supplied to the airbag and personal injury may result if the airbag is accidentally deployed.*

1.4 To disconnect battery power from the vehicle on convertibles and sedans, remove the nut from the ground stud on the left strut tower, then push the plastic hole on the cable insulator over the stud to secure the cable

2   Battery - emergency jump starting

Refer to the *Booster battery (jump) starting* procedure at the front of this manual.

3   Battery - check and replacement

Warning: *Hydrogen gas is produced by the battery, so keep open flames and lighted cigarettes away from it at all times. Always wear eye protection when working around a battery. Rinse off spilled electrolyte immediately with large amounts of water.*

Check

Refer to illustrations 3.1a, 3.1b and 3.1c

1   A battery cannot be accurately tested until it is at or near a fully charged state. Disconnect the negative battery cable from the battery and perform the following tests:

a) **Battery state of charge test** - *Visually inspect the indicator eye (if equipped) on the top of the battery. If the indicator eye is dark in color, charge the battery as described in Chapter 1. If the battery is equipped with removable caps, check the battery electrolyte. The electrolyte level should be above the upper edge of the plates. If the level is low, add distilled water. DO NOT OVERFILL. The excess electrolyte may spill over during periods of heavy charging. Test the specific gravity of the electrolyte using a hydrometer* **(see illustration).** *Remove the caps and extract a sample of the electrolyte and observe the float inside the barrel of the hydrometer. Follow the instructions from the tool manufacturer and determine the specific gravity of the electrolyte for each cell. A fully charged battery will indicate approximately 1.270 (green zone) at*

68-degrees F (20-degrees C). If the specific gravity of the electrolyte is low (red zone), charge the battery as described in Chapter 1.

b) **Open circuit voltage test** - *Using a digital voltmeter, perform an open circuit voltage test* **(see illustration).** *Connect the negative probe of the voltmeter to the negative battery post and the positive probe to the positive battery post. The battery voltage should be greater than 12.5 volts. If the battery is less than the specified voltage, charge the battery before proceeding to the next test. Do not proceed with the battery load test until the battery is fully charged.*

c) **Battery load test** - *An accurate check of the battery condition can only be performed with a load tester (available at most auto parts stores). This test evaluates the ability of the battery to operate the starter and other accessories during periods of heavy amperage draw (load). Install a special battery load testing tool onto the battery terminals* **(see illustration).** *Load test the battery according to the tool manufacturer's instructions. This tool utilizes a carbon pile to increase the load demand (amperage draw) on the battery. Maintain the load on the battery for 15 seconds and observe that the battery voltage does not drop below 9.6 volts. If the battery condition is weak or defective, the tool will indicate this condition immediately.* **Note:** *Cold temperatures will cause the minimum voltage requirements to drop slightly. Follow the chart given in the tool manufacturer's instructions to compensate for cold climates. Minimum load voltage for freezing temperatures (32 degrees F/0-degrees C) should be approximately 9.1 volts.*

d) **Battery drain test** - *This test will indicate whether there's a constant drain on the*

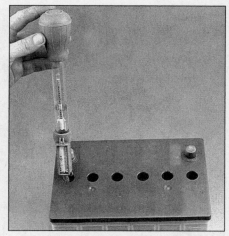

3.1a Use a battery hydrometer to draw electrolyte from the battery cell - this hydrometer is equipped with a thermometer to make temperature corrections

vehicle's electrical system that can cause the battery to discharge. Make sure all accessories are turned Off. If the vehicle has an underhood light, verify it's working properly, then disconnect it. Connect one lead of a digital ammeter to the disconnected negative battery cable clamp and the other lead to the negative battery post. A drain of approximately 100 milliamps or less is considered normal (due to the engine control computers, clocks, digital radios and other components which normally cause a key-off battery drain). An excessive drain (approximately 500 milliamps or more) will cause the battery to discharge. The problem circuit or component can be located by removing the fuses, one at a time, until the excessive drain stops and normal drain is indicated on the meter.

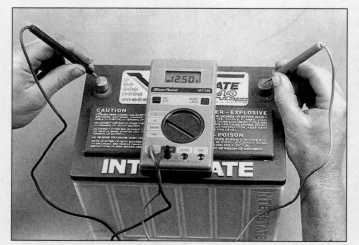

3.1b To test the open circuit voltage of the battery, connect the black probe of the voltmeter to the negative terminal and the red probe to the positive terminal of the battery - a fully charged battery should indicate approximately 12.5 volts depending on the outside air temperature

3.1c Some battery load testers are equipped with an ammeter which enables the battery load to be precisely dialed in, as shown - less expensive testers have a load switch and a voltmeter only

3.3 Slide the rubber protective cover from the positive terminal for access to the clamp nut

3.6 Location of the battery tray mounting bolts (arrows)

Replacement

Caution: *Always disconnect the negative cable first and hook it up last or the battery may be shorted by the tool being used to loosen the cable clamps.*

Coupes

Refer to illustrations 3.3 and 3.6

2   Loosen the cable clamp nut and remove the negative battery cable from the negative battery post. Isolate the cable end to prevent it from accidentally coming into contact with the battery post.

3   Loosen the cable clamp nut and remove the positive battery cable from the positive battery post **(see illustration)**.

4   Remove the battery hold-down clamp nuts.

5   Lift out the battery. Be careful - it's heavy.

Note: *Battery straps and handlers are available at most auto parts stores for a reasonable price. They make it easier to remove and carry the battery.*

6   While the battery is out, inspect the battery tray for corrosion **(see illustration)**. If corrosion exists, clean the deposits with a mixture of baking soda and water to prevent further corrosion. Flush the area with plenty of clean water and dry thoroughly.

7   If you are replacing the battery, make sure you replace it with a battery with the identical dimensions, amperage rating, cold cranking rating, etc.

8   When installing the battery, make sure the center notch in the battery foot is aligned with the cut-out in the battery tray. Install the hold-down clamp nuts and tighten them securely. Do not over-tighten the bolt.

9   The remainder of installation is the reverse of removal.

Convertibles and sedans

Refer to illustrations 3.12, 3.13, 3.14a, 3.14b and 3.16

10   Disconnect the negative battery cable from the remote ground terminal on the left shock tower (see Section 1).

11   Loosen the left front wheel lug nuts, raise the vehicle and support it securely on jackstands. Remove the wheel.

12   Remove the battery cover/splash shield from the wheel well by turning the four plastic fasteners 1/4-turn counterclockwise **(see illustration)**.

13   Using a box-end wrench or socket, disconnect the negative cable from the battery first, then the positive cable **(see illustration)**.

3.12 Remove the battery cover/splash shield from the left front wheel well

14   Remove the bolt and nut securing the battery strap and hold-down bracket, then remove them **(see illustrations)** from the vehicle.

15   Vehicles manufactured with the cold weather package option (Alaska, Canada and northern USA) are equipped with a battery blanket heater. If equipped, disconnect the blanket heater electrical connector.

3.13 Always disconnect the negative battery cable first and attach it last!

3.14a Removing the battery strap and hold-down bracket bolt

3.14b Removing the battery strap upper nut

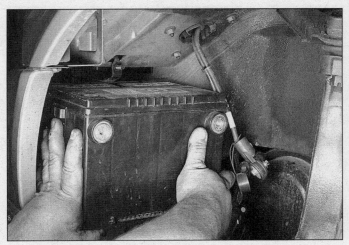

3.16 Position the cables out of the way and slide the battery out of the fenderwell - be careful, it's heavy!

4.4a Note the routing of the positive battery cable (convertible and sedan models shown)

16   Remove the battery from the vehicle (see illustration). Be careful - it's heavy. Note: Battery handling tools are available at most auto parts stores for a reasonable price. They make it easier to remove and carry the battery.

17   If equipped, remove the battery blanket heater from around the battery.

18   While the battery is removed, inspect the tray, strap, hold-down bracket and related fasteners for corrosion or damage.

19   If corrosion is evident on the battery tray, unscrew the mounting bolts and remove it. Use baking soda/water solution to clean corroded parts to prevent further oxidation. Repaint parts as necessary using rust resistant paint.

20   Clean and service the battery and cables (see Chapter 1).

21   If you are replacing the battery, make sure you purchase one that is identical to yours, with the same dimensions, amperage rating, cold cranking amps rating, etc. Make sure it is fully charged prior to installation in the vehicle.

22   Installation is the reverse of removal. Make sure you connect the negative cable last.

23   Tighten the wheel lug nuts to the torque given in the Chapter 1 Specifications.

All models

24   After connecting the cables to the battery, apply a light coating of petroleum jelly or grease to the connections to help prevent corrosion.

4   Battery cables - replacement

Refer to illustrations 4.4a, 4.4b and 4.4c

1   Periodically inspect the entire length of each battery cable for damage, cracked or burned insulation and corrosion. Poor battery cable connections can cause starting problems and decreased engine performance.

2   Check the cable-to-terminal connections at the ends of the cables for cracks, loose wire strands and corrosion. The presence of white, fluffy deposits under the insulation at the cable terminal connection is a sign that the cable is corroded and should be replaced. Check the terminals for distortion, missing mounting bolts and corrosion.

3   When removing the cables, always dis-

connect the negative cable from the negative battery post first and hook it up last or the battery may be shorted by the tool used to loosen the cable clamps. Even if only the positive cable is being replaced, be sure to disconnect the negative cable from the negative battery post first (see Chapter 1 for further information regarding battery cable maintenance).

4   Disconnect the old cables from the battery, then disconnect them from the opposite end. Detach the cables from the starter solenoid, the relay and fuse box and ground terminals, as necessary (see illustrations). Note the routing of each cable to ensure correct installation.

5   If you are replacing either or both of the battery cables, take them with you when buying new cables. It is vitally important that you replace the cables with identical parts. Cables have characteristics that make them easy to identify: Positive cables are usually red and larger in cross-section; ground cables are usually black and smaller in cross-section.

6   Clean the threads of the starter solenoid or ground connection with a wire brush to remove rust and corrosion. Apply a light coat of battery terminal corrosion inhibitor or petro-

4.4b Follow the negative battery cable to the remote ground terminal (convertible and sedan models shown)

4.4c The negative battery cable is grounded onto the transaxle (arrow) (coupe models shown)

leum jelly to the threads to prevent future cor-rosion.

7   Attach the cable to the terminal and tighten the mounting nut/bolt securely.

8   Before connecting a new cable to the battery, make sure that it reaches the battery post without having to be stretched.

9   After installing the cables, connect the negative cable to the negative battery post.

5   Ignition system - general information

1   All models are equipped with an elec-tronic ignition system. The ignition system consists of the ignition switch, the battery, the coil, the primary (low voltage) and secondary (high voltage) wiring circuits, the ignition wires and spark plugs, the camshaft position sen-sor, the crankshaft position sensor, the power transistor and the Powertrain Control Module (PCM). The PCM controls the ignition timing and spark advance characteristics for the engine. The ignition timing is not adjustable.

2   There are two different types of electronic ignition systems on these models depending upon year and model. The 2.5L and 3.0L V6 engines are equipped with a conventional electronic distributor-type ignition system. All other models are equipped with a distributor-less ignition system.

Conventional electronic ignition system

3   The 2.5L and 3.0L V6 engines are equipped with a conventional type electronic ignition system. The 2.5L V6 distributor igni-tion system is slightly different than the 3.0L V6 distributor ignition system.

4   A conventional type distributor with a rotor is used to send the ignition voltage to the proper cylinder in the firing order. The distribu-tor is located on the rear of the cylinder head near the transaxle and driven by the camshaft. On 2.5L V6 engines, the distributor incorpo-rates the power transistor, the ignition coil and camshaft position sensor. The crankshaft sen-sor is mounted on the bellhousing near the transaxle. On 3.0L V6 engines, the distributor incorporates the ignition coil and the camshaft position sensor. The crankshaft sensor is mounted above the crankshaft sprocket under the timing belt cover.

5   The crankshaft sensor and camshaft sensor generate voltage pulses that are sent to the PCM. The PCM then determines the crankshaft position, injector sequence and ignition timing. The PCM supplies battery volt-age to the ignition coil through the Automatic Shutdown Relay (ASD). The PCM also con-trols the ground circuit for the coil.

6   If the PCM does not receive a signal from the crankshaft or camshaft position sensors, the PCM signals the ASD relay and fuel pump relay to shut down the ignition and fuel deliv-

ery systems respectively. Refer to Chapter 6 for replacement procedures for the crankshaft and camshaft sensors.

Distributorless ignition systems

7   There are two different types of distribu-torless ignition systems on these models. 2.0L, 2.4L DOHC and 2.4L SOHC engines use coil packs with ignition wires. These engines incorporate the "waste spark" system. The 2.7L V6 engines are designed with sepa-rate coil/power transistor assemblies mounted over each cylinder. The 2.7L V6 ignition sys-tem does not use ignition wires; the PCM fires each coil "sequentially" along with the injector firing order.

DIS with coil packs and ignition wires (2.0L, 2.4L DOHC and 2.4L SOHC models)

8   2.0L, 2.4L DOHC and 2.4L SOHC engines are equipped with an early version of DIS. The DIS system includes the cam-shaft position sensor, the crankshaft posi-tion sensor, coil pack(s) (one coil for a pair of cylinders), the power transistor and the PCM (computer). The coil and power transistor are built into one unit (coil packs) and mounted near the valve cover. The PCM generates cylinder identification signals which allow the power transistor to trigger the correct coil. The power transistor distributes the signal to the proper coil driver circuit and determines dwell period based on coil primary current flow. This DIS system uses a "waste spark" method of spark distribution. Each cylinder is paired with its companion cylinder in the firing order, 1-4, 3-2; the cylinder under compression fires simultaneously with its companion cylinder, which is on the exhaust stroke. Since the cyl-inder on the exhaust stroke requires very little of the available voltage to fire its spark plug, most of the voltage is used to fire the plug of the cylinder on the compression stroke.

9   The coil packs are mounted near the valve covers. Secondary ignition wires run to each spark plug from the coil packs. 2001 and later coupe models with 2.4L DOHC engines have a coil/power transistor assem-bly over cylinders 2 and 4, with spark plug wires connected to them and cylinders 1 and 3. These are also designed to fire the companion cylinders using the "waste spark" system.

DIS with coil/power transistor assemblies (2.7L V6 models)

10   2.7L V6 engines are equipped with the latest version of DIS. This DIS system includes the camshaft position sensor, the crankshaft position sensor, a coil/power transistor/spark plug assembly for each cylinder and the PCM (computer). The coil, the power transis-tor and spark plug are built into one unit and mounted over each cylinder. The crankshaft and camshaft generate cylinder identification

signals which allow the igniter to trigger the correct coil. The PCM distributes the signal to the proper coil driver circuit and determines dwell period based on coil primary current flow. The spark is direct (cylinder specific) and sequenced to the engine's firing order. There is no "waste spark" effect with this system.

All models

11   When working on the ignition system, take the following precautions:

a) *Do not keep the ignition switch on for more than 10 seconds if the engine will not start.*

b) *Always connect a tachometer in accor-dance with the manufacturer's instruc-tions. Some tachometers may be incom-patible with this ignition system. Consult an auto parts counterperson before buy-ing a tachometer for use with this vehi-cle.*

c) *Never allow the ignition coil terminals to touch ground. Grounding the coil could result in damage to the power transistor and/or the ignition coil.*

d) *Do not disconnect the battery when the engine is running.*

6   Ignition system - check

Warning: *Because of the very high voltage generated by the ignition system (approxi-mately 40,000 volts), extreme care should be taken whenever an operation is performed involving ignition components. This not only includes the coil and spark plug wires, but related items connected to the system as well, such as the electrical connectors, tachometer and any test equipment.*

Note: *The ignition system components on these models are expensive and difficult to diagnose. In the event of ignition system fail-ure, if the checks do not clearly indicate the source of the ignition system problem, have the vehicle tested by a dealer service depart-ment or other qualified auto repair facility.*

1   If a malfunction occurs and the vehicle won't start, do not immediately assume that the ignition system is causing the problem. First, check the following items:

a) *Make sure the battery cable clamps, where they connect to the battery, are clean and tight.*

b) *Test the condition of the battery (see Section 3). If it does not pass all the tests, replace it with a new battery.*

c) *Check the external ignition coil (if equipped) wiring and connections.*

d) *Check the related fuses inside the fuse box (see Chapter 12). If they're burned, determine the cause and repair the cir-cuit.*

2   If the engine turns over but won't start, make sure there is sufficient secondary igni-tion voltage to fire the spark plug.

2.7L V6 engines

Refer to illustration 6.3

3   Remove an ignition coil/power transistor assembly (see Section 7) and attach a calibrated ignition tester (available at most auto parts stores). Connect the clip on the tester to a bolt or metal bracket on the engine **(see illustration)**.

All other engines

Refer to illustration 6.4

4   Disconnect the spark plug wire from any spark plug and attach it to a calibrated ignition tester (available at most auto parts stores) **(see illustration)**. Connect the clip on the tester to a bolt or metal bracket on the engine. **Note:** *2001 and later coupe models with the 2.4L SOHC engines have a coil/power transistor assembly over cylinders 2 and 4, with spark plug wires connected to them and cylinders 1 and 3. Make sure that you test the secondary voltage to both cylinders.*

All models

5   Relieve the fuel pressure (see Chapter 4). Keep the fuel system disabled while performing the ignition system checks.

6   Crank the engine and watch the end of the tester to see if bright blue, well-defined sparks occur (weak spark or intermittent spark is the same as no spark).

7   If sparks occur, sufficient voltage is reaching the spark plug to fire it (repeat the check at the remaining spark plug wires to verify that all the ignition coils are functioning). However, the plugs themselves may be fouled, so remove and check them as described in Chapter 1 or install new ones.

8   If no sparks or intermittent sparks occur, check for battery voltage to the ignition coils. Refer to the wiring diagrams at the end of Chapter 12. If battery voltage is present, check the coil resistance (see Section 7).

9   Also, if no sparks or intermittent sparks occur, check the ignition wires to each spark plug (see Chapter 1).

10   If the checks are all correct, there may

6.3 Remove one coil power transistor assembly and install the calibrated ignition tester, making sure the clip is installed onto a suitable ground (2.7L V6 engine)

6.4 Remove one ignition wire and install a calibrated ignition tester to visually verify spark is reaching the spark plug (2.5L V6 engine)

be a defective camshaft position sensor and/or crankshaft position sensor (see Chapter 6), or ignition coil.

---

7   Ignition coil - check and replacement

Check

Note 1: *Because of the circuit design, it is not possible to check the coil primary resistance on 2.4L DOHC engines. There are no specifications available for the ignition system on 2001 and later 2.0L DOHC, 2.4L DOHC or 2.7L V6 engines.*

Note 2: *The following checks should be made with the engine cold. If the engine is hot, the resistance will be greater.*

2.0L, 2.4L DOHC (1999 and earlier) and 2.4L SOHC models

Refer to illustrations 7.3 and 7.4

1   Clearly label the spark plug wires and

detach them from the coil pack.

2   Disconnect the primary wiring electrical connector from the coil pack.

3   Measure each coil primary resistance. Connect an ohmmeter between the center terminal (B+) and one of the outer terminals and note the resistance **(see illustration)**. Repeat the check with the probe connected to the other outer terminal. Compare the measured resistances with the coil primary resistance value listed in this Chapter's Specifications. Replace the coil if the primary resistance is out of tolerance.

4   Next, measure the secondary resistance of each coil. Connect an ohmmeter between the spark plug wire terminals 1 and 4 and note the resistance **(see illustration)**. Repeat the check on terminals 2 and 3. Compare the measured resistances with the secondary resistance value listed in this Chapter's Specifications. Replace the coil if the secondary resistance is out of tolerance. **Note:** *On 2.4L SOHC engines, remove the coil/power transistor assembly from the engine (see Steps 18 through 21) and check the second-*

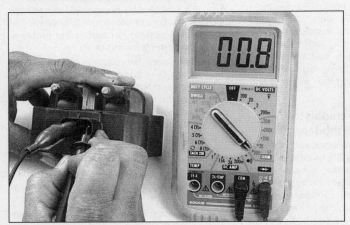

7.3 Test each coil's primary resistance by connecting one probe of the ohmmeter to the center terminal and the other probe to each end terminal. The primary resistance of each coil should be within specifications

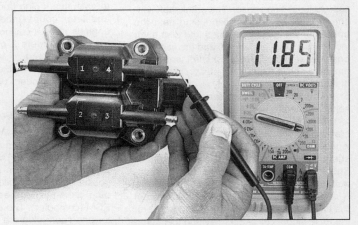

7.4 Checking the secondary resistance of coil "1 and 4" - repeat the test for coil "2 and 3". The secondary resistance of each coil should be within specifications

ary resistance between the secondary voltage terminal and the outer terminals of the primary connector.

5   Install the spark plug wires in their proper locations and connect the primary wiring electrical connector.

2.5L and 3.0L V6 models
Refer to illustration 7.10

6   Remove the air filter housing (see Chapter 4).

7   Remove the EGR pipe (see Chapter 6), if necessary.

8   Label each spark plug wire on the distributor cap and then disconnect them.

9   Loosen the two screws and remove the distributor cap **(see illustration 29.15 in Chapter 1)**.

10   Disconnect the primary wiring electrical connector from the distributor **(see illustration)**.

11   Measure the coil primary resistance. Connect an ohmmeter across the terminal numbers 1 and 2 of the connector on the distributor and note the resistance. Compare the measured resistance with the coil primary resistance value listed in this Chapter's Specifications. If the coil primary resistance is out of tolerance, the entire distributor must be replaced - the coil is not serviceable.

12   Measure the coil secondary resistance. Measure the resistance between the coil secondary terminal and terminal numbers 1 and 2 on the connector. Compare the measured resistances with the secondary resistance value listed in this Chapter's Specifications. If the coil secondary resistance is out of tolerance, the entire distributor must be replaced - the coil is not serviceable.

13   Install the distributor cap and related components in the reverse order of removal.

Replacement

14   Disconnect the cable from the negative battery terminal or the remote ground terminal (see Chapter 5).

7.16 After disconnecting the wiring harness electrical connector, remove the coil pack mounting nuts and lift the coil from the valve cover

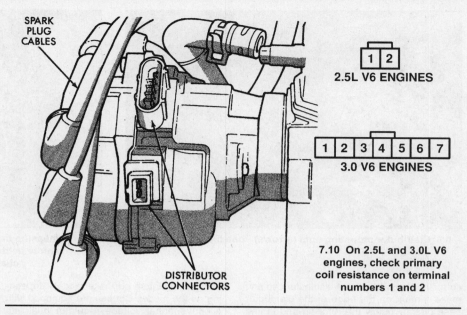

7.10 On 2.5L and 3.0L V6 engines, check primary coil resistance on terminal numbers 1 and 2

2.0L and 2.4L DOHC (1999 and earlier) and 2.4L SOHC models
Refer to illustration 7.16

15   Disconnect the ignition coil harness electrical connector. Label the connector for proper assembly. Label and detach the spark plug wires.

16   Remove the bolts from the mounting bracket and separate the coil pack from the engine **(see illustration)**.

17   Installation is the reverse of the removal.

2.4L SOHC (2001 and later) and 2.7L V6 models
Refer to illustration 7.21

18   Disconnect the coil/power transistor electrical connector from each coil/power transistor assembly.

19   Label each connector so they don't get mixed up.

20   On 2.4L SOHC (2001 and later) engines, label and detach the spark plug wires for the companion cylinders from the two coil/power transistor assemblies.

21   Remove the bolt(s) securing the coil/power transistor assemblies **(see illustration)**.

22   Installation is the reverse of removal.

2.5L and 3.0L V6 models

23   Remove the distributor (see Section 8).

24   The coil on these models is not serviceable. Install a new or rebuilt distributor.

25   Installation is the reverse of removal.

8   Distributor (2.5L and 3.0L V6 models) - removal and installation

Removal
Refer to illustration 8.9

1   Disconnect the cable from the negative battery terminal or the remote ground terminal (see Chapter 5).

2   Remove the air inlet resonator (if equipped) and the air filter housing (see Chapter 4).

3   Remove the EGR pipe, if necessary (see Chapter 6).

4   Disconnect the electrical connector(s) from the distributor.

5   Look for a raised "1" on the distributor cap. This marks the location for the number one cylinder spark plug wire terminal. If the cap does not have a mark for the number one terminal, locate the number one spark plug and trace the wire back to the terminal on the cap. Refer to the firing order schematics in the Specifications in Chapter 1.

6   Remove the bolt from the transaxle dipstick and remove the dipstick from the engine compartment.

7   Remove the distributor cap **(see illustration 29.15 in Chapter 1)** and turn the engine over until the rotor is pointing toward the number one spark plug terminal (see locating TDC procedure in Chapter 2B).

8   Mark the distributor base and the engine block to ensure that the distributor is installed

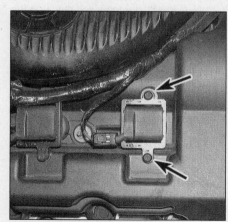

7.21 Coil power transistor assembly mounting bolts (arrows)

8.9 Distributor mounting nuts (arrows) - one hidden from view

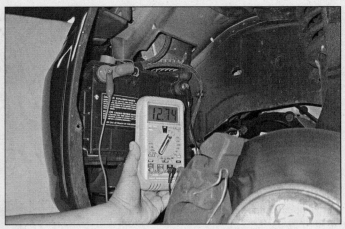

10.2 To measure battery voltage, attach the voltmeter leads to the remote battery terminals (engine OFF) - to measure charging voltage, start the engine

correctly. Also, remove the distributor cap and make a mark on the edge of the distributor base directly below the rotor tip and in line with it.

9   Remove the distributor hold-down nuts **(see illustration)**, then pull the distributor straight out to remove it. **Caution:** *DO NOT turn the crankshaft while the distributor is out of the engine, or the alignment marks will be useless.*

Installation

Note: *If the crankshaft has been moved while the distributor is out, locate Top Dead Center (TDC) for the number one piston (see Chapter 2B) and position the distributor and the rotor accordingly.*

10   Install a new distributor O-ring.
11   Align the housing mating mark with the gear mating mark.
12   Insert the distributor into the engine in exactly the same relationship to the block that it was in when removed.
13   If the distributor does not seat completely, recheck the alignment marks between the distributor base and the block to verify that the distributor is in the same position it was in before removal. Also, check the rotor to see if it's aligned with the mark you made on the edge of the distributor base.
14   Tighten the distributor hold-down nuts securely.
15   The remainder of installation is the reverse of removal.

9   Charging system - general information and precautions

The charging system includes the alternator, a charge indicator light, the battery, the Powertrain Control Module (PCM), the ASD relay, a fusible link and the wiring between all the components. The charging system supplies electrical power to maintain the battery at its full charge capacity. The alternator is driven by a drivebelt on the front of the engine.

There are two different types of alternator

voltage regulators on these models depending on the model. Coupes are equipped with a conventional voltage regulator built into the alternator. Convertibles and sedans are equipped with the Electronic Voltage Regulator (EVR) built into the PCM. The EVR varies the battery charge rate depending on electric load, vehicle speed, engine coolant temperature, battery temperature, accessories (air conditioning system, radio, cruise control etc.) and the intake air temperature. The PCM will adjust the amount of voltage generated, creating less load on the engine.

The purpose of the voltage regulator is to limit the alternator's voltage to a preset value thereby regulating the battery charging rate. This prevents power surges, circuit overloads, etc., during peak voltage output. On convertibles and sedans, since the EVR is contained within the PCM, the PCM must be replaced in the event of EVR failure.

The alternator is not serviceable and therefore must be replaced as a unit in the event of failure.

The charging system doesn't ordinarily require periodic maintenance. However, the drivebelt, battery, wires and connections should be inspected at the intervals outlined in Chapter 1.

The dashboard warning light should illuminate when the ignition key is turned to ON, but it should go off immediately after the engine is started. If it remains on, there is a malfunction in the charging system which must be diagnosed (see Section 10).

Be very careful when making electrical circuit connections to a vehicle equipped with an alternator and note the following:

a) *When reconnecting wires to the alternator from the battery, be sure to note the polarity.*
b) *Before using arc welding equipment to repair any part of the vehicle, disconnect the wiring from the alternator and the cables from the battery.*
c) *Never start the engine with a battery charger connected.*

d) *Always disconnect both battery cables before using a battery charger.*
e) *The alternator is turned by an engine drivebelt which could cause serious injury if your hands, hair or clothes become entangled in it with the engine running.*
f) *Because the alternator is connected directly to the battery, it could arc or cause a fire if overloaded or shorted out.*

10   Charging system - check

Refer to illustration 10.2
Note: *Convertibles and sedans are equipped with an Electronic Voltage Regulator (EVR) with the On Board Diagnostic (OBD-II) system that is useful for detecting charging system problems. This system incorporates a battery temperature sensor mounted near the front bumper next to the battery. Due to the special equipment necessary to diagnose the charging system on these models, it is recommended that the vehicle be tested by a dealer service department or other qualified automotive repair facility.*

1   If a malfunction occurs in the charging circuit, do not immediately assume that the alternator is causing the problem. First, check the following items:

a) *Make sure the battery cable clamps, where they connect to the battery, are clean and tight.*
b) *Test the condition of the battery (see Section 3). If it does not pass all the tests, replace it with a new battery.*
c) *Check the external alternator wiring and connections.*
d) *Check the drivebelt condition and tension (see Chapter 1).*
e) *Check the alternator mounting bolts for tightness.*
f) *Run the engine and check the alternator for abnormal noise.*
g) *Check the fusible links (if equipped) in the engine compartment fuse box (see Chapter 12). If they're burned, determine the cause and repair the circuit.*

11.10 Alternator electrical connections (arrows) - 2.4L DOHC (2001 and later) engines

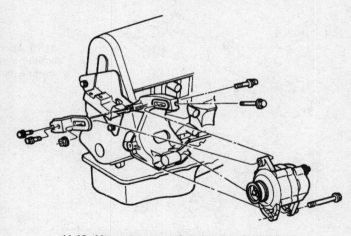

11.12 Alternator mounting details - 2.4L DOHC (1999 and earlier) engine

h) Check the charge light on the dash. It should illuminate when the ignition key is turned ON (engine not running). If it does not, check the circuit from the alternator to the charge light on the dash.

i) Check all the fuses that are in series with the charging system circuit. The location of these fuses and fusible links may vary from year and model but the designations are generally the same. Refer to the wiring schematics at the end of Chapter 12 for additional information.

2   With the ignition key off, check the battery voltage with no accessories operating **(see illustration)**. It should be approximately 12.5 volts. It may be slightly higher if the engine had been operating within the last hour.

3   Start the engine and check the battery voltage again. It should now be greater than the voltage recorded in Step 2, but not more than 14.5 volts. Turn On all the vehicle accessories (air conditioning, rear window defogger, blower motor, etc.) and increase the engine speed to 2,000 rpm - the voltage should not

11.16 Alternator electrical connections (arrows) - 2.5L V6 engine (convertible models)

drop below the voltage recorded in Step 2.

4   If the indicated voltage is greater than the specified charging voltage, replace the voltage regulator. **Note:** On coupes, it is recommended to replace the alternator/voltage regulator as a complete unit, using either a rebuilt or new alternator.

5   If the indicated voltage reading is less than the specified charging voltage, the alternator is probably defective. Have the charging system checked at a dealer service department or other properly equipped repair facility. **Note:** Many auto parts stores will bench test an alternator off the vehicle. Refer to your local auto parts store regarding their policy; many will perform this service free of charge.

11 Alternator - removal and installation

Note: Although some of the models are equipped with an alternator that can be removed from above the engine compartment, many of the brackets and components surrounding the alternator can be accessed from below the engine compartment.

Removal

1   Disconnect the cable from the negative battery terminal or the remote ground terminal (see Section 3).

2   Raise the vehicle and support it on jackstands.

3   Remove the engine protection cover from below the engine compartment.

4   Remove the alternator drivebelt(s) (see Chapter 1).

2.0L, 2.4L SOHC and 2.4L DOHC engines

Refer to illustrations 11.10 and 11.12

5   On 1999 and earlier 2.4L DOHC engines equipped with anti-lock brakes (ABS), disconnect the electrical connector and remove the

two lower plate mounting bolts securing the ABS controller and withdraw it from the vehicle (see Chapter 9).

6   On 1999 and earlier 2.4L DOHC engines, remove the engine coolant reservoir (see Chapter 3).

7   On 2001 and later 2.4L DOHC engines, remove the MAP sensor from the intake manifold (see Chapter 6).

8   On 2.4L SOHC engines, remove the transaxle fluid pressure and return line hose clamps and position the fluid cooling hoses out of the way.

9   On 2.0L engines equipped with cruise control, remove the cruise control actuator without disconnecting the cables and position the assembly off to the side.

10   Disconnect the electrical connector and B+ cable from the alternator **(see illustration)**.

11   On 2.0L engines, loosen the alternator brace bolts. It will be necessary to remove the brace along with the alternator.

12   Remove the pivot bolt and spacer **(see illustration)**.

13   While supporting the alternator, remove the adjustment nut and bolt, then separate the alternator from the bracket. Maneuver the alternator carefully, angling the assembly away from air conditioning lines, vacuum lines, etc. and remove it from the engine compartment.

2.5L and 2.7L V6 engines (convertible models)

Refer to illustrations 11.16 and 11.18

14   On 2.7L V6 engines, disconnect the air conditioning high pressure switch and the compressor clutch connector (see Chapter 3).

15   On 2.7L V6 engines, remove the engine oil dipstick.

16   Disconnect the electrical connector and B+ cable from the alternator **(see illustration)**.

17   Loosen the upper mounting bolt and nut.

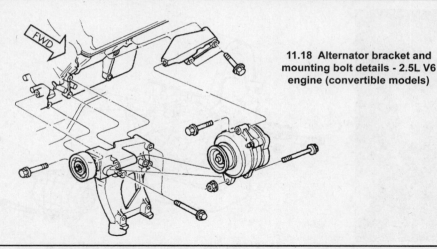

11.18 Alternator bracket and mounting bolt details - 2.5L V6 engine (convertible models)

11.28 Alternator upper mounting bolt (arrow) - 2.5L V6 engine (coupe models)

18   Loosen the lower mounting bolts **(see illustration)**.
19   Remove the lower mounting bolt and spacer. On 2.5L V6 engines, be careful not to drop the spacer or nut.
20   On 2.5L V6 engines, while supporting the alternator, remove the two bolts securing the alternator upper bracket to the cylinder head.
21   Remove the upper mounting bolt(s). On 2.5L V6 engines, separate the bracket from the alternator.

2.5L V6 engines (coupe models)
Refer to illustrations 11.28 and 11.29
22   Remove the engine coolant reservoir (see Chapter 3).
23   Remove the air conditioning compressor drivebelt (see Chapter 1).
24   Remove the power steering oil pump (see Chapter 10). Position the assembly off to the side without disconnecting the power steering lines.
25   Remove the intake manifold (see Chapter 2B).
26   Remove the drivebelt tensioner pulley bracket.
27   Remove the electrical connector and B+ cable from the alternator.
28   Loosen the upper mounting bolt and bracket bolt **(see illustration)**.

29   Remove the lower mounting bolts **(see illustration)**.
30   Remove the alternator lower bracket bolts, spacer and bracket.

Installation - all models
31   If you are replacing the alternator, take the old alternator with you when purchasing a replacement unit. Make sure that the new/rebuilt unit is identical to the old alternator. Look at the terminals - they should be the same in number, size and locations as the terminals on the old alternator. Finally, look at the identification markings - they will be stamped in the housing or printed on a tag or plaque affixed to the housing. Make sure that these numbers are the same on both alternators.
32   Many new/rebuilt alternators do not have a pulley installed, so you may have to switch the pulley from the old unit to the new/rebuilt one. When buying an alternator, find out the shop's policy regarding installation of pulleys - some shops will perform this service free of charge.
33   Installation is the reverse of removal.
34   Adjust the drivebelt tension (see Chapter 1).
35   Check the charging voltage to verify proper operation of the alternator (see Section 10).

12   Starting system - general information and precautions

Refer to illustration 12.3
There are two different types of starter motor assemblies used on these models; a planetary gear reduction type or an offset gear reduction type. The starter motor/solenoid for all models is not serviceable and is sold strictly as a complete assembly.
The starting system consists of the battery, the starter motor, the starter solenoid, the starter relay, the clutch start switch (manual transaxles), the Park/Neutral position switch (automatic transaxles), ignition switch and the wires that connect the components. The solenoid is located on the starter motor which is located on the side of the engine mounted to the transaxle bellhousing towards the front of the vehicle.
When the ignition key is turned to the Start position, the starter solenoid is actuated through the starter control circuit which includes a starter relay. The starter relay is located near the center console (2000 and earlier coupes) or in the fuse/relay center **(see illustration)** in the engine compartment (all other models). The starter solenoid then connects the battery to the starter. The battery supplies the electrical energy to the starter motor, which does the actual work of cranking the engine.
The starter motor on a vehicle equipped with a manual transaxle can be operated only when the clutch pedal is depressed. The starter on a vehicle equipped with an automatic transaxle can be operated only when the transaxle selector lever is in Park or Neutral.
Always observe the following precautions when working on the starting system:
a)   *Excessive cranking of the starter motor can overheat it and cause serious damage. Never operate the starter motor for more than 15 seconds at a time without pausing for at least two minutes to allow it to cool.*

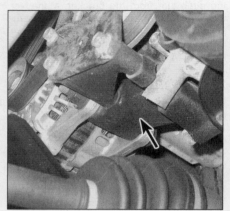

11.29 Alternator lower bracket (arrow) mounting details - 2.5L V6 engine (coupe models)

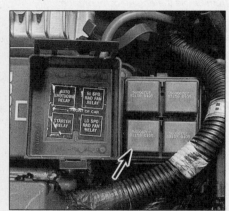

12.3 The starter relay (arrow) is located in the Power Distribution Center inside the engine compartment on most models

b) The starter is connected directly to the battery and could arc or cause a fire if mishandled, overloaded or short circuited.

c) Always detach the negative battery cable from the negative terminal on the battery (coupes) or remote ground terminal (convertibles and sedans) before working on the starting system.

13 Starter motor - in-vehicle check

Refer to illustration 13.3

1 If a malfunction occurs in the starting circuit, do not immediately assume that the starter is causing the problem. First, check the following items:

a) Make sure the battery cable clamps, where they connect to the battery, are clean and tight.

b) Check the condition of the battery cables (see Section 4). Replace any defective battery cables with new parts.

c) Test the condition of the battery (see Section 3). If it does not pass all the tests, replace it with a new battery.

d) Check the starter solenoid wiring and connections. Refer to the wiring diagrams at the end of Chapter 12.

e) Check the starter mounting bolts for tightness.

f) Check the fusible links (if equipped) exiting the engine compartment fuse box (see Chapter 12). If they're burned, determine the cause and repair the circuit. Also, check the ignition switch circuit for correct operation (see Chapter 12).

g) Check the operation of the Park/Neutral Position switch (automatic transaxle) or clutch start switch (manual transaxle). Make sure the shift lever is in PARK or NEUTRAL (automatic transaxle) or the clutch pedal is pressed (manual transaxle). Refer to Chapter 7 for the Park/Neutral Position switch check and adjustment procedure. Refer to Chapter 12 wiring diagrams, if necessary, when performing circuit checks. These systems must operate correctly to provide battery voltage to the ignition solenoid.

h) Check the operation of the starter relay. The starter relay is located either near the center console (2000 and earlier coupes) or in the fuse/relay box (all other models) inside the engine compartment. Refer to Chapter 12 for the testing procedure.

2 If the starter does not actuate when the ignition switch is turned to the start position, check for battery voltage to the solenoid. This will determine if the solenoid is receiving the correct voltage signal from the ignition switch. Connect a test light or voltmeter to the starter solenoid positive terminal and while an assistant turns the ignition switch to the start position. If voltage is not available, refer to the wiring diagrams in Chapter 12 and check all

13.3 To use an inductive ammeter, simply hold the ammeter over the positive or negative cable (whichever cable has better clearance)

the fuses and relays in series with the starting system. If voltage is available but the starter motor does not operate, remove the starter from the engine compartment (see Section 14) and bench test the starter (see Step 4).

3 If the starter turns over slowly, check the starter cranking voltage and the current draw from the battery. This test must be performed with the starter assembly on the engine. Crank the engine over (for 10 seconds or less) and observe the battery voltage. It should not drop below 8.0 volts on manual transaxle models or 8.5 volts on automatic transaxle models. Also, observe the current draw using an amp meter **(see illustration)**. It should not exceed 400 amps or drop below 250 amps. **Caution:** *The battery cables may be excessively heated because of the large amount of amperage being drawn from the battery. Discontinue the testing until the starting system has cooled down.* If the starter motor cranking amp values are not within the correct range, replace it with a new unit. There are several conditions that may affect the starter cranking potential. The battery must be in good condition and the battery cold-cranking rating must not be under-rated for the particular application. Be sure to check the battery specifications carefully. The battery terminals and cables must be clean and not corroded. Also, in cases of extreme cold temperatures, make sure the battery and/or engine block is warmed before performing the tests.

4 If the starter is receiving voltage but does not activate, remove and check the starter/solenoid assembly on the bench. Most likely the solenoid is defective. In some rare cases, the engine may be seized so be sure to try and rotate the crankshaft pulley (see Chapter 2A or 2B) before proceeding. With the starter/solenoid assembly mounted in a vise on the bench, install one jumper cable from the negative battery terminal to the body of the starter. Install the other jumper cable from the positive battery terminal to the B+ terminal on the starter. Install a starter switch and apply battery voltage to the solenoid S ter-

14.6 Starter motor mounting bolt locations - 2.4L DOHC engine

minal (for 10 seconds or less) and see if the solenoid plunger, shift lever and overrunning clutch extends and rotates the pinion drive. If the pinion drive extends but does not rotate, the solenoid is operating but the starter motor is defective. If there is no movement but the solenoid clicks, the solenoid and/or the starter motor is defective. If the solenoid plunger extends and rotates the pinion drive, the starter/solenoid assembly is working properly.

14 Starter motor - removal and installation

Note: *Although some of the models are equipped with a starter that can be removed from above the engine compartment, many of the brackets and components surrounding the starter can be accessed from below the engine compartment.*

1 Disconnect the cable from the negative battery terminal or the remote ground terminal (see Section 3).

2 Raise the vehicle and support it on jackstands.

3 Remove the engine protection cover from below the engine compartment.

Removal

Four-cylinder engines

Refer to illustrations 14.6 and 14.7

4 Remove the air filter housing (see Chapter 4).

5 On vehicles equipped with automatic transaxles, remove the transmission control module (TCM) from its mounting and position it out of the way. **Note:** *DO NOT disconnect the electrical connector from the TCM.*

6 Remove the starter motor upper mounting bolt **(see illustration)**.

7 Clearly label and disconnect the wires from the terminals on the starter motor solenoid **(see illustration)**.

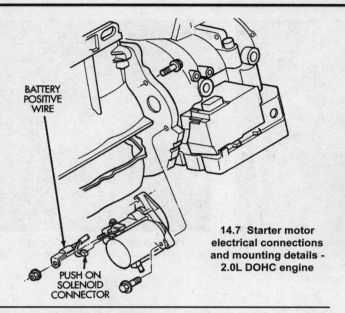

14.7 Starter motor electrical connections and mounting details - 2.0L DOHC engine

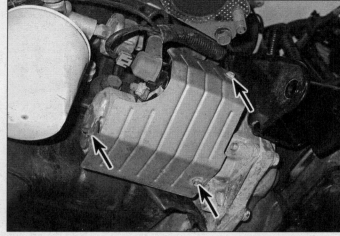

14.11a Starter motor heat shield mounting bolts (arrows) - 2.5L V6 engine (coupe models)

8   While supporting the starter motor, remove the lower mounting bolt and withdraw the starter motor from the vehicle.

2.5L and 3.0L V6 engines

Refer to illustrations 14.11a, 14.11b and 14.12

9   On convertibles, remove the oil filter (see Chapter 1).

10   On coupes, remove the front exhaust pipe (see Chapter 4).

11   Disconnect the wires from the terminals on the starter motor solenoid **(see illustrations)**.

12   While supporting the starter motor, remove the three bolts securing it to the transaxle bellhousing **(see illustration)** and remove the starter motor from the vehicle.

2.7L V6 engines

Refer to illustration 14.16

13   Disconnect the oxygen sensor connector and remove the O2 sensor from the exhaust pipe (see Chapter 6).

14   Remove the front engine mount through-bolt and front engine mount bracket from the engine compartment (see Chapter 2C).

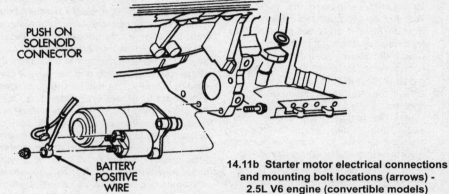

14.11b Starter motor electrical connections and mounting bolt locations (arrows) - 2.5L V6 engine (convertible models)

15   Disconnect the wires from the terminals on the starter motor solenoid.

16   While supporting the starter motor, remove the three bolts securing it to the transaxle bellhousing **(see illustration)** and remove the starter motor from the vehicle.

Installation

All models

17   Installation is the reverse of removal. Tighten the starter motor mounting bolts to the torque listed in this Chapter's Specifications.

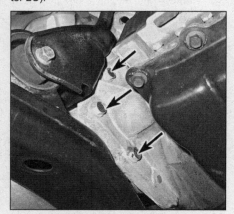

14.12 Starter motor mounting bolts (arrows) - 2.5L V6 engine (coupe models)

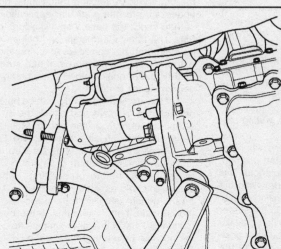

14.16 Starter motor mounting details - 2.7L V6 engine

Chapter 6
Emissions and engine control systems

Contents

1 General information

Refer to illustrations 1.1a, 1.1b, 1.1c and 1.6

To prevent pollution of the atmosphere from incompletely burned and evaporating gases, and to maintain good driveability and fuel economy, a number of emission control systems are incorporated **(see illustrations)**. They include the:

On-Board Diagnostic (OBD) II system
Electronic Fuel Injection (EFI) system

Exhaust Gas Recirculation (EGR) system
Evaporative Emissions Control (EVAP) system
Positive Crankcase Ventilation (PCV) system
Catalytic converter

The Sections in this Chapter include general descriptions, checking procedures within the scope of the home mechanic and component replacement procedures (when possible) for each of the systems listed above.

Before assuming that an emissions control system is malfunctioning, check the fuel and ignition systems carefully. The diagnosis of some emission control devices requires specialized tools, equipment and training. If checking and servicing become too difficult or if a procedure is beyond your ability, consult a dealer service department or other repair shop. Remember, the most frequent cause of emissions problems is simply a loose or broken wire or vacuum hose, so always check the hose and wiring connections first.

1.1a Typical emission control components - 1998 coupe 2.5L V6 engine

1	*IAT sensor*	*4*	*IAC valve*	*6*	*ECT sensor*
2	*MAP sensor*	*5*	*TPS*	*7*	*Powertrain Control Module*
3	*EGR pipe at intake manifold*				

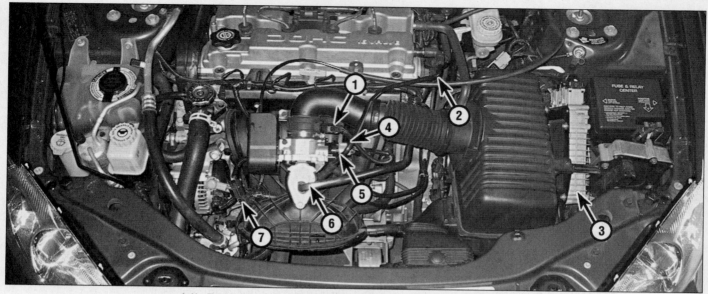

1.1b Typical emission control components - 2001 2.4L DOHC engine

1	*IAT sensor*	4	*IAC valve*	6	*EGR pipe*
2	*CMP sensor*	5	*TPS*	7	*MAP sensor*
3	*Powertrain Control Module*				

This doesn't mean, however, that emissions control systems are particularly difficult to maintain and repair. You can quickly and easily perform many checks and do most of the regular maintenance at home with common tune-up and hand tools. **Note:** *Because of a Federally mandated warranty which covers the emissions control system components, check with your dealer about warranty coverage before working on any emissions-related systems. Once the warranty has expired, you may wish to perform some of the component checks and/or replacement procedures in this Chapter to save money.*

Pay close attention to any special precautions outlined in this Chapter. It should be noted that the illustrations of the various systems may not exactly match the system installed on your vehicle because of changes made by the manufacturer during production or from year-to-year.

A Vehicle Emissions Control Information (VECI) label is attached to the underside of the hood **(see illustration)**. This label contains important emissions specifications and adjustment information. Part of this label, the Vacuum Hose Routing Diagram, provides a

1.1c Typical emission control components - 2001 2.7L V6 engine

1	*Manifold Tuning Valve*	4	*IAT sensor*	7	*PCV valve*
2	*MAP sensor*	5	*EGR pipe*	8	*Upstream O2 sensor*
3	*ECT sensor*	6	*Powertrain Control Module*		

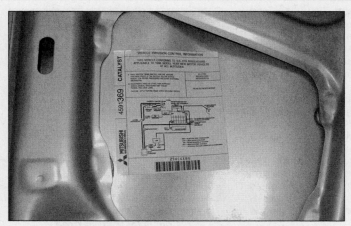

1.6 The Vehicle Emission Control Information (VECI) label contains such essential information as the types of emission control systems installed on the engine, and a vacuum diagram

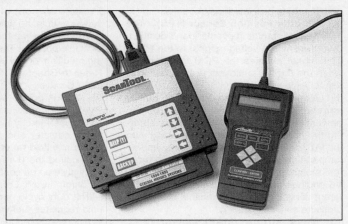

2.1 Scanners like the Actron Scantool and the AutoXray XP240 are powerful diagnostic aids - programmed with comprehensive diagnostic information, they can tell you just about anything you want to know about your engine management system

vacuum hose schematic with emissions components identified. When servicing the engine or emissions systems, the VECI label and the vacuum hose routing diagram in your particular vehicle should always be checked for up-to-date information.

2   On-Board Diagnostic (OBD) system and trouble codes

Scan tool information

Refer to illustrations 2.1 and 2.2

1   Hand-held scanners are the most powerful and versatile tools for analyzing engine management systems used on later model vehicles **(see illustration)**. Early model scanners handle codes and some diagnostics for many systems. Each brand scan tool must be examined carefully to match the year, make and model of the vehicle you are working on. Often, interchangeable cartridges are available to access the particular manufacturer (Ford, GM, Chrysler, Toyota etc.). Some manufacturers will specify by continent (Asia, Europe, USA, etc.). **Note:** *An aftermarket generic scanner should work with any model covered by this manual. However, some early OBD-II models, although technically classified as OBD-II compliant by the manufacturer and by the federal government, might not be fully compliant with all SAE standards for OBD-II. Some generic scanners are unable to extract all the codes from these early OBD-II models. Before purchasing a generic scan tool, contact the manufacturer of the scanner you're planning to buy and verify that it will work properly with the OBD-II system you want to scan. If necessary, of course, you can always have the codes extracted by a dealer service department or an independent repair shop with a professional scan tool.*

2   With the arrival of the Federally mandated emission control system (OBD-II), a specially designed scanner has been developed. Sev-

eral tool manufacturers have released OBD-II scan tools for the home mechanic **(see illustration)**. Ask the parts salesman at a local auto parts store for additional information concerning dates and costs.

OBD system general description

3   All models are equipped with the second generation OBD-II system. This system consists of an on-board computer known as the Powertrain Control Module (PCM), and information sensors, which monitor various functions of the engine and send data to the PCM. This system incorporates a series of diagnostic monitors that detect and identify fuel injection and emissions control systems faults and store the information in the computer memory. This updated system also tests sensors and output actuators, diagnoses drive cycles, freezes data and clears codes. This powerful diagnostic computer must be accessed using the new OBD-II scan tool and 16 pin Data Link Connector (DLC) located under the driver's dash area.

4   The PCM is the "brain" of the electronically controlled fuel and emissions system. It receives data from a number of sensors and other electronic components (switches, relays, etc.). Based on the information it receives, the PCM generates output signals to control various relays, solenoids (i.e. fuel injectors) and other actuators. The PCM is specifically calibrated to optimize the emissions, fuel economy and driveability of the vehicle.

5   It isn't a good idea to attempt diagnosis or replacement of the PCM or emission control components at home while the vehicle is under warranty. Because of a Federally mandated warranty which covers the emissions system components and because any owner-induced damage to the PCM, the sensors and/or the control devices may void this warranty, take the vehicle to a dealer service department if the PCM or a system component malfunctions.

2.2 Trouble code readers like the Actron OBD-II diagnostic tester simplify the task of extracting the trouble codes

Information sensors

6   **Oxygen sensors (O2S) -** The O2S generates a voltage signal that varies with the difference between the oxygen content of the exhaust and the oxygen in the surrounding air.

7   **Crankshaft Position (CKP) sensor -** The crankshaft sensor provides information on crankshaft position and the engine speed signal to the PCM.

8   **Camshaft Position (CMP) sensor -** The camshaft position sensor produces a signal in which the PCM uses to identify number 1 cylinder and to time the sequential fuel injection. The camshaft position sensor is built into the distributor on 2.5L and 3.0L V6 models.

9   **Engine Coolant Temperature (ECT) sensor -** The coolant temperature (ECT) sensor monitors engine coolant temperature and sends the PCM a voltage signal that affects PCM control of the fuel mixture, ignition timing, and EGR operation.

10   **Intake Air Temperature (IAT) sensor -** The IAT sensor provides the PCM with intake air temperature information. The PCM uses this information to control fuel flow, ignition timing, and EGR system operation. 2.4L SOHC and 3.0L V6 models are equipped with

an IAT sensor built into the MAF sensor.

11   **Throttle Position Sensor (TPS) -** The TPS senses throttle movement and position, then transmits a voltage signal to the PCM. This signal enables the PCM to determine when the throttle is closed, in a cruise position, or wide open.

12   **Manifold Absolute Pressure (MAP) sensor -** The MAP sensor measures the amount (volume) of the intake airflow entering the engine. The MAP sensor along with the IAT sensor, provide airflow volume and air temperature information for the most precise fuel metering. The 2.4L SOHC and the 3.0L V6 engines are equipped with a slightly different version called the manifold differential pressure sensor.

13   **Mass Airflow (MAF) sensor (2.4L SOHC and 3.0L V6 models) -** The mass airflow sensor measures the mass of the intake air by detecting volume and weight of the air from samples passing over the hot wire element.

14   **Vehicle Speed Sensor (VSS) -** The vehicle speed sensor provides information to the PCM to indicate vehicle speed.

15   **Leak Detection Pump -** The leak detection pump is part of the evaporative emission control system and is used to monitor vapor pressure in the EVAP system. The PCM uses this information to turn on and off the vacuum switching valves (VSV) of the evaporative emission system.

16   **Power Steering Pressure (PSP) switch -** The PSP sensor is used to increase engine idle speed during low-speed vehicle maneuvers.

17   **Transaxle sensors -** In addition to the vehicle speed sensor, the PCM receives input signals from the following sensors inside the transaxle or connected to it: (a) the input speed sensor (b) the output speed sensor.

Output actuators

18   **Auto Shutdown relay -** The auto shutdown relay activates power to the fuel injectors, the alternator field, the ignition coil and the heating elements in the O2 sensors. The PCM will deactivate power to the ASD relay if it does not receive signals from the crankshaft sensor and the camshaft sensor. Refer to Chapter 4 or your owner's manual for more information on relay location.

19   **Fuel injectors -** The PCM opens the fuel injectors individually in firing order sequence. The PCM also controls the time the injector is open, called the "pulse width." The pulse width of the injector (measured in milliseconds) determines the amount of fuel delivered. For more information on the fuel delivery system and the fuel injectors, including injector replacement, refer to Chapter 4.

20   **Power transistor -** The power transistor triggers the ignition coil and determines proper spark advance based on inputs from the PCM. The power transistor is mounted in various locations depending on the type of electronic ignition system used on the engine. Refer to Chapter 5 for more information on the power transistor.

21   **Idle air control (IAC) valve -** The IAC valve controls the amount of air to bypass the throttle plate when the throttle valve is closed or at idle position. The IAC valve opening and the resulting airflow is controlled by the PCM. Refer to Chapter 4 for more information on the IAC valve.

22   **EVAP purge control solenoid -** The EVAP vacuum switching valve is a solenoid valve, operated by the PCM to purge the fuel vapor canister and route fuel vapor to the intake manifold for combustion. This valve is also called the purge control solenoid. The early style purge control solenoids operate as an on/off switch. Later models are equipped with a duty cycle purge solenoid. This solenoid regulates fuel vapor flow to the canister at a constant proportion.

23   **Intake manifold tuning valve (2.7L models) -** The intake manifold tuning valve operates a valve which opens a crossover passage inside the intake manifold providing acoustical tuning for improved intake charges.

Obtaining OBD-II system trouble codes

Refer to illustration 2.25

Note: *All models covered by this manual are equipped with the OBD-II system. Generic trouble codes on 1997 and earlier models can be accessed using the ignition key method. It is necessary to use a SCAN tool to read trouble codes on 1998 and later models. Before outputting the trouble codes, thoroughly inspect ALL electrical connectors and hoses. Make sure all electrical connections are tight, clean and free of corrosion; make sure all hoses are properly connected, fit tightly and are in good condition (no cracks or tears).*

24   The PCM will illuminate the CHECK ENGINE light (also called the Malfunction Indicator Light) on the dash if it recognizes a component fault for two consecutive drive cycles. It will continue to set the light until the PCM does not detect any malfunction for three or more consecutive drive cycles.

25   The self-diagnosis information contained in the PCM can be accessed either by the ignition key (1997 and earlier models) or by using a scan tool. This tool is attached to the diagnostic connector **(see illustration)** located under the left (driver's) side of the instrument panel in the passenger compartment and reads the codes and parameters on the digital display screen. The tool is expensive and most home mechanics prefer to use the alternate method. The drawback with the ignition key method is that it does not access all the available codes for display. If the information cannot be obtained readily, have the vehicle's self-diagnosis system analyzed by a dealer service department or other qualified repair shop.

Ignition key method

26   To obtain the codes using the ignition key method, first set the parking brake and put the shift lever in Park. Raise the engine speed to approximately 2,500 rpm and slowly let the

2.25 Location of the 16-pin Data Link Connector (DLC) (arrow)

speed down to idle. Also, if equipped, cycle the air conditioning system (on briefly, then off). Next, on models equipped with an automatic transaxle, apply the brakes and select each position on the transmission (Reverse, Drive, Low etc.), finally bring the shifter back to Park and turn off the engine. This will allow the computer to obtain any fault codes that might be linked to any of the sensors controlled by the transmission, engine speed or air conditioning system.

27   To display the codes on the instrument panel (CHECK ENGINE light or Malfunction Indicator Light), with the engine NOT running, turn the ignition key ON, OFF, ON, OFF and finally ON (must be done within 5 seconds). The codes will begin to flash. The light will blink the number of the first digit then pause and blink the number of the second digit. For example: Code 23, air temperature sensor circuit, would be indicated by two flashes, pause, three flashes.

Scan tool method

28   The diagnostic codes for the OBD-II system can be extracted from the PCM by plugging a generic OBD-II scan tool **(see illustrations 2.1 and 2.2)** into the PCM's data link connector **(see illustration 2.25)**, which is located under the left end of the dash.

29   Plug the scan tool into the 16-pin data link connector (DLC), and then follow the instructions included with the scan tool to extract all the diagnostic codes.

Clearing trouble codes

1996 and 1997 models

30   To erase trouble codes from the PCM memory on these models, detach the negative cable from the battery or the remote ground terminal for at least ten seconds. **Caution:** *To prevent damage to the PCM, the ignition switch must be in the Off position when disconnecting the cable.*

1998 and later models

31   On these models, trouble codes must be cleared from the PCM memory using the scan tool. Follow the instructions on the scan tool menu to clear any stored codes.

Trouble codes - 1995 through 1997 models

Trouble code	Code identification
Code 11	Intermittent loss of crankshaft and/or camshaft position sensor signals to PCM.
Code 12	Problem with the battery connection. Direct battery input to PCM disconnected within the last 50 ignition key-on cycles.
Code 13**	Problem with the MAP sensor circuit.
Code 14**	MAP sensor voltage out of normal range.
Code 15**	A problem with the Vehicle Speed Sensor signal. No Vehicle Speed Sensor signal detected during road load conditions.
Code 16	No input signal from knock sensor.
Code 17	Engine is cold too long. Engine coolant temperature remains below normal operating temperatures during initial operation (check the thermostat).
Code 21**	Problem with oxygen sensor signal circuit. Sensor voltage to computer not fluctuating.
Code 22**	Engine coolant temperature sensor voltage out of normal range.
Code 23**	Intake air temperature sensor voltage out of normal range.
Code 24**	Throttle position sensor voltage high or low. Test the throttle position sensor.
Code 25**	Idle Air Control (IAC) valve circuits. A shorted condition is detected in one or more of the IAC valve circuits. Or a vacuum leak is detected.
Code 27	One of the injector control circuit output drivers does not respond properly to the control signal. Check the circuits.
Code 31**	EVAP system fault.
Code 32**	An open or shorted condition detected in the EGR solenoid circuit. Possible air/fuel ratio imbalance not detected during diagnosis.
Code 33	Air conditioning clutch relay circuit. An open or shorted condition detected in the compressor clutch relay circuit.
Code 34	Open or shorted condition detected in the speed control vacuum or vent solenoid circuits.
Code 35	Open or shorted condition detected in the radiator fan high or low speed relay circuits.
Code 36	Open or shorted condition detected in the secondary air Injection solenoid circuit (manual transaxle models).
Code 37**	Transaxle Park/Neutral switch failure.
Code 41***	Problem with the charging system. An open or shorted condition detected in the alternator field control circuit.
Code 42	Fuel pump relay or auto shutdown relay (ASD) control circuit indicates an open or shorted circuit condition.
Code 42	Fuel level sending unit circuit problem detected. Check fuel level sensor and circuit.
Code 43**	Multiple cylinder misfire detected. Peak primary circuit current not achieved with the maximum dwell time.
Code 44**	Battery temperature sensor voltage circuit.
Code 45	Transaxle fault present in transmission control module - automatic transaxles.
Code 46***	Charging system voltage too high. Computer indicates that the battery voltage is not properly regulated.
Code 47***	Charging system voltage too low. Battery voltage sensor input below target charging voltage during engine operation and no significant change in voltage detected during active test of alternator output.
Code 51**	Oxygen sensor signal input indicates lean fuel/air ratio condition during engine operation.
Code 52**	Oxygen sensor signal input indicates rich fuel/air ratio condition during engine operation.
Code 53**	Internal PCM failure detected.
Code 54**	No camshaft position sensor signal. Problem with the camshaft sensor synchronization circuit.
Code 55	Completion of fault code display on CHECK ENGINE light. This is the end of stored codes.
Code 61	MAP sensor out of range.
Code 62	Unsuccessful attempt to update EMR mileage in the controller EEPROM.
Code 63**	Controller failure. EEPROM write denied. Check the PCM.
Code 64**	Catalytic converter efficiency below required level.
Code 65**	Power steering switch failure or no release of brake switch detected.
Code 66	Transmission control module (TCM) or body control module (BCM) not sensed by PCM.
Code 71	PCM output voltage low.
Code 72**	Catalytic converter efficiency below required level.
Code 77	Speed Control relay fault.
Code 87	Speed Control switch fault.

** On convertibles, these codes illuminate the CHECK ENGINE light on the instrument panel during engine operation once the trouble code has been recorded.

*** On convertibles, these codes illuminate the charging system light (battery) on the instrument panel during engine operation once the trouble code has been recorded.

Trouble codes - 1998 and later models

Trouble code	Code identification
P0101	Airflow sensor circuit out of range
P0102	Airflow sensor circuit low input
P0102	Mass Airflow (MAF) sensor circuit low input
P0103	Airflow sensor circuit high input
P0103	Mass Airflow (MAF) sensor circuit high input
P0106	Barometric pressure out of range
P0107	Manifold Absolute Pressure (MAP) sensor voltage too low
P0107	Barometric Pressure sensor voltage too low
P0108	Manifold Absolute Pressure (MAP) sensor voltage too high
P0108	Barometric Pressure sensor voltage too high
P0111	Intake Air Temperature (IAT) sensor circuit out of range
P0112	Intake Air Temperature (IAT) sensor circuit low input
P0113	Intake Air Temperature (IAT) sensor circuit high input
P0115	Electronic Coolant Temperature (ECT) sensor circuit high input
P0116	Electronic Coolant Temperature (ECT) sensor circuit out of range
P0117	Electronic Coolant Temperature (ECT) sensor circuit low input
P0118	Electronic Coolant Temperature (ECT) sensor circuit high input
P0121	Throttle Position Sensor (TPS) circuit out of range
P0122	Throttle Position Sensor (TPS) circuit low input
P0123	Throttle Position Sensor (TPS) circuit high input
P0125	Coolant thermostat malfunction
P0128	Coolant thermostat malfunction
P0130	Upstream heated O2 sensor circuit fault (Bank 1)
P0131	Upstream heated O2 sensor circuit low voltage (Bank 1)
P0132	Upstream heated O2 sensor shorted to voltage
P0133	Upstream heated O2 sensor circuit slow response (Bank 1)
P0134	Upstream O2 sensor neither rich or lean
P0135	Upstream heated O2 sensor heater circuit fault (Bank 1)
P0136	Downstream heated O2 sensor fault (Bank 1)
P0137	Downstream heated O2 sensor shorted to ground
P0138	Downstream heated O2 sensor open or shorted circuit
P0139	Downstream heated O2 sensor slow response
P0140	Downstream heated O2 sensor - neither rich nor lean condition detected
P0141	Downstream heated O2 sensor heater circuit fault (Bank 1)
P0143	Downstream heated O2 sensor circuit fault (Bank 1)
P0144	Downstream heated O2 sensor circuit fault (Bank 1)
P0145	Downstream heated O2 sensor slow response (Bank 1)
P0146	Downstream heated O2 sensor neither rich nor lean mixture (Bank 1)
P0147	Downstream heated O2 sensor heater circuit fault (Bank 1)
P0150	Upstream heated O2 sensor circuit fault (Bank 2)
P0151	Upstream heated O2 sensor circuit low voltage (Bank 2)
P0152	Upstream heated O2 sensor circuit fault (Bank 2)
P0153	Upstream heated O2 sensor circuit slow response (Bank 2)
P0154	Upstream heated O2 sensor neither rich nor lean mixture (Bank 2)
P0155	Upstream heated O2 sensor heater circuit fault (Bank 2)
P0156	Downstream heated O2 sensor fault (Bank 2)
P0157	Downstream heated O2 sensor circuit fault (Bank 2)
P0158	Downstream heated O2 sensor circuit fault (Bank 2)

Trouble code	Code identification
P0159	Downstream heated O2 sensor slow response (Bank 2)
P0160	Downstream heated O2 sensor neither rich nor lean mixture (Bank 2)
P0161	Downstream heated O2 sensor heater circuit fault (Bank 2)
P0165	Starter relay control circuit open or shorted circuit
P0171	System Adaptive fuel too lean (Bank 1)
P0172	System Adaptive fuel too rich (Bank 1)
P0174	System Adaptive fuel too lean (Bank 2)
P0175	System Adaptive fuel too rich (Bank 2)
P0178	Water in fuel sensor voltage signal high
P0179	Flexible fuel sensor voltage signal high
P0182	CNG temperature sensor voltage signal low
P0183	CNG temperature sensor voltage signal high
P0191	Injector Pressure sensor system performance
P0192	Injector Pressure sensor circuit low input
P0193	Injector Pressure sensor circuit high input
P0201	Injector no. 1 output driver not responding properly
P0202	Injector no. 2 output driver not responding properly
P0203	Injector no. 3 output driver not responding properly
P0204	Injector no. 4 output driver not responding properly
P0205	Injector no. 5 output driver not responding properly
P0206	Injector no. 6 output driver not responding properly
P0220	Fuel pump relay circuit fault
P0300	Multiple cylinder misfiring detected
P0301	Cylinder no. 1 misfire detected
P0302	Cylinder no. 2 misfire detected
P0303	Cylinder no. 3 misfire detected
P0304	Cylinder no. 4 misfire detected
P0305	Cylinder no. 5 misfire detected
P0306	Cylinder no. 6 misfire detected
P0320	No crankshaft sensor signal detected during engine cranking
P0325	Knock sensor circuit fault
P0326	Knock sensor circuit performance
P0330	Knock sensor circuit fault
P0335	No crankshaft sensor signal detected at PCM
P0340	No camshaft sensor signal detected during engine cranking
P0350	Ignition coil drawing too much current
P0351	Ignition coil no. 1 primary circuit fault
P0352	Ignition coil no. 2 primary circuit fault
P0353	Ignition coil no. 3 primary circuit fault
P0354	Ignition coil no. 4 primary circuit fault
P0355	Ignition coil no. 5 primary circuit fault
P0356	Ignition coil no. 6 primary circuit fault
P0400	EGR flow fault
P0401	EGR insufficient flow detected
P0402	EGR excessive flow detected
P0403	EGR transducer circuit open or shorted
P0404	EGR valve position sensor circuit fault
P0405	EGR valve position sensor voltage signal low
P0406	EGR valve position sensor voltage signal high

Trouble codes - 1998 and later models (continued)

Trouble code	Code identification
P0412	Secondary air solenoid circuit open or shorted
P0420	Catalyst system efficiency below threshold (Bank 1)
P0421	Catalyst system efficiency below threshold (Bank 1)
P0430	Catalyst system efficiency below threshold (Bank 2)
P0431	Catalyst system efficiency below threshold (Bank 2)
P0432	Catalyst system efficiency below threshold (Bank 2)
P0441	EVAP monitor detects insufficient vapor flow
P0442	EVAP small leak detected
P0443	EVAP VMV circuit fault
P0446	EVAP vent control solenoid circuit fault
P0450	EVAP pressure sensor malfunction
P0451	EVAP pressure sensor out of range
P0452	EVAP fuel tank pressure sensor low input
P0453	EVAP fuel tank pressure sensor high input
P0455	Leak in EVAP system detected
P0456	Leak in EVAP system detected
P0460	Fuel level sending unit - no movement detected
P0462	Fuel level sending unit - low voltage indicated
P0463	Fuel level sending unit - high voltage indicated
P0500	VSS fault
P0505	IAC valve system fault
P0506	IAC valve system fault
P0507	IAC valve system fault
P0522	Oil pressure sensor input voltage low
P0523	Oil pressure sensor input voltage high
P0551	Power steering switch failure detected
P0600	PCM internal fault
P0601	PCM internal fault
P0603	PCM Keep Alive Memory test error
P0605	PCM Read Only Memory test error
P0622	Alternator field circuit open or shorted
P0645	A/C clutch relay circuit open or shorted
P0700	Automatic transmission fault detected
P0703	Brake switch stuck open or closed
P1192	Intake air temperature voltage low
P1193	Intake air temperature voltage high
P1281	Engine not reaching operating temperature within correct limits
P1289	Manifold tuning valve circuit out of range
P1297	MAP sensor values not indicating start-up condition
P1299	Vacuum leak detected
P1388	Auto Shutdown relay circuit open or shorted
P1389	No Auto Shutdown relay voltage indicated at PCM
P1391	Camshaft position sensor and/or crankshaft position sensor signal loss
P1489	High speed fan relay circuit open or shorted
P1490	Low speed fan relay circuit open or shorted
P1493	Ambient battery temperature sensor circuit voltage low
P1594	Charging system voltage indicates high output
P1682	Charging system voltage indicates low output
P1899	Park/Neutral switch stuck in Park or in gear

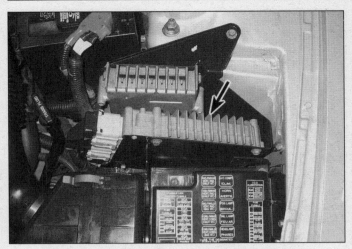

3.1a Location of the PCM (arrow) on a 2.5L V6 model

3.1b Location of the PCM (arrow) on a 2.7L V6 model

3 Powertrain Control Module (PCM) - removal and installation

Refer to illustrations 3.1a and 3.1b
Warning: *The models covered by this manual are equipped with Supplemental Restraint systems (SRS), more commonly known as airbags. Always disable the airbag system before working in the vicinity of any airbag system components to avoid the possibility of accidental deployment of the airbag, which could cause personal injury (see Chapter 12).*
Caution: *To avoid electrostatic discharge damage to the PCM, handle the PCM only by its case. Do not touch the electrical terminals during removal and installation. If available, ground yourself to the vehicle with an anti-static ground strap, available at computer supply stores.*
1   The Powertrain Control Module (PCM) is located behind the glovebox (2001 and later coupes) or in the engine compartment (all other models) next to the air filter housing **(see illustrations)**.

2   Disconnect the cable from the negative battery terminal or the remote ground terminal (see Chapter 5).

2001 and later coupes
3   Remove the lower trim panels from the dash area (see Chapter 11).
4   Remove the glovebox (see Chapter 11).
5   Unplug the electrical connectors from the PCM.
6   Remove the retaining bolts from the PCM bracket.
7   Carefully remove the PCM. **Note:** *Avoid any static electricity damage to the computer by grounding yourself to the body before touching the PCM and using a special anti-static pad to store the PCM on once it is removed.*
8   Installation is the reverse of removal.

All other models
Refer to illustrations 3.9 and 3.11
9   Unplug the electrical connectors from the PCM **(see illustration)**.

10   Remove the air filter housing (see Chapter 4).
11   Remove the retaining bolts from the PCM bracket **(see illustration)**.
12   Carefully remove the PCM. **Note:** *Avoid any static electricity damage to the computer by grounding yourself to the body before touching the PCM and using a special anti-static pad to store the PCM on once it is removed.*
13   Installation is the reverse of removal.

4 Throttle Position Sensor (TPS) - replacement

Refer to illustrations 4.1a, 4.1b and 4.5
Note: *After installing a new TPS, it will be necessary to have the TPS adjusted by a dealer service department or other qualified auto repair facility using a scan tool.*
1   The Throttle Position Sensor (TPS) is located on the end of the throttle shaft on the

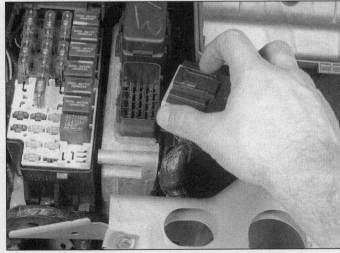

3.9 Disconnect the PCM electrical connectors

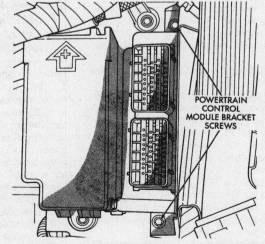

POWERTRAIN CONTROL MODULE BRACKET SCREWS

3.11 Remove the nuts from the PCM mounting brackets

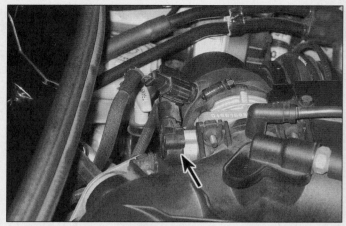

4.1a Location of the TPS (arrow) on a 2.5L V6 model

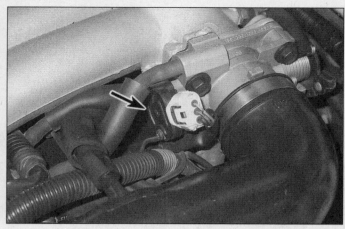

4.1b Location of the TPS (arrow) on a 2.7L V6 model

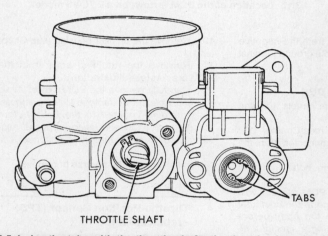

THROTTLE SHAFT

TABS

4.5 Index the tabs with the throttle shaft - the throttle plate should close and the TPS must be rotated clockwise into position

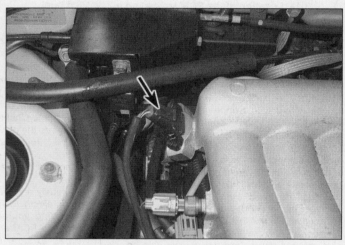

5.1a Location of the MAP sensor (arrow) on a 2.5L V6 model

throttle body **(see illustrations)**. By monitoring the output voltage from the TPS, the PCM can determine fuel delivery based on throttle valve angle (driver demand). A broken or loose TPS can cause intermittent bursts of fuel from the injectors and an unstable idle because the PCM thinks the throttle is moving. A problem with the TPS circuits will set a diagnostic trouble code (see Section 2).
2   Make sure the ignition key is in the OFF position.
3   Disconnect the electrical connector from the TPS.
4   Remove the throttle body (see Chapter 4), if necessary. On some models, it will be necessary to remove the throttle body to gain access to the TPS mounting screws.
5   Remove the screws that retain the TPS to the throttle body and remove the TPS **(see illustration)**.
6   To install the TPS, index the tabs on the TPS onto the throttle shaft. After the TPS is installed, the TPS should rotate clockwise a few degrees to line up the screw holes with the screw holes in the throttle body.
7   After installing the TPS, the throttle plate should be closed. If the throttle plate opens

slightly, the tabs on the TPS are indexed incorrectly (180 degrees off).
8   Tighten the TPS mounting screws.
9   Installation is the reverse of removal.

5   Manifold Absolute Pressure (MAP) sensor (2.0L, 2.4L DOHC and 2.5L/2.7L V6 engines) - replacement

Refer to illustrations 5.1a and 5.1b
1   The MAP sensor is mounted on the intake manifold **(see illustrations)**. The Manifold Absolute Pressure (MAP) sensor monitors the intake manifold pressure changes resulting from changes in engine load and speed and converts the information into a voltage output. The PCM uses the MAP sensor to control fuel delivery and ignition timing. The PCM will receive information as a voltage signal that will vary from 1.9 to 2.1 volts at closed throttle (high vacuum) and 0.3 to 0.5 volt at wide open throttle (low vacuum). The voltage range values will vary slightly according to changes in altitude. A problem in any of the MAP sensor circuits will set a diagnostic

trouble code (see Section 2).
2   Make sure the ignition key is in the OFF position.
3   Disconnect the electrical connector from the MAP sensor.
4   Remove the bolts that retain the MAP sensor to the intake manifold. Remove the MAP sensor.
5   Installation is the reverse of removal.

5.1b Location of the MAP sensor (arrow) on a 2.7L V6 model

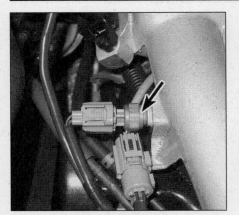

7.1a The intake air temperature sensor is located in the intake manifold (arrow) on 2.5L V6 models

7.1b The intake air temperature sensor is located in the air intake duct (arrow) on 2.7L V6 models

8.1a Location of the ECT sensor (arrow) on 2.5L V6 models

6 Mass Airflow (MAF) sensor (2.4L SOHC and 3.0L V6 engines) - replacement

1   The mass airflow sensor is located on the air intake duct. The MAF system circuit consists of a platinum hot wire, a thermistor and a control circuit inside a plastic housing. The sensor uses a hot wire sensing element to measure the molecular mass (weight) of air entering the engine. As the throttle opens, increasing volume of air passes over the hot wire, which cools the wire. The MAF sensor circuit is designed to maintain the hot wire at a constant preset temperature by controlling the current flow through the hot wire. So, as the wire cools, the PCM increases the flow of current through the hot wire in order to maintain the wire at a constant temperature. The output voltage signal of the MAF sensor varies in accordance with this current flow. This voltage signal is measured by the PCM, which converts this signal into a digital wave form, calculates the fuel injector pulse width (duration) and turns the injectors on and off accordingly. A problem in the MAF sensor circuit will set a diagnostic trouble code (see Section 2).
2   Make sure the ignition key is in the OFF position.

3   Disconnect the electrical connector from the MAF sensor.
4   Remove the air filter housing (see Chapter 4).
5   Remove the sensor retaining bolts and remove the MAF sensor.
6   Installation is the reverse of removal. Be sure to install a gasket between the MAF sensor and the intake duct, if equipped.

7 Intake Air Temperature (IAT) sensor - replacement

Refer to illustrations 7.1a and 7.1b
Note: *2.4L SOHC and 3.0L V6 engines are equipped with an IAT sensor that is built into the MAF sensor.*
1   The intake air temperature sensor is mounted either on the intake manifold **(see illustration)** or the air intake duct **(see illustration)**. The intake air temperature (IAT) sensor is a thermistor (a resistor which varies the value of its resistance in accordance with temperature changes). The change in the resistance values will directly affect the voltage signal from the sensor to the PCM. As the sensor temperature DECREASES, the resistance values will INCREASE. As the sensor temperature INCREASES, the resistance val-

ues will DECREASE. A problem in any of the IAT sensor circuits will set a diagnostic trouble code.
2   Make sure the ignition key is in the OFF position.
3   Disconnect the electrical connector from the IAT sensor.
4   Remove the IAT sensor from the air filter housing.
5   Installation is the reverse of removal.

8 Engine Coolant Temperature (ECT) sensor - replacement

Refer to illustrations 8.1a, 8.1b, 8.1c and 8.5
Warning: *Wait until the engine has cooled completely before beginning this procedure.*
1   The engine coolant temperature sensor is mounted near the thermostat housing **(see illustrations)**. The engine coolant temperature (ECT) sensor is a thermistor. The thermistor is a resistor which varies the value of its resistance in accordance with temperature changes. The change in the resistance values will directly affect the voltage signal from the sensor to the PCM. As the sensor temperature DECREASES, the resistance values will INCREASE. As the sensor temperature INCREASES, the resistance values

8.1b Location of the ECT sensor (arrow) on 2.7L V6 models

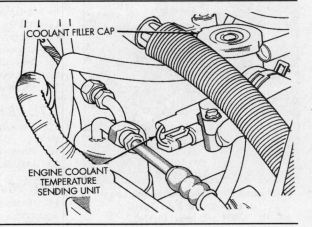

8.1c Location of the ECT sensor (arrow) on the 2.4L DOHC model

COOLANT FILLER CAP

ENGINE COOLANT TEMPERATURE SENDING UNIT

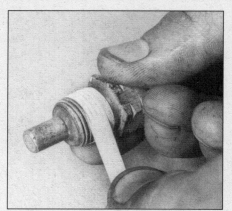

8.5 Wrap the threads of the ECT sensor with Teflon tape to prevent leakage

9.1a Location of the crankshaft sensor (arrow) on the 2.0L DOHC model

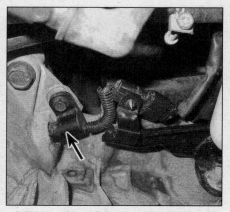

9.1b Location of the crankshaft sensor (arrow) on the 2.5L V6 model

will DECREASE. A problem in any of the ECT sensor circuits will set a diagnostic trouble code.

2   Make sure the ignition key is in the OFF position.

3   Drain approximately one gallon from the cooling system (see Chapter 1).

4   Disconnect the electrical connector and carefully unscrew the sensor.

5   Wrap the threads of the new sensor with Teflon sealing tape to prevent leakage and thread corrosion **(see illustration)**.

6   Installation is the reverse of removal.
Caution: *Handle the coolant sensor with care. Damage to this sensor will affect the operation of the entire fuel injection system.*

7   Refill the cooling system (see Chapter 1).

9   Crankshaft position (CKP) sensor - replacement

Refer to illustrations 9.1a, 9.1b and 9.1c

1   The crankshaft position sensor (CKP) determines the timing on each cylinder for the fuel injectors and ignition system. The crankshaft sensor is mounted in several different places depending on the year and model **(see illustrations)**.

9.1c Location of the crankshaft sensor (arrow) on the 2.4L DOHC (2001 and later) model

a) On 2.0L and 2.4L DOHC (1999 and earlier) engines, the crankshaft sensor is mounted above the oil filter.

b) On 2.4L DOHC (2001 and later) engines, the crankshaft sensor is mounted on the rear side of the engine block.

c) On 2.4L SOHC and 3.0L V6 engines, the crankshaft sensor is mounted behind the timing belt cover next to the crankshaft sprocket.

d) On 2.5L V6 engines, the crankshaft sensor is mounted under the distributor near the transaxle bellhousing.

e) On 2.7L V6 engines, the crankshaft sensor is mounted on the transaxle bellhousing near the air filter housing.

A problem in the crankshaft sensor circuit will set a diagnostic trouble code (see Section 2).

2   Make sure the ignition key is in the OFF position.

3   Raise the vehicle and support it securely on jackstands.

2.0L and 2.4L DOHC models

4   Working under the vehicle, disconnect the crankshaft position sensor electrical connector.

5   Remove the bolt and detach the sensor.

6   Installation is the reverse of removal.

2.4L SOHC and 3.0L V6 models

7   The timing belt cover must be removed to access the crankshaft sensor. Refer to Chapter 2A or 2B for the timing belt cover removal procedure.

8   Disconnect the crankshaft position sensor electrical connector.

9   Remove the bolt and detach the sensor.

10   Installation is the reverse of removal.

2.7L V6 models

11   Remove the air filter housing (see Chapter 4).

12   Remove the bolt and detach the sensor.

13   Installation is the reverse of removal.

2.5L V6 models

14   Remove the cruise control actuator, if equipped.

15   Disconnect the crankshaft position sensor electrical connector.

16   Remove the bolt and detach the sensor.

17   Installation is the reverse of removal.

10   Camshaft position (CMP) sensor - replacement

Refer to illustration 10.1

1   The camshaft position (CMP) sensor determines the position of the cylinder for ignition start-up signals and for sequential fuel injection signals to each cylinder. The camshaft position sensor is mounted in several different places depending on the model.

a) On 2.0L and 2.4L DOHC engines, the camshaft sensor is mounted at the back of the cylinder head **(see illustration)**.

b) On 2.4L SOHC engines, the camshaft sensor is mounted on the camshaft housing located on the end of the cylinder head.

c) On 2.5L and 3.0L V6 engines, the camshaft sensor is mounted in the distributor.

d) On 2.7L V6 engines, the camshaft sensor is mounted on the front of the cylinder head.

A problem in the camshaft sensor circuit will set a diagnostic trouble code (see Section 2).

2   Make sure the ignition key is in the OFF position.

2.0L and 2.4L DOHC models

3   Remove the PCV hose and position it out of the way (see Section 16).

4   Disconnect the electrical connector from the camshaft position sensor.

5   Remove the bolts and detach the sensor.

6   Installation is the reverse of removal.

2.4L SOHC models

7   Carefully mark and disconnect any vacuum hose that may interfere with the camshaft position sensor removal.

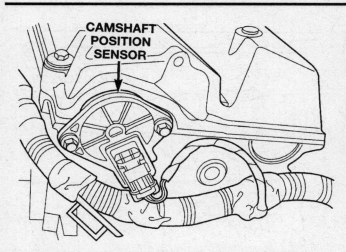

10.1 The camshaft position (CMP) sensor on the 2.0L and 2.4L DOHC models is located on the end of the cylinder head

11.2a Location of the upstream oxygen sensor (arrow) on a 2.5L V6 model

8   Remove the bolts and detach the sensor.
9   Installation is the reverse of removal.

2.7L V6 models

10   Disconnect the electrical connector from the camshaft position sensor.
11   Remove the bolts and detach the sensor.
12   Installation is the reverse of removal.

2.5L and 3.0L V6 models

13   Remove the distributor (see Chapter 5).
14   The camshaft sensor is not sold as an individual component. Replace the distributor as a complete unit.
15   Installation is the reverse of removal.

11   Oxygen sensor - general information and replacement

General information

Refer to illustrations 11.2a and 11.2b
1   All vehicles covered by this manual have On-Board Diagnostics II (OBD-II) engine management systems, which means they have the ability to verify the accuracy of the basic feedback loop between the oxygen sensor and the PCM. They accomplish this by using an oxygen sensor in front of the catalytic converter and an oxygen sensor behind the catalytic converter. By sampling the exhaust gas before and after the catalytic converter, the PCM can determine the efficiency of the converter and can even predict when it will fail.
2   The primary (upstream) oxygen sensor is located in the exhaust manifold and the secondary (downstream) oxygen sensor is located behind the catalytic converter The upstream **(see illustration)** and downstream **(see illustration)** oxygen sensors on all models is a heated oxygen sensor. The PCM uses a supply wire and ground wire to control the power to the O2 sensor heater during warm-

up. The automatic shutdown relay supplies battery voltage to the heater while the ground is controlled by the PCM.
3   Special care must be taken whenever a sensor is serviced.
  a) *Oxygen sensors have a permanently attached pigtail and an electrical connector which should not be removed from the sensor. Damage or removal of the pigtail or electrical connector can adversely affect operation of the sensor.*
  b) *Grease, dirt and other contaminants should be kept away from the electrical connector and the louvered end of the sensor.*
  c) *Do not use cleaning solvents of any kind on an oxygen sensor.*
  d) *Do not drop or roughly handle an oxygen sensor.*
  e) *The silicone boot must be installed in the correct position to prevent the boot from being melted and to allow the sensor to operate properly.*

Replacement

Refer to illustration 11.7
Note: *Because it is installed in the exhaust manifold or pipe, which contracts when cool,*

the oxygen sensor may be very difficult to loosen when the engine is cold. Rather than risk damage to the sensor, assuming you are planning to reuse it in another manifold or pipe, start and run the engine for a minute or two, then shut it off. Be careful not to burn yourself during the following procedure.*
4   Make sure the ignition key is in the OFF position.
5   If you're replacing the downstream sensor, raise the vehicle and secure it on jackstands. Access the oxygen sensor harness and then unplug the electrical connector.
6   The upstream sensor can be replaced without raising the vehicle. Unplug the sensor electrical connector.
7   Unscrew the sensor from the exhaust manifold or exhaust pipe **(see illustration)**. **Note:** *The best tool for removing an oxygen sensor is a special slotted socket, especially if you're planning to reuse a sensor. If you don't have this tool, and you plan to reuse the sensor, be extremely careful when unscrewing the sensor.*
8   Apply anti-seize compound to the threads of the sensor to facilitate future removal. The threads of new sensors should already be coated with this compound, but if

11.2b Location of the downstream oxygen sensor (arrow) on a 2.5L V6 model

11.7 Use a slotted socket to remove the oxygen sensor

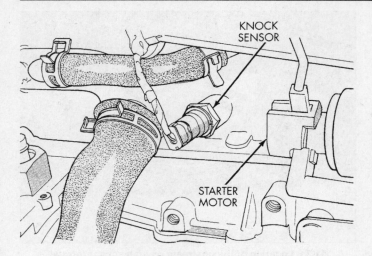

12.5 Location of the knock sensor on 2.4L DOHC models

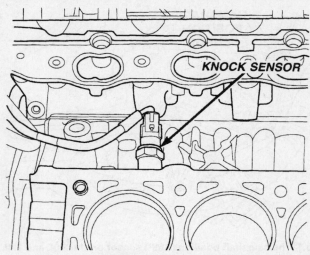

12.9 Location of the knock sensor on 2.7L V6 models

you're planning to reuse an old sensor, recoat the threads. Install the sensor and tighten it securely.

9   Reconnect the electrical connector of the pigtail lead to the main wiring harness.

10   Lower the vehicle (if it was raised), test drive the car and verify that no trouble codes have been set.

12   Knock sensor - replacement

Warning: *Wait for the engine to cool completely before performing this procedure.*

1   The knock control system is designed to reduce spark knock during periods of heavy detonation. This allows the engine to use optimal spark advance to improve driveability. The knock sensor detects abnormal vibration in the engine and produces a voltage output which increases with the severity of the knock. The voltage signal is monitored by the PCM, which retards ignition timing until the detonation ceases. The knock sensor is located on the backside of the engine block on four-cylinder engines or under the intake manifold on 2.7L and 3.0L V6 models. The 2.5L V6 engine

is not equipped with a knock sensor.

2   Make sure the ignition key is in the OFF position.

3   Drain the cooling system (see Chapter 1).

Four-cylinder models

Refer to illustration 12.5

4   Raise the vehicle and secure it on jackstands.

5   Disconnect the electrical connector from the knock sensor **(see illustration)**.

6   Use a special tool such as a crowfoot socket to remove the knock sensor.

V6 models

Refer to illustration 12.9

Note: *The 2.5L V6 engine is not equipped with a knock sensor.*

7   Remove the intake manifold (see Chapter 2B or 2C).

8   On 2.7L V6 engines, remove the cylinder head from the right bank (the side closest to the firewall) (see Chapter 2C).

9   Disconnect the electrical connector and remove the knock sensor **(see illustration)**.

All models

10   If you're going to reuse the old sensor, coat the threads with thread sealant. New sensors are pre-coated with thread sealant, do not apply any additional sealant or the operation of the sensor may be affected.

11   Install the knock sensor and tighten it securely. Don't overtighten the sensor or damage may occur.

12   Plug in the electrical connector, refill the cooling system and check for leaks.

13   Vehicle Speed Sensor (VSS) - replacement

Check

Refer to illustrations 13.1a and 13.1b

1   The Vehicle Speed Sensor (VSS) **(see illustrations)** is located on the transaxle. This sensor is an electronic component that produces a pulsing voltage signal whenever the sensor shaft is rotated. These voltage pulses are monitored by the PCM, which uses this information to help control the fuel and igni-

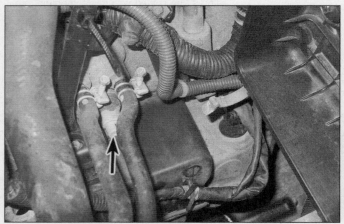

13.1a Location of the vehicle speed sensor (arrow) on the 2.5L V6 model

13.1b Location of the vehicle speed sensor (arrow) on the 2.7L V6 model

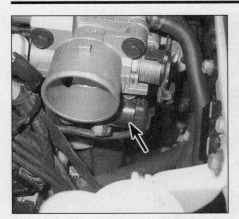

14.1a Location of the IAC valve (arrow) on a 2.5L V6 model

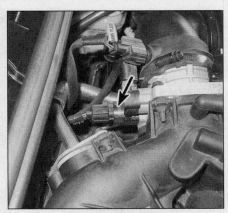

14.1b Location of the IAC valve (arrow) on a 2.7L V6 model

14.4 Remove the Torx drive screws (arrows) and separate the IAC valve from the throttle body - 2.5L V6 model shown

tion systems and transaxle shifting.
2   Make sure the ignition key is in the OFF position.
.3   Disconnect the electrical connector from the VSS.
4   Remove the VSS out of the transaxle.
5   Replace the O-ring, if equipped.
6   Installation is the reverse of removal.

14   Idle Air Control (IAC) valve - replacement

Refer to illustrations 14.1a, 14.1b and 14.4
Note: *The minimum idle speed is pre-set at the factory and should not require adjustment under normal operating conditions. However if the throttle body has been replaced or you suspect the minimum idle speed has been tampered with (for example, if the idle speed screw was removed from the throttle body), have the vehicle checked by a dealer service department or other qualified automotive repair shop.*
1   The engine idle speed is controlled by the Idle Air Control (IAC) valve **(see illustra-**

tions). The IAC valve controls the amount of air that bypasses the throttle plate into the intake manifold. The IAC valve is controlled by the PCM in accordance with the demands on the engine (air conditioning, power steering) and the operating conditions (cold or warmed up).
2   Make sure the ignition key is in the OFF position.
3   Remove the throttle body (see Chapter 4).
4   Remove the mounting screws **(see illustration)** and detach the IAC valve and gasket.
5   Installation is the reverse of removal. Be sure to use a new gasket when installing the IAC valve.

15   Intake manifold tuning system (2.7L V6 models)

General information
Refer to illustration 15.1
1   The 2.7L V6 models are equipped with an intake manifold tuning system **(see illus-**

tration). The intake manifold tuning system consists of a manifold tuning valve located in the upper intake manifold.
2   The manifold tuning valve opens a cross-over passage between the two sides of the upper intake manifold plenum, improving the acoustical tuning qualities of the intake manifold. The PCM energizes the manifold tuning valve solenoid during wide-open throttle operation.
3   A scan tool is required for complete testing of the manifold tuning valve and circuit.

Component replacement
Manifold tuning valve
Refer to illustration 15.6
4   Make sure the ignition key is in the OFF position.
5   Disconnect the electrical connector from the manifold tuning valve.
6   Remove the mounting bolts and withdraw the manual tuning valve from the upper intake manifold **(see illustration)**.
7   Installation is the reverse of removal.

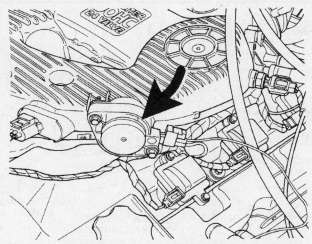

15.1 The intake manifold tuning valve (arrow) is located in the upper intake manifold housing

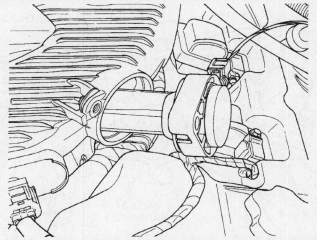

15.6 Remove the intake manifold tuning valve from the upper intake manifold

16.1 Typical PCV valve (arrow) and hose - 2.5L V6 model

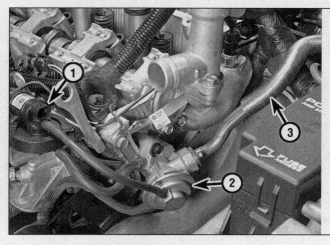

17.2 Typical EGR system and components on a 2.5L V6 model

1   *EGR solenoid/ transducer assembly*
2   *EGR valve*
3   *EGR pipe*

16   Positive Crankcase Ventilation (PCV) system

Refer to illustration 16.1

1   The Positive Crankcase Ventilation (PCV) system **(see illustration)** reduces hydrocarbon emissions by scavenging crankcase vapors. It does this by circulating fresh air from the air cleaner through the crankcase, where it mixes with blow-by gases and is then rerouted through a PCV valve to the intake manifold.

2   The main components of the PCV system are the PCV valve, a blow-by filter and the vacuum hoses connecting these two components with the engine. Refer to Chapter 1 for locations of the PCV valve.

3   To maintain idle quality, the PCV valve restricts the flow when the intake manifold vacuum is high. If abnormal operating conditions (such as piston ring problems) arise, the system is designed to allow excessive amounts of blow-by gases to flow back through the crankcase vent tube into the air cleaner to be consumed by normal combustion.

4   Checking and replacement of the PCV valve is covered in Chapter 1.

17   Exhaust Gas Recirculation (EGR) system

General description

Refer to illustration 17.2

1   The EGR system reduces oxides of nitrogen (NOx) by recirculating exhaust gases from the exhaust ports through the EGR valve and back into the intake manifold for recirculation into the engine which lowers the peak flame temperature during combustion.

2   The EGR system consists of the EGR valve, the EGR solenoid/transducer assembly, the Powertrain Control Module (PCM) and various related sensors **(see illustration)**. The PCM uses the solenoid to control vacuum to the transducer. The transducer is controlled by exhaust system back-pressure which in turn regulates the amount of vacuum applied to the EGR valve. When exhaust system back-pressure becomes high enough, it fully closes a bleed valve in the transducer. Then the PCM de-energizes the solenoid and allows vacuum to flow through the transducer to operate the EGR valve. Turning the solenoid ON-and-OFF provides the correct amount of exhaust gas to

be introduced into the engine for combustion. **Note:** *2.4L SOHC and 3.0L V6 models are equipped with a slightly different type of EGR system. The EGR valve is vacuum controlled using an EGR solenoid which is controlled by the computer. The PCM uses information from the MAF sensor, the ECT sensor and the CKP sensor to determine proper EGR control.*

Replacement

EGR valve

3   Disconnect the cable from the negative battery terminal or the remote ground terminal (see Chapter 5).

2.0L, 2.4L DOHC and 2.5L V6 models

Refer to illustrations 17.4a, 17.4b, 17.8a, 17.8b, 17.8c and 17.9

Note: *Because the EGR valve and solenoid/ transducer is a calibrated unit, it must be replaced as an assembly.*

4   Disconnect the electrical connector and vacuum hoses from the solenoid/transducer assembly **(see illustrations)**.

5   On 2.4L DOHC (2001 and later) engines, remove the air filter housing (see Chapter 4).

6   Remove the mounting bolts and the sole-

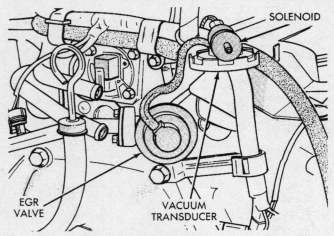

17.4a Location of the EGR valve and the solenoid/transducer assembly on a 2.4L DOHC engine

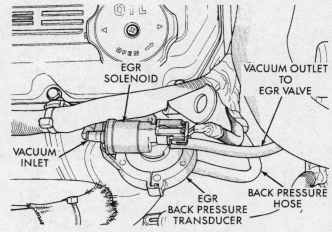

17.4b Location of the EGR valve and the solenoid/transducer assembly on a 2.4L DOHC engine

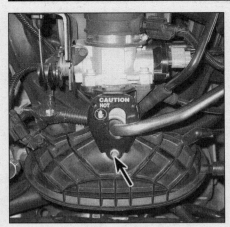

17.8a Remove the mounting bolt (arrow) from the EGR pipe flange and separate the EGR pipe from the intake manifold - 2.4L DOHC 2001 and later shown

17.8b Location of the EGR pipe mounting bolts (arrows) at the intake manifold on a 2.5L V6 model

noid/transducer assembly from its mounting.

7   On 2.5L V6 engines, remove the Transmission Control Module from the bracket and position it out of the way. **Note:** *Do not disconnect the electrical connector from the TCM.*

8   Remove the EGR pipe mounting bolts from the EGR valve and intake manifold **(see illustrations).**

9   Remove the EGR valve mounting bolts **(see illustration)** and then remove the EGR valve and pipe.

10   Clean the gasket surfaces of the EGR valve, the EGR pipe and the intake manifold. If the EGR valve is to be reinstalled, clean the gasket surfaces and, if necessary, remove any carbon build-up that may be present. If carbon build-up is excessive, replace the EGR valve and solenoid/transducer assembly.

11   Loosely assemble the EGR valve and pipe, using new gaskets. Hand tighten all the bolts. Next, tighten the EGR pipe bolts. Finish by tightening the EGR valve bolts.

12   On 2.5L V6 engines, place the TCM in

it's proper position and secure it with the mounting screws.

13   Install the solenoid/transducer and tighten the mounting bolts.

14   Connect the vacuum hoses and electrical connector to the solenoid/transducer assembly.

2.4L SOHC and 3.0L V6 models

15   Remove the air filter housing (see Chapter 4).

16   Remove the intake manifold (see Chapter 2A or 2B).

17   Disconnect the vacuum hose(s) from the EGR valve assembly.

18   Remove the EGR pipe mounting bolts from the EGR valve and the intake manifold.

19   Remove the EGR valve mounting bolts and then remove the EGR valve.

20   Clean the gasket surfaces of the EGR valve, the EGR pipe and the intake manifold. If the EGR valve is to be re-installed, clean the gasket surfaces and, if necessary, remove any carbon build-up that may be present.

If carbon build-up is excessive, replace the EGR valve and solenoid.

21   Installation is the reverse of removal.

2.7L V6 models

Note: *Because the EGR valve and solenoid/ transducer is a calibrated unit, it must be replaced as an assembly.*

22   Remove the air filter housing (see Chapter 4).

23   Remove the accelerator cable and the shield (see Chapter 4).

24   Remove the EGR pipe upper mounting bolts from the EGR valve.

25   Raise the vehicle and support it securely on jackstands.

26   Remove the bolts for the lower section of the EGR pipe.

27   Disconnect the electrical connector and vacuum hoses from the solenoid/transducer assembly.

28   Remove the mounting bolts and the solenoid/transducer assembly.

29   Remove the EGR valve mounting bolts and then remove the EGR valve and the EGR pipe.

30   Clean the gasket surfaces of the EGR valve, the EGR pipe and the intake manifold. If the EGR valve is to be re-installed, clean the gasket surfaces and, if necessary, remove any carbon build-up that may be present. If carbon build-up is excessive, replace the EGR valve and solenoid/transducer assembly.

31   Installation is the reverse of removal. Be sure to use new gaskets

EGR solenoid - 2.4L SOHC and 3.0L V6 models

32   Locate the EGR solenoid on the side of the intake manifold. Unplug the electrical connector from the EGR solenoid.

33   Clearly label and disconnect the vacuum hoses attached to the EGR solenoid.

34   Remove the EGR solenoid from its mounting bracket.

35   Installation is the reverse of removal.

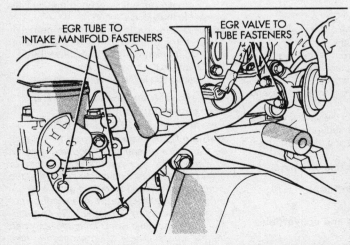

17.8c EGR pipe mounting bolt locations on the 2.4L DOHC engine

EGR TUBE TO INTAKE MANIFOLD FASTENERS

EGR VALVE TO TUBE FASTENERS

17.9 EGR pipe mounting bolt locations at the EGR valve (arrows) on 2.5L V6 models

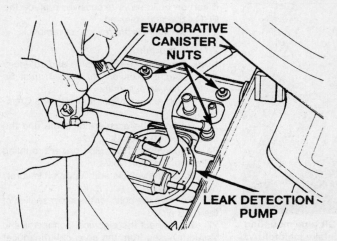

18.17 Remove the three nuts securing the canister to the leak detection pump bracket

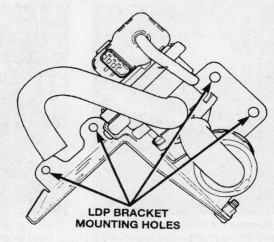

18.20 Location of the leak detection pump mounting bolt holes on convertibles

18 Evaporative emissions control (EVAP) system

General description

1   The function of the evaporative emissions control system is to prevent fuel vapors from escaping the fuel system and being released into the atmosphere. Vapors are trapped inside the fuel tank until the pressure overcomes the pressure-relief/rollover valve and is then routed to a charcoal canister via hoses for temporary storage. The Powertrain Control Module (PCM) monitors the engine operating parameters and then activates the EVAP purge control solenoid according to a programmed schedule which allows the fuel vapors from the canister to be drawn into the intake manifold and burned in the combustion process.

2   The charcoal canister on 1999 and earlier convertibles and 1997 and earlier coupes is mounted to a bracket in the right front corner of the engine compartment near the windshield washer reservoir. On 1998 and later coupes and 2000 and later convertibles and sedans, it's located on top of the fuel tank. The canisters are maintenance-free and should last the life of the vehicle.

3   The most common symptom of a fault in the evaporative emissions system is a strong fuel odor or raw fuel leaking from the canister. These indications are usually more prevalent during hot temperatures. Most models are equipped with a pressurized leak detection pump. The leak detection pump is located next to the charcoal canister. If normal system pressure cannot be achieved by the LDP, which indicates a leak, the PCM will store the appropriate fault code and illuminate the CHECK ENGINE light on the instrument panel. The most common cause of system pressure loss is a loose or poor sealing fuel filler cap. If the CHECK ENGINE light is illuminated, check the fuel filler cap first!

4   The fuel filler cap is equipped with a two-way pressure-vacuum relief valve as a safety device. If the pressure inside the tank exceeds approximately 1.5 to 2 psi, the relief valve vents the fuel vapors to the atmosphere. If the vacuum inside the tank becomes greater than approximately 0.6 in-Hg, the relief valve allows fresh air to be drawn into the tank.

5   All models are equipped with two rollover valves, which are mounted on the top of the fuel tank. The rollover valves are designed to close the fuel vapor vent ports in case the vehicle should flip upside down. The rollover valves are not serviceable.

6   Early models are equipped with a purge control solenoid that operates from a vacuum signal. The early style purge control solenoids operate as an on/off switch. Later models are equipped with a duty cycle purge solenoid. This solenoid regulates fuel vapor flow to the canister at a constant proportion.

Replacement
Charcoal canister
1995 models

7   Remove the fuel filler cap to relieve the pressure inside the fuel tank.

8   Loosen the right front wheel lug nuts. Raise the vehicle and place it securely on jackstands. Remove the wheel.

9   Remove the right front wheel inner and lower splash shields.

10   Label and disconnect the vacuum hoses, remove the nut and bolt securing the canister to the support bracket and then withdraw it from the vehicle.

11   Installation is the reverse of removal.

Charcoal canister and leak detection pump
1996 and 1997 coupes and convertibles through 1999
Refer to illustrations 18.17 and 18.20
Note: *1996 and 1997 coupes are not equipped with a leak detection pump. On*

1996 and 1997 coupes, remove the charcoal canister and the purge control solenoid as a single unit.

12   Remove the fuel filler cap to relieve the pressure inside the fuel tank.

13   On 1996 and 1997 convertibles, remove the right headlight assembly (see Chapter 12).

14   On coupes and 1998 and 1999 convertibles, raise the vehicle and place it securely on jackstands.

15   On coupes and 1998 and 1999 convertibles, remove the right front wheel inner and lower splash shields.

16   Label and disconnect the hoses from the leak detection pump or canister purge solenoid and charcoal canister.

17   On 1996 and 1997 convertibles, remove the nuts securing the canister to the upper brace **(see illustration)**.

18   Disconnect the electrical connector from the leak detection pump or the canister purge solenoid.

19   Remove the bolts securing the canister bracket to the vehicle.

20   Remove the leak detection pump or canister purge solenoid, with the bracket attached, from the vehicle **(see illustration)**.

21   Remove the charcoal canister.

22   Installation is the reverse of removal.

1998 and later coupes and 2000 and later convertibles and sedans
Refer to illustration 18.23a and 18.23b
Warning: *Gasoline is extremely flammable, so take extra precautions when you work on any part of the fuel system. Don't smoke or allow open flames or bare light bulbs near the work area, and don't work in a garage where a gas-type appliance (such as a water heater or a clothes dryer) is present. Since gasoline is carcinogenic, wear latex gloves when there's a possibility of being exposed to fuel, and if you spill any on your skin, rinse it off immediately with soap and water. Mop up any spills immediately and do not store fuel-*

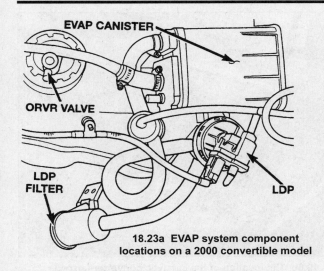

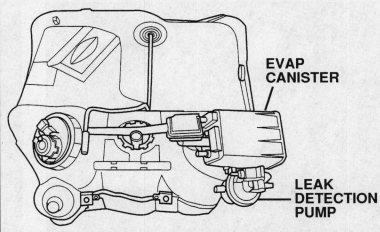

18.23a EVAP system component locations on a 2000 convertible model

18.23b EVAP system component locations on a 2001 convertible model

soaked rags where they could ignite. The fuel system is under constant pressure, so, if any fuel lines are to be disconnected, the pressure must be relieved first. When you perform any kind of work on the fuel system, wear safety glasses and have a Class B type fire extinguisher on hand.

23 The charcoal canister and leak detection pump on these models mount to a bracket located on top of the fuel tank (see illustrations).

24 Remove the fuel filler cap to relieve the pressure inside the fuel tank.

25 Perform the fuel pressure relief procedure (see Chapter 4).

26 Drain and remove the fuel tank (see Chapter 4).

27 Label and disconnect the vapor hoses connected to the canister.

28 Withdraw the push-pin securing the canister to the bracket and remove it from the fuel tank.

29 Remove the bracket and leak detection pump, then remove the leak detection pump from the bracket.

30 Since they are accessible, check the condition of all EVAP system hoses and electrical connections at this time and repair or replace as necessary.

31 Installation is the reverse of removal.

Canister purge control solenoid

Refer to illustrations 18.32a, 18.32b and 18.32c

Note: *The EVAP purge control solenoid must be installed with the solenoid electrical connector UP in order to operate properly.*

32 The purge control solenoid is mounted in various places depending on year and model:

a) *On 1996 and 1997 convertibles, the purge control solenoid is mounted on the left (driver's) side of the engine compartment on the shock tower near the brake master cylinder* (see illustration).

b) *On 1995 through 2000 coupes and 1998 through 2000 convertibles, the purge control solenoid is mounted on the passenger side of the engine compartment on the fender panel near the windshield washer fluid reservoir* (see illustration).

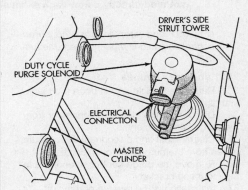

18.32a The purge control solenoid on 1996 and 1997 convertibles is located near the master cylinder

c) *On 2001 and later convertibles and sedans, the purge control solenoid is mounted near the cruise control actuator in the left side of the engine compartment* (see illustration).

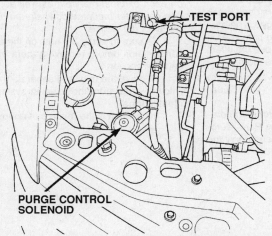

18.32b The purge control solenoid on 1998 convertibles is located near the coolant reservoir

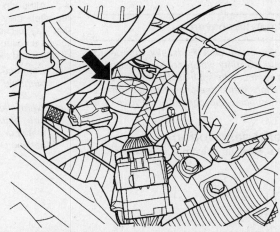

18.32c The purge control solenoid on 2001 convertibles and sedans is located near the cruise control actuator

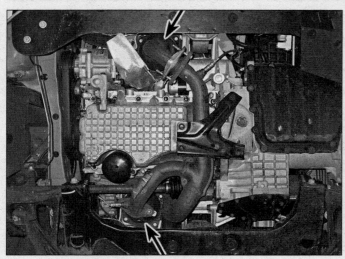

19.6a The catalytic converters (arrows) on the 2.7L V6 models are mounted directly below each exhaust manifold

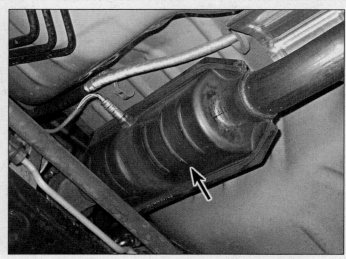

19.6b The location of the catalytic converter (arrow) on 2.5L V6 models

d) *On 2001 and later coupes, the purge control solenoid is mounted near the fuel tank.*

2001 and later coupes

33   Raise the vehicle and support it on jack-stands.
34   Disconnect the electrical connector from the purge control solenoid.
35   Clearly label and disconnect the vacuum hoses from the purge control solenoid.
36   Remove the purge control solenoid from the mounting bracket.
37   Installation is the reverse of removal.

All other models

38   On 2001 and later convertibles and sedans, remove the air filter housing (see Chapter 4).
39   Disconnect the electrical connector from the purge control solenoid.
40   Clearly label and disconnect the vacuum hoses from the purge control solenoid.
41   Remove the purge control solenoid from the mounting bracket.
42   Installation is the reverse of removal.

---

19   Catalytic converter

Note: *Because of a Federally mandated extended warranty which covers emissions-related components such as the catalytic converter, check with a dealer service department before replacing the converter at your own expense.*

General description

1   The catalytic converter is an emission control device added to the exhaust system to reduce pollutants from the exhaust gas stream. There are two types of converters. The conventional oxidation catalyst reduces the levels of hydrocarbon (HC) and carbon monoxide (CO). The three-way catalyst lowers the levels of oxides of nitrogen (NOx) as well as hydrocarbons (HC) and carbon monoxide (CO). These models are equipped only with three-way catalytic converters.

Check

2   The test equipment for a catalytic converter is expensive and highly sophisticated. If you suspect that the converter on your vehicle is malfunctioning, take it to a dealer or authorized emissions inspection facility for diagnosis and repair.
3   Whenever the vehicle is raised for servicing of underbody components, check the converter for leaks, corrosion, dents and other damage. Check the welds/flange bolts that attach the front and rear ends of the converter to the exhaust system. If damage is discovered, the converter should be replaced.
4   Although catalytic converters don't break too often, they can become plugged. The easiest way to check for a restricted converter is to use a vacuum gauge to diagnose the effect of a blocked exhaust on intake vacuum.

a) *Connect a vacuum gauge to an intake manifold vacuum source (see Chapter 2D).*
b) *Warm the engine to operating temperature, place the transaxle in Park (automatic) or Neutral (manual) and apply the parking brake.*
c) *Note and record the vacuum reading at idle.*
d) *Quickly open the throttle to near full throttle and release it shut. Note and record the vacuum reading.*
e) *Perform the test three more times, recording the reading after each test.*
f) *If the reading after the fourth test is more than one in-Hg lower than the reading recorded at idle, the exhaust system may be restricted (the catalytic converter could be plugged or an exhaust pipe or muffler could be restricted).*

Replacement

Refer to illustrations 19.6a and 19.6b
Note 1: *The catalytic converter on 2.7L V6 models is mounted together with the exhaust manifold as a complete unit. Remove the exhaust manifold(s) (see Chapter 2C) and separate the catalytic converter(s) mounting bolts.*
Note 2: *The 3.0L V6 is equipped with a front exhaust pipe/catalytic converter unit mounted on each exhaust manifold as well as a catalytic converter mounted downstream near the center of the vehicle.*
5   Be sure to spray the nuts on the exhaust flange studs before removing them from the catalytic converter.
6   Remove the nuts and separate the catalytic converter from the exhaust system **(see illustrations)**.
7   Installation is the reverse of removal.

Chapter 7 Part A
Manual transaxle

Contents

Specifications

Torque specifications

	Ft-lbs
Centermember support bolts (coupes only)	
1999 and earlier	58
2001 and later	
Front	69
Rear	55
Transaxle-to-engine bolts	
Coupes	
1995 through 2000	70
2001 and later	
2.4L	36
3.0L	54
Sedans	70
Structural collar mounting bolts	See Chapter 2

1   General information

The vehicles covered in this manual are equipped with either a 5-speed manual, or a 4-speed automatic transaxle. Information on the manual transaxles is included in this Part of Chapter 7. Service procedures for the automatic transaxles are contained in Chapter 7, Part B.

The manual transaxle is a compact, two-piece, lightweight aluminum alloy housing containing both the transmission and differential assemblies.

Because of the complexity, unavailability of replacement parts and special tools necessary, internal repair procedures for the manual transaxle are beyond the scope of this manual. The bulk of information in this Chapter is devoted to removal and installation procedures.

2   Shift cables - removal, installation and adjustment

Removal
Coupes
Refer to illustrations 2.5, 2.6, 2.7 and 2.10

1   Disconnect the cable from the negative

2.5 Remove the cotter pins from the selector and shift cables, and slide the cable ends off of the lever pins

battery terminal or the remote ground terminal (see Chapter 5).

2   Working inside the vehicle, unscrew the gearshift knob and remove the boot assembly.

3   Remove the center console (see Chapter 11).

4   For 2002 model sedans go to Step 13.

5   On early model Coupes, remove the cotter pins from the shift and selector cables,

2.6 Pry the cable retaining clips out with a screwdriver

and slide the cables off of the lever ends **(see illustration)**. On 2001 and later model coupes, disconnect the shift cable by carefully spreading the fingers of the wire retainer clip and pivot it upward to free the cable end from the shift lever. Remove the selector cable by removing the cotter pin and an sliding the cable off of the lever.

6   Remove both cable retaining clips and remove the cables from the bracket **(see illustration)**.

2.7 Remove the forward retainer bolts, detach the retainer from the firewall and pull the cable grommet through the firewall

2.10 Remove the cotter pins and the retainer clips

7   At the firewall remove the forward retainer bolts **(see illustration)**.

8   Remove the air filter housing assembly (see Chapter 4).

9   If necessary remove the battery and battery tray (see Chapter 5).

10   At the transaxle, remove the cotter pins from the select and shift cables, and remove the cable retaining clips **(see illustration)**.

11   Pry the cable grommet out of the firewall and pull the cables through the firewall from the engine compartment side and remove the cable assembly from the vehicle.

2002 model sedans

Refer to illustration 2.12 and 2.15

12   Use a two flat blade screwdrivers and carefully pry the shifter and selector cables from the shifter levers at the transaxle side **(see illustration)**.

13   Remove both cable retaining clips and remove the cables from the bracket.

14   Remove the cable retaining clips at the shifter and detach the cables from the bracket.

15   Using a flat blade screwdriver, carefully pry the selector cable and the shift cable from the shift lever assembly **(see illustration)**.

16   Raise the vehicle and place it securely on jackstands.

17   Working under the vehicle, remove the cable grommet from the floor pan and pull the cable assembly out from under vehicle.

Installation and adjustment

Refer to illustration 2.30

18   Installation is the reverse of removal.

19   Install new cable retaining clips and make sure they are properly seated in the cable grooves.

2000 and earlier Coupe models

20   Place the transaxle levers in the neutral position (if they're not already there). Also place the shift lever in the passenger compartment in the neutral position.

21   Connect the select cable to the select lever in the passenger compartment so the flange side of the bushing is downward on the select lever.

22   When connecting the shift cable to the shift lever in the passenger compartment, make sure the slit in the bushing is straight up or straight down.

23   Shift the transaxle into all gear positions to make sure the cable is functioning properly. No adjustment is necessary.

2001 and later Coupe models

24   Measure the gap between the fingers on the wire retainer shift cable retainer clip. If it's more than 3/8-inch, squeeze the ends together until the gap narrows to 3/16 to 5/16 inch.

25   Connect the select cable to the select lever in the passenger compartment so the flange side of the bushing is downward on the select lever.

26   Place the transaxle shift lever in the neutral. Also place the shift lever in the passenger compartment in the neutral position.

27   The paint marks on the cables (white and yellow) at the transaxle should face the cotter pins.

28   Shift the transaxle into all gear positions to make sure the cable is functioning properly. No adjustment is necessary.

2002 model sedans

29   Place the gear shift lever in the neutral position (allow the shifter to self-center in its proper location).

30   Without moving the gear shift lever from its neutral position, tighten the crossover cable adjusting screw **(see illustration)**.

31   Shift the transaxle into all gear positions to make sure the cable is functioning properly. Readjust if necessary.

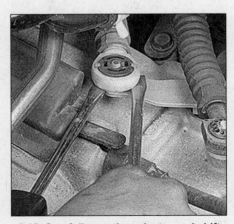

2.12 Carefully pry the selector and shift cables off of the levers

2.15 Use a flat blade screwdriver to carefully pry the selector cable and the shifter cable from the shifter

2.30 Tighten the crossover cable adjusting nut

4.1 The back-up light switch is located on top of the transaxle

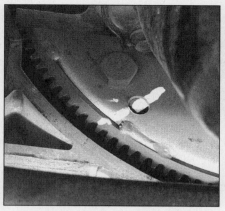

5.19a Match-mark the modular clutch assembly to the driveplate

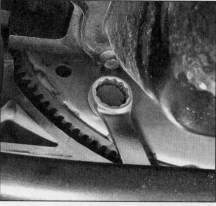

5.19b Rotate the engine to gain access to the clutch bolts and remove the bolts

3 Shift lever - removal and installation

1 Disconnect the cable from the negative battery terminal or the remote ground terminal (see Chapter 5).
2 Remove the center console assembly (see Chapter 11).
3 Disconnect the select and shift cables.
4 Unbolt the shift lever bracket bolts and remove the shift lever.
5 Installation is the reverse of removal.

4 Back-up light switch - replacement

Refer to illustration 4.1

1 The back-up light switch is located on top of the transaxle **(see illustration)**.

Replacement

2 Disconnect the electrical connector from the back-up light switch.
3 Unscrew the switch from the case.
4 Wrap the threads of the new switch with Teflon tape, or equivalent.
4 Screw in the new switch and tighten it securely.
5 Connect the electrical connector.
6 Check the operation of the back-up lights.

5 Manual transaxle - removal and installation

Removal

Coupes

Refer to illustrations 5.19a and 5.19b

1 Open the hood and place protective covers on the front fenders and cowl. Special fender covers are available, but an old bedspread or blankets will also work.
2 Disconnect both the negative and positive battery cable (negative cable first) and remove the battery (see Chapter 5).
3 If necessary, remove the air cleaner

assembly (see Chapter 4).
4 Disconnect the shift cables from the transaxle (see Section 2).
5 Disconnect the shifter cables from the transaxle (see Section 2).
6 Disconnect the harness connectors from the vehicle speed sensor and back-up light switch.
7 Remove the starter (see Chapter 5).
8 Remove the clutch release cylinder (see Chapter 8).
9 Remove the left side transaxle mounting bracket.
10 Remove the transaxle-to-engine upper bolts.
11 Loosen the driveaxle hub nuts (see Chapter 8) and front wheel lug nuts. Raise the vehicle and place it securely on jackstands. Remove both front wheels.
12 On the center member assembly, remove the rear roll stopper bracket mounting bolts.
13 Support the engine from above with a hoist, or place a floor jack under the oil pan. Place a wood block on the jack head to spread the load on the oil pan.
14 Drain the transaxle fluid (see Chapter 1).
15 Remove the driveaxles (see Chapter 8).
16 If equipped, remove the two supports at the transaxle lower inspection cover.
17 Remove the lower inspection cover.
18 On 2001 and later models, the transaxle uses a conventional type clutch. Remove the service hole plug on the bottom of the transaxle and insert a flat-tipped screwdriver between the release bearing and the wedge collar on the clutch fingers. Twist the screwdriver 90 degrees while pushing the clutch release lever in the direction away from the engine block.
19 All other models with a modular type clutch, if the modular clutch assembly is to be reinstalled, match-mark the clutch assembly to the driveplate **(see illustration)**. Remove the four modular clutch assembly-to-driveplate bolts **(see illustration)**. To gain access to each bolt, rotate the engine from the drivebelt end of the engine using the crankshaft damper/pulley bolt. Remove all four bolts and discard them. Use a screwdriver placed in the ring gear of the driveplate to keep the crank-

shaft from turning during removal of the bolts.
20 After removing the clutch module mounting bolts, push the modular clutch assembly into the transaxle clutch housing as far as possible.
21 Remove any exhaust components which will interfere with transaxle removal (see Chapter 4).
22 Remove the front roll stopper through bolt and remove the four bolts on the center member assembly.
23 Remove the center member assembly.
24 Support the transaxle with a transmission jack, if available, or use a floor jack. Secure the transaxle to the jack using straps or chains so it doesn't fall off during removal.
25 Make a final check that all wires, hoses and brackets have been disconnected from the transaxle, then with the engine properly supported, remove upper transaxle mount, and lower the engine transaxle assembly.
26 Remove the lower transaxle clutch housing-to-engine bolts. Make sure all clutch housing-to-engine bolts are removed.
27 Carefully lower the transaxle and remove it from under the vehicle. Make sure you keep the transaxle level as you maneuver it or the modular clutch assembly may fall out. **Note 1:** *If necessary have someone help with the removal procedure.* **Note 2:** *Reinstalling the clutch housing lower cover after the transaxle clears the flywheel will help hold the clutch assembly in place.*

Sedans

Refer to illustration 5.45

Note: *There are different gear ratios available with this transaxle. If you are going to replace this transaxle or obtain a rebuilt unit, check the metal identification tag mounted to the rear cover before purchasing a new or rebuilt transaxle to ensure you're getting the correct gear ratio for your particular application.*

28 Open the hood and place protective covers on the front fenders and cowl. Special fender covers are available, but an old bedspread or blankets will also work.
29 Disconnect the cable from the negative battery terminal or the remote ground terminal (see Chapter 5).

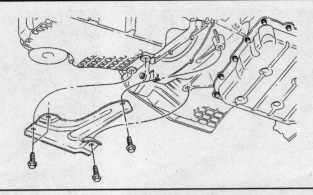

5.45 Remove the bolts that secure the structural collar

30   Remove the air cleaner assembly (see Chapter 4).
31   Disconnect the shifter cables from the transaxle (see Section 2).
32   On 2.7L models, remove the throttle body support bracket.
33   On 2.7L models, remove the connector for the crankshaft position sensor and remove sensor from transaxle case.
34   On Sedans equipped with a clutch cable remove the cable from the release lever (see Chapter 8).
35   On 2.7L models remove the starter heat shield.
36   Remove the upper clutch housing bolts.
37   Remove the rear mount bracket-to-transaxle mount and through bolt (see Chapter 2).
38   Remove the three rear mount-to-crossmember bolts (see Chapter 2).
39   Remove the front mount through bolt and bracket (see Chapter 2).
40   Loosen the driveaxle hub nuts (see Chapter 8) and front wheel lug nuts. Raise the vehicle and place it securely on jackstands. Remove both front wheels.
41   Drain the transaxle fluid (see Chapter 1).
42   Remove the driveaxles (see Chapter 8).
43   Remove the starter motor (see Chapter 5).
44   Remove the splash shield from the left front wheel well (see Chapter 11). Extract the push-in fasteners and remove the transaxle splash shield.
45   Remove the oil pan-to-transaxle structural collar and transaxle clutch housing lower cover **(see illustration)**.
46   Remove the transaxle clutch housing lower cover.
47   On 2.7L models disconnect the clutch hydraulic line and remove the clutch release cylinder (see Chapter 8).
48   If the modular clutch assembly is to be reinstalled, match-mark the clutch assembly to the driveplate **(see illustration 5.19a)**.
49   Remove the four modular clutch assembly-to-driveplate bolts **(see illustration 5.19b)**. To gain access to each bolt, rotate the engine from the drivebelt end of the engine using the crankshaft damper/pulley bolt. Remove all four bolts and discard them. Use a screwdriver placed in the ring gear of the driveplate to keep the crankshaft from turning during removal of the bolts.
50   After removing the clutch module mounting bolts, push the modular clutch assembly

into the transaxle clutch housing as far as possible.
51   Support the transaxle with a transmission jack, if available, or use a floor jack. Secure the transaxle to the jack using straps or chains so it doesn't fall off during removal.
52   Support the engine from above with a hoist, or place a floor jack under the oil pan. Place a wood block on the jack head to spread the load on the oil pan.
53   Make a final check that all wires, hoses and brackets have been disconnected from the transaxle, then with the engine properly supported, remove upper transaxle mount, and lower the engine transaxle assembly.
54   Remove the lower transaxle clutch housing-to-engine bolts. Make sure all transaxle-to-engine bolts are removed.
Remove the left transaxle mount.
55   Carefully lower the transaxle and remove it from under the vehicle. Make sure you keep the transaxle level as you maneuver it or the modular clutch assembly may fall out. **Note 1:** *If necessary have someone help with the removal procedure.* **Note 2:** *Reinstalling the clutch housing lower cover after the transaxle clears the flywheel will help hold the clutch assembly in place.*

Installation
Coupes
56   Installation of the transaxle is the reverse of the removal procedure, but note the following points:
a) *Check the mounts and replace them if necessary.*
b) *Tighten all fastners securely, or to the specified tourque where given.*
c) *The front roll stopper should be temporaraly tightened during installation, and then fully tightened after the vehicle is on the ground and with the full weight of the engine on the body.*
d) *Replace modular clutch bolts with new ones (see Chapter 8).*
e) *Refill the transaxle to the specified level (see Chapter 1).*
f) *On completion, refer to Section 2 and check the shift linkage adjustment.*

Sedans
57   Installation of the transaxle is the reverse of the removal procedure, but note the following points:

a) *Check the mounts and replace them if necessary.*
b) *Tighten all fastners securely, or to the specified tourque where given.*
c) *Replace modular clutch bolts with new ones (see Chapter 8).*
d) *Refill the transaxle to the specified level (see Chapter 1).*
e) *On completion, refer to Section 2 and check the shift linkage adjustment.*

6   Manual transaxle overhaul - general information

1   Overhauling a manual transaxle unit is a difficult and involved job for the home mechanic. In addition to dismantling and reassembling many small parts, clearances must be precisely measured and, if necessary, changed by selecting shims and spacers. Internal transaxle components are also often difficult to obtain and in many instances, extremely expensive. Because of this, if the transaxle develops a fault or becomes noisy, the best course of action is to have the unit overhauled by a transmission specialist or to obtain an exchange reconditioned unit.
2   Nevertheless, it is not impossible for the more experienced mechanic to overhaul the transaxle if the special tools are available and the job is carried out in a deliberate step-by-step manner, to ensure that nothing is overlooked.
3   The tools necessary for an overhaul include internal and external snap-ring pliers, bearing pullers, a slide hammer, a set of pin punches, a dial test indicator and possibly a hydraulic press. In addition, a large, sturdy workbench and a vise will be required.
4   During dismantling of the transaxle, make careful notes of how each component is fitted to make reassembly easier and accurate.
5   Before disassembling the transaxle, it will help if you have some idea of where the problem lies. Certain problems can be closely related to specific areas in the transaxle which can make component examination and replacement easier. Refer to the *Troubleshooting* Section in this manual for more information.

7   Transaxle mounts - check and replacement

1   Insert a large screwdriver or prybar between the mount and the transaxle and pry up.
2   The transaxle should not move excessively away from the mount. If it does, replace the mount.
3   To replace a mount, support the transaxle with a jack, remove the nuts and bolts and remove the mount. It may be necessary to raise the transaxle slightly to provide enough clearance to remove the mount.
4   Installation is the reverse of removal.

Chapter 7 Part B
Automatic transaxle

Contents

Specifications

Torque specifications

	Ft-lbs
Structural collar mounting bolts	See Chapter 2
Torque converter-to-driveplate bolts	
Coupes	
2000 and earlier	55
2001 and later	37
Sedans and Convertibles	55
Transaxle-to-engine bolts	
Coupes	
2000 and earlier	70
2001 and later	
2.4L	36
3.0L	65
Sedans and Convertibles	70

1 General information

All information on the automatic transaxle is included in this Part of Chapter 7. Information for the manual transaxle can be found in Part A of this Chapter.

The automatic transaxle and the differential are housed in a compact, lightweight, two-piece aluminum alloy housing. Operation of the transaxle is controlled electronically by the Transmission Control Module (TCM) which is the "brain" of the transaxle. The TCM monitors engine and transaxle operating parameters through numerous sensors and then generates output signals to various relays and solenoids to regulate hydraulic pressures, optimize driveability, provide efficient torque management and maintain maximum fuel economy. The TCM is part of the On-Board Diagnostic system OBD-II. For more information see Chapter 6. **Note:** *If the power*

has been interrupted (battery disconnected or has failed) the transaxle will shift roughly for the first few gear progressions while the TCM relearns the engine and transaxle parameters.

Because of the complexity of the automatic transaxles and the specialized equipment necessary to perform most service operations, this Chapter contains only those procedures related to general diagnosis, routine maintenance, adjustment and removal and installation.

If the transaxle requires major repair work, it should be left to a dealer service department or an automotive or transmission repair shop. Once properly diagnosed you can, however, remove and install the transaxle yourself and save the expense, even if the repair work is done by a transmission shop.

2 Diagnosis - general

1 Automatic transaxle malfunctions may be caused by five general conditions:

a) *Poor engine performance*
b) *Improper adjustments*
c) *Hydraulic malfunctions*
d) *Mechanical malfunctions*
e) *Malfunctions in the computer or its signal network*

2 Diagnosis of these problems should always begin with a check of the easily repaired items: fluid level and condition (see Chapter 1), shift cable adjustment and shift lever installation. Next, perform a road test to determine if the problem has been corrected or if more diagnosis is necessary. If the problem persists after the preliminary tests and corrections are completed, additional diagnosis should be performed by a dealer service department or other qualified transmission

repair shop. Refer to the *Troubleshooting* section at the front of this manual for information on symptoms of transaxle problems.

Preliminary checks

3   Drive the vehicle to warm the transaxle to normal operating temperature.

4   Check the fluid level as described in Chapter 1:

a) *If the fluid level is unusually low, add enough fluid to bring the level within the designated area of the dipstick, then check for external leaks (see following).*

b) *If the fluid level is abnormally high, drain off the excess, then check the drained fluid for contamination by coolant. The presence of engine coolant in the automatic transmission fluid indicates that a failure has occurred in the internal radiator oil cooler walls that separate the coolant from the transmission fluid (see Chapter 3).*

c) *If the fluid is foaming, drain it and refill the transaxle, then check for coolant in the fluid, or a high fluid level.*

5   Check the engine idle speed. **Note:** *If the engine is malfunctioning, do not proceed with the preliminary checks until it has been repaired and runs normally.*

6   Check and adjust the shift cable, if necessary (see Section 4).

7   If hard shifting is experienced, inspect the shift cable under the center console and at the manual lever on the transaxle (see Section 4).

Fluid leak diagnosis

8   Most fluid leaks are easy to locate visually. Repair usually consists of replacing a seal or gasket. If a leak is difficult to find, the following procedure may help.

9   Identify the fluid. Make sure it's transmission fluid and not engine oil or brake fluid (automatic transmission fluid is a deep red color).

10   Try to pinpoint the source of the leak. Drive the vehicle several miles, then park it over a large sheet of cardboard. After a minute or two, you should be able to locate the leak by determining the source of the fluid dripping onto the cardboard.

11   Make a careful visual inspection of the suspected component and the area immediately around it. Pay particular attention to gasket mating surfaces. A mirror is often helpful for finding leaks in areas that are hard to see.

12   If the leak still cannot be found, clean the suspected area thoroughly with a degreaser or solvent, then dry it thoroughly.

13   Drive the vehicle for several miles at normal operating temperature and varying speeds. After driving the vehicle, visually inspect the suspected component again.

14   Once the leak has been located, the cause must be determined before it can be properly repaired. If a gasket is replaced but the sealing flange is bent, the new gasket will not stop the leak. The bent flange must be straightened.

3.3 Using a large screwdriver or prybar, carefully pry the oil seal out of the transaxle (you may need to obtain a special seal removal tool - available at most auto parts stores - to do the job)

15   Before attempting to repair a leak, check to make sure that the following conditions are corrected or they may cause another leak. **Note:** *Some of the following conditions cannot be fixed without highly specialized tools and expertise. Such problems must be referred to a qualified transmission shop or a dealer service department.*

Gasket leaks

16   Check the pan periodically. Make sure the bolts are tight, no bolts are missing, the gasket is in good condition and the pan is flat (dents in the pan may indicate damage to the valve body inside).

17   If the pan gasket is leaking, the fluid level or the fluid pressure may be too high, the vent may be plugged, the pan bolts may be too tight, the pan sealing flange may be warped, the sealing surface of the transaxle housing may be damaged, the gasket may be damaged or the transaxle casting may be cracked or porous. If sealant instead of gasket material has been used to form a seal between the pan and the transaxle housing, it may be the wrong type of sealant.

Seal leaks

18   If a transaxle seal is leaking, the fluid level or pressure may be too high, the vent may be plugged, the seal bore may be damaged, the seal itself may be damaged or improperly installed, the surface of the shaft protruding through the seal may be damaged or a loose bearing may be causing excessive shaft movement.

19   Make sure the dipstick tube seal is in good condition and the tube is properly seated. Periodically check the area around the sensors for leakage. If transmission fluid is evident, check the seals for damage.

Case leaks

20   If the case itself appears to be leaking, the casting is porous and will have to be repaired or replaced.

21   Make sure the oil cooler hose fittings are tight and in good condition.

3.5 Using a seal installer, drive the new seal squarely into the bore and make sure that it's completely seated

Fluid comes out vent pipe or fill tube

22   If this condition occurs the possible causes are, the transaxle is overfilled, there is coolant in the fluid, the case is porous, the dipstick is incorrect, the vent is plugged or the drain-back holes are plugged.

---

3   Driveaxle oil seals - replacement

Refer to illustration 3.3 and 3.5

1   The driveaxle oil seals are located on the sides of the transaxle, where the inner ends of the driveaxles are splined into the differential side gears. If you suspect that a driveaxle oil seal is leaking, raise the vehicle and support it securely on jackstands. If the seal is leaking, you'll see lubricant on the side of the transaxle, below the seal.

2   Remove the driveaxle (see Chapter 8).

3   Using a screwdriver or prybar, carefully pry the oil seal out of the transaxle bore **(see illustration)**. **Note:** *Driveaxle oil seals on the right side of the transaxle may require a slide hammer equipped with a hook-type tool for removal.*

4   If the oil seal cannot be removed with a screwdriver or prybar, a special oil seal removal tool (available at auto parts stores) will be required.

5   Using a seal installer, install the new oil seal. Drive it into the bore squarely until it bottoms **(see illustration)**.

6   Install the driveaxle (see Chapter 8).

---

4   Shift cable - removal, installation and adjustment

Note: *If the power has been interrupted (battery disconnected or has failed) the transaxle will shift roughly for the first few gear progressions while the TCM relearns the engine and transaxle parameters.*

1   Raise the hood and place a blanket over the left (driver's) fender to protect it.

2   Disconnect the cable from the negative

4.9 Remove the cotter pin and pull the cable off of the pin

4.10 Use pliers to remove the shift cable retaining clip

battery terminal or the remote ground terminal (see Chapter 5).

3   Remove the air cleaner assembly (see Chapter 4).

Removal

Note: *If the power has been interrupted (battery disconnected or has failed) the transaxle will shift roughly for the first few gear progressions while the TCM relearns the engine and transaxle parameters.*

Coupes
Refer to illustrations 4.9 and 4.10

4   On 1997 through 2000 models, remove the Transmission Control Module (see Section 6).

5   On 2001 and later models remove the battery and battery tray (see Chapter 5).

6   On 2000 and earlier models, remove the nut securing the shift cable to the shift lever at the transaxle, and on 2001 and later models, remove the cotter pin that attaches the shift cable to the shift lever.

7   Using a pair of pliers, remove the shift cable retaining clip.

8   Working inside the vehicle, remove the center console (see Chapter 11).

9   On 2000 and earlier models, remove the cotter pin that attaches the shift cable to the shifter lever **(see Illustration)** and on 2001 and later models, use a flat blade screwdriver to carefully pry the shift cable from the gearshift lever pin.

10   Using pliers, remove the shift cable retaining clip **(see illustration)** and remove the cable from the bracket.

11   If necessary remove the knee bolster (see Chapter 11).

12   Remove the fasteners that attach the cable grommet at the firewall.

13   Remove the shift cable assembly from the vehicle.

Sedans and Convertibles
Refer to illustration 4.16

14   On 2000 and earlier models, remove the

Transmission Control Module (see Section 6), and remove the Power Distribution Center from its mounting and position it out of the way.

15   Using two flat blade screwdrivers, carefully pry the shift cable from the manual lever on the transaxle. To avoid damaging the cable isolator bushing, pry up with equal force on both sides of the shift cable end.

16   Remove the bolt securing the shift cable bracket to the transaxle and detach the cable from the transaxle **(see illustration)**.

17   Working inside the vehicle, remove the center console (see Chapter 11).

18   Using a flat blade screwdriver, carefully pry the shift cable from the gearshift lever pin.

19   Using pliers, remove the shift cable retaining clip and remove the cable from the bracket.

20   Raise the vehicle and support it securely on jackstands.

21   'Working under the vehicle, remove the shift cable grommet from the floorpan.

22   Carefully remove the shift cable through the floorpan opening, unfold the cable retaining clips as you go along.

23   Remove the shift cable assembly from the vehicle.

Installation and adjustment

Coupes
24   Installation is the reverse of removal.

25   Place the shift lever and neutral start switch in the Neutral position inside the vehicle attach the new shift cable to the shifter.

26   Working at the transaxle, with the adjusting nut loosened pull forward lightly on the end of the cable until the cable is taught and fasten the nut securely.

27   Verify that the shifter operates correctly and the transaxle end of the cable functions in the range which corresponds to each position of the shift lever.

Sedans and Convertibles
Refer to illustration 4.30

28   Installation is the reverse of removal.

29   Place the gearshift lever in the PARK position.

30   Loosen the gearshift cable adjusting nut at the gearshift lever **(see illustration)**.

31   Working in the engine compartment, place the manual shift lever at the transaxle in the PARK position. The PARK sprag must be engaged when adjusting the cable. Rock the vehicle back and forth to ensure PARK sprag

4.16 Remove the bolt securing the shift cable

4.30 Shift cable adjusting nut

6.3 Remove the electrical connector

7.19 Removing a lateral strut bracket

engagement. The vehicle should not be able to move.

32   Tighten the shift cable adjusting nut securely.

33   Check the shift lever for proper operation. It should operate smoothly without binding

5   Park/Neutral Position (PNP) switch - replacement and adjustment

Removal

1   Disconnect the shift cable from the shift lever (see Section 4).

2   Remove the shift lever, the switch mounting bolts and remove the switch.

3   Installation is the reverse of removal. Be sure to adjust the switch when you're done (see below).

Adjustment

4   Place the shift lever in the Neutral position.

5   Loosen the adjusting nut on the shift cable.

6   Make sure the shift lever on the transaxle is in the Neutral position.

7   Loosen the switch mounting bolts.

8   Align the hole in the end of the manual control lever with the hole in the switch body, then tighten the switch body mounting bolts securely.

9   Adjust the shift cable (see Section 4, Step 25).

6   Transmission Control Module (TCM) - removal and installation

Note: *Do not interchange TCM's from different year vehicles. After replacing a TCM take the vehicle to your local dealer service department or other qualified transmission shop to have the TCM calibrated for your vehicle.*
Caution: *The TCM is an Electro-Static Dis-*

charge (ESD) sensitive electronic device, meaning a static electricity discharge from your body could possibly damage electrical components. Make sure to properly ground yourself and the TCM before handling it. Avoid touching the electrical terminals of the TCM unless absolutely necessary.

Removal

Refer to illustration 6.3

1   Disconnect the cable from the negative battery terminal or the remote ground terminal (see Chapter 5).

2   Remove the air cleaner assembly (see Chapter 4).

3   Detach the electrical connector from the TCM **(see illustration)**.

4   Remove the mounting screws and withdraw the TCM from the vehicle.

Installation

5   Installation is the reverse of removal.

7   Automatic transaxle - removal and installation

Removal

Refer to illustrations 7.19 and 7.22

1   Disconnect the cable from the negative battery terminal or the remote ground terminal (see Chapter 5).

2   Remove the air cleaner and air intake duct assembly (see Chapter 4).

3   Remove the transmission Control Module if equipped (see Section 6).

4   Clearly label, then unplug, all electrical connectors.

5   Disconnect the shift cable from the manual lever (see Section 5).

6   Remove the transaxle dipstick tube.

7   Loosen the hose clamps and disconnect the oil cooler hoses. Plug the hoses to prevent contamination and leaks.

8   Remove the starter motor (see Chapter 5).

9   Remove the upper transaxle-to-engine bolts.

10   Remove the left upper transaxle mounting bracket top bolts.

11   Loosen the wheel lug nuts, raise the vehicle and support it securely on jackstands. Remove the wheels.

12   Remove any exhaust components which will interfere with transaxle removal (see Chapter 4).

13   Drain the transaxle fluid (see Chapter 1).

14   Remove both driveaxle assemblies (see Chapter 8).

15   Support the engine from above with a hoist or place a jack and a block of wood under the oil pan to spread the load.

16   Support the transaxle with a transmission jack (a special jack made for this purpose), if available, or with a floor jack. Safety chains will help steady the transaxle on the jack.

17   Remove the remaining left upper transaxle mount bolts.

18   Remove the front motor mount bracket (see Chapter 2).

19   Remove the center member bolts and the front and back lateral bending strut brackets **(see illustration).**

20   Remove any remaining chassis or suspension components which will interfere with transaxle removal.

21   Remove the torque converter cover.

22   Mark the relationship of the torque converter to the driveplate so they can be installed in the same position **(see illustration)**.

23   Remove all three torque converter-to-driveplate bolts. Turn the crankshaft 120-degrees at a time for access to each bolt. After all three bolts are removed, push the torque converter into the bellhousing so it doesn't stay with the engine when the transaxle is removed.

24   If equipped, remove the oil pan collar bracket.

25   On 2000 and earlier Convertible and Sedan models, remove the sway bar mounts (see Chapter 10) and loosen the right side steering gear and suspension crossmember bolts, then remove the left side bolts of the

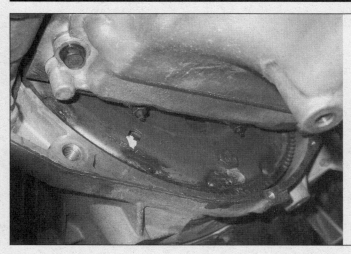

7.22 Before removing the driveplate-to-torque converter bolts, find a hole in the drive plate and match-mark the driveplate to the torque converter

steering gear and suspension crossmember bolts. Move crossmember reward during the transaxle lowering process.

26   Remove the lower engine-to-transaxle bolts.

27   Make sure the torque converter is detached from the driveplate. Secure the torque converter to the transaxle so that it will not fall out during removal. Lower the transaxle from the vehicle.

Installation

Note: *If the power has been interrupted (battery disconnected or has failed) the transaxle will shift roughly for the first few gear progressions while the TCM relearns the engine and transaxle parameters.*

28   Install the fluid filler tube, if it was removed. Make sure the torque converter hub is securely engaged in the pump prior to installation. This can be confirmed by pushing on the torque converter and turning it (if it isn't seated completely, it will drop into place as this is done, evidenced by one or more "clunks").

29   With the transaxle secured to the jack, raise it into position. Be sure to keep it level so the torque converter does not slide forward.

30   Move the transaxle carefully into place until the dowel pins are engaged and the torque converter is engaged.

31   Turn the torque converter to line up the bolt holes with the holes in the driveplate. The match marks on the torque converter and driveplate, made during step 16, must line up.

32   Install the lower engine-to-transaxle bolt and the transaxle-to-engine bolts and tighten them to the torque listed in this Chapter's Specifications.

33   Install the torque converter-to-driveplate bolts and tighten them to the torque listed in this Chapter's Specifications. **Note:** *Install all of the bolts before tightening any of them.*

34   Install all suspension components that were removed. Tighten all suspension fasteners to the torque listed in the Chapter 10 Specifications.

35   Remove the jacks supporting the transaxle and the engine. Install any exhaust system components that were removed (see Chapter 4).

36   Install the wheels, remove the jack stands and lower the vehicle.

37   Install the upper transaxle-to-engine bolts and tighten them to the torque listed in this Chapter's Specifications.

38   Install the transaxle mounting bracket and tighten the bolts securely.

39   Install the starter motor (see Chapter 5).

40   Unplug the oil cooler hoses and reattach them to the transaxle.

41   Reconnect the shift cable to the manual lever (see Section 5).

42   Plug in all electrical connectors.

43   The rest of installation is the reverse of removal.

44   Fill the transaxle (see Chapter 1). Run the vehicle and check for fluid leaks.

---

8   Automatic transaxle overhaul - general information

In the event of a problem occurring, it will be necessary to establish whether the fault is electrical, mechanical or hydraulic in nature, before repair work can be contemplated. Diagnosis requires detailed knowledge of the transaxle's operation and construction, as well as access to specialized test equipment, and so is deemed to be beyond the scope of this manual. It is therefore essential that problems with the automatic transaxle are referred to a dealer service department or other qualified repair facility for assessment.

Note that a faulty transaxle should not be removed before the vehicle has been diagnosed by a knowledgeable technician equipped with the proper tools, as troubleshooting must be performed with the transaxle installed in the vehicle.

Notes

Chapter 8
Clutch and driveaxles

Contents

Specifications

Torque specifications

	Ft-lbs
Center bearing bracket bolts	30
Clutch cover to driveplate bolts	
Coupes	
1999 and earlier	55
2001 and later	14
Sedans	65
Driveaxle/hub nut	
Coupes	167
Convertibles and sedans	110
Driveplate	See Chapter 2

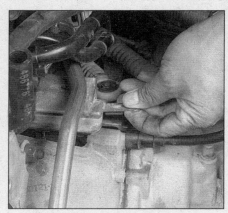

3.3 Remove the clutch cable inspection cover

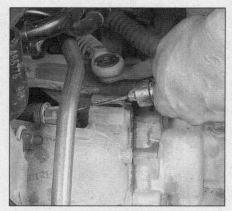

3.4 Grab onto the clutch cable housing, pull it back and pass the clutch cable through the slot in the bellhousing, then disconnect it from the release lever

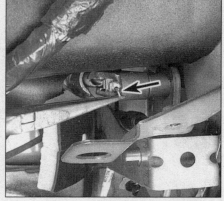

3.6a Working inside the vehicle slightly depress the clutch pedal for access to the clutch cable, then remove the clip (arrow) securing the up-stop/spacer to the clutch pedal pivot pin . . .

1   General Information

The information in this Chapter deals with the components from the rear of the engine to the front wheels, except for the transaxle, which is covered with in Chapter 7. For the purposes of this Chapter, these components are grouped into two categories: Clutch and driveaxles. Separate Sections within this Chapter offer general descriptions and checking procedures for both groups.

Most models covered by this manual are equipped with a single-unit modular clutch that is serviced as a complete assembly. The 2001 and later Sebring coupe and Stratus coupe models are equipped with a conventional-type clutch.

Since nearly all the procedures covered in this Chapter involve working under the vehicle, make sure it's securely supported on sturdy jackstands or a hoist where the vehicle can be easily raised and lowered.

2   Clutch - description and check

1   All vehicles with a manual transaxle use a single dry plate, diaphragm spring type clutch. The clutch disc has a splined hub which allows it to slide along the splines of the transaxle input shaft. The clutch and pressure plate are held in contact by spring pressure exerted by the diaphragm in the pressure plate. Most of the vehicles are equipped with a modular clutch assembly that includes a clutch assembly where the clutch pressure plate and friction disc are an integral unit. While 2001 and later Coupe models, have a conventional clutch assembly.

2   The clutch release system is operated by hydraulic pressure on most models; a mechanical system is used on other models. The hydraulic release system consists of the clutch pedal, a master cylinder, the hydraulic line, a slave cylinder which actuates the clutch release lever and the clutch release (or throw-out) bearing. The mechanical release system includes the clutch pedal with a self-adjuster

mechanism on the cable, a clutch cable that actuates the clutch release lever and the release (or throw-out) bearing.

3   When pressure is applied to the clutch pedal to release the clutch, hydraulic or mechanical pressure is exerted against the outer end of the clutch release lever. As the lever pivots, the shaft fingers push against the release bearing. The bearing pushes against the fingers of the diaphragm spring of the pressure plate assembly, which in turn releases the clutch plate.

4   Other than to replace components with obvious damage, some preliminary checks should be performed to diagnose a clutch system failure.

a)   *The first check should be of the fluid level in the clutch master cylinder. If the fluid level is low, add fluid as necessary and inspect the hydraulic clutch system for leaks. If the master cylinder reservoir has run dry, bleed the system as described in Section 6 and re-test the clutch operation.*

b)   *On vehicles with mechanical release systems, a clutch pedal that is difficult to operate is most likely caused by a faulty clutch cable. Check the cable where it enters the casing for fraying, rust or other signs of corrosion. If it looks good, lubricate the cable with penetrating oil. If pedal operation improves, the cable is worn out and should be replaced.*

c)   *To check "clutch spin down time," run the engine at normal idle speed with the transaxle in Neutral (clutch pedal up - engaged). Disengage the clutch (pedal down), wait nine seconds and shift the transaxle into Reverse. No grinding noise should be heard. A grinding noise would most likely indicate a problem in the pressure plate or the clutch disc.*

d)   *To check for complete clutch release, run the engine (with the parking brake on to prevent movement) and hold the clutch pedal approximately 1/2-inch from the floor. Shift the transaxle between 1st*

gear and Reverse several times. If the shift is not smooth, component failure is indicated. On vehicles with a hydraulic release system, measure the slave cylinder pushrod travel. With the clutch pedal depressed completely the slave cylinder pushrod should extend 7/16-inch minimum. If the pushrod doesn't meet this requirement, check the fluid level in the clutch master cylinder.

e)   *Visually inspect the clutch pedal bushing at the top of the clutch pedal to make sure there is no sticking or excessive wear.*

3   Clutch cable - removal, installation and adjustment

Removal

Refer to illustrations 3.3, 3.4, 3.6a, 3.6b, 3.6c and 3.8

1   Raise the hood and place a blanket over the left (driver's) fender to protect it.

2   Disconnect the cable from the negative battery terminal or the remote ground terminal (see Chapter 5).

3   Remove the air cleaner assembly (see Chapter 4) and clutch cable inspection cover from the bellhousing **(see illustration).**

4   Pull back on the clutch cable housing and disengage it from the slot in the bellhousing, then disconnect it from the release lever **(see illustration).**

5   Working inside the vehicle, if necessary, remove the steering column lower cover and the knee bolster (see Chapter 11).

6   Slightly depress the clutch pedal, to allow access to the clutch cable up-stop/spacer. Remove the retaining clip securing the up-stop/spacer to the clutch pedal pivot pin **(see illustration).** Wedge a narrow flat-blade screwdriver between the clutch pedal pivot pin and the up-stop/spacer retaining tab, then remove the up-stop/spacer from the pivot pin **(see illustration).** Remove the up-

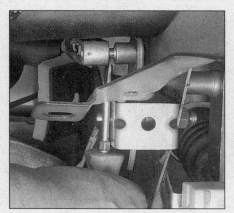

3.6b . . . next, wedge a narrow flat-blade screwdriver between the up-stop spacer retainer and the clutch pedal pivot pin, then slide the up-stop/spacer off the pivot pin . . .

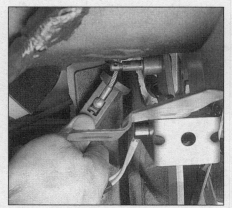

3.6c . . . and remove the up-stop/spacer from the clutch cable end

3.8 Working in the engine compartment, carefully remove the clutch cable and grommet from the firewall

stop/spacer from the clutch cable end (**see illustration**).

7   If necessary loosen the four brake booster to dash panel nuts.

8   **Caution:** *Do not pull on the clutch cable while removing it from the dash panel as the cable self-adjuster may be damaged.* Working inside the engine compartment, hold onto the grommet and, using a slight twisting motion, carefully remove the clutch cable grommet from the firewall and clutch bracket (**see illustration**). If necessary, carefully use a screwdriver to free the grommet from the firewall opening. Remove the clutch cable assembly from the vehicle.

Installation and adjustment

9   To help ease installation, apply a little petroleum jelly to the clutch cable grommet.

10   Working inside the engine compartment, insert the self-adjusting end of the clutch cable through the firewall and into the clutch bracket using a slight twisting motion. Make sure the cable grommet is fully seated in the firewall.

11   Working inside the vehicle, seat the cylindrical part of the grommet into the firewall opening and clutch bracket. Make sure the self-adjuster is firmly seated against the clutch bracket to ensure the adjuster will function properly.

12   Install the up-stop/spacer onto the clutch cable end, then install the up-stop/spacer onto the clutch pedal pivot pin. Install the retaining clip and make sure it is properly seated.

13   Working inside the engine compartment, using slight pressure, pull the clutch cable end to draw the cable taut. Push the cable housing toward the firewall with less than 25 lbs of pressure. The cable housing should move about 1 to 2 inches - this indicates proper adjuster operation. If the cable does not adjust (move), make sure the self- adjuster mechanism is properly seated in the bracket.

14   Connect the cable to the release lever making sure the cupped washer seats securely on the release lever tangs.

15   Pull back on the clutch cable housing and insert it into the bellhousing.

16   Install the clutch cable inspection cover onto the bellhousing.

17   The remainder of installation is the reverse of removal.

---

4   Clutch master cylinder - removal and installation

Removal

Refer to illustration 4.8

1   Disconnect the cable from the negative battery terminal or the remote ground terminal (see Chapter 5).

2   Working inside the vehicle, if necessary, remove the steering column lower cover and the knee bolster (see Chapter 11), remove the clip that secures the master cylinder pushrod to the clutch pedal and slide the pushrod off the clutch pedal pin.

3   To avoid spillage during removal, verify that the cap on the clutch fluid reservoir is tight. **Caution:** *Don't allow brake fluid to come into contact with paint, as it will damage the finish.*

4   On some vehicles, it may be necessary to remove the master cylinder reservoir for easier access to the master cylinder. Clamp a pair of locking pliers onto the clutch fluid feed hose, a couple of inches downstream of the clutch fluid reservoir. The pliers should be just tight enough to prevent fluid flow when the hose is disconnected. Disconnect the reservoir hose from the clutch master cylinder. Have some rags handy to absorb any fluid lost as the line is removed.

5   Remove the retainer-to-firewall fasteners and remove the reservoir from the vehicle.

6   Some master cylinders are bolted in place. Others are locked by turning. If fastened by hardware, disconnect the hydraulic line at the clutch master cylinder. If available, use a flare-nut wrench on the fitting to prevent the fitting from being rounded off.

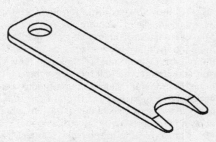

4.8 Tool for separating the quick-disconnect fitting on the clutch hydraulic line

7   Working in the engine compartment, remove the fasteners, which secure the master cylinder to the firewall. Remove the master cylinder, again being careful not to spill any of the fluid.

8   On master cylinders locked in place, the hydraulic line is equipped with a quick-disconnect fitting located on the hydraulic line midway between the release cylinder and the master cylinder. A special tool is required for separation (**see illustration**).

9   Raise the vehicle and support it securely on jackstands.

10   Working under the vehicle, separate the hydraulic line using the special tool (or an equivalent substitute).

11   Lower the vehicle.

12   Working in the engine compartment, rotate the master cylinder counter-clockwise about a 1/4 turn and remove it from the dash panel/clutch pedal bracket.

13   Using care not to damage the hydraulic line, work the master cylinder and line from the engine compartment.

Installation

14   Place the master cylinder pushrod through the firewall and install the fasteners finger tight.

15   Connect the hydraulic line to the master cylinder, moving the cylinder slightly as necessary to thread the fitting properly into the bore. Don't cross-thread the fitting.

5.4 Remove the release cylinder mounting bolts

16   Tighten the mounting nuts and the hydraulic line fitting securely.

17   On master cylinders that lock into place, route the hydraulic line into position and place the master cylinder pushrod through firewall and the dash panel/clutch pedal bracket. Index the master cylinder counter-clockwise about a 1/4 turn, and then rotate the master cylinder clockwise about a 1/4 turn while applying pressure towards the dash panel.

18   Working inside the vehicle, connect the master cylinder pushrod to the clutch pedal pin and install a new clip.

19   On master cylinders that lock into place, connect the release cylinder hydraulic line to the master cylinder hydraulic line at the quick-connect fitting. Verify proper connection by an audible click and then pulling outward on the connection.

20   The remainder of installation is the reverse of removal.

21   Fill the clutch master cylinder reservoir with the brake fluid conforming to the specifications listed in the Chapter 1 Specifications and bleed the clutch system (see Section 6).

22   Wash off any spilled brake fluid with water. **Caution:** *Don't allow brake fluid to come into contact with paint, as it will damage the finish.*

23   Check and, if necessary, adjust the clutch pedal height and free-play (see Chapter 1). Connect the negative battery cable.

---

5   Clutch release cylinder - removal and installation

Removal

Refer to illustration 5.4

1   Disconnect the cable from the negative battery terminal or the remote ground terminal (see Chapter 5).

2   Raise the vehicle and support it securely on jackstands.

3   On some vehicles a quick connect fitting is used to connect the release cylinder to the master cylinder located on the hydraulic line midway between the release cylinder and

the master cylinder. On others, a flare-nut fitting directly connects the hydraulic line to the release cylinder. If a flare-nut is used, disconnect the hydraulic line by using a flare-nut wrench. Have a small can and rags handy, as some fluid will be spilled as the line is removed. **Caution:** *Don't allow brake fluid to come into contact with paint, as it will damage the finish.* Plug the line to prevent excessive fluid loss.

4   Remove the release cylinder mounting bolts **(see illustration).**

5   On release cylinders with a quick-connect fitting, disconnect the lines at the fitting (see Section 4, Step 8).

6   Using a small screwdriver lift up on the nylon tab, and while depressing the cylinder inward rotate the cylinder counter-clockwise approximately 60-degrees. Remove the release cylinder.

Installation

7   Installation is the reverse of removal, with the following points:

a)   *Install the release cylinder on the clutch housing and install the bolts, but leave them a little loose until after the hydraulic line fitting threads have been started. Apply a layer of Multi-purpose grease to the contact point of the release cylinder pushrod and release fork. Make sure the pushrod is then seated in the release fork pocket.*

b)   *Connect the hydraulic line fitting to the release cylinder, using your fingers only at this time (since the cylinder is still a bit loose, it'll be easier to start the threads into the cylinder).*

c)   *Tighten the mounting bolts and hydraulic fitting securely.*

d)   *On release cylinders with a quick-connect fitting, verify proper installation of release cylinder by the nylon locating tab should rest in the transaxle case cutout and the hydraulic tube should be vertical. Connect the release cylinder hydraulic line to the master cylinder hydraulic line at the quick-connect fitting. Verify proper connection by an audible click and then pulling outward on the connection. Check for proper clutch pedal operation, and depress the clutch pedal approximately (10) times to purge any air from system.*

e)   *Check the fluid level in the reservoir, adding fluid until the level is correct.*

f)   *On all other hydraulic systems, bleed the system as described in Section 6, then recheck the fluid level.*

g)   *Lower the vehicle and connect the negative battery cable.*

---

6   Clutch hydraulic system - bleeding

1   Bleed the hydraulic system whenever any part of the system has been removed or the fluid level has fallen so low that air has been drawn into the master cylinder. The

bleeding procedure is very similar to bleeding a brake system.

2   Fill the brake master cylinder reservoir with new brake fluid conforming to DOT 3 specifications. **Caution:** *Do not re-use any of the fluid coming from the system during the bleeding operation or use fluid that has been inside an open container for an extended period of time.*

3   Raise the vehicle and support it securely on jackstands to gain access to the release cylinder, which is located on the front of the transaxle.

4   Remove the dust cap that fits over the bleeder valve and push a length of plastic hose over the valve. Place the other end of the hose into a clear container with about two inches of brake fluid. The hose end must be in the fluid at the bottom of the container.

5   Have an assistant depress the clutch pedal and hold it. Open the bleeder valve on the release cylinder, allowing fluid to flow through the hose. Close the bleeder valve when the flow of fluid (and bubbles) ceases. Once closed, have your assistant release the pedal.

6   Continue this process until all air is evacuated from the system, indicated by a solid stream of fluid being ejected from the bleeder valve each time with no air bubbles in the hose or container. Keep a close watch on the fluid level inside the clutch master cylinder reservoir - if the level drops too far, air will get into the system and you'll have to start all over again.

7   Install the dust cap and lower the vehicle. Check the brake fluid level again, and add some, if necessary, to bring it to the appropriate level. Check carefully for proper operation before placing the vehicle into normal service.

---

7   Clutch components - removal, inspection and installation

Note: *Most of the vehicles are equipped with a modular clutch assembly that includes a clutch assembly where the clutch pressure plate and friction disc are an integral unit. While 2001 and later Coupes, have a conventional clutch assembly.*

Warning: *Dust produced by clutch wear and deposited on clutch components is hazardous to your health. DO NOT blow it out with compressed air and DO NOT inhale it. DO NOT use gasoline or petroleum-based solvents to remove the dust. Brake system cleaner should be used to flush the dust into a drain pan. After the clutch components are wiped clean with a rag, dispose of the contaminated rags and cleaner in a covered, marked container.*

Removal

Access to the clutch components is normally accomplished by removing the transaxle, leaving the engine in the vehicle. If the engine is being removed for major overhaul,

7.8 Mark the relationship of the pressure plate to the flywheel (in case you're going to re-use the same pressure plate)

7.10 Hold onto the clutch disc and pull it away from the flywheel, then remove the clutch cover and the clutch disc

then the opportunity should always be taken to check the clutch for wear and replace worn components as necessary. However, the relatively low cost of the clutch components compared to the time and labor involved in gaining access to them warrants their replacement any time the engine or transaxle is removed, unless they are new or in near-perfect condition. The following procedure assumes that the engine will remain in the vehicle.

Modular clutch

Note: *The modular clutch can only be serviced as an assembly.*

1   Remove the transaxle from the vehicle (see Chapter 7A). Support the engine while the transmission is out. Preferably, an engine hoist should be used to support it from above. However, if a jack is used underneath the engine, make sure a piece of wood is used between the jack and oil pan to spread the load. **Caution:** *The pick-up for the oil pump is very close to the bottom of the oil pan. If the pan is bent or distorted in any way, engine oil starvation may occur.* **Note:** *The modular clutch assembly remains on the transaxle input shaft during the removal process.*

2   Remove the modular clutch assembly

from the transaxle input shaft. Handle it carefully to avoid contaminating the friction surfaces.

3   Remove the clutch release bearing and lever (Section 8).

4   Inspect the flywheel for cracks, heat checking, score marks and other damage. If the imperfections are slight, a machine shop can resurface it.

5   The release bearing should be replaced along with the clutch disc.

Conventional type clutch

Refer to illustrations 7.8 and 7.10

6   Remove the transaxle from the vehicle (see Chapter 7). Support the engine while the transaxle is out. Preferably, an engine hoist should be used to support it from above. However, if a jack is used underneath the engine, make sure a piece of wood is used between the jack and oil pan to spread the load. **Caution:** *The pick-up for the oil pump is very close to the bottom of the oil pan. If the pan is bent or distorted in any way, engine oil starvation may occur.*

7   The release lever and release bearing can remain attached to the transaxle; how-

ever, you should inspect them (see Section 8) while the transaxle is removed.

8   Carefully inspect the flywheel and pressure plate for indexing marks. The marks are usually an X, an O or a white letter. If they cannot be found, scribe marks yourself so the pressure plate and the flywheel will be in the same alignment during installation **(see illustration)**. Of course, this won't be necessary if you're planning to replace the pressure plate with a new one.

9   Slowly, loosen the pressure plate-to-flywheel bolts. Work in a criss-cross pattern and loosen each bolt a little at a time until all spring pressure is relieved.

10   Hold the pressure plate securely and completely remove the bolts, followed by the pressure plate and clutch disc **(see illustration)**.

Inspection (conventional type clutch only)

Refer to illustrations 7.13, 7.15a and 7.15b

11   Ordinarily, when a problem occurs in the clutch, it can be attributed to wear of the clutch driven plate assembly (clutch disc). However, all components should be inspected at this time.

12   Inspect the flywheel for cracks, heat checking, score marks and other damage. If the imperfections are slight, a machine shop can resurface it to make it flat and smooth. Refer to Chapter 2 for the flywheel removal procedure.

13   Inspect the lining on the clutch disc. There should be at least 1/16-inch of lining above the rivet heads. Check for loose rivets, distortion, cracks, broken springs and other obvious damage **(see illustration)**. As mentioned above, ordinarily the clutch disc is replaced as a matter of course, so if in doubt about the condition, replace it with a new one.

14   The release bearing should be replaced along with the clutch disc (see Section 8).

15   Check the machined surface and the

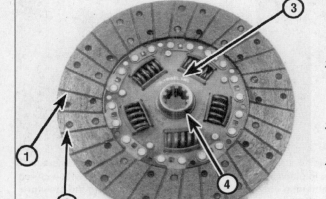

7.13 Conventional type clutch disc

1   *Lining* - this will wear down in use

2   *Rivets* - these secure the lining and will damage the flywheel or pressure plate if allowed to contact the surfaces

3   *Markings* - "Flywheel side" or something similar

4   *Hub* - Be sure this is installed facing the proper direction (see the text)

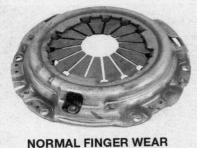
NORMAL FINGER WEAR

EXCESSIVE WEAR →
EXCESSIVE FINGER WEAR

BROKEN OR BENT FINGERS

7.15a Replace the pressure plate if excessive wear is noted (conventional type clutch)

7.15b Examine the pressure plate friction surface for score marks, cracks and evidence of overheating (conventional type clutch)

7.20a Position and center the clutch disc onto the flywheel and hold it in place . . .

7.20b . . . hold the clutch disc in place and install the pressure plate against the flywheel while aligning the plate to the flywheel dowel pins. Insert your thumb through the spring fingers of the pressure plate to keep the clutch centered and move the pressure plate against the flywheel and onto the dowel pins (conventional type clutch)

diaphragm spring fingers of the pressure plate **(see illustrations)**. If the surface is grooved or otherwise damaged, replace the pressure plate assembly. Also, check for obvious damage, distortion, cracking, etc. Light glazing can be removed with emery cloth or sandpaper. If a new pressure plate is indicated, new or factory rebuilt units are available.

Installation

Modular clutch

16   Before installation, carefully wipe the flywheel and pressure plate machined surfaces clean with brake system cleaner. It's important that no oil or grease is on these surfaces or the lining of the clutch disc. Handle these parts only with clean hands.

17   Install the clutch release bearing and lever (see Section 8).

18   Install the modular clutch assembly onto the transaxle input shaft.

19   Install the transaxle onto the vehicle (see Chapter 7A). **Note:** *Be sure to install new bolts when attaching a modular clutch to the driveplate.* Tighten the bolts to the torque listed in this Chapter's specifications.

Conventional type clutch

Refer to illustrations 7.20a, 7.20b, 7.21a and 7.21b

20   Position the clutch disc against the flywheel and center it **(see illustration)**, while holding the disc in place, install the pressure

plate against the flywheel **(see illustration)**.

21   Hold the pressure plate in place and install the mounting bolts and tighten only finger tight at this time **(see illustration)**. Install an alignment tool **(see illustration)**. Make sure it's installed properly (most replacement clutch plates will be marked "flywheel side" or something similar - if not marked, install the clutch disc with the damper springs or cushions toward the transaxle).

22   Center the clutch disc by ensuring the alignment tool is through the splined hub and

7.21a Hold the pressure plate in place and install the mounting bolts, tightening only finger tight at this time (conventional type clutch)

into the recess in the crankshaft. Wiggle the tool up, down or side-to-side as needed to bottom the tool. Tighten the pressure plate-to-flywheel bolts a little at a time, working in a criss-cross pattern to prevent distortion of the cover. After all of the bolts are snug, tighten them to the torque listed in this Chapter's

7.21b Center the clutch disc with a clutch alignment tool, then tighten the pressure plate bolts a little at a time, in a criss-cross pattern (conventional type clutch)

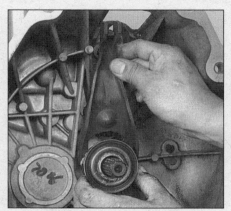

8.5 Hold the release bearing in place, disengage the clip and pull the release lever from the pivot stud. Then slide the release lever up to disengage it from the release bearing

8.7 Hold the bearing by the outer race and rotate the inner race while applying pressure - if the bearing doesn't turn smoothly or if it's noisy, it must be replaced (it's a good idea to replace the bearing even if it checks out good)

8.11a Using high-temperature grease, lubricate the release lever ends . . .

Specifications. Remove the alignment tool.

23   Using moly-base grease, lubricate the inner surface of the release bearing and the face of the bearing where it contacts the fingers of the pressure plate diaphragm spring. Also place grease on the release lever contact areas and the transaxle input shaft. **Caution:** *Don't use too much grease.*

24   Install the clutch release bearing and lever (see Section 8).

25   Install the transaxle (see Chapter 7A) and all components removed previously, tightening all fasteners to the proper torque specifications.

8   Clutch release bearing and lever - removal, inspection and installation

Warning: *Dust produced by clutch wear and deposited on clutch components may contain asbestos, which is hazardous to your health. DO NOT blow it out with compressed air and DO NOT inhale it. DO NOT use gasoline or petroleum-based solvents to remove the dust. Brake system cleaner should be used to flush it into a drain pan. After the clutch components are wiped clean with a rag, dispose of the contaminated rags and cleaner in a labeled, covered container.*

Removal

Refer to illustration 8.5

1   Disconnect the cable from the negative battery terminal or the remote ground terminal (see Chapter 5).

2   Remove the transaxle (see Chapter 7A).

3   On Vehicles with a modular clutch assembly remove the clutch assembly from the transaxle (see Section 7). Handle it carefully to avoid contaminating the friction surfaces.

4   Working on the transaxle, position the release lever and bearing so the lever is at a right angle to the input shaft. Grasp the

release lever on each side of the pivot ball socket and pull; the release lever will pop off the pivot stud. **Caution:** *Do not use a screwdriver or pry bar to disengage the lever, as the spring clips on the underside of the release lever will be damaged.* If you're working on a 3.0L V6 engine, separate the release bearing from the lever. If you need to remove the lever from the bell housing, unscrew the pivot shaft lockbolt and remove the shaft, release fork, springs, and seals.

5   Slide the release bearing and lever off the bearing sleeve **(see illustration)**.

6   Separate the fork from the bearing, being careful not to damage the return spring or retention tabs on the bearing.

Inspection

Refer to illustration 8.7

7   Hold the bearing by the outer race and rotate the inner race while applying pressure **(see illustration)**. If the bearing doesn't turn smoothly or if it's noisy, replace the bearing assembly with a new one. Wipe the bearing with a clean rag and inspect it for damage, wear and cracks. Don't immerse the bearing in solvent - it's sealed for life and to do so

would ruin it. **Note:** *Because of the difficulty involved in removing the transaxle for release bearing replacement, we recommend routinely replacing the release bearing when the clutch assembly is replaced.*

8   Check the release lever fork for cracks or distortion. Replace if necessary.

9   Inspect the pivot ball spring clips on the backside of the lever. If they're cracked or broken, replace the lever.

10   Clean any dirt off the pivot ball and pocket in the release fork. Examine them for damage or excessive wear. Replace if necessary. If you're working on a 3.0L V6 engine, inspect the pivot bushings in the release lever for wear or damage. If necessary, press the old bushings out and press new ones in. Install new bushings whenever the old ones are removed.

Installation

Refer to illustrations 8.11a, 8.11b, 8.11c, 8.12, and 8.15

11   Lightly lubricate the release lever ends, the inner diameter of the release bearing and the input shaft with high-temperature grease **(see illustrations).**

8.11b . . . the inner splines of the release bearing . . .

8.11c . . . and the sleeve around the input shaft

12   Also place a light coat of high-temperature grease to the release lever contact areas
(see illustration). Note: *Some models have
a release lever with a Teflon coated pivot ball
pocket and should be installed WITHOUT any
grease. Applying grease to the pocket or pivot
ball stud would break down the Teflon coating.*
13   Attach the release bearing to the release
lever.
14   Slide the release bearing onto the transaxle input shaft front bearing retainer while
passing the end of the release lever through
the opening in the clutch housing. Push the
clutch release lever onto the pivot ball stud
until it's firmly seated.
15   If you're working on a 3.0L V6 engine,
in addition to (Step 11), apply a light coat of
high-temperature grease to the pivot bushings
on the release lever and the release cylinder
pushrod pocket **(see illustration)**. Position
the release lever in the bell housing, and then
install the pivot shaft, seals and springs.
16   The remainder of installation is the
reverse of removal.

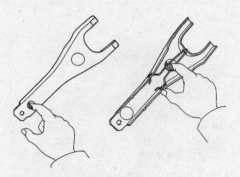

**8.12 Lubricate the release cylinder
pushrod pocket and release lever pivot
ball pocket with high temperature grease**

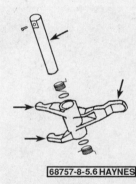

68757-8-5.6 HAYNES

**8.15 Exploded view of the clutch release
lever and shaft (3.0L engine)**

---

9   Clutch start switch - check and replacement

Note: *Two different types of switches are
used by the vehicles in this manual, an adjustable switch on vehicles with a hydraulic clutch
system, and a non-adjustable switch (secured
by wing tabs) is used on vehicles with a clutch
cable.*

Check

1   The clutch start switch is located on the
clutch pedal bracket.
2   Verify that the engine will not start when
the clutch pedal is depressed all teh way.
4   If the clutch start switch doesn't perform
as described above, check switch continuity.
5   If necessary, remove the steering column cover and knee bolster (see Chapter
11). Unplug the electrical connector from
the switch and verify that there is continuity
between the two clutch stat switch terminals
when the edal is depressed.
6   Verify that no continuity exists between
the seitch terminals when the pedal is
released.
7   If the switch fails either of these continuity tests, replace it.

Replacement

Refer to illustration 9.14
8   Disconnect the cable from the negative
battery terminal or the remote ground terminal
(see Chapter 5).
9   If necessary, remove the lower steering
column cover and knee bolster (see Chapter 11).
10   The switch is mounted vertically at the
upper end of the clutch pedal lever.
11   Unplug the connector from the position
switch or wiring harness.
12   For non-adjustable switches, depress the

wing tabs on the switch and push it from the
mounting bracket. For adjustable switches,
loosen the adjustment nut and unscrew the
switch from its mounting bracket.
13   Installation is the reverse of removal.
14   On switches with an adjustment nut,
loosen the locknut and turn the switch in or
out, as necessary to achieve the correct measurement **(see illustration)**.

10   Driveaxles - general information and inspection

1   Power is transmitted from the transaxle
to the wheels through a pair of driveaxles. The
inner end of each driveaxle is splined into its
corresponding differential side gear inside the
transaxle; the outer end of each driveaxle has
a stub shaft that is splined to the front hub and
bearing assembly and locked in place with a
large nut and cotter pin combination.
2   The inner ends of the driveaxles are
equipped with sliding tripod-type Constant
Velocity (CV) joints, which are capable of both
angular and axial motion. Each inner tripod
CV joint assembly consists of a tripod-type
bearing and a housing in which the joint is
free to slide in-and-out as the driveaxle moves
up-and-down with the wheel. On some models the drive axles are equipped with a tuned
rubber damper weight. **Note:** *If the driveaxle
is equipped with a damper, when replacing
the driveaxle, be sure the replacement has
the same damper weight as the orignal.* On
vehicles equipped with an Antilock Brake System (ABS), the outer CV joints are equipped
with a tone wheel that is used to determine
the vehicle speed for proper ABS operation.
3   The outer ends of the driveaxles are
equipped with Rzeppo-type Constant Velocity (CV) joints, which permits the high move-
ments of steering maneuvers. Each outer CV
joint has ball bearings that run between an
inner race and an outer cage.
4   The boots should be inspected periodically for damage and leaking lubricant. Torn
joint boots must be replaced immediately or
the joints will be damaged. If either boot of a

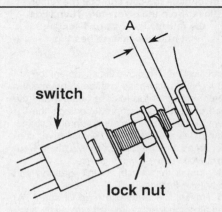

**9.14 With the clutch pedal depressed at
full stroke the measurement for distance
"A" is approximately 3.5mm**

driveaxle is damaged, that driveaxle must be
removed in order to replace the boot. **Note
1:** *Some auto parts stores carry "split" type
replacement boots, which can be installed
without removing the driveaxle from the vehicle. This is convenient, but we recommend that
the driveaxle be removed and the joint disassembled and cleaned to ensure that the joint
is free from contaminants, such as moisture
and dirt, which will accelerate joint wear.* **Note
2:** *The inner tripod joint boots on the vehicles
covered in this manual are constructed from
different materials: The inner boot is made
from a high-temperature application silicone;
for regular temperature applications, the boot
is made from Hytrel thermoplastic. Make sure
you obtain a boot made of the correct material
for the joint boot you're replacing.*
5   Should a boot be damaged, the joint can
be disassembled and cleaned, but if any parts
are damaged, the entire driveaxle assembly
must be replaced as a unit.
6   The most common symptom of worn or
damaged CV joints, besides lubricant leaks, is
a clicking noise in turns, a clunk when accel-
erating after coasting and vibration at highway
speeds. To check for wear in the CV joints and
axleshafts, grasp each axle (one at a time)
and rotate it in both directions while holding

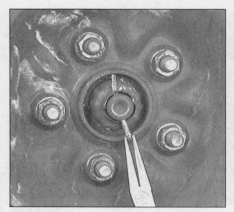

11.2a Remove the hub nut cotter pin . . .

11.2b . . . then remove the lock and spring washer

11.3 Loosen the driveaxle/hub nut - DO NOT remove the nut - it holds the wheel hub/bearing assembly together

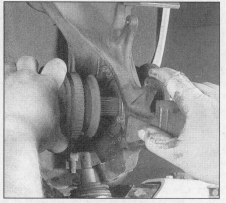

11.6a Angle the steering knuckle as required and pull the driveaxle from the wheel hub

the joint housings, feeling for play indicating worn splines or sloppy joints. Also, check the axleshafts for cracks, dents and distortion. The driveaxles are equipped with tuned rubber damper weights. The damper weight on the right side (if equipped) is a single clamp style damper. The damper weight on the left is a double clamp style damper. When replac-

ing a driveaxle, be sure that the replacement driveaxle has the same damper weight as the original.

11   Driveaxle - removal and installation

Removal

Refer to illustrations 11.2a, 11.2b, 11.3, 11.6a, 11.6b, 11.7, 11.8 and 11.9

1   Disconnect the cable from the negative battery terminal or the remote ground terminal (see Chapter 5).
2   Remove the cotter pin, nut lock, and spring washer from the stub axle **(see illustrations)**. **Note:** Some *models may only be equipped with a cotter pin and a front hub nut.*
3   Loosen (but do not remove) the front hub nut **(see illustration)**.
4   Raise the vehicle and support it securely on jackstands.
5   Separate the tie rod end and the ball joint stud from the steering knuckle (see Chapter 10).

6   Remove the hub nut and pull the steering knuckle out and away from the outer CV joint of the driveaxle **(see illustration)**. If the driveaxle proves difficult to remove, tap the end of the driveaxle with a soft-faced hammer or a hammer and a brass punch **(see illustration)**. If the driveaxle is stuck in the hub splines and won't move, it may be necessary to push it from the hub with a two-jaw puller.
7   On left axles with a center-bearing bracket, remove the two bolts that secure the bracket to the block, and then gently tap the bearing bracket with a plastic hammer to separate the inner shaft from the transaxle **(see illustration)**.
8   On right axles and left axles without a center bearing, support the outer end of the driveaxle and insert a pry bar between the inner tripod CV joint and the transaxle case **(see illustration)**. Pry out sharply to disengage the inner tripod CV joint from the transaxle. Make sure you have a drain pan under the transaxle, as some oil will leak out. It may be necessary to remove the brake caliper and disc (see Chapter 9), if the proper clearance cannot be obtained because of the brake line.

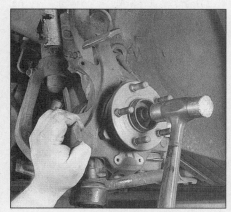

11.6b To loosen the driveaxle from the hub splines, tap the end of the driveaxle with a soft-faced hammer

11.7 On axles with a center-bearing bracket, separate the inner shaft from the transaxle by gently tapping the center support bracket

11.8 Using a large pry bar, pry the inner tripod CV joint out sharply to disengage the differential gears inside the transaxle

11.9 When withdrawing the the inner tripod CV joint from the transaxle, be careful not to damage the oil seal with the splines

12.4 Remove the boot from the inner CV joint and slide the tripod from the joint housing

9   Carefully withdraw the inner tripod CV joint from the transaxle **(see illustration)**. Do not let the spline or the snap-ring drag across the sealing lip of the driveaxle-to-transaxle oil seal. **Caution:** *The driveaxle acts as a bolt, when installed, that secures the front hub/ bearing assembly. If the vehicle must be supported or moved with the driveaxle removed, a proper sized bolt and nut must be secured through the front hub. Tighten the bolt and nut to the torque listed in this Chapter's Specifications.*

Installation
10   Installation is the reverse of the removal procedure, noting the following additional points:
a) *Thoroughly clean the splines and bearing shield on the outer CV joint. This is very important, as the bearing shield protects the wheel bearings from water and contamination. Also clean the wheel bearing area of the steering knuckle.*
b) *Thoroughly clean the splines and oil seal sealing surface on the inner tripod CV joint. Apply an even bead of multi-purpose grease around the oil seal sealing surface of the tripod CV joint.*
c) *When installing the driveaxle, push it sharply in to seat the snap-ring on the tri-*

pod CV joint stub shaft into its groove in the differential gears inside the transaxle. Pull out sharply to ensure it's seated.
d) *Tighten the driveaxle/hub nut to the torque listed in this Chapter's Specifications.*
e) *Install the wheel and lug nuts, lower the vehicle and tighten the lug nuts to the torque listed in the Chapter 1 Specifications.*
f) *The steering knuckle to ball joint stud clamping bolt and nut should not be reused. A new clamping bolt and nut should always be used.*

---

12   Driveaxle boot replacement and CV joint inspection

Note 1: *If the CV joints or boots must be replaced, explore all options before beginning the job. Complete, rebuilt driveaxles may be available on an exchange basis, eliminating much time and work. Whichever route you choose to take, check on the cost and availability of parts before disassembling the vehicle.*
Note 2: *The inner and outer boots on the vehicles covered in this manual are constructed from different materials: The inner boots are*

made from either high-temperature application silicone material or Hytrel thermoplastic; the outer boot is made of Hytrel thermoplastic. Make sure you obtain a boot made of the correct material for the CV joint boot you're replacing.

Inner Tripod joint
1   Remove the driveaxle (see Section 12).
2   Mount the driveaxle in a vise with wood-lined jaws (to prevent damage to the axleshaft). Check the CV joints for excessive play in the radial direction, which indicates worn parts. Check for smooth operation throughout the full range of motion for each CV joint. If a boot is torn, the recommended procedure is to disassemble the joint, clean the components and inspect for damage due to loss of lubrication and possible contamination by foreign matter. If the CV joint is in good condition, lubricate it with CV joint grease and install a new boot.

Disassembly
Refer to illustrations 12.4, 12.5, 12.6, 12.7
3   Cut the boot clamps with side-cutters, remove and discard them.
4   Using a screwdriver, carefully pry up on the edge of the CV boot, pull it off the CV joint housing and slide it down the axleshaft, exposing the tripod spider assembly. To separate the axleshaft and spider assembly from the inner Tripod joint housing, simply pull them straight out **(see illustration)**. **Note:** *When removing the spider assembly, hold the rollers in place on the spider trunion to protect the rollers and the needle bearings from falling free.*
5   Remove the spider assembly snap-ring with a pair of snap-ring pliers **(see illustration)**.
6   Mark the tripod to the axleshaft to ensure that they are reassembled properly **(see illustration)**.
7   Use a hammer and a brass drift to drive the spider assembly from the axleshaft **(see illustration)**.
8   Slide the boot off the shaft.

12.5 Remove the snap-ring with a pair of snap-ring pliers

12.6 Mark the relationship of the tripod bearing assembly to the axleshaft

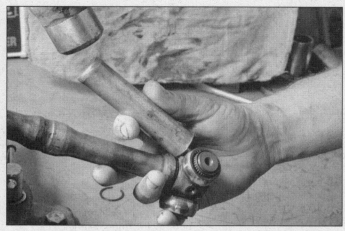

12.7 Drive the tripod joint off the axleshaft with a brass punch and hammer; be careful not to damage the bearing surfaces or the splines on the shaft

12.10a Wrap the axleshaft splines with electrical tape to prevent damaging the boot as it's slid onto the shaft

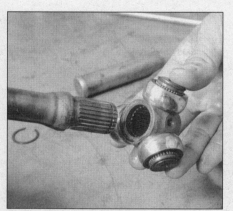

12.10b Install the tripod spider on the axleshaft (make sure your match mark is facing out)

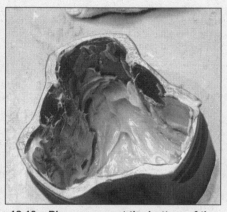

12.10c Place grease at the bottom of the CV joint housing

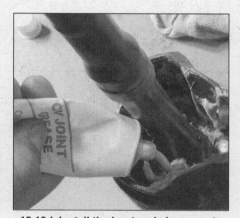

12.10d Install the boot and clamps onto the axleshaft, then insert the tripod into the housing, followed by the rest of the grease

Inspection

9   Thoroughly clean all components with solvent until the old CV joint grease is completely removed. Inspect the bearing surfaces of the inner tripods and housings for cracks, pitting, scoring and other signs of wear. If any part of the inner CV joint is worn, you must replace the entire driveaxle assembly (inner Tripod joint, axleshaft and outer CV joint). The only components that can be purchased separately are the boots themselves and the boot clamps.

Reassembly

Refer to illustrations 12.10a, 12.10b, 12.10c, 12.10.d, 12.11a, 12.11b, 12.13, 12.15a, 12.15b,12.15c and 12.15d

10   Wrap the splines on the inner end the axleshaft with electrical or duct tape to protect the boots from the sharp edges of the splines and slide the clamps and boot onto the axleshaft **(see illustration)**. Remove the tape and place the tripod spider on the axleshaft with the chamfer toward the shaft **(see illustration)**. Tap the spider onto the shaft with a brass drift until it's seated and install the snap ring. Apply grease to the tripod assem-

bly and inside the housing **(see illustration)**. Insert the tripod into the housing and pack the remainder of the grease around the tripod **(see illustration)**.
11   Slide the boot into place; making sure the raised bead on the inside of the seal boot is

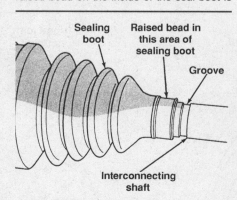

12.11a Slide the boot into place, making sure the small end seats in the flat spot on the axleshaft between the locating shoulders

positioned in the groove on the interconnecting shaft **(see illustration)**. If the driveaxle has multiple locating grooves on the shaft, position the boot so only one of the grooves (the thinnest) is exposed **(see illustration)**.

12.11b Make sure that the thinnest groove on the axleshaft is the only one showing

12   Position the sealing boot into the groove on the tripod housing retaining groove.

13   Equalize the pressure inside the boot by inserting a small, dull, flat screwdriver tip between the boot and the CV joint housing **(see illustration)**. Then remove the screwdriver tip.

14   Make sure each end of the boot is seated properly, and the boot is not distorted.

15   Two types of clamps are used on the inner CV joint. If a crimp-type clamp is used, clamp the new boot clamps onto the boot with a special crimping tool (available at most automotive parts stores). Place the crimping tool over the bridge of each new boot clamp, then tighten the nut on the crimping tool until the jaws are closed **(see illustrations)**. If a low profile latching type clamp is used, place the prongs of the clamping tool (available at most automotive parts stores) in the holes of the clamp and squeeze the tool together until the top band latches behind the tabs of the lower band **(see illustrations)**.

16   The driveaxle is now ready for installation (see Section 11).

Outer CV joint

Note 1: *On 1997 and earlier convertible models, the outer CV joint cannot be removed from the axleshaft, eliminating the ability for boot replacement. These driveaxles must be serviced as a quarter shaft if the CV joint or boot fails.*

1998 and later convertibles and all sedans

Disassembly

Refer to illustrations 12.20, 12.21a and 12.21b

17   Remove the driveaxle (see Section 11) and mount it in a vise with wood-lined jaws (to prevent damage to the axleshaft). Check the CV joints for excessive play in the radial direction, which indicates worn parts. Check for smooth operation throughout the full range of motion for each CV joint. If a boot is torn, the recommended procedure is to disassemble the joint, clean the components and inspect for damage due to loss of lubrication and possible contamination by foreign matter. If the CV joint is in good condition, lubricate it with

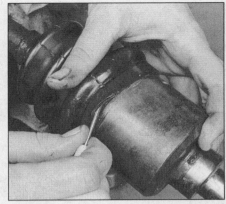

12.13 Equalize the pressure inside the boot by inserting a small, <u>Dull</u> screwdriver between the boot and the CV joint housing

CV joint grease and install a new boot.

18   Cut the boot clamps with side-cutters, remove and discard them.

19   Slide the boot away from the outer CV

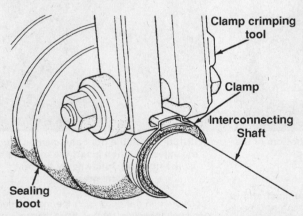

12.15a Clamp the new boot clamps onto the boot with a crimping tool such as this one (available at most auto parts stores). Place the crimping tool over the bridge of each new boot clamp . . .

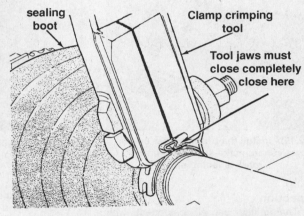

12.15b . . . then tighten the nut on the crimping tool until the jaws are closed

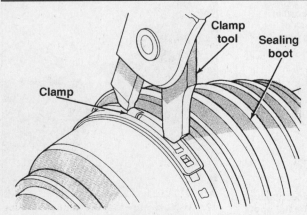

12.15c For the low profile latching type boot clamp, place the prongs of the clamping tool in the holes of the clamp . . .

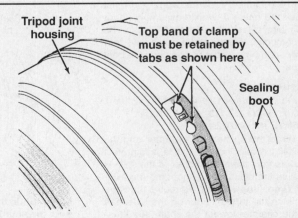

12.15d . . . and squeeze the tool together until the top band latches behind the tabs of the lower band

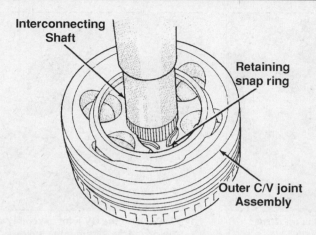

12.20 If the CV joint has a snap-ring like this one, use a pair of snap-ring pliers to release the snap-ring

12.21a Strike the edge of the CV joint housing sharply with a soft-faced hammer to dislodge the CV joint from the shaft

joint, and clean the CV joint and the interconnecting parts.

20   Some models axleshafts have a snap-ring that secures the CV joint to the axle shaft **(see illustration)**. Once the boot for the outer CV joint has been slid back out of the way and some grease is wiped off, check to see if a snap-ring is buried in there, if equipped use a pair of snap-ring pliers to release the snap-ring, then slide the outer CV joint assembly off the axleshaft. If a snap-ring is not found, refer to the next step for removal.

21   Strike the edge of the CV joint housing sharply with a soft-faced hammer to dislodge the outer CV joint housing from the axleshaft **(see illustration)**. Remove the circlip from the shaft **(see illustration)**.

22   Slide the outer CV joint and the sealing boot off the axleshaft.

Inspection

23   Thoroughly clean all components with solvent until the old CV grease is completely removed. Inspect the bearing surfaces of the inner tripods and housings for cracks, pitting, scoring, and other signs of wear. If any part of the outer CV joint is worn, you must replace the entire driveaxle assembly (inner CV joint, axleshaft and outer CV joint).

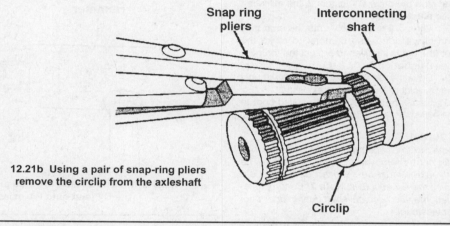

12.21b Using a pair of snap-ring pliers remove the circlip from the axleshaft

Reassembly

Refer to illustrations 12.25a, 12.25b, 12.26a, 12.26b, 12.26c, 12.27 and 12.28

24   Slide a new sealing boot clamp and sealing boot onto the axleshaft. **Note:** *The sealing boot must be positioned on the shaft so the raised bead on the inside of the boot is in the groove on the shaft.*

25   On axleshafts with a cir-clip, replace the cir-clip onto the axle shaft. On shafts equipped with a snap-ring, use needle-nose pliers to place the retaining ring into the groove on the outer CV joint housing **(see illustrations)**.

26   Place half the grease provided in the sealing boot kit into the outer CV joint assembly housing **(see illustration)**. Put the remaining grease into the sealing boot **(see illustrations)**.

27   Align the splines on the axleshaft with the splines on the outer CV joint assembly

12.25a Use needle-nose pliers to lower the snap-ring into the groove . . .

12.25b . . . then seat it into the groove with snap-ring pliers

12.26a Pack the outer CV joint assembly with grease . . .

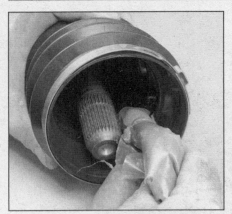

12.26b Install a small clamp and the new boot on the driveaxle, then apply grease to the inside of the boot until . . .

12.26c . . . the level is up to the end of the axle

12.27 Position the CV joint assembly on the driveaxle, aligning the splines

and start the outer CV joint onto the axleshaft **(see illustration)**.

28   Thread a nut loosely onto the stub axle and use a soft-faced hammer to strike the nut (the nut is installed to protect the threads) **(see illustration)**.

29   Drive the CV joint onto the axleshaft until the CV joint is seated to the axleshaft.

30   Install the outer CV joint sealing boot to the axleshaft (see Steps 11 through 16).

Coupes

Note 1: *On Coupe models, the outer CV joint can not be removed from the axleshaft. The driveaxles must be serviced as a complete unit if the CV joint fails.* **Note 2:** *Boot replacement may be accomplished during inner boot replacement.*

Note 2: *Make sure you check the availability of replacement boots before attempting the following procedure.*

Disassembly

31   Remove the driveaxle (see Section 11).

32   Following Steps 3 through 8, remove the inner CV joint from the axleshaft.

33   If the driveaxle is equipped with a dynamic damper, scribe or paint a location mark on the axleshaft along the outer edge of the damper (the side facing the outer CV joint), cut the retaining clamp and slide the damper off.

34   Remove the outer CV joint boot clamps by prying up the boot clamp retaining tabs with a small screwdriver and slide the boot off the axleshaft.

Inspection

Refer to illustration 12.36

35   Thoroughly wash the inner and outer CV joints in clean solvent and blow them dry with compressed air, if available. **Warning:** *Wear eye protection when using compressed air.*

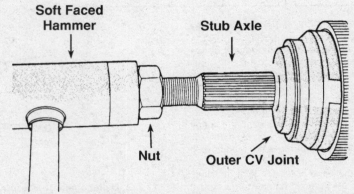

12.28   Thread a nut onto the stub axle to protect the shaft threads and drive the CV joint onto the axleshaft with a soft-faced hammer

Note: *Because the outer joint cannot be disassembled, it is difficult to wash away all the old grease and to rid the bearing of solvent once it's clean. But it is imperative that the job be done thoroughly, so take your time and do it right.*

36   Bend the outer CV joint housing at an angle to the driveaxle to expose the bearings, inner race and cage **(see illustration)**. Inspect the bearing surfaces for signs of wear. If the bearings are damaged or worn, replace the driveaxle.

Reassembly

37   Slide the new outer boot onto the axleshaft. It's a good idea to wrap tape around the splines of the shaft to prevent damage to the boot. When the boot is in position, add the specified amount of grease to the outer joint and the boot (see Step 26). Slide the boot on the rest of the way and install the new clamps (see Steps 11 through 16).

38   Install the dynamic dampner and clamps if necessary.

12.36 Rotate the joint housing through its full range of motion and inspect the bearing surfaces for wear and damage

39   Clean and reassemble the inner CV joint by following Steps 9 through 15, then install the driveaxle as outlined in Section 11.

Chapter 9   Brakes

Contents

Specifications

General

Brake fluid type	See Chapter 1
Power brake booster pushrod-to-master cylinder piston clearance (2000 and earlier coupe models) (see Section 9)	
1995 models	0.0 to 0.010 inch
1996 through 2000 models	0.025 to 0.033 inch
Power brake booster pushrod protrusion (2001 and later models) (see Section 9)	0.404 to 0.415 inch

Disc brakes

Minimum pad lining thickness	See Chapter 1
Disc minimum thickness	Cast into disc
Disc runout limit	
Coupe models	
2000 and earlier	0.0031 inch
2001 and later	
Front	0.002 inch
Rear	0.003 inch
Convertible and sedan models	
2001 and earlier models	0.005 inch
2002 and later models	0.004 inch
Maximum disc thickness variation (parallelism)	
Coupe models	0.0006 inch
Convertible and sedan models	0.0005 inch

Drum brakes

Shoe lining minimum thickness	See Chapter 1
Maximum drum diameter	Cast into drum

Torque specifications

Ft-lbs (unless otherwise indicated)

Note: *One foot pound (ft-lb) of torque is equivalent to 12 inch-pounds (in-lbs) of torque. Torque values below approximately 15 ft-lbs are expressed in inch-pounds, since most foot-pound torque wrenches are not accurate at these smaller values.*

Caliper guide pin/lock pin (mounting) bolts
    Coupe models
        Front
            2000 and earlier 54
            2001 and later 28
        Rear
            2000 and earlier 54
            2001 and later 32
    Convertible and sedan models
        2000 and earlier models 16
        2001 and later models 26
Caliper mounting bracket bolts
    Coupe models
        Front
            2000 and earlier 65
            2001 and later 74
        Rear 41
    Convertible and sedan models
        2000 and earlier models 55
        2001 through 2003 models 60
        2004 and later models 80
Brake hose inlet fitting bolts
    Coupe models
        1999 and earlier .... 132 in-lbs
        2000 and later 22
    Convertible and sedan models
        2000 and earlier 35
        2001 and later 26
Master cylinder-to-brake booster nuts
    Coupe models
        2001 and earlier .... 84 in-lbs
        2002 and later .... 111 in-lbs
    Convertible and sedan models
        2000 and earlier 21
        2001 and later 19
Power brake booster mounting nuts
    Coupe models .... 120 in-lbs
    Convertible and sedan models
        2000 and earlier models 27
        2001 and later models 21
Wheel cylinder mounting bolts
    Coupe models .... 84 in-lbs
    Convertible and sedan models .... 115 in-lbs

1 General information

The vehicles covered by this manual are equipped with a hydraulically operated brake system. The front brakes are disc type and the rear brakes are either drum or disc type. Both the front and rear disc brakes automatically compensate for disc and pad wear. As the pads wear down, the pistons gradually protrude farther from the calipers, but don't retract as far, automatically compensating for the thinner pads. Rear drum brakes have automatic adjusters which compensate for wear of the brake shoes.

Hydraulic system

The hydraulic system consists of two separate circuits that are diagonally split (one circuit operates the left front and right rear brakes, while the other circuit operates the right front and left rear brakes). The master cylinder has separate reservoirs for the two circuits, and, in the event of a leak or failure in one hydraulic circuit, the other circuit will remain operative. A dual proportioning valve on the firewall (coupe models) or on the front suspension crossmember (sedan models) provides brake balance between the front and rear brakes.

Power brake booster

The power brake booster, which is mounted on the firewall, utilizes engine manifold vacuum and atmospheric pressure to provide assistance to the hydraulically operated brakes.

Parking brake

The parking brake operates the rear brakes only, through cable actuation. It's activated by a lever mounted in the center console. The parking brake on rear disc brake models uses brake shoes and small brake drums integral with the rear brake discs.

Service

After completing any operation involving disassembly of any part of the brake system, always test drive the vehicle to check for

2.2a The ABS hydraulic unit on 2000 and earlier coupe models is located forward of the left front wheelwell, under the fuse/relay box (bumper cover removed for clarity)

proper braking performance before resuming normal driving. When testing the brakes, perform the tests on a clean, dry, flat surface. Conditions other than these can lead to inaccurate test results.

Test the brakes at various speeds with both light and heavy pedal pressure. The vehicle should stop evenly without pulling to one side or the other. Avoid locking the brakes, because this slides the tires and diminishes braking efficiency and control of the vehicle.

Tires, vehicle load and wheel alignment are factors which also affect braking performance.

2 Anti-lock Brake System (ABS) - general information and speed sensor removal and installation

General information
Refer to illustrations 2.2a, 2.2b and 2.2c
1   The anti-lock brake system is designed to maintain vehicle steerability, directional stability and optimum deceleration under severe braking conditions on most road surfaces. It does

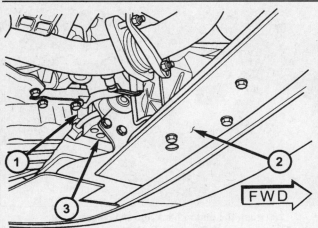

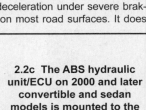

2.2c The ABS hydraulic unit/ECU on 2000 and later convertible and sedan models is mounted to the left side of the radiator crossmember

1   *Electrical connector*
2   *Radiator crossmember*
3   *ABS hydraulic unit*

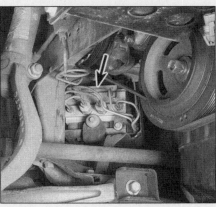

2.2b The ABS hydraulic unit/ECU on 1999 and earlier convertible and sedan models is mounted to the right side of the front suspension crossmember

so by monitoring the rotational speed of each wheel and controlling the brake line pressure to each wheel during braking. This prevents the wheels from locking up.
2   The ABS system has three main components - the wheel speed sensors, the electronic control unit (ECU) and the hydraulic unit **(see illustrations)**. Four wheel speed sensors - one at each wheel - send a variable voltage signal to the control unit, which monitors these signals, compares them to its program and determines whether a wheel is about to lock up. When a wheel is about to lock up, the control unit signals the hydraulic unit to reduce hydraulic pressure (or not increase it further) at that wheel's brake caliper. Pressure modulation is handled by electrically-operated solenoid valves.
3   If a problem develops within the system, an "ABS" warning light will glow on the dashboard. Sometimes, a visual inspection of the ABS system can help you locate the problem. Carefully inspect the ABS wiring harness. Pay particularly close attention to the harness and connections near each wheel. Look for signs of chafing and other damage caused by incorrectly routed wires. If a wheel sensor harness is damaged, the sensor must be replaced. **Warning:** *Do NOT try to repair an ABS wiring harness. The ABS system is sensitive to even the smallest changes in resistance. Repairing the harness could alter resistance values and cause the system to malfunction. If the ABS wiring harness is damaged in any way, it must be replaced.* **Caution:** *Make sure the ignition is turned off before unplugging or reattaching any electrical connections.*

Diagnosis and repair
4   If a dashboard warning light comes on and stays on while the vehicle is in operation, the ABS system requires attention. Although special electronic ABS diagnostic testing tools are necessary to properly diagnose the system, you can perform a few preliminary checks before taking the vehicle to a dealer service department.

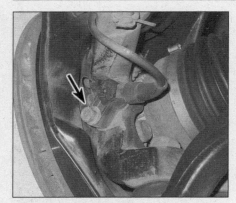

2.9a Wheel speed sensor mounting bolt - coupe model

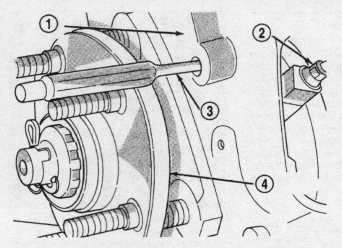

2.9b If a front wheel speed sensor locating pin is stuck in the steering knuckle, remove the brake disc and tap it out with a punch (convertible and sedan models only)

1 *Steering knuckle*
2 *Speed sensor*
3 *Punch*
4 *Hub and bearing assembly*

a) *Check the brake fluid level in the reservoir.*
b) *Verify that the computer electrical connectors are securely connected.*
c) *Check the electrical connectors at the hydraulic control unit.*
d) *Check the fuses.*
e) *Follow the wiring harness to each wheel and verify that all connections are secure and that the wiring is undamaged.*

5   If the above preliminary checks do not rectify the problem, the vehicle should be diagnosed by a dealer service department or other qualified repair shop. Due to the complex nature of this system, all actual repair work must be done by a qualified automotive technician.

Wheel speed sensor - removal and installation

Refer to illustrations 2.9a and 2.9b

6   Loosen the wheel lug nuts, raise the vehicle and support it securely on jackstands. Remove the wheel.
7   Make sure the ignition key is turned to the Off position.
8   Trace the wiring back from the sensor, detaching all brackets and clips while noting its correct routing, then disconnect the electrical connector.
9   Remove the mounting bolt and carefully

pull the sensor out from the knuckle or brake backing plate **(see illustrations)**.
10   Installation is the reverse of the removal procedure. If you're working on a convertible or sedan model, apply a light film of multi-purpose grease to the locating pin. Tighten the mounting bolt securely.
11   Install the wheel and lug nuts, tightening them securely. Lower the vehicle and tighten the lug nuts to the torque listed in the Chapter 1 Specifications.

---

3 Disc brake pads - replacement

Preliminary steps (all models)

Refer to illustrations 3.4 and 3.5
Warning: *Disc brake pads must be replaced on both front or rear wheels at the same time - never replace the pads on only one wheel. Also, the dust created by the brake system is harmful to your health. Never blow it out with compressed air and don't inhale any of it. An approved filtering mask should be worn when working on the brakes. Do not, under any circumstances, use petroleum-based solvents to clean brake parts. Use brake system cleaner only!*
Caution: *Don't depress the brake pedal with*

the caliper removed.
1   Remove the cap from the brake fluid reservoir. Remove about two-thirds of the fluid from the reservoir, then reinstall the cap. **Warning:** *Brake fluid is poisonous - never siphon it by mouth. Use a suction gun or old poultry baster. If a baster is used, never again use it for the preparation of food.* **Caution:** *Brake fluid will damage paint. If any fluid is spilled, wash it off immediately with plenty of clean, cold water.*
2   Loosen the wheel lug nuts, raise the end of the vehicle you're working on and support it securely on jackstands. Block the wheels that remain on the ground.
3   Remove the wheels. Work on one brake assembly at a time, using the assembled brake for reference if necessary.
4   Position a drain pan under the brake assembly and clean the caliper and surrounding area with brake system cleaner **(see illustration)**.
5   Push the piston back into its bore using a C-clamp **(see illustration)**. As the piston(s) is depressed to the bottom of the caliper bore, the fluid level in the master cylinder will rise as the brake fluid is displaced. Make sure it doesn't overflow. If necessary, siphon off some more of the fluid.

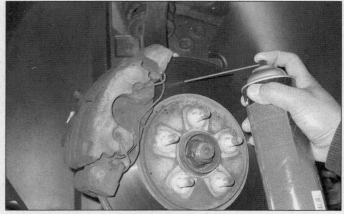

3.4 Always wash the brakes with brake system cleaner before working on them

3.5 Push the piston back into the caliper bore with a large C-clamp

Coupe models

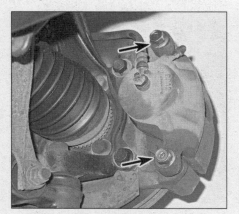

3.6a Remove the caliper guide pin (lower arrow) - it's only necessary to remove the lock pin (upper arrow) if you're removing the caliper

3.6b Swing the caliper up like this . . .

3.6c . . . and support it in this position with a piece of wire

3.6d Remove the inner pad and shim(s)

3.6e Remove the outer pad and shim(s)

3.6f Remove the anti-rattle clips, paying close attention to how they're installed in the torque plate (mounting bracket)

Coupe models

Refer to illustrations 3.6a through 3.6l and 3.9

6   To replace the brake pads, follow the accompanying photos, beginning with **illustration 3.6a**. Be sure to stay in order and read the caption under each illustration.

7   While the pads are removed, inspect the caliper for brake fluid leaks and ruptures of the piston dust boot. Replace the caliper if necessary (see Section 4). Also inspect the brake disc carefully (see Section 5). If machining is necessary, follow the information in that Section to remove the disc. Inspect the brake hoses for damage and replace if necessary

(see Section 10).

8   Before installing the caliper guide pin, clean the pin boots and check them for corrosion and damage. If they're significantly corroded or damaged, replace them.

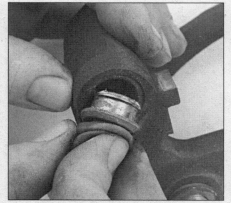

3.6g Remove the dust boots from the torque plate, inspect them for cracks and tears, and replace as necessary

3.6h Install the anti-rattle clips in the torque plate - make sure both are fully seated

3.6i Apply anti-squeal compound (available at auto parts stores - follow the label instructions) to the back of the brake pads and install the anti-squeal shim(s)

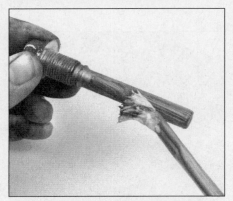

3.6j Lubricate the guide pin with multi-purpose grease before installing it

3.6k Install the inner pad . . .

3.6l . . . and the outer pad into the torque plate - make sure both pads are fully seated, then swing the caliper down into place, install the guide pin and tighten it to the torque listed in this Chapter's Specifications

9   If you removed both the guide pin and the lock pin, be sure to reinstall them in the correct locations **(see illustration)**. Tighten the guide pin and lock pin to the torque listed in this Chapter's Specifications.

10   Repeat the procedure on the opposite wheel, then install the wheels and lug nuts, lower the vehicle and tighten the lug nuts to the torque listed in the Chapter 1 Specifications.

11   Add the specified type of brake fluid to the reservoir until it's full (see Chapter 1).

12   Pump the brake pedal a few times to bring the pads into contact with the disc. Check the level of the brake fluid, adding some if necessary.

13   Check the operation of the brakes carefully before placing the vehicle into normal service. Try to avoid heavy brake application until the brakes have been applied lightly several times to seat the pads.

Convertible and sedan models

Front (2000 and earlier models) and rear (all model years)

Refer to illustrations 3.14a through 3.14l

14   To replace the brake pads, follow the accompanying photos, beginning with **illustration 3.14a**. Be sure to stay in order and read the caption under each illustration.

15   While the pads are removed, inspect the caliper for brake fluid leaks and ruptures of the piston dust boot. Replace the caliper if necessary (see Section 4). Also inspect the brake disc carefully (see Section 5). If machining is necessary, follow the information in that Section to remove the disc. Inspect the brake hoses for damage and replace if necessary (see Section 10).

16   Before installing the caliper guide pins, clean the pin boots and check them for corrosion and damage. If they're significantly corroded or damaged, replace them. Be sure to tighten them to the torque listed in this Chapter's Specifications

17   Repeat the procedure on the opposite wheel, then install the wheels and lug nuts, lower the vehicle and tighten the lug nuts to the torque listed in the Chapter 1 Specifications.

18   Add the specified type of brake fluid to the reservoir until it's full (see Chapter 1).

19   Pump the brake pedal a few times to bring the pads into contact with the disc. Check the level of the brake fluid, adding

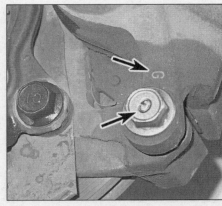

3.9 If you removed the guide pin and lock pin, install them in the correct locations by referring to the letters stamped in the ends of the pins - they correspond with the letters cast into the caliper body. Note: *On rear calipers they might not be marked*

Convertible and sedan models

Front (2000 and earlier models) and rear (all model years)

3.14a To remove the front brake caliper, remove the two guide pin bolts (arrows)

3.14b Lift the caliper off the steering knuckle and remove the outer pad from the caliper

3.14c Remove the inner pad from the caliper

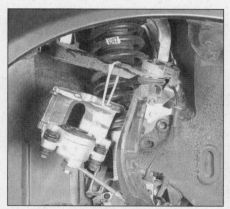

3.14d Hang the caliper from the upper control arm - don't let it hang by the brake hose

3.14e Remove the guide pin bushings

3.14f Remove the bushing boots, inspect them for damage and replace if necessary

3.14g Lubricate the guide pin bushings with high-temperature grease before installing them

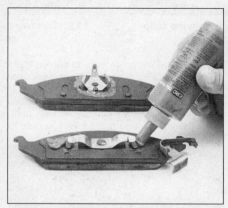

3.14h Apply an anti-squeal compound to the back of the pads where they mate with the caliper and piston

3.14i Install the inner brake pad - make sure the retaining spring is fully seated into the piston bore

some if necessary.

20   Check the operation of the brakes carefully before placing the vehicle into normal service. Try to avoid heavy brake application until the brakes have been applied lightly several times to seat the pads.

Front (2001 and later models)

Refer to illustrations 3.21a through 3.21n

21   To replace the brake pads, follow the accompanying photos, beginning with **illustration 3.21a**. Be sure to stay in order and read the caption under each illustration.

22   While the pads are removed, inspect the caliper for brake fluid leaks and ruptures of the piston dust boot. Replace the caliper if necessary (see Section 4). Also inspect the brake disc carefully (see Section 5). If machining is necessary, follow the information in that

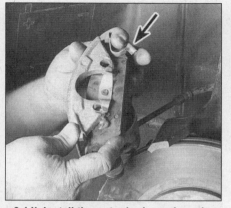

3.14j Install the outer brake pad - make sure the retaining spring is properly engaged with the caliper body and the wear indicator (arrow) on the pad is positioned at the top of the caliper as shown

3.14k Place the caliper/brake pad assembly onto the steering knuckle (make sure the upper ends of the pads seat properly, and the spring [arrow] seats under the steering knuckle boss)

3.14l Install the guide pin bolts and tighten them to the torque listed in this Chapter's Specifications

Convertible and sedan models

Front (2001 and later models)

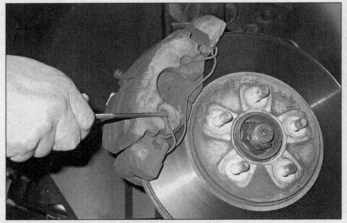

3.21a Unclip the anti-rattle spring and remove it from the caliper

3.21b Remove the end caps from the guide bushings to gain access to the caliper guide pins

Section to remove the disc. Inspect the brake hoses for damage and replace if necessary (see Section 10).

23   Before installing the caliper guide pins, clean and check them for corrosion and damage. If they're significantly corroded or damaged, replace them. Be sure to tighten them to the torque listed in this Chapter's Specifications

24   Repeat the procedure on the opposite wheel, then install the wheels and lug nuts, lower the vehicle and tighten the lug nuts to the torque listed in the Chapter 1 Specifications.

25   Add the specified type of brake fluid to the reservoir until it's full (see Chapter 1).

26   Pump the brake pedal a few times to bring the pads into contact with the disc.

3.21c Unscrew the caliper guide pins and lift the caliper off the mounting bracket

3.21d Hang the caliper from the coil spring with a piece of wire - don't let it hang by the hose

3.21e Unclip the inner pad from the caliper piston . . .

3.21f . . . and remove the outer pad from the mounting bracket

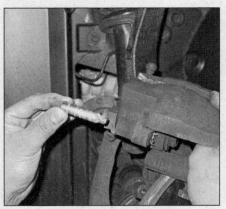

3.21g Remove the guide pins and inspect them for wear and corrosion

3.21h Also remove the pin boots and check them for wear or damage

3.21i Lubricate the guide pin bushings with high-temperature grease before installing them

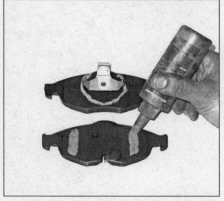

3.21j Apply an anti-squeal compound to the back of the pads where they mate with the caliper and piston

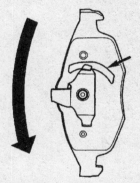

3.21k Before installing the inner pad, be sure to select the proper one from the pad replacement kit; they're marked L and R, and the slot on the insulator must be positioned toward the top of the caliper when installed

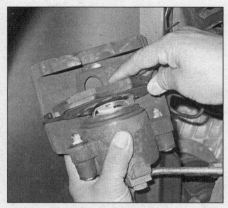

3.21l Install the inner brake pad - make sure the retaining spring is fully seated into the piston bore

3.21m Install the outer brake pad in the caliper mounting bracket

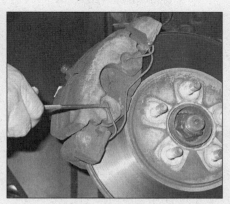

3.21n Install the caliper and guide pins, tightening them to the torque listed in this Chapter's Specifications, then install the end caps. Finally, install the anti-rattle spring, lifting the ends of the spring into the holes in the caliper frame

Check the level of the brake fluid, adding some if necessary.

27   Check the operation of the brakes carefully before placing the vehicle into normal service. Try to avoid heavy brake application until the brakes have been applied lightly several times to seat the pads.

4   Disc brake caliper - removal and installation

Warning: *Dust created by the brake system is harmful to your health. Never blow it out with compressed air and don't inhale any of it. An approved filtering mask should be worn when working on the brakes. Do not, under any circumstances, use petroleum-based solvents to* clean brake parts. Use brake system cleaner only.

Note: *If replacement is indicated (usually because of fluid leakage), it is recommended that the calipers be replaced, not overhauled. New and factory rebuilt units are available on an exchange basis. Always replace the calipers in pairs - never replace just one of them.*

Removal

Refer to illustrations 4.2a and 4.2b

1   Loosen the wheel lug nuts, raise the vehicle and support it securely on jackstands. Remove the wheel.

2   If you're removing a front caliper on a coupe model or any caliper on a convertible or sedan model, remove the fitting bolt and disconnect the brake hose from the caliper. Plug the brake hose to keep contaminants out of the brake system and to prevent losing any more brake fluid than is necessary **(see illustration)**. Discard the sealing washers - new ones should be used during installation **(see illustration)**. **Note:** *If the caliper is being removed for access to another component, don't disconnect the hose.*

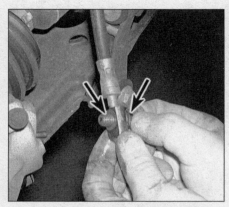

4.2a There is a sealing washer on either side of the brake hose inlet fitting; be sure to replace these with new ones when reconnecting the hose

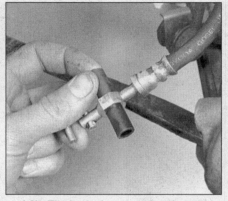

4.2b The brake hose can be plugged using a snug-fitting piece of tubing

5.3 The brake pads on this vehicle were obviously neglected - they wore down to the rivets and cut deep grooves into the disc (wear this severe means the disc must be replaced)

5.4a Use a dial indicator to measure disc runout - if the reading exceeds the maximum allowable runout limit, the disc will have to be machined or replaced

5.4b Using a swirling motion, remove the glaze from the disc surface with sandpaper or emery cloth

3   If you're removing a rear caliper on a coupe model, remove the rear brake hose (see Section 10).

4   Refer to Section 3 for the caliper removal procedure (it's part of the brake pad replacement procedure). If the caliper is being removed for access to another component, hang it from the coil spring with a piece of wire **(see illustration 3.14d)**.

Installation

5   Install the caliper by reversing the removal procedure. Remember to replace the sealing washers at the brake hose-to-caliper connection. Tighten the caliper guide/lock pins to the torque listed in this Chapter's Specifications.

6   Bleed the brake circuit according to the procedure in Section 11 (only if the brake hose was disconnected. Make sure there are no leaks from the hose connections. If you didn't disconnect the hose, be sure to pump the brake pedal several times to bring the pads into contact with the disc.

7   Test the brakes carefully before returning the vehicle to normal service.

5   Brake disc - inspection, removal and installation

Note: *This procedure applies to both front and rear brake discs.*

Inspection

Refer to illustrations 5.3, 5.4a, 5.4b, 5.5a and 5.5b

1   Loosen the wheel lug nuts, raise the vehicle and support it securely on jackstands. Remove the wheel and reinstall the lug nuts to hold the disc in place (washers may be required). If the rear brake disc is being worked on, release the parking brake.

2   Remove the brake caliper and pads (see Section 3) but don't disconnect the brake hose from the caliper, or you'll have to bleed the brakes when everything is reassembled. After removing the caliper bolts, suspend the caliper out of the way with a piece of wire **(see illustration 3.14d)**.

3   Visually inspect the disc surface for score marks and other damage. Light scratches and shallow grooves are normal after use and may not always be detrimental to brake operation, but deep scoring requires disc removal and refinishing by an automotive machine shop. Be sure to check both sides of the disc **(see illustration)**. If pulsating has been noticed during application of the brakes, suspect disc runout.

4   To check disc runout, place a dial indicator at a point about 1/2-inch from the outer edge of the disc **(see illustration)**. Set the indicator to zero and turn the disc. The indicator reading should not exceed the specified allowable runout limit. If it does, the disc should be refinished by an automotive machine shop. **Note:** *The discs should be resurfaced regardless of the dial indicator reading, as this will impart a smooth finish and ensure a perfectly flat surface, eliminating any brake pedal pulsation or other undesirable symptoms related to questionable discs. At the very least, if you elect not to have the discs resurfaced, remove the glaze from the surface with emery cloth using a swirling motion (see illustration).*

5   It's absolutely critical that the disc not be machined to a thickness under the specified minimum allowable thickness. The minimum

5.5a The minimum wear dimension is cast into the back side of the disc (typical)

5.5b Use a micrometer to measure disc thickness

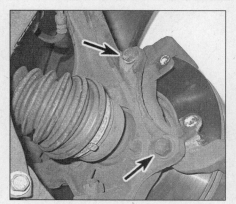

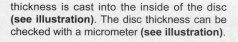

5.6a Caliper mounting bracket (also known as the "torque plate") bolts (front shown, rear similar)

5.6b Using two bolts to force a stuck disc off the hub flange

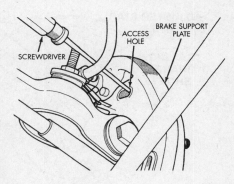

6.2 If the drum binds on the brake shoes, insert a screwdriver through the hole in the backing plate and turn the adjuster wheel to retract the shoes

thickness is cast into the inside of the disc **(see illustration)**. The disc thickness can be checked with a micrometer **(see illustration)**.

Removal

Refer to illustrations 5.6a and 5.6b

6   Remove the caliper mounting bracket, on models so equipped **(see illustration)**. Remove the lug nuts which were put on to hold the disc in place and remove the disc from the hub. Some models are equipped with threaded holes in the hub portion of the disc; if the disc sticks to the hub, screw in two bolts of the proper size and thread pitch and tighten them to force the disc off the hub **(see illustration)**.

Installation

7   Place the disc in position over the wheel studs. Install the mounting bracket (if equipped), tightening the bolts to the torque listed in this Chapter's Specifications.
8   Install the brake pads and caliper (see Section 3). Tighten the caliper guide pin/lock pin to the torque listed in this Chapter's Specifications.

9   Install the wheel, lower the vehicle and tighten the lug nuts. Tighten the lug nuts to the torque listed in the Chapter 1 Specifications.
10   Pump the brake pedal a few times to bring the brake pads into contact with the disc. Bleeding won't be necessary unless the brake hose was disconnected from the caliper. Check the operation of the brakes carefully before driving the vehicle.

6   Drum brake shoes - replacement

Refer to illustrations 6.2, 6.3, 6.4, 6.5, 6.6, 6.7, 6.8, 6.12 and 6.13
Warning: *Drum brake shoes must be replaced on both wheels at the same time - never replace the shoes on only one wheel. Also, the dust created by the brake system is harmful to your health. Never blow it out with compressed air and don't inhale any of it. An approved filtering mask should be worn when working on the brakes. Do not, under any circumstances, use petroleum-based solvents to clean brake parts. Use brake system cleaner only!*

Convertible models (except 2003 through 2005)

1   Loosen the rear wheel lug nuts, raise the rear end of the vehicle and support it securely on jackstands. Block the front wheels to keep the vehicle from rolling. Release the parking brake and remove the rear wheels.
2   Remove the brake drum. If the drum won't come off, the brake shoes must be retracted from their fully adjusted position. Insert a screwdriver through the adjuster hole in the brake backing plate and turn the adjuster wheel to retract the shoes **(see illustration)**.
3   Once the drum is removed, clean the brake assembly with brake system cleaner **(see illustration)**.
4   Using locking pliers, unhook the lever return spring from the adjuster lever and brake shoe **(see illustration)**. **Note:** *On convertible and sedan models this spring connects to the lever at the top and to the trailing shoe at the bottom. On coupe models this spring connects to the lever and stretches across to the leading shoe.*

6.3 Before disassembling the brake shoe assembly, spray it with brake cleaner to remove brake dust; DO NOT blow brake dust off with compressed air

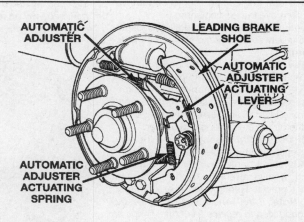

6.4 Remove the spring from the automatic adjuster lever, then detach the lever from the shoe (convertible and sedan models shown)

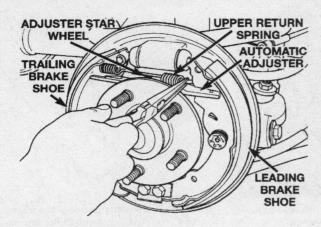

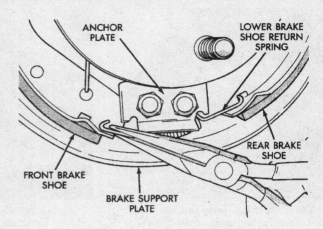

6.5 Unhook the upper return spring from the shoes

6.6 Detach the lower return spring from the shoes

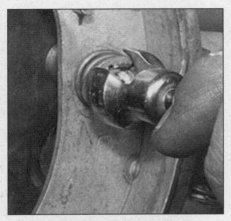

6.7 Remove the hold-down spring and retainer from the leading shoe (push the retainer in and turn it 90-degrees to release it from the pin)

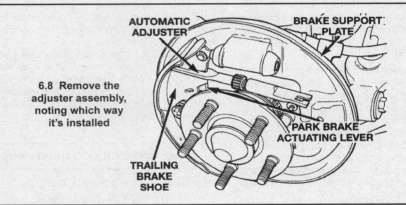

6.8 Remove the adjuster assembly, noting which way it's installed

5   Unhook and remove the upper return spring **(see illustration)**.

6   Unhook and remove the lower return spring **(see illustration)**.

7   Remove the hold-down spring and retainer from the leading shoe **(see illustration)**. Remove the leading shoe.

8   Remove the automatic adjuster assembly from between the brake shoes **(see illustration)**.

9   Pry the retainer on the parking brake lever open just far enough to remove it, then remove the hold-down spring and retainer and separate the trailing shoe from the parking brake lever. Don't lose the wave washer from the pin on the parking brake lever.

10   If necessary, disengage the parking brake lever from the cable.

11   Check all parts for wear and damage, paying special attention to metal-to-metal contact points. Replace worn or damaged parts. **Note:** *If the vehicle has high mileage, it's a good idea to replace all of the springs as well as any parts that have visible problems.*

12   Check the brake drum for score marks, cracks, deep scratches and hard spots, which will appear as small discolored areas. If the

hard spots cannot be removed with emery cloth or if any of the other conditions are seen, the drum must be resurfaced by an automotive machine shop. **Note:** *Professionals recommend resurfacing the drum whenever a brake job is performed. Resurfacing will correct out-of-roundness in the drums as well as removing visible problems. If the drums are so worn that they can't be resurfaced without exceeding the maximum allowable diameter stamped into the drum* **(see illustration)**, *then new ones will be required. At the very least, if*

6.12 The maximum allowable diameter is stamped into the drum (typical)

you don't have the drums resurfaced, remove the glazing from the surface with emery cloth or sandpaper using a swirling motion.

13   Apply a small amount of high-temperature brake grease to the shoe contact areas of the backing plate **(see illustration)**, the moving parts of the adjuster assembly and where the adjuster contacts the brake shoes.

14   Install the wave washer and attach the parking brake lever to the new brake shoe. Place the retainer in the pin groove and secure it with pliers.

6.13 Apply a small amount of high-temperature grease to the areas where the brake shoes contact the backing plate

6.23 Unhook the return spring from the automatic adjuster lever . . .

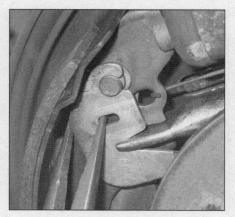

6.24 . . . then remove the adjuster lever

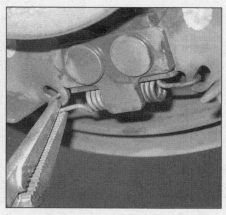

6.25 Unhook the retainer spring from the lower ends of the brake shoes

15   Reverse the removal steps to install the brake shoes. Expand the shoes, using the adjuster screw, until the drum will just fit over them.

16   Now, working through the backing plate, turn the adjuster screw wheel until the shoes drag on the drum when the drum is turned. Finally, back off the adjuster screw wheel so the shoes don't drag. Depress the brake pedal firmly several times, then rotate the drum to ensure that the brakes are not dragging. If they are, back off the star wheel a little more. Install the rubber plug in the hole in the backing plate.

17   Install the wheel and lug nuts. Lower the vehicle and tighten the lug nuts to the torque listed in the Chapter 1 Specifications.

18   Start the engine, pump the brake pedal and operate the parking brake lever several times to actuate the automatic adjusters.

19   Carefully test brake operation before driving the vehicle in traffic.

Coupe models (except 2003 through 2005)

Refer to illustrations 6.23, 6.24, 6.25, 6.26, 6.27 and 6.28

Caution: *Whenever the brake shoes are replaced, the hold-down springs should also*

be replaced. Due to the continuous heating/cooling cycle that the springs are subjected to, they lose their tension over a period of time and may allow the shoes to drag on the drum and wear at a much faster rate than normal. **Note:** *Work on one brake assembly at a time, using the assembled brake for reference if necessary.*

20   Loosen the rear wheel lug nuts, raise the rear of the vehicle and support it securely on jackstands. Block the front wheels to keep the vehicle from rolling. Release the parking brake and loosen and remove the rear wheels.

21   Remove the brake drum. If the drum won't come off, loosen the parking brake adjusting nut to remove the tension on the brake shoes (see Section 13).

22   Once the drum is removed, clean the brake assembly with brake system cleaner **(see illustration 6.3)**.

23   Using locking pliers, unhook the lever return spring from the adjuster lever and brake shoe **(see illustration)**.

24   Remove the adjuster lever **(see illustration)**.

25   Unhook the retainer spring from the lower ends of the brake shoes **(see illustration)**.

26   Using locking pliers, unhook the upper return spring **(see illustration)**.

27   Note the orientation of the automatic adjuster assembly, then remove the adjuster from between the brake shoes **(see illustration)**.

28   Remove the hold-down retainer and spring from each shoe **(see illustration)**.

29   Remove the leading shoe from the backing plate.

30   Remove the trailing shoe from the backing plate, then pry the retainer on the parking brake lever open just far enough to remove it. Detach the lever from the trailing shoe. Be careful not to lose the wave washer.

31   Check all parts for wear and damage, paying special attention to metal-to-metal contact points. Replace worn or damaged parts. **Note:** *If the vehicle has high mileage, it's a good idea to replace all of the springs as well as any parts that have visible problems.*

32   Check the brake drum for score marks, cracks, deep scratches and hard spots, which will appear as small discolored areas. If the hard spots cannot be removed with sandpaper or emery cloth or if any of the other conditions are seen, the drum must be resurfaced by an automotive machine shop. **Note:** *Professionals recommend resurfacing the drum whenever a brake job is performed. Resurfacing will correct taper and out-of-roundness in the drums as well as removing visible prob-*

6.26 Unhook the upper return spring from the upper ends of the shoes

6.27 Note which way the automatic adjuster assembly is installed, then remove it from between the shoes

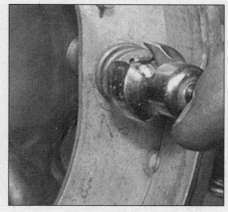

6.28 Using a hold-down spring tool, remove each hold-down spring retainer by pushing in and rotating it 1/4-turn

6.47a Using locking pliers, grasp the lower return spring and detach it from the leading brake shoe (left hand brake assembly shown)

6.47b Remove the lower return spring - note that the shorter spring end is towards the trailing brake shoe

6.47c Using locking pliers, grasp the upper return spring and detach it from the trailing brake shoe

lems. If the drums are so worn that they can't be resurfaced without exceeding the maximum allowable diameter stamped into the drum **(see illustration 6.12)**, *then new ones will be required. At the very least, if you don't have the drums resurfaced, remove the glazing from the surface with emery cloth or sandpaper using a swirling motion.*

33   Apply a small amount of high-temperature brake grease to the shoe contact areas of the backing plate **(see illustration 6.13)**, the moving parts of the adjuster assembly and where the adjuster contacts the brake shoes.

34   Install the wave washer and attach the parking brake lever to the new trailing brake shoe. Place the retainer in the pin groove and secure it with pliers.

35   Reverse the removal steps to install the brake shoes. Expand the shoes, using the adjuster screw, until the drum will just fit over them.

36   Turn the drum and listen for the shoes dragging on the drum as it is turned. If they do rub, remove the drum and back-off the adjuster screw a little and try it again. Repeat this step until you don't hear any drag.

37   Install the drum, depress the brake pedal firmly several times, then rotate the drum to

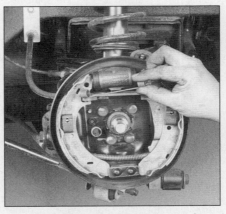

6.47d Unhook the upper return spring from the leading brake shoe

ensure that the brakes are not dragging. If they are, back off the star wheel a little more.

38   Repeat the brake shoe replacement procedure on the other rear wheel.

39   Install the wheels and lug nuts. Lower the vehicle and tighten the lug nuts to the torque listed in the Chapter 1 Specifications.

6.47e Using locking pliers, detach the automatic self-adjuster spring from the adjuster

40   Adjust the parking brake (see Section 13).

42   Start the engine, pump the brake pedal and operate the parking brake lever several times to actuate the automatic adjusters.

43   Carefully test brake operation before driving the vehicle in traffic.

6.47f Compress the retaining clip, remove the pin . . .

6.47g . . . and separate the leading brake shoe and the automatic self-adjuster from the backing plate

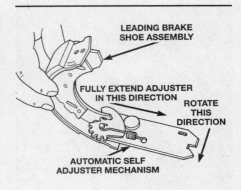

LEADING BRAKE
SHOE ASSEMBLY

FULLY EXTEND ADJUSTER
IN THIS DIRECTION

ROTATE
THIS
DIRECTION

AUTOMATIC SELF
ADJUSTER MECHANISM

6.47h To remove the adjuster from the shoe, pull it outward, then rotate it toward the reinforced side of the shoe

6.47i Compress the retaining clip, then remove the pin and clip from the trailing shoe

6.47j Detach the parking brake cable from the actuating lever - DO NOT try to separate the actuating lever from the brake shoe

6.47k Before installing the brake shoes, apply a small amount of high-temperature grease to all areas where the brake shoes make contact with the backing plate

6.47l Obtain the correct replacement trailing brake shoe (they are unique for each side of the vehicle, RH or LH and the parking brake actuating lever should be permanently attached) and install the parking brake cable onto the actuating lever

6.47m Correctly position the trailing shoe in place on the backing plate (parking brake actuating lever toward the inside) and secure it with a new pin and retaining clip

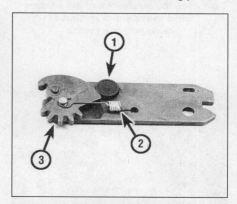

6.47n Inspect the automatic self-adjuster for damage and replace if necessary

1 Knurled pin - check to see it is firmly attached and the teeth are not damaged or excessively worn
2 Quadrant spring - inspect for damage and verify it hasn't lost its tension
3 Quadrant - verify the quadrant is free to slide within its mounting slot and can rotate through the entire tooth range

Sedan models (except 2003 through 2005)

Refer to illustrations 6.47a through 6.47v
Caution: *Whenever the brake shoes are replaced, the hold-down springs should also be replaced. Due to the continuous heating/ cooling cycle that the springs are subjected to, they lose their tension over a period of time and may allow the shoes to drag on the drum and wear at a much faster rate than normal.*
Note: *Work on one brake assembly at a time, using the assembled brake for reference if necessary.*
44   Loosen the wheel lug nuts 1/4-turn, raise the rear of the vehicle and support it securely on jackstands. Block the front wheels to keep the vehicle from rolling. Release the parking brake. Remove the wheel. **Note:** *The brake shoes on both wheels must be replaced at the same time. The drum brake assemblies on these models are unique for each side of the vehicle (left hand only - right hand only) so to avoid mixing up parts, service one brake assembly at a time.*
45   Remove the brake drum. If the drum

won't come off, the brake shoes must be retracted from their fully adjusted position by inserting a screwdriver through the adjuster hole in the backing plate. Locate the adjuster access hole and remove the plug. Insert a screwdriver through the access hole and engage the adjuster quadrant teeth. Using the screwdriver, move the adjuster quadrant teeth fully toward the FRONT of the vehicle. The drum should now come off. Wash the brake assembly with brake system cleaner **(see illustration 6.3)**.
46   Remove the wheel hub/bearing assembly (see Chapter 10). **Note:** *Removal of the wheel hub/bearing assembly is not mandatory, but it makes the job a lot easier.*
47   Follow **illustrations 6.47a through 6.47v** for inspection and replacement of the brake shoes. Be sure to stay in order and read the caption under each illustration.
48   Before reinstalling the drum, carefully examine it for cracks, score marks, deep scratches and hard spots, which will appear as small discolored areas. If the hard spots cannot be removed with fine emery cloth or if any of the other conditions listed above exist, the drum must be taken to an auto- motive machine shop to have it resurfaced.

Note: *Professionals recommend resurfacing the drums whenever a brake job is performed. Resurfacing will eliminate the possibility of out-of-round drums. If the drums are worn so much that they can't be resurfaced without exceeding the maximum allowable diameter (stamped into the drum)* **(see illustration 6.12)**, *then new ones will be required. At the very least, if you elect not to have the drums resurfaced, remove the glazing from the sur- face with emery cloth or sandpaper using a swirling motion.*
49   Install the wheel hub/bearing assembly (with a new hub nut), if removed (see Chap- ter 10).
50   Install the brake drum, mount the wheel and install the lug nuts.
51   Repeat the procedure for the opposite wheel.
52   Lower the vehicle and tighten the lug nuts to the torque listed in the Chapter 1 Specifications.

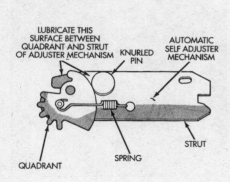

6.47o Before installing the adjuster on the leading brake shoe, lubricate the area between the quadrant and the adjuster strut with a small amount of multi-purpose grease

6.47p Install the automatic self-adjuster onto the proper leading brake shoe (they are unique for each side of the vehicle, RH or LH and are marked on the reinforcement plate) - after installation the quadrant teeth should be on the reinforced side of the brake shoe

6.47q Place the leading brake shoe (with adjuster installed) in position on the backing plate, making sure to match up the notch in the adjuster strut with the notch in the trailing brake shoe

6.47r Install the new pin and retaining clip

6.47s Compress the retaining clip and turn the pin 90-degrees to retain the brake shoe

6.47t Install the adjuster spring into the trailing brake shoe, then attach it to the adjuster

6.47u Install the upper return spring

6.47v Install the lower return spring, positioned as shown

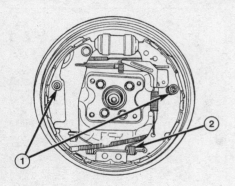

6.59 Rear brake shoe assembly (2003 through 2005 models)

1   Hold-down springs and retainers
2   Lower return spring

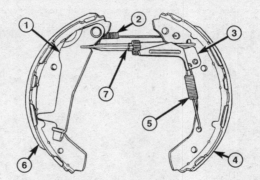

6.62 Rear brake shoe assembly details (2003 through 2005 models)

1   Lever
2   Upper return spring
3   Lever pawl
4   Leading shoe
5   Adjuster spring
6   Trailing shoe
7   Adjuster

53   To adjust the brakes, start the engine and fully depress the brake pedal two or three times to activate the automatic adjusters.

54   Carefully test brake operation before driving the vehicle in traffic.

2003 through 2005 models

Refer to illustrations 6.59 and 6.62

55   Loosen the wheel lug nuts 1/4-turn, raise the rear of the vehicle and support it securely on jackstands. Block the front wheels to keep the vehicle from rolling. Release the parking brake. Remove the wheel. **Note:** *The brake shoes on both wheels must be replaced at the same time. The drum brake assemblies on these models are unique for each side of the vehicle (left hand only - right hand only) so to avoid mixing up parts, service one brake assembly at a time.*

56   Remove the brake drum. If the drum won't come off, the brake shoes must be retracted from their fully adjusted position by inserting a screwdriver through the adjuster hole in the backing plate. Locate the adjuster access hole and remove the plug. Insert a screwdriver through the access hole and turn the adjuster wheel to retract the shoes. The drum should now come off. Wash the brake assembly with brake system cleaner **(see illustration 6.3)**.

57   Remove the wheel hub/bearing assembly (see Chapter 10). **Note:** *Removal of the wheel hub/bearing assembly is not mandatory, but it makes the job a lot easier.*

58   Compress the parking brake cable return spring with a pair of pliers **(see illustration 6.47j)** and disconnect the parking brake cable from the parking brake lever.

59   Remove the hold-down retainer and spring **(see illustration)** from each shoe. If you're unfamiliar with this procedure, refer to **illustration 6.28**.

60   Unhook the lower return spring from the brake shoes **(see illustration 6.59)**.

61   Remove both brake shoes and the other parts from the brake backing plate as a single assembly.

62   Unhook the adjuster spring from the lever pawl and from the leading brake shoe **(see illustration)**.

63   Remove the lever pawl from the pivot on the leading shoe and slide it out from under the adjuster **(see illustration 6.62)**.

64   Remove the adjuster and upper spring **(see illustration 6.62)**.

65   Check all parts for wear and damage, paying special attention to metal-to-metal contact points. Replace worn or damaged parts. **Note:** *If the vehicle has high mileage, it's a good idea to replace all of the springs as well as any parts that have visible problems.*

66   Check the brake drum for score marks, cracks, deep scratches and hard spots, which will appear as small discolored areas. If the hard spots cannot be removed with sandpaper or emery cloth or if any of the other conditions are seen, the drum must be resurfaced by an automotive machine shop. **Note:** *Professionals recommend resurfacing the drum whenever a brake job is performed. Resurfacing will correct taper and out-of-roundness in the drums as well as removing visible problems. If the drums are so worn that they can't be resurfaced without exceeding the maximum allowable diameter stamped into the drum* **(see illustration 6.12)**, *then new ones will be required. At the very least, if you don't have the drums resurfaced, remove the glazing from the surface with emery cloth or sandpaper using a swirling motion.*

67   Apply a small amount of high-temperature brake grease to the shoe contact areas of the backing plate **(see illustration 6.13)**, the moving parts of the adjuster assembly and where the adjuster contacts the brake shoes.

68   Install the wave washer and attach the parking brake lever to the new trailing brake shoe. Place the retainer in the pin groove and secure it with pliers.

69   Reverse the removal steps to install the brake shoes. Expand the shoes, using the adjuster screw, until the drum will just fit over them.

70   Turn the drum and listen for the shoes dragging on the drum as it is turned. If they do rub, remove the drum and back-off the adjuster screw a little and try it again. Repeat this step until you don't hear any drag.

71   Install the drum, depress the brake pedal firmly several times, then rotate the drum to ensure that the brakes are not dragging. If they are, back off the star wheel a little more.

72   Repeat the brake shoe replacement procedure on the other rear wheel.

73   Install the wheels and lug nuts. Lower the vehicle and tighten the lug nuts to the torque listed in the Chapter 1 Specifications.

74   Adjust the parking brake (see Section 13).

75   Start the engine, pump the brake pedal and operate the parking brake lever several times to actuate the automatic adjusters.

76   Carefully test brake operation before driving the vehicle in traffic.

7   Wheel cylinder - removal and installation

Refer to illustration 7.2

Note: *If replacement is warranted (usually because of fluid leakage or sticky operation) explore all options before beginning the job. New wheel cylinders are available, which makes this job quite easy. Never replace only one wheel cylinder. Always replace both of them at the same time.*

Removal

1   Remove the rear brake shoes (see Section 6).

2   Using a flare-nut wrench (if available), disconnect the brake line fitting from the wheel cylinder **(see illustration)**. Plug the end of the brake line to prevent fluid loss and contamination.

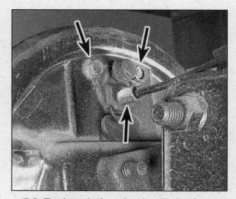

7.2 To detach the wheel cylinder from the brake backing plate, disconnect the brake line fitting, then remove the wheel cylinder bolts

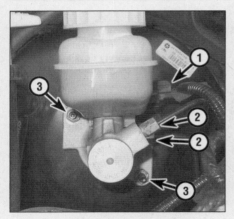

**8.6a Master cylinder mounting details -
convertible and sedan models**

1   *Electrical connector for fluid level
     switch*
2   *Brake line fittings*
3   *Mounting nuts*

3   Remove the two bolts securing the wheel
cylinder to the backing plate and remove the
wheel cylinder.

Installation

4   Installation is the reverse of removal.
Tighten the wheel cylinder mounting bolts to
the torque listed in this Chapter's Specifications. Tighten the line fitting securely.
5   Install the brake shoes, wheel hub/bear-
ing assembly, if removed (see Chapter 10)
and brake drum (see Section 6).
6   Bleed the brakes (see Section 11). Carefully test brake operation before resuming
normal operation.

8   Master cylinder - removal and
     installation

Removal

Refer to illustrations 8.6a and 8.6b

1   The master cylinder, which is located
in the engine compartment, is mounted on
the power brake booster. On 1995 through
2000 coupe models the remote reservoir is
mounted on the firewall, next to the booster.
On 2001 and later coupes and all convertible
and sedan models the reservoir is mounted
directly on the master cylinder.
2   If you're working on a convertible or
sedan model, disconnect the cable from the
remote ground terminal (see Chapter 5, Section 1). If you're working on a coupe model,
remove the battery (see Chapter 5).
3   Using a syringe or equivalent, siphon the
brake fluid from the master cylinder reservoir
and dispose of it properly. **Caution:** *Brake fluid
will damage paint. Cover all painted surfaces
and avoid spilling fluid during this procedure.*
4   If you're working on a 2000 or earlier
coupe model, remove the windshield washer
fluid reservoir. If you're working on a convertible or sedan model, remove the cruise control
servo and, on V6 models, the air intake duct.

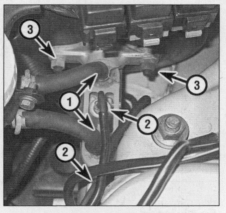

**8.6b Master cylinder mounting details -
coupe models**

1   *Reservoir hoses*
2   *Brake line fittings*
3   *Mounting nuts*

If equipped, unplug the electrical connector
from the fluid level warning switch.
5   If the vehicle has a remote reservoir,
place rags under the fittings and prepare caps
or plastic bags to cover the ends of the lines
once they're disconnected. **Caution:** *Brake
fluid will damage paint. Cover all body parts
and be careful not to spill fluid during this procedure.* Loosen the clamps that attach the
brake hoses to the reservoir. Pull the fluid
hoses away from the reservoir and plug the
ends to prevent contamination.
6   Disconnect the fluid lines from the master cylinder with a flare nut wrench **(see illustrations)**.
7   Remove the nuts attaching the master
cylinder to the power booster and pull the
master cylinder off the studs. Again, be careful not to spill the fluid as this is done.

Installation

Refer to illustration 8.9

8   Bench bleed the master cylinder before
installing it. Mount the master cylinder in a
vise, with the jaws of the vise clamping on the
mounting flange.
9   Attach a pair of master cylinder bleeder
tubes to the outlet ports of the master cylinder
(see illustration).
10   Fill the reservoir with brake fluid of the
recommended type (see Chapter 1).
11   Slowly push the pistons into the master
cylinder (a large Phillips screwdriver can be
used for this) - air will be expelled from the
pressure chambers and into the reservoir.
Because the tubes are submerged in fluid, air
can't be drawn back into the master cylinder
when you release the pistons.
12   Repeat the procedure until no more air
bubbles are present.
13   Remove the bleed tubes, one at a time,
and install plugs in the open ports to prevent
fluid leakage and air from entering. Install the
reservoir cap.
14   Install the master cylinder over the studs
on the power brake booster and tighten the
nuts only finger-tight at this time. On models

**8.9 The best way to bleed the master
cylinder before installing it on the vehicle
is with a pair of bleeder tubes that direct
fluid into the reservoir during bleeding**

with a remote reservoir, connect the reservoir hoses to the inlet fittings and install the
clamps.
15   Thread the brake line fittings into the
master cylinder. Since the master cylinder is
still a bit loose, it can be moved slightly so the
fittings thread in easily. Don't strip the threads
as the fittings are tightened.
16   Tighten the mounting nuts to the torque
listed in this Chapter's Specifications. Tighten
the brake line fittings securely.
17   Fill the master cylinder reservoir with
fluid, then bleed the master cylinder and the
rest of the brake system (see Section 11). To
bleed the master cylinder on the vehicle, have
an assistant depress the brake pedal and hold
it down. Loosen the fitting to allow air and fluid
to escape. Tighten the fitting, then allow your
assistant to return the pedal to its rest position. Repeat this procedure on the other fittings until the fluid is free of air bubbles.
18   Reinstall any components that were
removed for access to the master cylinder.
19   Re-check the brake fluid level, then
check the operation of the brake system carefully before driving the vehicle in traffic.

9   Power brake booster - check,
     removal and installation

Operating check

1   Depress the brake pedal several times
with the engine off and make sure that there is
no change in the pedal reserve distance.
2   Depress the pedal and start the engine.
If the pedal goes down slightly, operation is
normal.

Airtightness check

3   Start the engine and turn it off after one
or two minutes. Depress the brake pedal
several times slowly. If the pedal goes down
farther the first time but gradually rises after
the second or third depression, the booster is
airtight.

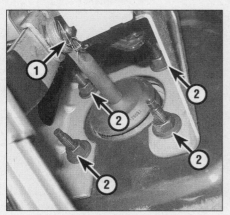

9.16 Power brake booster mounting details (as viewed from under the dash) - convertible and sedan models

1   *Pushrod retaining clip*
2   *Booster mounting nuts*

9.26 Remove the retaining clip from the pushrod clevis pin . . .

9.27 . . . then remove the four booster-to-firewall nuts

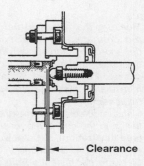

9.31a If there is there is too much clearance between the booster pushrod and the master cylinder piston, there will be excessive brake pedal travel, if there is interference between the two, the brakes may drag

4   Depress the brake pedal while the engine is running, then stop the engine with the pedal depressed. If there is no change in the pedal reserve travel after holding the pedal for 30 seconds, the booster is airtight.

5   The power brake booster unit requires no special maintenance apart from periodic inspection of the vacuum hoses and the case. The booster is not serviceable. If a problem develops, it must be replaced with a new one.

Convertible and sedan models

Removal

Refer to illustration 9.16

6   Disconnect the negative battery cable from the ground stud on the left shock tower (see Chapter 5, Section 1). Remove the air intake resonator and the related ducting between the throttle body and the air cleaner (see Chapter 4).

7   If equipped, unplug the cruise control servo electrical connector. Detach the servo from the shock tower and position it out of the way.

8   On V6 engines, detach the accelerator/cruise control cable bracket from the intake manifold and position it out of the way (the cable(s) may remain attached to bracket).

9   Label and detach the electrical connector and vacuum hose from the canister purge solenoid. Remove the purge solenoid from the vehicle.

10   Disconnect the vacuum hose from the power brake booster vacuum fitting.

11   Label and disconnect the vacuum hoses and electrical connector from the EGR valve transducer (see Chapter 6). Remove the EGR valve transducer.

12   Disconnect the fluid level sensor connector from the master cylinder reservoir (see Section 8).

13   On models with four-cylinder engines, it is not necessary to disconnect the brake lines from the master cylinder; simply remove the mounting nuts (see Section 8) and slide the master cylinder off the studs and let it rest on

the top of the transaxle (just make sure you don't kink the metal brake lines).

14   On models with a V6 engine, remove the master cylinder from the vehicle (see Section 8).

15   On V6 engines equipped with automatic transaxles, remove the transaxle fluid dipstick tube. Cover the dipstick tube hole in the transaxle with duct tape to prevent the entry of foreign debris.

16   Working inside the vehicle under the dash, disconnect the power brake pushrod from the top of the brake pedal by prying off the retaining clip **(see illustration)**. For safety reasons, discard the old pushrod retaining clip and buy a new clip for reassembly.

17   Remove the nuts attaching the booster to the firewall.

18   Working inside the engine compartment, carefully withdraw the power brake booster unit from the firewall and out of the engine compartment.

Installation

19   To install the booster, place it into position on the firewall and tighten the retaining nuts to the torque listed in this Chapter's Specifications. Connect the pushrod to the brake pedal. **Warning:** *Use a new retainer clip. DO NOT reuse the old clip.*

20   The remaining installation steps are the reverse of removal.

21   If the brake lines were detached from the master cylinder, bleed the brake hydraulic system (see Section 11).

22   Carefully test the operation of the brakes before placing the vehicle in normal operation.

Coupe models

Removal

Refer to illustrations 9.26 and 9.27

23   If the vehicle is equipped with a manual transaxle, remove the clutch fluid reservoir bracket (see Chapter 8).

24   Remove the battery (see Chapter 5).

25   Remove the brake master cylinder (see Section 8).

26   Locate the pushrod clevis connecting the

booster to the brake pedal **(see illustration)**. It's accessible from inside the vehicle, under the dash on the driver's side. Remove the clevis pin retaining clip with pliers and pull out the pin.

27   Remove the four nuts holding the brake booster to the firewall **(see illustration)**.

28   Disconnect the hose leading from the engine to the booster. Be careful not to damage the hose when removing it from the booster fitting.

29   Slide the booster straight out from the firewall until the studs clear the holes.

Installation

30   Installation procedures are basically the reverse of removal. Tighten the clevis locknut securely (if loosened) and the booster mounting nuts to the torque listed in this Chapter's Specifications. **Note:** *Apply a film of multi-purpose grease to the clevis pin before installing it.*

2000 and earlier models

Refer to illustrations 9.31a, 9.31b, 9.31c, 9.31d and 9.31e

31   If a new power brake booster unit is being installed, check the pushrod clearance **(see illustration)** as follows:

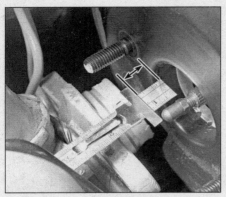

9.31b Measure the distance that the pushrod protrudes from the brake booster at the master cylinder mounting surface (including the gasket, *if* one is used)

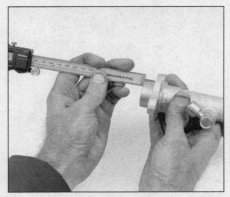

9.31c Measure the distance from the mounting flange to the end of the master cylinder

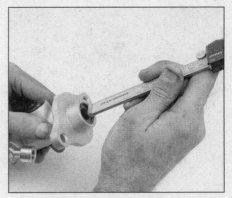

9.31d Measure the distance from the piston pocket to the end of the master cylinder

a) *Measure the distance that the push-rod protrudes from the master cylinder mounting surface on the front of the power brake booster, including the gasket, if one is used. Write down this measurement (see illustration). This is "dimension A."*

b) *Measure the distance from the mounting flange to the end of the master cylinder (see illustration). Write down this measurement. This is "dimension B."*

c) *Measure the distance from the end of the master cylinder to the bottom of the pocket in the piston (see illustration). Write down this measurement. This is "dimension C."*

d) *Subtract measurement B from measurement C, then subtract measurement A from the difference between B and C. This the pushrod clearance.*

e) *Compare your calculated pushrod clearance to the pushrod clearance listed in this Chapter's Specifications. If necessary, adjust the pushrod length to achieve the correct clearance (see illustration).*

f) *Proceed to Step 33.*

2001 and later models

32   On these models, the only measurement that has to be taken is the amount the booster pushrod protrudes from the face of the booster **(see illustration 9.31b)**, with a vacuum of 19.6 in-Hg applied to the booster with a hand-held vacuum pump. Compare this dimension with the value listed in this Chapter's Specifications. If it doesn't fall within the specified range, adjust the length of the pushrod **(see illustration 9.31e)**.

All coupe models

33   After the final installation of the master cylinder and brake hoses and lines, the brake pedal height and freeplay must be adjusted and the system must be bled. See the appropriate Sections of this Chapter for the procedures.

9.31e To adjust the length of the booster pushrod, hold the serrated portion of the rod with a pair of pliers and turn the adjusting screw in or out, as necessary, to achieve the desired setting

10   Brake hoses and lines - inspection and replacement

Inspection

1   Whenever the vehicle is raised and supported securely on jackstands, the rubber hoses which connect the steel brake lines with the front and rear brake assemblies should be inspected for cracks, chafing of the outer cover, leaks, blisters and other damage. These are important and vulnerable parts of the brake system and inspection should be thorough. A light and mirror will be helpful for a complete check. If a hose exhibits any of the above conditions, renew it immediately.

Flexible hose replacement

Refer to illustration 10.3

2   Clean all dirt away from the hose fittings.
3   Using a flare-nut wrench, disconnect the metal brake line from the hose fitting **(see illustration)**. Be careful not to bend the frame bracket or line. If the threaded fitting is cor-

10.3 Loosening a brake line fitting from a front brake hose

roded, spray it with penetrating oil and allow it to soak in for about 10 minutes, then try again. If you try to break loose a fitting nut that's frozen, you will kink the metal line, which will then have to be replaced.

4   Remove the brake hose from the bracket (some are secured to a bracket with a retaining clip, others have an integral bracket/fitting). Detach the brake hose from the bracket or bracket from the vehicle as applicable. Immediately plug the metal line to prevent excessive leakage and contamination.

5   If you're removing a rear brake hose on a drum-brake model, use a flare-nut wrench to loosen the line fitting at the wheel cylinder and remove the hose.

6   On hoses that are attached to the caliper with an inlet fitting bolt, unscrew the fitting bolt at the caliper and remove the hose, discarding the sealing washers on either side of the fitting.

7   If you're removing a rear hose on a coupe model with disc brakes, remove the clip securing the hose to the bracket, then unscrew the hose from the caliper.

8   Attach the new brake hose to the caliper or wheel cylinder as applicable. **Note:** *When replacing the front brake hoses, always use new sealing washers.* Tighten the fitting bolt to

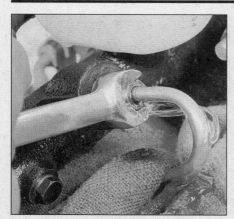

11.7 Have an assistant depress the brake pedal and hold it down, then loosen the fitting nut, allowing air and brake fluid to escape; repeat this procedure on the other fitting(s) until the fluid is clear of air bubbles

11.9 When bleeding the brakes, a hose is connected to the bleed screw at the caliper or wheel cylinder and then submerged in clean brake fluid - air will be seen as bubbles exiting the tube (all air must be expelled before moving to the next wheel)

the torque listed this Chapter's Specifications.

9   Insert the other end of the new hose through the bracket or loosely attach the fitting/bracket to the vehicle as applicable making sure the hose isn't kinked or twisted. Then fit the metal line to the hose (or hose fitting), tighten the hose bracket (if applicable) and tighten the brake tube fitting nut securely.

10   Carefully check to make sure the suspension or steering components don't make contact with the hose. Have an assistant push down on the vehicle while you watch to see whether the hose interferes with suspension operation. If you're replacing a front hose, have your assistant turn the steering wheel lock-to-lock while you make sure the hose doesn't interfere with the steering linkage or the steering knuckle.

11   After installation, check the master cylinder fluid level and add fluid as necessary. Bleed the brakes (see Section 11). Carefully test brake operation before resuming normal operation.

Metal brake lines

12   When replacing brake lines, be sure to use the correct parts. Do not use copper tubing for any brake system components. Purchase steel brake lines from a dealer parts department or auto parts store.

13   Prefabricated brake line, with the tube ends already flared and fittings installed, is available at auto parts stores and dealer parts departments. If it is necessary to bend a line, use a tubing bender to prevent kinking the line.

14   When installing the new line make sure it's well supported in the brackets and has plenty of clearance between moving or hot components. Make sure you tighten the fittings securely.

15   After installation, check the master cylinder fluid level and add fluid as necessary. Bleed the brakes (see Section 11). Carefully test brake operation before resuming normal operation.

11   Brake hydraulic system - bleeding

Refer to illustrations 11.7 and 11.9

Warning 1: *The following procedure is a manual bleeding procedure. This is the only bleeding procedure which can be performed at home without special tools. However, if air has found its way into the hydraulic control unit of a convertible or a sedan model, the entire system must be bled manually, then with a DRB scan tool, then manually a second time. If the brake pedal feels "spongy" even after bleeding the brakes, or the ABS light on the instrument panel does not go off, or if you have any doubts whatsoever about the effectiveness of the brake system, have the vehicle towed to a dealer service department or other repair shop equipped with the necessary tools for bleeding the system.*

Warning 2: *Wear eye protection when bleeding the brake system. If the fluid comes in contact with your eyes, immediately rinse them with water and seek medical attention.*

Note: *Bleeding the hydraulic system is necessary to remove any air that manages to find its way into the system when it's been opened during removal and installation of a hydraulic component.*

1   It will be necessary to bleed the complete system if air has entered the system due to low fluid level, or if the brake lines have been disconnected at the master cylinder.

2   If a brake line was disconnected only at a wheel, then only that caliper or wheel cylinder must be bled.

3   If a brake line is disconnected at a fitting located between the master cylinder and any of the brakes, that part of the system served by the disconnected line must be bled. The following procedure describes bleeding the entire system, however.

4   Remove any residual vacuum from the brake power booster by applying the brake several times with the engine off.

5   Remove the cap from the master cylinder reservoir and fill the reservoir with brake fluid. Reinstall the cap(s). **Note:** *Check the fluid level often during the bleeding operation and add fluid as necessary to prevent the fluid level from falling low enough to allow air bubbles into the master cylinder.*

6   Have an assistant on hand, as well as a supply of new brake fluid, a clear container partially filled with clean brake fluid, a length of clear tubing to fit over the bleeder valve and a wrench to open and close the bleeder valve.

7   Begin the bleeding process by bleeding the master cylinder **(see illustration)**.

8   Moving to the first wheel in the bleeding sequence, loosen the bleeder valve slightly, then tighten it to a point where it is snug but can still be loosened quickly and easily. The bleeding sequence is as follows:

> **Coupe models**
> Right rear
> Left front
> Left rear
> Right front
> **Convertible and sedan models**
> Left rear
> Right front
> Right rear
> Left front

9   Place one end of the hose over the bleeder valve and submerge the other end in brake fluid in the container **(see illustration)**.

10   Have the assistant push the brake pedal slowly to the floor, then hold the pedal firmly depressed.

11   While the pedal is held depressed, open the bleeder valve just enough to allow a flow of fluid to leave the valve. Watch for air bubbles to exit the submerged end of the tube. When the fluid flow slows after a couple of seconds, close the valve and have your assistant release the pedal.

12   Repeat Steps 10 and 11 until no more air is seen leaving the tube, then tighten the bleeder valve and proceed to bleed the other calipers/wheel cylinders, in the proper sequence, using the same procedure. Be sure to check the fluid in the master cylinder reservoir frequently.

13   Never use old brake fluid. It contains moisture which can boil, rendering the brakes inoperative.

14   Refill the master cylinder with fluid at the end of the operation.

15   Check the operation of the brakes. The pedal should feel solid when depressed, with no sponginess. If necessary, repeat the entire process. **Warning:** *If, after bleeding the system you do not have a firm brake pedal, or if the ABS light on the instrument panel does not go off, or if you have any doubts whatsoever about the effectiveness of the brake system, have it towed to a dealer service department or other repair shop to have the system bled.*

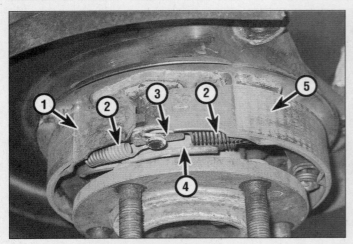

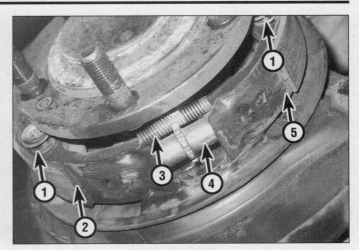

12.4a Parking brake shoe details (right side, viewed from above) - coupe models

1	Trailing shoe	4	Strut
2	Upper return spring	5	Leading shoe
3	Anchor plate		

12.4b Parking brake shoe details (right side, viewed from below) - coupe models

1	Hold-down spring and retainer	3	Lower return spring
2	Trailing shoe	4	Adjuster screw assembly
		5	Leading shoe

12 Parking brake shoes (models with rear disc brakes) - replacement

Warning: *Parking brake shoes must be replaced on both wheels at the same time - never replace the shoes on only one wheel. Also, the dust created by the brake system is harmful to your health. Never blow it out with compressed air and don't inhale any of it. An approved filtering mask should be worn when working on the brakes. Do not, under any circumstances, use petroleum-based solvents to clean brake parts. Use brake system cleaner only!*

Coupe models

Refer to illustrations 12.4a and 12.4b

1　Loosen the rear wheel lug nuts, raise the rear end of the vehicle and support it securely on jackstands. Block the front wheels to keep the vehicle from rolling. Release the parking brake and remove the rear wheels.

2　Remove the brake caliper, torque plate and brake disc (see Section 5).

3　Once the disc is removed, clean the parking brake assembly with brake system cleaner.

4　Using locking pliers, unhook and remove the springs **(see illustrations)**.

5　Remove the adjuster assembly (noting which end is facing forward) and strut from between the brake shoes.

6　Grasp one of the shoe hold-down cups with pliers and push it toward the brake backing plate to compress the hold-down spring. Twist the cup 1/4-turn to align the slot in the hold-down pin with the cup, then release the spring pressure (the pin will pass through the cup slot) and take off the cup and spring. Repeat this with the cup and spring on the other parking brake shoe.

7　Take the shoes off the backing plate. Disengage the parking brake lever from the cable.

8　Check all parts for wear and damage, paying special attention to metal-to-metal contact points. Replace worn or damaged parts.

The parking brake lever is integral with the shoe it's attached to. **Note:** *If the vehicle has high mileage, it's a good idea to replace all of the springs as well as any parts that have visible problems.*

9　Check the parking brake drum surface inside the brake disc for score marks, cracks, deep scratches and hard spots, which will appear as small discolored areas. If the hard spots cannot be removed with emery cloth or if any of the other conditions are seen, the drum must be resurfaced by an automotive machine shop. **Note:** *If you don't have the drums resurfaced, remove the glazing from the surface with emery cloth or sandpaper using a swirling motion.*

10　Apply a small amount of high-temperature brake grease to the friction points of the backing plate and adjuster screw assembly **(see illustration 6.13)**.

11　Reverse the removal steps to install the brake shoes. The shoe-to-anchor spring with the paint mark is installed with the paint mark toward the rear of the vehicle (for both left

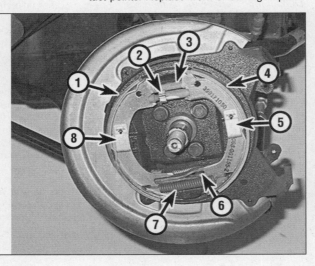

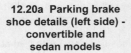
12.20a Parking brake shoe details (left side) - convertible and sedan models

1　Leading shoe
2　Adjuster screw assembly
3　Upper return spring
4　Trailing shoe
5　Hold-down clip
6　Adjuster lever
7　Lower return spring
8　Hold-down clip

12.20b Squeeze the hold-down clip on the trailing shoe with pliers and turn the pin 90-degrees, then remove the clip

12.20c Pull the trailing shoe back and remove the adjuster screw assembly (note how it's installed; it must be reinstalled the same way)

12.20d Remove the upper return spring

12.20e Unhook the lower return spring and remove the trailing shoe

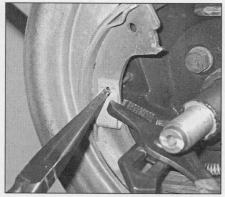

12.20f Remove the hold-down clip from the leading shoe and remove the shoe from the backing plate

12.20g Detach the parking brake cable from the adjuster lever

12.20h Clean the backing plate, then apply a thin coat of high-temperature grease to the shoe contact points on the backing plate (also clean and lubricate the friction surfaces of the adjuster screw assembly)

and right sides). Expand the shoes, using the automatic adjuster, until the drum will just fit over them.

12   Install the brake disc and caliper. Remove the rubber plug in the hub portion of the disc, then turn the adjuster screw until the disc will not turn. Now turn the adjuster in the opposite direction five notches.

13   Adjust the parking brake (see Section 13).

14   Install the wheel and lug nuts. Lower the vehicle and tighten the lug nuts to the torque listed in the Chapter 1 Specifications.

15   Check the operation of the parking brake.

Convertible and sedan models

Refer to illustrations 12.20a through 12.20o and 12.23

16   Loosen the rear wheel lug nuts, raise the rear of the vehicle and support it securely on jackstands. Block the front wheels and remove the rear wheels. Release the parking brake.

17   Remove the rear calipers (see Section 4). Support the caliper assemblies with a coat hanger or heavy wire and don't disconnect the brake line from the caliper.

18   Remove the rear discs (see Section 5). Remove the rear hub and bearing assemblies (see Chapter 10).

19   Clean the parking brake assembly with brake system cleaner.

20   Follow the accompanying sequence of

photos to replace the parking brake shoes **(see illustrations)**. Be sure to stay in order and read the caption under each illustration.

12.20i Connect the adjuster lever to the cable, mount the leading shoe on the backing plate, making sure the notch in the shoe engages with the adjuster lever . . .

12.20j . . . and secure the shoe with the hold-down clip

12.20k Connect the lower return spring to the bottom of each shoe . . .

12.20l . . . Engage the adjuster lever with the notch in the trailing shoe . . .

12.20m . . . then secure the shoe with the hold-down clip

12.20n Install the upper return spring

21 Inspect the drum surface inside the disc for score marks, deep grooves, hard spots (which will appear as small, discolored areas) and cracks. If the disc/drum is worn, scored or out of round, it will have to be resurfaced by an automotive machine shop, or replaced.

22 Install the hub and bearing assemblies (see Chapter 10).
23 Before installing the disc, rotate the star wheel on the adjuster until the distance across the friction surfaces of the parking brake shoes is 6-3/4 inches **(see illustration)**.
24 Install the disc/drum over the shoes.

Using a screwdriver or brake adjusting tool, turn the star wheel on the parking brake shoe adjuster until the shoes slightly drag as the disc is turned, then back-off the adjuster until the shoes don't drag.
25 Install the caliper (see Section 4).
26 Repeat this sequence for the other parking brake shoes at the other rear wheel.
27 Adjust the parking brake (see Section 13).

13   Parking brake - adjustment

Coupe models
Refer to illustration 13.3

1 The parking brake lever, when properly adjusted, should travel five to seven clicks (rear drum brakes) or three to five clicks (rear disc brakes) when a moderate pulling force is applied. If it travels less than specified, there's a chance the parking brake might not be releasing completely and might be dragging on the drum. If the lever can be pulled up more than specified, the parking brake may

12.20o Spread the shoes apart and install the adjuster screw assembly

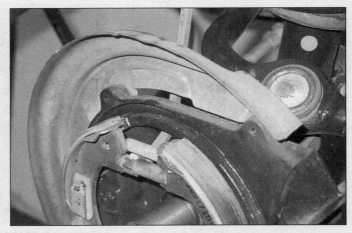

12.23 Turn the adjuster screw star wheel until the span across the shoes is 6-3/4 inches (tool is inserted through the backing plate to illustrate how the shoes can be adjusted with the disc in place)

13.3 With the center console removed, the parking brake cable adjuster nut is accessible (coupe model shown)

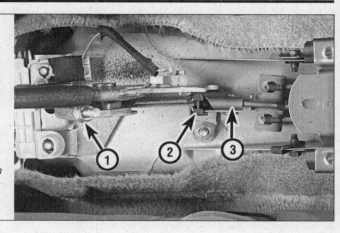

13.12 Parking brake lever and cable details (convertible and sedan models)

1   *Output cable/ adjusting nut*
2   *Output cable retaining clip*
3   *Rear cable tension equalizer*

not hold adequately on an incline, allowing the car to roll.

2   To gain access to the parking brake cable adjuster, remove the center console (see Chapter 11).

3   Turn the adjusting nut on the parking brake cable all the way to the end of the cable **(see illustration)**.

4   If you're working on a vehicle with rear drum brakes, press the brake pedal firmly several times to operate the rear brake adjusters. The pedal stroke should change, then stop changing, as the pedal is pumped. If the automatic adjusters are working properly, this will adjust the parking brake, too.

5   If you're working on a vehicle with rear disc brakes, loosen the rear wheel lug nuts, raise the rear of the vehicle and remove the rear wheels. Insert a screwdriver into the hole in the hub portion of the disc and turn the adjuster to lock the brake disc. Turn the adjuster back five notches. Install the rear wheels and leave the rear end jacked up.

6   Loosen or tighten the adjusting nut **(see illustration 13.3)** until the desired travel is attained. Tighten the nut. Make sure there's no play between the adjusting nut and the pin in the nut holder.

7   On drum brake models, jack up the rear end and support the vehicle on jackstands. Spin the rear wheels by hand and make sure the rear brakes don't drag. Lower the vehicle.

8   On rear disc brake models, install the wheel and lug nuts, then lower the vehicle and tighten the lug nuts to the torque listed in the Chapter 1 Specifications.

9   Install the console.

Convertible and sedan models (2001 and later models)

Refer to illustration 13.12

Note 1: *On 2000 and earlier convertible and sedan models, the parking brake is adjusted automatically. If the parking brake won't hold the vehicle on an incline, check to see if the parking brake shoes (models with disc brakes) or the rear brake shoes (models with drum brakes) are properly adjusted (see Section 6 [drum brakes] or Section 12 [disc brakes]).*

Note: *Anytime the parking brake cable requires adjustment, the cable tension equalizer must be replaced to ensure proper adjustment.*

10   Remove the center console (see Chapter 11).

11   Place the parking brake lever in the fully released position (down).

12   Tighten the output cable adjusting nut

until 26 mm (approximately 1-inch) of threads are protruding from the nut **(see illustration)**.

13   Pull the lever back as far as it will travel - one time only. Fully actuating the lever in this manner stretches the portion of the cable tensioner which automatically provides the correct tension on the cables.

14   After adjustment, verify that the rear brakes are not dragging on the drums and the parking brake lever does not exhibit any free play. If either condition exists, tighten or loosen the output cable adjusting nut as required.

15   Install the center console (see Chapter 11).

14   Brake light switch - check, replacement and adjustment

Refer to illustrations 14.1a and 14.1b

Check

1   The brake light switch is located on the brake pedal mounting bracket **(see illustrations)**. The switch activates the brake lights at the rear of the vehicle when the pedal is depressed. To gain access to the switch, remove the left-side under-dash panel and the heater/air conditioning duct.

14.1a Brake light switch - coupe models

14.1b Brake light switch - convertible and sedan models

2   If the brake lights are inoperative, check the fuse first (see Chapter 12).

3   If the fuse is good, check for voltage to the switch on the feed wire (refer to the wiring diagrams at the end of this manual for the proper color wire to check). If no voltage is present, repair the wire between the switch and the fuse box.

4   If voltage is present, depress the brake pedal and check for voltage at the output wire terminal (again, refer to the wiring diagrams). If no voltage is present, replace the switch.

5   If voltage is present, check for power on the brake light wires at the tail light housings (with the brake pedal depressed). If voltage is not present, repair the circuit between the switch and the brake lights.

6   If voltage is present, check for a bad ground; using a jumper wire connected to a good ground, probe the ground wire terminal at the tail light connector. If the brake lights go on, repair the ground circuit (follow the ground wire from the tail light housing).

7   Keep in mind that the brake light bulbs *could* be burned out, but the likelihood of all the bulbs being burned out is very slim.

Replacement and adjustment
Coupe models

8   Disconnect the electrical connector from the brake light switch **(see illustration 14.1a)**

9   Rotate the switch counterclockwise slightly, so it unlocks from its holder, then pull it out of the holder.

10   To install the switch, insert it into its holder (canted slightly counterclockwise as during removal) and push it in until the switch body contacts the bracket on the brake pedal, then pull it back so there is approximately 3/64-inch (1 mm) clearance between the switch body and the bracket on the pedal. Rotate the switch clockwise to lock it into place.

11   Plug the electrical connector into the switch.

Convertible and sedan models

12   Depress and hold the brake pedal, then rotate the brake light switch about 30-degrees in a counterclockwise direction **(see illustration 14.1b)** and remove it from the mounting bracket.

13   Unplug the electrical connector from the switch and remove it from the vehicle.

14   Grasp the switch plunger and pull it outward until it has ratcheted to it's fully extended position.

15   Depress the brake pedal as far as it will go, then install the switch in the bracket by aligning the index key on the switch with the slot at the top of the square hole in the mounting bracket. When the switch is fully installed in the bracket, rotate the switch clockwise about 30-degrees to lock the switch into the bracket.

16   Gently pull back on the brake pedal until the pedal stops moving. The switch plunger will ratchet backward to the correct position. **Caution:** *Don't use excessive force when pulling back on the brake pedal to adjust the switch. If you use too much force, you will damage the switch or the striker.*

17   Plug the electrical connector into the switch.

Chapter 10
Suspension and steering systems

Contents

Specifications

Torque specifications

Ft-lbs (unless otherwise indicated)

Front suspension (2000 and earlier coupe models)

Shock absorber	
Upper mounting nuts	44
Damper fork-to-shock absorber pinch bolt	75
Damper fork-to-lateral arm bolt/nut	64
Damper rod nut	18
Stabilizer bar	
Bracket bolts	28
Link nuts	28
Compression lower arm	
Balljoint nut	43 to 51
Pivot shaft bolts	60
Lateral lower arm	
Balljoint nut	43 to 51
To damper fork bolt	64
Pivot bolt/nut	64
Upper control arm	
Shaft-to-body nuts	62
Pivot bolt nuts	41
Balljoint nut	20

Torque specifications

Ft-lbs (unless otherwise indicated)

Note: *One foot pound (ft-lb) of torque is equivalent to 12 inch-pounds (in-lbs) of torque. Torque values below approximately 15 ft-lbs are expressed in inch-pounds, since most foot-pound torque wrenches are not accurate at these smaller values.*

Front suspension (2000 and earlier coupe models) (continued)

Hub and bearing assembly-to-steering knuckle bolts	65
Stiffener plate bolts	55
Driveaxle/hub nut	See Chapter 8

Front suspension (2001 and later coupe models)

Strut
Upper mounting nuts	33
Damper rod nut	47
Strut-to-steering knuckle bolts/nuts	221

Stabilizer bar
Bracket bolts	33
Link nuts	33

Control arm
Clamp-to-body bolts	60
Pivot bolt nut	80
Balljoint-to-steering knuckle pinch bolt/nut	80
Hub and bearing assembly-to-steering knuckle bolts	65
Driveaxle/hub nut	See Chapter 8

Front suspension (convertible and sedan models)

Shock absorber

Upper mounting bolts
1996	70
1997 and later	75
Damper fork-to-shock absorber pinch bolt	65
Damper fork-to-lower control arm bolt/nut	65
Damper rod nut	40

Stabilizer bar
Bracket bolts	45
Link nuts	75

Lower control arm
Balljoint nut	55
To damper fork bolt	65

Front pivot bolt/nut
1995 through 2003 models	135
2004 and later models	104

Control arm-to-crossmember rear bolt
1995 through 2003 models	70
2004 and later models	55

Upper control arm

Balljoint nut
2001 and earlier models	40
2002 and later models	20

Pivot bolts
1996 models	70
1997 and later models	66
Hub and bearing assembly-to-steering knuckle bolts	80
Crossmember-to-body bolts	120
Driveaxle/hub nut	See Chapter 8

Rear suspension (coupe models)

Rear stabilizer bar

Clamp bolts
2000 and earlier models	108 to 168 in-lbs
2001 and later	33
Link nuts	28

Shock absorber
To body nuts	33

Lower mounting bolt/nut
2000 and earlier models	71
2001 and later models	73
Damper rod nut	16
Trailing arm-to-body bolt/nut	109
Trailing arm-to-knuckle bolt	94

Torque specifications   Ft-lbs (unless otherwise indicated)

Note: *One foot pound (ft-lb) of torque is equivalent to 12 inch-pounds (in-lbs) of torque. Torque values below approximately 15 ft-lbs are expressed in inch-pounds, since most foot-pound torque wrenches are not accurate at these smaller values.*

Rear suspension (coupe models) (continued)

Upper control arm-to-knuckle bolt/nut	71
Upper control arm-to-bracket pivot bolts/nuts	41
Upper control arm bracket-to-body bolts	28
Lower arm-to-crossmember bolt	71
Lower arm-to-knuckle bolt/nut	71
Toe control arm-to-crossmember bolt/nut	55
Toe control arm balljoint nut	20
Rear hub-to-knuckle bolts	60
Rear suspension crossmember-to-body nuts	64

Rear suspension (convertible and sedan models)

Balljoint-to-knuckle castle nut	
1996 through 2001 models	63
2002 and later models	20
Crossmember-to-body bolts	80
Control arm pivot bar-to-crossmember	
1995 through 2003	80
2004 and later	70
Hub and bearing assembly-to-knuckle retaining nut	185
Lateral link-to-knuckle bolts/nuts	
1995 through 2003	80
2004 and later	90
Lateral link jam nuts	
1996 through 1999 models	48
2000 and later models	70
Lateral link-to-crossmember bolts	70
Shock absorber mounting bracket-to-body nuts	40
Shock absorber-to-knuckle bolts/nuts	70
Shock absorber rod-to-upper mount nut	40
Stabilizer bushing clamp bolts	23
Stabilizer-to-lateral link nuts	26
Trailing link shaft nuts (both ends)	
1995 through 2003	73
2004 and later	85
Trailing link bracket-to-body bolts	25

Steering system (coupe models)

Airbag bolts	
1995 through 2000 models	48 in-lbs
2001 and later models	78 in-lbs
Steering wheel nut	30
Steering gear mounting bolts	51
Steering column mounting bolts	108 in-lbs
Intermediate shaft pinch bolt	156 in-lbs
Tie-rod end-to-steering knuckle nut	21

Steering system (convertible and sedan models)

Airbag-to-steering wheel bolts	
1996 through 2000 models	90 in-lbs
2001 models	73 in-lbs
2002 and later models	85 in-lbs
Steering wheel nut or bolt	
1996 through 2000	45
2001 and later	40
Steering gear mounting bolts	50
Steering column mounting nuts	
1996 through 1999 models	105 in-lbs
2000 and later models	150 in-lbs
Intermediate shaft pinch bolt	
1996 through 2000 models	20
2001 and later models	32
Tie-rod end-to-steering knuckle nut	
1996 through 2000 models	45
2001 and later models	40

1.1 Front suspension and steering components - 2000 and earlier coupe models

1	Upper control arm	4	Lateral arm	7	Steering gear boot
2	Shock absorber/coil spring assembly	5	Steering knuckle	8	Stabilizer bar
3	Damper fork	6	Compression arm		

1   General information

Refer to illustrations 1.1, 1.2, 1.3a and 1.3b

The front suspension on 2000 and earlier coupe models uses a single upper and two lower control arms connected by a steering knuckle. Damping is provided by a coil spring/ shock absorber unit, which is attached to the body at the top and through a damper fork to the compression lower control arm at the bottom **(see illustration)**.

The front suspension on convertible and sedan models is similar, but uses only one lower control arm **(see illustration)**.

The front suspension on 2001 and later coupes is a MacPherson strut design. The upper end of each strut is attached to the vehicle body. The lower end of the strut is connected to the upper end of the steering knuckle. The steering knuckle is attached to a balljoint in the outer end of the control arm.

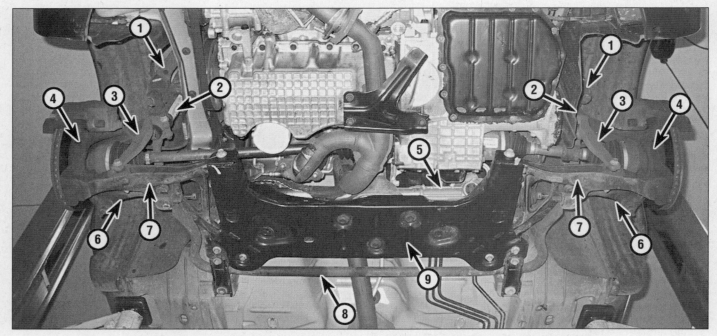

1.2 Front suspension and steering components - Sebring convertible and sedan models

1	Upper control arm	4	Steering knuckle	7	Lower control arm
2	Shock absorber/coil spring assembly	5	Steering gear	8	Stabilizer bar
3	Damper fork	6	Tie-rod end	9	Crossmember

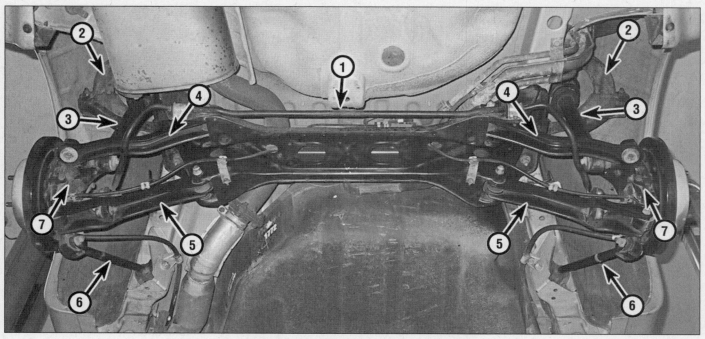

1.3a Rear suspension components - coupe models

1	Stabilizer bar	4	Toe control arm	6	Trailing arm
2	Upper control arm	5	Lower control arm	7	Rear knuckle
3	Shock absorber/coil spring assembly				

On all models, a front stabilizer bar is attached to the lower control arms to minimize body roll during cornering.

The rear suspension on all models also uses shock absorber/coil spring assemblies. The upper end of each shock is attached to the vehicle body. The lower end of the shock is attached to the rear knuckle. The knuckle is located by an upper control arm at the top, and two lateral links and a trailing arm at the bottom. The basic design of the rear suspension is the same for all model years covered in this manual. The shapes of some components differ between models, but the overall design is the same **(see illustrations)**.

The rack-and-pinion steering gear is located below and behind the engine/ transaxle assembly on the crossmember and actuates

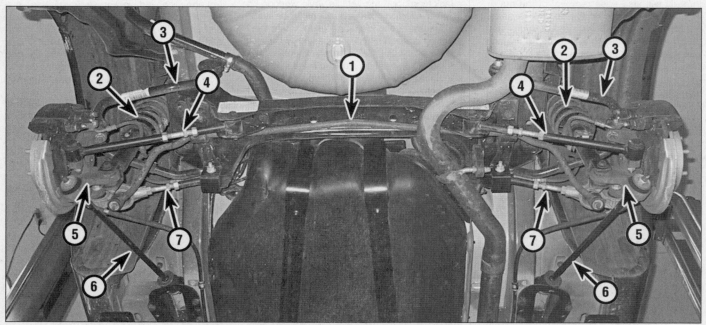

1.3b Rear suspension components - convertible and sedan models

1	Stabilizer bar	4	Rear lateral link	6	Trailing arm
2	Shock absorber/coil spring assembly	5	Rear knuckle	7	Forward lateral link
3	Upper control arm				

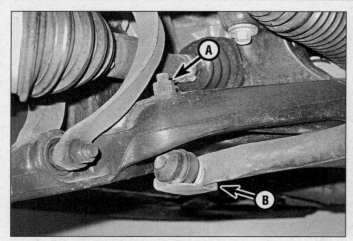

2.2a Remove the stabilizer bar link-to-lower control arm nut (A); it's a good idea to loosen the link-to-bar nut (B) now so it can be detached and checked for wear (convertible and sedan models)

2.2b On 2000 and earlier coupe models the stabilizer bar link is connected to the damper fork

the tie-rods, which are attached to the steering knuckles. The steering column is designed to collapse in the event of an accident.

Frequently, when working on the suspension or steering system components, you may come across fasteners which seem impossible to loosen. These fasteners on the underside of the vehicle are continually subjected to water, road grime, mud, etc., and can become rusted or "frozen," making them extremely difficult to remove. In order to unscrew these stubborn fasteners without damaging them (or other components), be sure to use lots of penetrating oil and allow it to soak in for a while. Using a wire brush to clean exposed threads will also ease removal of the nut or bolt and prevent damage to the threads. Sometimes a sharp blow with a hammer and punch will break the bond between a nut and bolt threads, but care must be taken to prevent the punch from slipping off the fastener and ruining the threads. Heating the stuck fastener and surrounding area with a torch sometimes helps too, but isn't recommended because of the obvious dangers associated with fire. Long breaker bars and extension,

or "cheater," pipes will increase leverage, but never use an extension pipe on a ratchet - the ratcheting mechanism could be damaged. Sometimes tightening the nut or bolt first will help to break it loose. Fasteners that require drastic measures to remove should always be replaced with new ones.

Since most of the procedures dealt with in this Chapter involve jacking up the vehicle and working underneath it, a good pair of jackstands will be needed. A hydraulic floor jack is the preferred type of jack to lift the vehicle, and it can also be used to support certain components during various operations. Warning: Never, under any circumstances, rely on a jack to support the vehicle while working on it. Whenever any of the suspension or steering fasteners are loosened or removed they must be inspected and, if necessary, replaced with new ones of the same part number or of original equipment quality and design. Torque specifications must be followed for proper reassembly and component retention. Never attempt to heat or straighten any suspension or steering components. Instead, replace any bent or damaged part with a new one.

2   Stabilizer bar and bushings (front) - removal, inspection and installation

Removal

Refer to illustrations 2.2a, 2.2b, 2.2c, 2.3a, 2.3b and 2.4

1   Loosen the front wheel lug nuts, raise the front of the vehicle and support it securely on jackstands. Apply the parking brake and block the rear wheels to keep the vehicle from rolling off the stands. Remove the front wheels.

2   Remove the nuts and the stabilizer bar attaching link assemblies from the lower control arms (convertible and sedan models), the damper forks (2000 and earlier coupe models) or the strut (2001 and later coupe models) **(see Illustrations)**. **Note:** *Use an Allen wrench to prevent the ballstud from turning when removing the attaching link nut.*

3   Remove the stabilizer bar bushing retainer bolts **(see illustration)**.

4   Remove the stabilizer bar from the vehicle. On some models it'll be necessary to unbolt the center member (see Chapter 2).

2.2c Link-to-strut nut (2001 and later coupe models)

2.3a Remove the stabilizer bar bushing retainer bolts; this is a Sebring convertible . . .

2.3b . . . and this is an Avenger coupe

2.4 The stiffener plates will have to be removed, on models so equipped, to allow removal of the stabilizer bar or steering gear (left side shown)

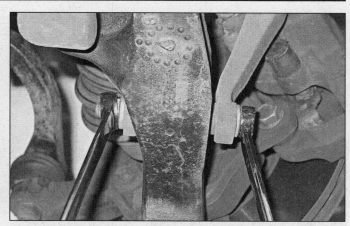

3.4 Unscrew the nut from the damper fork-to-control arm bolt, then drive the bolt out with a hammer and punch

and stiffener plates from between the cross-member and the floorpan to allow removal of the bar **(see illustration)**.

Inspection

5   Inspect for cracked, torn, or distorted stabilizer bar bushings, bushing retainers, and worn or damaged stabilizer bar links. On convertible and sedan models, damaged stabilizer bar links must be replaced before re-installing the stabilizer bar.

6   To replace damaged stabilizer bar bushings, remove the retainer, open the bushing slit and peel the bushing from the stabilizer bar. On some models it will be necessary to bend back the tabs holding the retainer together. **Caution:** *Install the new bushings with the slits facing the same way that the original bushing slits faced.*

Installation

7   Guide the stabilizer bar into position. Install the retainer bolts, tightening them to the torque listed in this Chapter's Specifications.

8   Connect the stabilizer bar links to the lower control arms, damper forks or struts, as applicable, and install the retaining nuts.

Tighten the nuts to the torque in this Chapter's Specifications.

9   Install the wheels and lug nuts. Lower the vehicle and tighten the lug nuts to the torque listed in the Chapter 1 Specifications.

---

3   Shock absorber/coil spring assembly (front) (convertible, sedan and 2000 and earlier coupe models) - removal, inspection and installation

Removal

Refer to illustrations 3.4 and 3.6

1   Loosen the wheel lug nuts, raise the front of the vehicle, support it securely on jackstands and remove the front wheels.

2   Mark the shock absorbers LEFT and RIGHT if you're going to remove both of them at the same time. Unbolt the brake hose bracket and the ABS wheel speed sensor bracket from the steering knuckle, as applicable.

3   On 2000 and earlier coupe models, remove the nut and detach the stabilizer bar link from the damper fork **(see illustration 2.2b)**.

4   Remove the pinch bolt that secures the lower end of the shock absorber to the damper fork. Also remove the nut and through-bolt that secures the lower end of the damper fork to the suspension arm **(see illustration)**. **Note:** *After removing the nut, drive the bolt out with a hammer and punch (don't turn it, because it has a serrated shoulder).*

5   If you're working on a convertible or sedan model, separate the upper control arm from the steering knuckle (see Section 6).

6   Remove the upper mounting nuts that secure the shock absorber to the body **(see illustration)**. **Warning:** *Do not remove the shock absorber damper rod nut (the nut in the center of the upper mount).* Separate the damper fork from the shock absorber, using a brass hammer if necessary, and remove them both from the vehicle. It may be necessary to push down on the steering knuckle/lower control arm(s), but be careful not to strain the brake hose. **Note:** *If you're working on a convertible or sedan model, the upper control arm will come out with the shock absorber assembly.*

Inspection

7   Check the shock absorber/coil spring assembly for leaking fluid, dents, cracks and other obvious damage which would warrant replacement.

8   Check the coil spring for chips and corrosion. Replace it if any undesirable symptoms are found. See Section 5 for the shock absorber or coil spring replacement procedure.

Installation

Refer to illustration 3.9

9   Installation is the reverse of the removal steps. When installing the damper fork to the shock absorber, make sure it is properly aligned and fully seated against the locating tab on the shock absorber body **(see illustration)**. Tighten the fasteners to the torque values listed in this Chapter's Specifications. Tighten the lug nuts to the torque listed in the Chapter 1 Specifications.

3.6 Shock absorber upper mounting nuts (2000 and earlier coupe model shown; convertibles and sedans have only three upper mounting nuts)

3.9 When installing the damper fork to the shock absorber, make sure the tab on the shock engages with the slot in the fork, and that it seats completely

4.2 Remove the clip and detach the brake hose from the strut (not visible here); unbolt the ABS speed sensor from the strut, if equipped; remove the two large nuts and drive out the strut-to-knuckle bolts

5.3 Install the spring compressor following the tool manufacturer's instructions; compress the spring until all pressure is relieved from the spring seat

4   Strut assembly (front) (2001 and later coupe models) - removal, inspection and installation

Removal

Refer to illustration 4.2

1   Loosen the wheel lug nuts, raise the vehicle and support it securely on jackstands. Remove the wheel.

2   Detach the brake hose from the strut. If the vehicle is equipped with ABS, also detach the speed sensor wiring harness from the strut **(see illustration)**.

3   Remove the strut-to-knuckle nuts and knock the bolts out with a hammer and punch. **Note:** *Mark the locations of the bolts, as special camber adjusting bolts may have been installed at some point. Also mark the relationship of the strut to the steering knuckle.*

4   Separate the strut from the steering knuckle. Be careful not to overextend the inner CV joint. Also make sure you don't push down too far on the control arm or you could overextend - and damage - the ABS speed sensor wiring harness and the brake hose. **Caution:** *Don't allow the steering knuckle and hub assembly to swing outward as this could strain the brake hose also.*

5   Support the strut and spring assembly with one hand and remove the three strut upper mounting nuts. Remove the assembly from the fenderwell.

Inspection

6   Check the strut body for leaking fluid, dents, cracks and other obvious damage which would warrant repair or replacement.

7   Check the coil spring for chips or cracks in the spring coating (this will cause premature spring failure due to corrosion). Inspect the spring seat for cuts, hardness and general deterioration.

8   If any undesirable conditions exist, pro-

ceed to the strut disassembly procedure (see Section 5).

Installation

9   Guide the strut assembly up into the fenderwell and insert the three mounting studs through the holes in the strut tower. Once the three studs protrude from the shock tower, install the nuts so the strut won't fall back through. This is most easily accomplished with the help of an assistant, as the strut is quite heavy and awkward.

10   Slide the steering knuckle into the strut flange and insert the two bolts. Install the nuts, line-up the marks you made on the strut and the knuckle, then tighten the nuts to the torque listed in this Chapter's Specifications.

11   Attach the brake hose to the strut. If the vehicle is equipped with ABS, attach the speed sensor wiring harness bracket.

12   Install the wheel and lug nuts, then lower the vehicle and tighten the lug nuts to the torque listed in the Chapter 1 Specifications.

13   Tighten the upper mounting nuts to the torque listed in this Chapter's Specifications.

14   It's a good idea to have the front end alignment checked and, if necessary, adjusted.

5   Shock absorber/strut or coil spring - replacement

1   If the shock absorbers/struts or coil springs exhibit the telltale signs of wear (leaking fluid, loss of damping capability, chipped, sagging or cracked coil springs) explore all options before beginning any work. The strut/shock absorber portions of the assemblies are not serviceable and must be replaced if a problem develops. The coil springs and strut/shock absorber assemblies can be replaced separately, using the procedures in this Section. In the case of struts, you'll need a special tool or equivalent to hold the spring seat while

you unscrew the nut. Strut/shock absorber assemblies complete with springs may be available on an exchange basis, which eliminates much time and work. Whichever route you choose to take, check on the cost and availability of parts before disassembling your vehicle. **Warning:** *Disassembling a strut/shock absorber assembly is potentially dangerous and utmost attention must be directed to the job, or serious injury may result. Use only a high quality spring compressor and carefully follow the manufacturer's instructions furnished with the tool. After removing the coil spring, set it aside in a safe, isolated area.*

Disassembly

Refer to illustrations 5.3, 5.5, 5.6, 5.7, 5.8a, 5.8b and 5.9

2   Remove the front shock absorber/coil spring assembly (see Section 3), the strut and spring assembly (see Section 4) or the rear shock absorber/coil spring assembly (see Section 14). Mount the assembly in a vise. Line the vise jaws with wood or rags to prevent damage to the unit and don't tighten the vise excessively.

3   Following the tool manufacturer's instructions, install the spring compressor (which can be obtained at most auto parts stores or equipment yards on a daily rental basis) on the spring and compress it sufficiently to relieve all pressure from the spring seats insulator **(see illustration)**. This can be verified by wiggling the spring.

4   If you're working on a shock absorber/coil spring assembly, hold the flat on the damper rod with a wrench and unscrew the nut with another wrench.

5   If you're working on a strut, you'll probably have to use a special tool with pins that engage with the holes in the spring seat to prevent the damper rod from turning while unscrewing the nut. Loosen the damper rod nut with a socket wrench **(see illustration)**.

6   Remove the nut and the upper mount

5.5 Remove the damper rod nut (you'll probably have to prevent the rod from turning by holding the spring seat with a pin spanner type tool that engages with the holes in the seat)

5.6 Lift the upper mount off the rod

5.7 Remove the upper spring seat and the upper pad from the damper rod

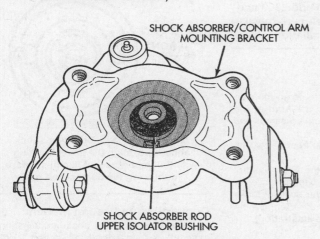

SHOCK ABSORBER/CONTROL ARM MOUNTING BRACKET

SHOCK ABSORBER ROD UPPER ISOLATOR BUSHING

5.8a Remove the upper isolator bushing . . .

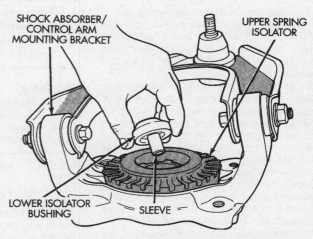

SHOCK ABSORBER/ CONTROL ARM MOUNTING BRACKET

UPPER SPRING ISOLATOR

LOWER ISOLATOR BUSHING

SLEEVE

5.8b . . . and the lower isolator bushing and sleeve (Sebring convertible or 2001 or later Sebring/Stratus Sedan front shock absorber)

(see illustration). Inspect the bearing in the mount for smooth operation. If it doesn't turn smoothly, replace the mount. Inspect the rubber portion of the mount for cracking and general deterioration. If there is any separation of the rubber, replace it.

7   Lift the upper spring seat and upper pad from the damper rod (see illustration). Check the spring seat for cracking and hardness, replacing it if necessary.

8   If you're working on a Sebring convertible or a 2001 or later Sebring or Stratus Sedan front shock absorber, mark and remove the upper isolator bushing and the lower isolator bushing and sleeve from the upper mount/ control arm mounting bracket (see illustrations).

9   Carefully lift the compressed spring from the assembly (see illustration) and set it in a safe place. **Warning:** *Never place your head near the end of the spring!* Slide the rubber bumper and dust cover off the damper rod.

Reassembly

Refer to illustrations 5.12, 5.13, 5.14a and 5.14b

10   If the lower insulator is being replaced, set it into position with the dropped portion seated in the lowest part of the seat.

11   Extend the damper rod to its full length and install the rubber bumper and dust cover.

12   Carefully place the coil spring onto the lower insulator, with the end of the spring resting in the lowest part of the insulator (see illustration).

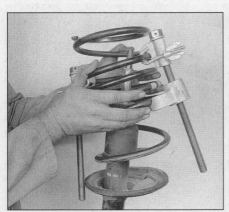

5.9 Remove the compressed spring from the strut/shock absorber assembly - keep the ends of the spring pointed away from your body

5.12 When installing the spring, make sure the end fits into the recessed portion of the lower seat

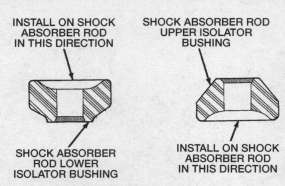

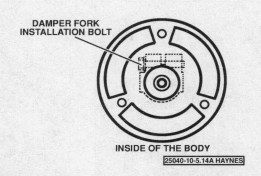

5.13 Upper and lower isolator bushing identification and positioning (Sebring convertibles and 2001 or later Sebring or Stratus Sedan front shock absorbers)

5.14a On 2000 and earlier coupe model front shock absorbers the damper fork bolt must align with the three upper mounting studs like this

13   Install the upper pad and spring seat. If you're working on a Sebring convertible or a 2001 or later Sebring or Stratus Sedan front shock absorber, install the upper and lower isolator bushings in the proper orientation **(see illustration)**.

14   Install the upper mount onto the damper shaft. If you're working on a front shock absorber of a 2000 or earlier coupe model, make sure the studs of the upper mount are aligned correctly with the pinch bolt that secures the damper fork to the shock absorber body **(see illustration)**. If you're working on a rear shock absorber assembly on a coupe model (any year), make sure the upper mount bracket is properly aligned with the lower mounting bushing of the shock absorber **(see illustration)**. On convertible and sedan models, make sure the upper mounting studs are properly lined-up with the lower mounting bolt hole

15   Install the damper rod nut and tighten it to the torque listed in this Chapter's Specifications. Slowly release the spring compressor.

16   Install the strut/shock absorber and coil spring assembly following the procedure in Section 3, 4 or 14.

6   Upper control arm (front) (convertible, sedan and 2000 and earlier coupe models) - removal, inspection and installation

Removal

Refer to illustration 6.3

1   Loosen the wheel lug nuts on the side to be disassembled, raise the front of the vehicle, support it securely on jackstands and remove the wheel.

2   Support the suspension from below with a jack.

3   Loosen the nut from the upper control arm balljoint stud. Using a two-jaw puller or balljoint separator, break the balljoint loose from the steering knuckle, then remove the nut and detach the arm **(see illustration)**.

2000 and earlier coupe models

Refer to illustration 6.4

4   Working in the engine compartment, remove the nuts from the control arm shafts **(see illustration)** and remove the control arm.

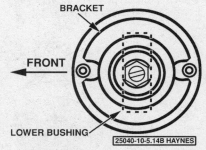

5.14b On coupe model rear shock absorbers, align the lower bushing with the upper bracket like this before tightening the damper rod nut

Convertible and sedan models

5   Remove the shock absorber/coil spring assembly as described in Section 3 (the upper control arm is connected to the shock absorber upper mount). Then refer to Section 5 and compress the coil spring, remove the damper rod nut and detach the shock absorber upper mount/upper control arm. The control arm can now be unbolted from the mount.

6.3 Use a two-jaw puller to break the ball joint loose from the steering knuckle. Loosen the nut a few turns, but leave it in place to prevent a violent separation

6.4 Upper control arm-to-body nuts (2000 and earlier coupe models)

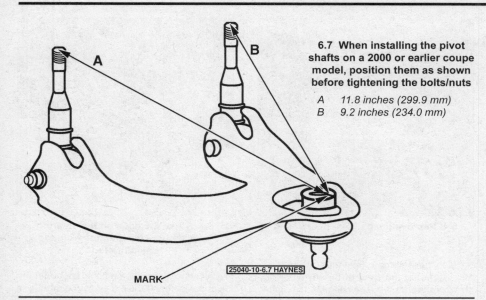

6.7 When installing the pivot shafts on a 2000 or earlier coupe model, position them as shown before tightening the bolts/nuts

A   11.8 inches (299.9 mm)
B   9.2 inches (234.0 mm)

3   Remove the nut from the balljoint stud on the arm you're removing (see **illustration**). Using a large ball peen hammer (and wearing goggles to protect your eyes), give the steering knuckle a few good whacks in the vicinity of the balljoint stud to break the stud loose from the knuckle. Use a prybar to disconnect the control arm from the steering knuckle. If that doesn't work, use a tie-rod or balljoint separator. These tools can usually be rented from rental outlets and some auto parts stores.
4   To remove the compression lower arm, remove its bushing bolts and separate it from the vehicle (see **illustration**).
5   To remove the lateral lower arm, remove the nut and bolt that secure it to the damper fork (see **illustration 3.4**), then remove the pivot bolt and nut (see **illustration**). Work the arm free of its pivot point in the body and take it out of the vehicle.

Inspection

6   Check the control arms for distortion and the bushings for wear. If the arm is bent or any of the bushings are cracked, torn or worn out, replace the control arm. These parts are not replaceable and you can't straighten a bent control arm. Also check the balljoint (see Section 10). If a balljoint is worn out, you'll have to replace the control arm; the balljoint is not available separately.

Installation

7   Installation is the reverse of removal. Do NOT reuse self-locking nuts. Replace them with new ones. Tighten all of the fasteners to the torque values listed in this Chapter's Specifications. **Note:** *Before tightening the lateral lower arm pivot bolt, raise the outer end of the arm with a floor jack to simulate normal ride height, then tighten the pivot bolt/nut to the specified torque.*
8   Install the wheel and lug nuts, lower the vehicle and tighten the lug nuts to the torque listed in the Chapter 1 Specifications.
9   It's a good idea to have the front wheel alignment checked, and if necessary, adjusted after this job has been performed.

Inspection

6   Check the control arm for distortion and the pivot bushings (convertible and sedan models), pivot bolts (and shafts, on 2000 and earlier coupe models) for wear. If the arm is bent or the pivot shafts or bolts are worn, replace them. Don't try to straighten a bent control arm. Also check the balljoint (see Section 10). If a balljoint is worn out, you'll have to replace the control arm; the balljoint is not available separately. **Note:** *If you remove the pivot bolts, be sure to install them facing in the correct direction (with the bolt heads facing towards each other.*

Installation

Refer to illustration 6.7
Warning: *The manufacturer recommends replacing self-locking nuts with new ones whenever they are removed.*
7   If you're working on a 2000 or earlier coupe model and have removed the pivot bolts, the pivot shafts must be installed in a certain position before tightening the nuts (see **illustration**).

8   Installation is the reverse of removal. Tighten all of the fasteners to the torque values listed in this Chapter's Specifications.
9   Install the wheel and lug nuts, lower the vehicle and tighten the lug nuts to the torque listed in the Chapter 1 Specifications.
10   It's a good idea to have the front wheel alignment checked, and if necessary, adjusted after this job has been performed.

7   Lower control arms (front) (2000 and earlier coupe models) - removal, inspection and installation

Refer to illustrations 7.3, 7.4 and 7.5
1   These models have two lower control arms; a lateral lower arm and a compression lower arm.

Removal

2   Loosen the wheel lug nuts on the side to be disassembled, raise the front of the vehicle, support it securely on jackstands and remove the wheel.

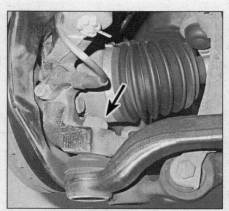

7.3 Compression lower arm-to-steering knuckle nut (2000 and earlier coupe models)

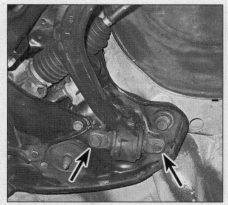

7.4 Compression lower arm-to-body bolts (2000 and earlier coupe models)

7.5 Lateral lower arm-to-crossmember bolt/nut (2000 and earlier coupe models)

8 Lower control arm (front) (convertible and sedan models) - removal, inspection and installation

Refer to illustrations 8.4, 8.6, 8.12a, and 8.12b

Removal and inspection

1   Loosen the wheel lug nuts, raise the front of the vehicle, support it securely on jackstands and remove the wheel.

2   Remove the brake caliper (see Chapter 9) and support it with a piece of wire - don't let it hang from the brake hose.

3   Remove the brake disc from the front hub/bearing assembly.

4   Remove the two bolts and detach the balljoint heat shield from the steering knuckle, if so equipped **(see illustration)**.

5   Remove the cotter pin and loosen the lower balljoint castle nut a few turns.

6   Use a hammer to strike the boss on the steering knuckle until it separates from the lower balljoint stud **(see illustration)**. **Caution:** *Do not hit the lower control arm or the balljoint grease seal, be careful not to separate the inner C/V joint and **do not** pry the lower balljoint from the steering knuckle.* Once the balljoint stud has been released from the steering knuckle, remove the castle nut.

7   Remove the shock absorber damper fork-to-lower control arm bolt and separate the fork from the lower control arm **(see illustration 3.4)**.

8   Detach the stabilizer bar link from the lower control arm (see Section 2).

9   Remove the bolts attaching the stabilizer bar bushing clamp to the front suspension crossmember and the body of the vehicle.

10   Lower one side of the stabilizer bar away from the lower control arm.

11   Remove the nut and bolt attaching the rear of the lower control arm to the front suspension crossmember.

12   Remove the nut and bolt attaching the front of the lower control arm to the front sus-

8.4 Remove the balljoint heat shield

8.6 Strike the boss on the steering knuckle until it separates from the balljoint stud

pension crossmember **(see illustrations)**.

13   Separate the front of the lower control arm from the front suspension crossmember. **Caution:** *Be careful not to damage the balljoint seal against the steering knuckle when lowering it from the crossmember.*

14   Remove the rear of the lower control arm from the front suspension crossmember. Be careful to keep the rear bushing from binding on the crossmember. Check the bushings in the lower control arm for cracking and other signs of deterioration. If necessary, take the control arm to an automotive machine shop to have the bushings replaced.

Installation

15   Install the rear, and then the front of the lower control arm into the front suspension cradle. Do not tighten the bolts at this time.

16   Connect the lower balljoint to the steering knuckle, tightening the castle nut to the torque listed in this Chapter's Specifications. Install a new cotter pin.

17   Installation of the remaining components is the reverse of removal. **Caution:** *Be sure to install the balljoint heat shield. If the heat shield is not installed, the boot may fail due to excessive heat from the brake disc.*

18   After installing the damper fork on the

lower control arm, place a floor jack under the lower balljoint and raise the lower control arm to simulate normal ride height. Tighten the lower control arm-to-crossmember bolts and the damper fork-to-lower control arm bolt/nut to the values listed in this Chapter's Specifications.

19   Install the brake disc and caliper. Tighten the caliper mounting bolts to the torque listed in the Chapter 9 Specifications.

20   Tighten the wheel lug nuts to the torque listed in the Chapter 1 Specifications.

21   Have the front wheel alignment checked, and if necessary, adjusted after this job has been performed.

9 Control arm (front) (2001 and later coupe models) - removal, inspection and installation

Removal

Refer to illustrations 9.2 and 9.3

1   Loosen the wheel lug nuts on the side to be disassembled, raise the front of the vehicle, support it securely on jackstands and remove the wheel.

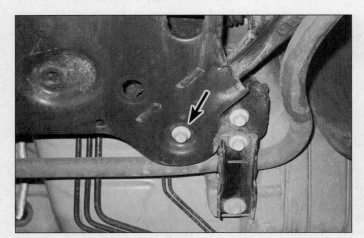

8.11 Lower control arm rear mounting bolt (nut not visible) - convertible and sedan models

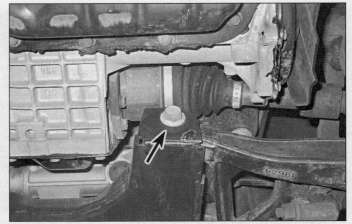

8.12 Lower control arm front mounting bolt (nut not visible) - convertible and sedan models

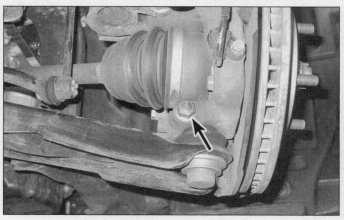

9.2 Unscrew the nut and remove the pinch bolt completely (2001 and later coupe models)

9.3 Control arm pivot bolt (left) and clamp bolts (right) (2001 and later coupe models)

2   Completely remove the nut and pinch bolt from the balljoint stud that's connected to the steering knuckle **(see illustration)**. Use a prybar to disconnect the control arm from the steering knuckle.

3   Remove the nut and washer from the control arm forward pivot bolt **(see illustration)**. Pull out the pivot bolt.

4   Remove the two nuts and two bolts from the clamp for the rear control arm bushing **(see illustration 8.4)**.

5   Remove the control arm and rear clamp from the vehicle.

Inspection

6   Remove the nut that secures the rear clamp and bushing to the control arm. Slide the bushing off the control arm stud.

7   Check the control arm for distortion and the bushings for wear. If the arm is bent or the forward bushing is cracked, torn or worn out, replace the control arm. These parts are not replaceable and you can't straighten a bent control arm.

8   If the bushing in the clamp is worn or damaged, have it pressed out and a new one pressed in by a dealer service department or machine shop.

9   Also check the balljoint (see Section 10). If a balljoint is worn out, you'll have to replace the control arm; the balljoint is not available separately.

Installation

10   Installation is the reverse of removal. Do NOT reuse self-locking nuts. Replace them with new ones. Tighten all of the fasteners to the torque values listed in this Chapter's Specifications. **Note:** *Before tightening the control arm pivot bolt, raise the outer end of the control arm with a floor jack to simulate normal ride height.*

11   Install the wheel and lug nuts, lower the vehicle and tighten the lug nuts to the torque listed in the Chapter 1 Specifications.

12   Have the front wheel alignment checked, and if necessary, adjusted after this job has been performed.

10 Balljoints - check and replacement

Check

Lower balljoint(s)

1   Raise the front of the vehicle and support it securely on jackstands. Apply the parking brake and block the rear wheels to keep the vehicle from rolling off the jackstands.

2   If you're working on a convertible, sedan or 2000 or earlier coupe, remove the damper fork-to-control arm nut and bolt.

3   Place a large prybar under the balljoint and resting on the wheel, then try to pry the balljoint up while feeling for movement between the balljoint and steering knuckle. Now, pry between the control arm and the steering knuckle and try to lever the control arm down while feeling for movement between the balljoint and steering knuckle. If any movement is evident in either check, the balljoint is worn.

4   Have an assistant grasp the tire at the top and bottom and move the top of the tire in-and-out. Touch the balljoint stud nut. If any looseness is felt, suspect a worn balljoint stud or a widened hole in the steering knuckle boss. If the latter problem exists, the steering knuckle should be replaced as well as the balljoint/control arm.

Upper balljoint (convertible, sedan and 2000 and earlier coupe models only)

5   Loosen the wheel lug nuts, raise the front of the vehicle and support it securely on jackstands. Remove the wheel.

6   Place a floor jack under the lower balljoint(s) and raise it slightly.

7   Using a prybar, attempt to pry the upper control arm up and down while feeling for play in the balljoint. If any play is felt, replace the control arm.

All balljoints

8   Separate the control arm from the steering knuckle (Section 6, 7, 8 or 9). Using your fingers (don't use pliers), try to twist the stud in the socket. If the stud turns, replace the balljoint.

Replacement

Note: *On 1998 and later models, upper ball joints are replaceable. Contact your local auto parts store for availability.*

9   The balljoints are not replaceable separately (the entire control arm must be replaced).

10   The balljoint dust boot can be replaced separately. This should not be done if the dust boot has cracked or been damaged while the vehicle is in use, since dirt has probably gotten into the balljoint. However, if the dust boot was damaged during removal of the control arm, the dust boot can be replaced. To do this, pry off the old dust boot. Grease the balljoint stud and the upper lip of the dust boot. Push the dust boot onto the balljoint with a special tool or a socket the same diameter as the dust boot. If you're working on a 2001 or later coupe model, push the dust boot upper lip down with a smaller socket until it locks into the groove in the bottom of the balljoint stud.

11   Install the wheel and lug nuts (if removed) and lower the vehicle. Tighten the lug nuts to the torque listed in the Chapter 1 Specifications.

11 Hub and bearing assembly (front) - removal and installation

Refer to illustration 11.5

Warning: *Dust created by the brake system is harmful to your health. Never blow it out with compressed air and don't inhale any of it. Do not, under any circumstances, use petroleum-based solvents to clean brake parts. Use brake system cleaner only.*

1   Loosen the wheel lug nuts, raise the vehicle and support it securely on jackstands. Remove the wheel.

2   Remove the driveaxle/hub nut (see Chapter 8).

11.5 With the driveaxle out of the way, unscrew the hub-to-steering knuckle bolts

13.2a Stabilizer bar link bolt - convertible and sedan models

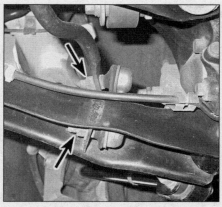

13.2b Stabilizer bar link nuts - coupe models

3   Remove the brake caliper and support it with a piece of wire as described in Chapter 9. Remove the caliper torque plate and separate the brake disc from the hub.

4   Separate the lower balljoint(s) from the steering knuckle (see Section 7 or 8). Pivot the knuckle outward and push the driveaxle from the hub to provide removal access for the hub mounting bolts. Support the end of the driveaxle with a piece of wire.

5   Unbolt the hub from the knuckle **(see illustration)**. Remove the hub from the vehicle.

6   If necessary, remove the brake disc shield from the knuckle.

7   Check the hub bearing for wear or damage. Spin it with fingers and check for rough, loose or noisy rotation. The bearing can't be replaced separately, so if the bearing is bad or any other problems are found, replace the hub as an assembly.

8   Installation is the reverse of removal. Tighten the hub bolts and balljoint fasteners to the torque listed in this Chapter's Specifications. Tighten the driveaxle/hub nut to the torque listed in the Chapter 8 Specifications (and on models so equipped, be sure to use a new cotter pin), the brake fasteners to the torque listed in Chapter 9 and the wheel lug nuts to the torque listed in Chapter 1.

12   Steering knuckle - removal and installation

Warning: *Dust created by the brake system is harmful to your health. Never blow it out with compressed air and don't inhale any of it. Do not, under any circumstances, use petroleum-based solvents to clean brake parts. Use brake system cleaner only.*

Removal

1   Loosen the wheel lug nuts, raise the vehicle and support it securely on jackstands. Remove the wheel.

2   Remove the brake caliper and support it with a piece of wire as described in Chap-

13.3a Stabilizer bar clamp bolts - convertible and sedan models

ter 9. If the vehicle is equipped with ABS, unbolt and remove the wheel speed sensor from the knuckle. Remove the caliper torque plate, separate the brake disc from the hub, then remove the driveaxle/hub nut (see Chapter 8).

3   Separate the tie-rod end from the steering knuckle arm (see Section 22).

4   Separate the control arm(s) from the knuckle (see Sections 6 and 7 [2000 and earlier coupe models], Sections 6 and 8 [convertible and sedan models] or Section 9 [2001 and later coupe models]).

5   Push the driveaxle from the hub as described in Chapter 8. Support the end of the driveaxle with a piece of wire.

6   If you're working on a 2001 or later coupe model, remove the bolts and carefully separate the steering knuckle from the strut (see Section 4).

7   If necessary, unbolt the hub from the knuckle.

Installation

8   Installation is the reverse of the removal steps. Tighten all suspension and steering fasteners to the torque values listed in this Chapter's Specifications. Tighten the driveaxle/hub nut to the torque listed in the Chapter 8 Specifications (and be sure to use a new cotter pin), the brake fasteners to the

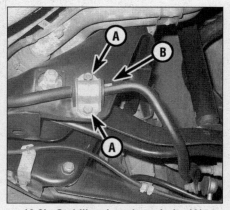

13.3b Stabilizer bar clamp bolts (A); approximately 13/32-inch (10 mm) of the alignment mark (B) must be showing past the outside of each bushing when installing the bar - coupe models

torque listed in Chapter 9 and the wheel lug nuts to the torque listed in Chapter 1.

13   Stabilizer bar and bushings (rear) - removal, inspection and installation

Removal

Refer to illustrations 13.2a, 13.2b, 13.3a and 13.3b

1   Loosen the wheel lug nuts, raise the vehicle and support it securely on jackstands. Remove the wheels.

2   Remove the nuts attaching the stabilizer links to the stabilizer and lower control arm **(see illustration)**.

3   Unbolt the stabilizer bar clamps from the crossmember **(see illustration)**. Remove the stabilizer bar from the vehicle.

Inspection

4   Inspect the stabilizer bushings for cracks and tears. If the bushings are damaged, distorted or excessively worn, replace them. Also, inspect the link balljoints for damage or excessive looseness.

14.3a Shock absorber upper mounting nuts - coupe model

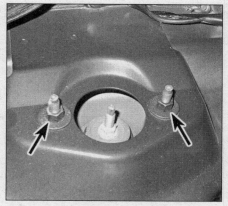

14.3b Shock absorber upper mounting nuts - convertible model

14.4a Shock absorber lower mounting bolt - coupe model

14.4b Shock absorber lower mounting bolt/nut - convertible model shown, sedan similar

15.2 Use an open-end wrench to hold the trailing arm from rotating while removing the nut and washer at the knuckle

15.3 Unbolt the trailing arm bracket bolts to remove the forward end of the trailing arm

Installation

5   Installation is the reverse of the removal steps. If you're working on a coupe model, position the stabilizer bar in the brackets so its alignment mark is within the specified distance of the bushing (see illustration 12.3b). Tighten all fasteners to the torque listed in this Chapter's Specifications.

---

14 Shock absorber/coil spring assembly (rear) - removal, inspection and installation

Removal

Refer to illustrations 14.3a, 14.3b, 14.4a and 14.4b

1   Loosen the wheel lug nuts, raise the vehicle and support it securely on jackstands. Remove the wheel.
2   On coupe models, remove the package tray for access to the upper shock mount (see Chapter 11). On convertible models, raise the top fully and remove the plastic trim panel from the convertible top storage well (see Chapter 11). If you're working on a sedan, open the trunk, peel back the carpet for access to the upper mount.

3   Support the trailing arm with a floor jack. Raise the jack just enough to take the load off the shock absorber, then remove the two shock absorber upper mounting nuts (see illustrations). **Warning:** *Don't remove the nut from the damper rod (the center nut).*
4   Remove the shock absorber lower mounting bolt and remove the shock (see illustration).

Inspection

5   Follow the inspection procedures described in Section 3. If the shock absorber assembly must be disassembled for replacement of the shock or the coil spring, refer to Section 5.

Installation

6   Maneuver the shock absorber assembly up into the fenderwell and insert the mounting studs through the holes in the body. Install the nuts, but don't tighten them yet.
7   If you're working on a 2001 or later coupe model, position the lower end of the shock so the flanged portion of the bushing is toward the outside of the vehicle. On all other models, push the lower end of the shock into its bracket on the knuckle, install the bolt (and nut, on convertible and sedan models) and

tighten them to the torque listed in this Chapter's Specifications.
8   Install the wheel and lug nuts, lower the vehicle and tighten the lug nuts to the torque listed in the Chapter 1 Specifications.
9   Tighten the two upper mounting nuts to the torque listed in this Chapter's Specifications. Reinstall the trim panels.

---

15 Rear suspension arms (convertible and sedan models) - removal and installation

1   Loosen the rear wheel lug nuts, raise the vehicle and support it securely on jackstands. Block the front wheels and remove the rear wheel.

Trailing arm

Refer to illustrations 15.2 and 15.3

2   At the rear knuckle, remove the nut, bushing retainer, and outer trailing arm bushing from the trailing arm (see illustration).
3   Remove the four bolts from the trailing arm bracket which attach the bracket to the body and frame rail (see illustration).
4   Remove trailing arm and mounting bracket as an assembly from the vehicle.

**15.8 Forward lateral link-to-rear knuckle bolt
(convertible and sedan models)**

**15.9 Forward lateral link-to-crossmember bolt
(convertible and sedan models)**

5   If separating the trailing arm from the mounting bracket, note the location and positions of the bushings and retainer for correct reinstallation.

6   Installation is the reverse of the removal procedure. Be sure to tighten the bolts and nuts to the torque listed in this Chapter's Specifications.

Lateral links

Refer to illustrations 15.8, 15.9, 15.11 and 15.12

Removal

Forward lateral link

7   Remove rear stabilizer bar attaching link from the forward lateral link (**see illustration 12.2a**).

8   Remove the nut, bolt and washer attaching the lateral link to the knuckle (**see illustration**).

9   Remove the nut, bolt and washer attaching the forward lateral link to the suspension crossmember (**see illustration**).

10   Remove the forward lateral link from the vehicle. **Note:** *Lateral links are replaced as a unit - do not repair or straighten a lateral link. Do not apply heat to the lateral link adjusting screws or jam nuts to loosen them.*

Rear lateral link

11   Remove the nut, bolt and washer attaching the rear lateral link to the knuckle (**see illustration**).

12   Remove the bolt and washer attaching the rear lateral link to the suspension crossmember (**see illustration**).

13   Remove the rear lateral link from the vehicle. **Note:** *Lateral links are replaced as a unit - do not repair or straighten a lateral link. Do not apply heat to the lateral link adjusting screws or jam nuts to loosen them.*

Installation

14   Installation is the reverse of removal. Install the front lateral link crossmember bolt with the head of the bolts are toward the front of the vehicle. Install the rear lateral link crossmember bolt with the head of the bolts facing toward the rear of the vehicle. For the forward lateral link, make sure the cup in the cast portion faces downward and toward the rear knuckle when installed. For the rear lateral link, install with the adjusting screw toward the knuckle, not toward the suspension crossmember. Raise the rear knuckle with a floor jack to simulate normal ride height and tighten the bolts/nuts to the torque listed in this Chapter's Specifications.

15   Install the wheel and lug nuts, then lower the vehicle to the ground. Tighten the wheel lug nuts to the torque listed in the Chapter 1 Specifications.

Upper control arm

Refer to illustrations 15.20, 15.23 and 15.27

16   Remove the shock absorber clevis bracket bolt and nut from both sides of the vehicle (**see illustration 14.4b**).

17   Remove the muffler support bracket from the rear frame rail.

18   Remove the rear exhaust pipe hangar from the suspension crossmember, then ease the exhaust system while it drops down as far as possible.

19   Remove the cotter pin and loosen the castle nut attaching the upper control arm balljoint to the knuckle.

20   With the castle nut loosened a few turns, detach the balljoint stud from the knuckle using a puller (**see illustration**).

21   Support the suspension crossmember with a hydraulic jack and a wooden block on the jack. If the vehicle has ABS (Anti-lock Brake System), remove the routing clips for the wheel speed sensor cable from brackets on the upper control arm.

22   Remove the nuts and bolts on each side

**15.11 Remove the rear lateral link-to-
knuckle bolt and nut**

**15.12 Remove the rear lateral link bolt/nut
from the rear suspension crossmember**

**15.20 Use a puller to detach the upper
control arm balljoint from the rear knuckle**

15.23 Remove the suspension crossmember mounting bolts

15.27 Use a drift inserted in the alignment holes to line-up the crossmember with the threaded holes in the frame rails

of the vehicle which attach both rear lateral links and both front lateral links to the knuckles.

23   Remove the bolts attaching the suspension crossmember to the rear frame rails **(see illustration)**.

24   Lower the suspension crossmember using the hydraulic jack a sufficient distance to remove the upper control arm pivot bolts which attach the control arm pivot bar to the crossmember.

25   Remove the two upper control arm mounting bolts from the suspension crossmember. Remove the upper control arm from the crossmember.

26   The upper control arm, bushings, and pivot bar are serviced as a complete assembly. Only the balljoint and balljoint seal are replaceable. If the balljoint is in need of replacement, take the upper control arm to an automotive machine shop to have the old one pressed out and a new one pressed in.

27   Installation is the reverse of removal. When installing the suspension crossmember, install a drift **(see illustration)** into the positioning holes (one positioning hole in each

side of the crossmember and frame rail) to line-up the bolt holes. Tighten fasteners to the torque listed in this Chapter's Specifications. Remove the drifts.

28   Have the rear wheel alignment checked and, if necessary, adjusted.

16   Rear suspension arms (coupe models) - removal and installation

1   Loosen the wheel lug nuts, raise the vehicle and support it securely on jackstands. Remove the wheels.

Trailing arm

Refer to illustrations 16.2 and 16.3

2   Remove the nut, washer and bolt that attach the rear end of the trailing arm to the rear knuckle **(see illustration)**.

3   Remove the plug at the front end of the trailing arm **(see illustration)**. Remove the nut, washer and bolt that attach the front end of the trailing arm to the body, then remove

the trailing arm.

4   Inspect the bushings in the front end of the trailing arm and in the knuckle for cracks and deterioration. Replace parts as necessary.

5   Installation is the reverse of removal. Make sure you install the bolts with the heads facing outward. Raise the rear knuckle with a floor jack to simulate normal ride height and tighten the bolts/nuts to the torque listed in this Chapter's Specifications.

6   Tighten the lug nuts to the torque listed in the Chapter 1 Specifications.

Lower and toe control arms
Removal

Refer to illustrations 16.9a, 16.9b, 16.10 and 16.11

Lower control arm

7   Remove the nut that connects the stabilizer bar link to the lower control arm **(see illustration 12.2b)**.

8   If you're working on a vehicle equipped with ABS, unbolt the clamp that secures the wheel speed sensor wiring harness.

16.2 Trailing arm-to-rear knuckle nut/bolt

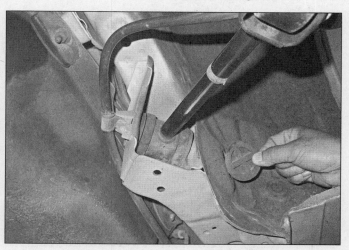

16.3 Remove this plug for access to the trailing arm pivot bolt nut

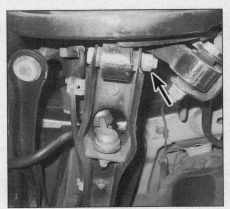

16.9a Lower control arm-to-rear knuckle nut/bolt (coupe models)

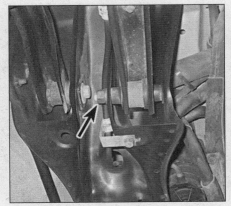

16.9b Lower control arm inner pivot bolt/ nut (coupe models)

16.10 Mark the position of the toe adjuster cam to the rear crossmember (when installing the toe control arm, line-up these marks)

9   Remove the nut, lockwasher and bolt that secure the outer end of the lower control arm to the knuckle. Do the same thing at the inner end, then remove the control arm from the vehicle **(see illustrations)**.

Toe control arm

10   Mark the position of the eccentric at the inner end of the toe control arm before removing it **(see illustration)**.

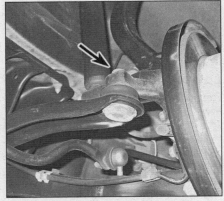

16.11 Toe control arm balljoint-to-knuckle nut (coupe models)

11   Loosen the nut on the toe control arm balljoint **(see illustration)**. Strike the knuckle in the vicinity of the balljoint several times with a hammer to free the balljoint stud, then pry it loose with a pry bar. If that doesn't work, use a tie-rod or balljoint separator.

12   Remove the toe control arm pivot bolt, lockwasher and nut and take the arm out.

Inspection

13   Check the bushing in the inner end of each arm, and the lower control arm bushing in the knuckle, for wear or damage. Replace parts as necessary.

14   Refer to Section 10 to inspect the balljoint in the outer end of the toe control arm.

Installation

15   Installation is the reverse of the removal steps. Raise the rear knuckle with a floor jack to simulate normal ride height and tighten the bolts/nuts to the torque listed in this Chapter's Specifications.

16   Tighten the lug nuts to the torque listed in the Chapter 1 Specifications.

17   Have the rear wheel alignment checked and, if necessary, adjusted.

Upper control arm

Removal

Refer to illustrations 16.19 and 16.20

18   Loosen the wheel lug nuts, raise the vehicle and support it securely on jackstands. Remove the wheels.

19   Remove the bolt, nut and washer that attach the upper control arm to the knuckle **(see illustration)**.

20   Unscrew the bolts that attach the upper control arm pivots to the body **(see illustration)**. Remove the upper control arm from the vehicle. Don't allow the knuckle to fall outward - the brake hose or CV joint (4WD models) could be damaged.

21   If necessary, remove the pivot bolts and nuts and separate the brackets from the control arm.

Inspection

Refer to illustration 16.23

22   Check the control arm for cracks or bending and check the bushings for wear or damage. Replace the control arm and bushings as an assembly if any problems are found.

16.19 Upper control arm-to-rear knuckle nut/bolt (coupe models)

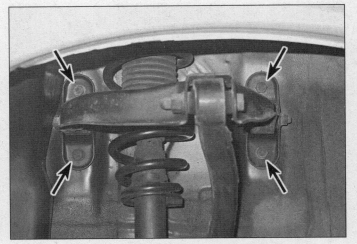

16.20 Upper control arm-to-body bolts (coupe models)

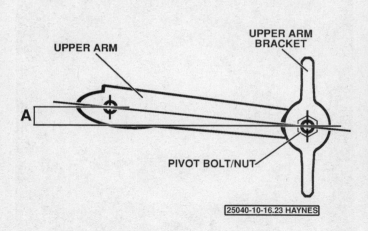

16.23 With the upper arm mounting brackets positioned properly, the vertical distance between the pivots (dimension A) should be 1.46 +/- 0.080 inch

17.3 Tap off the rear hub/bearing dust cap with a hammer and chisel (convertible and sedan models)

23   If the brackets have been separated from the arm, place them at the correct angle **(see illustration)**. The vertical distance between the outer control arm pivot point and the inner pivot point should be 1.46 +/-0.080 inch. With this distance set correctly, tighten the pivot bolts and nuts to the torque listed in this Chapter's Specifications.

Installation

24   Installation is the reverse of the removal steps. Install the arm and tighten the mounting bracket bolts to the torque listed in this Chapter's Specifications. Raise the rear knuckle with a floor jack to simulate normal ride height and tighten the arm-to-knuckle bolt/nut to the torque listed in this Chapter's Specifications.
25   Tighten the lug nuts to the torque listed in the Chapter 1 Specifications.

17   Hub and bearing assembly (rear) - removal and installation

Warning: *Dust created by the brake system is harmful to your health. Never blow it out with compressed air and don't inhale any of it. Do not, under any circumstances, use petroleum-based solvents to clean brake parts. Use brake system cleaner only.*

Convertible and sedan models
Refer to illustrations 17.3, 17.4 and 17.5
1   Loosen the wheel lug nuts, raise the vehicle and support it securely on jackstands. Remove the wheel.
2   Remove the brake drum or disc from the rear hub/bearing (see Chapter 9).
3   Remove the dust cap **(see illustration)**.
4   Remove the hub/bearing rear hub retaining nut **(see illustration)**. Discard the nut - a new one must be used upon installation.
5   Pull the hub/bearing assembly off of the rear spindle **(see illustration)**.

6   Installation is the reverse of removal. Use a new spindle retaining nut - do not reuse the old spindle retaining nut. Tighten the spindle nut to the torque listed in this Chapter's Specifications.
7   Install the wheel and lug nuts. Lower the vehicle and tighten the lug nuts to the torque listed in the Chapter 1 Specifications.

Coupe models
Refer to illustration 17.10
8   Loosen the wheel lug nuts, raise the vehicle and support it securely on jackstands. Remove the wheel.
9   Remove the rear brake caliper and disc or rear brake drum and shoes and, on vehicles equipped with an ABS braking system, remove the rear wheel speed sensor (see Chapter 9).
10   Remove the hub bolts **(see illustration)** and detach the hub from the knuckle.
11   Check the hub bearing for wear or damage. Spin it with your fingers and check for rough, loose or noisy rotation. The bearing can't be replaced separately, so if the bear-

17.4 Remove the hub retaining nut (convertible and sedan models)

ing is bad or any other problems are found, replace the hub as an assembly.
12   Installation is the reverse of removal. Tighten the hub bolts to the torque listed in this Chapter's Specifications.
13   Install the wheel and lug nuts. Lower the vehicle and tighten the lug nuts to the torque listed in the Chapter 1 Specifications.

17.5 Slide the hub and bearing assembly off the spindle (convertible and sedan models)

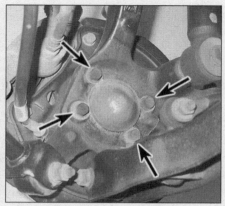

17.10 Hub and bearing assembly-to-rear knuckle bolts (coupe models)

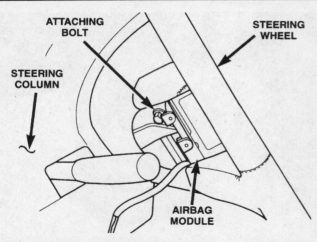

20.3a On 1997 through 2000 convertible models, the airbag is retained to the steering wheel by two bolts, accessible from each side of the steering wheel after the cruise control switches have been removed

20.3b On 2001 and later convertible and sedan models, the airbag is retained to the steering wheel by two bolts, accessible from the front of the steering wheel after the cruise control switches have been removed

18 Knuckle (rear) - removal, inspection and installation

Removal

1   If the vehicle is equipped with ABS, remove the rear wheel speed sensor (see Chapter 9).

2   Remove the rear brake caliper, bracket and disc (disc brakes) or brake drum and shoes (drum brakes) (see Chapter 9).

3   Remove the rear hub and bearing assembly (see Section 17).

4   Disconnect the shock absorber, trailing arm, lower control arm and toe control arm (coupe models), lateral links (convertible and sedan models), and the upper control arm from the knuckle as described elsewhere in this Chapter. Remove the knuckle from the vehicle.

Inspection

5   Check the bushings in the knuckle for wear and damage. Replace the knuckle if problems are found.

6   Check the knuckle for cracks or bending. Don't try to repair any damage; replace the knuckle if there are visible problems.

7   Refer to Section 10 to inspect the balljoint at the outer end of the toe control arm.

Installation

8   Installation is the reverse of the removal steps. Tighten all suspension fasteners to the torque listed in this Chapter's Specifications. Tighten the brake fasteners to the torque listed in the Chapter 9 Specifications. Note: Before tightening the pivot bolts that attach the suspension arms to the knuckle, raise the suspension with a floor jack to simulate normal ride height, then tighten the fasteners to the specified torque.

9   Tighten the lug nuts to the torque listed in the Chapter 1 Specifications.

19 Steering system - general information

All models are equipped with power rack-and-pinion steering. The steering gear is bolted to the crossmember and operates the steering arms via tie-rods. The inner ends of the tie-rods are protected by rubber boots which should be inspected periodically for secure attachment, tears and leaking lubricant.

The power assist system consists of a belt-driven pump and associated lines and hoses. The fluid level in the power steering pump reservoir should be checked periodically (see Chapter 1).

The steering wheel operates the steering shaft, which actuates the steering gear through universal joints. Looseness in the steering can be caused by wear in the steering shaft universal joints, the steering gear, the tie-rod ends and loose retaining bolts.

20 Steering wheel - removal and installation

Removal

Refer to illustrations 20.3a, 20.3b, 20.5a, 20.5b, 20.8 and 20.9

Warning 1: *These models have airbags. Always disable the airbag system before working in the vicinity of the impact sensors, steering column or instrument panel to avoid the possibility of accidental deployment of the airbag, which could cause personal injury (see Chapter 12).*

Warning 2: *Do not use a memory saving device to preserve the ECM's memory when working on or near airbag system components.*

1   Park the vehicle with the front wheels pointing straight ahead.

2   Disconnect the cable from the negative terminal of the battery or from the remote ground terminal (see Chapter 5, Section 1). Wait at least two minutes before proceeding (the airbag system has a back-up capacitor that must fully discharge).

3   Remove the airbag retaining bolts. There are several ways that airbags have been mounted on the vehicles covered by this manual, depending on model and year:

2000 and earlier coupe models - Unscrew the four bolts from the back side of the steering wheel.

2001 and later coupe models - Unscrew the Torx bolt from each side of the steering wheel, but don't attempt to remove it from its casing.

1996 convertible models - Unscrew the two bolts from the back side of the steering wheel.

1997 through 2000 convertible models - Remove the cruise control switches from the sides of the steering wheel (see Chapter 12), then unscrew the airbag mounting bolt from each side of the steering wheel **(see illustration)**.

2001 and later convertible and sedan models - Remove the cruise control switches from the sides of the steering wheel (see Chapter 12), then unscrew the two airbag mounting bolts from the front of the steering wheel (one bolt underneath each switch **(see illustration)**.

4   Remove the airbag module from the steering wheel.

5   Remove the lock from the airbag clockspring electrical connector and disconnect the electrical connector from the back of the airbag module **(see illustrations)**. **Warning:** *When handling the airbag module, make sure that at no time any source of electricity is allowed near the inflator on the back of the airbag module; when carrying the airbag module, the trim cover must be pointed away from your body or any other person; if the airbag*

20.5a Disengage the connector lock . . .

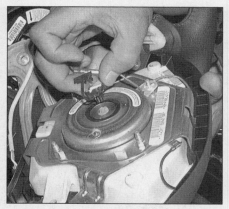

20.5b . . . then unplug the electrical connector from the airbag module

20.8 Use a steering wheel puller to remove the steering wheel from the shaft

module is placed on a workbench or any other surface, the trim cover must face upwards. When removing the airbag module, tag or mark all fasteners, screws, bolts, and other parts for the airbag module with their location as removed, for correct installation later.

6   Disconnect the airbag clockspring and horn wires from the airbag mounting bracket. On coupe models also unbolt the cruise control switch and disconnect its electrical connector.

7   Remove the steering wheel retaining nut or bolt. Mark the steering column shaft and the steering wheel for correct positioning when reinstalling later.

8   Remove the steering wheel with a steering wheel puller - do not bump or hammer on the steering wheel or steering column in an attempt to remove the wheel **(see illustration)**.

9   If necessary for access to other components, remove the airbag clockspring **(see illustration)**. **Note:** *The steering column covers will have to be removed first (see Chapter 11).* **Warning:** *Don't allow the steering shaft to rotate with the steering wheel removed.*

Installation

10   Before installing the steering wheel, make sure the front wheels are pointing straight ahead and the airbag clockspring is centered, as follows:

   2000 and earlier coupe models - Turn the clockspring rotor clockwise by hand until it stops (don't apply too much force), then turn the rotor counterclockwise approximately 3-1/8 turns until the arrows on the clockspring body and rotor are in alignment.

   2001 and later coupe models - Depress the locking pin and turn the clockspring rotor clockwise by hand until it stops (don't apply too much force), then turn the rotor counterclockwise approximately 3 turns until the arrows on the clockspring body and rotor are in alignment.

   2000 and earlier convertible models - Push in on the two locking pins to disengage the locking mechanism. While continuing to depress the pins, turn the clockspring rotor clockwise until it stops (don't turn it with too much force or you could damage it). Slowly

turn the rotor counterclockwise until yellow appears in the centering window. The arrow on the rotor of the clockspring should now be pointing at the yellow window on the clockspring. Release the locking pins to engage the locking mechanism.

   2001 and later convertible and sedan models - Depress the locking pin and turn the clockspring rotor clockwise by hand until it stops (don't apply too much force). Slowly rotate the clockspring counterclockwise until the yellow mark appears in the centering window and the locking pin is aligned with the arrow on the clockspring label. Release the locking pin and engage the clockspring into the locked position.

11   Lower the steering wheel into position, feeding the clockspring wiring harness through the opening in the wheel.

12   Place the steering wheel on the shaft, aligning the marks. Install the nut or bolt and tighten it to the torque listed in this Chapter's Specifications.

13   Correctly route and reconnect electrical connectors such as the cruise control switch electrical leads from the clockspring to switch openings in the steering wheel.

14   Plug in the horn and airbag module electrical connectors. Press the cruise control wires into the retaining channels on the steer-

20.9 Airbag clockspring mounting screws (coupe model shown, others similar)

ing wheel, if applicable.

15   Install the airbag module electrical lead from the clockspring into the connector on the airbag module. Insert the locking tab in the back of the airbag module connector. **Warning:** *Make sure the electrical connector from the clockspring is securely latched into the airbag module connector. The fasteners, screws, bolts, and other parts for the airbag module are specifically designed and must never be replaced with anything other than genuine factory part number replacements.*

16   Install the airbag module into the center of the steering wheel and install the mounting bolts, tightening them to the torque listed in this Chapter's Specifications.

17   Connect the cable to the negative terminal of the battery or to the remote ground terminal.

---

21   Steering column - removal and installation

Refer to illustrations 21.8, 21.9, 21.10a and 21.10b

Warning: *These models are equipped with airbags. Always disable the airbag system before working in the vicinity of any airbag system component to avoid the possibility of accidental deployment of the airbag(s), which could cause personal injury (see Chapter 12).*
Warning: *Do not use a memory saving device to preserve the ECM's memory when working on or near airbag system components.*

Removal

1   Park the vehicle with the wheels in the straight-ahead position. Disconnect the cable from the negative terminal of the battery or from the remote ground terminal (see Chapter 5, Section 1). Wait at least two minutes before proceeding (the airbag system has a back-up capacitor that must fully discharge).

2   Remove the steering wheel (see Section 20).

3   Remove the lower instrument panel trim (under the steering column), the knee bolster and the heater/air conditioning duct (see Chapter 11).

21.8 Remove the nut and pull out the pinch bolt securing the intermediate shaft to the steering gear (convertible and sedan models)

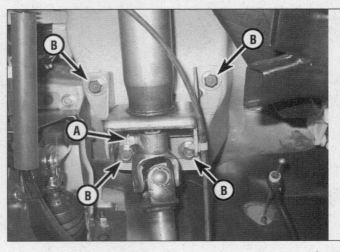

21.9 Steering column shaft-to-intermediate shaft pinch bolt (A) and column lower mounting bolts (B) - coupe models

4   Remove the steering column covers (see Chapter 11).
5   Remove the airbag system clockspring (see Section 20).
6   Remove the multi-function switch (see Chapter 12).
7   On models equipped with an automatic transmission, detach the shift interlock cable from the ignition lock cylinder (see Chapter 7B).
8   If you're working on a convertible or sedan model, remove the cover, mark the relationship of the steering shaft lower universal joint to the steering gear input shaft, then remove the nut from the pinch bolt securing the universal joint **(see illustration)**. Remove the bolt and separate the universal joint from the steering gear input shaft.
9   If you're working on a coupe model, mark the relationship of the steering column shaft to the intermediate shaft, then remove the pinch bolt **(see illustration)**.
10   **Caution:** *If you're working on a 2000 or earlier convertible model with tilt steering, lock the tilt mechanism as shown in Chapter 11,* **illustration 22.17** *before loosening the*

coumn mounting nuts. Remove the steering column mounting fasteners **(see illustration 21.9 and the accompanying illustrations)**, then guide the column out from the instrument panel. **Note:** *On convertible and sedan models the intermediate shaft will be removed along with the steering column.*

Installation

11   Guide the column into position, connecting the U-joint with the steering gear input shaft (convertible and sedan models) or with the intermediate shaft (coupe models). Be sure to align the marks made in Steps 8 or 9.
12   Install the mounting bolts/nuts, tightening them to the torque listed in this Chapter's Specifications.
13   Install the pinch bolt and tighten it to the torque listed in this Chapter's Specifications. On convertible and sedan models be sure to install the retention clip. **Note:** *The manufacturer recommends installing a new nut and bolt (convertible and sedan models).*
14   The remainder of installation is the reverse of the removal procedure. When installing the steering wheel, be sure the airbag clockspring is centered (see Sec-

tion 20), and tighten the steering wheel nut or bolt to the torque listed in this Chapter's Specifications. Also tighten the airbag mounting bolts to the torque listed in this Chapter's Specifications.

22 Tie-rod ends - removal and installation

Refer to illustrations 22.2, 22.4a and 22.4b

Removal

1   Loosen the wheel lug nuts, raise the front of the vehicle and support it securely on jackstands. Apply the parking brake and block the rear wheels to keep the vehicle from rolling off the jackstands. Remove the wheel.
2   Loosen the tie-rod end jam nut **(see illustration)**.
3   Mark the relationship of the tie-rod end to the threaded portion of the tie-rod. This will ensure the toe-in setting is restored when reassembled. If you're working on a coupe model, remove the cotter pin from the ball-stud.
4   Loosen the nut from the tie-rod end ball-stud a few turns, while holding the ballstud

21.10a Steering column mounting nuts - convertible and sedan models

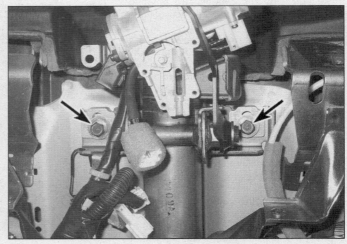

21.10b Steering column upper mounting bolts - coupe models

22.2 Loosen the tie-rod end jam nut far enough to mark its position on the tie-rod

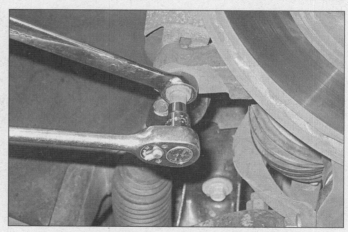

22.4a While holding the ballstud with a wrench to prevent it from turning, loosen the nut

with a wrench **(see illustration)**. Disconnect the tie-rod end from the steering knuckle arm with a puller **(see illustration)**.

5   Remove the nut from the ballstud, separate the tie-rod end from the steering knuckle, then unscrew the tie-rod end from the tie-rod.

Installation

6   Thread the tie-rod end onto the tie-rod to the marked position and connect the tie-rod end to the steering arm. Install the nut on the ballstud and tighten it to the torque listed in this Chapter's Specifications while holding the ballstud with a wrench to prevent it from turning. If you're working on a coupe model, install a new cotter pin.

7   Tighten the jam nut securely and install the wheel. Lower the vehicle and tighten the lug nuts to the torque listed in the Chapter 1 Specifications.

8   Have the front end alignment checked and, if necessary, adjusted.

23 Steering gear boots - replacement

1   Loosen the lug nuts, raise the vehicle and support it securely on jackstands. Remove the wheel.

2   Remove the tie-rod end and jam nut (see Section 22).

3   Remove the steering gear boot clamps and slide the boot off. **Note:** *Check for the presence of power steering fluid in the boot. If there is a substantial amount, it means the rack seals are leaking and the power steering gear should be replaced with a new or rebuilt unit.*

4   Before installing the new boot, wrap the threads and serrations on the end of the steering rod with a layer of tape so the small end of the new boot isn't damaged.

5   Slide the new boot into position on the steering gear until it seats in the grooves, then install new clamps.

6   Remove the tape and install the tie-rod end (see Section 22).

7   Install the wheel and lug nuts. Lower the vehicle and tighten the lug nuts to the torque listed in the Chapter 1 Specifications.

8   Have the front end alignment checked and, if necessary, adjusted.

24 Steering gear - removal and installation

Warning: *These models are equipped with airbags. Always disable the airbag system before working in the vicinity of airbag system components (see Chapter 12). Make sure the steering column shaft is not turned while the steering gear is removed or you could damage the airbag system clockspring. To prevent the shaft from turning, turn the ignition key to the lock position before beginning work, and run the seat belt through the steering wheel and clip it into its latch.*

Convertible and sedan models
Removal

Refer to illustrations 24.7, 24.16a and 24.16b

1   Disconnect the negative battery cable from the remote ground terminal (see Chapter 5, Section 1).

22.4b Using a puller, separate the ballstud from the steering knuckle

2   Drain the power steering fluid from the remote power steering reservoir. This can be accomplished with a suction gun or large syringe, or by disconnecting the fluid hose and draining the fluid into a container.

3   From inside the vehicle under the dashboard, slide the steering shaft boot up from the firewall and remove the intermediate shaft pinch bolt **(see illustration 20.8)**.

4   Mark the intermediate shaft and the steering gear shaft with alignment markings for later installation, then separate the intermediate shaft coupler from the steering gear shaft.

5   Loosen the front wheel lug nuts. Raise the vehicle and place it securely on jackstands. Remove both front wheels.

6   Detach the tie-rod ends from the steering knuckles (see Section 22).

7   Mark the relationship of the front suspension crossmember to the body **(see illustration)**. Be sure to mark each side, at the front and at the rear.

8   Remove the front stabilizer bar clamp-to-body bolts. It is not necessary to remove the stabilizer bar clamp-to-front suspension crossmember bolts.

9   For ABS-equipped vehicles, remove the bolts attaching the Anti-lock Brake System hydraulic control unit to the front suspension

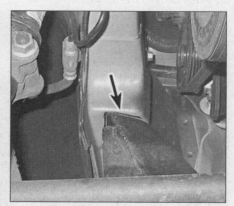

24.7 Mark the position of the suspension crossmember to the body

crossmember. Using a length of wire, hang the hydraulic control unit from the body/engine.

10 Detach the left and right shock absorber damper forks from the lower control arms (see Section 3).

11 Remove the two bolts from the engine support bracket attaching to the front edge of the suspension crossmember, and the two bolts attaching the rear support bracket at the rear of the suspension crossmember.

12 Remove the bolt attaching the engine support bracket to the transaxle mounting bracket.

13 Using a transmission jack or two floor jacks, support the front suspension crossmember. Lower the crossmember sufficiently to allow the steering gear to be removed. **Note:** *Make sure you support the crossmember and do not allow it to hang from the lower control arms at any time.*

14 Place a drain pan under the steering gear and detach the power steering pressure and return lines. Cap the ends to prevent excessive fluid loss and contamination.

15 Disconnect the pressure switch wiring harness connector from the steering gear. On models equipped with the electronic speed sensing/variable assist steering, disconnect the speed sensing/variable assist module and solenoid control valve electrical connectors. If equipped with a heat shield, unbolt and remove it.

16 Remove the two steering gear mounting bolts and isolators at the crossmember and then remove the two steering gear-to-crossmember clamp bolts **(see illustrations)**.

17 Remove the steering gear from the vehicle.

Installation

18 Center the steering gear before installing it. To do this, turn the steering gear input shaft counterclockwise until it stops, then count the number of turns as you turn the shaft clockwise until it stops. Divide that number by two, then turn the shaft counterclockwise that amount.

19 Installation is the reverse of removal. Make sure you align the steering gear assembly with the positioning marks scribed before removal. Gently tap the front suspension crossmember into place, lining up the marks

24.16a Steering gear-to-crossmember clamp bolt

made during removal. Use a new steering gear intermediate shaft coupler retaining pinch bolt, and make sure the retention pin is installed in the bolt after tightening the pinch bolt to the torque listed in this Chapter's Specifications.

20 Install the wheel and lug nuts. Lower the vehicle and tighten the lug nuts to the torque listed in the Chapter 1 Specifications.

21 Refill the power steering with power steering fluid (see Chapter 1), and bleed the system (see Section 25). **Warning:** *Do not use automatic transaxle fluid.*

22 Have the front wheel alignment checked and, if necessary, adjusted.

Coupe models

Removal

Refer to illustration 24.31

23 Disconnect the cable from the negative terminal of the battery.

24 Remove the windshield washer fluid reservoir.

25 Loosen the front wheel lug nuts, raise the front of the vehicle and support it securely on jackstands. Apply the parking brake and remove the wheels.

26 Remove the front exhaust pipe (see Chapter 4).

27 Remove the stiffener plates from under the steering gear **(see illustration 2.4)**. Also remove the transaxle rear roll stopper (mount)

24.16b Steering gear-to-crossmember mounting bolt

and center member (see Chapter 2) and the stabilizer bar (see Section 2).

28 Mark the relationship of the lower universal joint to the steering gear input shaft. Remove the lower intermediate shaft pinch bolt **(see illustration 20.9)**.

29 Place a drain pan under the steering gear. Detach the power steering pressure and return lines and cap the ends to prevent excessive fluid loss and contamination.

30 Separate the tie-rod ends from the steering knuckle arms (see Section 22).

31 Support the steering gear and remove the steering gear-to-crossmember mounting bolts and clamps **(see illustration)**. Separate the intermediate shaft from the steering gear input shaft and guide it out from under the vehicle.

32 Check the steering gear mounting grommets for excessive wear or deterioration, replacing them if necessary.

Installation

33 Center the steering gear before installing it. To do this, turn the steering gear input shaft counterclockwise until it stops, then count the number of turns as you turn the shaft clockwise until it stops. Divide that number by two, then turn the shaft counterclockwise that amount.

34 Raise the steering gear into position and connect the U-joint, aligning the marks.

35 Install the mounting brackets and bolts and tighten them to the torque listed in this Chapter's Specifications.

36 Connect the tie-rod ends to the steering knuckle arms (see Section 22).

37 Install the U-joint pinch bolt and tighten it to the torque listed in this Chapter's Specifications.

38 Connect the power steering pressure and return hoses to the steering gear and fill the power steering pump reservoir with the recommended fluid (see Chapter 1).

39 The remainder of installation is the reverse of the removal steps.

40 Lower the vehicle and bleed the steering system (see Section 26).

41 Tighten the lug nuts to the torque listed in the Chapter 1 Specifications.

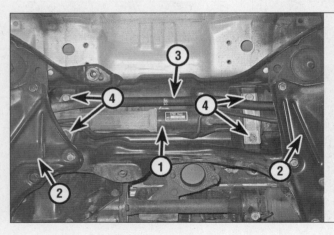

24.31 Steering gear details (coupe models)

1 Steering gear
2 Stiffener plates
3 Stabilizer bar
4 Mounting bolts

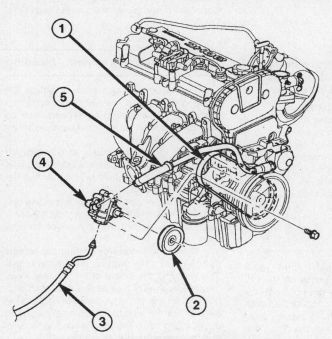

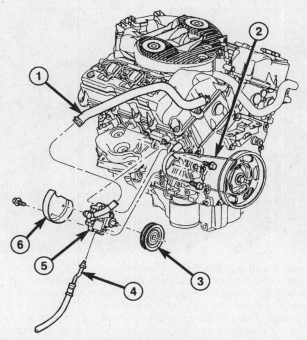

25.8a Power steering pump mounting details -
2.4L four-cylinder engine

1	Drivebelt	4	Power steering pump
2	Pulley	5	Feed hose
3	Pressure hose		

25.8b Power steering pump mounting details - 2.7L V6 engine

1	Feed hose	4	Pressure hose
2	Drivebelt	5	Power steering pump
3	Pulley	6	Heat shield

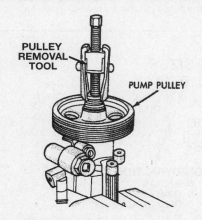

25.10a If you're installing a new pump,
you'll need a special puller to remove
the pulley from the old pump . . .

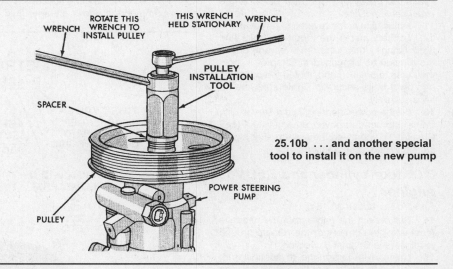

25.10b . . . and another special
tool to install it on the new pump

25 Power steering pump - removal and installation

2.4L four-cylinder, 2.7L and 3.0L V6 engines

Refer to illustrations 25.8a, 25.8b, 25.10a and 25.10b

1 Disconnect the cable from the negative terminal of the battery or the remote ground terminal (see Chapter 5, Section 1).

2 Using a large syringe or suction gun, suck as much fluid out of the power steering fluid reservoir as possible.

3 Loosen the right front wheel lug nuts. Raise the vehicle and support it securely on jackstands.

4 Remove the right front wheel. Also remove the right front wheel splash shield.

5 Place a drain pan under the vehicle to catch any fluid that spills out when the hoses are disconnected.

6 Disconnect the power steering pump hoses. Cap the hoses and the power steering pump ports.

7 On models with a pump-mounted pressure switch, unplug the electrical connector from the switch.

8 Loosen the pump mounting bolts and

remove the drivebelt **(see illustrations)**. **Note:** *Some models have mounting bolts at the rear of the pump as well as the front. Also, access to the upper mounting bolt on some models is through a hole in the inner fender panel.*

9 Unscrew the mounting bolts and remove the power steering pump and mounting bracket as an assembly through the area between the rear of the engine, driveaxle and front suspension crossmember.

10 If you're installing a new pump, you'll need a special puller to remove the pulley from the old pump and another special tool to install it on the new pump **(see illustrations)**. These tools are available at most auto parts

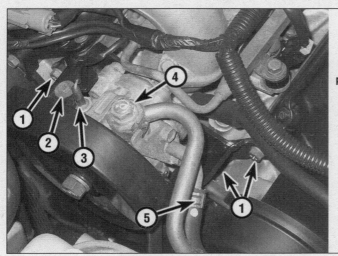

25.16 Power steering pump mounting details - 2.5L V6 engine

1 Mounting bolt
2 Cover bolt
3 Pressure switch electrical connector
4 Pressure line fitting
5 Feed hose clamp

stores. **Caution:** *Although generic pulley removal and installation tools can be used, the factory tool has a calibrated spacer that is placed between the hub of the pulley and the installer tool; this spacer ensures that the pulley is installed to the correct position on the shaft, which is critical for drivebelt alignment. If you are using a generic installer tool, measure the distance from the pulley hub to the end of the shaft using a vernier or dial caliper (or some other type of depth gauge) before you remove the pulley from the old pump. Press the pulley onto the new pump to the exact same position.*

11   Installation is the reverse of removal.

12   Loosely install the mounting bolts and hose fittings. Install the drivebelt and adjust the tension as described in Chapter 1, hold the pump in position and tighten the adjusting and pivot bolts securely. Tighten the line fittings securely.

13   Fill the power steering fluid reservoir with the recommended power steering fluid (see Chapter 1), and bleed the system after lowering the vehicle (see Section 26).

2.0L four-cylinder and 2.5L V6 engines

Refer to illustration 25.16

14   Disconnect the cable from the negative terminal of the battery or the remote ground terminal (see Chapter 5, Section 1).

15   Using a large syringe or suction gun, suck as much fluid out of the power steering fluid reservoir as possible.

16   Unplug the electrical connector from the power steering pressure switch (**see illustration**). On 2.5L V6 models remove the cover from the pump.

17   Remove the drivebelt (see Chapter 1).

18   Detach the pressure and feed lines from the pump. Discard the pressure line sealing washers; new ones should be used when reinstalling the pump.

19   Remove the pump mounting bolts and detach the pump from the engine. If you're working on a 2.5L V6 model, unbolt the pump from the mounting bracket.

20   If you're installing a new pump, you'll probably have to take the pulley off the old pump and install it on the new one. To do this, insert a punch through one of the holes in the pulley to prevent it from turning, then unscrew the pulley nut. When installing the pulley, immobilize using the same method, then tighten the nut securely.

21   Installation is the reverse of removal. Install the drivebelt and adjust the tension as described in Chapter 1. Tighten the pump mounting bolts securely.

22   Fill the power steering fluid reservoir with the recommended power steering fluid (see

Chapter 1), and bleed the system (see Section 26).

26   Power steering system - bleeding

1   Following any operation in which the power steering fluid lines have been disconnected, the power steering system must be bled to remove all air and obtain proper steering performance.

2   With the front wheels in the straight ahead position, check the power steering fluid level and, if low, add fluid until it reaches the Cold mark on the dipstick.

3   Start the engine and allow it to run at fast idle. Recheck the fluid level and add more if necessary to reach the Cold mark on the dipstick.

4   Bleed the system by turning the wheels from side to side, without hitting the stops. This will work the air out of the system. Keep the reservoir full of fluid as this is done.

5   When the air is worked out of the system, return the wheels to the straight ahead position and leave the vehicle running for several more minutes before shutting it off.

6   Road test the vehicle to be sure the steering system is functioning normally and noise free.

7   Recheck the fluid level to be sure it is up to the Hot mark on the dipstick while the engine is at normal operating temperature. Add fluid if necessary (see Chapter 1).

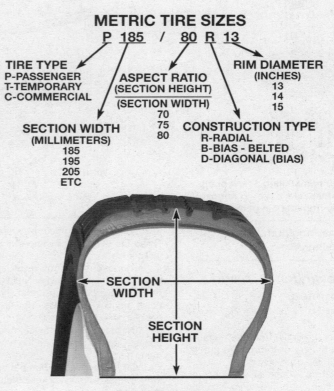

27.1 Metric tire size code

27 Wheels and tires - general information

Refer to illustration 27.1

1   Vehicles covered by this manual are equipped with metric-sized radial tires **(see illustration)**. Use of other size or type of tires may affect the ride and handling of the vehicle. Don't mix different types of tires, such as radials and bias belted, on the same vehicle as handling may be seriously affected. It's recommended that tires be replaced in pairs on the same axle, but if only one tire is being replaced, be sure it's the same size, structure and tread design as the other.

2   Because tire pressure has a substantial effect on handling and wear, the pressure on all tires should be checked at least once a month or before any extended trips (see Chapter 1).

3   Wheels must be replaced if they are bent, dented, leak air, have elongated bolt holes, are heavily corroded, out of vertical symmetry or if the lug nuts won't stay tight. Wheel repairs that use welding or peening are not recommended.

4   Tire and wheel balance is important in the overall handling, braking and performance of the vehicle. Unbalanced wheels can adversely affect handling and ride characteristics as well as tire life. Whenever a tire is installed on a wheel, the tire and wheel should be balanced by a shop with the proper equipment.

28 Wheel alignment - general information

Refer to illustration 28.1

    A wheel alignment refers to the adjustments made to the wheels so they are in proper angular relationship to the suspension and the ground. Wheels that are out of proper alignment not only affect vehicle control, but also increase tire wear.

    The front end should be measured for camber, caster and toe-in **(see illustration)**. Toe-in can be adjusted by turning the tie-rods in or out. On convertible and sedan models, front camber and caster is adjustable by loosening the upper control arm/shock absorber mount bolts and moving the mount in relation to the body. On 2000 and earlier coupe models, front camber and caster is not adjustable; if camber and caster aren't within the specified dimensions, suspension parts are bent or worn and must be replaced. On 2001 and later coupe models, camber can be adjusted by installing special bolts in the strut-to-steering knuckle lower mounting holes, but caster isn't adjustable.

    The rear should be measured for camber and toe-in. Toe-in on coupe models is adjusted by an eccentric cam at the inner end of the toe control arm. On convertible and sedan models it's adjusted by altering the

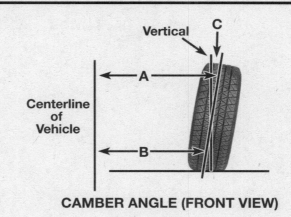

CAMBER ANGLE (FRONT VIEW)

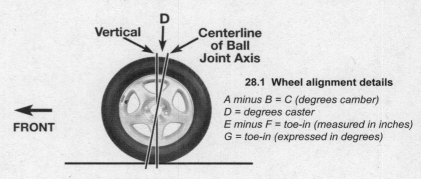

28.1 Wheel alignment details

A minus B = C (degrees camber)
D = degrees caster
E minus F = toe-in (measured in inches)
G = toe-in (expressed in degrees)

CASTER ANGLE (SIDE VIEW)

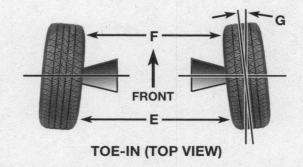

TOE-IN (TOP VIEW)

length of the threaded lateral links. Camber and caster is adjustable on convertible and sedan models, but not on coupe models.

    Getting the proper wheel alignment is a very exacting process, one in which complicated and expensive machines are necessary to perform the job properly. Because of this, you should have a technician with the proper equipment perform these tasks. We will, however, use this space to give you a basic idea of what is involved with a wheel alignment so you can better understand the process and deal intelligently with the shop that does the work.

    Toe-in is the turning in of the wheels. The purpose of a toe specification is to ensure parallel rolling of the wheels. In a vehicle with zero toe-in, the distance between the front edges of the wheels will be the same as the distance between the rear edges of the

wheels. The actual amount of toe-in is normally only a fraction of an inch. Incorrect toe-in will cause the tires to wear improperly by making them scrub against the road surface.

    Camber is the tilting of the wheels from vertical when viewed from one end of the vehicle. When the wheels tilt out at the top, the camber is said to be positive (+). When the wheels tilt in at the top the camber is negative (-). The amount of tilt is measured in degrees from vertical and this measurement is called the camber angle. This angle affects the amount of tire tread which contacts the road and compensates for changes in the suspension geometry when the vehicle is cornering or traveling over an undulating surface.

    Caster is the tilting of the front steering axis from the vertical. A tilt toward the rear is positive caster and a tilt toward the front is negative caster.

Notes

Chapter 11   Body

Contents

1   General information

The models covered by this manual feature a "unibody" layout, using a floor pan with front and rear frame side rails which support the body components, front and rear suspension systems and other mechanical components. Certain components are particularly vulnerable to accident damage and can be unbolted and repaired or replaced. Among these parts are the body moldings, bumpers, front fenders, the hood and trunk lids and all glass. Only general body maintenance practices and body panel repair procedures within the scope of the do-it-yourselfer are included in this Chapter.

2   Body - maintenance

1   The condition of the vehicle's body is very important, because the resale value depends a great deal on it. It's much more difficult to repair a neglected or damaged body than it is to repair mechanical components. The hidden areas of the body, such as the wheel wells, the frame and the engine compartment, are equally important, although they don't require as frequent attention as the rest of the body.

2   Once a year, or every 12,000 miles, it's a good idea to have the underside of the body steam cleaned. All traces of dirt and oil will be removed and the area can then be inspected carefully for rust, damaged brake lines, frayed electrical wires, damaged cables and other problems. The front suspension components should be greased after completion of this job.

3   At the same time, clean the engine and the engine compartment with a steam cleaner or water-soluble degreaser.

4   The wheel wells should be given close attention, since undercoating can peel away and stones and dirt thrown up by the tires can cause the paint to chip and flake, allowing rust to set in. If rust is found, clean down to the bare metal and apply an anti-rust paint.

5   The body should be washed about once a week. Wet the vehicle thoroughly to soften the dirt, then wash it down with a soft sponge and plenty of clean soapy water. If the surplus dirt is not washed off very carefully, it can wear down the paint.

6   Spots of tar or asphalt thrown up from the road should be removed with a cloth soaked in solvent.

7   Once every six months, wax the body and chrome trim. If a chrome cleaner is used to remove rust from any of the vehicle's plated parts, remember that the cleaner also removes part of the chrome, so use it sparingly.

3   Vinyl trim - maintenance

Don't clean vinyl trim with detergents, caustic soap or petroleum-based cleaners. Plain soap and water works just fine, with a soft brush to clean dirt that may be ingrained. Wash the vinyl as frequently as the rest of the vehicle. After cleaning, application of a high-quality rubber and vinyl protectant will help prevent oxidation and cracks. The protectant can also be applied to weatherstripping, vacuum lines and rubber hoses, which often fail as a result of chemical degradation, and to the tires.

4   Upholstery and carpets - maintenance

1   Every three months remove the floor mats and clean the interior of the vehicle (more frequently if necessary). Use a stiff whisk broom to brush the carpeting and loosen dirt and dust, then vacuum the upholstery and carpets thoroughly, especially along seams and crevices.

2   Dirt and stains can be removed from carpeting with basic household or automotive carpet shampoos available in spray cans. Follow the directions and vacuum again, then use a stiff brush to bring back the "nap" of the carpet.

3   Most interiors have cloth or vinyl upholstery, either of which can be cleaned and maintained with a number of material-specific cleaners or shampoos available in auto supply stores. Follow the directions on the product for usage, and always spot-test any upholstery cleaner on an inconspicuous area (like the bottom edge of a back seat cushion) to ensure that it doesn't cause a color shift in the material.

4   After cleaning, vinyl upholstery should be treated with a protectant. **Note:** *Make sure the protectant container indicates the product can be used on seats - some products make may a seat too slippery.* **Caution:** *Do not use a protectant on vinyl-covered steering wheels.*

5   Leather upholstery requires special care. It should be cleaned regularly with saddle soap or leather cleaner. Never use alcohol, gasoline, nail polish remover or thinner to clean leather upholstery.

6   After cleaning, regularly treat leather upholstery with a leather conditioner, rubbed in with a soft cotton cloth. Never use car wax on leather upholstery.

7   In areas where the interior of the vehicle is subject to bright sunlight, cover leather seating areas of the seats with a sheet if the vehicle is to be left out for any length of time.

5   Body repair

Minor damage

Repair of scratches

1   If the scratch is superficial and does not penetrate to the metal of the body, repair is very simple. Lightly rub the scratched area with a fine rubbing compound to remove loose paint and built up wax. Rinse the area with clean water.

2   Apply touch-up paint to the scratch, using a small brush. Continue to apply thin layers of paint until the surface of the paint in the scratch is level with the surrounding paint. Allow the new paint at least two weeks to harden, then blend it into the surrounding paint by rubbing with a very fine rubbing compound. Finally, apply a coat of wax to the scratch area.

3   If the scratch has penetrated the paint and exposed the metal of the body, causing the metal to rust, a different repair technique is required. Remove all loose rust from the bottom of the scratch with a pocket knife, then apply rust inhibiting paint to prevent the formation of rust in the future. Using a rubber or nylon applicator, coat the scratched area with glaze-type filler. If required, the filler can be mixed with thinner to provide a very thin paste, which is ideal for filling narrow scratches. Before the glaze filler in the scratch hardens, wrap a piece of smooth cotton cloth around the tip of a finger. Dip the cloth in thinner and then quickly wipe it along the surface of the scratch. This will ensure that the surface of the filler is slightly hollow. The scratch can now be painted over as described earlier in this Section.

Repair of dents

See photo sequence

4   When repairing dents, the first job is to pull the dent out until the affected area is as close as possible to its original shape. There is no point in trying to restore the original shape completely as the metal in the damaged area will have stretched on impact and cannot be restored to its original contours. It is better to bring the level of the dent up to a point which is about 1/8-inch below the level of the surrounding metal. In cases where the dent is very shallow, it is not worth trying to pull it out at all.

5   If the back side of the dent is accessible, it can be hammered out gently from behind using a soft-face hammer. While doing this, hold a block of wood firmly against the opposite side of the metal to absorb the hammer blows and prevent the metal from being stretched.

6   If the dent is in a section of the body which has double layers, or some other factor makes it inaccessible from behind, a different technique is required. Drill several small holes through the metal inside the damaged area, particularly in the deeper sections. Screw long, self tapping screws into the holes just enough for them to get a good grip in the metal. Now the dent can be pulled out by pulling on the protruding heads of the screws with locking pliers.

7   The next stage of repair is the removal of paint from the damaged area and from an inch or so of the surrounding metal. This is easily done with a wire brush or sanding disk in a drill motor, although it can be done just as effectively by hand with sandpaper. To complete the preparation for filling, score the surface of the bare metal with a screwdriver or the tang of a file or drill small holes in the affected area. This will provide a good grip for the filler material. To complete the repair, see the subsection on *filling and painting*.

Repair of rust holes or gashes

8   Remove all paint from the affected area and from an inch or so of the surrounding metal using a sanding disk or wire brush mounted in a drill motor. If these are not available, a few sheets of sandpaper will do the job just as effectively.

9   With the paint removed, you will be able to determine the severity of the corrosion and decide whether to replace the whole panel, if possible, or repair the affected area. New body panels are not as expensive as most people think and it is often quicker to install a new panel than to repair large areas of rust.

10   Remove all trim pieces from the affected area except those which will act as a guide to the original shape of the damaged body, such as headlight shells, etc. Using metal snips or a hacksaw blade, remove all loose metal and any other metal that is badly affected by rust. Hammer the edges of the hole on the inside to create a slight depression for the filler material.

11   Wire brush the affected area to remove the powdery rust from the surface of the metal. If the back of the rusted area is accessible, treat it with rust inhibiting paint.

12   Before filling is done, block the hole in some way. This can be done with sheet metal riveted or screwed into place, or by stuffing the hole with wire mesh.

13   Once the hole is blocked off, the affected area can be filled and painted. See the following subsection on *filling and painting*.

Filling and painting

14   Many types of body fillers are available, but generally speaking, body repair kits which contain filler paste and a tube of resin hardener are best for this type of repair work. A wide, flexible plastic or nylon applicator will be necessary for imparting a smooth and contoured finish to the surface of the filler material. Mix up a small amount of filler on a clean piece of wood or cardboard (use the hardener sparingly). Follow the manufacturer's instructions on the package, otherwise the filler will set incorrectly.

15   Using the applicator, apply the filler paste to the prepared area. Draw the applicator across the surface of the filler to achieve the desired contour and to level the filler surface. As soon as a contour that approximates the original one is achieved, stop working the paste. If you continue, the paste will begin to stick to the applicator. Continue to add thin layers of paste at 20-minute intervals until the level of the filler is just above the surrounding metal.

16   Once the filler has hardened, the excess can be removed with a body file. From then on, progressively finer grades of sandpaper should be used, starting with a 180-grit paper and finishing with 600-grit wet-or-dry paper. Always wrap the sandpaper around a flat rubber or wooden block, otherwise the surface of the filler will not be completely flat. During the sanding of the filler surface, the wet-or-dry paper should be periodically rinsed in water. This will ensure that a very smooth finish is produced in the final stage.

17   At this point, the repair area should be surrounded by a ring of bare metal, which in turn should be encircled by the finely feathered edge of good paint. Rinse the repair area with clean water until all of the dust produced by the sanding operation is gone.

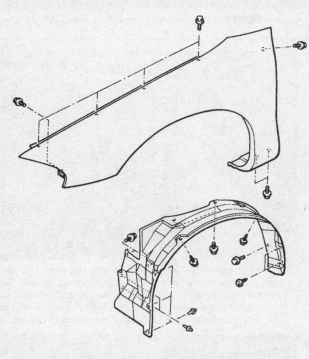

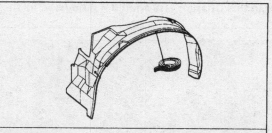

Sealant:
MOPAR Silicon Rubber Sealer Part No.
4026070 or Auto Glass Adhesive and Sealer
Part No.2298825 or equivalent

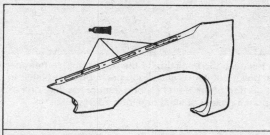

Sealant:
MOPAR Silicon Rubber Sealer Part No.
4026070 or equivalent

8.2 Front fender mounting details (typical)

18   Spray the entire area with a light coat of primer. This will reveal any imperfections in the surface of the filler. Repair the imperfections with fresh filler paste or glaze filler and once more smooth the surface with sandpaper. Repeat this spray-and-repair procedure until you are satisfied that the surface of the filler and the feathered edge of the paint are perfect. Rinse the area with clean water and allow it to dry completely.

19   The repair area is now ready for painting. Spray painting must be carried out in a warm, dry, windless and dust free atmosphere. These conditions can be created if you have access to a large indoor work area, but if you are forced to work in the open, you will have to pick the day very carefully. If you are working indoors, dousing the floor in the work area with water will help settle the dust which would otherwise be in the air. If the repair area is confined to one body panel, mask off the surrounding panels. This will help minimize the effects of a slight mismatch in paint color. Trim pieces such as chrome strips, door handles, etc., will also need to be masked off or removed. Use masking tape and several thickness of newspaper for the masking operations.

20   Before spraying, shake the paint can thoroughly, then spray a test area until the spray painting technique is mastered. Cover the repair area with a thick coat of primer. The thickness should be built up using several thin layers of primer rather than one thick one. Using 600-grit wet-or-dry sandpaper, rub down the surface of the primer until it is very smooth. While doing this, the work area

should be thoroughly rinsed with water and the wet-or-dry sandpaper periodically rinsed as well. Allow the primer to dry before spraying additional coats.

21   Spray on the top coat, again building up the thickness by using several thin layers of paint. Begin spraying in the center of the repair area and then, using a circular motion, work out until the whole repair area and about two inches of the surrounding original paint is covered. Remove all masking material 10 to 15 minutes after spraying on the final coat of paint. Allow the new paint at least two weeks to harden, then use a very fine rubbing compound to blend the edges of the new paint into the existing paint. Finally, apply a coat of wax.

Major damage

22   Major damage must be repaired by an auto body shop specifically equipped to perform unibody repairs. These shops have the specialized equipment required to do the job properly.

23   If the damage is extensive, the body must be checked for proper alignment or the vehicle's handling characteristics may be adversely affected and other components may wear at an accelerated rate.

24   Due to the fact that all of the major body components (hood, fenders, etc.) are separate and replaceable units, any seriously damaged components should be replaced rather than repaired. Sometimes the components can be found in a auto salvage or wrecking yard that specializes in used vehicle components, often at considerable savings over the cost of new parts.

6   Hinges and locks - maintenance

Once every 3000 miles, or every three months, the hinges and latch assemblies on the doors, hood and trunk should be given a few drops of light oil or lock lubricant. The door latch strikers should also be lubricated with a thin coat of grease to reduce wear and ensure free movement. Lubricate the door and trunk locks with spray-on graphite lubricant.

7   Windshield and fixed glass - replacement

Replacement of the windshield and fixed glass requires the use of special fast-setting adhesive/caulk materials and some specialized tools and techniques. These operations should be left to a dealer service department or a shop specializing in glass work.

8   Front fender - removal and installation

Refer to illustration 8.2

1   Remove the headlight, turn signal light and front bumper (see Chapter 12 and Section 12).

2   Remove the screws and detach the splash shield **(see illustration)**.

3   Remove the bolts and detach the fender.

These photos illustrate a method of repairing simple dents. They are intended to supplement *Body repair - minor damage* in this Chapter and should not be used as the sole instructions for body repair on these vehicles.

1 If you can't access the backside of the body panel to hammer out the dent, pull it out with a slide-hammer-type dent puller. In the deepest portion of the dent or along the crease line, drill or punch hole(s) at least one inch apart . . .

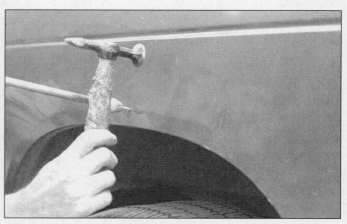

2 . . . then screw the slide-hammer into the hole and operate it. Tap with a hammer near the edge of the dent to help 'pop' the metal back to its original shape. When you're finished, the dent area should be close to its original contour and about 1/8-inch below the surface of the surrounding metal

3 Using coarse-grit sandpaper, remove the paint down to the bare metal. Hand sanding works fine, but the disc sander shown here makes the job faster. Use finer (about 320-grit) sandpaper to feather-edge the paint at least one inch around the dent area

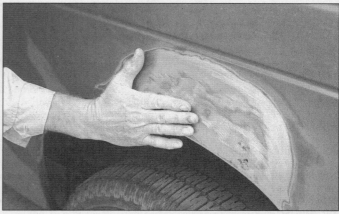

4 When the paint is removed, touch will probably be more helpful than sight for telling if the metal is straight. Hammer down the high spots or raise the low spots as necessary. Clean the repair area with wax/silicone remover

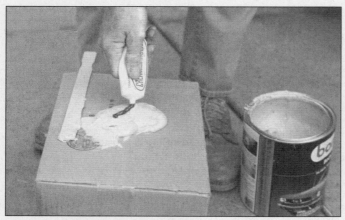

5 Following label instructions, mix up a batch of plastic filler and hardener. The ratio of filler to hardener is critical, and, if you mix it incorrectly, it will either not cure properly or cure too quickly (you won't have time to file and sand it into shape)

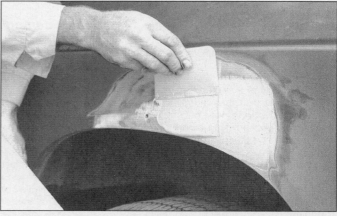

6 Working quickly so the filler doesn't harden, use a plastic applicator to press the body filler firmly into the metal, assuring it bonds completely. Work the filler until it matches the original contour and is slightly above the surrounding metal

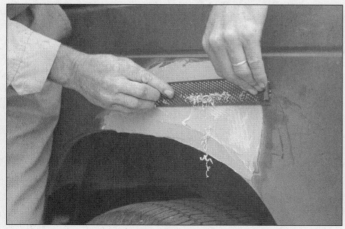

7 Let the filler harden until you can just dent it with your fingernail. Use a body file or Surform tool (shown here) to rough-shape the filler

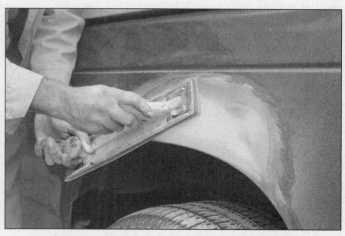

8 Use coarse-grit sandpaper and a sanding board or block to work the filler down until it's smooth and even. Work down to finer grits of sandpaper - always using a board or block - ending up with 360 or 400 grit

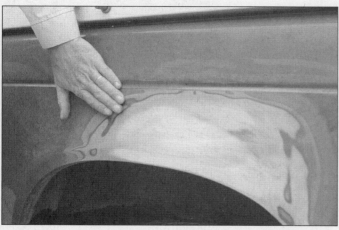

9 You shouldn't be able to feel any ridge at the transition from the filler to the bare metal or from the bare metal to the old paint. As soon as the repair is flat and uniform, remove the dust and mask off the adjacent panels or trim pieces

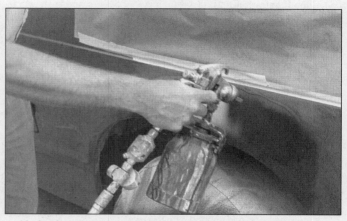

10 Apply several layers of primer to the area. Don't spray the primer on too heavy, so it sags or runs, and make sure each coat is dry before you spray on the next one. A professional-type spray gun is being used here, but aerosol spray primer is available inexpensively from auto parts stores

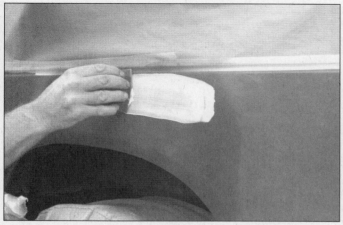

11 The primer will help reveal imperfections or scratches. Fill these with glazing compound. Follow the label instructions and sand it with 360 or 400-grit sandpaper until it's smooth. Repeat the glazing, sanding and respraying until the primer reveals a perfectly smooth surface

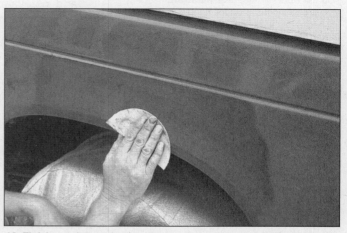

12 Finish sand the primer with very fine sandpaper (400 or 600-grit) to remove the primer overspray. Clean the area with water and allow it to dry. Use a tack rag to remove any dust, then apply the finish coat. Don't attempt to rub out or wax the repair area until the paint has dried completely (at least two weeks)

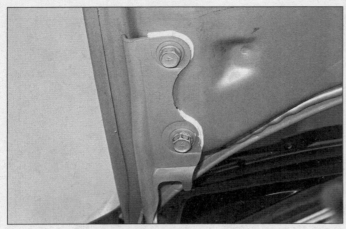

9.3 Paint or mark around the hood hinge before removing the bolts

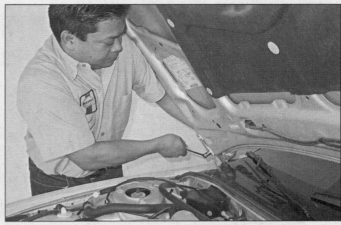

9.5 Support the hood with your shoulder while removing the hood bolts

4   Prior to installation, apply silicone sealant to the contact surfaces of the fender and body **(see illustration 8.2)**. Installation is the reverse of removal.

9 Hood - removal, installation and adjustment

Note: *The hood is heavy and somewhat awkward to remove and install - at least two people should perform this procedure.*

Removal

Refer to illustration 9.3 and 9.5

1   Use blankets or pads to cover the cowl area of the body and both fenders. This will protect the body and paint as the hood is lifted off.
2   Open the hood and support it on the prop rod.
3   Scribe alignment marks around the bolt heads and hinges to aid alignment during installation (a permanent-type felt-tip marker also will work for this) **(see illustration)**.
4   Disconnect the under hood lamp electrical connector (if equipped).
5   Have an assistant support one side of the hood while you support the other. Simultaneously remove the hinge-to-hood bolts **(see illustration)**.
6   Lift off the hood. **Note:** *A good place to store the hood is on the roof of the vehicle. Place blankets or pads on the roof first and lay the hood painted side down on the blankets.*

Installation

7   Installation is the reverse of removal. Align the marks around the hinges and bolts (one side at a time) and then check for proper clearance. Readjust as necessary (see below).

Adjustment

8   Fore-and-aft and side-to-side adjustment of the hood is done by moving the hood in relation to the hinge plate after loosening the bolts. The hood must be aligned so there is a 5/32-inch gap (approximate) to the front fenders and flush with the top surface.
9   Scribe or trace a line around the entire hinge plate so you can judge the amount of movement **(see illustration 9.3)**.
10   Loosen the bolts and move the hood into correct alignment. Move it only a little at a time. Tighten the hinge bolts and carefully lower the hood to check the alignment.
11   Adjust the hood bumpers on the radiator support so the hood is flush with the fenders when closed.
12   The hood latch assembly can also be adjusted up-and-down and side-to-side after loosening the nuts. Make sure you place alignment marks around the hood latch assembly before loosening the mounting nuts.
13   The hood latch assembly, as well as the hinges, should be periodically lubricated with white lithium-base grease to prevent sticking and wear.

10 Hood latch and cable - removal and installation

Warning: *These models have airbags. Always disable the airbag system before working in the vicinity of any airbag system components to avoid the possibility of accidental deployment of the airbag, which could cause personal injury* (see Chapter 12).

Latch

Removal

Refer to illustrations 10.2 and 10.3

1   Open the hood and support it on the prop rod.
2   Scribe alignment marks around the hood latch assembly to aid alignment during installation (a permanent-type felt-tip marker or paint will also work for this) **(see illustration)**.
3   Remove the bolts/nuts detach the latch assembly from the radiator support, then disconnect the release cable from the hood latch assembly **(see illustration)**.

10.2 For a reference point at installation, outline the hinges on the hood with a felt tip marker or white paint

Installation

4   Installation is the reverse of removal. Align the hood latch assembly with the marks on the radiator support and then tighten the nuts. Check hood latch operation. Readjust as necessary.

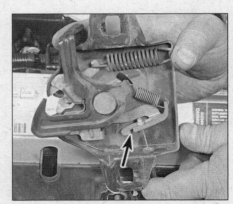

10.3 Slide the cable housing from the key-hole slot in the hood latch, then slide the cable through the slot (arrow) in the release arm and separate the cable from the hood latch assembly (convertible and sedan)

Cable

Removal

Refer to illustration 10.8a and 10.8b

5   Disconnect the release cable from the hood latch (see Steps 1 through 3).

6   Detach the cable from the clips securing it to the radiator support.

7   On sedan and convertible models, inside the vehicle remove the left front kick panel to gain access to the hood release handle bolts.

8   Remove the bolts securing the hood release handle/cable assembly to the cowl panel **(see illustrations)**.

9   Under the dash, locate and disengage the push-in retainer and cable grommet from the firewall.

10   Connect a piece of heavy string or flexible wire to the engine compartment end of the cable, then from inside the vehicle, pull the cable with string or wire attached through the firewall into the vehicle. Disconnect the string or wire from the old cable.

Installation

11   Connect the string or wire to the new cable and carefully pull it through the firewall into the engine compartment.

12   The remaining installation steps are the reverse of removal.

11   Radiator grille - removal and installation

Refer to illustration 11.3

Warning: *These models have airbags. Always disable the airbag system before working in the vicinity of any airbag system components to avoid the possibility of accidental deployment of the airbag, which could cause personal injury (see Chapter 12).*

Removal

1   Open the hood and support it on the prop rod.

2   Remove the front bumper with grille attached (see Section 12).

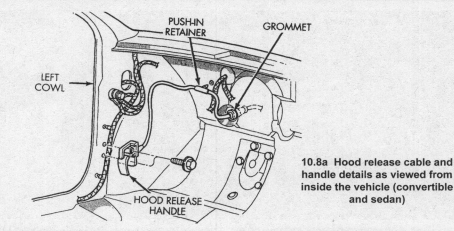

10.8a Hood release cable and handle details as viewed from inside the vehicle (convertible and sedan)

3   Remove the screws, nuts or fasteners securing the grille to the bumper and separate the grille from the bumper **(see illustration)**.

Installation

4   Installation is the reverse of removal. The grille can be reattached to the bumper using rivets (if available) or screws, nuts and washers. If threaded fasteners are used, apply thread locking compound to the screw threads.

12   Bumpers - removal and installation

Warning: *These models have airbags. Always disable the airbag system before working in the vicinity of any airbag system components to avoid the possibility of accidental deployment of the airbag, which could cause personal injury (see Chapter 12).*

Front bumper

Removal

Refer to illustrations 12.3, 12.5a, 12.5b, 12.6a, 12.6b and 12.9

1   Open the hood and support it on the prop rod.

10.8b On coupe models, lift up the release lever for access to the retaining screws

2   On coupe models disconnect the negative battery cable from the battery, or on convertible and sedan models from the ground stud on the left shock tower (see Chapter 5, Section 1).

3   Remove the fasteners securing the front fender inner splash shields to the lower section of the bumper cover **(see illustration)**.

11.3 To remove push-in fasteners, pry out the center stud, then remove the outer housing

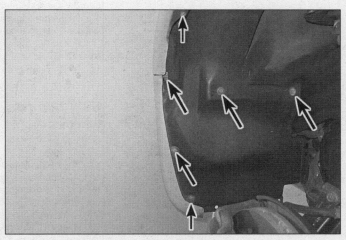

12.3 Remove the fasteners holding the fender inner splash panel to the bumper cover (arrows) (coupe model shown)

12.5a Sedan model upper bumper cover fasteners (arrows)

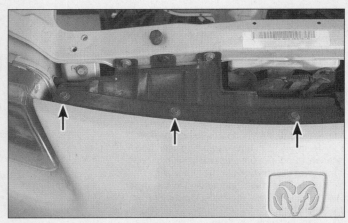

12.5b Remove the bolts along the top of the front bumper cover (arrows) (coupe model shown)

12.6a Remove the fasteners (arrows) along the bottom of the front bumper cover

12.6b Coupe model lower bumper cover fasteners (arrows)

4   Pull the splash shields away from the fender well as necessary to remove the bolts securing the bumper cover to the front fender.

5   Remove the fasteners securing the top of the bumper cover **(see illustrations)**.

6   Remove the fasteners securing the bottom edge of the bumper cover to the chassis **(see illustrations)**.

12.9 To detach the front bumper bar, disconnect any electrical connectors and remove the bolts (arrows) at each end of the bar (sedan shown)

7   If equipped, disconnect the foglight wiring harness connectors.

8   Disengage the bumper cover from the front fenders (both sides) and remove the bumper from the vehicle. **Note:** *If you are performing this job alone, place some blankets or other suitable padding on the ground below the bumper to protect the paint should the bumper fall during removal.*

9   If required, the bumper bar can be removed at this time **(see illustration)**.

Installation
10   Installation is the reverse of removal.

Rear bumper
Removal
Refer to illustrations 12.13a, 12.13b, 12.14a 12.14b and 12.14c

11   Open the trunk lid.

12   On some models, it may be necessary to remove one or both rear tail lights and disconnect the license plate light wiring from the tail lamp assembly.

13   Remove the rear tail light(s) inside the tail light cavities if necessary, remove the push-in fasteners or bolts securing the bum-

per cover to each rear quarter panel **(see illustrations)**.

14   Remove the bolts or fasteners securing the top, bottom and the center of the rear bumper cover **(see illustrations)**.

15   Remove the screws holding bumper cover to each rear wheel well splash shield.

16   Remove the bolts securing the bumper cover to the rear quarter panel in each wheel well.

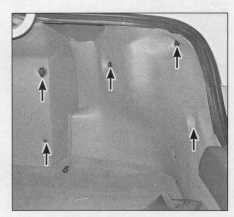

12.13a Remove the trim panels in the trunk area . . .

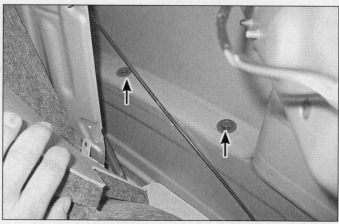

12.13b . . . for access to the bumper cover bolts (coupe shown)

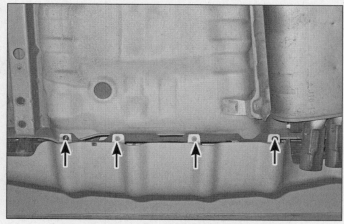

12.14a Remove the bolts along the bottom of the bumper cover (coupe)

12.14b Remove the bolts located behind the license plate (coupe)

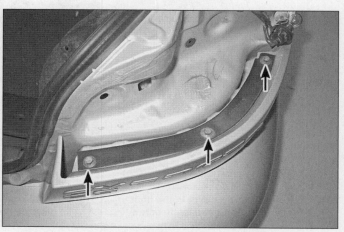

12.14c On coupe models, there are retaining bolts (arrows) on each side of the bumper

17   Slide the bumper cover rearward to dis-engage any hooks securing it to the bottom of each quarter panel and remove it from the vehicle. **Note:** *If you are performing this job alone, place some blankets or other suitable padding on the ground below the bumper to protect the paint should the bumper cover fall during removal.*

18   If required, the bumper bar can be removed at this time, however, before removal use a felt tip pen to mark the position of the nuts on the bar to aid with installation.

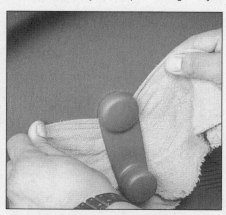

13.2 If you don't have a window crank removal tool (which is available at most auto parts stores and relatively inexpensive), place a shop cloth behind the window crank handle and work it back-and-forth to dislodge the retaining clip

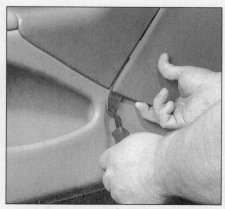

13.3 Carefully pry off the speaker grille (convertible models)

Installation

19   Installation is the reverse of removal.

13   Door trim panel - removal and installation

Removal

Refer to illustration 13.2

Note: *This procedure applies to both the front and rear doors.*

1   Open the door and completely lower the window glass.

2   On manual window models, remove the window crank using a special tool (available at most auto parts stores) or by working a cloth back-and-forth behind the handle to dislodge the retaining clip **(see illustration).**

Convertible and sedan models

Refer to illustration 13.3, 13.4, 13.5a, 13.5b, 13.6, 13.7, 13,8 and 13.9

3   Carefully pry off the speaker grille **(see illustration).**

4   Inside the speaker opening, remove the three screws securing the trim panel to the

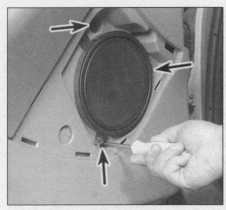

13.4 Remove the screws (arrows) that secure the panel to the door

13.5a Pry off the screw cover in the pull handle area . . .

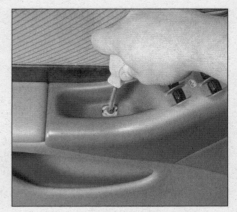

13.5b . . . and remove the screw

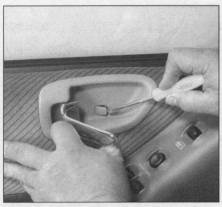

13.6 Pry off the screw cover in the door latch handle trim and remove the screw

13.7 Remove the door trim panel screw near the upper door hinge

13.8 Carefully pry around the door panel to disengage it from the retaining clips

door **(see illustration)**.

5   On the pull handle, pry off the screw cover and remove the screw **(see illustrations)**.

6   Pry the screw cover from the door handle latch trim and remove the screw **(see illustration)**.

7   Remove the screw securing the door trim panel near the upper door hinge **(see illustration)**.

8   Carefully pry around the door trim panel to disengage it from the retaining clips **(see illustration)**.

9   Grasp the trim panel and pull up sharply to detach it from the retainer channel in the window sill **(see illustration)**.

10   Position the trim panel slightly away from the door and disengage the clip holding the door latch linkage to the door handle.

11   On models so equipped, disconnect the electrical connectors from the speaker, power door lock switch, the mirror switch and power

window switch and then remove the trim panel. **Caution:** *Do not allow the trim panel to hang from the electrical wires.*

Coupe models
Refer to illustration 13.12a, 13.12b, 13.13a, 13.13a, 13.14a, 13.14b, 13.15 and 13.17

12   Remove the screws at the front edge and the rear edge of the trim panel of the door trim panel **(see illustrations)**.

13   In the pull handle pocket, pry off the

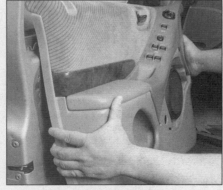

13.9 Grasp the door trim panel and lift it up sharply to detach it from the retainer channel in the window sill, then separate it from the door just far enough to disconnect the electrical connectors

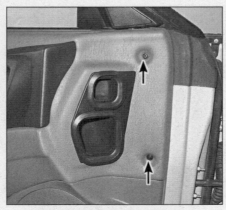

13.12a Remove the screws from the front edge . . .

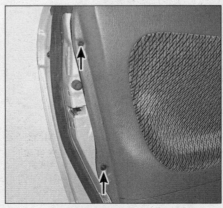

13.12b . . . and the rear edge of the door trim panel (coupe models)

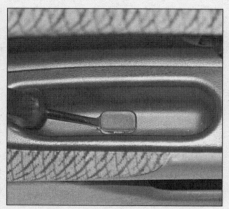

13.13a Pry off the screw cover in the pull handle pocket area . . .

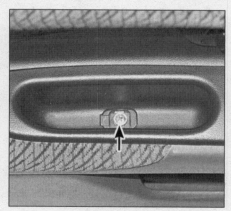

13.13b . . . and remove the screw (arrow) (coupe models)

13.14a Pry off the cover in the pull handle pocket area, remove the screw . . .

13.14b . . . and lift out the cover (coupe models)

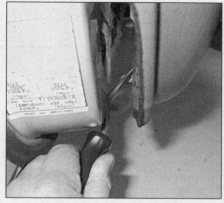

13.15 Disengage the door panel by carefully prying around it (coupe models)

13.17 Disconnect the electrical connector (arrow) from the door trim panel (coupe models)

screw cover and remove the screw **(see illustrations)**.

14   Pull the inner door handle away, remove the screw and detach the cover from the opening **(see illustrations)**.

15   Carefully pry around the door trim panel to disengage it from the retaining clips **(see illustration)**.

16   Grasp the trim panel and pull up sharply to detach it from the retainer channel in the window sill.

17   Disconnect the electrical connector **(see**

illustration) and then remove the trim panel.
Caution: *Do not allow the trim panel to hang from the electrical wires.*

Installation
All models

18   Reconnect any electrical connectors and install the latch linkage into the door handle. Secure it with the retaining clip.

19   Engage the top of the trim panel into the window sill retainer channel and press it into

place and seating all clip fasteners.

20   The remaining installation steps are the reverse of removal.

---

14   Door latch, outside handle and lock cylinder - removal, installation and adjustment

---

Note: *This procedure applies to both the front and rear doors.*

Latch
Removal

Refer to illustrations 14.4a, 14.4b and 14.6

1   Remove the door trim panel (see Section 13), except on vehicles equipped with electric windows, close the window before disconnecting the door trim panel electrical connectors.

2   On vehicles with manual windows, install the window crank (without the retaining clip) and roll up the window.

3   If you are removing a rear door latch, remove the window glass lower rear run channel.

4   Disconnect the lock cylinder, lock button and latch release operating rods from the door latch **(see illustrations)**.

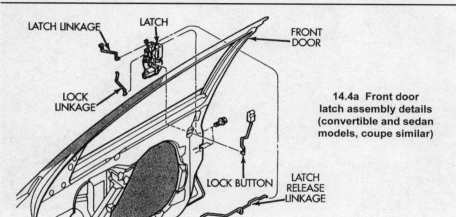

14.4a Front door latch assembly details (convertible and sedan models, coupe similar)

LATCH LINKAGE

LATCH

FRONT DOOR

LOCK LINKAGE

LOCK BUTTON

LATCH RELEASE LINKAGE

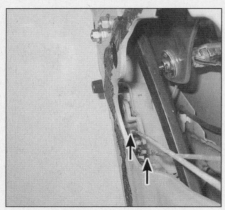

14.4b Coupe model door latch linkage rod connections (arrows)

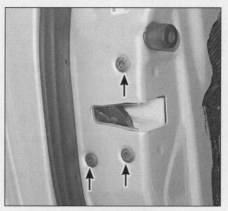

14.6 The door latch is retained by three screws (arrows)

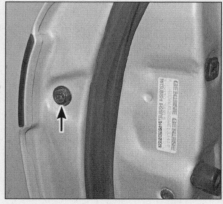

14.17a Remove the bolt from the end . . .

5   On vehicles equipped with central door locks, disconnect the electrical connector from the lock actuator.

6   Remove the three mounting screws from the end of the door and remove the door latch **(see illustration)**.

Installation

7   Place the latch in position, install the screws and tighten them securely.

8   Connect the operating rods to the latch and secure with retaining clips. **Caution:** *On convertible and some sedan models, do not close the door until the latch has been properly adjusted* (see below), *otherwise it may not reopen.*

Adjustment - convertible and sedan models

9   Insert a hex-wrench through the elongated hole in the end of the door near the latch.

10   Engage the wrench in the socket head screw located on the side of the door latch linkage and loosen it a couple of turns.

11   Lift the outside door handle all the way up and then release it.

12   Tighten the socket head screw on the door latch linkage and check door operation.

Outside handle

Removal

13   Remove the door trim panel (see Section 13). **Note:** *Close the window before disconnecting the door trim panel electrical connectors.*

14   On vehicles with manual windows, install the window crank (without the retaining clip) and roll up the window.

Convertible and sedan models

15   On vehicles so equipped, disconnect the central locking electrical connector.

16   Disconnect the operating rod, remove the mounting nuts and withdraw the handle from the door.

Coupe models

Refer to illustrations 14.17a and 14.17b

17   Remove the two bolts, one in the end of the door and the other inside it **(see illustrations)**.

18   Withdraw the handle from the door and disconnect the electrical connector.

Installation

19   Installation is the reverse of removal.

Lock cylinder

Removal

20   Remove the outside door handle (see Steps 13 through 18).

21   Detach the operating rod retaining clip and operating rod from the lock cylinder.

22   Disconnect the electrical connector (if equipped).

23   Using a screwdriver, pry off the lock cylinder retainer and withdraw it from the door or handle.

Installation

24   Installation is the reverse of removal.

---

15   Door window glass - removal and installation

Removal

Refer to illustrations 15.2a, 15.2b, 15.3, 15.9, 15.10a and 15.10b

1   Remove the door trim panel (see Section 13).

2   Carefully remove the plastic water shield from the door **(see illustrations)**.

3   Remove the inner belt weatherstrip from

14.17b . . . and the bolt inside the door, then withdraw the outside door handle (coupe models)

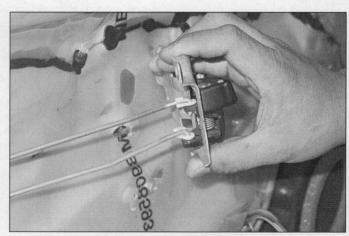

15.2a Remove the screws and detach the inner door handle . . .

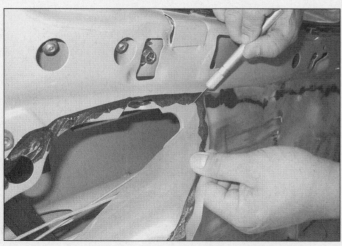

15.2b ... and carefully peel the plastic water shield from the door

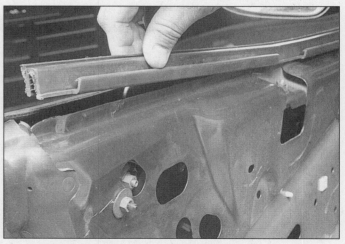

15.3 Remove the inner belt weatherstrip from the door window sill (convertible shown)

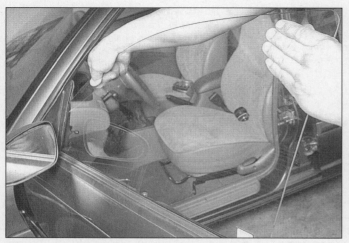

15.9 Carefully maneuver the glass out of the opening in the top of the door (convertible and sedan)

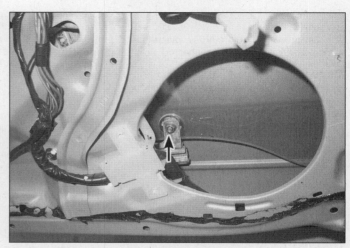

15.10a Remove the nut (arrow) securing the front regulator arm to the glass

the window sill **(see illustration)**.

4   If you are removing the rear door glass, remove the window glass lower rear run channel.

5   On vehicles equipped with power windows, remove the switch from the door trim

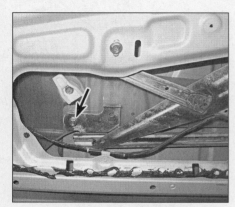

15.10b Remove the rear regulator arm-to-glass nut (arrow)

panel and connect it to the wiring harness. This will allow you to move the window as necessary.

6   On vehicles with manual windows, install the window crank (without the retaining clip). This will allow you to move the window as necessary.

7   Lower the window for access to two inches from the bottom of its travel.

Convertible and sedan models

8   Loosen the screws that secure the glass to the regulator roller channel.

9   While supporting the glass, slide the roller channel rearward and pass the screw heads through the key-hole slots in the channel, then maneuver the glass out of the opening in the top of the door **(see illustration)**.

Coupe models

10   Remove the nuts securing the regulator to the glass then maneuver the glass out of the opening in the top of the door **(see illustrations)**.

Installation

11   Installation is the reverse of removal. Make sure there is enough adhesive remaining on the water shield to seal properly, replace adhesive if necessary.

---

16   Door window regulator - removal and installation

Note: *This procedure applies to both the front and rear doors and both manual and power operated windows.*

Removal

Refer to illustrations 16.4 and 16.6

Warning: *On power window models, do not remove the motor from the regulator assembly without first clamping the sector gear to the mounting plate or serious personal injury may result.*

1   Remove the door trim panel (see Section 13).

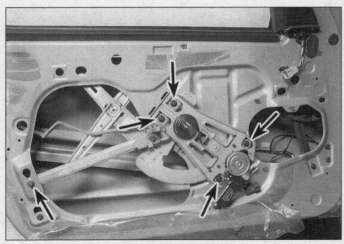

16.4 Remove these bolts (arrows) to remove the convertible and sedan window regulator

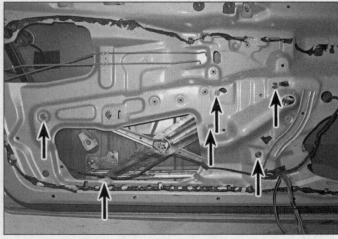

16.6 Coupe model window regulator retaining bolts (arrows)

2   Remove the door window glass (see Section 15).

3   On power window models, disconnect the window motor electrical connector.

Convertible and sedan models

4   Remove the bolts securing the window regulator to the inner door panel **(see illustration)**.

5   Slide the window regulator rearward and then rotate forward end of the lower roller channel through the access hole in the door and remove the regulator.

Coupe models

6   Remove the retaining bolts and remove the regulator assembly through the access hole in the door **(see illustration)**.

Installation

7   Installation is the reverse of removal.

---

17   Door - removal and installation

Note 1: *This procedure applies to both the front and rear doors.*
Note 2: *The door is heavy and somewhat awkward to remove and install - at least two people should perform this procedure.*

Removal

Refer to illustrations 17.1 and 17.4

1   Open the door and disconnect the wiring harness connector at the door pillar **(see illustration)**.

2   Remove the bolt/pin and detach the check strap from the door pillar. Detach the electrical connection.

3   Place a jack under the door or have an assistant on hand to support it when the hinge pins or bolts are removed. **Note:** *If a jack is used, place a rag and a piece of wood between it and the door to protect the door's painted surfaces.*

4   On early convertible models, remove the E-clips from the hinge pins, then remove the upper, then lower hinge pin and remove the

door **(see illustration)**. On all other models, mark around the hinges, then remove the nuts/bolts and remove the door **(see illustration)**. **Note:** *Place scribe marks around the hinges before loosening the bolts to maintain a reference point.*

Installation

5   Installation is the reverse of removal. On convertible models, make sure both hinge pin E-clips are properly secured in the hinge pins. On other models, install the bolts/nuts and tighten them securely. Check door fit and adjust if necessary by loosening the hinge bolts.

---

18   Trunk lid and support strut - removal, installation and adjustment

Trunk lid

Note: *The trunk lid is heavy and somewhat awkward to remove and install - at least two people should perform this procedure.*

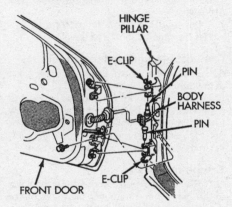

17.1 Convertible door hinge assembly details

Removal

Refer to illustration 18.3

1   Open the trunk lid and cover the edges of the trunk compartment with pads or cloths to protect the painted surfaces when the lid is removed.

2   Disconnect any electrical connectors attached to the trunk latch and center brake light. To aid with installation, attach a length of flexible wire to the connector end of the harness and then carefully pull it out of the trunk lid. Disconnect the guide wire from the harness and secure it at both openings of the trunk lid.

3   Use a permanent type marking pen to make alignment marks around the hinges **(see illustration)**.

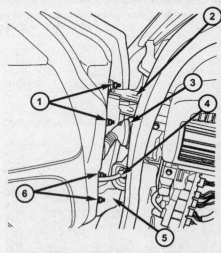

17.4 Typical later model convertible and sedan door hinge assembly details

1   *Upper hinge nuts*
2   *Upper door hinge*
3   *Electrical connection*
4   *Check strap*
5   *Lower hinge*
6   *Lower hinge nuts*

4   Have an assistant support one side of the trunk lid while you support the other. Simultaneously remove the hinge-to-trunk lid bolts.
5   Lift off the trunk lid.

Installation

6   Installation is the reverse of removal.
Note: *When reinstalling the trunk lid, align the hinge bolt heads with the marks made during removal.* After installation, close the lid and see if it's in proper alignment with the surrounding panels and adjust if necessary.

Adjustment

7   Fore-and-aft and side-to-side adjustments of the lid are controlled by the position of the hinge bolts in the holes. To adjust it, loosen the hinge bolts, reposition the lid and retighten the bolts. Make sure to mark the position of the hinges before loosening the bolts.
8   The height of the lid in relation to the surrounding body panels when closed can be adjusted on convertible and sedan models by loosening the lock striker bolts, repositioning the striker and retightening the bolts. Make sure to mark the position of the striker before loosening the bolts. On coupe models the closed height can be further adjusted by screwing the trunk lid bumpers in or out.

Support strut

Removal

9   Open the trunk.
10   Remove the lock caps from the support struts.
11   Remove support strut from the mounting studs.

Installation

12   Installation is the reverse of removal.

19 Instrument panel top cover (convertible and sedan models) - removal and installation

Warning: *These models have airbags. Always disable the airbag system before working in the vicinity of the impact sensors, steering column or instrument panel to avoid the possibility of accidental deployment of the airbag, which could cause personal injury (see Chapter 12).*
Caution: *The cover can be easily scratched or bent, take care in removing the top cover to avoid damage.*
1   Disconnect the negative battery cable from the ground stud on the left shock tower (see Chapter 5, Section 1).

Removal

Refer to illustrations 19.3a and 19.3b
2   Remove the end caps (see Section 20). On some models it will be necessary to remove a screw retaining the end of the top cover.

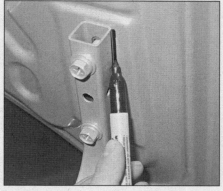

18.3 For a reference point at installation, outline the hinges on the trunk lid with a felt tip marker

3   Using a screwdriver with a taped tip to avoid damage, disengage the clips along the rear edge of the top cover starting from the right side and proceeding to the left. To avoid damage, do not pry on the top cover during removal **(see illustrations)**.

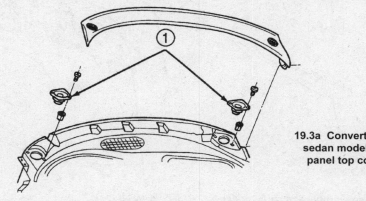

19.3a Convertible and early sedan model instrument panel top cover details

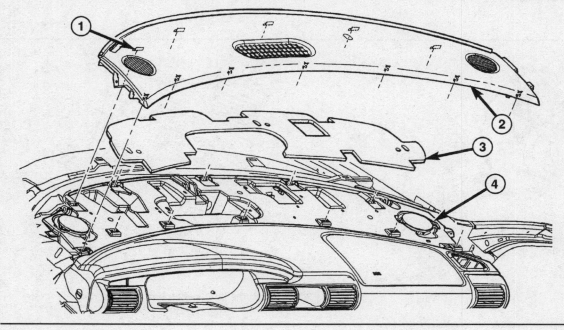

19.3b Later model sedan instrument panel top cover details

1   *Clip locations*
2   *Top cover*
3   *Pad*
4   *Instrument panel*

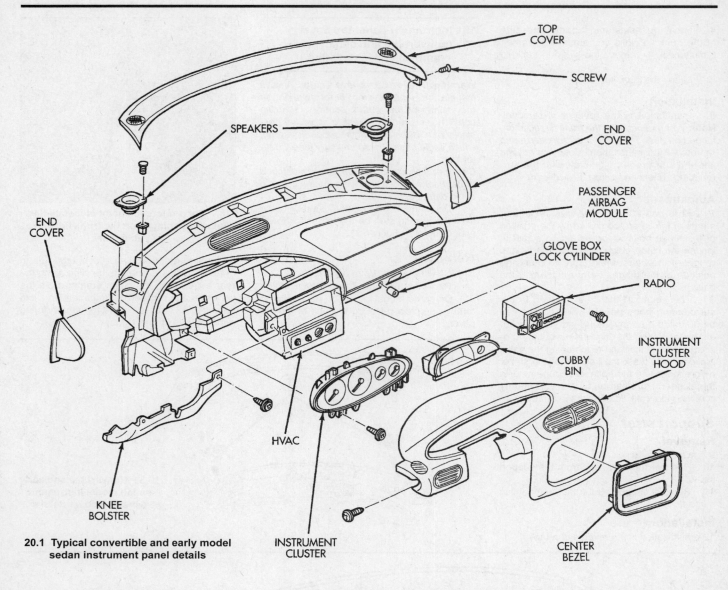

20.1 Typical convertible and early model sedan instrument panel details

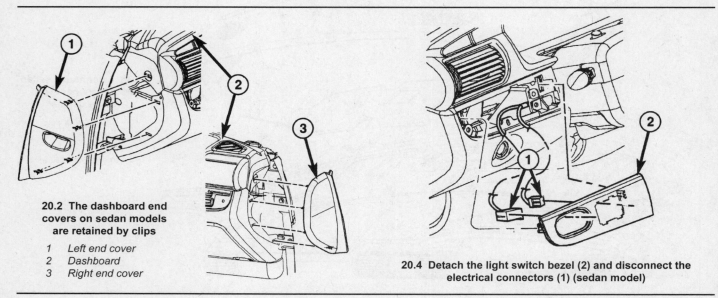

20.2 The dashboard end covers on sedan models are retained by clips

1   *Left end cover*
2   *Dashboard*
3   *Right end cover*

20.4 Detach the light switch bezel (2) and disconnect the electrical connectors (1) (sedan model)

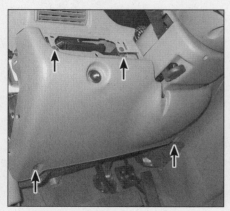

20.5 Knee bolster bolt locations (arrows) (sedan model shown)

4   Lift the rear edge and slide the top cover rearward to disengage the clips, then remove the top cover.

Installation

5   Installation is the reverse of removal, except engage the top cover into the two center clips first. Place your thumb in the Vehicle Identification Number (VIN) slot and pull the top cover towards pad to ensure VIN alignment. If a gap exists between the top cover and the pad after installation, check for a damaged retaining clip and replace as necessary.

20   Dashboard trim panels and glove box - removal and installation

Warning: *These models have airbags. Always disable the airbag system before working in the vicinity of the impact sensors, steering column or instrument panel to avoid the possibility of accidental deployment of the airbag, which could cause personal injury (see Chapter 12).*
Caution: *The following trim covers can be*

20.8 To remove the center bezel, simply grasp it securely and pull it out evenly

easily scratched, take care in removing them to avoid damage.

Convertible and sedan models
Dashboard end covers
Removal

Refer to illustrations 20.1 and 20.2

1   On convertible models, remove the left end cover by swinging it open, then pulling it rearward to disengage it from the clips. Remove the right cover by opening the glove box door, then pulling rearward to detach it **(see illustration)**.
2   On sedan models use a screwdriver to carefully detach the end covers **(see illustration)**.

Installation

3   Installation is the reverse of removal.

Light switch bezel

Refer to illustration 20.4

4   Carefully pry around the edges to detach the bezel, then disconnect the electrical connectors **(see illustration)**.

Installation

5   Installation is the reverse of removal.

Knee bolster

Refer to illustration 20.5

6   After detaching the light switch bezel and left end cover, remove the bolts and lower the bolster **(see illustration)**.

Installation

7   Installation is the reverse of removal.

Center bezel
Removal

Refer to illustration 20.8

8   Grasp the bezel on each side and pull it out evenly to remove it **(see illustration)**.

Installation

9   Installation is the reverse of removal.

Glove box

10   Open the glove box, squeeze the sidewalls in and hinge the glove box door all the way down.

Installation

11   Installation is the reverse of removal.

Coupe models
Knee bolster

Refer to illustration 20.12

Removal

12   Remove the bolts, detach the knee bolster and lower it from the dashboard **(see illustration)**.

Installation

13   Place the bolster in position and install the bolts and bolt covers.

Center bezel
Removal

Refer to illustration 20.14

14   Grasp the bezel securely, pull out sharply on the upper edge to detach the clips then rotate it away from the dash **(see illustration)**.

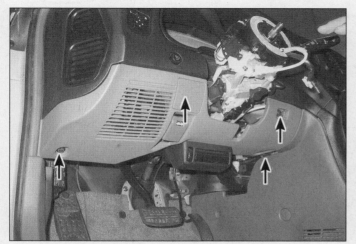

20.12 Coupe model knee bolster bolt locations (arrows)

20.14 Pull out sharply on the upper edge of the center bezel to detach it from the dash (coupe model)

Installation

15   Place the bezel in position and press it in until the clips engage.

Glove box

Removal

Refer to illustration 20.16

16   Open the glove box, detach the stoppers by pushing them rearward, then lower the glove box fully for access to the two hinge screws. Remove the screws and lower the glove box from the dash.

Installation

17   Installation is the reverse of removal.

21   Instrument cluster hood/bezel - removal and installation

Warning: *These models have airbags. Always disable the airbag system before working in the vicinity of any airbag system components to avoid the possibility of accidental deployment of the airbag, which could cause personal injury (see Chapter 12).*

Convertible and sedan model hood/bezel assembly

Removal

Refer to illustrations 21.3, 21.6a and 21.6b

1   Disconnect the negative battery cable from the ground stud on the left shock tower (see Chapter 5, Section 1).
2   Remove the dashboard left end cover (see Section 20).
3   At the left end of the hood/bezel on convertible models, remove the screw securing the assembly to the instrument panel (see illustration).
4   Position the tilt steering wheel to its lowest position.
5   Remove the dashboard center bezel (see Section 20).
6   Remove the screws attaching the hood/bezel to the instrument panel (see illustrations).

20.16 Rotate each stopper rearward and pull them out, then lower the glove box for access to the retaining screws

21.3 Removing the screw securing the left side of the instrument cluster hood/bezel (convertible and early sedan models)

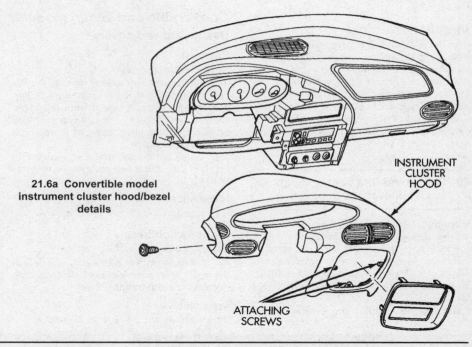

21.6a Convertible model instrument cluster hood/bezel details

INSTRUMENT CLUSTER HOOD

ATTACHING SCREWS

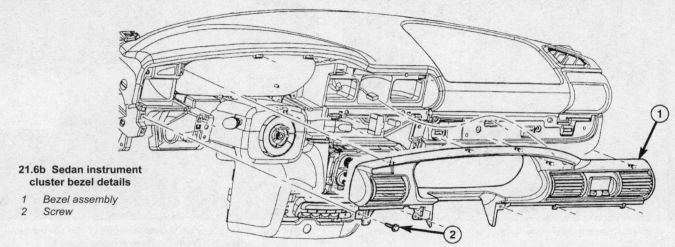

21.6b Sedan instrument cluster bezel details

1   *Bezel assembly*
2   *Screw*

7   Pull the hood/bezel straight back to disengage the clips.

8   Remove the instrument cluster hood/bezel.

Installation

9   Installation is the reverse of removal. Keep the forward edge of the hood down on the instrument panel while sliding the hood/bezel forward to engage the retaining clips.

Coupe models

Refer to illustration 21.11

10   Disconnect the negative battery cable.

11   Remove the screws securing the bezel to the top of the cluster, detach the clips at the lower edge and remove the bezel **(see illustration)**.

12   Place the bezel in position, press in until the clips engage, then install the retaining screws.

22   Instrument panel - removal and installation

Warning: *These models have airbags. Always disable the airbag system before working in the vicinity any airbag system components to avoid the possibility of accidental deployment of the airbag, which could cause personal injury (see Chapter 12).*

Note: *It is not necessary, but it is suggested to remove both front seats to allow additional working space and lessen the chance of damage to the seats during this procedure.*

Convertible and sedan models

Removal

Refer to illustrations 22.17, 22.18, 22.22a, 22.22b and 22.22c

1   Disconnect the negative battery cable from the ground stud on the left shock tower (see Chapter 5, Section 1).

2   Remove the dashboard right and left end trim panels (see Section 20).

3   Remove the floor console (see Section 24).

21.11 Remove the retaining screws at the top, then detach the clips at the lower edge of the bezel (coupe model)

4   Disconnect the electrical connector from the Airbag Control Module.

5   Remove the instrument cluster bezel (see Section 21).

6   Remove the two screws securing the cubby (storage) bin and withdraw it from the forward console **(see illustration 20.1)**.

7   Remove the knee bolster mounting screws and remove the knee bolster (see Section 20).

8   Remove the glove box (see Section 20). Remove the passenger airbag module (see Chapter 12). **Warning:** *Carry the airbag with the trim cover side FACING AWAY from your body to minimize injury if the airbag module accidentally deploys. Store the airbag module aside in a safe, isolated location with the trim cover side facing UP.*

9   Remove the forward floor console attaching screws and fasteners at forward driver's side.

10   Remove the forward floor console (see Section 24).

11   Pull the driver's side under panel silencer outboard off the distribution duct.

12   Remove the instrument panel top cover (see Section 19).

13   Remove the heating and air conditioning control module (see Chapter 3). Remove the radio (see Chapter 12).

14   Remove the center distribution duct

screws from behind the radio and duct.

15   Locate and remove the three heating and air conditioning unit attaching screws securing the duct and instrument panel. Remove the three screws securing the heating and air conditioning unit to the cross-car beam.

16   Remove the screws attaching the instrument panel frame to the air distribution duct and the two fasteners at the air duct below the steering column.

17   The steering column must be lowered, but before loosening the steering column mounting nuts on a 2000 and earlier model equipped with a tilt steering wheel, use the following procedure to lock the tilt mechanism or it will not operate correctly when installed **(see illustration)**.

a)   *Place the steering wheel straight ahead and ensure the tilt mechanism is fully locked.*

b)   *Insert two 5/32-inch drill bits into the two locking pin holes on the steering column mounting bracket.*

c)   *Loosen the two upper steering column mounting nuts.*

d)   *Loosen the two lower steering column mounting nuts.*

18   Remove the steering column mounting nuts **(see illustration)**. Lower and support the column securely.

19   Disconnect the engine and body wiring

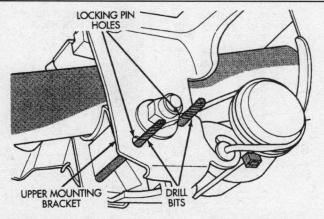

22.17 Before loosening the steering column mounting nuts on 2000 and earlier convertible models equipped with a tilt steering wheel, insert two drill bits into the locking pin holes

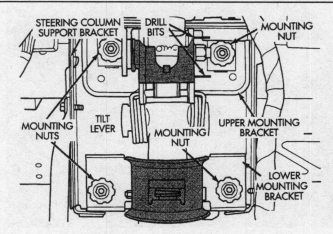

22.18 Steering column mounting nut locations

22.22a Remove the bolts (arrows) from the left end . . .

22.22b . . . and right end (arrows) of the instrument panel (sedan model shown)

harness from the junction block.

20   Remove the fasteners securing the instrument panel to the cross-car beam.

21   Remove the fastener at the glove box hinge to cowl area.

22   Remove the remaining fasteners retaining the instrument panel **(see illustrations)**.

23   Remove the screw attaching the rear of the heating and air conditioning unit to the center support bracket.

24   Lift up the instrument panel and pull rearward and withdraw it from the vehicle.

Installation

Refer to illustration 22.25

25   Installation is the reverse of removal noting the following points **(see illustration)**:

a) *Raise the steering column onto the support bracket and loosely install the four nuts.*

b) *Snugly tighten the lower nuts and ensure the plastic capsules are seated in the*

slots in the upper mounting bracket and the studs are centered in the plastic capsules.

c) *Tighten the upper mounting nuts until the upper mounting bracket is seated.*

d) *Tighten the four steering column mounting nuts to the torque listed in the Chapter 10 Specifications.*

e) *On 2000 and earlier models equipped with a tilt steering wheel, remove the drill bits from the locking pin holes.*

f) *Turn the ignition switch to the Off position, then turn it to the On position. Check that the instrument cluster AIRBAG lamp illuminates for six to eight seconds and then goes out indicating the airbag system is functioning properly. If the lamp fails to light, blinks on and off or stays on, there is a malfunction in the airbag system. If any of these conditions exist, the vehicle should be diagnosed by a dealer service department or other qualified repair shop.*

Coupe models
Removal

Refer to illustrations 22.37a, 22.37b, 22.38, 22.39 and 22.40

26   Disconnect the battery cable from the negative battery terminal.

27   Remove the center console (see Section 24).

28   Remove the steering column covers (see Section 23).

29   Remove the airbag and the steering wheel (see Chapter 10).

30   Remove the instrument cluster (see Chapter 12).

31   Remove the console side cover and the radio (see Chapter 12).

32   Remove the dashboard trim panels and glove box (see Section 20).

33   Remove the passenger side airbag (see Chapter 10). **Warning:** *Carry the airbag with the trim cover side FACING AWAY from your body to minimize injury if the airbag module*

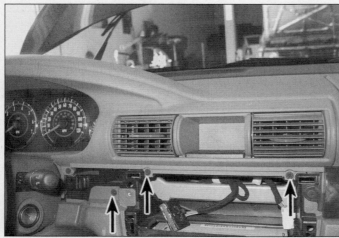

22.22c Remove the bolts (arrows) retaining the center of the instrument panel (sedan)

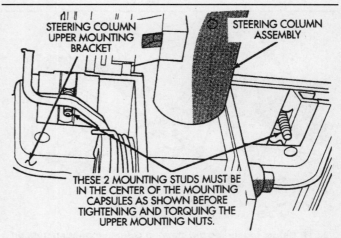

22.25 When installing the steering column, ensure that the two upper mounting studs are centered before tightening the nuts

22.37a Pry off the covers and remove the speakers . . .

22.37b . . . then remove the bolts retaining the instrument panel

the instrument panel center console base to the floor **(see illustration)**.

40 Remove the mounting bolts in the instrument cluster opening **(see illustration)**.

41 Remove any remaining fasteners.

42 Disconnect the instrument panel wiring harness connectors.

43 Lift up the instrument panel and pull rearward and withdraw it from the vehicle.

Installation

44 Installation is the reverse of removal.

45 Turn the ignition switch to the Off position, then turn it to the On position. Check that the instrument cluster AIRBAG lamp illuminates for six to eight seconds and then goes out indicating the airbag system is functioning properly. If the lamp fails to light, blinks on and off or stays on, there is a malfunction in the airbag system. If any of these conditions exist, the vehicle should be diagnosed by a dealer service department or other qualified repair shop.

accidentally deploys. Store the airbag module aside in a safe, isolated location with the trim cover side facing UP.

34 Remove the hood latch release lever and the driver's side under panel.

35 Remove the center air outlet and heating and air conditioning control module (see Chapter 3).

36 Remove the dash lighting rheostat and

the right side undercover panel.

37 Remove the speaker covers and speakers for access then remove the screws from the top of the instrument panel **(see illustrations)**.

38 Remove the instrument panel retaining screws in the glove box opening **(see illustration)**.

39 Locate and remove the bolts attaching

23 Steering column covers - removal and installation

Refer to illustrations 23.3a and 23.3b

Warning: *These models have airbags. Always disable the airbag system before working in the vicinity of the impact sensors, steering column or instrument panel to avoid the possibility of accidental deployment of the airbag, which could cause personal injury (see Chapter 12).*

Caution: *These covers can be easily scratched; take care when removing them to avoid damage.*

1 On convertible and sedan models, disconnect the negative battery cable from the ground stud on the left shock tower (see Chapter 5, Section 1). On coupe models disconnect the battery cable from the negative battery terminal.

2 Remove the instrument hood/bezel (see Section 21) and the knee bolster (see Section 21).

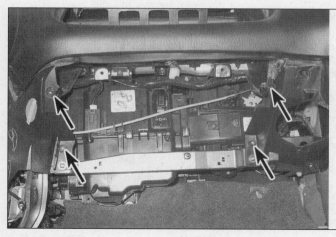

22.38 Remove the instrument panel bolts in the glove box opening (arrows)

22.39 Remove the console-to-floor retaining bolts (arrows)

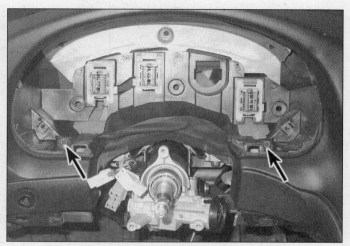
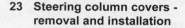

22.40 Instrument panel-to-cluster opening bolt locations (arrows)

23.3a After removing the two screws from the lower cover, the covers can then be separated from the steering column (convertible and sedan models)

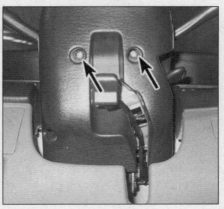

23.3b On coupe models, remove the two lower screws (arrows) and the one upper screw and separate the steering column covers

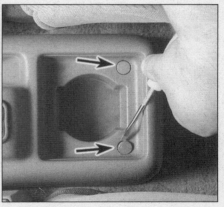

24.5 Pry off the trim plugs (arrows) to access the console rear attaching screws

3   Remove the two screws from the lower steering column cover (coupe models also have an upper screw) and separate the covers **(see illustrations)**.
4   Installation is the reverse of removal.

---

24   Center console - removal and installation

Warning: *These models have airbags. Always disable the airbag system before working in the vicinity of the impact sensors, steering column or instrument panel to avoid the possibility of accidental deployment of the airbag,*

which could cause personal injury (see Chapter 12).
Caution: *The center console can be easily scratched; take care in removing the assembly to avoid damage.*
Note: *The center console on these vehicles is composed of two separate sections.*

Convertible and sedan models
Floor console
Refer to illustrations 24.5 and 24.7
1   Disconnect the negative battery cable from the ground stud on the left shock tower (see Chapter 5, Section 1).
2   Completely raise the parking brake lever.

3   On vehicles equipped with a manual transaxle, pull the gear shift boot down away from the knob to expose the knob retaining clips. Pry the clips away from the shift lever and remove the gear shift knob. Grasp the base of the boot at the floor console and squeeze it together, then remove it from the gear shift lever.
4   On vehicles equipped with an automatic transaxle, remove the shift lever set screw and lift the handle assembly off the shift lever. Using a screwdriver, carefully pry the shift position indicator bezel from the floor console and disconnect the electrical connector.
5   Remove the two screws securing the front of the console.
6   At the rear of the floor console, pry off the trim plugs and remove the two screws

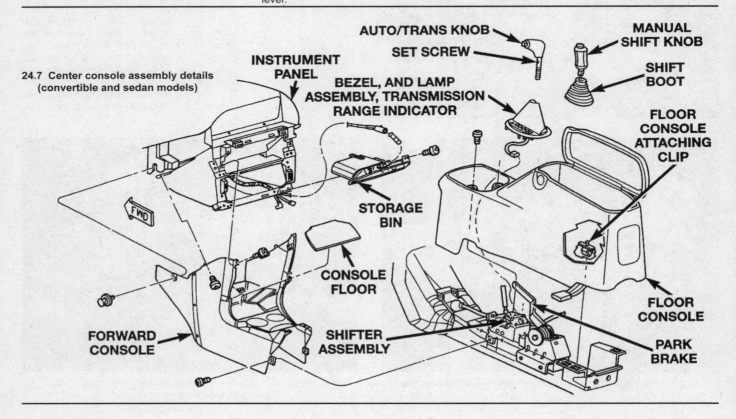

24.7 Center console assembly details (convertible and sedan models)

AUTO/TRANS KNOB
SET SCREW
MANUAL SHIFT KNOB
SHIFT BOOT
INSTRUMENT PANEL
BEZEL, AND LAMP ASSEMBLY, TRANSMISSION RANGE INDICATOR
FLOOR CONSOLE ATTACHING CLIP
STORAGE BIN
CONSOLE FLOOR
FWD
FORWARD CONSOLE
SHIFTER ASSEMBLY
FLOOR CONSOLE
PARK BRAKE

24.22a Detach the clips at the rear . . .

24.22b . . . and the front of the console shift panel and lift it out

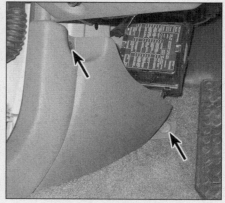

24.26a Remove the screws on the right . . .

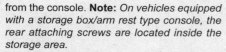

from the console. **Note:** *On vehicles equipped with a storage box/arm rest type console, the rear attaching screws are located inside the storage area.*

7   Maneuver the floor console up and over the shift lever and parking brake handle and remove it from vehicle **(see illustration)**.

8   Installation is the reverse of removal.

Forward console

9   Remove the floor console (see above).

10   Remove the dashboard center bezel (see Section 20).

11   Unscrew the screws securing the storage bin and remove it from the console **(see illustration 24.7)**

12   Remove the two screws securing the forward console to the gear selector mount bracket.

13   Remove the screws holding the console to the instrument panel at each side of the heater/air conditioning controls, storage bin area and panel support braces.

14   With all fasteners removed, carefully withdraw the forward console from the vehicle.

15   Installation is the reverse of removal.

Coupe models

Floor console

Refer to illustrations 24.22a and 24.22b

16   Disconnect the negative cable from the battery.

17   Completely raise the parking brake lever.

18   Remove the instrument panel center bezel (see Section 20).

19   On vehicles equipped with a manual transaxle, pull the boot down and unscrew the gear shift knob.

20   On vehicles equipped with an automatic transaxle, remove the shift lever set screw and lift the handle assembly off the shift lever.

21   Open the center console and detach the inner box.

22   Use a screwdriver to release the clips and remove the console shift panel **(see illustrations)**.

23   Remove the screws retaining the floor console, maneuver it up and over the shift

lever and parking brake handle and remove it from vehicle.

24   Installation is the reverse of removal.

Forward console

Refer to illustrations 24.26a and 24.26b

25   Remove the floor console (see above).

26   Remove the screws holding the console to the instrument panel at each side of the heater/air conditioning controls, storage bin area and panel support braces **(see illustrations)**.

27   With all fasteners removed, carefully withdraw the forward console from the vehicle.

28   Installation is the reverse of removal.

---

25   Mirrors - removal and installation

Interior

Refer to illustration 25.1

1   On convertible and sedan models, use a Phillips head screwdriver to remove the screws, lower the mirror from the header panel and disconnect the electrical connector **(see illustration)**. On coupe models, insert a small flat blade screwdriver into the notch in the mirror bracket, push up toward the top of

24.26b . . . and the left side of the front console (arrows)

the windshield to release the internal spring and remove the mirror. On sunroof-equipped coupe models, a special forked tool is required to detach the clip retaining the mirror.

2   Installation is the reverse of removal.

Exterior

Refer to illustrations 25.4a, 25.4b, 25.4c, 25.7, 25.8a and 25.8b

3   Remove the door trim panel (see Section 13).

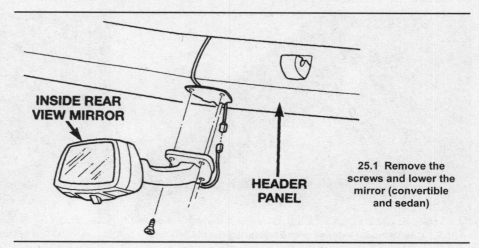

25.1 Remove the screws and lower the mirror (convertible and sedan)

25.4a On convertible and sedan models, remove the exterior mirror cover mounting screws (arrows) . . .

25.4b . . . then separate it from the door

25.4c On coupe models, pry the mirror cover off with a small screwdriver

4   Remove the mirror cover from the door **(see illustrations)**.

5   On vehicles equipped with standard mirrors, loosen the set screw holding the mirror adjuster cable to the bezel and separate the adjuster from the bezel.

6   On vehicles equipped with power mirrors, detach the mirror electrical connector from its mounting on the door.

7   On convertible and sedan models, pry the caps from the mirror nut access holes **(see illustration)**.

8   Remove the three nuts **(see illustration)** and detach the mirror from the door.

9   Installation is the reverse of removal.

25.7 On convertible and sedan models, pry off the caps from the exterior mirror mounting nut access holes (arrows) . . .

25.8a then remove the mirror mounting nuts through these holes

---

26 Cowl cover - removal and installation

Refer to illustration 26.2

1   Remove the plastic trim caps from the windshield wiper arms (see Chapter 1), then detach the wiper arm retaining nuts and remove the wiper arms.

2   Peel off the hood rubber sealing strip from the cowl edge **(see illustration)**.

3   Remove the retaining screws on each side of the cowl cover and carefully lift it from the vehicle.

4   Installation is the reverse of removal.

---

27 Seats - removal and installation

Warning: *Some of the models covered by this manual are equipped with side-impact airbags located in the seat backs. Some are also equipped with seat belt pre-tensioners, which are pyrotechnic (explosive) devices which tighten the seat belts during an impact of sufficient force. Be sure to disarm the airbag system when working in the*

vicinity of any of the airbag system or seat belt pre-tensioner components (see Chapter 12).

Front

Refer to illustrations 27.1 and 27.2

1   Move the seat fully rearward and remove the seat track front bolts **(see illustration)**.

2   Move the seat fully forward and remove the seat track rear bolts **(see illustration)**.

3   If the vehicle is equipped with power

25.8b Coupe model exterior mirror mounting details (arrows)

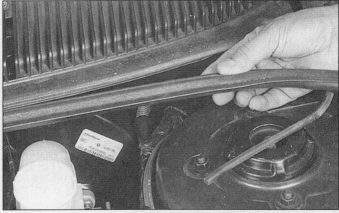

26.2 Peel the rubber weatherstrip from the cowl

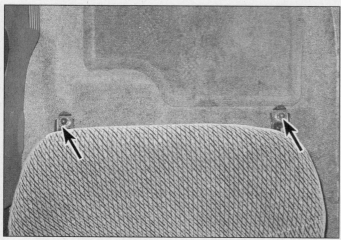

27.1 Front seat - front mounting bolts

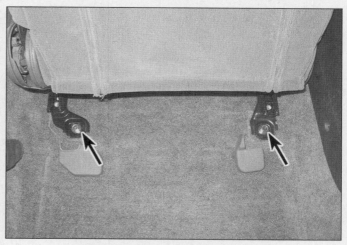

27.2 Front seat - rear mounting bolts

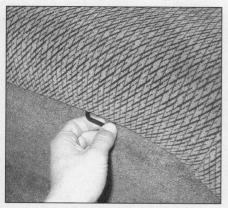

27.5 On coupe models, pull out on the rear seat cushion release levers and remove the cushion

seats, side impact airbags and/or seat belt pre-tensioners, disconnect the electrical connector(s) and lift the seat out of the vehicle.

4   Installation is the reverse of removal.

Rear

Seat cushion

Refer to illustration 27.5

5   On convertible and sedan models, remove the seat cushion by grasping the front edge securely, then pulling up sharply to detach the cushion from the retainer cups in the floorpan. On coupe models, pull out on the two release tabs at the bottom edge and detach the seat cushion **(see illustration)**.

6   Installation is the reverse of removal. Press down firmly over the seat retainers to

ensure they are fully engaged in the floorpan.

Seat back

7   On convertible and sedan models, remove the seat cushion, then remove the seat belts. Remove the nuts along the lower edge of the seat back, detach the clips along the upper edge and remove the seat back assembly.

8   Installation is the reverse of removal. Press firmly over the seat retainers to ensure they are fully engaged.

9   On coupe models, remove the seat cushion, then remove the bolts and detach the seat back and side cushions.

10   Installation is the reverse of removal. Press firmly over the seat retainers to ensure they are fully engaged.

28 Rear parcel shelf - removal and installation

Sedan models

Refer to illustration 28.1

1   Remove the push-in fasteners securing the parcel shelf to the trunk closure panel **(see illustration)**.

2   Pull the parcel shelf forward to disengage the clip securing parcel shelf to the trunk closure panel and remove it from the vehicle.

3   Installation is the reverse of removal.

Coupe models

4   Remove the seat back and cushions.

5   Remove the speaker covers and speakers and detach the parcel shelf.

6   Installation is the reverse of removal.

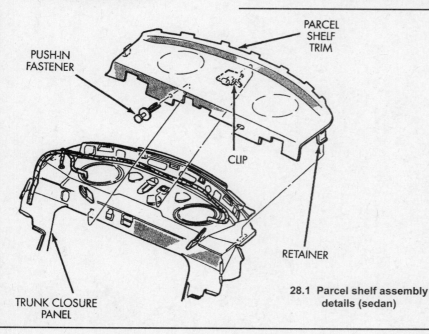

PARCEL
SHELF
TRIM

PUSH-IN
FASTENER

CLIP

RETAINER

TRUNK CLOSURE
PANEL

28.1 Parcel shelf assembly details (sedan)

Notes

Chapter 12
Chassis electrical system

Contents

1 General information

The electrical system is a 12-volt, negative ground type. Power for the lights and all electrical accessories is supplied by a lead/acid-type battery which is charged by the alternator.

This Chapter covers repair and service procedures for the various electrical components not associated with the engine. Information on the battery, alternator, distributor and starter motor can be found in Chapter 5.

It should be noted that when portions of the electrical system are serviced, the cable should be disconnected from the negative battery terminal or the remote ground terminal (see Chapter 5) to prevent electrical shorts and/or fires.

2 Electrical troubleshooting - general information

Refer to illustrations 2.5a, 2.5b, 2.6 and 2.9

A typical electrical circuit consists of an electrical component, any switches, relays, motors, fuses, fusible links or circuit breakers related to that component and the wiring and connectors that link the component to both the battery and the chassis. To help you pinpoint an electrical circuit problem, wiring diagrams are included at the end of this Chapter.

Before tackling any troublesome electrical circuit, first study the appropriate wiring diagrams to get a complete understanding of what makes up that individual circuit. Trouble spots, for instance, can often be narrowed down by noting if other components related to the circuit are operating properly.

If several components or circuits fail at one time, chances are the problem is in a fuse or ground connection, because several circuits are often routed through the same fuse and ground connections.

Electrical problems usually stem from simple causes, such as loose or corroded connections, a blown fuse, a melted fusible link or a failed relay. Visually inspect the condition of all fuses, wires and connections in a problem circuit before troubleshooting the circuit.

If test equipment and instruments are going to be utilized, use the diagrams to plan ahead of time where you will make the necessary connections in order to accurately pinpoint the trouble spot.

The basic tools needed for electrical troubleshooting include a circuit tester or

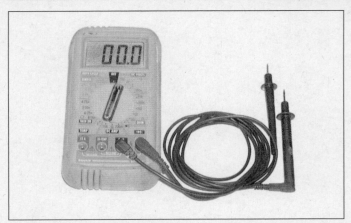

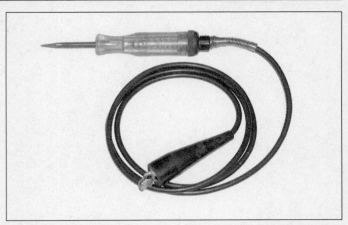

2.5a The most useful tool for electrical troubleshooting is a digital multimeter that can check volts, amps, and test continuity

2.5b A simple test light is a very handy tool for testing voltage

voltmeter (a 12-volt bulb with a set of test leads can also be used), a continuity tester, which includes a bulb, battery and set of test leads, and a jumper wire, preferably with a circuit breaker incorporated, which can be used to bypass electrical components **(see illustrations)**. Before attempting to locate a problem with test instruments, use the wiring diagram(s) to decide where to make the connections.

Voltage checks

Voltage checks should be performed if a circuit is not functioning properly. Connect one lead of a circuit tester to either the negative battery terminal or a known good ground. Connect the other lead to a connector in the circuit being tested, preferably nearest to the battery or fuse **(see illustration)**. If the bulb of the tester lights, voltage is present, which means that the part of the circuit between the connector and the battery is problem free. Continue checking the rest of the circuit in the same fashion. When you reach a point at which no voltage is present, the problem lies

between that point and the last test point with voltage. Most of the time the problem can be traced to a loose connection. **Note:** *Keep in mind that some circuits receive voltage only when the ignition key is in the Accessory or Run position.*

Finding a short

One method of finding shorts in a live circuit is to remove the fuse and connect a test light in place of the fuse terminals (fabricate two jumper wires with small spade terminals, plug the jumper wires into the fuse box and connect the test light). There should be voltage present in the circuit. Move the suspected wiring harness from side-to-side while watching the test light. If the bulb goes off, there is a short to ground somewhere in that area, probably where the insulation has rubbed through.

Ground check

Perform a ground test to check whether a component is properly grounded. Disconnect the battery and connect one lead of a continuity tester or multimeter (set to the ohms

scale), to a known good ground. Connect the other lead to the wire or ground connection being tested. If the resistance is low (less than 5 ohms), the ground is good. If the bulb on a self-powered test light does not go on, the ground is not good.

Continuity check

A continuity check is done to determine if there are any breaks in a circuit - if it is passing electricity properly. With the circuit off (no power in the circuit), a self-powered continuity tester or multimeter can be used to check the circuit. Connect the test leads to both ends of the circuit (or to the "power" end and a good ground), and if the test light comes on the circuit is passing current properly **(see illustration)**. If the resistance is low (less than 5 ohms), there is continuity; if the reading is 10,000 ohms or higher, there is a break somewhere in the circuit. The same procedure can be used to test a switch, by connecting the continuity tester to the switch terminals. With the switch turned On, the test light should come on (or low resistance should be indicated on a meter).

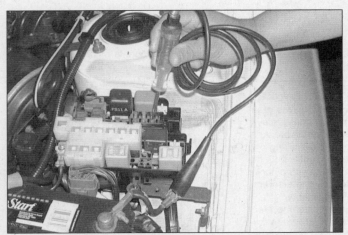

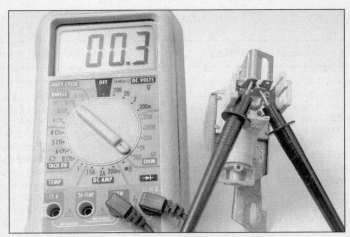

2.6 In use, a basic test light's lead is clipped to a known good ground, then the pointed probe can test connectors, wires or electrical sockets - if the bulb lights, the circuit being tested has battery voltage

2.9 With a multimeter set to the ohms scale, resistance can be checked across two terminals - when checking for continuity, a low reading indicates continuity, a high reading or infinity indicates lack of continuity

3.1a The main engine compartment fuse/relay box on a 2001 convertible

Finding an open circuit

When diagnosing for possible open circuits, it is often difficult to locate them by sight because the connectors hide oxidation or terminal misalignment. Merely wiggling a connector on a sensor or in the wiring harness may correct the open circuit condition. Remember this when an open circuit is indicated when troubleshooting a circuit. Intermittent problems may also be caused by oxidized or loose connections.

Electrical troubleshooting is simple if you keep in mind that all electrical circuits are basically electricity running from the battery, through the wires, switches, relays, fuses and fusible links to each electrical component (light bulb, motor, etc.) and to ground, from which it is passed back to the battery. Any electrical problem is an interruption in the flow of electricity to and from the battery.

Connectors

Most electrical connections on these vehicles are made with multiwire plastic connectors. The mating halves of many connectors are secured with locking clips molded into the plastic connector shells. The mating halves of large connectors, such as some of those under the instrument panel, are held together by a bolt through the center of the connector.

To separate a connector with locking clips, use a small screwdriver to pry the clips apart carefully, then separate the connector halves. Pull only on the shell, never pull on the wiring harness as you may damage the individual wires and terminals inside the connectors. Look at the connector closely before trying to separate the halves. Often the locking clips are engaged in a way that is not immediately clear. Additionally, many connectors have more than one set of clips.

Each pair of connector terminals has a male half and a female half. When you look at the end view of a connector in a diagram, be sure to understand whether the view shows the harness side or the component side of the connector. Connector halves are mirror images of each other, and a terminal shown on the right side end-view of one half will be on the left side end view of the other half.

3 Fuses and fusible links - general information

Fuses

Refer to illustrations 3.1a, 3.1b and 3.3

The electrical circuits of the vehicle are protected by a combination of fuses, circuit breakers and fusible links. Fuse blocks are located under the instrument panel (coupes) or behind a cover at the left end of the instrument panel, (convertibles and sedans) and in the engine compartment **(see illustrations)**.

Each of the fuses is designed to protect a specific circuit, and the various circuits are identified on the fuse panel cover.

Miniaturized fuses are employed in the fuse blocks. These compact fuses, with blade terminal design, allow fingertip removal and replacement. If an electrical component fails, always check the fuse first. The best way to check a fuse is with a test light. Check for power at the exposed terminal tips of each fuse. If power is present on one side of the fuse but not the other, the fuse is blown. A blown fuse can also be confirmed by visually inspecting it **(see illustration)**.

Be sure to replace blown fuses with the correct type. Fuses of different ratings are physically interchangeable, but only fuses of the proper rating should be used. Replacing a fuse with one of a higher or lower value than specified is not recommended. Each electrical circuit needs a specific amount of protection. The amperage value of each fuse is molded into the fuse body.

If the replacement fuse immediately fails, don't replace it again until the cause of the problem is isolated and corrected. In most cases, this will be a short circuit in the wiring caused by a broken or deteriorated wire.

Fusible links

Some circuits are protected by fusible links. The links are used in circuits which are not ordinarily fused, or which carry high current.

Cartridge type fusible links are located in the engine compartment fuse/relay link box and are similar to a large fuse. After disconnecting the negative battery cable or remote ground terminal, simply unplug and replace a fusible link of the same amperage.

4 Circuit breakers - general information

Circuit breakers protect certain circuits, such as the power windows or heated seats. Depending on the vehicle's accessories, there may be one or two circuit breakers, located in the fuse/relay box in the engine compartment **(see illustration 3.1a)**.

Because the circuit breakers reset automatically, an electrical overload in a circuit-breaker-protected system will cause the cir-

3.1b On convertible and sedan models, the interior fuse box is located on the left end of the instrument panel

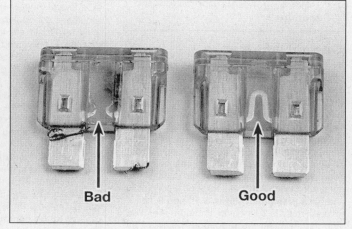

Bad   Good

3.3 When a fuse blows, the element between the terminals melts

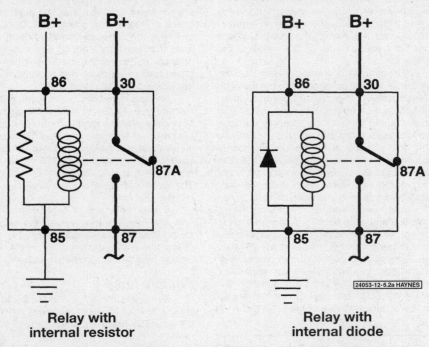

Relay with internal resistor

Relay with internal diode

5.2a Typical ISO relay designs, terminal numbering and circuit connections

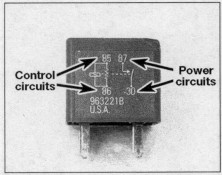

5.2b Most relays are marked on the outside to easily identify the control circuits and the power circuits - four-terminal type shown

cuit to fail momentarily, then come back on. If the circuit does not come back on, check it immediately.

For a basic check, pull the circuit breaker up out of its socket on the fuse panel, but just far enough to probe with a voltmeter. The breaker should still contact the sockets.

With the voltmeter negative lead on a good chassis ground, touch each end prong of the circuit breaker with the positive meter probe. There should be battery voltage at each end. If there is battery voltage only at one end, the circuit breaker must be replaced.

Some circuit breakers must be reset manually.

5   Relays - general information and testing

General information

1   Several electrical accessories in the vehicle, such as the fuel injection system, horns, starter, and fog lamps use relays to transmit the electrical signal to the component. Relays use a low-current circuit (the control circuit) to open and close a high-current circuit (the power circuit). If the relay is defective, that component will not operate properly. Most relays are mounted in the engine compartment fuse/relay box, with some specialized relays located above the interior fuse box in the dash (see illustrations 3.1a and 3.1b). If a faulty relay is suspected, it can be removed and tested using the procedure below or by a dealer service department or a repair shop. Defective relays must be replaced as a unit.

Testing

Refer to illustrations 5.2a and 5.2b

2   Most of the relays used in these vehicles are of a type often called "ISO" relays, which refers to the International Standards Organization. The terminals of ISO relays are numbered to indicate their usual circuit connections and functions. There are two basic layouts of terminals on the relays used in the covered vehicles **(see illustrations)**.

3   Refer to the wiring diagram for the circuit to determine the proper connections for the relay you're testing. If you can't determine the correct connection from the wiring diagrams, however, you may be able to determine the test connections from the information that follows.

4   Two of the terminals are the relay control circuit and connect to the relay coil. The other relay terminals are the power circuit. When the relay is energized, the coil creates a magnetic field that closes the larger contacts of the power circuit to provide power to the circuit loads.

5   Terminals 85 and 86 are normally the control circuit. If the relay contains a diode, terminal 86 must be connected to battery positive (B+) voltage and terminal 85 to ground. If the relay contains a resistor, terminals 85 and 86 can be connected in either direction with respect to B+ and ground.

6   Terminal 30 is normally connected to the battery voltage (B+) source for the circuit loads. Terminal 87 is connected to the circuit leading to the component being powered. If the relay has several alternate terminals for load or ground connections, they usually are numbered 87A, 87B, 87C, and so on.

7   Use an ohmmeter to check continuity through the relay control coil.

  a) *Connect the meter according to the polarity shown in the illustration for one check; then reverse the ohmmeter leads and check continuity in the other direction.*

  b) *If the relay contains a resistor, resistance will be indicated on the meter, and should be the same value with the ohmmeter in either direction.*

  c) *If the relay contains a diode, resistance should be higher with the ohmmeter in the forward polarity direction than with the meter leads reversed.*

  d) *If the ohmmeter shows infinite resistance in both directions, replace the relay.*

8   Remove the relay from the vehicle and use the ohmmeter to check for continuity between the relay power circuit terminals. There should be no continuity between terminal 30 and 87 with the relay de-energized.

9   Connect a fused jumper wire to terminal 86 and the positive battery terminal. Connect another jumper wire between terminal 85 and ground. When the connections are made, the relay should click.

10   With the jumper wires connected, check for continuity between the power circuit terminals. Now, there should be continuity between terminals 30 and 87.

11   If the relay fails any of the above tests, replace it.

6   Turn signal and hazard flasher - check and replacement

Refer to illustrations 6.4a and 6.4b
Warning: *The models covered by this manual are equipped with Supplemental Restraint Systems (SRS), more commonly known as airbags. Always disable the airbag system before working in the vicinity of any airbag system components to avoid the possibility of accidental deployment of the airbags, which could cause personal injury (see Section 27).*

1   The turn signal and hazard flasher is a single combination unit.

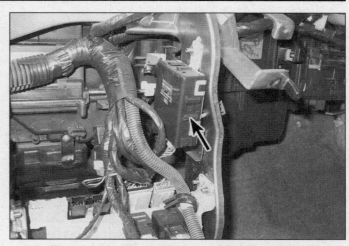

6.4a The turn signal/hazard flasher unit is located in the steering column and mounted behind the multi-function switch on convertibles and sedans

6.4b The turn signal/hazard flasher unit is located behind the center console on coupes - it will be necessary to remove the radio for access to it (instrument panel removed for clarity)

2   When the flasher unit is functioning properly, an audible click can be heard during its operation. If the turn signals fail on one side or the other and the flasher unit does not make its characteristic clicking sound, or if a bulb on one side of the vehicle flashes much faster than normal but the bulb at the other end of the vehicle (on the same side) doesn't light at all, a faulty turn signal bulb may be indicated.

3   If both turn signals fail to blink, the problem may be due to a blown fuse, a faulty flasher unit, a defective switch or a loose or open connection. If a quick check of the fuse box indicates that the turn signal fuse has blown, check the wiring for a short before installing a new fuse.

4   To replace the flasher, disconnect the electrical connector and remove the flasher unit from its mounting bracket. The flasher is located in the steering column behind the multi-function switch on convertibles and sedans **(see illustration)** or behind the center console in coupes **(see illustration)**.

5   Make sure that the replacement unit is identical to the original. Compare the old one to the new one before installing it.

6   Installation is the reverse of removal.

7   Steering column switches - replacement

Refer to illustrations 7.5a, 7.5b and 7.5c
Warning: *The models covered by this manual are equipped with Supplemental Restraint Systems (SRS), more commonly known as airbags. Always disable the airbag system before working in the vicinity of any airbag system components to avoid the possibility of accidental deployment of the airbags, which could cause personal injury (see Section 27).*
Note: *Convertibles and sedans are equipped with a multi-function switch. This assembly is removed from the steering column as a complete unit. Coupes are equipped with steering column switches that can be removed separately. In the event of problems with the main switch body (i.e. defective canceling cam) on coupes, it will be necessary to remove the steering wheel for replacement.*

1   The multi-function switch (steering column switches) is located on the steering column. It incorporates the turn signals, the hazard warning, the headlights, the headlight beam select (Hi/Lo), the headlight flasher, the

instrument panel dimmer switch, the windshield wiper and windshield washer functions. There are two levers on the multi-function switch, the left side controls the signaling and the lighting, the right side controls the wipers and washer system.

2   Disconnect the cable from the negative battery terminal or the remote ground terminal (see Chapter 5).

3   Remove the steering column covers (see Chapter 11).

4   Disconnect the electrical connectors from the backside of the switch.

5   Remove the multi-function switch retaining screws **(see illustrations)**.

6   Remove the multi-function switch. On convertibles and sedans, slide the switch off the column and lift the assembly **(see illustration 6.4a)**.

7   Insert the connectors into the new multi-function switch, pushing in until they are securely locked in place.

8   The remainder of installation is the reverse of removal.

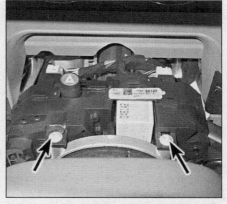

7.5a Location of the turn signal switch mounting screws (arrows) on a 1998 coupe

7.5b Location of the washer/wiper switch mounting screws (arrows) on a 1998 coupe

7.5c Location of the multi-function switch mounting screws (arrows) on a 2001 convertible

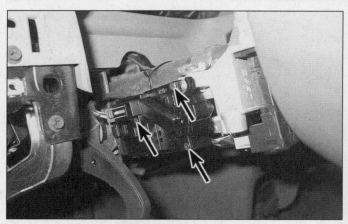

8.10 Location of the ignition switch mounting screws (arrows) on a 2001 convertible

8.19 Location of the ignition switch mounting screws (arrows) on a 1998 coupe

8   Ignition switch and key lock cylinder - replacement

Warning: *The models covered by this manual are equipped with Supplemental Restraint Systems (SRS), more commonly known as airbags. Always disable the airbag system before working in the vicinity of any airbag system components to avoid the possibility of accidental deployment of the airbags, which could cause personal injury (see Section 27).*

Ignition switch
Removal

1   Disconnect the cable from the negative battery terminal or the remote ground terminal (see Chapter 5).

Convertibles and sedans

Refer to illustration 8.10

2   Remove the instrument cluster hood (see Chapter 11).

3   Remove the center bezel (see Chapter 11).

4   Remove the lower knee bolster (see Chapter 11).

5   Remove the steering column covers (see Chapter 11).

6   Tilt the steering wheel lever down and slide the upper steering column cover off the steering column.

7   Remove the key lock cylinder (see Steps 21 through 24).

8   On models with a key reminder switch, disconnect the switch and remove the assembly from the ignition switch and key lock cylinder. **Note:** *On models equipped with the anti-theft system, disconnect the key ring antenna and remove the immobilizer ECU harness from the below the dash.*

9   Disconnect the electrical connector from the ignition switch.

10   Remove the screw securing the switch to the steering column **(see illustration)**.

11   Depress the retaining tabs, then detach the switch and lower it from the steering column.

Coupes

Refer to illustration 8.19

12   Remove the steering column covers (see Chapter 11).

13   Remove the dash kick panel adjacent to the steering column (see Chapter 11).

14   Remove the steering wheel (see Chapter 10).

15   Remove the clockspring (see Chapter 10).

16   Disconnect the electrical connector from the ignition switch.

17   Remove the key lock cylinder (see Steps 21 through 24).

18   On models with a key reminder switch, disconnect the switch and remove the assembly from the ignition switch and the lock cylinder. **Note:** *On models equipped with the anti-theft system, disconnect the key ring antenna and remove the immobilizer ECU harness from the below the dash.*

19   Remove the screws securing the switch to the steering column **(see illustration)**.

Installation

20   Installation is the reverse of removal. Make sure the switch and lock cylinder are in

the RUN position (convertibles and sedans) or the ACC position (coupes) before installation. Tighten the switch mounting screws securely.

Lock cylinder
Removal

Refer to illustrations 8.24a and 8.24b

21   Disconnect the cable from the negative battery terminal or the remote ground terminal (see Chapter 5).

22   Remove the steering column covers (see Chapter 11).

23   Insert the ignition key and turn the switch to the RUN position (convertibles and sedans) or the ACC position (coupes).

24   Depress the retaining tab with a small screwdriver and then withdraw the lock cylinder from the housing **(see illustrations)**.

Installation

Refer to illustration 8.25

25   Make sure the slot in the ignition switch is in the RUN position (convertibles and sedans) or the ACC position (coupes) and insert the lock cylinder into the housing until the retain-

8.24a With the lock cylinder in the RUN position, depress the retaining pin with a thin tool, then pull straight out to remove the lock cylinder - 2001 convertible

8.24b With the lock cylinder in the ACC position, depress the retaining pin with a thin tool, then pull straight out to remove the lock cylinder - 1998 coupe

ing tab locates the housing **(see illustration)**. Check key operation.

26   The remaining installation steps are the reverse of removal. **Note:** *On models equipped with the anti-theft system, if the immobilizer ECU is replaced, attach a new immobilizer serial number identification sticker onto the steering column under the steering column covers.*

9   Instrument panel switches - replacement

Warning: *The models covered by this manual are equipped with Supplemental Restraint Systems (SRS), more commonly known as airbags. Always disable the airbag system before working in the vicinity of any airbag system components to avoid the possibility of accidental deployment of the airbag(s), which could cause personal injury (see Section 27).*

Hazard warning switch

Note: *Convertibles and sedans are equipped with a hazard warning switch built into the multi-function switch. Refer to Section 7 for the multi-function switch replacement procedure.*

1995 through 2000 coupes

Refer to illustrations 9.2 and 9.4

1   Remove the glovebox (see Chapter 11).
2   Remove the center air outlet assembly **(see illustration)**.
3   Disconnect the cool air bypass lever and air bypass damper lever from the center air outlet assembly.
4   Disconnect the electrical connector from the hazard warning switch **(see illustration)**.
5   Separate the hazard warning switch from the center air outlet assembly.
6   Installation is the reverse of removal.
7   Turn the cool air bypass lever down and the air bypass damper lever toward the front position to install the cables.

2001 and later coupes

8   Remove the center bezel assembly (see Chapter 11).
9   Remove the hazard warning switch from the center bezel assembly.
10   Installation is the reverse of the removal procedure.

Power mirror/fog light/cruise control switch

Refer to illustrations 9.11a, 9.11b, 9.12a and 9.12b

Note 1: *Convertibles and sedans are equipped with a fog light switch built into the multi-function switch. Refer to Section 7 for the multi-function switch replacement procedure.*

Note 2: *On convertibles and sedans, the cruise control switch pods are located on the steering wheel. The cruise control switches are part of the vehicle's multiplexing communication system with the PCM, and send/receive information through the steering wheel's airbag clockspring connector. Standard troubleshooting will not give a true pic-*

8.25 Make sure the slot in the switch (arrow) is positioned the exact same angle as the ignition key lock cylinder

9.2 Carefully pry the center air outlet assembly from the instrument panel using a flat-bladed screwdriver

9.4 Disconnect the hazard switch electrical connector (arrow)

ture of the switch operation. If you suspect a problem with either cruise control switch pod, have the system checked with a factory scan tool at a dealership service department.

11   Carefully pry the switch assembly from the instrument panel **(see illustrations)**.

9.11a Carefully pry the the power mirror/fog light/cruise control switch assembly from the instrument panel using a flat-bladed screwdriver - 1998 coupe

9.11b Pry the lower instrument panel bezel from the instrument panel to access the power mirror switch - 2001 convertible

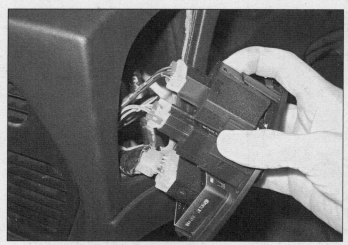

9.12a Disconnect the electrical connectors from the back side of the assembly - 1998 coupe

9.12b Disconnect the power mirror switch from the back side of the bezel - 2001 convertible

12   Disconnect the electrical connector (**see illustrations**) and remove the switch.
13   Installation of the is the reverse of the removal procedure.

Instrument panel light control switch

Note: *Convertibles and sedans are equipped with an instrument panel light control switch built into the multi-function switch. Refer to Section 7 for the multi-function switch replacement procedure.*
14   On 1995 through 2000 coupes, remove the instrument panel lower dash panel (see Chapter 11).
15   On 2001 and later coupes, remove the instrument cluster trim panel (see Chapter 11).
16   Disconnect the electrical connector and remove the switch.
17   Installation is the reverse of the removal procedure.

10   Instrument cluster - removal and installation

Warning: *The models covered by this manual are equipped with Supplemental Restraint Systems (SRS), more commonly known as airbags. Always disable the airbag system before working in the vicinity of any airbag system components to avoid the possibility of accidental deployment of the airbag(s), which could cause personal injury (see Section 27).*
1   Disconnect the cable from the negative battery terminal or the remote ground terminal (see Chapter 5).

Coupes

Refer to illustrations 10.3 and 10.4
2   Remove the instrument cluster trim panel (see Chapter 11).
3   Remove the cluster mounting screws (**see illustration**) and pull the instrument cluster towards the steering wheel.
4   Disconnect any electrical connectors that

would interfere with removal (**see illustration**).
5   Cover the steering column with a cloth to protect the trim covers, then remove the instrument cluster from the vehicle.
6   Installation is the reverse of removal.

Convertibles and sedans

7   Remove the instrument cluster hood (see Chapter 11).
8   Remove the cluster mounting screws (see Chapter 11) and separate the instrument cluster from the instrument panel.
9   Disconnect any electrical connectors that would interfere with removal.
10   Installation is the reverse of removal.

11   Wiper motor - check and replacement

Wiper motor circuit check

Note: *Refer to the wiring diagrams for wire colors in the following checks. When checking*

10.3 Remove the instrument cluster mounting screws (arrows) - 2001 convertible

10.4 Disconnect the instrument cluster harness connector (arrow)

11.7   Paint an alignment mark over the stud and the wiper arm for correct reassembly

11.9a   Wiper motor/linkage mounting bolts, left side (arrows) on a 1998 convertible

for voltage, probe a grounded 12-volt test light to each terminal at a connector until it lights; this verifies voltage (power) at the terminal. If the following checks fail to locate the problem, have the system diagnosed by a dealer service department or other properly equipped repair facility.

1   If the wipers work slowly, make sure the battery is in good condition and has a strong charge (see Chapter 5). If the battery is in good condition, remove the wiper motor (see below) and operate the wiper arms by hand. Check for binding linkage and pivots. Lubricate or repair the linkage or pivots as necessary. Reinstall the wiper motor. If the wipers still operate slowly, check for loose or corroded connections, especially the ground connection. If all connections look OK, replace the motor.

2   If the wipers fail to operate when activated, check the fuse (see Section 3). If the fuse is OK, connect a jumper wire between the wiper motor's ground terminal and ground, then retest. If the motor works now, repair the ground connection. If the motor still doesn't

work, turn the wiper switch to the HI position and check for voltage at the motor. **Note:** *The cowl cover will have to be removed* (see Chapter 11) *to access the electrical connector.*

3   If there's voltage at the connector, remove the motor and check it off the vehicle with fused jumper wires from the battery. If the motor now works, check for binding linkage (see Step 1). If the motor still doesn't work, replace it. If there's no voltage to the motor, check for voltage at the wiper control relays. If there's voltage at the wiper control relays and no voltage at the wiper motor, have the switch tested. If the switch is OK, the wiper control relay is probably bad. See Section 5 for relay testing.

4   If the interval (delay) function is inoperative, check the continuity of all the wiring between the switch and wiper control module.

5   If the wipers stop at the position they're in when the switch is turned off (fail to park), check for voltage at the park feed wire of the wiper motor connector when the wiper switch is OFF but the ignition is ON. If no voltage is

present, check for an open circuit between the wiper motor and the fuse panel.

Replacement

Refer to illustrations 11.7, 11.9a, 11.9b and 11.11

6   Disconnect the cable from the negative battery terminal or the remote ground terminal (see Chapter 5).

7   Mark the positions of the wiper arm(s) **(see illustration)**, then remove the wiper arm(s).

8   Remove the windshield cowl cover (see Chapter 11).

9   Disconnect the wiper motor harness connector and remove the windshield wiper motor/linkage assembly mounting bolts **(see illustrations)**.

10   Lift the windshield wiper motor assembly from the cowl area.

11   Remove the wiper motor mounting nuts and separate the motor from the linkage **(see illustration)**.

12   Installation is the reverse of removal.

11.9b   Wiper motor/linkage mounting bolt, right side (arrow) on a 1998 convertible

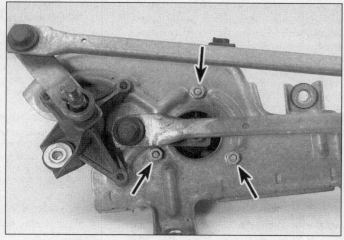

11.11   Location of the wiper motor mounting nuts (arrows) on a 1998 convertible

12.3a Location of the radio mounting screws (arrows) on a 1998 coupe

12.3b Location of the radio mounting screws (arrows) on a 2001 convertible

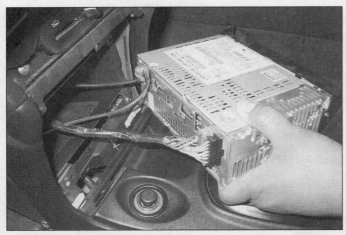

12.3c Pull the radio forward, then disconnect the antenna lead and the electrical connector

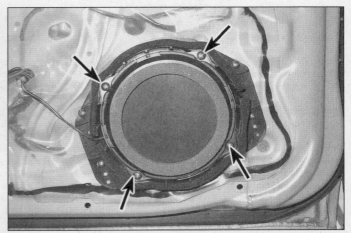

12.6a Remove the speaker screws (arrows)

12   Radio and speakers - removal and installation

Warning: *The models covered by this manual are equipped with Supplemental Restraint Systems (SRS), more commonly known as airbags. Always disable the airbag system before working in the vicinity of any airbag system components to avoid the possibility of accidental deployment of the airbag(s), which could cause personal injury* (see Section 27).
Note: *The amplifier is located under the passenger seat on convertibles, sedans and 2001 and later coupes or under the rear parcel shelf on 2000 and earlier coupes.*

1   Disconnect the cable from the negative battery terminal or the remote ground terminal (see Chapter 5).

Radio

Refer to illustrations 12.3a, 12.3b and 12.3c

2   Access the radio by removing the dash panel surrounding the radio (see Chapter 11).
3   Remove the retaining screws **(see illustrations)** and pull the radio outward to access the backside, then disconnect the electrical

connectors and the antenna lead **(see illustration)**.
4   Installation is the reverse of removal.

Door speakers

Refer to illustrations 12.6a and 12.6b

5   Remove the door trim panel (see Chapter 11).
6   Remove the speaker screws **(see illustration)**. Disconnect the electrical connector and the antenna lead and remove the speaker from the vehicle **(see illustration)**.
7   Installation is the reverse of removal.

Dash speakers

8   Remove the dash pad (see Chapter 11).
9   Remove the speaker screws. Disconnect the electrical connector and remove the speaker from the vehicle.
10   Installation is the reverse of removal.

Rear parcel shelf speakers

11   Remove the rear pillar trim panels (see Chapter 11).
12   Remove the lower trim panels behind the rear seats (see Chapter 11).

13   Remove the rear parcel shelf trim screws and lift the trim cover (see Chapter 11).
14   Remove the speaker screws. Disconnect the electrical connector and remove the speaker from the vehicle.
15   Installation is the reverse of removal.

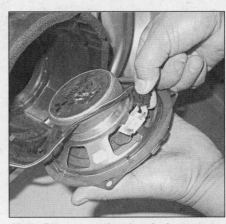

12.6b Disconnect the electrical connector to remove the speaker from the vehicle

13.1 Unscrew the antenna rod from the base

13.3 Working in the fenderwell, disconnect the antenna lead from the base

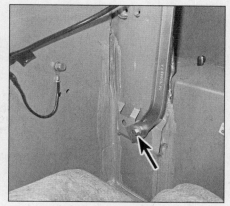

13.4 Remove the antenna bolt (arrow) working in the fenderwell

13 Antenna - replacement

Warning: *The models covered by this manual are equipped with Supplemental Restraint Systems (SRS), more commonly known as airbags. Always disable the airbag system before working in the vicinity of any airbag system components to avoid the possibility of accidental deployment of the airbag(s), which could cause personal injury (see Section 27).*

Fixed antenna
Removal
Refer to illustrations 13.1, 13.3 and 13.4

1   Use a small open-end wrench and unscrew the antenna mast from the body **(see illustration)**.
2   Working inside the trunk, detach the liner from the side of the trunk.
3   Disconnect the antenna lead from the base of the antenna body **(see illustration)**.
4   Remove the mounting bolt securing the antenna body to the rear quarter panel **(see illustration)**.
5   Withdraw the antenna body from the rear quarter panel.

Installation
6   Installation is the reverse of removal.

Power antenna
Removal
Refer to illustration 13.9

7   Disconnect the cable from the negative battery terminal or the remote ground terminal (see Chapter 5).
8   Working inside the trunk, detach the liner from the side of the trunk.
9   Detach the drain hose from the antenna **(see illustration)**.
10   Disconnect the antenna lead from the power antenna harness.
11   Disconnect the electrical connector from the antenna motor.
12   Remove the bolt securing the ground strap and the cap nut securing the antenna brace to the rear quarter panel.
13   Withdraw the antenna from the rear quarter panel.

Installation
14   Installation is the reverse of removal. Make sure that the fender grommet locating tab is in line with the slot in the body before installing the antenna. Make sure the ball of the antenna body is fully seated in the grommet.

Power antenna mast - convertibles
Removal
Refer to illustrations 13.15 and 13.17

15   Remove the cap nut **(see illustration)**.
16   Turn the ignition key to the ACCESSORY position.
17   Turn the radio ON and while the antenna is moving UP, grab the mast and pull it out of the antenna body. The antenna mast, contact spring and drive rod should all come out at this time **(see illustration)**.

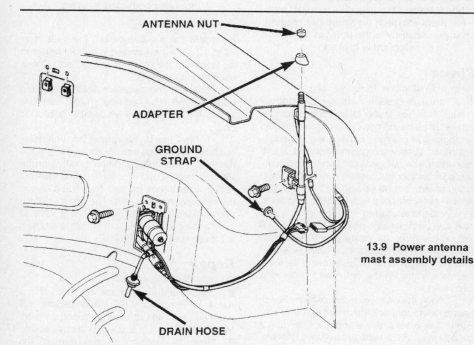

ANTENNA NUT

ADAPTER

GROUND STRAP

DRAIN HOSE

13.9 Power antenna mast assembly details

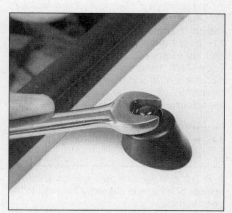

13.15 Remove the power antenna cap nut

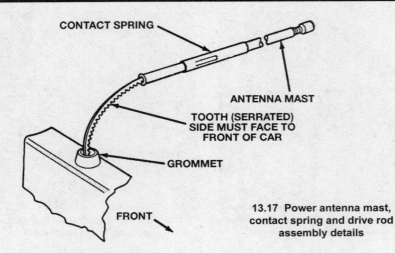

13.17 Power antenna mast,
contact spring and drive rod
assembly details

14.4 When measuring the voltage at the
rear window defogger grid, wrap a piece
of aluminum foil around the positive probe
of the voltmeter and press the foil against
the wire with your finger

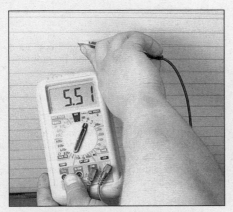

14.5 To determine if a heating element
has broken, check the voltage at the
center of each element - if the voltage is 5
or 6-volts, the element is unbroken - if the
voltage is 10 or 12-volts, the element is
broken between the center and the ground
side - if there is no voltage, the element
is broken between the center and the
positive side

14.7 To find the break, place the voltmeter
negative lead against the defogger ground
terminal, place the voltmeter positive
lead with the foil strip against the heating
element at the positive terminal end and
slide it toward the negative terminal end
- the point at which the voltmeter reading
changes abruptly is the point at which the
element is broken

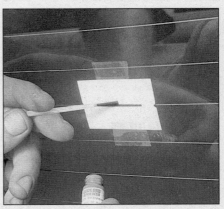

14.13 To use a defogger repair kit, apply
masking tape to the inside of the window
at the damaged area, then brush on the
special conductive coating

Installation

18   Insert the new antenna mast, contact spring and drive rod into the body with the drive rod teeth facing toward the antenna motor (remove the trunk lining if necessary).
19   Turn the radio OFF and guide the drive rod into the body.
20   Install the cap nut. **Note:** *The antenna may not completely retract after initial installation. Turn the radio ON-and-OFF to cycle the antenna up-and-down. The mast should completely retract after raising and lowering the antenna a few times.*

14   Rear window defogger - check and repair

1   The rear window defogger consists of a number of horizontal elements baked onto the glass surface.
2   Small breaks in the element can be repaired without removing the rear window.

Check

Refer to illustrations 14.4, 14.5 and 14.7
3   Turn the ignition switch and defogger system switches to the ON position. Using a voltmeter, place the positive probe against the defogger grid positive terminal and the negative probe against the ground terminal. If battery voltage is not indicated, check the fuse, defogger switch and related wiring. If voltage is indicated, but all or part of the defogger doesn't heat, proceed with the following tests.
4   When measuring voltage during the next two tests, wrap a piece of aluminum foil around the tip of the voltmeter positive probe and press the foil against the heating element with your finger **(see illustration)**. Place the negative probe on the defogger grid ground terminal.
5   Check the voltage at the center of each heating element **(see illustration)**. If the voltage is 5 or 6-volts, the element is okay (there is no break). If the voltage is 0-volts, the element is broken between the center of the ele-

ment and the positive end. If the voltage is 10 to 12-volts the element is broken between the center of the element and ground. Check each heating element.
6   Connect the negative lead to a good body ground. The reading should stay the same. If it doesn't, the ground connection is bad.
7   To find the break, place the voltmeter negative probe against the defogger ground terminal. Place the voltmeter positive probe with the foil strip against the heating element at the positive terminal end and slide it toward the negative terminal end. The point at which the voltmeter deflects from several volts to zero is the point at which the heating element is broken **(see illustration)**.

Repair

Refer to illustration 14.13
8   Repair the break in the element using a repair kit specifically recommended for this purpose, available at most auto parts stores. Included in this kit is plastic conductive epoxy.
9   Prior to repairing a break, turn off the

TACHOMETER …6000 rpm SPEEDOMETER …100mph (220 kmh) FUEL GAUGE pointer ON …F TEMPERATURE GAUGE pointer ON …H
TACHOMETER …3000 rpm SPEEDOMETER …75mph (120 kmh) FUEL GAUGE pointer ON …1/2 TEMPERATURE GAUGE pointer ON …midscale
TACHOMETER …3000 rpm SPEEDOMETER …55mph (100 kmh) FUEL GAUGE pointer ON …1/2 TEMPERATURE GAUGE pointer ON …midscale
TACHOMETER …1000 rpm SPEEDOMETER …20mph (40 kmh) FUEL GAUGE pointer ON …E TEMPERATURE GAUGE pointer ON …C

15.5a Instrument cluster CHEC 1 chart

CHECK ENGINE
SEAT BELT
AIRBAG
CHARGING SYSTEM
LOW FUEL
HIGH BEAM INDICATOR
ENGINE TEMPERATURE
CRUISE

15.5b Instrument cluster CHEC 2 chart

system and allow it to cool off for a few minutes.

10   Lightly buff the element area with fine steel wool, then clean it thoroughly with rubbing alcohol.

11   Use masking tape to mask off the area being repaired.

12   Thoroughly mix the epoxy, following the instructions provided with the repair kit.

13   Apply the epoxy material to the slit in the masking tape, overlapping the undamaged area about 3/4-inch on either end **(see illustration)**.

14   Allow the repair to cure for 24 hours before removing the tape and using the system.

15   Instrument cluster self-diagnosis (convertibles and sedans)

General description

1   The instrument cluster is equipped with a self-diagnosis feature. When activated, the electronic display, odometer/transmission range indicator and all indicator lamps will illuminate in a specific sequence.

2   If the instrument cluster is not receiving power from the CCD bus, the cluster will appear non-functional except the airbag indicator lamp will illuminate and a NO BUS message will be displayed. If this message is displayed, further diagnosis should be performed by a dealer service department or other qualified repair shop.

Starting the self-diagnosis

Refer to illustrations 15.5a, 15.5b, 15.5c, 15.5d, 15.5e and 15.5f

Note: *2001 and later convertibles are equipped with a slightly different self-diagnosis system for the instrument cluster. The access procedure is the same but the instrument cluster will display the diagnostic message.*

3   While depressing the odometer/trip reset button, turn the ignition key to the OFF/RUN/START position.

4   This will initiate an electronic display system check and the illumination (in sequence) of all CCD bus activated instrument cluster warning indicators. Due to the complexity of replacing the instrument cluster circuit board, gauges and transmission range indicator, the

home mechanic should limit service to bulb replacement (see Section 20). If the instrument cluster circuit board, gauge or transmission range indicator replacement is indicated, take the vehicle to a dealer service department or other qualified repair shop for service.

5   There are four check (CHEC) functions **(see illustrations)**:

a) *CHEC 1 - Gauges: If all gauges fail to move or do not indicate at the proper locations, the instrument cluster circuit board is faulty and should be replaced. If any one gauge fails to move or indicate properly, have it replaced.*

b) *CHEC 2 - Warning lamps: If any lamp listed in Step 1 does not illuminate, check the bulb operation. If the bulb is OK, the instrument cluster circuit board is faulty and should be replaced.*

c) *CHEC 3 - Odometer/trip meter: If any LED does not illuminate, have it replaced.*

d) *CHEC 4 - Transmission range indicator/Autostick indicator: If any LED does not illuminate, have it replaced.*

TRIP
ODOMETER CENTER
ODOMETER LOWER RIGHT
ODOMETER BOTTOM
ODOMETER LOWER LEFT
ODOMETER UPPER LEFT
ODOMETER TOP
ODOMETER UPPER RIGHT
ALL ODOMETER V/F DISPLAY DIGIT SEGMENTS ON

15.5c Instrument cluster CHEC 3 chart

PRND3L
PRND3L AND BOX AROUND P
PRND3L AND BOX AROUND R
PRND3L AND BOX AROUND N
PRND3L AND BOX AROUND D
PRND3L AND BOX AROUND 3
PRND3L AND BOX AROUND L
PRND3L AND ALL BOXES
END

15.5d Instrument cluster CHEC 4 chart - automatic transaxle models without the Autostick option

CHEC 4 - TRANSMISSION RANGE INDICATOR LED DISPLAY		CHEC 4 - TRANSMISSION RANGE INDICATOR LED DISPLAY
AUTOSTICK		**AUTOSTICK**
PRND AS 1 AND AS BOX		PRND1234 AND BOX AROUND 1
PRND AS 2 AND AS BOX		PRND1234 AND BOX AROUND 2
PRND AS 3 AND AS BOX		PRND1234 AND BOX AROUND 3
PRND AS 4 AND AS BOX		PRND1234 AND BOX AROUND 4
PRND AS AND BOX AROUND P		PRND1234 AND BOX AROUND P
PRND AS AND BOX AROUND R		PRND1234 AND BOX AROUND R
PRND AS AND BOX AROUND N		PRND1234 AND BOX AROUND N
PRND AS AND BOX AROUND D		PRND1234 AND BOX AROUND D
PRND AS 1234 AND ALL BOXES		PRND1234 AND ALL BOXES
END		END

15.5e Instrument cluster CHEC 4 chart - 1997 and earlier automatic transaxle models with the Autostick option

15.5f Instrument cluster CHEC 4 chart - 1998 and later automatic transaxle models with the Autostick option

16.1 Rotate the sealing cover counterclockwise to access the bulb

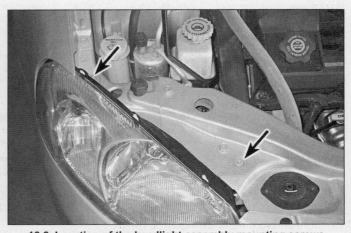

16.6 Location of the headlight assembly mounting screws (arrows) on a 2001 convertible

16   Headlight bulb - replacement

Warning: *Halogen gas filled bulbs are under pressure and may shatter if the surface is scratched or the bulb is dropped. Wear eye protection and handle the bulbs carefully, grasping only the base whenever possible.*

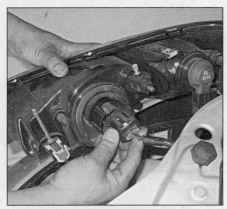

16.7 Disconnect the bulb electrical connector

Do not touch the surface of the bulb with your fingers because the oil from your skin could cause it to overheat and fail prematurely. If you do touch the bulb surface, clean it with rubbing alcohol.

Coupes

Refer to illustration 16.1

1   Reach behind the headlight assembly and rotate the sealing cover counterclockwise **(see illustration)** to remove it from the head-light housing.
2   Remove the bulb locking spring.
3   Disconnect the bulb electrical connector.
4   Pull straight out on the bulb to remove from it from the bulb holder. **Note:** *Don't touch the surface of the bulb with your fingers because the oil from your skin could cause it to overheat and fail prematurely. If you happen to touch the bulb surface, clean it with rubbing alcohol.* Insert the new bulb assembly into the headlight housing and secure it with the locking spring.
5   Plug in the electrical connector and install the cover.

Convertibles and sedans

Refer to illustrations 16.6, 16.7 and 16.8

6   Remove the headlight assembly **(see illustration)**.
7   Disconnect the bulb electrical connector **(see illustration)**.

16.8 Rotate bulb retaining ring counterclockwise and remove the bulb from the holder to replace it

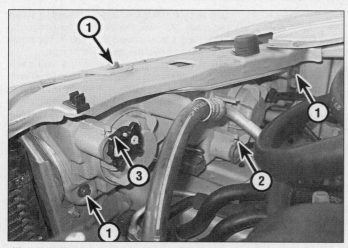

17.1 Headlight mounting and adjustment details on a 1998 coupe

1   *Headlight assembly mounting screws*
2   *Vertical position adjusting screw*
3   *Horizontal position indicator/adjuster*

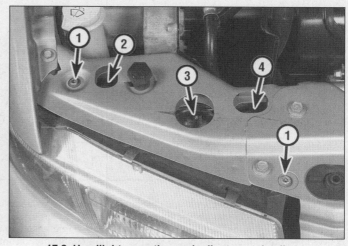

17.2 Headlight mounting and adjustment details on a 1998 convertible

1   *Headlight assembly mounting screws*
2   *Vertical position adjusting screw*
3   *Vertical position indicator (bubble level)*
4   *Horizontal position indicator/adjuster*

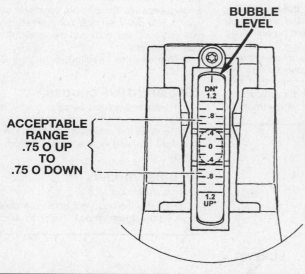

BUBBLE LEVEL

DN° 1.2
.8
.4
0
.4
.8
1.2 UP°

ACCEPTABLE RANGE .75 O UP TO .75 O DOWN

17.6 Headlight vertical position indicator - Do not tamper with the screw located on the indicator or calibration will be lost. When properly adjusted, the bubble should be in the range shown

ment screw located on the rear (end) of the headlight housing and a vertical screw located on the rear (middle) of the headlight housing **(see illustration)**. Insert a Phillips screwdriver into the gear-drive mechanism to turn the screw.

Convertibles
Refer to illustration 17.2

2   These models have a horizontal and vertical adjustment screw located on the top of each headlight housing **(see illustration)**. Insert a Phillips screwdriver into the gear-drive mechanism to turn the screw.

All models

Using the built-in indicators (2000 and earlier models)
Refer to illustrations 17.6 and 17.8

3   The headlight assemblies have built-in horizontal and vertical position indicators which are calibrated at the factory.
4   Adjustment should be made with the vehicle on a level surface, with a full gas tank and a normal load in the vehicle.
5   Rock the vehicle side-to-side three times, then push down on the front bumper to jounce the front suspension up-and-down three times. This will allow the suspension to stabilize prior to adjustment.
6   Open the hood and check the vertical indicators on the headlight assemblies. The bubble in the vial should be centered over the zero **(see illustration)**. **Note:** *A bubble located anywhere between 0.75 degrees UP and 0.75 degrees DOWN is also acceptable.*
7   If the bubble is not within the 0.75 degrees UP to 0.75 degrees DOWN range, adjust the vertical aiming screw **(see illustrations 17.1 and 17.2)** as required to bring the bubble back to the centered location. **Caution:** *Do not tamper with the screw on the vial itself or calibration will be lost.*

8   Grasp the headlight bulb holder retaining ring and rotate it counterclockwise and remove the bulb holder from the headlight assembly **(see illustration)**.
9   Grasp the bulb and pull it out of the holder.
10   Using gloves or a clean shop towel, insert the new bulb into the holder. **Note:** *Don't touch the surface of the bulb with your fingers because the oil from your skin could cause it to overheat and fail prematurely. If you happen to touch the bulb surface, clean it with rubbing alcohol.*
11   Install the bulb holder in the headlight assembly and rotate it clockwise to lock it in place. Attach the electrical connectors to the bulb holders.
12   Install the headlight assembly and adjust if necessary (see Section 17).

17   Headlights - adjustment

Note: *The headlights must be aimed correctly. If adjusted incorrectly they could blind the driver of an oncoming vehicle and cause a serious accident or seriously reduce your ability to see the road. The headlights should be checked for proper aim every 12 months and any time a new headlight is installed or front end body work is performed. It should be emphasized that the following procedure is only an interim step which will provide temporary adjustment until the headlights can be adjusted by a properly equipped shop.*
Note: *2000 and earlier models are equipped with built-in leveling indicators.*

Coupes
Refer to illustration 17.1

1   These models have a horizontal adjust-

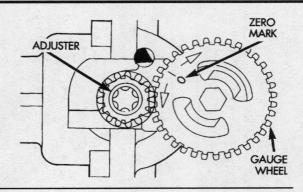

17.8 Headlight horizontal position indicator - When properly adjusted, the arrow on the adjuster should be pointing to the zero mark on the gauge wheel (convertible)

8   Next, check the horizontal indicators. The arrow on the adjuster should be pointing to the zero mark on the gauge wheel on convertibles **(see illustration)** or the stopper on coupes **(see illustration 17.1)**. **Note:** *On coupes, if the mating marks do not coincide, rotate the stopper clockwise to disengage the mechanism, then use a screwdriver to adjust the mating mark. After the alignment mark is correct, rotate the stopper to its original position.*
9   If the arrow is not pointing to the zero mark, adjust the horizontal aiming screw as required to align the horizontal marks.

Using the alignment screen
Refer to illustration 17.11
10   There are several methods of adjusting the headlights. The simplest method requires masking tape, a blank wall and a level floor.
11   Position masking tape vertically on the wall in reference to the vehicle centerline and the centerlines of both headlight bulbs **(see illustration)**.
12   Position a horizontal tape line in reference to the centerline of all the headlights. **Note:** *It may be easier to position the tape on the wall with the vehicle parked only a few inches away.*
13   Adjustment should be made with the vehicle parked 25 feet from the wall, sitting level, the gas tank half-full and no unusually heavy load in the vehicle.
14   Starting with the low beam adjustment, position the high intensity zone so it is two inches below the horizontal line and two inches to the side of the headlight vertical line, away from oncoming traffic. Adjustment is made by turning the vertical adjusting screw to raise or lower the beam. The horizontal adjusting screw should be used in the same manner to move the beam left or right.
15   With the high beams on, the high intensity zone should be vertically centered with the exact center just below the horizontal line. **Note:** *It may not be possible to position the headlight aim exactly for both high and low beams. If a compromise must be made, keep in mind that the low beams are the most used and have the greatest effect on driver safety.*
16   Have the headlights adjusted by a dealer service department or service station at the earliest opportunity.

18   Headlight housing - replacement

Warning: *These vehicles are equipped with halogen gas-filled headlight bulbs which are under pressure and may shatter if the surface is damaged or the bulb is dropped. Wear eye protection and handle the bulbs carefully, grasping only the base whenever possible. Do not touch the surface of the bulb with your fingers because the oil from your skin could cause it to overheat and fail prematurely. If you do touch the bulb surface, clean it with rubbing alcohol.*
1   Remove the headlight bulb (see Section 16).

1995 and 1996 coupes
2   Remove the front bumper (see Chapter 11).
3   Remove the retaining bolts, detach the headlight housing and withdraw it from the vehicle.

All other models
Refer to illustration 18.4
4   Remove the headlight housing mounting screws **(see illustration)**. Refer to illustra-

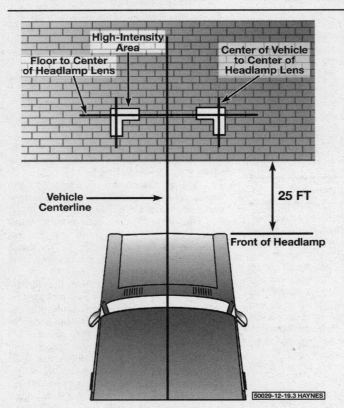

17.11 Headlight adjustment details

High-Intensity Area

Floor to Center of Headlamp Lens

Center of Vehicle to Center of Headlamp Lens

Vehicle Centerline

25 FT

Front of Headlamp

50029-12-19.3 HAYNES

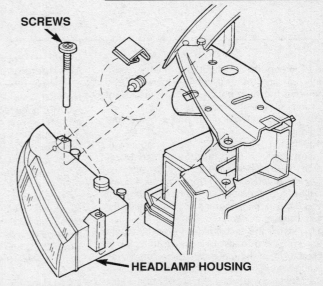

SCREWS

HEADLAMP HOUSING

18.4 Exploded view of the headlight housing and surrounding components on a 1999 convertible

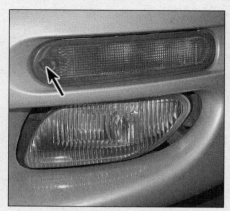

20.1 Remove the mounting screw (arrow) on the side of the park/turn signal assembly, then rotate the housing outward to access the bulb

tion 17.1 for headlight mounting screw locations on 1997 through 2000 coupes.

5   Detach the headlight housing and withdraw it from the vehicle. **Note:** *2001 and later coupes will require a special tool to access the headlight housing mounting screws. Have the housing removed by a dealer service department.*

All models

6   Installation is the reverse of removal. Be sure to check headlight adjustment (see Section 17).

19   Horn - check and replacement

Warning: *The models covered by this manual are equipped with Supplemental Restraint Systems (SRS), more commonly known as airbags. Always disable the airbag system before working in the vicinity of any airbag system components to avoid the possibility of accidental deployment of the airbag(s), which could cause personal injury (see Section 27).*

Check

Note: *Check the fuses before beginning electrical diagnosis.*

1   Disconnect the electrical connector from the horn.

20.11 Rotate the bulb holder 1/4 turn counterclockwise and remove

2   To test the horn, connect battery voltage to the horn terminal with a jumper wire. If the horn doesn't sound, replace it.

3   If the horn does sound, check for voltage at the terminal when the horn button is depressed. If there's voltage at the terminal, check for a bad ground at the horn.

4   If there's no voltage at the horn, check the relay (see Section 5).

5   If the relay is OK, check for voltage to the relay power and control circuits. If either of the circuits is not receiving voltage, inspect the wiring between the relay and the fuse panel.

6   If both relay circuits are receiving voltage, depress the horn button and check the circuit from the relay to the horn button for continuity to ground. If there's no continuity, check the circuit for an open. If there's no open circuit, replace the horn button.

7   If there's continuity to ground through the horn button, check for an open or short in the circuit from the relay to the horn.

Replacement

8   Access the horns:

a) On 2000 and earlier coupes, the horns are located behind the front bumper mounted on the frame rail. Remove the front bumper (see Chapter 11).

b) On 2000 and later coupes, the horns are located in the engine compartment near the headlight housing(s).

c) On 2000 and earlier convertibles, the horn is located on the right front frame rail. Raise the vehicle and secure it on jackstands. Remove the right front splash shield (see Chapter 11).

d) On 2001 and later convertibles and sedans, the horns are located behind the headlight housing(s). Remove the headlight housing(s) (see Section 16) and the vacuum tank to access the horn(s).

9   To replace the horn(s), disconnect the electrical connector and remove the bracket bolt.

10   Installation is the reverse of removal.

20   Bulb replacement

Front park/turn signal lights
Coupes

1995 through 2000 models
Refer to illustration 20.1

1   Remove the turn signal light assembly **(see illustration)**.

2   Rotate the turn signal bulb holder counterclockwise and pull it out of the light housing.

3   Remove the bulb from the holder.

4   Installation is the reverse of removal.

2001 and later models

5   Remove the horn from the left side of the engine compartment, if necessary (see Section 19).

6   Rotate the turn signal bulb holder counterclockwise and pull it out of the light housing.

7   Disconnect the bulb electrical connector.

8   Remove the bulb from the bulb holder.

9   Installation is the reverse of removal.

Convertibles and sedans
Refer to illustration 20.11

10   Remove the headlight assembly (see Section 16).

11   Grasp the bulb holder and rotate it counterclockwise 1/4 turn **(see illustration)**.

12   Disconnect the electrical connector and remove the bulb.

13   Install the new bulb into the holder.

14   Attach the electrical connector to the bulb holder.

15   Install the headlight assembly (see Section 16) and adjust headlight if necessary (see Section 19).

Rear tail light/brake light/turn signal
Refer to illustrations 20.18a, 20.18b, 20.20a and 20.20b

16   Open the trunk.

17   Separate the trunk lining from the rear tail light assembly.

18   Unscrew and remove the nuts securing the tail light assembly to the quarter panel **(see illustrations)**.

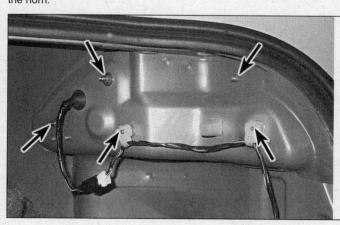

20.18a Location of the tail light assembly mounting nuts (arrows) on a 1998 coupe

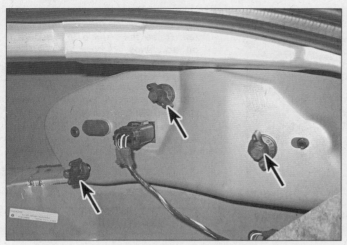

20.18b Location of the tail light assembly wing nuts (arrows) on a 2001 convertible

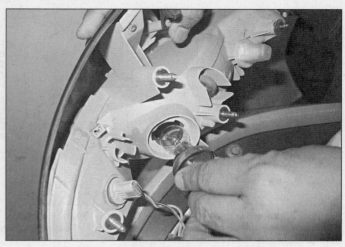

20.20a Removing a tail light bulb on a 1998 coupe

19   Withdraw the tail light assembly from the quarter panel and disconnect the wiring harness connector from the tail lamp assembly.
20   To replace a bulb, rotate the bulb holder counterclockwise and withdraw it from the assembly, then pull the bulb from the holder **(see illustrations)**.
21   Installation is the reverse of removal.

High-mounted brake light
Refer to illustration 20.23

22   Open the trunk and unclip the trunk latch cover for the high-mounted brake light (see Chapter 11). **Note:** *On Stratus models, remove the tail lid garnish to access the high mounted brake light assembly.*
23   Twist the bulb holder counterclockwise **(see illustration)** to remove it, then pull the bulb straight out of the holder.
24   Installation is the reverse of removal.

Instrument cluster lights
Refer to illustrations 20.26a and 20.26b

25   To gain access to the instrument cluster illumination bulbs, the instrument cluster will have to be removed (see Section 10). The

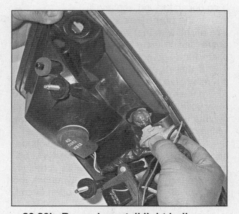

20.20b Removing a tail light bulb on a 2001 convertible

bulbs can then be removed and replaced from the rear of the cluster.
26   Rotate the bulb counterclockwise to remove it **(see illustrations)**.
27   Installation is the reverse of removal.

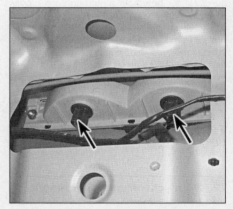

20.23 Rotate the bulbholder(s) (arrows) and remove it from the high-mounted brake light assembly

Reading light
Refer to illustration 20.28

28   Pry the interior lens off the reading light housing **(see illustration)**.
29   Remove the bulb.
30   Installation is the reverse of removal.

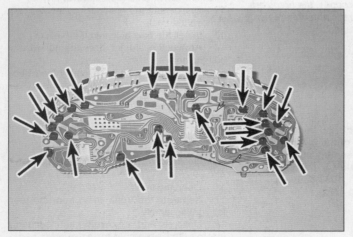

20.26a Instrument cluster bulb locations (arrows) on a 1998 coupe

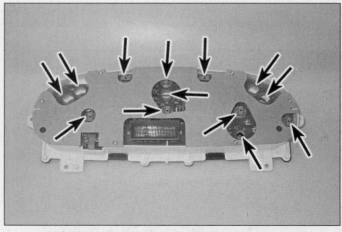

20.26b Instrument cluster bulb locations (arrows) on a 2001 convertible

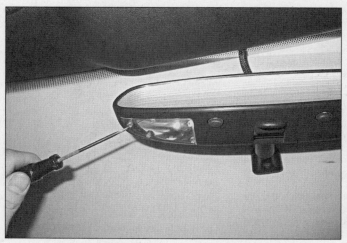

20.28 Carefully pry off the reading light lens using a flat-bladed screwdriver

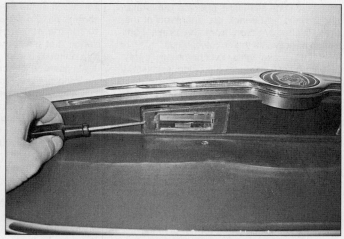

20.31a Carefully pry the license plate light assembly using a flat-bladed screwdriver - 2001 convertible

License plate light

Refer to illustrations 20.31a and 20.31b

31   Remove the license plate light assembly **(see illustrations)** and remove the license plate bulb. Replace the bulbs.
32   Installation is the reverse of removal.

Fog light

Refer to illustration 20.34

33   Raise the vehicle and secure it on jack-stands.
34   Remove the bulb **(see illustration)**.
Note: *On some models it will be necessary to remove the fog light assembly to access the bulb.*
35   Installation is the reverse of the removal.

21   Electric side view mirrors - description

1   Most electric rear view mirrors use two motors to move the glass; one for up and down adjustments and one for left-right adjustments.

2   The control switch has a selector portion which sends voltage to the left or right side mirror. With the ignition ON but the engine OFF, roll down the windows and operate the mirror control switch through all functions (left-right and up-down) for both the left and right side mirrors.
3   Listen carefully for the sound of the electric motors running in the mirrors.
4   If the motors can be heard but the mirror glass doesn't move, there's a problem with the drive mechanism inside the mirror.
5   If the mirrors do not operate and no sound comes from the mirrors, check the fuse (see Chapter 1).
6   If the fuse is OK, remove the mirror control switch. Have the switch continuity checked by a dealership service department or other qualified automobile repair facility.
7   Test the ground connections. Refer to the wiring diagrams at the end of Chapter 12.
8   If the mirror still doesn't work, remove the mirror and check the wires at the mirror for voltage.
9   If there's not voltage in each switch posi-

tion, check the circuit between the mirror and control switch for opens and shorts.
10   If there's voltage, remove the mirror and test it off the vehicle with jumper wires. Replace the mirror if it fails this test.

22   Cruise control system - description

Refer to illustration 22.5

1   The cruise control system maintains vehicle speed with an electronically controlled, vacuum operated servo located in the engine compartment, which is connected to the throttle body by a cable. The system consists of the cruise control servo, brake switch, control switches, the PCM and the vehicle speed sensor. Some features of the system require special testers and diagnostic procedures which are beyond the scope of this manual. Listed below are some general procedures that may be used to locate common problems.
2   Check the fuses (see Section 3).

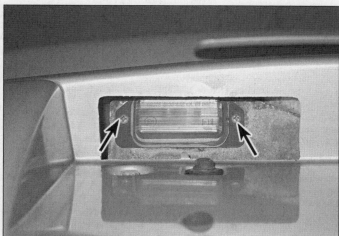

20.31b Remove the mounting screws (arrows) to access the license plate bulb - 1998 coupe

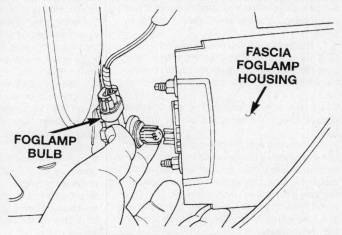

FASCIA FOGLAMP HOUSING

FOGLAMP BULB

20.34 Fog-light details on a 1999 convertible

3   Have an assistant operate the brake pedal while you check the operation of the brake lights (voltage from the brake light switch deactivates the cruise control).

4   If the brake lights don't come on or stay on all the time, correct the problem and retest the cruise control.

5   Inspect the control cable between cruise control servo and the throttle linkage for free movement **(see illustration)**. Replace it if necessary.

6   The cruise control system uses inputs from the Vehicle Speed Sensor (VSS). Refer to Chapter 6 for more information on the VSS.

7   Test drive the vehicle to determine if the cruise control is now working. If it isn't, take it to a dealer service department or an automotive electrical specialist for further diagnosis.

23   Power window system - description

1   The power window system operates electric motors, mounted in the doors, which lower and raise the windows. The system consists of the control switches, relays, the motors, regulators, glass mechanisms and associated wiring.

2   The power windows can be lowered and raised from the master control switch by the driver or by remote switches located at the individual windows. Each window has a separate motor that is reversible. The position of the control switch determines the polarity and therefore the direction of operation.

3   The circuit is protected by a fuse and a circuit breaker. Each motor is also equipped with an internal circuit breaker; this prevents one stuck window from disabling the whole system.

4   The power window system will only operate when the ignition switch is ON. In addition, many models have a window lockout switch at the master control switch that, when activated, disables the switches at the rear windows and, sometimes, the switch at the passenger's window also. Always check these items before troubleshooting a window problem.

5   These procedures are general in nature, so if you can't find the problem using them, take the vehicle to a dealer service department or other properly equipped repair facility.

6   If the power windows won't operate, always check the fuse and circuit breaker first.

7   If only the rear windows are inoperative, or if the windows only operate from the master control switch, check the rear window lockout switch for continuity in the unlocked position. Replace it if it doesn't have continuity.

8   Check the wiring between the switches and fuse panel for continuity. Repair the wiring, if necessary.

9   If only one window is inoperative from the master control switch, try the other control switch at the window. **Note:** *This doesn't apply to the driver's door window.*

10   If the same window works from one switch, but not the other, check the switch for continuity. Have the switch checked at a dealer service department or other qualified automobile repair facility.

11   If the switch tests OK, check for a short or open in the circuit between the affected switch and the window motor.

12   If one window is inoperative from both switches, remove the trim panel from the affected door and check for voltage at the switch and at the motor while the switch is operated.

13   If voltage is reaching the motor, disconnect the glass from the regulator (see Chapter 11). Move the window up and down by hand while checking for binding and damage. Also check for binding and damage to the regulator. If the regulator is not damaged and the window moves up and down smoothly, replace the motor. If there's binding or damage, lubricate, repair or replace parts, as necessary.

14   If voltage isn't reaching the motor, check the wiring in the circuit for continuity between the switches and motors. You'll need to consult the wiring diagram for the vehicle. If the circuit is equipped with a relay, check that the relay is grounded properly and receiving voltage.

24   Power door lock system - description

1   A power door lock system operates the door lock actuators mounted in each door. The system consists of the switches, actuators, a control unit and associated wiring. Diagnosis can usually be limited to simple checks of the wiring connections and actuators for minor faults that can be easily repaired.

2   Power door lock systems are operated by bi-directional solenoids located in the doors. The lock switches have two operating positions: Lock and Unlock. When activated, the switch sends a ground signal to the door lock control unit to lock or unlock the doors. Depending on which way the switch is activated, the control unit reverses polarity to the solenoids, allowing the two sides of the circuit to be used alternately as the feed (positive) and ground side.

3   Some vehicles may have an anti-theft system incorporated into the power locks. If you are unable to locate the trouble using the following general Steps, consult a dealer service department or other qualified repair shop.

4   Always check the circuit protection first. Some vehicles use a combination of circuit breakers and fuses.

5   Operate the door lock switches in both directions (Lock and Unlock) with the engine off. Listen for the click of the solenoids operating.

6   Test the switches for continuity. Remove the switches and have them checked by a

22.5 Cruise control servo on a 2001 convertible

dealer service department or other qualified automobile repair facility.

7   Check the wiring between the switches, control unit and solenoids for continuity. Repair the wiring if there's no continuity.

8   Check for a bad ground at the switches or the control unit.

9   If all but one lock solenoids operate, remove the trim panel from the affected door (see Chapter 11) and check for voltage at the solenoid while the lock switch is operated One of the wires should have voltage in the Lock position; the other should have voltage in the Unlock position.

10   If the inoperative solenoid is receiving voltage, replace the solenoid.

11   If the inoperative solenoid isn't receiving voltage, check the relay for an open or short in the wire between the lock solenoid and the control unit. **Note:** *It's common for wires to break in the portion of the harness between the body and door (opening and closing the door fatigues and eventually breaks the wires).*

Keyless entry system

Refer to illustration 24.14

12   The keyless entry system consists of a remote control transmitter that sends a coded infrared signal to a receiver which then operates the door lock system. On models so equipped, the transmitter may also engage the alarm system and provide a "panic" button which flashes the lights and blows the horn for emergencies.

13   Replace the transmitter batteries when the red LED light on the case doesn't light when the button is pushed. As the batteries deteriorate with age, the distance at which the remote transmitter operates will diminish.

14   Use a coin or small screwdriver to carefully separate the case halves for battery replacement **(see illustration)**.

15   Replace the two lithium batteries with the same type as originally installed, observing the polarity diagram on the case.

16   Snap the case halves together.

24.14 Separate the case halves on the remote transmitter (arrows) using a fine bladed screwdriver

25 Convertible top - general information

Note: *This information is general in nature, as it is intended to apply to all vehicle types, years and models.*

Adjustments

Note: *The following are typical adjustments. Some of these adjustments may not be provided for on your vehicle.*

Latches

The latches secure the convertible top frame to the upper edge of the windshield frame. If the latches are too loose, the top will rattle and move side to side. If the latches are too tight, they will be difficult or impossible to secure. The hooks on some latches are threaded so they can be screwed in or out to tighten or loosen the latch; pliers are often necessary, so make sure you protect the finish of the hook with a rag. Other latches have set-screws that lock the hooks in place - loosen the set-screws (usually with an Allen wrench), position the hooks as desired, then tighten the set-screws.

Also keep in mind that weatherstrip is attached to the front edge of the top. As this weatherstrip deteriorates over time, it will cause the latches and the front edge of the convertible top to become loose. The proper fix for this problem is to replace the deteriorated weatherstrip, which will also reduce wind noise.

Assist springs

Assist springs are attached between the rear of the top framework and the vehicle body. The springs allow the top to be raised and lowered slowly and evenly, without excessive effort in either direction. If the springs are too loose or too tight, they can cause the top to move very quickly in one direction and very slowly in the other direction. Often, the springs can be loosened or tightened by turning threaded adjusters. The springs are sometimes difficult to locate, especially when they travel into the trunk area or are covered by fabric. Search along the rear portion of the

framework and remove any access covers.

Some newer vehicles use gas-filled assist struts in place of springs. These struts are similar in design to the gas-filled support struts used to raise and support the hood on many newer vehicles. While these struts are not adjustable, they do lose their gas charge over time and become less effective. Replace the struts if they are not doing their job.

Center joint

On most vehicles, the center joints of the top framework can be adjusted to align the top weatherstrip with the side windows. This adjustment also slightly affects the forward "reach" of the top. The center-joint adjustment changes the angle between the forward and rear sections of the top framework at each side.

To visualize this adjustment, imagine a standard, flat door hinge lying flat on a table top. If you grasp the hinge on each side at its center pivot and lift slightly, the hinge will flex and appear as an arch, with only its ends touching the table - this also shortens the overall length of the hinge. In this analogy, the hinge plates are the front and rear framework sections and the lifting of the center pivot is the center-joint adjustment.

To make this adjustment, it is usually necessary to position the top at approximately its mid-point between raised and lowered. The adjustment mechanism is located at the joint between the front and rear frame sections on each side. The adjuster usually looks like a notched wheel with a set-screw that secures it in position, although some adjusters are a simple screw-and-locknut setup. Mark the position of the adjuster (in case you have to return to the original setting), then loosen or remove the set-screw or locknut. Rotate the wheel or screw, which will sometimes require an Allen wrench. Usually, you'll make the adjustments in the same small increments, side-to-side, until the correct adjustment is achieved. Raise and lower the top after each small adjustment to check alignment.

If the top alignment is not equal side-to-side (compare the alignment of the top to the upper edges of the side windows on each side), adjust one side more than the other to get the proper adjustment.

Adjusting the center joints also changes the height of the top's front edge, so it is usually necessary to adjust the control link after making a center-joint adjustment.

Control link

This adjustment affects both the forward "reach" of the top and the height of the front edge of the top (how high it sits above the windshield frame before the latches are secured). The control link is located at the rear of the top assembly, usually near the main pivot point. Various methods are used to provide adjustment at the control link, such as slotted mounting screw holes and wheel-type adjusters.

With the top down, locate the adjusters, mark their positions, then remove the set-

screws or loosen the mounting bolts. Raise the top, then move the adjusters to provide a slight gap between the front edge of the top and the window frame. Walk all around the vehicle to make sure the adjustment is even from side to side. If it is not even, adjust the low side up until it is even. When adjustment is complete, tighten the set-screws or mounting bolts.

Front frame

Some models have separate framework at the forward end of the top assembly that is adjustable by virtue of slotted mounting bolt holes. If, after all other adjustments are carried out, the alignment pins on the top are too far forward or backward to properly engage the holes in the windshield frame, adjust the frame as follows:

Retract the top part-way, loosen the bolts, slide the framework evenly forward or backward, tighten the bolts, then raise the top and check alignment again. Repeat this process until correct alignment is achieved.

Power-top troubleshooting

Power tops are operated by two hydraulic cylinders that are mounted between the vehicle body (at the rear) and the convertible-top framework. The cylinders receive hydraulic pressure from an electric motor/pump assembly that is usually mounted behind the rearmost seat or in the trunk. When the switch is pressed to raise the top, the motor drives the pump in a direction that sends hydraulic pressure to the bottom end of each hydraulic cylinder, driving the pistons out of the cylinders, which raises the top. When the switch is pressed to lower the top, the motor turns in the opposite direction, sending hydraulic pressure to the top of each cylinder, driving the pistons down and lowering the top.

As a first step in troubleshooting, listen for the whirring sound of the motor as the switch is pressed. If there is no sound from the motor, proceed to *Electrical Troubleshooting.* If you can hear the motor running but the top does not raise, proceed to *Hydraulic/mechanical troubleshooting.*

Hydraulic/mechanical troubleshooting

Mechanical and hydraulic problems will cause the top to not open (or close) or to get stuck part-way through the process. If the motor is operating normally, there are generally two possible causes for these problems: 1) A hydraulic system malfunction (low fluid level, air in the system, inadequate pump pressure) or 2) A mechanical binding in the top framework.

Hydraulic system fluid level check

Locate the hydraulic motor/pump attached to the floor behind the rearmost seat or in the trunk. The motor/pump is usually a canister-shaped assembly, approximately 12-inches long. It will have an electrical connector and hoses attached to it. On the side or end of the motor/pump assembly will be a

27.1a The driver's side airbag (arrow) is located in the steering column horn pad

27.1b The passenger's airbag (arrow) is located on the dashboard above the glove box

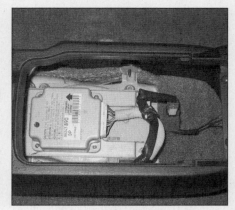

27.1c The airbag control module is located under the center console and mounted to the floorpan

screw-type check plug. Place rags underneath the check plug. Unscrew the plug and verify the fluid level is within 1/4-inch of the bottom of the check-plug hole (the procedure is very much like checking differential fluid level). If necessary, add fluid through the check-plug hole to bring the fluid level to normal. Check your owner's manual for specific fluid recommendations, but generally, Dexron III Automatic Transmission Fluid (ATF) is used. If you find a low fluid level, check for leaks at the pump, hoses and hydraulic cylinders.

Hydraulic system bleeding

Air can get into the hydraulic system through leaks and if the fluid level is too low. Air in the system will generally cause excess noise and, in extreme cases, will cause the top to raise or lower only part-way.

To bleed the hydraulic system, first check the fluid level, then start the engine and raise and lower the top. If the fluid has excessive air, the top might not raise or lower, so you will need an assistant to hold the switch while you raise and lower the top slowly by hand. Raise and lower the top several times to work out all the air. Check the fluid level again, since it will likely drop as the air is expelled.

Checking for binding

If the hydraulic system seems to be operating properly, disconnect the hydraulic cylinders from the top framework and operate the top by hand. The top should go up and down smoothly, without excessive effort.
If the top binds during manual operation, make sure all adjustments are correct and spray penetrating lubricant on all framework joints.

If the top is operating smoothly during manual operation but will not raise properly with the hydraulic cylinders connected, suspect a pump/motor assembly that is not providing adequate pressure.

Electrical troubleshooting

If you cannot hear the motor running when the switch is pressed, first check for

blown fuses and fusible links. If the fuses and fusible links are all OK, disconnect the electrical connector at the motor. Connect a 12-volt test-light to ground and probe each terminal of the disconnected wiring-harness connector while an assistant operates the switch. There should be power (light will illuminate) at one terminal with the switch in the TOP UP position and power at the other terminal with the switch in the TOP DOWN position.

If there is power, but the motor does not operate, check the ground circuit. On most models, there is a third wire from the motor that is attached to ground somewhere near the motor. It is common for this ground connection to become loose or corroded, causing the motor to stop functioning. If the motor is receiving power and has a good ground, but it is still not functioning, the motor itself is the problem. **Note:** O*n some models, there is no separate ground connection. A relay in the system alternately grounds one wire and powers the other, depending on switch position. On models with this system, check for a solid ground at the relay.*

If there is no power at the motor, check for power at the three switch terminals by backprobing with the electrical connector still attached. There should be power at one of the switch terminals with the switch in neutral position, and power at two of the terminals with the switch in either the TOP UP or TOP DOWN position. If there is no power at the switch, the problem lies in the wiring between the battery and the switch. If there is power at only one terminal in the TOP UP or TOP DOWN position, the switch is bad. If the switch tests are OK, the problem lies in the relay(s) (if equipped) or the wiring.

26 Daytime Running Lights (DRL) - general information

The Daytime Running Lights (DRL) system used on Canadian models illuminates the headlights whenever the engine is running. The only exception is with the engine run-

ning and the parking brake engaged. Once the parking brake is released, the lights will remain on as long as the ignition switch is on, even if the parking brake is later applied.

The DRL system supplies reduced power to the headlights so they won't be too bright for daytime use, while prolonging headlight life.

27 Airbag system - general information

General information

Refer to illustrations 27.1a, 27.1b and 27.1c

1   All models are equipped with a Supplemental Restraint System (SRS), more commonly known as an airbag. This system is designed to protect the driver, and the front seat passenger, from serious injury in the event of a head-on or frontal collision. It consists of airbag sensors mounted on the front unibody frame members and a sensing/diagnostic module mounted in the center of the vehicle, near the floor console. The airbag assemblies are mounted on the steering wheel **(see illustration)** and the right side top surface of the passenger's side dash **(see illustration)**. Some later models are equipped with side-impact airbags located in the sides of the seat backs, and "curtain" airbags located in the headliner side rails. The airbag control module is mounted in the center console **(see illustration)**. **Note:** *Only 1995 and 1996 models are equipped with front airbag sensors mounted on the front of the frame. All other models incorporate a safing G sensor and an analog G sensor within the airbag control module to detect G force impact.*

Airbag module
Driver's side

2   The airbag inflator module contains a housing incorporating the cushion (airbag) and inflator unit, mounted in the center of the steering wheel The inflator assembly is mounted on the back of the housing over a

hole through which gas is expelled, inflating the bag almost instantaneously when an electrical signal is sent from the system. A spiral cable assembly on the steering column under the steering wheel carries this signal to the module.

3   This spiral cable assembly can transmit an electrical signal regardless of steering wheel position. The igniter in the airbag converts the electrical signal to heat and ignites the powder, which inflates the bag.

Passenger's side

4   The airbag is mounted above the glove compartment and is designated by the letters SRS (Supplemental Restraint System). It consists of an inflator containing an igniter, a bag assembly, a reaction housing and a trim cover.

5   The airbag is considerably larger than the steering wheel-mounted unit and is supported by the steel reaction housing. The trim cover is textured and painted to match the instrument panel and has a molded seam which splits when the bag inflates.

Sensing and diagnostic module

6   The sensing and diagnostic module supplies the current to the airbag system in the event of the collision, even if battery power is cut off. It checks this system every time the vehicle is started, causing the "SRS" light to go on then off, if the system is operating properly. If there is a fault in the system, the light will go on and stay on, flash, or the dash will make a beeping sound. If this happens, the vehicle should be taken to your dealer immediately for service.

Disarming the system and other precautions

Refer to illustration 27.10

Warning: *Failure to follow these precautions could result in accidental deployment of the airbag and personal injury.*

7   Whenever working in the vicinity of the steering wheel, steering column or any of the other SRS system components, the system must be disarmed. To disarm the system:

a) *Point the wheels straight ahead and turn the key to the Lock position.*

b) *Disconnect the cable from the negative battery terminal or remote ground terminal, then the positive cable from the positive battery terminal or the remote positive jump-start connections (see Chapter 5, Section 1).*

c) *Wait at least two minutes for the back-up power supply to be depleted.*

8   Whenever handling an airbag module, always keep the airbag opening (the trim side) pointed away from your body. Never place the airbag module on a bench or other surface with the airbag opening facing the surface. Always place the airbag module in a safe location with the airbag opening facing up.

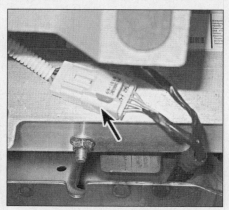

27.10 Location of the passenger side airbag yellow connector (arrow)

9   Never measure the resistance of any SRS component. An ohmmeter has a built-in battery supply that could accidentally deploy the airbag.

10   Never use electrical welding equipment on a vehicle equipped with an airbag without first disconnecting the yellow airbag connector, located under the steering column near the combination switch connector (driver's airbag) and behind the glove box (passenger's airbag) **(see illustration)**.

11   Never dispose of a live airbag module. Return it to a dealer service department or other qualified repair shop for safe deployment and disposal.

Component removal and installation

Driver's side airbag module and spiral cable

12   Refer to Chapter 10, *Steering wheel - removal and installation*, for the driver's side airbag module and spiral cable removal and installation procedures.

Passenger's side airbag module

Refer to illustration 27.15

13   Disarm the airbag system as described previously in this Section.

14   If you're working on a 2001 or later coupe, remove the glovebox (see Chapter 11). The airbag fasteners are now accessible. Remove the fasteners, unplug the electrical connector and detach the airbag module from the instrument panel. Be sure to heed the precautions outlined previously in this Section.

15   On all other models, lower glovebox door fully to gain access to the airbag, then unplug the electrical connector and remove the airbag module mounting fasteners **(see illustration)**. Be sure to heed the precautions outlined previously in this Section.

16   Installation is the reverse of the removal procedure. Tighten the airbag module mounting fasteners securely.

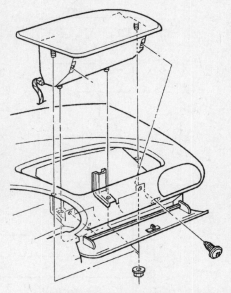

27.15 Passenger side airbag details on a 1999 convertible

Curtain airbag

17   This procedure will require the headliner to be removed. Have the curtain airbag replaced by a dealer service department.

28   Wiring diagrams - general information

Since it isn't possible to include all wiring diagrams for every year covered by this manual, the following diagrams are those that are typical and most commonly needed.

Prior to troubleshooting any circuits, check the fuse and circuit breakers (if equipped) to make sure they're in good condition. Make sure the battery is properly charged and check the cable connections (see Chapter 1).

When checking a circuit, make sure that all connectors are clean, with no broken or loose terminals. When unplugging a connector, do not pull on the wires. Pull only on the connector housings themselves. **Note:** *You may find that some of the wire colors in the wiring diagrams do not exactly match those on your vehicle. This is due to running changes made by the manufacturer from year-to-year and model-to-model. However, the circuitry, components and their terminals still function as shown on the diagrams; if you encounter a wire on your vehicle whose color doesn't match the corresponding circuit on the wiring diagram, pencil in the correct color on the diagram to help you avoid confusion.*

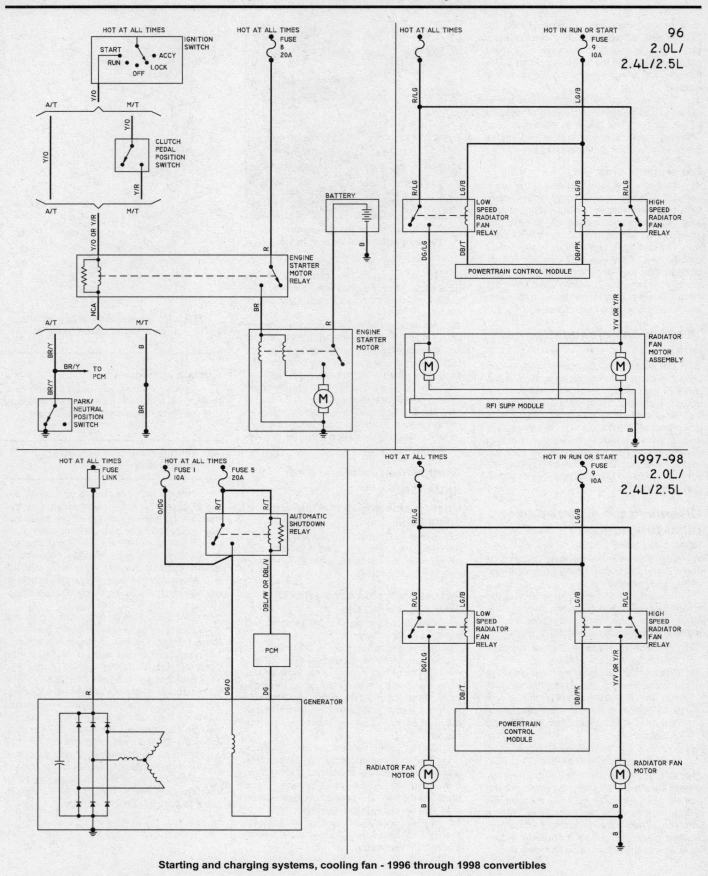

Starting and charging systems, cooling fan - 1996 through 1998 convertibles

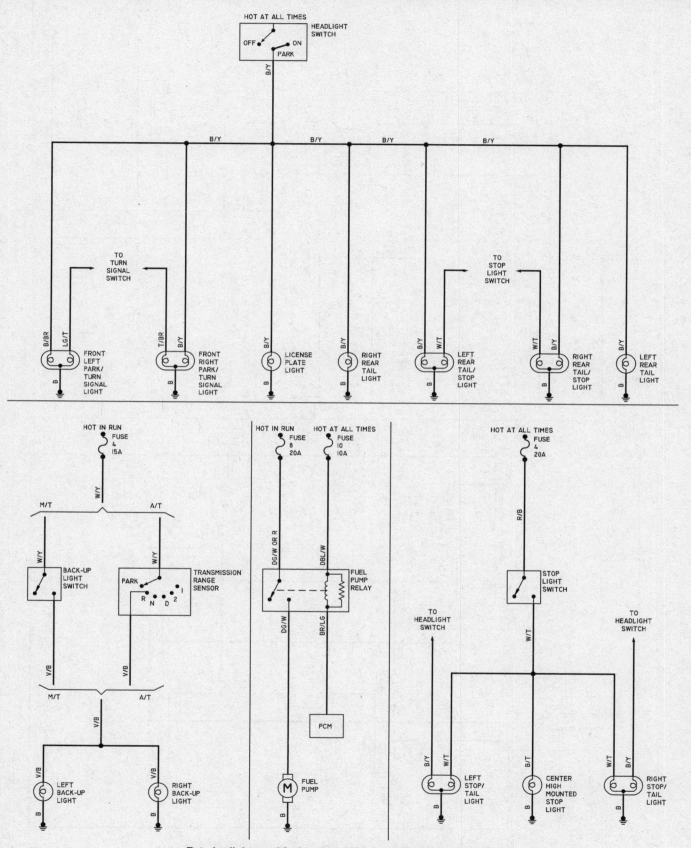

Exterior lights and fuel pump - 1996 through 1998 convertibles

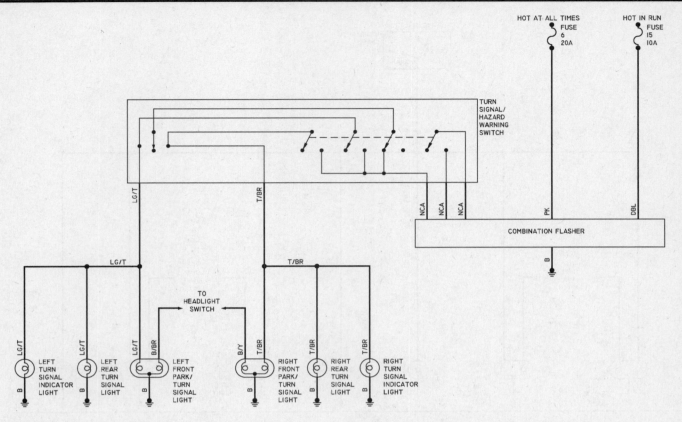

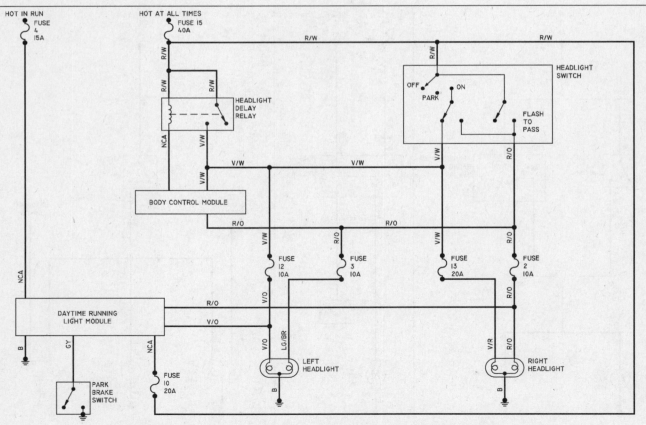

Turn signal/hazard warning lights, headlights - 1996 through 1998 convertibles

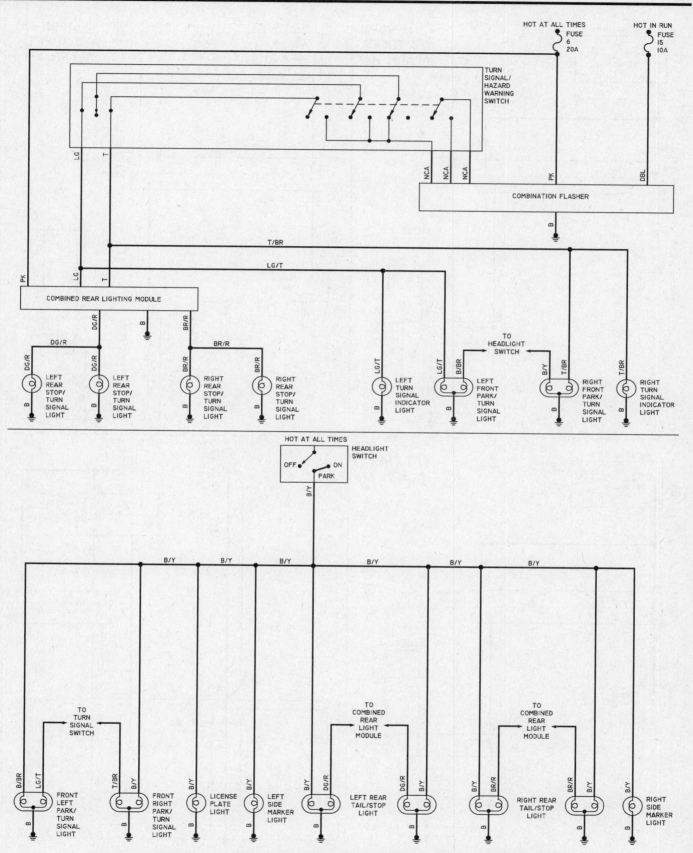

Turn signal/hazard warning lights, parking lights, brake lights - 1996 through 1998 convertibles

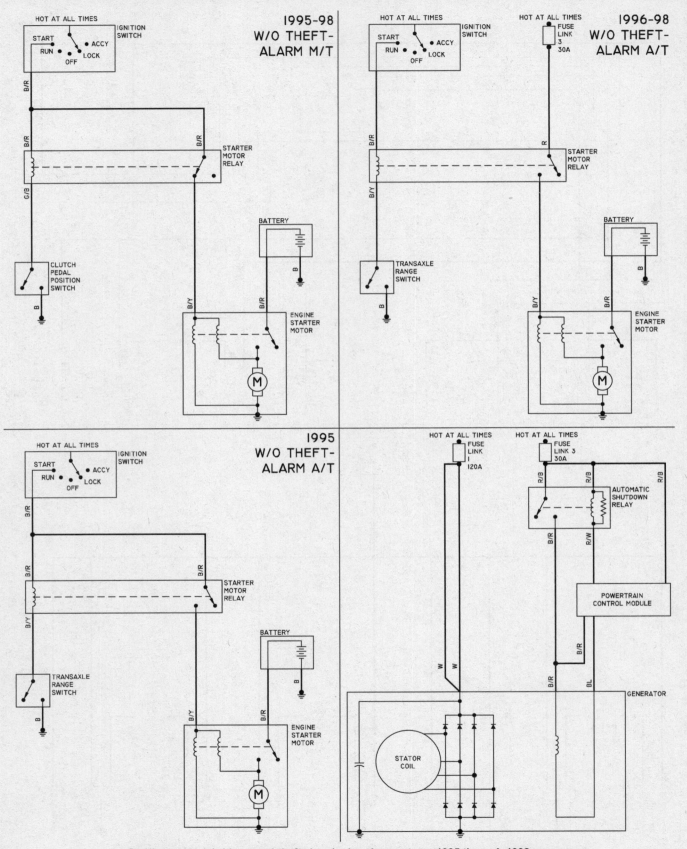

Starting system (without anti-theft alarm), charging system - 1995 through 1998 coupes

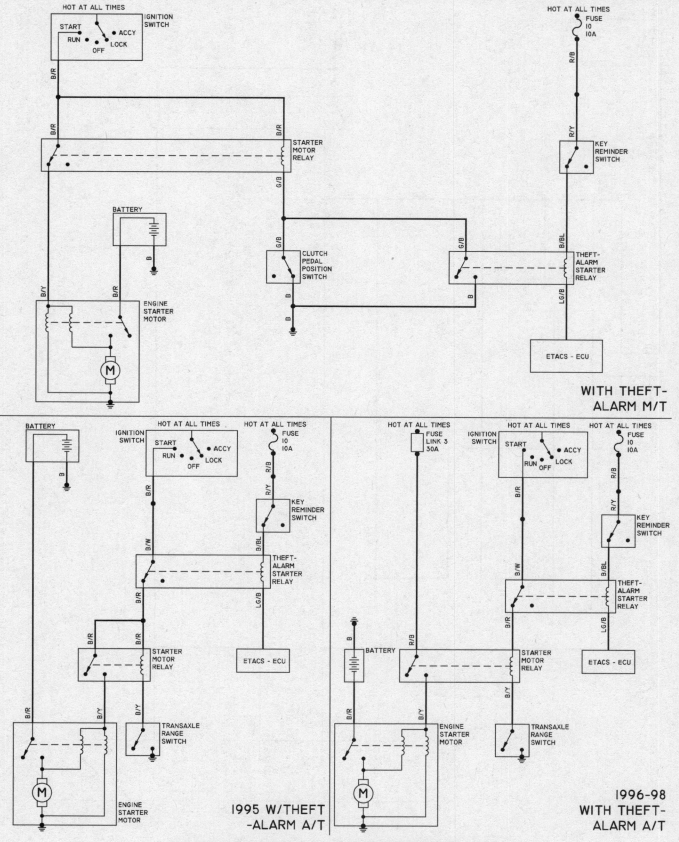

Starting system (with anti-theft alarm) - 1995 through 1998 coupes

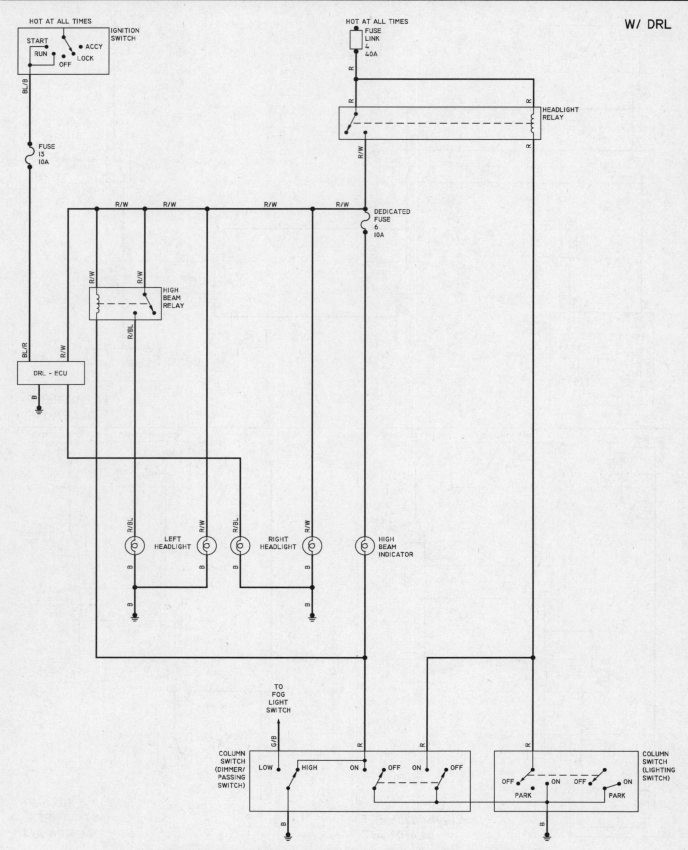

Headlight system (with Daytime Running Lights) - 1995 through 1998 coupes

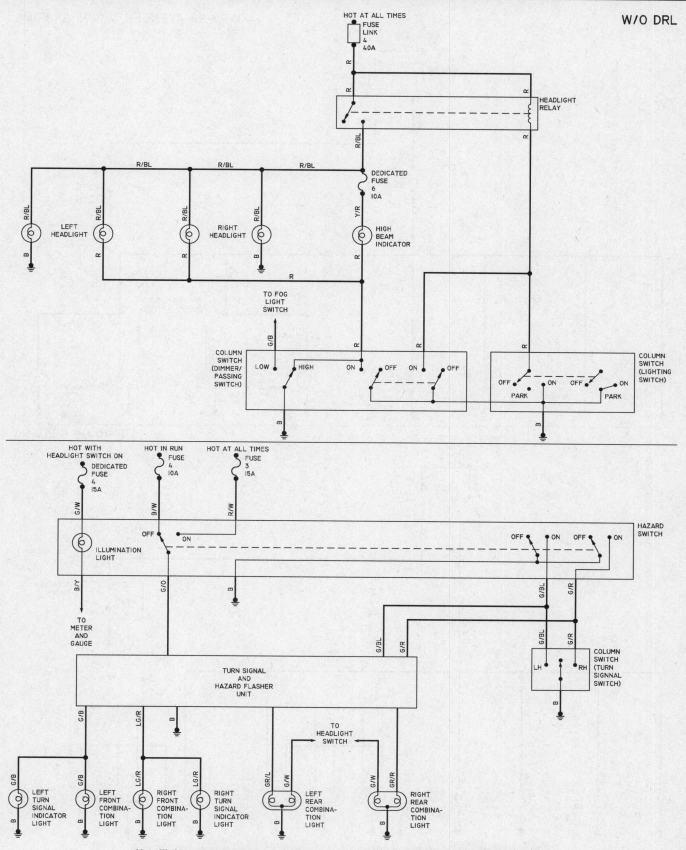

Headlight system (without Daytime Running Lights) - 1995 through 1998 coupes

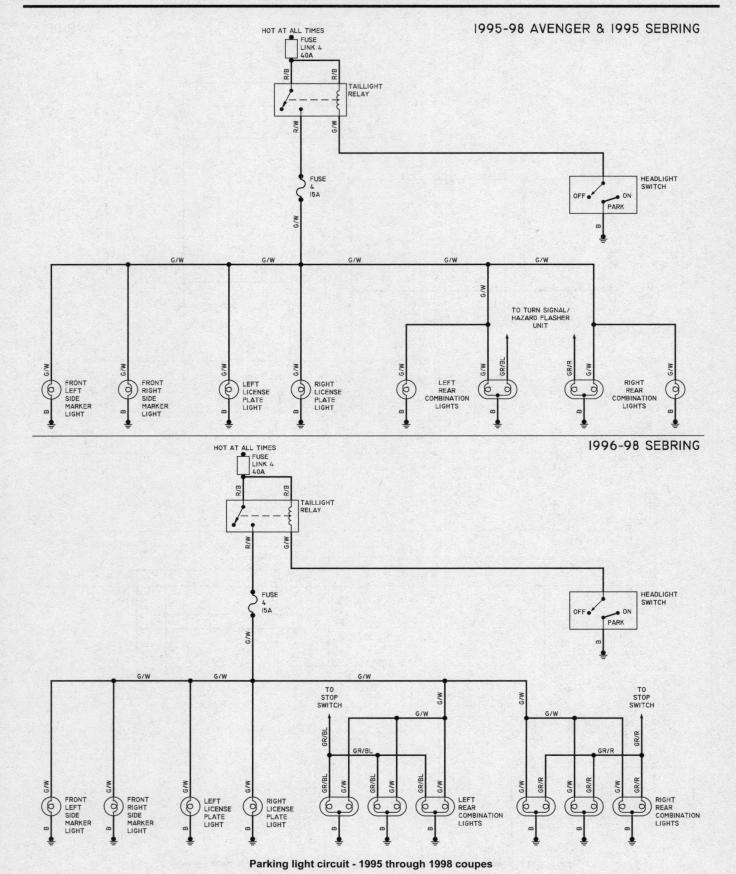

Parking light circuit - 1995 through 1998 coupes

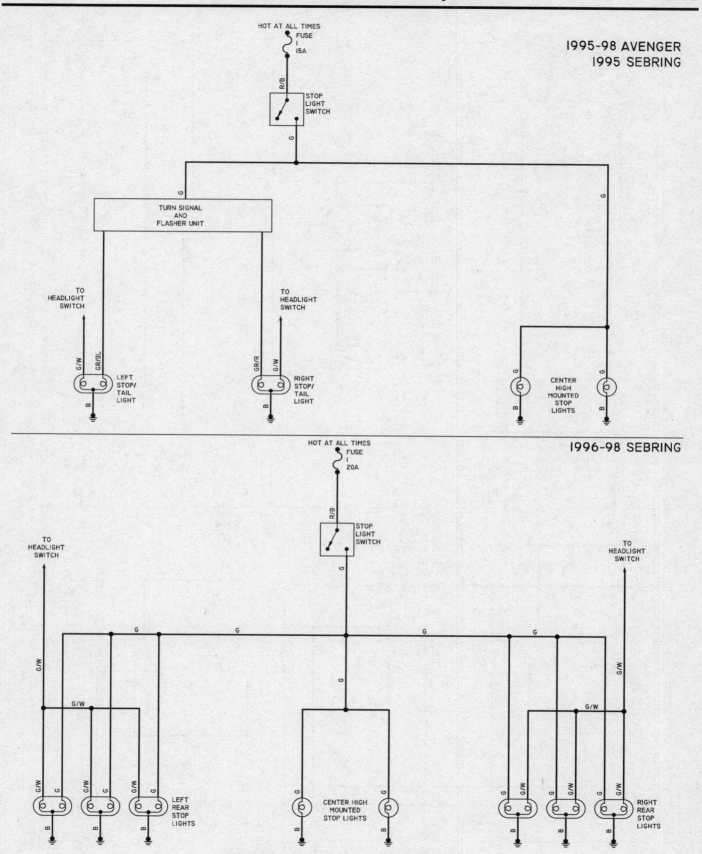

Brake light circuit - 1995 through 1998 coupes

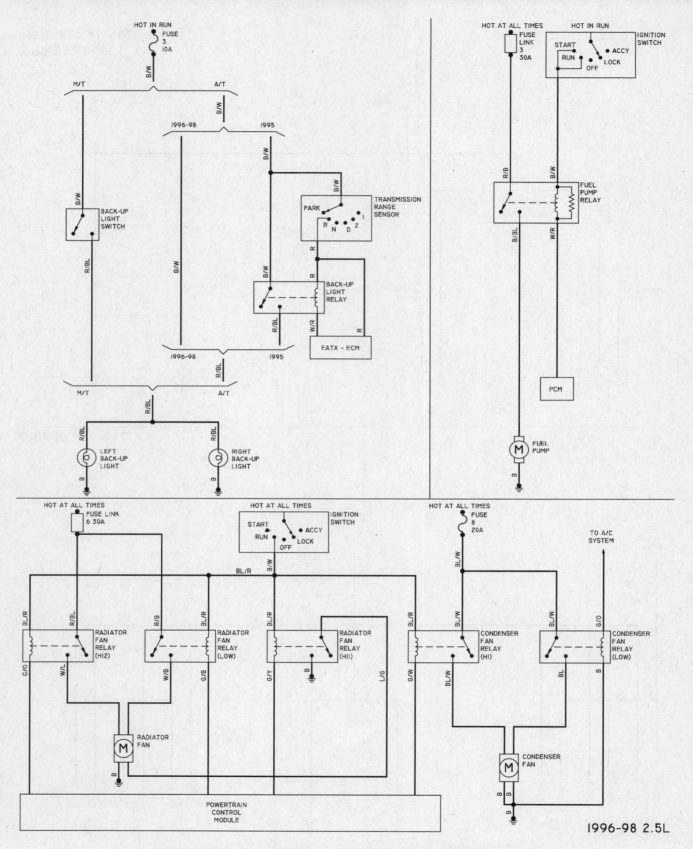

Back-up lights, fuel pump, engine cooling fan(s) - 1995 through 1998 coupes

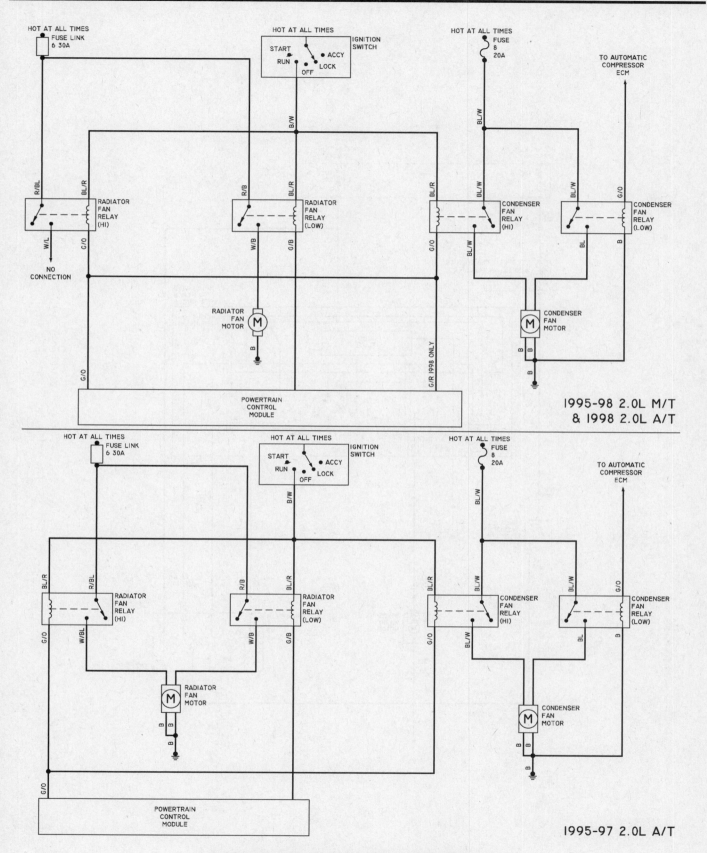

1995-98 2.0L M/T
& 1998 2.0L A/T

1995-97 2.0L A/T

Engine cooling fan(s) circuit - 1995 through 1998 coupes

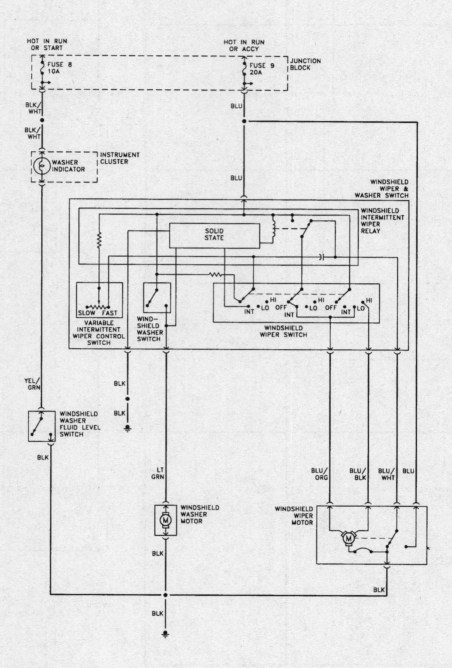

Wiper and washer systems - 1999 and 2000 coupe models

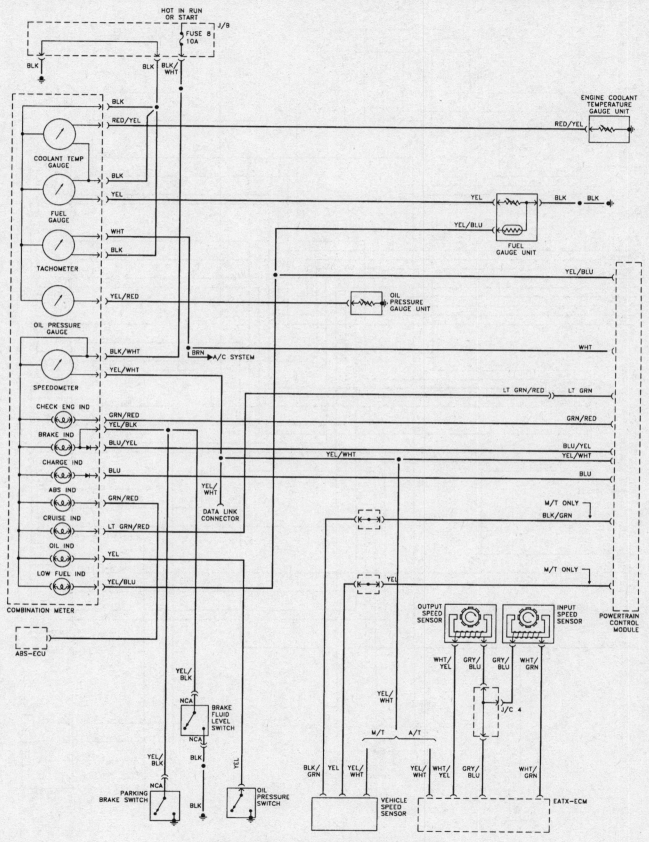

Warning systems - 1999 and 2000 coupe models

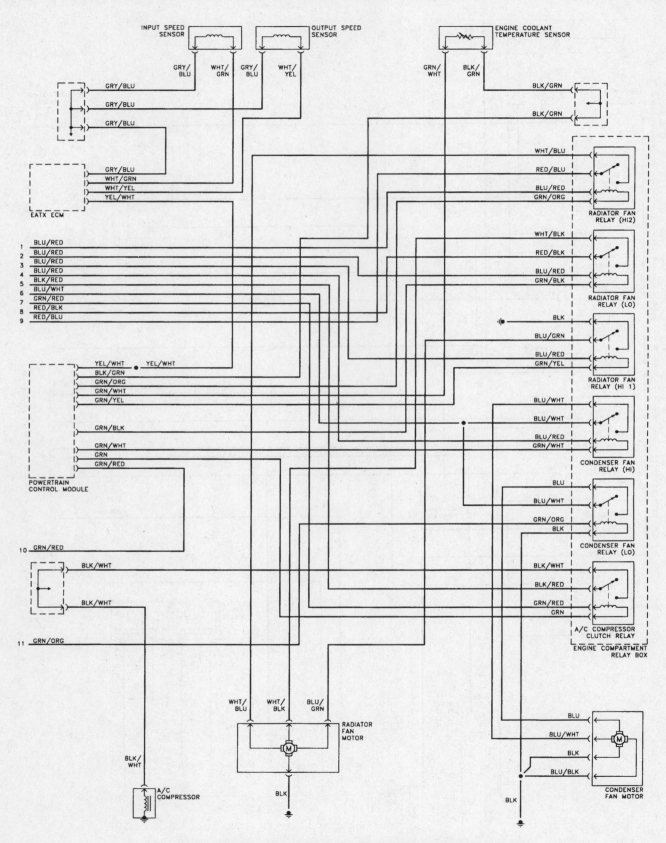

Air conditioning system - 1999 and 2000 2.5L V6 coupe models (1 of 2)

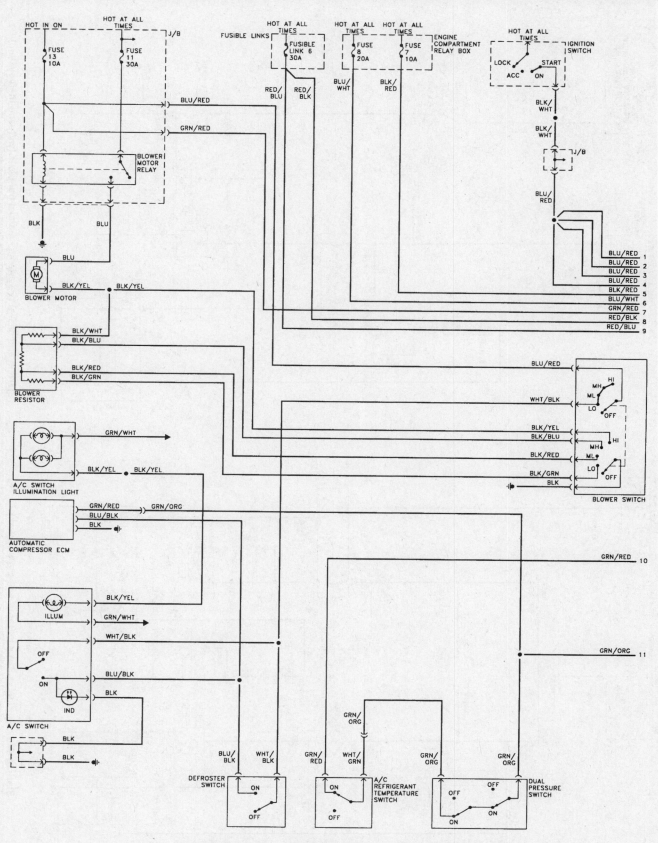

Air conditioning system - 1999 and 2000 2.5L V6 coupe models (2 of 2)

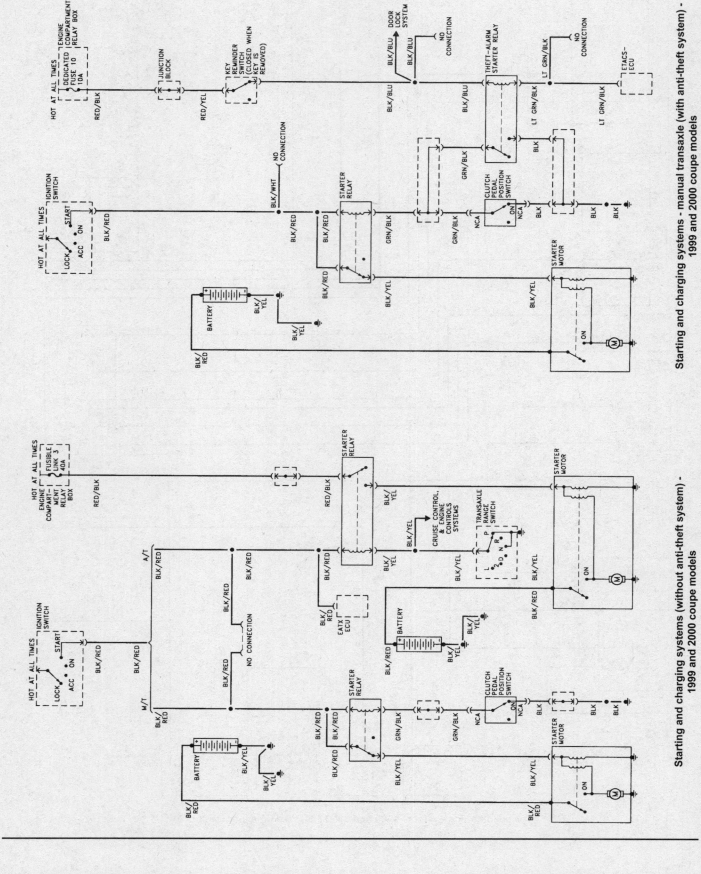

Starting and charging systems - manual transaxle (with anti-theft system) - 1999 and 2000 coupe models

Starting and charging systems (without anti-theft system) - 1999 and 2000 coupe models

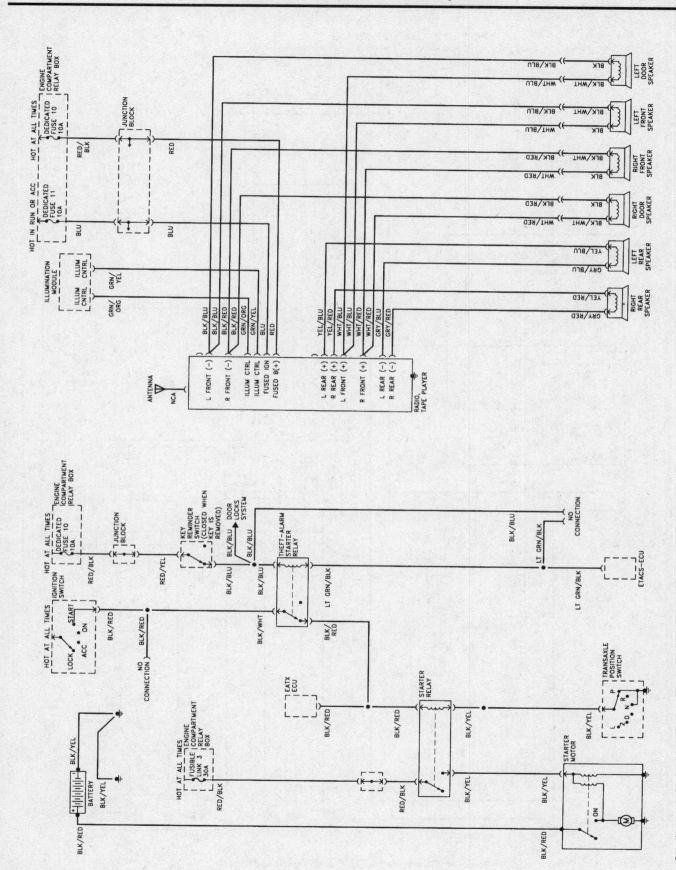

Radio system - 1999 and 2000 coupe models

Starting and charging systems - automatic transaxle (with anti-theft system) - 1999 and 2000 coupe models

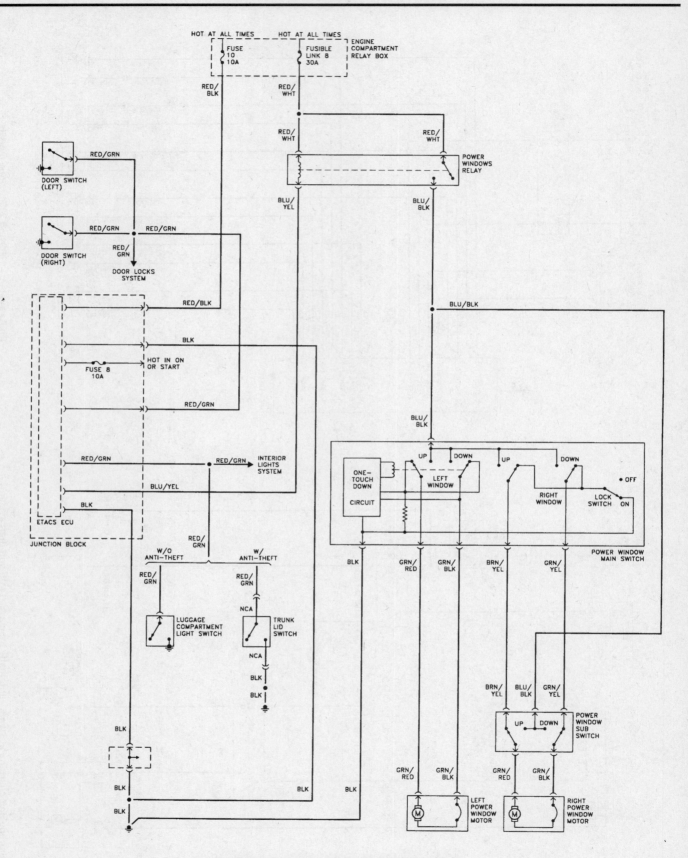

Power window systems - 1999 and 2000 coupe models

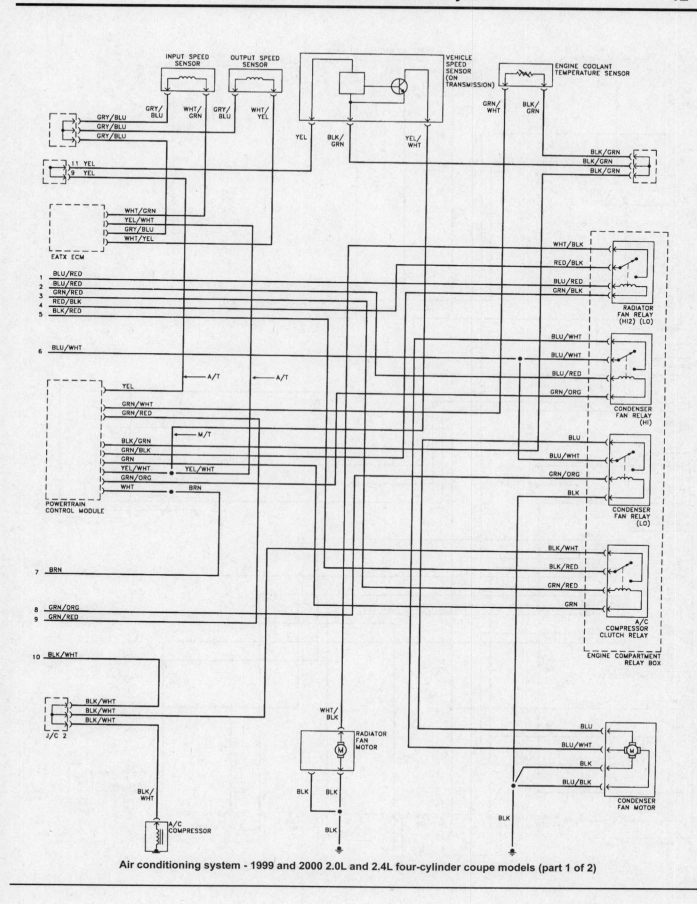

Air conditioning system - 1999 and 2000 2.0L and 2.4L four-cylinder coupe models (part 1 of 2)

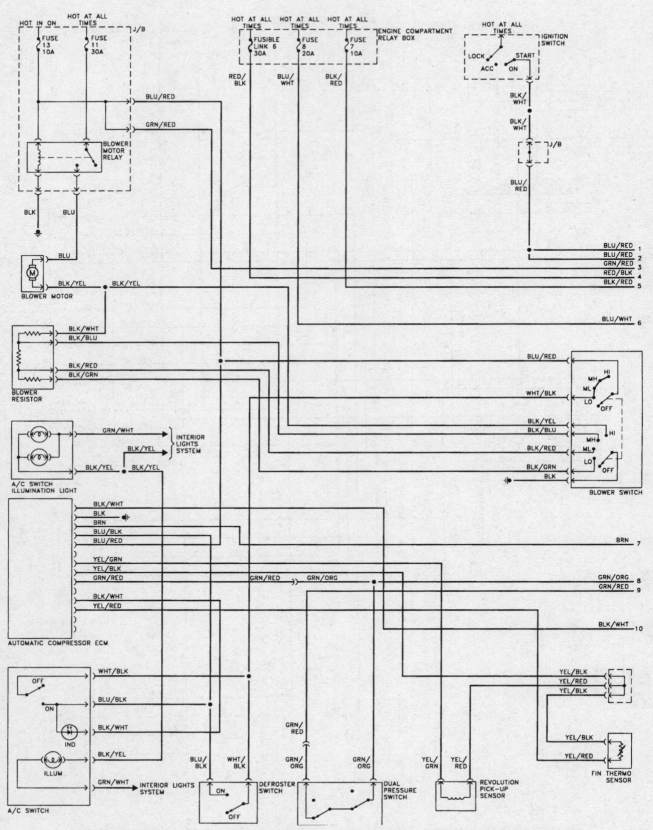

Air conditioning system - 1999 and 2000 2.0L and 2.4L four-cylinder coupe models (part 2 of 2)

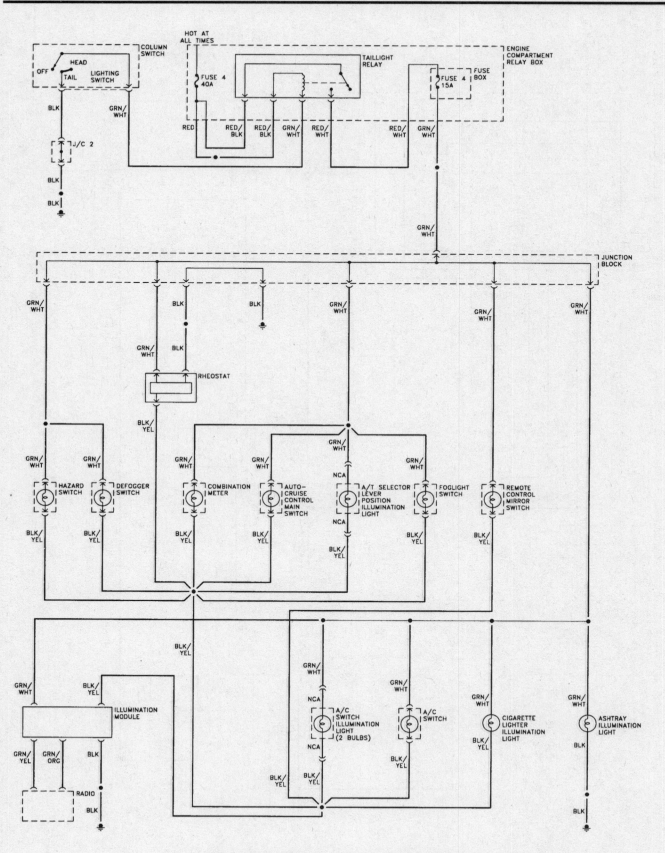

Instrument panel illumination system - 1999 and 2000 coupe models

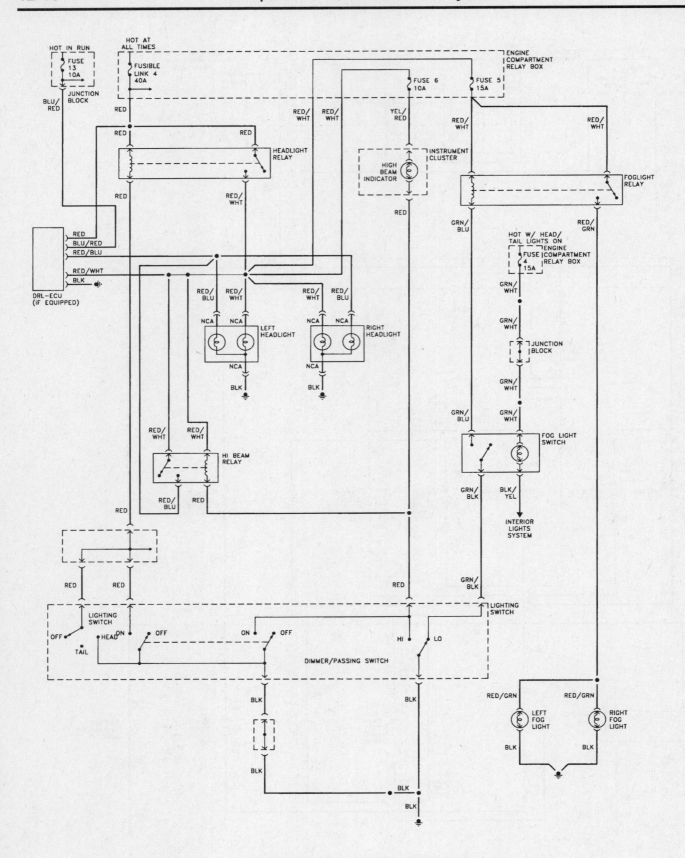

Headlight system - 1999 and 2000 coupe models

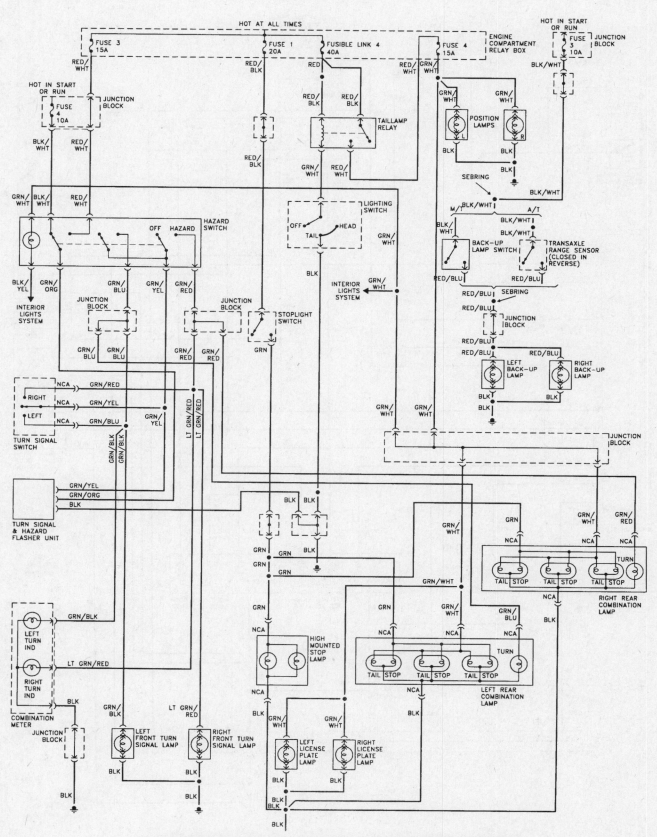

Exterior lighting system (except headlights) - 1999 and 2000 coupe models

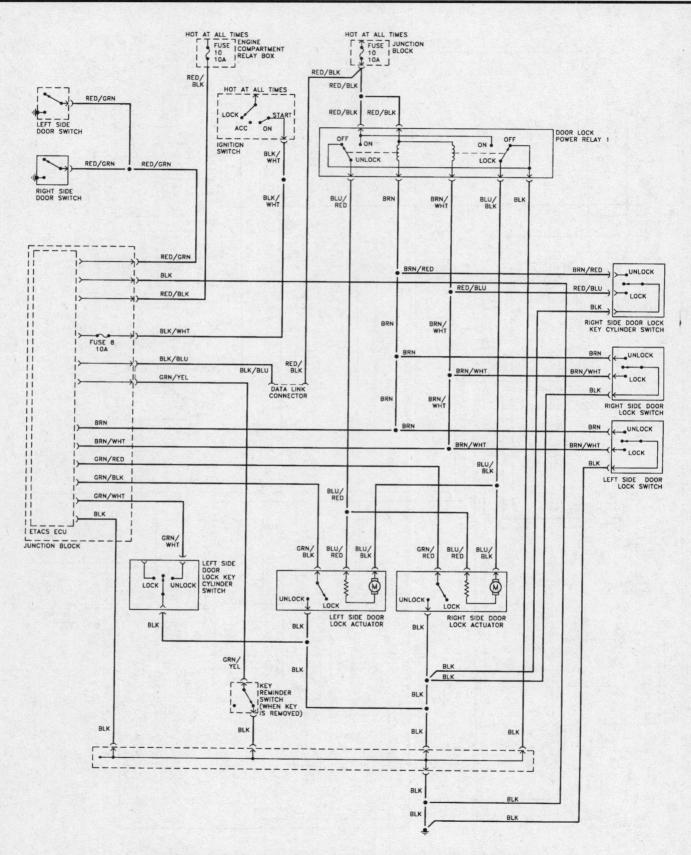

Power door lock system (without keyless entry) - 1999 and 2000 coupe models

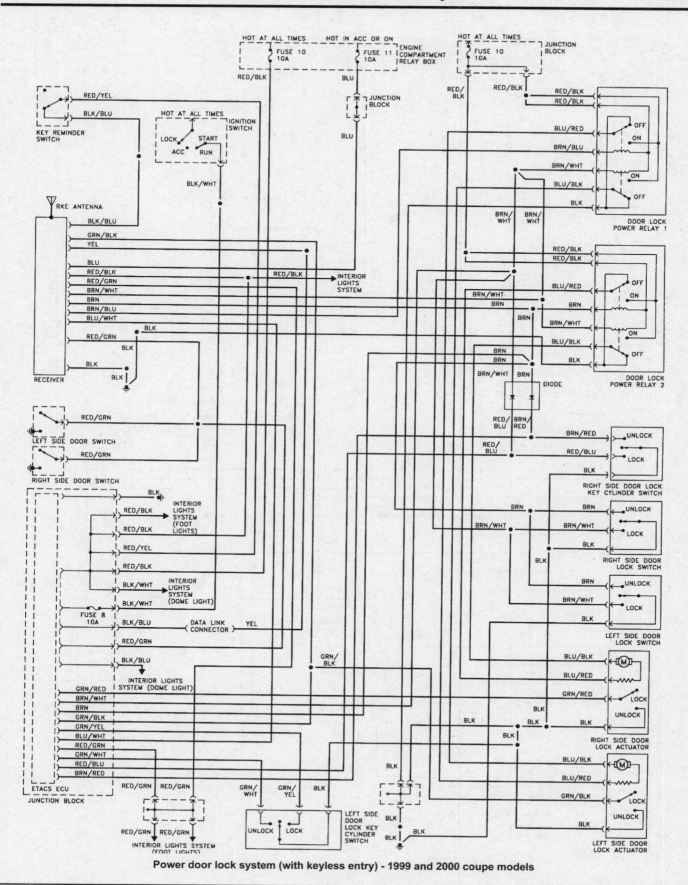

Power door lock system (with keyless entry) - 1999 and 2000 coupe models

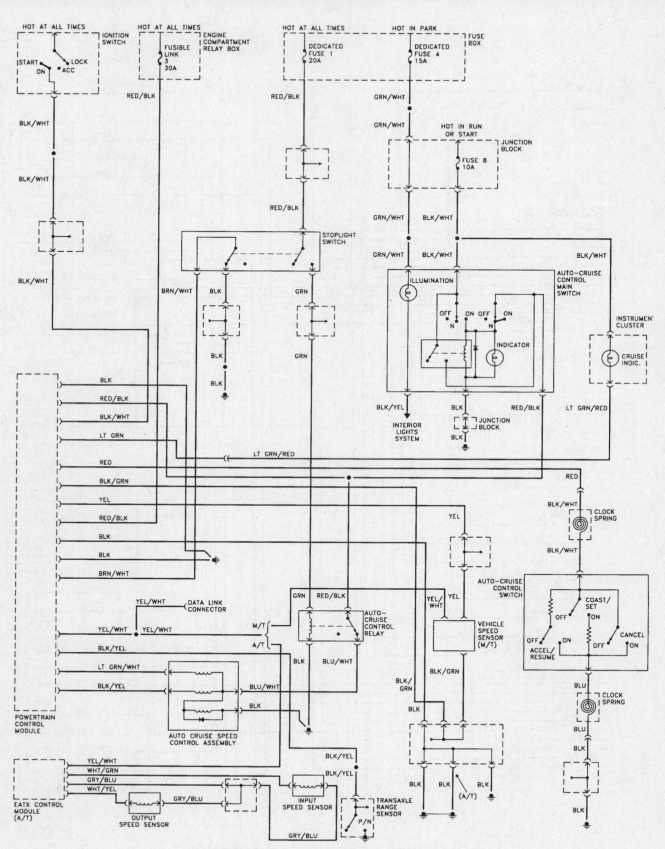

Cruise control system - 1999 and 2000 coupe models

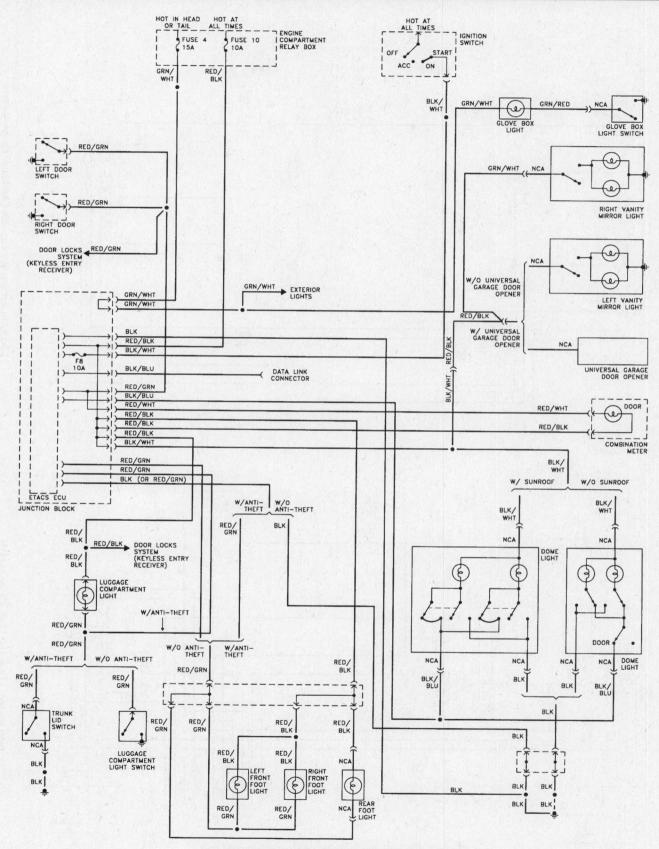

Courtesy light system - 1999 and 2000 coupe models

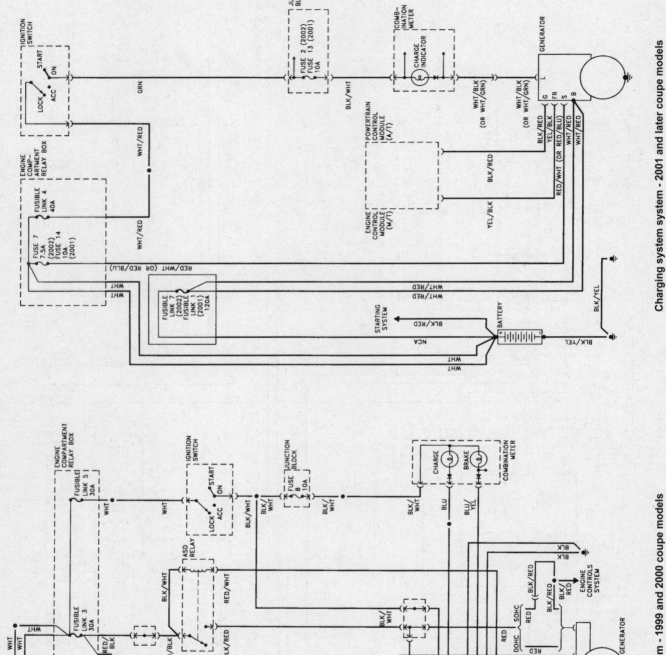

Charging system system - 2001 and later coupe models

Charging system - 1999 and 2000 coupe models

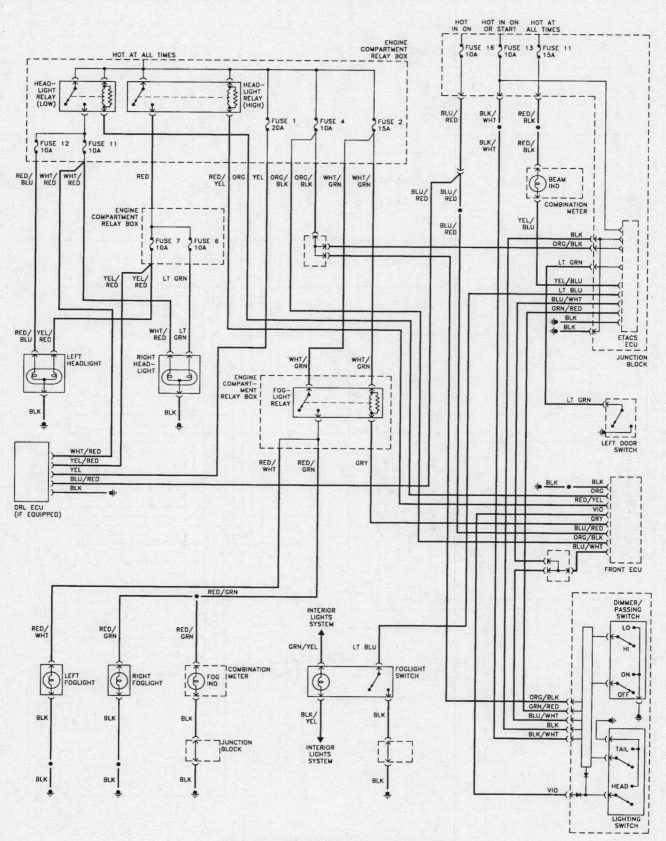

Exterior lighting system - 2001 coupe models

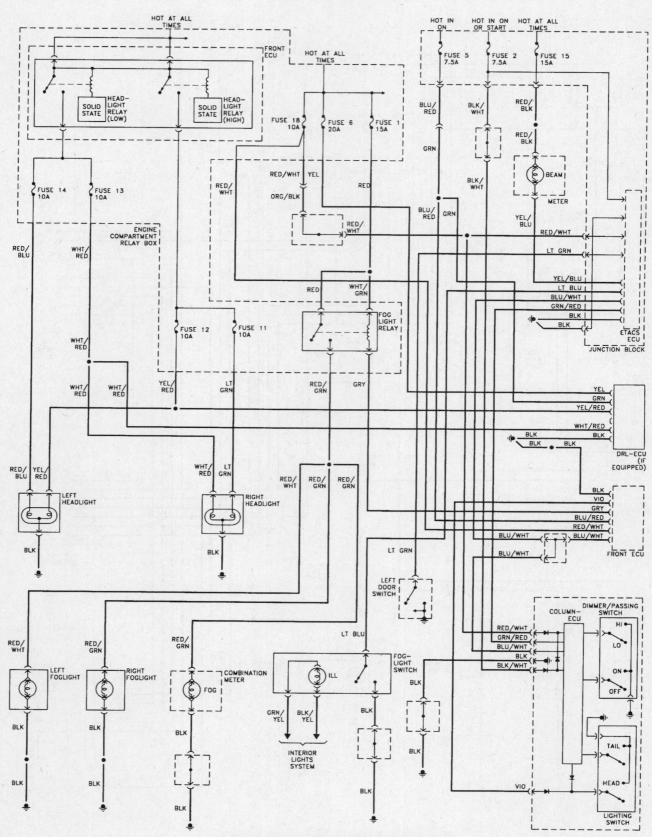

Exterior lighting system - 2002 coupe models

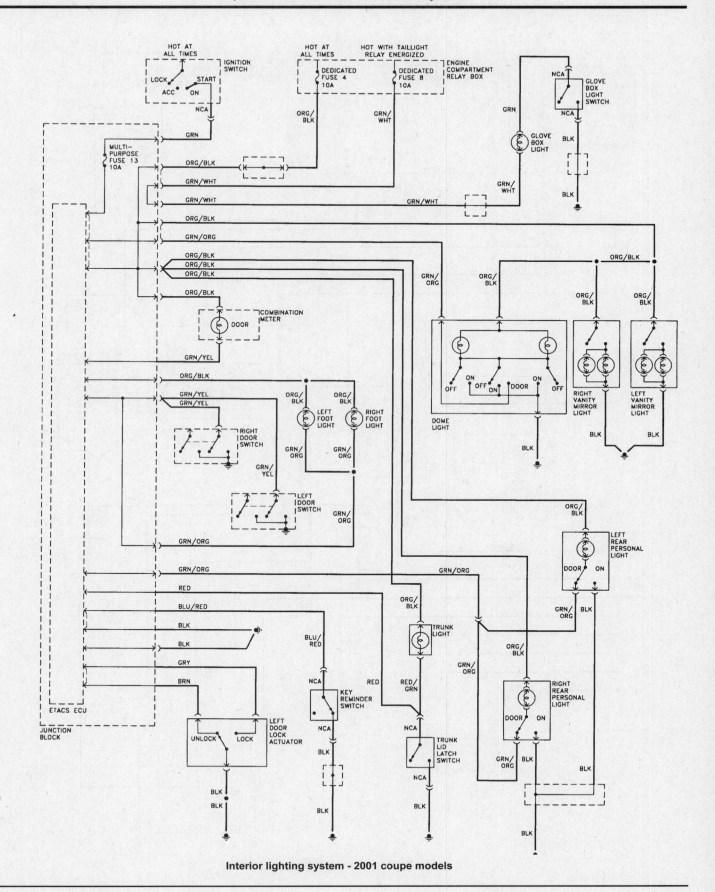

Interior lighting system - 2001 coupe models

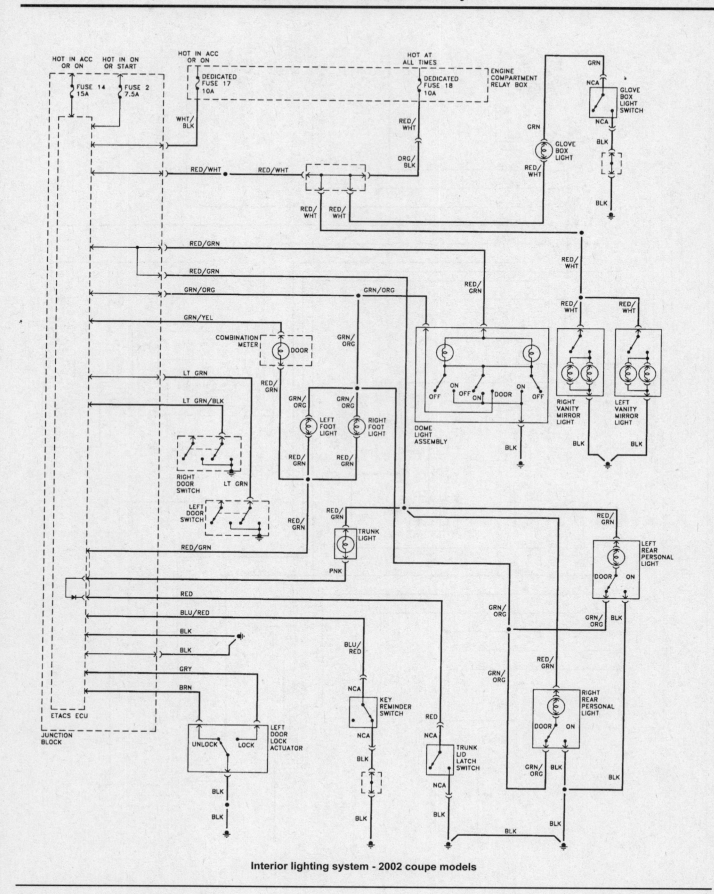

Interior lighting system - 2002 coupe models

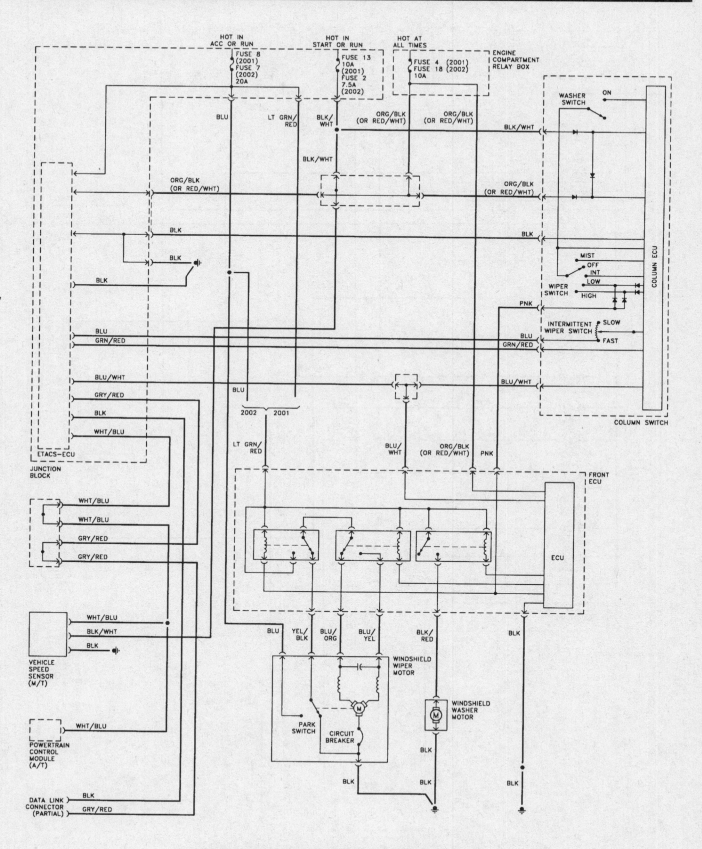

Wiper and washer systems - 2001 and later coupe models

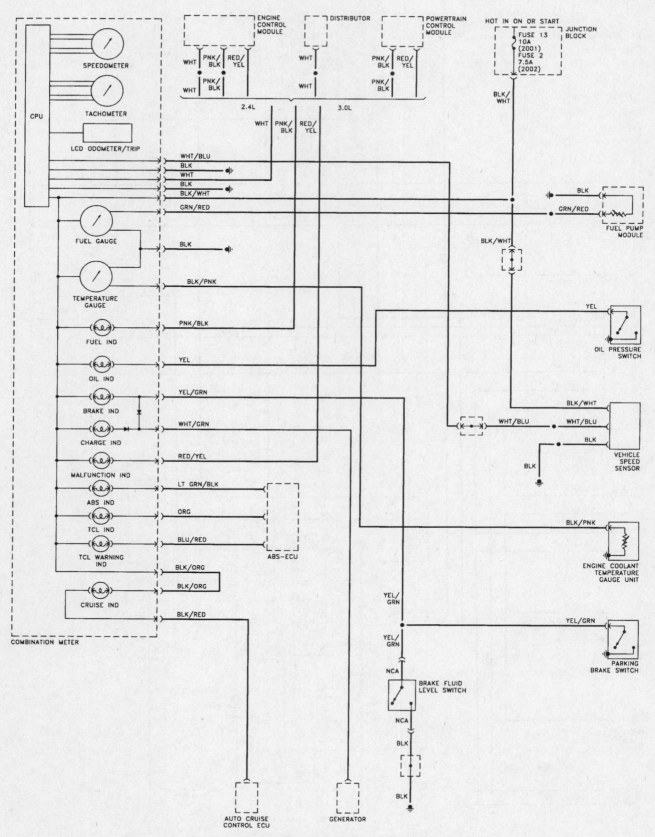

Warning systems - 2001 and later coupe models

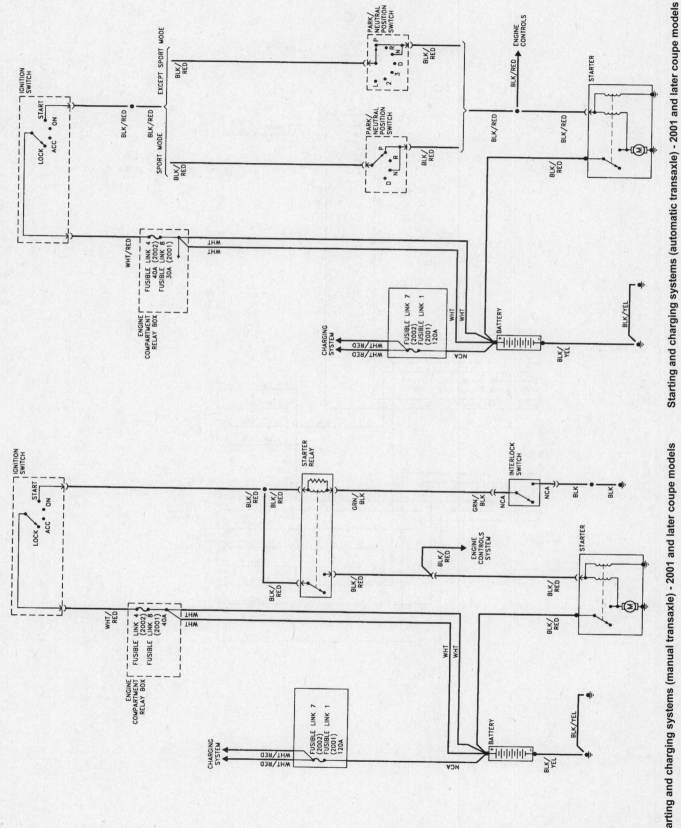

Starting and charging systems (automatic transaxle) - 2001 and later coupe models

Starting and charging systems (manual transaxle) - 2001 and later coupe models

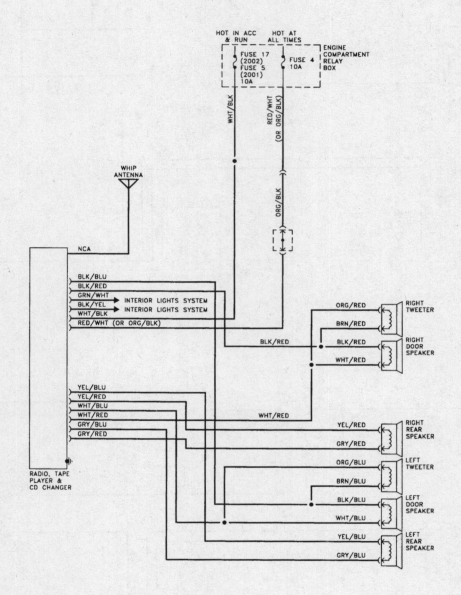

Radio system - 2001 and later coupe models

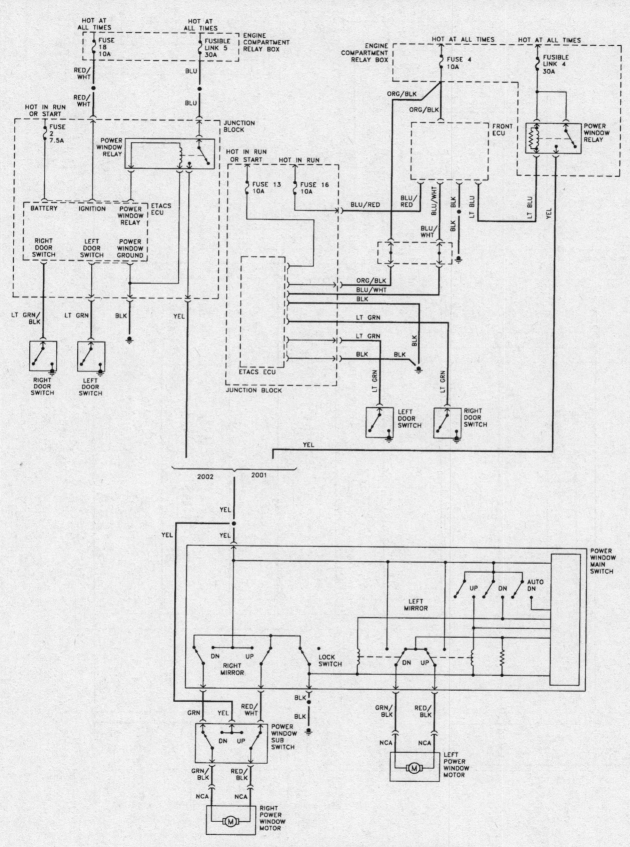

Power window system - 2001 and later coupe models

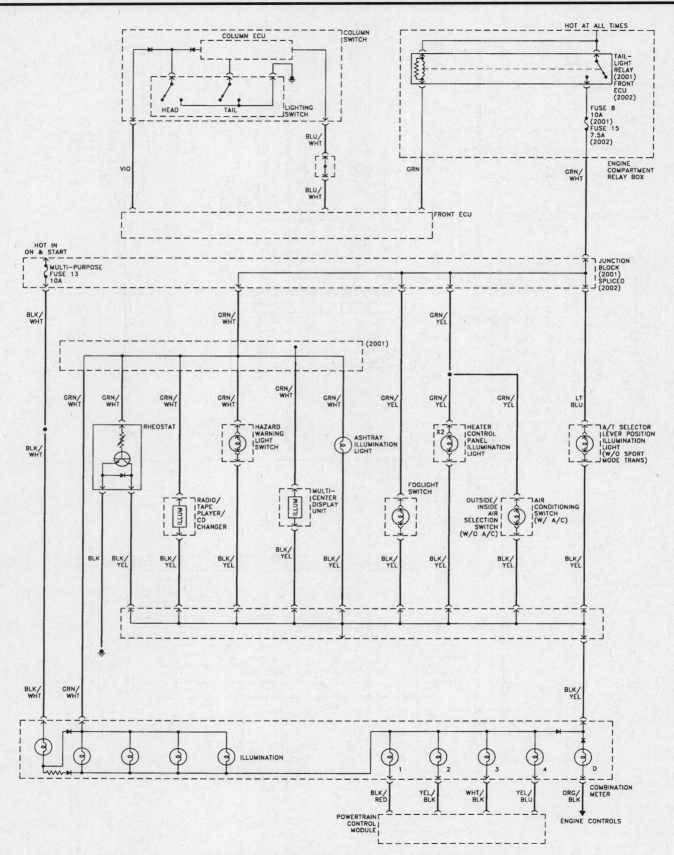

Interior lighting system - 2001 and later coupe models

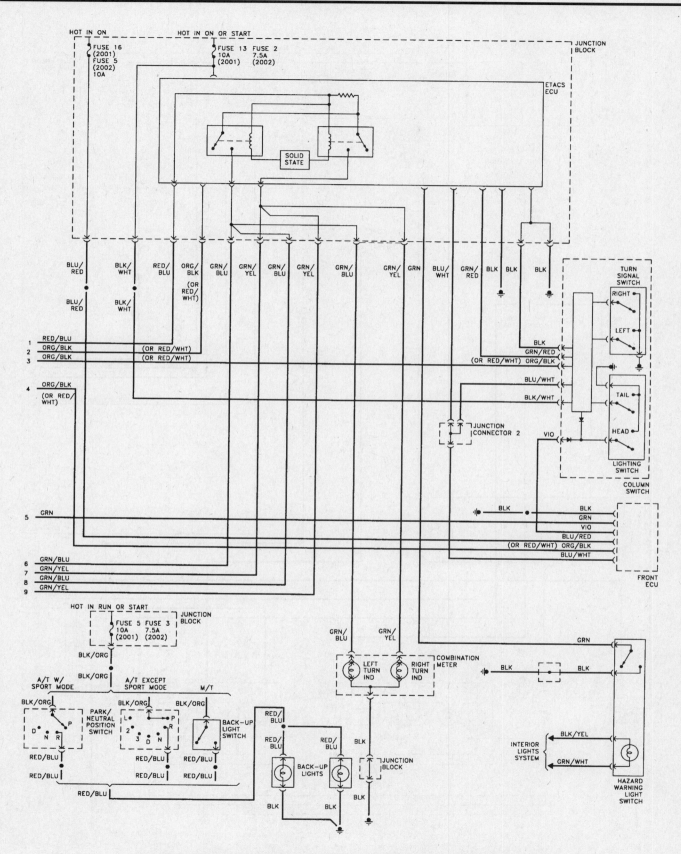

Exterior lighting system (except headlights) - 2001 and later coupe models (1 of 2)

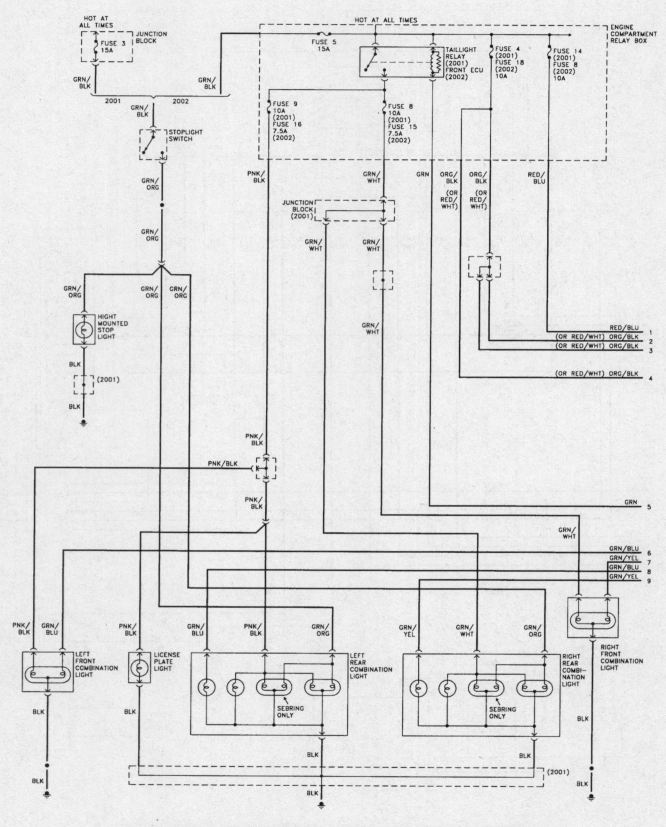

Exterior lighting system (except headlights) - 2001 and later coupe models (2 of 2)

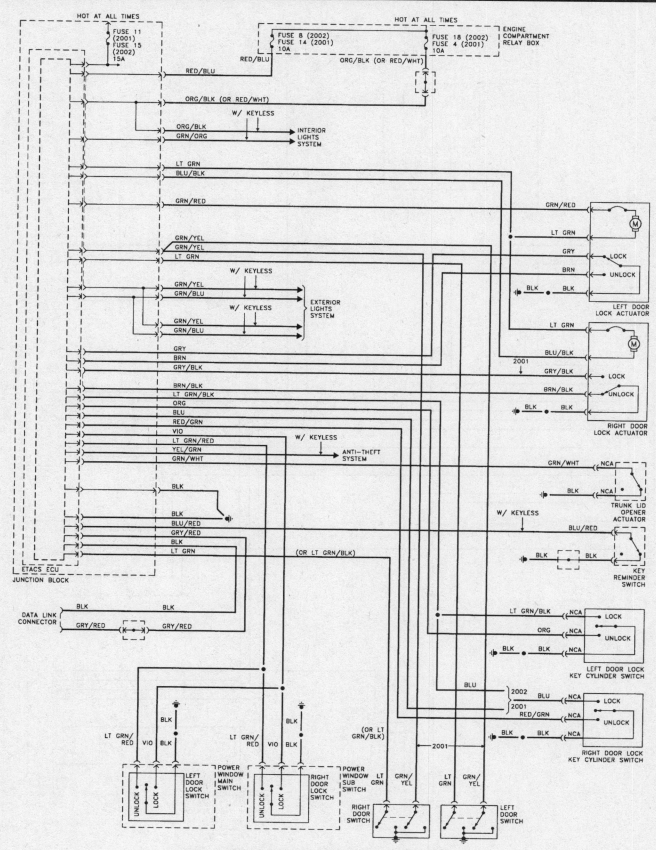

Power door lock system - 2001 and later coupe models

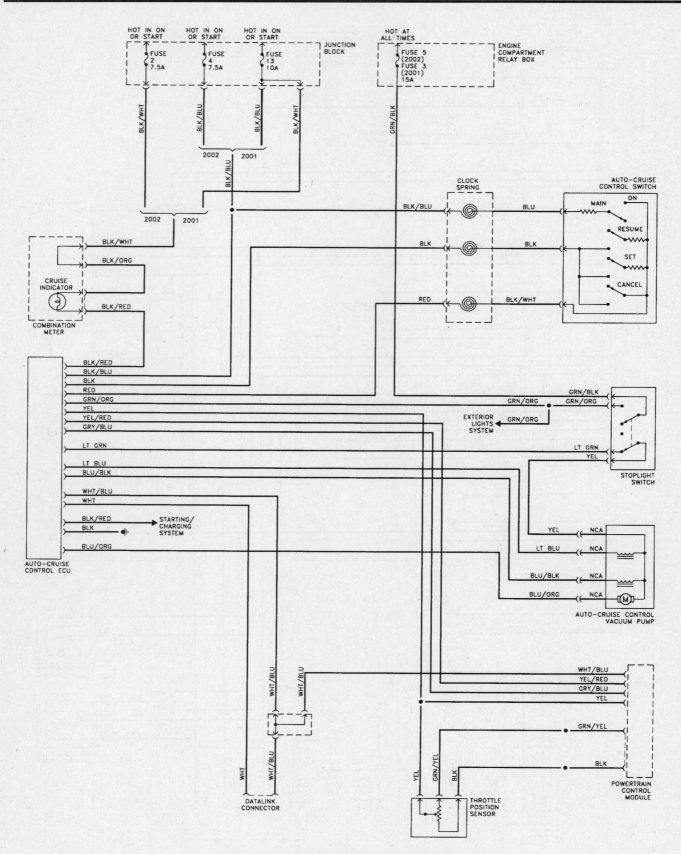

Cruise control system - 2001 and later coupe models

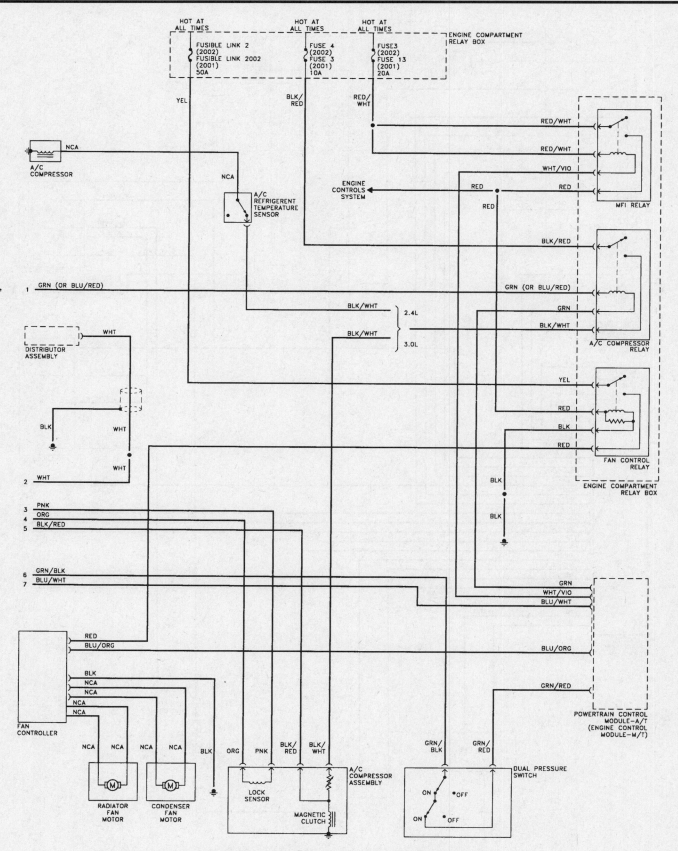

Air conditioning system - 2001 and later coupe models (1 of 2)

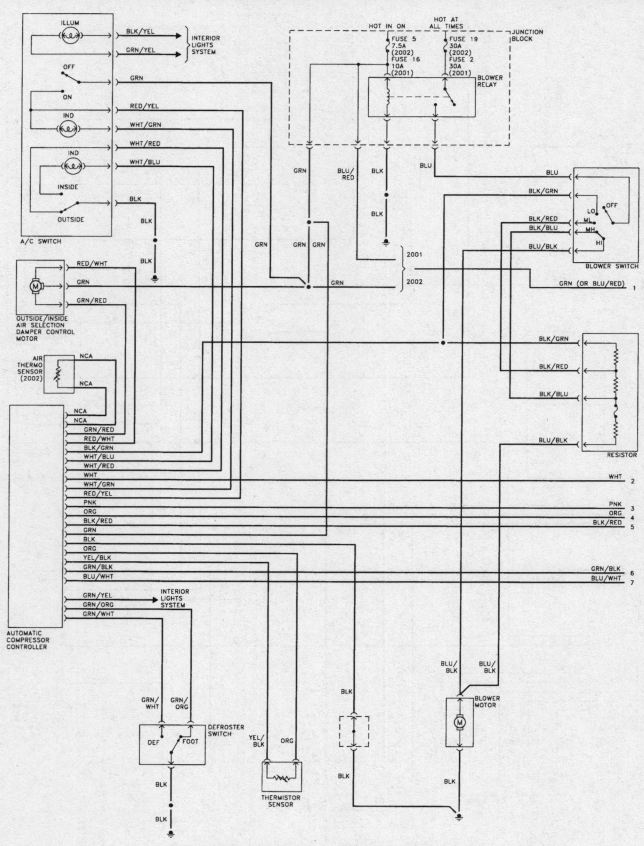

Air conditioning system - 2001 and later coupe models (2 of 2)

Index

Haynes Automotive Manuals

ACURA
- **12020** Integra '86 thru '89 & Legend '86 thru '90
- **12021** Integra '90 thru '93 & Legend '91 thru '95
  Integra '94 thru '00 - see HONDA Civic (42025)
  MDX '01 thru '07 - see HONDA Pilot (42037)
- **12050** Acura TL all models '99 thru '08

AMC
  Jeep CJ - see JEEP (50020)
- **14020** Mid-size models '70 thru '83
- **14025** (Renault) Alliance & Encore '83 thru '87

AUDI
- **15020** 4000 all models '80 thru '87
- **15025** 5000 all models '77 thru '83
- **15026** 5000 all models '84 thru '88
  Audi A4 '96 thru '01 - see VW Passat (96023)
- **15030** Audi A4 '02 thru '08

AUSTIN-HEALEY
  Sprite - see MG Midget (66015)

BMW
- **18020** 3/5 Series '82 thru '92
- **18021** 3-Series incl. Z3 models '92 thru '98
- **18022** 3-Series incl. Z4 models '99 thru '05
- **18023** 3-Series '06 thru '10
- **18025** 320i all 4 cyl models '75 thru '83
- **18050** 1500 thru 2002 except Turbo '59 thru '77

BUICK
- **19010** Buick Century '97 thru '05
  Century (front-wheel drive) - see GM (38005)
- **19020** Buick, Oldsmobile & Pontiac Full-size (Front-wheel drive) '85 thru '05
  Buick Electra, LeSabre and Park Avenue; Oldsmobile Delta 88 Royale, Ninety Eight and Regency; Pontiac Bonneville
- **19025** Buick, Oldsmobile & Pontiac Full-size (Rear wheel drive) '70 thru '90
  Buick Estate, Electra, LeSabre, Limited, Oldsmobile Custom Cruiser, Delta 88, Ninety-eight, Pontiac Bonneville, Catalina, Grandville, Parisienne
- **19030** Mid-size Regal & Century all rear-drive models with V6, V8 and Turbo '74 thru '87
  Regal - see GENERAL MOTORS (38010)
  Riviera - see GENERAL MOTORS (38030)
  Roadmaster - see CHEVROLET (24046)
  Skyhawk - see GENERAL MOTORS (38015)
  Skylark - see GM (38020, 38025)
  Somerset - see GENERAL MOTORS (38025)

CADILLAC
- **21015** CTS & CTS-V '03 thru '12
- **21030** Cadillac Rear Wheel Drive '70 thru '93
  Cimarron - see GENERAL MOTORS (38015)
  DeVille - see GM (38031 & 38032)
  Eldorado - see GM (38030 & 38031)
  Fleetwood - see GM (38031)
  Seville - see GM (38030, 38031 & 38032)

CHEVROLET
- **10305** Chevrolet Engine Overhaul Manual
- **24010** Astro & GMC Safari Mini-vans '85 thru '05
- **24015** Camaro V8 all models '70 thru '81
- **24016** Camaro all models '82 thru '92
- **24017** Camaro & Firebird '93 thru '02
  Cavalier - see GENERAL MOTORS (38016)
  Celebrity - see GENERAL MOTORS (38005)
- **24020** Chevelle, Malibu & El Camino '69 thru '87
- **24024** Chevette & Pontiac T1000 '76 thru '87
  Citation - see GENERAL MOTORS (38020)
- **24027** Colorado & GMC Canyon '04 thru '10
- **24032** Corsica/Beretta all models '87 thru '96
- **24040** Corvette all V8 models '68 thru '82
- **24041** Corvette all models '84 thru '96
- **24045** Full-size Sedans Caprice, Impala, Biscayne, Bel Air & Wagons '69 thru '90
- **24046** Impala SS & Caprice and Buick Roadmaster '91 thru '96
  Impala '00 thru '05 - see LUMINA (24048)
- **24047** Impala & Monte Carlo all models '06 thru '11
  Lumina '90 thru '94 - see GM (38010)
- **24048** Lumina & Monte Carlo '95 thru '05
  Lumina APV - see GM (38035)
- **24050** Luv Pick-up all 2WD & 4WD '72 thru '82
  Malibu '97 thru '00 - see GM (38026)
- **24055** Monte Carlo all models '70 thru '88
  Monte Carlo '95 thru '01 - see LUMINA (24048)
- **24059** Nova all V8 models '69 thru '79
- **24060** Nova and Geo Prizm '85 thru '92
- **24064** Pick-ups '67 thru '87 - Chevrolet & GMC
- **24065** Pick-ups '88 thru '98 - Chevrolet & GMC

- **24066** Pick-ups '99 thru '06 - Chevrolet & GMC
- **24067** Chevrolet Silverado & GMC Sierra '07 thru '12
- **24070** S-10 & S-15 Pick-ups '82 thru '93, Blazer & Jimmy '83 thru '94,
- **24071** S-10 & Sonoma Pick-ups '94 thru '04, including Blazer, Jimmy & Hombre
- **24072** Chevrolet TrailBlazer, GMC Envoy & Oldsmobile Bravada '02 thru '09
- **24075** Sprint '85 thru '88 & Geo Metro '89 thru '01
- **24080** Vans - Chevrolet & GMC '68 thru '96
- **24081** Chevrolet Express & GMC Savana Full-size Vans '96 thru '10

CHRYSLER
- **10310** Chrysler Engine Overhaul Manual
- **25015** Chrysler Cirrus, Dodge Stratus, Plymouth Breeze '95 thru '00
- **25020** Full-size Front-Wheel Drive '88 thru '93
  K-Cars - see DODGE Aries (30008)
  Laser - see DODGE Daytona (30030)
- **25025** Chrysler LHS, Concorde, New Yorker, Dodge Intrepid, Eagle Vision, '93 thru '97
- **25026** Chrysler LHS, Concorde, 300M, Dodge Intrepid, '98 thru '04
- **25027** Chrysler 300, Dodge Charger & Magnum '05 thru '09
- **25030** Chrysler & Plymouth Mid-size front wheel drive '82 thru '95
  Rear-wheel Drive - see Dodge (30050)
- **25035** PT Cruiser all models '01 thru '10
- **25040** Chrysler Sebring '95 thru '06, Dodge Stratus '01 thru '06, Dodge Avenger '95 thru '00

DATSUN
- **28005** 200SX all models '80 thru '83
- **28007** B-210 all models '73 thru '78
- **28009** 210 all models '79 thru '82
- **28012** 240Z, 260Z & 280Z Coupe '70 thru '78
- **28014** 280ZX Coupe & 2+2 '79 thru '83
  300ZX - see NISSAN (72010)
- **28018** 510 & PL521 Pick-up '68 thru '73
- **28020** 510 all models '78 thru '81
- **28022** 620 Series Pick-up all models '73 thru '79
  720 Series Pick-up - see NISSAN (72030)
- **28025** 810/Maxima all gasoline models '77 thru '84

DODGE
  400 & 600 - see CHRYSLER (25030)
- **30008** Aries & Plymouth Reliant '81 thru '89
- **30010** Caravan & Plymouth Voyager '84 thru '95
- **30011** Caravan & Plymouth Voyager '96 thru '02
- **30012** Challenger/Plymouth Saporro '78 thru '83
- **30013** Caravan, Chrysler Voyager, Town & Country '03 thru '07
- **30016** Colt & Plymouth Champ '78 thru '87
- **30020** Dakota Pick-ups all models '87 thru '96
- **30021** Durango '98 & '99, Dakota '97 thru '99
- **30022** Durango '00 thru '03 Dakota '00 thru '04
- **30023** Durango '04 thru '09, Dakota '05 thru '11
- **30025** Dart, Demon, Plymouth Barracuda, Duster & Valiant 6 cyl models '67 thru '76
- **30030** Daytona & Chrysler Laser '84 thru '89
  Intrepid - see CHRYSLER (25025, 25026)
- **30034** Neon all models '95 thru '99
- **30035** Omni & Plymouth Horizon '78 thru '90
- **30036** Dodge and Plymouth Neon '00 thru '05
- **30040** Pick-ups all full-size models '74 thru '93
- **30041** Pick-ups all full-size models '94 thru '01
- **30042** Pick-ups full-size models '02 thru '08
- **30045** Ram 50/D50 Pick-ups & Raider and Plymouth Arrow Pick-ups '79 thru '93
- **30050** Dodge/Plymouth/Chrysler RWD '71 thru '89
- **30055** Shadow & Plymouth Sundance '87 thru '94
- **30060** Spirit & Plymouth Acclaim '89 thru '95
- **30065** Vans - Dodge & Plymouth '71 thru '03

EAGLE
  Talon - see MITSUBISHI (68030, 68031)
  Vision - see CHRYSLER (25025)

FIAT
- **34010** 124 Sport Coupe & Spider '68 thru '78
- **34025** X1/9 all models '74 thru '80

FORD
- **10320** Ford Engine Overhaul Manual
- **10355** Ford Automatic Transmission Overhaul
- **11500** Mustang '64-1/2 thru '70 Restoration Guide
- **36004** Aerostar Mini-vans all models '86 thru '97
- **36006** Contour & Mercury Mystique '95 thru '00
- **36008** Courier Pick-up all models '72 thru '82
- **36012** Crown Victoria & Mercury Grand Marquis '88 thru '10
- **36016** Escort/Mercury Lynx '81 thru '90
- **36020** Escort/Mercury Tracer '91 thru '02

- **36022** Escape & Mazda Tribute '01 thru '11
- **36024** Explorer & Mazda Navajo '91 thru '01
- **36025** Explorer/Mercury Mountaineer '02 thru '10
- **36028** Fairmont & Mercury Zephyr '78 thru '83
- **36030** Festiva & Mercury Aspire '88 thru '97
- **36032** Fiesta all models '77 thru '80
- **36034** Focus all models '00 thru '11
- **36036** Ford & Mercury Full-size '75 thru '87
- **36044** Ford & Mercury Mid-size '75 thru '86
- **36045** Fusion & Mercury Milan '06 thru '10
- **36048** Mustang V8 all models '64-1/2 thru '73
- **36049** Mustang II 4 cyl, V6 & V8 models '74 thru '78
- **36050** Mustang & Mercury Capri '79 thru '93
- **36051** Mustang all models '94 thru '04
- **36052** Mustang '05 thru '10
- **36054** Pick-ups & Bronco '73 thru '79
- **36058** Pick-ups & Bronco '80 thru '96
- **36059** F-150 & Expedition '97 thru '09, F-250 '97 thru '99 & Lincoln Navigator '98 thru '09
- **36060** Super Duty Pick-ups, Excursion '99 thru '10
- **36061** F-150 full-size '04 thru '10
- **36062** Pinto & Mercury Bobcat '75 thru '80
- **36066** Probe all models '89 thru '92
  Probe '93 thru '97 - see MAZDA 626 (61042)
- **36070** Ranger/Bronco II gasoline models '83 thru '92
- **36071** Ranger '93 thru '10 & Mazda Pick-ups '94 thru '09
- **36074** Taurus & Mercury Sable '86 thru '95
- **36075** Taurus & Mercury Sable '96 thru '05
- **36078** Tempo & Mercury Topaz '84 thru '94
- **36082** Thunderbird/Mercury Cougar '83 thru '88
- **36086** Thunderbird/Mercury Cougar '89 thru '97
- **36090** Vans all V8 Econoline models '69 thru '91
- **36094** Vans full size '92 thru '10
- **36097** Windstar Mini-van '95 thru '07

GENERAL MOTORS
- **10360** GM Automatic Transmission Overhaul
- **38005** Buick Century, Chevrolet Celebrity, Oldsmobile Cutlass Ciera & Pontiac 6000 all models '82 thru '96
- **38010** Buick Regal, Chevrolet Lumina, Oldsmobile Cutlass Supreme & Pontiac Grand Prix (FWD) '88 thru '07
- **38015** Buick Skyhawk, Cadillac Cimarron, Chevrolet Cavalier, Oldsmobile Firenza & Pontiac J-2000 & Sunbird '82 thru '94
- **38016** Chevrolet Cavalier & Pontiac Sunfire '95 thru '05
- **38017** Chevrolet Cobalt & Pontiac G5 '05 thru '11
- **38020** Buick Skylark, Chevrolet Citation, Olds Omega, Pontiac Phoenix '80 thru '85
- **38025** Buick Skylark & Somerset, Oldsmobile Achieva & Calais and Pontiac Grand Am all models '85 thru '98
- **38026** Chevrolet Malibu, Olds Alero & Cutlass, Pontiac Grand Am '97 thru '03
- **38027** Chevrolet Malibu '04 thru '10
- **38030** Cadillac Eldorado, Seville, Oldsmobile Toronado, Buick Riviera '71 thru '85
- **38031** Cadillac Eldorado & Seville, DeVille, Fleetwood & Olds Toronado, Buick Riviera '86 thru '93
- **38032** Cadillac DeVille '94 thru '05 & Seville '92 thru '04 Cadillac DTS '06 thru '10
- **38035** Chevrolet Lumina APV, Olds Silhouette & Pontiac Trans Sport all models '90 thru '96
- **38036** Chevrolet Venture, Olds Silhouette, Pontiac Trans Sport & Montana '97 thru '05
  General Motors Full-size Rear-wheel Drive - see BUICK (19025)
- **38040** Chevrolet Equinox '05 thru '09 Pontiac Torrent '06 thru '09
- **38070** Chevrolet HHR '06 thru '11

GEO
  Metro - see CHEVROLET Sprint (24075)
  Prizm - '85 thru '92 see CHEVY (24060), '93 thru '02 see TOYOTA Corolla (92036)
- **40030** Storm all models '90 thru '93
  Tracker - see SUZUKI Samurai (90010)

GMC
  Vans & Pick-ups - see CHEVROLET

HONDA
- **42010** Accord CVCC all models '76 thru '83
- **42011** Accord all models '84 thru '89
- **42012** Accord all models '90 thru '93
- **42013** Accord all models '94 thru '97
- **42014** Accord all models '98 thru '02
- **42015** Accord '03 thru '07
- **42020** Civic 1200 all models '73 thru '79
- **42021** Civic 1300 & 1500 CVCC '80 thru '83
- **42022** Civic 1500 CVCC all models '75 thru '79

(Continued on other side)

Haynes North America, Inc., 859 Lawrence Drive, Newbury Park, CA 91320-1514 • (805) 498-6703 • http://www.haynes.com

Haynes Automotive Manuals (continued)

NOTE: If you do not see a listing for your vehicle, consult your local Haynes dealer for the latest product information.

42023 **Civic** all models '84 thru '91
42024 **Civic & del Sol** '92 thru '95
42025 **Civic** '96 thru '00, **CR-V** '97 thru '01, **Acura Integra** '94 thru '00
42026 **Civic** '01 thru '10, **CR-V** '02 thru '09
42035 **Odyssey** all models '99 thru '10
    Passport - see *ISUZU Rodeo (47017)*
42037 **Honda Pilot** '03 thru '07, **Acura MDX** '01 thru '07
42040 **Prelude CVCC** all models '79 thru '89

HYUNDAI
43010 **Elantra** all models '96 thru '10
43015 **Excel & Accent** all models '86 thru '09
43050 **Santa Fe** all models '01 thru '06
43055 **Sonata** all models '99 thru '08

INFINITI
    G35 '03 thru '08 - see *NISSAN 350Z (72011)*

ISUZU
    Hombre - see *CHEVROLET S-10 (24071)*
47017 **Rodeo, Amigo & Honda Passport** '89 thru '02
47020 **Trooper & Pick-up** '81 thru '93

JAGUAR
49010 **XJ6** all 6 cyl models '68 thru '86
49011 **XJ6** all models '88 thru '94
49015 **XJ12 & XJS** all 12 cyl models '72 thru '85

JEEP
50010 **Cherokee, Comanche & Wagoneer Limited** all models '84 thru '01
50020 **CJ** all models '49 thru '86
50025 **Grand Cherokee** all models '93 thru '04
50026 **Grand Cherokee** '05 thru '09
50029 **Grand Wagoneer & Pick-up** '72 thru '91 **Grand Wagoneer** '84 thru '91, **Cherokee & Wagoneer** '72 thru '83, **Pick-up** '72 thru '88
50030 **Wrangler** all models '87 thru '11
50035 **Liberty** '02 thru '07

KIA
54050 **Optima** '01 thru '10
54070 **Sephia** '94 thru '01, **Spectra** '00 thru '09, **Sportage** '05 thru '10

LEXUS
    ES 300/330 - see *TOYOTA Camry (92007) (92008)*
    RX 330 - see *TOYOTA Highlander (92095)*

LINCOLN
    Navigator - see *FORD Pick-up (36059)*
59010 **Rear-Wheel Drive** all models '70 thru '10

MAZDA
61010 **GLC Hatchback** (rear-wheel drive) '77 thru '83
61011 **GLC** (front-wheel drive) '81 thru '85
61012 **Mazda3** '04 thru '11
61015 **323 & Protegé** '90 thru '03
61016 **MX-5 Miata** '90 thru '09
61020 **MPV** all models '89 thru '98
    Navajo - see *Ford Explorer (36024)*
61030 **Pick-ups** '72 thru '93
    Pick-ups '94 thru '00 - see *Ford Ranger (36071)*
61035 **RX-7** all models '79 thru '85
61036 **RX-7** all models '86 thru '91
61040 **626** (rear-wheel drive) all models '79 thru '82
61041 **626/MX-6** (front-wheel drive) '83 thru '92
61042 **626, MX-6/Ford Probe** '93 thru '02
61043 **Mazda6** '03 thru '11

MERCEDES-BENZ
63012 **123 Series Diesel** '76 thru '85
63015 **190 Series** four-cyl gas models, '84 thru '88
63020 **230/250/280** 6 cyl sohc models '68 thru '72
63025 **280 123 Series** gasoline models '77 thru '81
63030 **350 & 450** all models '71 thru '80
63040 **C-Class:** C230/C240/C280/C320/C350 '01 thru '07

MERCURY
64200 **Villager & Nissan Quest** '93 thru '01
    All other titles, see FORD Listing.

MG
66010 **MGB** Roadster & GT Coupe '62 thru '80
66015 **MG Midget, Austin Healey Sprite** '58 thru '80

MINI
67020 **Mini** '02 thru '11

MITSUBISHI
68020 **Cordia, Tredia, Galant, Precis & Mirage** '83 thru '93
68030 **Eclipse, Eagle Talon & Ply. Laser** '90 thru '94
68031 **Eclipse** '95 thru '05, **Eagle Talon** '95 thru '98
68035 **Galant** '94 thru '10
68040 **Pick-up** '83 thru '96 & **Montero** '83 thru '93

NISSAN
72010 **300ZX** all models including Turbo '84 thru '89
72011 **350Z & Infiniti G35** all models '03 thru '08
72015 **Altima** all models '93 thru '06
72016 **Altima** '07 thru '10
72020 **Maxima** all models '85 thru '92
72021 **Maxima** all models '93 thru '04
72025 **Murano** '03 thru '10
72030 **Pick-ups** '80 thru '97 **Pathfinder** '87 thru '95
72031 **Frontier Pick-up, Xterra, Pathfinder** '96 thru '04
72032 **Frontier & Xterra** '05 thru '11
72040 **Pulsar** all models '83 thru '86
    Quest - see *MERCURY Villager (64200)*
72050 **Sentra** all models '82 thru '94
72051 **Sentra & 200SX** all models '95 thru '06
72060 **Stanza** all models '82 thru '90
72070 **Titan pick-ups** '04 thru '10 **Armada** '05 thru '10

OLDSMOBILE
73015 **Cutlass** V6 & V8 gas models '74 thru '88
    For other OLDSMOBILE titles, see BUICK, CHEVROLET or GENERAL MOTORS listing.

PLYMOUTH
    For PLYMOUTH titles, see DODGE listing.

PONTIAC
79008 **Fiero** all models '84 thru '88
79018 **Firebird** V8 models except Turbo '70 thru '81
79019 **Firebird** all models '82 thru '92
79025 **G6** all models '05 thru '09
79040 **Mid-size Rear-wheel Drive** '70 thru '87
    Vibe '03 thru '11 - see *TOYOTA Matrix (92060)*
    For other PONTIAC titles, see BUICK, CHEVROLET or GENERAL MOTORS listing.

PORSCHE
80020 **911** except Turbo & Carrera 4 '65 thru '89
80025 **914** all 4 cyl models '69 thru '76
80030 **924** all models including Turbo '76 thru '82
80035 **944** all models including Turbo '83 thru '89

RENAULT
    Alliance & Encore - see *AMC (14020)*

SAAB
84010 **900** all models including Turbo '79 thru '88

SATURN
87010 **Saturn** all S-series models '91 thru '02
87011 **Saturn Ion** '03 thru '07
87020 **Saturn** all L-series models '00 thru '04
87040 **Saturn VUE** '02 thru '07

SUBARU
89002 **1100, 1300, 1400 & 1600** '71 thru '79
89003 **1600 & 1800** 2WD & 4WD '80 thru '94
89100 **Legacy** all models '90 thru '99
89101 **Legacy & Forester** '00 thru '06

SUZUKI
90010 **Samurai/Sidekick & Geo Tracker** '86 thru '01

TOYOTA
92005 **Camry** all models '83 thru '91
92006 **Camry** all models '92 thru '96
92007 **Camry, Avalon, Solara, Lexus ES 300** '97 thru '01
92008 **Toyota Camry, Avalon and Solara and Lexus ES 300/330** all models '02 thru '06
92009 **Camry** '07 thru '11
92015 **Celica Rear Wheel Drive** '71 thru '85
92020 **Celica Front Wheel Drive** '86 thru '99
92025 **Celica Supra** all models '79 thru '92
92030 **Corolla** all models '75 thru '79
92032 **Corolla** all rear wheel drive models '80 thru '87
92035 **Corolla** all front wheel drive models '84 thru '92
92036 **Corolla & Geo Prizm** '93 thru '02
92037 **Corolla** models '03 thru '11
92040 **Corolla Tercel** all models '80 thru '82
92045 **Corona** all models '74 thru '82
92050 **Cressida** all models '78 thru '82
92055 **Land Cruiser** FJ40, 43, 45, 55 '68 thru '82
92056 **Land Cruiser** FJ60, 62, 80, FZJ80 '80 thru '96
92060 **Matrix & Pontiac Vibe** '03 thru '11
92065 **MR2** all models '85 thru '87
92070 **Pick-up** all models '69 thru '78
92075 **Pick-up** all models '79 thru '95
92076 **Tacoma, 4Runner, & T100** '93 thru '04
92077 **Tacoma** all models '05 thru '09
92078 **Tundra** '00 thru '06 & **Sequoia** '01 thru '07
92079 **4Runner** all models '03 thru '09
92080 **Previa** all models '91 thru '95
92081 **Prius** all models '01 thru '08
92082 **RAV4** all models '96 thru '10
92085 **Tercel** all models '87 thru '94
92090 **Sienna** all models '98 thru '09
92095 **Highlander & Lexus RX-330** '99 thru '07

TRIUMPH
94007 **Spitfire** all models '62 thru '81
94010 **TR7** all models '75 thru '81

VW
96008 **Beetle & Karmann Ghia** '54 thru '79
96009 **New Beetle** '98 thru '11
96016 **Rabbit, Jetta, Scirocco & Pick-up** gas models '75 thru '92 & Convertible '80 thru '92
96017 **Golf, GTI & Jetta** '93 thru '98, **Cabrio** '95 thru '02
96018 **Golf, GTI, Jetta** '99 thru '05
96019 **Jetta, Rabbit, GTI & Golf** '05 thru '11
96020 **Rabbit, Jetta & Pick-up** diesel '77 thru '84
96023 **Passat** '98 thru '05, **Audi A4** '96 thru '01
96030 **Transporter 1600** all models '68 thru '79
96035 **Transporter 1700, 1800 & 2000** '72 thru '79
96040 **Type 3 1500 & 1600** all models '63 thru '73
96045 **Vanagon** all air-cooled models '80 thru '83

VOLVO
97010 **120, 130 Series & 1800 Sports** '61 thru '73
97015 **140 Series** all models '66 thru '74
97020 **240 Series** all models '76 thru '93
97040 **740 & 760 Series** all models '82 thru '88
97050 **850 Series** all models '93 thru '97

TECHBOOK MANUALS
10205 **Automotive Computer Codes**
10206 **OBD-II & Electronic Engine Management**
10210 **Automotive Emissions Control Manual**
10215 **Fuel Injection Manual** '78 thru '85
10220 **Fuel Injection Manual** '86 thru '99
10225 **Holley Carburetor Manual**
10230 **Rochester Carburetor Manual**
10240 **Weber/Zenith/Stromberg/SU Carburetors**
10305 **Chevrolet Engine Overhaul Manual**
10310 **Chrysler Engine Overhaul Manual**
10320 **Ford Engine Overhaul Manual**
10330 **GM and Ford Diesel Engine Repair Manual**
10333 **Engine Performance Manual**
10340 **Small Engine Repair Manual,** 5 HP & Less
10341 **Small Engine Repair Manual,** 5.5 - 20 HP
10345 **Suspension, Steering & Driveline Manual**
10355 **Ford Automatic Transmission Overhaul**
10360 **GM Automatic Transmission Overhaul**
10405 **Automotive Body Repair & Painting**
10410 **Automotive Brake Manual**
10411 **Automotive Anti-lock Brake (ABS) Systems**
10415 **Automotive Detailing Manual**
10420 **Automotive Electrical Manual**
10425 **Automotive Heating & Air Conditioning**
10430 **Automotive Reference Manual & Dictionary**
10435 **Automotive Tools Manual**
10440 **Used Car Buying Guide**
10445 **Welding Manual**
10450 **ATV Basics**
10452 **Scooters 50cc to 250cc**

SPANISH MANUALS
98903 **Reparación de Carrocería & Pintura**
98904 **Manual de Carburador Modelos Holley & Rochester**
98905 **Códigos Automotrices de la Computadora**
98906 **OBD-II & Sistemas de Control Electrónico del Motor**
98910 **Frenos Automotriz**
98913 **Electricidad Automotriz**
98915 **Inyección de Combustible** '86 al '99
99040 **Chevrolet & GMC Camionetas** '67 al '87
99041 **Chevrolet & GMC Camionetas** '88 al '98
99042 **Chevrolet & GMC Camionetas Cerradas** '68 al '95
99043 **Chevrolet/GMC Camionetas** '94 al '04
99048 **Chevrolet/GMC Camionetas** '99 al '06
99055 **Dodge Caravan & Plymouth Voyager** '84 al '95
99075 **Ford Camionetas y Bronco** '80 al '94
99076 **Ford F-150** '97 al '09
99077 **Ford Camionetas Cerradas** '69 al '91
99088 **Ford Modelos de Tamaño Mediano** '75 al '86
99089 **Ford Camionetas Ranger** '93 al '10
99091 **Ford Taurus & Mercury Sable** '86 al '95
99095 **GM Modelos de Tamaño Grande** '70 al '90
99100 **GM Modelos de Tamaño Mediano** '70 al '88
99106 **Jeep Cherokee, Wagoneer & Comanche** '84 al '00
99110 **Nissan Camioneta** '80 al '96, **Pathfinder** '87 al '95
99118 **Nissan Sentra** '82 al '94
99125 **Toyota Camionetas y 4Runner** '79 al '95

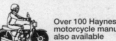

Over 100 Haynes motorcycle manuals also available

7-12